Iranun and Balangingi

Iranun and Balangingi

Globalization, Maritime Raiding and the Birth of Ethnicity

JAMES FRANCIS WARREN

SINGAPORE UNIVERSITY PRESS
NATIONAL UNIVERSITY OF SINGAPORE

© 2002 Singapore University Press
          Yusof Ishak House
          31 Lower Kent Ridge Road
          Singapore 119078

          Fax: (65) 6774-0652
          E-mail: supbooks@nus.edu.sg
          Website: http://www.nus.edu.sg/SUP

ISBN 9971-69-242-2 (Paper)

All rights reserved. This book, or parts thereof, may not be reproduced in any form or by any means, electronic or mechanical, including photocopying, recording or any information storage and retrieval system now known or to be invented, without written permission from the Publisher.

This edition for distribution worldwide except in the Philippines.

Printed by Seng Lee Press Pte Ltd, Singapore

For
my mother
Elsie Copeland-Warren
who first taught me the meaning of compassion and discipline
and my neurosurgeon
Richard Vaughan
whose skill and empathy gave me back my life and my vocation

CONTENTS

List of Tables viii
List of Maps viii
List of Illustrations viii
List of Appendices ix
Abbreviations x
Weights, Measures and Currencies xi
Preface xiii
Acknowledgments xx

Chapters
   1 The Iranun Age 1
   2 Maguindanao, Sulu and the Iranun Age 25
   3 The Iranun in the Sulu World 41
   4 The Raids, 1754-1838 53
   5 The Eastern Archipelago Defended, 1754-1838 86
   6 The Settlements and Bases 124
   7 The Expeditions 164
   8 The Crew 208
   9 The Raiding Ships 238
  10 Blood Upon the Sea and Sand 267
  11 The Captives 309
  12 Dispossession, Defeat and Diaspora 343
  13 Colonialism's Pirates: The 'Savage' Myth,
      Ethnic Identity and History 379

Appendices 419
Notes 449
Glossary 517
Bibliography 523
Index 565

List of Tables

1. The Iranun Communities in The Sulu Archipelago (1814), *51*
2. Slave Raiding and Population Variations
    in Nueva Caceres (1751-1815), *119*
3. Crew size of Balangingi fleets, 1838 and 1856, *172*

List of Maps

1. Sulu and Celebes Sea, *29*
2. Slave Raiding Outside the Philippines in Southeast Asia, *55*
3. Slave Raiding in the Philippines, 1768-1868, *75*
4. Spanish Colonial and Community Coastal Fortifications
    in the Philippines, *111*
5. Iranun–Balangingi Maritime Raiding and the Malay
    Archipelago in the first half of the nineteenth century, *127*
6. Balangingi Island, *147*

List of Illustrations

1. Iranun Sea Raider, *inside front cover*
2. Malay Chief, *195*
3. Entrance to Jolo town in the late 1830s, *196*
4. Street scene in Zamboanga in the late 1830s, *196*
5. Barangayan, *197*
6. Trading *prahu*, *197*
7. Portrait of Iranun warrior, *198*
8. Iranun Weapons, *199*
9. *Lanong (joanga)*, *199*
10. *Salisipan*, *200*
11. *Garay*, *201*
12. Iranun-Samal Weapons, *202*
13. Samal Laut, *203*
14. Slave Woman of Jolo, *203*
15. Muslim Woman from Cotabato, *204*
16. A *Vigia* or Castillo (village watchtower), *204*

17. Jesuit Church at Boac, Marinduque, *205*
18. Fortress walls of the Jesuit Church at Boac, Marinduque, *205*
19. Moluccan *Kora-Kora*, *206*
20. Spanish *Falua* (sailing gunboat), *206*
21. *Canonero* (steamer), *207*
22. Heavily armed Dyak from north Borneo, *213*
23. Late eighteenth century *joanga*, *243*
24. Balangingi *garay* or *panco* with two banks of oars under full sail, *247*
25. Spanish plans of the heavily fortified Samal stronghold (*kota*) of Sipac, *347*
26. Shipping note of Babalatchi, *397*
27. Painting depicting the 'Attack on the Island and Fort of Balangingi', *inside back cover*

List of Appendices

Appendix A	A Letter Soliciting Trade Between the United States and Sulu, *419*
Appendix B	The Coastal Defenses of the Bishopric of Cebu, 1799, *421*
Appendix C	An Inventory of the Land and Sea Defenses of Albay Province, 1799, *425*
Appendix D	Population Variation in Nueva Caceres between 1751-1780 and 1815, *426*
Appendix E	Statements of Balangingi Prisoners, 1838, *429*
Appendix F	The Statements of the Fugitive Captives of the Sulu Sultanate, 1836-1864, *431*

Abbreviations

AGI	Archivo General de Indias
AHN	Archivo Historico Nacional
AMAE	Archivo Ministerio Asuntos de Exteriores
ANRI	Arsip Nasional Republik Indonesia
AR	Algemeen Rijksarchief
ASJ	Archive Society of Jesus, Philippine Province
AUST	Archive University of Santo Tomas
BH-PCL	Beyer-Holleman collection of Original Sources in Philippine Customary Law
BIA	Bureau of Insular Affairs
BKI	Bijdragen tot de Taal- land- en Volkenkunde van Nederlandsch-Indie
BMGN	Bijdragen en Mededelingen Betreffende de Geschiedenis der Nederlanden
BRB	Borneo Research Bulletin
BRPI	Emma Blair and James A. Robertson, *The Philippine Islands, 1493-1898* (Cleveland, 1903-1909), 55 vols.
CO	Colonial Office, London
FO	Foreign Office, London
GCG	Governor Captain General
HDP	Historical Data Papers, Republic of the Philippines, Bureau of Public Schools
IOL	India Office Library
JIAEA	Journal of the Indian Archipelago and Eastern Asia
JMBRAS	Journal of the Malaysian Branch Royal Asiatic Society
JSEAS	Journal of Southeast Asian Studies
MN	Museo Naval
NBH	British North Borneo Herald and Official Gazette
PNA	Philippine National Archive
P.P.H.C.	Parliamentary Papers House of Commons
PRO	Public Records Office, London
SSJ	Sabah Society Journal
TBG	Tijdschrift voor Indische Taal-, Land- en Volkenkunde, uitgegeven door het (Koninklijk) Bataviaasch Genootschap van Kunsten en Wetenschappen

Weights, Measures and Currencies

Weights
Tahil (tahel) — 1.33 ounces
Kati (16 tahel) — 1.33 pounds
Picul (100 kati) — 133.33 pounds (Manila = 137.50lbs)
Bahar (3 picul) — 400 pounds
Koyan (40 picul) — 5,333.33 pounds
Quintal — 100-110 pounds

Measures
Gantang (4 kati) — 3.1 kilogrammes of rice
Cavan (25 gantang) — 44 kilogrammes of rice
Arroba — 25.36 pounds (5° arroba = picul)

Currencies
100 Spanish dollars
(pesos, duros) — 224° Company Rupees
                252.27 Dutch Guilders
                $366.97

PREFACE

The aim of *Iranun and Balangingi* is to explore ethnic, cultural and material changes in the transformative history of oceans and seas, commodities and populations, mariners and ships, and raiders and refugees in Southeast Asia, with particular reference to the Sulu-Mindanao region, or the 'Sulu Zone.' The oceans and seas of Asia, East by South, from Canton to Makassar, and from Singapore to the Birds Head coast of New Guinea, crossed by Iranun and Balangingi raiding and slaving ships, Southeast Asian merchant vessels and colonial warships have been the sites of extraordinary conflicts and changes often associated with the formation of ethnic groups and boundaries, political struggles and national histories. Examining the profound changes that were taking place in the Sulu-Mindanao region and elsewhere, this book, the companion volume to *The Sulu Zone*, charts an ethnohistorical framework for understanding the emerging interconnected patterns of global commerce, long-distance maritime raiding and the formation and maintenance of ethnic identity. I begin by tracing the evolution of Iranun maritime raiding from its late eighteenth century origins to support the English supplies of tea from China, into the nineteenth century's systematic, regional-based slaving and marauding activity. I then draw out the implications of that evolution for colonial systems of domination, development and discourse in the context of transoceanic trade, crosscultural commerce and empire building.

For several centuries, the Sulu-Mindanao region has been known for "piracy." In the early nineteenth century, entire ethnic groups specialized in the state sanctioned maritime raiding–Iranun and Balangingi–attacking Southeast Asian coastal settlements and trading vessels sailing for the fabled

Spice Islands, or for Singapore, Manila and Batavia. When people think of slavery in Southeast Asia, they imagine tens of thousands of peoples stolen from their villages across the region and sent directly to work the large fisheries and wilderness reserves of the Sulu Sultanate. The insatiable demands of the sultanate for labor to harvest and procure exotic natural commodities, such as sea cucumber and birds' nest, reached a peak in the first half of the nineteenth century as the China trade flourished. Now in this new globalized world, Jolo, Balangingi, Canton, and London were all intimately interconnected. A major feature of this emerging global economy was that over 200 years ago, Europe and the then emerging markets of East and Southeast Asia were tangled in a commercial and political web that was in many ways just as global as today's world economy. Yet another characteristic of late eighteenth and nineteenth century globalization was that it went hand in hand with degeneration and fragmentation. Even as economies of traditional trading states such as Sulu's integrated, others, for example the sultanates of Brunei and Cotabato, disintegrated, while regional populations across Southeast Asia in the process were fragmented, scattered and relocated. This book looks at the large-scale forced migrations of the unfortunate mass of captives and slaves caught in the cogs of the Sulu economy, which shaped the demographic origins of the Iranun and Balangingi and the overall population trends and settlement patterns of much of the Philippines and Eastern Indonesia well into the end of the nineteenth century.

Less than two centuries ago, few homes in Southeast Asia's vast patchwork of coastal settlements had been left unscathed by the "Illanun." Many people lost their kin and were forever haunted by their loss. Silent capture, swift retreat often marked the coastal slave raids by the Iranun and Balangingi in the nineteenth century, lying in wait along a path or creek to an isolated stretch of coast near a small settlement. Victims—especially women and children—were generally welcomed as new members of these maritime Muslim communities to which they were forcibly taken, often hundreds if not a thousand miles away. Most captives and slaves accepted their fate and new roles, large numbers replacing Iranun and Balangingi members lost to the hazards of nature, sea warfare and disease.

In a detailed analysis of the maritime raiding and slaving operations of the Iranun and Balangingi, as well as those of other seafaring groups like the Tobello, this book considers how, over a span of a century, the economy of the Sulu Sultanate expanded and was integrated into the modern world system as a result of interactions between European corporate trading enterprises, especially the British and the Dutch East India Companies, with China. The Sulu Sultanate was successful because it achieved global scale in particular types of commodity production, integrating labor acquisition and allocation—slaving and slavery—commodity production, marketing and other functions on a global-regional scale. The losers in this contest were traditional states and ethnic groups that neither achieved nor specialized on a global-regional scale, but relied on an entrenched position in their local markets for the bulk of their power and profits. *Iranun and Balangingi* also explains how this essentially market-determined commercial encounter in the latter part of the eighteenth century, as the entangled fateful relationship between Britain, China and Sulu was established, transformed the population and history of Southeast Asia. In their remorseless search for captives and slaves the Iranun and Balangingi brought the "border arcs," or moving frontiers of the margins of the Malayo-Muslim world and of the various colonial peripheries, home to the centers, striking back at the empire's heart around Batavia and Singapore, in the straits of Malacca and Manila Bay, and beyond, reaching right across the top of Northern Australia. These fearsome alien marauders originated from areas beyond the pale—unknown sites well outside the reach of colonial dominion. The Iranun and Balangingi profited from the expanding China trade, which they supplied with captives and slaves taken on the high seas and along the shores of Southeast Asia, in return for weapons and luxury goods. These sea raiders—the lords of the eastern seas—were the "shapers," a set of ethnic groups that specialized in long distance maritime raiding but did it on a regional scale. *Iranun and Balangingi* also details the complexities of relations in the struggle over power and autonomy on the seas, between the maritime Islamic world of the Iranun and Balangingi and the conflicting interests and machinations of the colonial western powers bent on controlling the oceans and sea lanes. The study further demonstrates how a pathology of physical and cultural violence associated with global macro-contact wars and empire building, particularly with political struggles between the English and Dutch in various parts of Southeast Asia, led to widespread conflicts and regional tragedies.

This ethnohistory also offers a range of insights about the process of ethnic self-definition and the meaning and constitution of "culture" in the modern world system. The problem of ethnic identity and the formation and maintenance of "cultures" are elusive, complex and contested processes, practises and attributes which defy simple explanations and definitions. This way of accounting for the Iranun and Balangingi and their history also provides a new conceptual framework for understanding the problem of ethnic self-definition and political processes and conflicts in the recent history of the Philippines, Indonesia and Malaysia.

Iranun and Balangingi seeks to probe these themes through an interdisciplinary approach, using archival sources and literature, as well as period testimony, interviews and fieldwork observations from sites primarily located in the Philippines, Indonesia and Malaysia. The alleged battle between savagism and civilization, with glory for the Spanish, British and Dutch and, ultimately, tragedy for the Iranun and Balangingi as its inevitable outcome, formed a major theme and metaphor of much of the official record and the literature–published and unpublished– depicting 'Malay Piracy' in the period under consideration here. By looking at both traditional and contemporary historical and visual texts and oral traditions that are indicative of such profound cultural confrontations and intersections, this ethnohistory explores both the "birth" and "death" of ethnicities and cultures that originated in the violent intimacies of the encounter between expansive global capital and maritime Muslim cultures in conflict; conflicts that also originated in the demographic origins of particular ecological landscapes intersecting with traditional maritime borders and the forceful imposition of state-imposed colonial political boundaries on those borders and "maritime spaces."

The broader issues of economic integration and identity formation that underpin this book also provide an apt backdrop to the current Muslim contestations and state and ethnic politics in the Philippines. Few other ethnic groups in Southeast Asia have developed such a notorious legacy of "piracy" than the Iranun and Balangingi. This book throws light on the principal fact that these maritime Muslim groups in the Sulu archipelago and southwestern Mindanao have always been very autonomous and led a free-roaring existence in Southeast Asian waters. These Vikings of Asia laid claim to being the true lords of the eastern seas in the age of sail. *Iranun and Balangingi* clearly demonstrates the economic motivation, geographical realities, cultural nexus, and religious impetus to 'piracy' in the area. Without that insight, it would be difficult to fully understand why Muslim autonomy remains such a burning issue in the Sulu archipelago and southwestern Mindanao today. While this ethnohistory deals with the historical legacy of 'piracy'–the book is also a pertinent reminder of how cultures and ethnic identities are embedded in sea-faring lifestyles and political processes that have not, in certain aspects, changed dramatically over the last two centuries. The Iranun and Balangingi remain marginalized from the Filipino nation state and their intractable cause has only emboldened them to fight for ethnic identity, progress and autonomous statehood.

The Making of a Series

I have had second thoughts about *The Sulu Zone 1768-1898*, or third thoughts, since the ideas associated with the book first came to me in the years between 1970 and 1975. Years later, working on a project at the Center for Southeast Asian Studies, Kyoto University, called 'The Sulu Zone, The World Capitalist Economy and the Historical Imagination,' I found the ethnohistory of the Iranun and Balangingi come alive for me in a way that had not been possible up until then. In order to set up *Iranun and Balangingi*, I had to re-present the original thinking and historical significance behind *The Sulu Zone 1768-1898* as an ethnohistory based on a critical blend of archival research, sophisticated social theory and solid ethnography; thus the small book *The Sulu Zone, The World Capitalist Economy and the Historical Imagination* came into existence in part so I could eventually write the ethnohistory *Iranun and Balangingi*. I have attempted to write a book that now forms part of an extended series which actually evolves and penetrates ever more deeply into particular conceptual frameworks, appropriate categories, structures, and processes. I never planned an extended series, but like many series the second volume is not a completely different kind of ethnohistory from the first. In *Iranun and Balangingi* I delve deeper and ever deeper into some of my original concepts and categories about the 'state,' 'piracy,' 'slavery,' 'ethnicities' and 'frontiers,' and 'border zones.'

In 1996, the Center for Southeast Asian Studies, Kyoto University, asked me to write either a lengthy article or a small book that explored various aspects of *The Sulu Zone 1768-1898* with particular reference to global-local cultural interconnections and interdependencies. After a hiatus of 15 years while I worked on other projects, I returned to the broad canvas of 'the Sulu Zone' to begin exploring the ethnohistory of the Iranun and the Balangingi anew, and also to inquire into the struggles and misunderstandings that linked patterns of consumption and 'frontiers' of desire in Europe, China and Southeast Asia with particular entangled commodities, maritime spaces and cultural geographies.

While there is a fundamental similarity between essential aspects of both works in *Iranun and Balangingi* there is increasing depth of insight into problems of globalization and maritime raiding and into the extraordinary personality of an individual like Panglima Taupan as the series proceeds. *Iranun and Balangingi* has been framed as a book as, part of a series that carries the reader through an evolutionary progression of historical concepts and insight into global-regional processes and the tension between integrative and disintegrative forces that produced one of Southeast Asia's most significant fault lines around the Sulu Zone in the first half of the nineteenth century. Here hundreds of thousands of lives were shaped and changed economically and culturally in terms of shifting ethnic identities. When I was invited to Japan, I found that I had not said all that I wanted to say about the subject of maritime raiding, slavery and the formation and maintenance of ethnicity, a position I had to recognize and accept, despite trying to move towards completion of another separate but related series, a trilogy on the social history of the Chinese in Singapore under colonial rule between 1870 and 1940. This ethnohistory titled, *Iranun and Balangingi*, is a sequel to *The Sulu Zone 1786-1898*, although it does cover some of the same ground, from the viewpoint of the same historian more than a quarter of a century after the earlier work was completed. Most importantly, I relied to a certain extent on the fine ethnographic and historical work published on the maritime world of Southeast Asia in the intervening years especially from the Philippines, to fill some of the less obvious gaps in space and time.

I hope that *Iranun and Balangingi* by design will advance some of the underlying concepts and categories concerning labor acquisition (maritime raiding); labor allocation (slavery); the manipulation of ethnically diverse groups; the meaning and constitution of 'culture'; and state formation. These two books combined with the little 'think piece,' *The Sulu Zone, The World Capitalist Economy and the Historical Imagination*, form a kind of triptych about a fascinating geographical, cultural and historical 'border zone,' centered around the Sulu and Celebes seas between 1768 and 1898, and its complex interactions with China and the West. This series looks deeply into the dynamics of a Malayo-Muslim maritime state and its reactions to the world capitalist economy and the rapid advance of colonialism and modernity; and as the series grows, I have also attempted to enhance our critical understanding of historiographical methods and models.

ACKNOWLEDGMENTS

In a very real sense *Iranun and Balangingi* grew out of a doctoral dissertation submitted to the Australian National University in 1975. The main research was carried out in 1972-1973, 1986 and 1999 in the United States, Europe and Southeast Asia. In the United States, the principal sources of information were the shipping records of the Peabody Museum, Salem; the G.W. Blunt White Library, Mystic Seaport Museum; and the Wood and Scott Collections of the Library of Congress. A number of important files were also examined in the United States National Archive. A major part of the field research over the years was carried out in Spain in the Archivo General de Indias, Sevilla; Archivo Historico Nacional, Madrid; Archivo de Ministerio de Asuntos Exteriores, Madrid; and the Museo Naval, Madrid. In England, in the India Office Library, London; the Public Records Office, London; the National Maritime Museum, Greenwich; and the Cambridge University Library, Cambridge. In the Netherlands, in the Algemeen Rijksarchief in Leiden; and the records of the Auxiliary Repository, Schaarsbergen. In the Philippines, many months were spent over the decades working in the Philippine National Archive, Manila; the Archive of the University of Santo Tomas, Manila; the Archive of the Society of Jesus, Philippine Province, Ateneo de Manila University, Quezon City; and the National Library of the Philippines, Manila. In Indonesia, the resources of the Arsip Nasional were made available. I want to thank the directors and all their staff in all these repositories and institutions for their kind assistance and constant help over the years.

Many people have contributed to this study. Major sources of inspiration remain the thought of John Smail, E.R. Leach and Eric

Wolf. I am particularly indebted to Rachel Drewry, my research assistant. In my efforts to come to grips with the globalized world of the Iranun and Balangingi, Ms. Drewry read and made a precis of items I flagged for her, and, as a valuable guide drew other sources in the literature to my attention. In this context, I also thank my research assistants in Manila, Ms. Rose Marie Mendoza and Ms. Cleofe Marpa who followed up items on my behalf that I had investigated earlier in the Philippine National Archive in several major record series. Thanks are also due to Ian Henderson, friend, student and retired architect, for his assistance and advice in reproducing the illustrations and maps and for helping me to create the artwork for the cover design.

I am indebted to the following colleagues and students for their interesting comments, criticisms and encouragement with respect to the publication of my earlier work on the Sulu Zone and this book–Jeremy Beckett, Carolyn Brewer, John Butcher, Bruce Cruikshank, Reynaldo Ileto, Adrian Lapian, John Legge, Alfred McCoy, Norman Owen, Anne L. Reber, Anthony Reid, John Schumacher, S.J., William Henry Scott, Kurt Stenross, Eric Tagliacozzo, Nicholas Tarling, and Esther Velthoen.

I am particularly grateful to Carolyn Brewer, colleague and friend. *Iranun and Balangingi* has benefited from her careful and thoughtful editing of the manuscript. I also appreciate the kind, intelligent and patient assistance of Ms. Irene Finlay, who has worked on my longhand drafts for many years, in preparing the manuscript in typed form for publication. A special note of thanks must go to my mother, Elsie Warren, who provided comfort and cheer on the opposite side of the globe, and allowed me to use her dining room table to write the first half of *Iranun and Balangingi* between February and June 1998.

Finally I want to express my gratitude to my wife, Carol, and my daughter Kristin, for their continued support and encouragement. Their own lives and work in Australia and Southeast Asia are bound up with a journey that first began for Carol and me in 1967 on the east coast of Borneo as Peace Corps Volunteers; a journey, and a turning point in our lives, that made this book possible.

> *Alungi Bisalla Alenyap na Bangsa –*
> Lost Language, Vanished People
>
> —an old Samal Bajau Laut adage

> Where are your monuments, your battles, martyrs?
> Where is your tribal memory? Sirs,
> in that grey vault. The sea. The sea
> has locked them up. The sea is History.
>
> —Derek Walcott
> "The Sea is History," 1979

CHAPTER ONE

THE IRANUN AGE

Lanun. The name struck fear into the hearts and minds of riverine and coastal populations across Southeast Asia two centuries ago. Recently, ethnohistorical research has also shown that where Iranun or Lanun raiding is concerned, old traditions die-hard. The terrors of the sudden harsh presence of these well-armed alien raiders lives on in the oral recollections, reminiscences, popular folk epics and drama of the victims' descendants in the Philippines, Indonesia and Malaysia, to this day.[1] Only in one part of the globe, in the latter part of the eighteenth century, did Europeans find 'piracy' flourishing extensively; pursued as a calling, not by individuals, as was the case with most of those who had followed the profession of buccaneering in the West, but by entire communities and states with whom it came to be regarded as the most honorable course of life–a vocation.

The Iranun were frequently the enemies of every community and nation stretching from the Birds Head coast of New Guinea and the Moluccas (among the most productive spice islands of the Netherlands East Indies) to mainland Southeast Asia. Over two centuries ago, a Bugis writer chronicled that 'Lanun' in double-decked *prahus* up to 90 or 100 feet long, rowed by more than 100 slaves and armed with intricately wrought swivel cannon cast in bronze, were plundering villages and robbing Malay fishers in the straits of Malacca and the Riau Islands. Among other victims of these marauders were the coastal inhabitants of Thailand and Vietnam.[2] They would also raid in the Philippines, where the central and northern sections of the archipelago were under the control of Spain.[3] Iranun squadrons regularly plundered villages and captured slaves. Their exploits and conquests had the immediate effect of either disrupting or destroying traditional trade routes. Chinese junks and traders were driven off from states such as Brunei and Cotabato, the erstwhile masters of the Iranun, robbing parts of the archipelago of the traditional trade and exchange of spices, birds' nests, camphor, rattans, and other valuable commodities.[4] The Iranun earned a fearsome reputation in an era of extensive world commerce and economic growth between the west and China.

By the 1780s maritime raiding or 'piracy' in Southeast Asian waters–although common in the past–began to occur far more frequently than colonial authorities cared to admit. The regularity of the Iranun sweeps led the authorities in Singapore and other straits settlements to refer to the months of August, September and October as the *musim lanun*.[5] No one at the time seemed to know for certain whether the intrusion of western traders in the affairs of China in the late eighteenth century helped create the 'Lanun' phenomena. No one seemed sure whether the mercantile capitalism of the European colonial powers was responsible for producing and reproducing the Muslim sea-warriors of the Sulu chain, southwestern Mindanao and north Borneo. Who were these sea raiders known as 'Lanun' and later as Balangingi, who made maritime slave raiding and plunder both a profession and a trade in the late eighteenth and nineteenth centuries?

A meaningful discussion of late eighteenth century Iranun maritime raiding must take into account several key factors, including the lack of an appropriate definition of the term 'piracy' and the difficulty of locating information about the acts committed by the 'lanun' or 'pirates.' Iranun attacks in late eighteenth century Southeast Asia were frequently mounted for private gain by individuals or a sovereign state on ships on the high seas. It involved "violence, illegal detention of persons or property, or the theft or destruction of goods."[6] But Iranun raiding at that time was not simply robbery or banditry made singular by the fact that incidents occurred only on the water. No clearer or more comprehensive definition of piracy, as established by the law of western nations, could be found than a quotation from the commentaries of the celebrated early American jurist, Chancellor Kent, who wrote of piracy and pirates thus: "Piracy is robbery, or a forcible depredation on the high seas without lawful authority, and done *animo furandi*, and in the spirit and intention of universal hostility."[7] However, this early nineteenth century definition of piracy did not include several provisos that made for subsequent difficulty in rendering precisely the legal definition of Iranun and Balangingi marauding and slave raiding. The first of these provisos is that an attack must be mounted for private gain. This caused problems with respect to the Iranun and Balangingi because sometimes the identity of the attackers was in doubt and their motives unclear. While it is apparent that Iranun maritime raiding was a real crime with real victims–robbery and violence certainly existed–a more practical definition that also takes into consideration political, economic or religiously inspired motives must be sought. The fact that many late eighteenth century Iranun assaults on villages and coastal dwellers came from or took place on land, often along the strand or beach head, while the attack vessels remained moored offshore and out of sight leads to the second area of difficulty with Kent's narrow definition of the location of the attacks. Piracy is only considered the same offense at sea as robbery on the land. Hence, a more suitable legal definition, from an ethnohistorical perspective, would define Iranun and Balangingi raiding or 'piracy' as "an act of boarding any vessel with the intent to commit theft or other crime and with the capability to use force against individuals and land based communities as well, in furtherance of these acts."[8]

The problems of Iranun and Balangingi marauding and slave raiding were complicated for late eighteenth and nineteenth century Europeans by their diverse modes of operation and geography. Whatever the exact cause for the sudden advent of large scale, long range Iranun maritime raiding, the geographical setting and opportunity or timing were right for these emergent seafaring peoples. The innumerable islands of Southeast Asia had been home to generations of people of Malay origin, who had progressively converted to Islam from the fifteenth century, and engaged in trading, raiding and warfare before the arrival of Europeans in the sixteenth century. Their exploits were recorded by early western explorers, travellers and merchants. More than two centuries later at the height of the China tea trade, marauding and maritime slave raiding were still going strong. The greatest threat to seaborne traders and the coastal populace came from the Iranun who operated from the mangrove-lined inlets, bays and reef strewn islets in the waters round the southern Philippines and Borneo, especially the Sulu and Celebes seas. They preyed on the increasingly rich shipping trade of the Spanish, Dutch and English, and Bugis and Chinese, and seized their cargoes of tin, opium, spices, munitions and slaves as the merchants headed to and from the trading centers of Manila, Makassar, Batavia, and Penang.[9]

The Iranun had a stranglehold on this trade across Southeast Asia because it was so exposed along its entire course through numerous hazardous straits and channels among countless islands–islands frequented by a fearless sea-going people of predatory tendencies possessed of swift sailing prahus–which offered every opportunity for stealth and surprise attack. More than a century and a half ago, as late as 1836, George Windsor Earl, a ship captain, colonial official, linguist, and lawyer in those parts, described in his most popular work, *The Eastern Seas*, the vast archipelago with its nest of islands curling around the Asian mainland as a breeding ground for sea predators. "The Malay pirates absolutely swarm in the neighbourhood of . . . the numerous islands in the vicinity, the intersecting channels of which are known only to themselves, affording them a snug retreat, whence they can pounce upon the defenceless native traders, and drag them into their lairs to plunder them at their leisure."[10] When small merchant prahus and Chinese junks made their halting voyages on the calm waters, the Iranun were never far away, striking at all sized craft like fishing boats, interisland coasters, trading junks as well as becalmed or grounded European vessels. They simply had to wait, sheltered behind a convenient island, headland or bay overlooking strategic sea routes, and sooner or later 'coastwise' targets, never straying out of sight of land, would cross their path. Nor were coastal villages spared, especially in the Philippines.

Expeditions against the raiders promised no lasting results because the points to which they could retire were innumerable and often off the charts. The Spanish officer, Don Jose Maria Halcon, providing naval intelligence about Iranun and Balangingi maritime raiding to an English officer at Manila in 1838, compared their haunts to extensive 'nests or banks of rats' where they could fly from one refuge to another, with impunity.[11] Europeans, he believed, could never succeed in annihilating them. A decade earlier, Edward Presgrave, Registrar of imports and exports at the newly founded British settlement of Singapore, astutely pointed out one of the major reasons why Iranun raiding was concentrated in that particular region of the world. He noted with some trepidation, "that piracy does exist to a very great extent even in the neighbourhood of our settlement . . . and the most casual view of a chart of these seas is sufficient to convince anyone that no corner of the globe is more favourably adapted for the secure and successful practice of piracy."[12] Hence, geography as destiny was a sinister friend, albeit an ally, of the Iranun and Balangingi in their protracted struggle against the West.

An ethnohistorically enigmatic case, the rise of Iranun-Balangingi maritime raiding, requires contextualizing within a cross-regional hemispheric framework. The period at the end of the eighteenth century was commonly recognized as the 'Age of the Iranun.' For 70 years or more, the fiercely independent raiders sallied forth from their bases in the Sulu and Celebes seas, and other parts of the archipelago, to prey upon the burgeoning intercontinental traffic sailing between Europe, India and China and the regional traffic from Penang and the ports of Batavia and Makassar to the east. The coasts of Borneo, Sumatra and Sulawesi harbored Iranun communities that specialized in the trade. But many Iranun raiders still continued to think of Mindanao and Sulu as their homeland and main bases. An ethnohistory of the late eighteenth century, which focuses on the Iranun as maritime raiders or 'Malay pirates' does not, for the most part, fit into conventional categories of historical analysis in the study of Southeast Asia. The Iranun-Balangingi presence in that critical half-century, was so bound up with world capitalist developments in Asia as to be almost inseparable, especially between the time of the establishment of the trading outpost of Penang in 1786 and the destruction of Balangingi in 1848. Similarly, the Sulu Sultanate's role is not intelligible if it is simply represented as a 'pirate' state, major haunt and outfitting center of the Iranun. Nor can it be separated intelligibly from global-local trade and economic growth between the west and Asia in the era of 'regional time' under consideration here.[13]

As in the case of *The Sulu Zone*, the only solution is to develop a more nuanced framework based on global-local interconnections and interdependencies within which Iranun-Balangingi slave raiding and marauding can be properly situated and understood. Hence, in the case of the sultanates of Cotabato and Sulu, cross-cultural trade and exchange involving China and the West and other such interactions would be major causative factors in the Iranun's sudden ascendancy, and in how and why the Sulu Zone developed its particular social and cultural forms. Here, greater scope must be established for understanding internal social and cultural transformation and interregional relations, as expressed in the form of common events, entangled commodities, patterns of consumption and desire, the meaning and constitution of culture and the construction of ethnicities linking slavery and slave raiding to the impact of capitalism and colonialism, and the rise of the Iranun. In this study, this viewpoint is a fundamental frame of reference. No ethnic group, even those as apparently misunderstood as the Iranun and Balangingi, can be studied in isolation from the maritime world(s) around and beyond them.[14] This ethnohistory of these so-called 'Malay pirates' will add to our knowledge of the maritime societies in which they lived and create a better understanding of the Southeast Asian world as a whole–as it was progressively integrated into the modern world system.

At the end of the eighteenth century, the Iranun maritime raids had a profound impact on Southeast Asia. The Iranun and Balangingi have been rightly blamed for demographic collapse, loss of agricultural productivity and economic decline, as well as the breakup of the Dutch stranglehold in the straits of Malacca and eastern Indonesia. But the driving force for this process was still global and economic: the Iranun profited from Spanish, Dutch and English internal colonial problems and expansion, but were not the cause of the problems. The Iranun usually came a poor second to the great power rivalries and concerns in the priorities of the Dutch and British colonial rulers, and they were sometimes even welcomed as allies in their macro-contact wars and regional struggles.[15] Until 1848, colonial measures taken against the Iranun and Balangingi were often perceived, by colonized subjects in the Netherland Indies and the Philippines, to be half-hearted. At the end of the eighteenth century, by demonstrating the particular ineffectiveness of Dutch and Spanish power, the Iranun were hastening European decline.

What exactly was the motivation of Iranun marauding and slave raiding and what were the underlying causes? Was it simply the lure of booty and slaves, or were there deeper motives that encouraged so many Iranun-Maranao and Samal-speaking men to embark on a life of roving and plunder? Iranun maritime raiding proved economically and politically important in the global-regional competition between local Malayo-Muslim states and European maritime powers–powers that did not hesitate to channel considerable naval and military equipment into it through key entrepots such as Cotabato and Sulu. European diplomats had little success in separating global-regional trade from warfare in the Eastern Hemisphere and wars continued throughout the Asian region. Because it was usually the weaker naval power, the British East India Company resorted to Iranun 'privateering' for commerce raiding against its Dutch counterpart. It is not often recognized that the Iranun played leading roles in a region-wide drama of many acts that pitted colonial expansionist forces against one another as they attempted to establish political and commercial dominion in Southeast Asia–in the straits of Malacca, around the coasts of Borneo, and especially among the smaller islands beyond Sulawesi. Feeling the Iranun squeeze, the Dutch East India Company evacuated the bulk of their forces from Riau just opposite the Singapore-Johore coast; an area which Lanun raiders conquered from the Dutch in 1787.[16]

An analysis of Iranun maritime raiding highlights the fact that most attacks took place in the waters of local principalities, and developing colonies–ports, towns and villages–close to the coast. Slave-taking and theft were the main motives. Their mobility, kinship and diplomatic connections, and, their capability to either protect or disrupt trade, enabled the Iranun to forge regional wide links, albeit a powerful fluid political confederation of sorts, that could make or break local states and destroy colonial trade networks and population centers.[17] James Brooke, the self-styled white rajah of Sarawak, an arch political rival and sworn enemy of the Iranun, who interviewed the commanders of an 'Illanun' fleet in 1841, described their wide-ranging raiding exploits as a "devastating system."[18]

In Sulu, the ethnohistorian can see at work the same extrinsic factors that gave rise to piracy and slave raiding elsewhere around the region. But here they play themselves out in the 'zone' in a somewhat different fashion owing to specific cultural-ecological factors and sociopolitical structures and circumstances arising from well-established patterns of ethnic interrelations, stratification and mobility. The Iranun and Balangingi needed a primary center from which to operate, somewhere to hide, and a means of converting their spoils, namely slaves, (as common purpose currency) for 'modern' trade commodities–especially firearms and textiles. To be successful, they also required a degree of cooperation from various indigenous rulers and colonial powers, or at least for local authorities on the spot to turn a blind eye and not take effective action.

Between 1780 and 1815, from the shores of the straits of Malacca to the coasts of the Moluccas, Iranun slave raiding and 'privateering,' a tacit substitute for war, dominated the history of relations between the colonial powers. While maritime raiding and slavery were a feature of many societies around the archipelago at the time, colonial officials and historians have encouraged us to see only the 'Lanun,' 'Maguindanao,' 'Moros,' and 'Sulu *Zeerovers*,' the pirates of Islam but especially the Iranun and Balangingi, while conveniently forgetting Europe's involvement in the compounding of the Iranun ascendancy.[19]

At the end of the seventeenth century, the Dutch, a new global maritime power, emerged along the cold grey coasts of the North Sea to challenge the mercantile supremacy of both the Spanish and the British throughout the ensuing centuries.[20] The larger international rivalries of these colonial powers–especially the British and Dutch–culminated in a protracted struggle for commercial dominance in the seas of Southeast Asia as both nations were inevitably drawn into the macro-contact wars of the eighteenth century. In this context, international economic and political considerations played their parts in aiding and abetting 'Lanun piracy'; considerations which were often hidden from view within the larger confidential diplomatic maneuverings of the Great European powers and their respective trading cartels.

What, for instance, can be made of the activities of the late eighteenth century English country traders? The powerful British East India Company of the period was instrumental in introducing a tacit system dominated by both the indiscriminate sale of arms and opium and intelligence gathering, to assist the Bengal-based business organization against its Dutch and Asian competitors.[21] The picture that emerges of Southeast Asia toward the end of the eighteenth century is one of a vast entrepot for the China trade and for foreign influence over almost every aspect of life including politics, economics, religion, and the social fabric. A large proportion of the population, including women, in Sulu, Brunei, Cotabato, Bone, Aceh, and elsewhere across the archipelago, were drawn into the magnetic force of the global Chinese market economy. Important trade decisions were based on analysis of economic and political intelligence culled from Europe as well as ship logs and journals of private English country traders who were circulating wealth and sowing seeds of discontent in the farthest outposts of the Dutch trading empire. As the small states of the fabled spice islands struggled to stand up to the Dutch (with their own political and economic bloc), the British East India Company took advantage of political instability, production shortages and sustained losses in one area–Sulawesi and the Moluccas–to eliminate the Dutch as competitors, while profiting in another–the straits of Malacca.

Thomas Forrest, during the space of 20 months from 1774 to 1776, undertook a successful voyage of discovery to the Moluccas and New Guinea in the *Tartar Galley*, a vessel of less than 10 tons burden. Later he put forward a secret proposal, subsequently abandoned as too risky, to sail to Sulawesi and instigate the Bugis sultan of Bone to declare war against the Dutch.[22] In 1782, just three years after he had made his name with the publication of his celebrated book about the voyage in the tiny *Tartar Galley*, Forrest hoped to set sail for Sulawesi. He was in the latter stages of his career as an accomplished country trader. The next phase of his life would be spent as a political emissary appointed by the British East India Company to gather sensitive information about Tidorese-Dutch relations and Acehnese-English relations, and the prospects for future navigation and commerce in the eastern archipelago and the straits of Malacca.[23] In his confidential dispatches he did not describe himself as a spy, but the fact is that the East India Company he served under was prepared to negotiate secretly with the Tidorese and Acehnese and the Bugis and their Iranun allies to clandestinely promote war against the Dutch trading empire in Southeast Asia. Captain Forrest, highly regarded by his company's powerful Committee of Secrecy, had been hand picked for this aborted dangerous mission because, as declared in a letter to Forrest, "it would have been impossible for me to have with hopes of success, sent any other person, . . . no other was conversant in the language and customs of the Eastern people; you had a genius and peculiar turn for business of that sort; which the person who undertook such ought to be endowed with."[24]

His confidential instructions which were meant to partially incite the Iranun leaving a trail of murder, sunken ships and burned coastal settlements in their wake as they cruised the coasts of the Moluccas and to the eastward over the next two decades, read, in part, as follows:

> Here on the coast of the King of Bone's Dominions, you are to collect what information you can respecting the terms on which he stands with the Dutch. In doing this you may pass for the commander of a vessel from Bencoolen bound on a trading voyage [and, more to the point], this letter will be delivered to you by Captain Thomas Forrest a person well acquainted with the country subordinate to you and for this reason he has received credentials from this Government to offer our friendship and good wishes to yourself and the other chiefs with whom you are in amity, and to intimate to you the successes which thru the will of divine providence we have had the good fortune to meet with against our enemies the French and Dutch, both in this country [India] and in Europe.[25]

European commercial expansion and geopolitical rivalry at the end of the eighteenth century, promoted the international trade of Sulu and its Bornean dependencies, and made the Iranun 'piracy' what it was. In the late 1780s, the Dutch East India Company was at its lowest ebb. The appearance of the British East India Company country traders, like Thomas Forrest, paved the way for the eventual English takeover, because of the contacts they established with local rulers in the Moluccas, Sulawesi, Sumatra, Mindanao, and Sulu. As the eighteenth century ended the activities of Forrest and his fellow ship captains trading in war stores, coupled with the growing Iranun expansion, meant an inevitable increase in shipping losses with yet more coastal raids throughout the Moluccas, the Celebes Sea and the Malacca Straits.

However, had Iranun mercenaries always operated according to the dictates of the English, the tacit 'privateering' system might well have functioned in the interest of the British and local Malay rulers. In practice, Iranun raiders proved too difficult to control, and once away from either the semiofficial scrutiny of East India Company traders or official representatives of various Malayo-Muslim states, their maritime raiding and plundering was frequently indiscriminate. They tended also to prey on the ports, towns and vessels of so-called friendly European nations, not just those of the enemy, as Francis Light, the founder of the British East India Company factory and settlement at Penang, learned, much to his dismay in the early 1790s, as did his counterparts in the Moluccas a decade later.[26]

To the Spanish the Iranun, irrespective of whether there was war or peace around the globe, were simply the arch-enemy–'moros,' '*piratas*' and '*contrabandistas.*'[27] However, because of Spain's involvement in the Seven Years War, the British attacked Manila in 1762. Taking full advantage of British intervention and friendship, Cotabato and Sulu-based Iranun maritime raiding increased. Avid for the gunpowder weapons of the English readily obtained at Jolo, the Iranun descended on coastal settlements throughout the central and northern parts of the Philippines and even ventured inland to pillage and burn churches and towns. Rampaging from one end of the archipelago to the other, they carried out "a pattern of tragedy so recurrent as to become almost tedious,"[28] as particular communities were repeatedly battered with a vengeance. They preyed on cargo-laden sailing vessels, colonial merchant ships and coastguard cruisers, disrupting interisland and regional trade and they turned Philippine waters into a vast Muslim lake. Between 1762 and 1848, no one in the coastal stretches of the Philippines was safe because of the global geopolitical drama that had begun to unfold in a series of acts involving the Seven Years War, Britain's entry into the China market, the sudden rise of the Sulu Sultanate as an entrepot for the Canton trade, and the widespread advent of the Iranun raiders.[29] A Spanish writer described the wholesale misery inflicted over the next 86 years by the Iranun on the inhabitants of the archipelago, as a chapter in the history of Spain in the Philippines "written in blood and tears and nourished in pain and suffering."[30]

Certainly no ethnohistory of the Iranun and Balangingi since the late eighteenth century, no description of the meaning and constitution of their 'cultures,' and no anthropologically informed historical analysis of the transformation of their societies can be undertaken without reference to the advent of the China trade and the rise of the Sulu Sultanate. Yet, despite their major historical importance, the Iranun and Balangingi, the infamous 'Illanoon' and 'Moros' still remain among the least known and most misunderstood ethnic groups in the modern history of Southeast Asia.

While there are occasional references to them in earlier histories, travel accounts, and official reports, historians have had to burrow deeper into the sources at the Archivo de Indias, the Rijksarchief, the Public Records Office, and various archives in Southeast Asia, especially the Philippine National Archive, in order to reconstruct a detailed historical account of these maritime peoples and their relationships to one another. As I have shown in *The Sulu Zone*, particular sources are of critical importance, but they are of little value unless the historian knows what to do with them.[31] The main impetus for fashioning a new understanding of the Iranun and Balangingi past has been the radical change in perspective that some historians have adopted to study the recent history of the region and its continuing integration within the world capitalist economy. These changes in perspective attempt to combine the historiographical approaches and ideas of the Annales historians with the conceptual framework of world system theorists and solid ethnography.[32] Here, I pay particular attention to the path breaking book Eric Wolf wrote in the early 1980s, *Europe and the People Without History*.[33] Wolf argues that no community or nation is or has been an island, and the world, a totality of interconnected processes or systems, is not and never has been a sum of self-contained human groups and cultures. The modern world-system, as it developed, never confined colonial capitalism to the political limitations of single states or empires. Wolf's postulations, if accepted, imply that an analysis of colonial capitalism not limited to the study of single states or empires will be more complete and, in certain ways, less static. The point is that history consists of the interaction of variously structured and geographically distributed social entities which mutually reshape each other. The transformation of the West and China and the rise of the Iranun in modern Southeast Asian history cannot be separated: each is the other's history.

The change in perspective to which I have been referring has also meant moving away from the 'Eurocentric' history, which had been practiced by colonial and postcolonial historians. This perspective was first challenged as early as the 1930s by J.C. Van Leur, advocating an 'Asia-centric' history of Southeast Asia.[34] By the mid-1950s in the new histories being written, despite some historians following Van Leur's direction—a direction in which the Iranun and Balangingi could have been seen as subjects worthy of consideration in their own right—the marauders still tended to fade into the background in the face of the European presence. In reviewing the writing of these new historians on the 'Malay' or 'moro' system of raiding, trading, slavery, and political organization, it is apparent that beginning with the latter part of the eighteenth century, the Iranun and Balangingi world was still usually "observed from the deck of the ship, the ramparts of the fortress, and the high gallery of the trading-house" and consequently this world remained "grey and undifferentiated."[35]

In the early 1980s, publication of *The Sulu Zone* enabled us to begin to understand the momentous changes which took place in the Mindanao-Sulu region and across Southeast Asia at the end of the eighteenth century. And whereas colonial officials and historians had seen the marauding of the Iranun and Balangingi throughout the island world as evidence of the decline of the Sulu Sultanate their activities can now be viewed as an integral part of the sultanate's economic vitality, as a major participant in the world capitalist economy, as they were drawn into contact with the West and the China trade. The numerous islands of the Sulu archipelago and coastal stretches of Southeast Asia were home to generations of Iranun and Balangingi 'pirates' several centuries ago. Their exploits were recorded by Spanish, Dutch and English naval officers, colonial officials, friars and merchant traders, and were often woven, myth-like, into the fabric of local folk tales and colonial national histories. These memories and histories commemorated attempts to eradicate the great Muslim threats of 'piracy' and slavery and invariably failed to place Iranun maritime raiding activity in a proper context. Past and present historians of the colonial period, in considering the Iranun-Balangingi slave raids, have uncritically adopted the interpretation perpetrated by interests "on the right side of the gunboat."[36] They have relied heavily on sources inherently antagonistic to the nature of the society and values of the Iranun and Samal raiders, such as the hostile accounts of the Spanish friars, the printed reports of Dutch and English punitive expeditions, and Sir Stamford Raffles and James Brooke's influential reports on 'Malay Piracy.' In these Euro-centered histories, which dwell on the activity of the Iranun and Balangingi at length, the term 'piracy' is conspicuously present in the titles.[37]

On the other hand, I have previously shown how the published accounts of Dampier, Dalrymple, Forrest, and Hunt provide a detailed picture from 'within' of key aspects of the lives and circumstance of these seafaring people in the Mindanao-Sulu area and their travels and maritime raiding. But there is another English eyewitness account of their way of life and exploits whose unpublished work is not as well known. Although he took part in the initial East India Company voyages of discovery and trade in the 1760s to the Mindanao-Sulu region described by Alexander Dalrymple, the celebrated company navigator and cartographer, the company official James Rennell, during the five months he stayed 'among the islands,' devoted much of his unpublished journal to descriptions of the Tausog and Samal and their material culture, as well as the fauna and flora of the islands.[38]

But it was Thomas Forrest who actually learned their languages, studied their history, customs, nautical skills and boat building, and later wrote, a remarkable account of aspects of the way of life of the Iranun and Magindanao in the mid-1770s–precisely at that moment in time when everything was beginning to change socially, politically and economically, because of the advent of the China trade. Forrest, a superb navigator and a gifted linguist and musician, first went to sea in 1751 in the service of the British East India Company as fifth mate of the *Essex*. His early voyages took him to Sumatra and Java in the western part of the archipelago. By 1762, he was a senior captain in the country trade stationed at Fort Malboro, Bencoolen, on the coast of West Sumatra. Over the next decade he held a series of commands, being sent in 1773, to the far-flung Company outpost of Balambangan in the Sulu archipelago. The following August, Forrest undertook, the extraordinary voyage to the eastward in the tiny *Tartar Galley*–a journey that was to last 20 months.[39]

The country traders were key players in the old-world struggle for supremacy in late eighteenth century Southeast Asia. They produced a rich body of knowledge—culturally-ecologically speaking—about Mindanao and Sulu and a key record of the Iranun and their exploits. Among them were a number of educated men who kept wonderful journals of their voyages and experiences. Several of these were published and they proved immensely popular in England and on the Continent, becoming best sellers. One of the richest sources on the Iranun was written by Forrest, who, like Rennell, lived on Balambangan and who, for several years, sailed to the east with the Maguindanao and Bugis—beyond the pale of the Dutch—as an explorer cum political emissary. What is fascinating about his published account of the voyage of the *Tartar Galley* is that it is more than simply tales of plundering expeditions and Iranun–Bugis sea battles against the Dutch. He also included meticulous descriptions of the new lands and new people encountered en route. Forrest vividly described the coasts and islands of Mindanao, Sulu, Sulawesi, parts of the Moluccas and New Guinea, and, like Rennell nearly two decades earlier, catalogued their rivers, harbors, exotic fauna and flora, as well as the culture and society of the inhabitants he met along the way—especially those of the Maguindanao and Iranun.[40]

Despite the invaluable writings about Mindanao and Sulu left by these earlier British explorers and company traders, and though having lived for years in a part of the archipelago under British dominion (nearest to the Sulu zone), British East India Company officials on Java and Singapore, at the beginning of the nineteenth century, possessed little understanding of the Iranun and Balangingi whose role and relationship to each other and to the Sulu Sultanate often seemed confusing, if not tenuous to them. By the late 1820s there was substantial local concern in the newly founded settlement of Singapore about the rising incidence of piracy in the straits of Malacca and the South China Sea. Raffles recognized that the growing danger of piracy would, out of fear, deter the archipelago coasting trade from attempting passage through the straits, resulting in sorely needed commerce and revenue being diverted to rival settlements and ports. Such worries had also increasingly preoccupied the European merchant settlers and local shipping community and their response was noisy but feeble. The full extent of the presence of Iranun and Balangingi marauding in the seas around Singapore was very difficult to gauge. The incomplete knowledge about their movements and their attacks on Singapore shipping highlighted cumbersome bureaucratic procedures and major security problems. The Strait was a major impediment for an antipiracy campaign that could coordinate the efforts of the British, the Dutch and the local states.

In 1828, Edward Presgrave, Registrar of imports and exports at Singapore, compiled one of the first detailed accounts of Malay 'piracy' in the straits of Malacca based on Dutch and Spanish reports and on information provided by local informants. He mentions the fierce reputation the Iranun had developed in recent years, but this was not balanced by new knowledge of Iranun enterprise in the fields of trade, exploration and settlement.[41] Ironically, in the late 1830s, the best information available on the subject of Sulu and Iranun or Balangingi maritime raiding still appeared to be a lengthy factual paper written in 1812 by J. Hunt to Stamford Raffles while he was Lieutenant Governor of Java. In 1837 this report was belatedly published in Singapore in a compendium of notices on the Indian archipelago.[42]

In an effort to lay out the wide ranging activities of these sea raiders–activities which extended from the Bay of Bengal to the Timor and Arafura seas–and to outline the structural basis of the system of social and political organization which united them, it is necessary to piece together a description of their way of life from a variety of sources. These include traveller's accounts, like that of Thomas Forrest, the captivity narratives of Ebenezer Edwards and Luis de Ibanez y Garcia, and oral recollections, as well as the vitally important *testimonio* of fugitive captives and the statements of Iranun and Balangingi prisoners.[43] The captivity narratives of Ebenezer Edwards and Luis de Ibanez y Garcia with the Balangingi, while highlighting motif images of the 'Illanoon' and 'Moros' as barbaric and uncivilized, also contain important personal introductions to the subject of captivity itself, and to the raiders' warlike activities. Significantly, Luis de Ibanez y Garcia, who travelled with the celebrated Balangingi leader Panglima Taupan nine years after the destruction of his people's stronghold at Balangingi, offers a bird's-eye view of how his small band of seafarers roamed the Visayan sea in search of slaves, plunder and revenge. The historical record rarely provides us with sufficient insight into the career and fate of individual leaders like Taupan, who achieved lasting fame through his daring exploits, travels and stubborn resistance against Spanish warships.[44] However, the orally transmitted local history of the exploits of such men, and women, in the Mindanao-Sulu region and the Cagayan Valley in northern Luzon, also provides the historian with additional rare information about their activities, followers and fate; detailed knowledge about aspects of global-local trade, slave raiding and the cultural-historical space between heredity and heritage, and the exploration of the temporal and physical sites of dislocation and relocation. These oral histories show how even peasants and fishers' narratives can shed light upon some of the region's darkest pages in modern history. They reveal to us not just the fear and suffering of the coastal populace across Southeast Asia, but also the impetus behind the forced relocation and disintegration of the entire traditional Samal Balangingi culture. While references to the oral narratives of the descendants of the exiled Samal Balangingi are not conclusive in themselves, the documenting of these memories by anthropologists and historians demonstrate the sea of unfished knowledge that is still extant within personal narratives today, despite the way state power both informs and reforms cultural and historical identity. The historian can, by studying also the statements of fugitive captives and captured slave raiders, comprehend the forces that shaped the way of life of the Iranun and Balangingi in the early nineteenth century and explore the uprooted lives and fate of those captured and enslaved. The statements of the fugitive captives [*cautivos fugados*] carry a self-affixed stamp of authenticity. Most statements and captivity narratives have a first person observer-narrator—an authentic voice of experience—attempting to present a narrative that usually shows similarities with other accounts dealing with the same subject(s), such as the dominant ways of organizing maritime life, slave raiding and marauding, and the forms and allocation of labor—and whether it fits into a widely accepted social and cultural pattern. Spanish and Dutch naval officers and colonial administrators, in their interrogations, invariably dealt in part one with the biography and circumstances of capture, the 'event' or plot, which usually pivoted or turned on seizure by the sea raiders or a shipwreck. The second part was generally descriptive recounting the captivity experience and the social organization of maritime raiding from the 'inside,' drawing a broader sketch of the society and culture of the Iranun and Balangingi.[45]

However, Haraway warns the historian about the difficulties of creating an ethnohistorical mosaic from sources such as specific statements of fugitive captives and slave raiders and the danger of 'appropriating the vision of the less powerful while claiming to see from their positions.'[46] In other words, the historian must question the authority of these statements and narratives, regarding insistence on truth and the exercise of historical representation. What is of central concern here is the historiographical issue and problem of how to create a point of entry or angle of vision from below, and whether a historian can resurrect voice(s) and/or reconstruct the world of maritime raiders and slaves, employing a nuanced ethnohistorical methodology.[47]

Many individual accounts, which add texture to the social-psychological portraits of the captives and the warriors of the raiding vessels, reaffirm the importance of this particular source as, the most convincing evidence on Sulu maritime raiding ever encountered. It does this despite the handicap of possible bias and distortion, having been specifically compiled as counterintelligence about the activities of the Iranun and Balangingi–as the 'nemesis' of virtually everybody in late eighteenth and early nineteenth century Southeast Asia. But the statements of the fugitive captives and captivity narratives do such an excellent job of humanizing the crews and slaves, of creating a tragic sense of bonding complete with tension that wrings one dry with an overpowering sense of the verisimilitude of their experiences. Which side somebody was on seems irrelevant. Set primarily in the years 1836 to 1864, at a time when the Balangingi were gradually losing the naval war on the seas of Southeast Asia, the testimony in the captive statements enables the historian to follow the Balangingi *garay* on their extended voyages.[48] The crews endure boredom, chase small fleets of *tripang* fishers, attack coasting ships, get attacked in return with thunderous broadsides from steam warships–all of it happening with a level of crushing realism as blood washes across the decks, among the splintered oars and carnage of dying slave rowers and raiders. These testimonies, if anything, evoke feelings as strong now as they did when written more than 150 years ago, such as, for example, in the case of the ill-fated Balangingi squadron swept away off the east coast of Malaya in the South China Sea in 1838.[49]

The content of practically all the statements of fugitive captives and captivity narratives–partially biographical, descriptive and ethnographic–suggests that coming to terms with the feelings aroused by Iranun and Balangingi raiding and the wholesale slaughter and captivity of tens of thousands of Southeast Asians were very traumatic for many of them. This was even more true with regard to the problem of an attack's aftermath; slavery and survivorship. Such events and experiences led colonial governments, especially naval officers, to encourage fugitive captives to give testimony and sometimes to write lengthy accounts as survivors about captivity–bearing witness to their lives as slaves under the Tausog or Samal, and celebrating their return to their own culture and political institutions. For example, Ebenezer Edward's 1843, widely read, autobiographical account of a whaler's experiences among the Balangingi contained invaluable information on the activities of the raiders, their vessels and armaments, trade transactions and division of booty. His account was published in both Dutch and English journals that focused on the 'piracy' and slave trade of the Indian Archipelago. Edwards was taken prisoner by the Balangingi, after going ashore from the whaler, *Sarah and Elizabeth*, on the Timor coast to take in a fresh supply of water. The raiders boarded the largely unmanned ship, took all its possessions and set it on fire. After five weeks in captivity Edwards escaped from the Balangingi, with the help of Bajau fishermen, and was able to supply detailed information about his extraordinary captivity experience, with a riveting terrifying, you-are-there-realism, not always matched by other such narratives, except perhaps for those of Lt. Col. Luis de Ibanez y Garcia and Capt. C. Z. Pieters.[50]

In 1838, five years before Ebenezer Edward's captivity, George Bonham, governor of the Straits Settlements, drew the Admiralty's attention to the significance of the testimony and narratives of captivity for gathering naval intelligence about long distance maritime raiding emanating from Mindanao and Sulu–statements that, in his estimation, met the test of authenticity. He wrote from Singapore regarding the recent destruction of a Balangingi fleet:

> From the depositions enclosed some conception of the extent and the varied form under which piracy is carried on by this lawless confederacy may be formed as by them it will be seen that on board the boat recently taken by the steamer no less than seven individuals were found who had shortly before been captured in separate boats and distinct places extending from Cavite which is situated in the Bay and within a few miles from the city of Manila to the immediate vicinity of this station.[51]

I now want to shift the discussion away from the sources to the historiographical problem of Malay piracy and the issue of historical representation. The heartland of piracy in Southeast Asia has been considered for centuries to be in the waters around the southern Philippines and Borneo, especially the Sulu and Celebes seas. The various Malayo-Muslim peoples who dominated the archipelago flanking mainland Southeast Asia, including what is now the southern Philippines, the east Malaysian state of Sabah, and the sultanate of Brunei, engaged in maritime raiding and warfare before the arrival of Europeans in the sixteenth century. But it was the intrusion of these alien traders, missionaries and colonizers–the Spaniards in the Philippines, the British along the coasts of Malaya and later north Borneo, the Portuguese and then the Dutch in the East Indies (now Indonesia)–that, because of their fatal impact in destroying traditional trade routes and triggering commercial decline, seemingly created a kind of pirate cult. Nicholas Tarling, the principal advocate of the decay and decline theory, described it in these terms:

> The old empires decayed, but were not replaced, and within their boundaries marauding communities appeared, led by adventurous sherifs, or deprived aristocracies, or hungry chiefs. The invasion of the Europeans did not destroy the native states, but it destroyed the dynamics (sic) of the state system; it reduced the old capitals from splendour to poverty and their chiefs from heroism to ambivalence, from constructiveness to stagnation.[52]

The establishment of Dutch outposts and British ports of trade and their interference with the traditional trade routes of rival entrepots had apparently contributed to a loss of commerce, revenue and power among traditional maritime states. According to this thesis, sultans, who were deprived of their usual sources of commercial income as Chinese junks and local traders were driven away, turned to piracy. Tarling argues that the Malays, allegedly reduced to poverty, learned to live by piracy: 'one result of the loss of commerce . . . was a shift to marauding on a more general scale than before; it became a way in which the Malay imperial aristocracy, deprived of other resources, could live from day to day. It became endemic, not epidemic.'[53]

This historical representation of the character, culture, and place of Malay piracy in the history of the Sulu Sultanate was widely accepted until quite recently. Most Spanish, British and Dutch colonial and postcolonial studies examined the history of European policy towards the Sulu Zone rather than the ethnohistory of the system of trading, raiding and slaving of the Zone itself, with its specific global-local interconnections and interdependencies. In particular, historians, of whom Nicholas Tarling and Cesar Majul are the most notable, have studied in great detail both British and Spanish efforts to suppress Sulu piracy.[54] Unlike his colonial predecessors, Tarling questioned the use of the term 'piracy' to describe the slave raiding and marauding activities of the Iranun and Balangingi. He suggested that in the eyes of those who pursued it, marauding came to be regarded as an honorable activity. But this somewhat tentative shift in viewpoint added little to our understanding of the place of maritime raiding in the statecraft and social structure of the Sulu Zone. Tarling conformed to the theory handed down from Raffles and Brooke that piracy, the stealthy nemesis of free trade and British dominion, was a sign of decay and decline in the Malayo-Muslim world, and that various sultans and chiefs had turned to marauding because their traditional local-regional trading activities and networks had been disrupted by the growing commercial strength and interference of Europeans. Aspiring empire builders, such as Stamford Raffles and James Brooke, had every reason to characterize the neighboring territories they hoped to rule or dominate in trade as areas of decadence, turmoil and decline, and whether or not they were sympathetic to colonial rule, later historians generally tended to adopt their view uncritically.

In the case of the historiography of the Sulu Sultanate, the Raffles' view was first seriously challenged by Anne Reber who traced the genesis of a historical misconception about British writings on Malay piracy with particular reference to Sulu. She argued that the commercial expansion of the British East India Company into China, with the likes of Dalrymple, Rennell and Forrest fanning out over the eastern archipelago in search of suitable commodities for the Canton market, brought with it a pronounced shift in political power and the system of trading and slaving in the Sulu archipelago.[55] In other words, by the end of the eighteenth century, it was European trade linked to China, and the insatiable desire for tea–a singular Chinese commodity–that made Iranun and Balangingi maritime raiding what it was. Tarling maintained that this global economic expansion, "scarcely reached these *piratical* regions, despite the efforts of Alexander Dalrymple and others."[56] More recently, I have shown the inextricable relationship between slave raiding and marauding, the economic and social structure of the Sulu Zone and its links to the world capitalist economy.[57] Whereas Tarling and others saw the maritime raiding of the Iranun and Balangingi throughout Southeast Asia as evidence of decadence of the Sulu Sultanate, slaving can now be read as an integral part of the sultanate's remarkable economic activity with the west and China. Iranun and Balangingi marauding was not the result of some sort of 'decay.' Indeed, I demonstrated that the Sulu Zone was an area of great economic vitality. This vitality was based on global-local links to the China trade. Commodities–marine and jungle products found within the zone–were highly desired on the Canton market, and, as Sulu chiefs prospered through regulation of the redistributive economy, they required more and more labor to collect and process these products. It was the Iranun and Balangingi, clients of the sultan of Sulu, who roamed about the island world in their swift raiding boats, finding slaves to meet this burgeoning labor demand. In the context of the world capitalist economy and the advent of the China trade, it should be understood that the slave raiding activities of the Iranun and Balangingi, so readily condemned in blanket terms as 'piracy' by European colonial powers and later historians, was a means of consolidating the economic base and political power of the sultan and Tausog coastal chiefs of Sulu, and which functioned as an integral, albeit critical, part of the emerging statecraft and sociopolitical structure of the zone. Thus, viewed from within the Sulu world of the eighteenth and early nineteenth centuries, the term 'piracy' is difficult to sustain. However, in its practical devastating effects, particularly when Iranun and Balangingi attacks were systematically directed against colonial coastal settlements and shipping, the Spanish, Dutch and English authorities could hardly be blamed for reacting to it in these terms, despite, from the late eighteenth century onwards, the word itself being bound up with larger colonial strategic policy implications and mythic resonances.

A different sort of 'decline theory' was proposed by Cesar Majul, and others following him, with respect to the history of the Maguindanao and Sulu Sultanates. For a period of four centuries, the Spanish attempted to colonize and Christianize Mindanao and areas of the Sulu archipelago. The earliest Spanish officials and friars referred to the various major ethnic groups–Tausog, Maguindanao, Iranun and Samal (Balangingi)–as 'Moros.' Frake notes that the word 'moro,' both in Spanish and in languages spoken by Philippine Christians, quickly became not only a religious label but an ethnic one as well; a label for social identity to which cultural behaviors, especially a propensity for piracy, and even physical features could be ascribed.[58]

The pejorative label 'Moro' provided a major intellectual and spiritual justification for Spanish retaliation and religious incursion against Mindanao and Sulu over the ensuing four centuries. Until recently, it was associated with ignorance, depravity and treachery. According to Luis Dery, as late as the 1950s, Kabikolan mothers continued to invoke the dreaded label, stereotypically saying, '*hala, iya-on na an mga Moros,*' [Watch out, the moros have come] which was enough to send their terrified children scurrying home.[59] The label 'moro,' by turning history into myth, in an epic struggle between civilization and 'savagism,' connoted Muslim people in the Sulu archipelago and Mindanao, who were considered in the eyes of most Spaniards and Filipinos to be savages or demons and pirates and slavers.[60] Thus, between the sixteenth and nineteenth centuries, Spaniards and others viewed Sulu's relations with Spain in the Philippines in terms of a pseudo-historical cycle, the 'moro-wars cycle,' according to which 'moro piracy' led to the repeated enslavement and humiliation of Christian

Filipinos, which in turn called for some form of consistent retaliation at once "punitive, imperial and morally imperative."[61]

Majul in his arguably classic, *The Muslims in the Philippines*, reiterated this version of cultural confrontation and 'Sulu piracy' while romanticizing it to a certain extent as a holy war–*jihad*–between the 'moros' and the Iberian infidel invaders, who slaughtered their kith and kin and blasphemed their sacred faith.[62] Though religious zealotry verging on fanaticism certainly existed in both camps, such an overall interpretation remains too simplistic to account for the dynamics of cultural-ecological transformation and the multifaceted changes that occurred in the Mindanao-Sulu region for over more than four centuries. It says little about the political economy and social organization of 'moro' maritime raiding in general or Iranun and Balangingi slave raiding in particular, and the processes of engagement with world commerce and economic growth. Iranun and Balangingi maritime raiding at the end of the eighteenth century was primarily a consequence of the onset of the China trade and never was a strictly Islamic enterprise. It was heavily commanded by Philippine and 'Malay' renegades in search of fortune and a new way of life and it used many European merchants, including Spaniards, as intermediaries who frequently traded war stores for the spoils and deployed the labor of ransomed captives for their private commerce.

Hence, two perspectives have dominated the historiography of the Sulu Zone and have tended to obscure the complex but integrated patterns of global-local trade, maritime raiding and slavery. On the one hand, the 'decay theory' has presented Iranun and Balangingi marauding and slaving as a symptom of the decline of traditional trade and the deterioration of the *kerajaan* or *negara*, the Malayo-Muslim state. On the other, Sulu slave raiding is interpreted within the framework of the 'moro wars' cycle as retaliation against Spanish colonial incursion and Christianity–holy confrontation. Both perspectives have underestimated and misunderstood the precise relationship between slavery, the advent of Iranun and Balangingi maritime raiding and the rise of the Sulu Sultanate, set within the wider framework of the intersections of the world capitalist economy in the years between 1768 and 1848, involving both China and the West, when Sulu became a crucial part of the global economic system.

CHAPTER TWO

MAGUINDANAO, SULU AND THE IRANUN AGE

The history of Sulu and Mindanao has always been shaped by its landscape and especially its relationship to the sea. The sea was a critical fact of life. The poverty of certain coastal areas and neighboring coral-sand atolls and islands made fishing and strand procurement an essential source of food and way of life, and the geography of the Mindanao-Sulu region meant that it was often easier to travel by water than land. Boat building and seamanship were essential skills, most obviously for the coastal Iranun and island-dwelling Samal Balangingi. Without superb sailing ships, the late eighteenth century Iranun expansion would have been impossible.[1]

The homeland of the Maranao-speaking Iranun and the Maguindanao was the southwestern interior and coast of Mindanao–a vast area of lakes, dense forests, rivers and mangrove swamps, which were a significant obstacle to travel and, until the second half of the nineteenth century, a natural barrier between the Iranun and the Spanish. While the Maranao encamped around the upland lake area of Lanao, the Maguindanao had the highest proportion of arable land. The sultanate of Cotabato, situated on the riverine plain of the Pulangi (Rio Grande de Mindanao) River, where it splits into two branches about 20 miles from the sea, was the wealthiest, most powerful and most politically advanced of the Mindanao Sultanates in the Iranun age. McKenna attributes the periodic inundation–flooding–of the valley floor as the source of the origin of the dominant ethnic group of the Cotabato Basin–the Maguindanaon. The word 'danao' refers to inundation by water, and 'Maguindanao,' or 'people of the flood plain,' is likely as a shortened form of 'Mag inged sa danao' or 'those residing at a flooded place.'[2] Laarhoven notes that the geography of Mindanao facilitated the maintenance of this precolonial state. That is, its prime down-river coastal position with access to harbors and major sea routes coupled with its central location in the Pulangi River valley, surrounded by large mountains, provided a favorable environment in terms of the economy, production, a certain demography and natural security. "It seems that trade and certain social mechanisms that were set up to attract people and absorb them were the main components of the successful consolidation of the sultanate started by Kudrat in 1645."[3] In southwestern Mindanao the impenetrable mangrove coastline and mountainous volcanic terrain of the Bukidnon-Lanao region made overland travel arduous. Sailing up the sheltered rivers was far quicker and safer, offering the best routes into the lakes and densely forested country.

The Iranun heartland was a large region stretching hundreds of miles from Lake Lanao in the southwestern interior to the maritime coasts of southern Mindanao and the eastern extremity of Ilana Bay: a heartland well beyond the *presidio* of Zamboanga and the pale of Spanish authority. In times of rapid population growth or natural catastrophe such as the devastating volcanic eruption of the mid-1760s, shortage of arable land became a serious problem. The advent of the 'Iranun age' after 1768 was a singular diasporic moment in time in which Maranao-speaking Iranun migrated in their thousands to the coasts of Mindanao and beyond in search of a new way of life and land to settle.

The Sulu archipelago is cut in pieces by the waves and currents of the Sulu and Celebes seas and has but few arable upland islands with relatively fertile soils. Of these Jolo, being one of the largest and centrally situated was the seat of the sultanate. Lying between Mindanao and Borneo, the Sulu archipelago was the gateway to the Philippines for trade coming from the East Indies, and the gateway to the Moluccas for trade going south from China. Away from Jolo to the west and south, clusters of low-lying small coral and sand islands, islets, rocks, reefs, and shoals, like Balangingi with its lagoons, mangrove swamp cover and particular pattern of tidal movements, stretched in an arc across the waters and merged like a seamless web into the seas of the Sulu Zone.

For the Iranun and Balangingi fortune was to be found on the sea.

Their maritime environment, seafaring traditions and the power struggles between rival states and colonial powers led them to raid and plunder their richer neighbors to the north and south. The pattern of Iranun and Balangingi marauding activity was strongly influenced by the monsoon trade-wind system, the major ocean current structure and the distribution of settlement locations and homelands of these seafaring peoples. Iranun expansion was mostly to the south and west–to Sulawesi, Borneo and ultimately to east Sumatra. The Samal Balangingi territory, a cluster of reef girdled islets, awash at high tide but exposed at low tide, straddled the main sea route midway between the South China Sea and the Celebes Sea, so it is not surprising that they first concentrated their raids on the Philippines and then spread to Makassar and Singapore.

Maritime raiding and cross-cultural commerce in this region of wind and water was a complex phenomenon involving a number of precolonial states, including the sultanates of Buayan, Cotabato, Sulu and a large number of local Iranun statelets and transitory raiding syndicates located in separate regional orbits. Mindanao had only two extensive states apart from numerous smaller Iranun principalities: Buayan at the headwaters of the Pulangi river to the north and Maguindanao or Cotabato in the south near the coast. Because of the distance and rival political interests between them, they became competing power centers.[4]

The geopolitical setting of the Mindanao-Sulu region was characterized by a competitive, multicentered political situation where Maguindanao, Maranao, Samal, Tausog, and the Europeans engaged one another in rival processes of state formation, economic development and colonization. The Tausog were dominant in the Sulu Sultanate, which encompassed north Borneo, southern Palawan, and parts of the southern Mindanao coast. The Maguindanao were territorially distributed among a number of sultanates, but only two were important: Buayan and Cotabato. However, the Iranun-Maranao, as Mednick notes, were very segmented. In 1776 Forrest listed no less than 33 sultanates dividing up a population of some 61,000 persons.[5] He noted that the Iranun or 'Illanon' resided near the 'great Lano' and were 'piratically inclined.' Forrest in his account of the Iranun also observed that 'on the banks of the Lano, are no fewer than 17 titled rajahs, and 16 who take the title of sultan, besides those on the coast.'[6] Ethnic groups such as the Samal

Laut and Yakan had no political sovereignty and were considered subject or client peoples.[7]

The Maguindanao homeland is in the lowland basin of the Rio Grande in the Cotabato Valley itself in southwestern Mindanao. The settlements of Tumbao, Dulawan or Datu Piang (once the site of the Buayan Sultanate) and Cotabato (capital of the Maguindanao Sultanate) emerged as the three major sovereign centers along the Pulangi. This fact is contrary to many historical reports which hold that there was only one center of power–the coastal population center of Cotabato, the traditional seat of the Maguindanao Sultanate.[8] In this geopolitical, physical, cultural, and regional setting, control of the seas and global-local trade were major preoccupations. The relative size and power of the various southwestern Mindanao sultanates illustrate this point. Mednick observed that it was no accident that the jurisdiction of the largest and most powerful southern sultanates, namely Maguindanao and later Sulu, extended far beyond what the eye could see.[9] There was a concerted effort by these states to spread Maguindanao and Tausog influence into non-state areas; areas with no previous foothold, for the belief was that the profits to be made from world commerce and economic growth were potentially far greater than those to be generated from within. While the sultanates of Maguindanao and Sulu controlled coastal areas, and sat athwart key trade routes, similar conditions did not prevail in Buayan, 35 miles up-stream, or among the Maranao of the lake region, where throughout most of their history control of the sea and coastal trade had not always been a major concern. Hence, the Maranao, cut off as a whole from coastal and seaborne trade, did not develop larger sultanates.[10] Much of this state building activity and internal transformation in southwestern Mindanao occurred in the seventeenth and eighteenth centuries in a region of increasing economic interdependence with the Spanish, Dutch and English colonizers and seafarers. Dulawan in the interior (*sa-raya* 'upper valley') and Cotabato on the coast (*sa-ilud* 'lower valley') came to be regarded as rival centers.

Early Spanish sources (late sixteenth century), however, show that Buayan was originally the principal settlement. The upriver center was believed to have fertile agricultural highlands and a ready source of labor power as the traditional upland agricultural horticulturalists in the

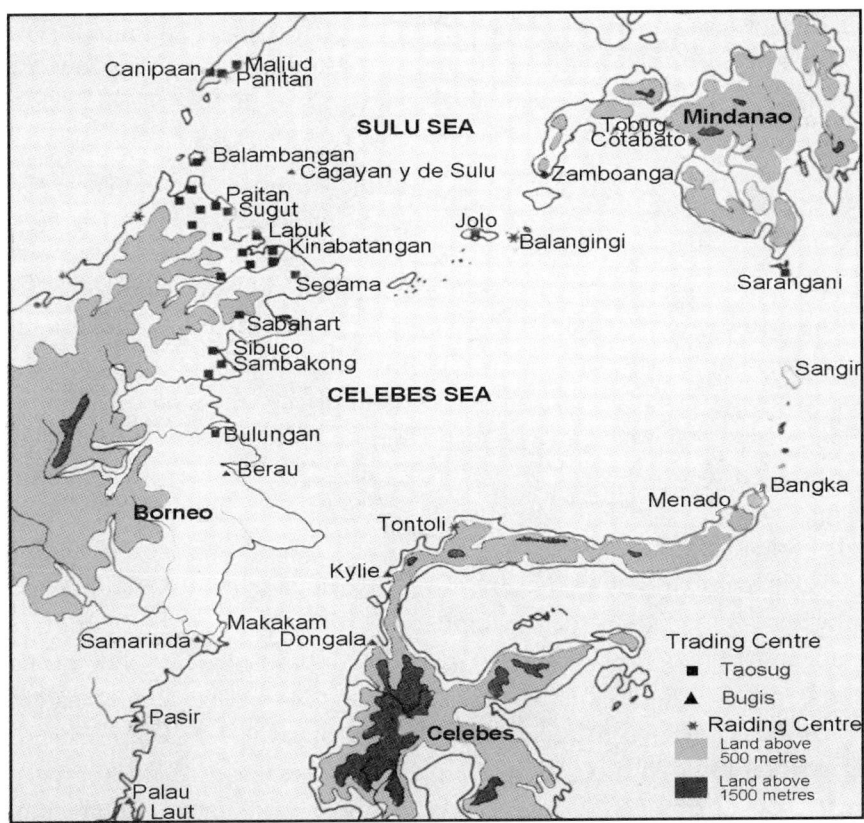

Sulu and Celebes Seas

Map 1. The Sulu Zone constituted a southeast Asian economic region with a multiethnic, precolonial, Malayo-Muslim state and an ethnically heterogenous set of societies of diverse political backgrounds and alignments. These diverse ethnic groups could be set within a strategic hierarchy of kinship-oriented stateless societies, maritime, nomadic fishers, and forest dwellers. In terms of world commerce and economic growth, the "Sulu Zone" was not an important region until the end of the eighteenth century.

remote forests of the highlands were regularly raided for slaves. The latter were used as tillers of the soil, bodyguards and objects of social reproduction and trade. For Ileto it was this combination of agriculture and labor-power which allowed for the "development of a wealthy ruling class in Buayan" and "would account for its early paramountcy."[11] The Spanish records note the military might of the Buayan cultural core. As an example they give an account of an expedition in 1596, led by Capt. Rodriguez de Figuero, which "met with a crushing defeat."[12]

Control of the coast and seas was not a central preoccupation of Buayan. However, when they attempted to do so, the goal was more to limit the ability of the coastal region and outside world to interfere unduly, rather than to harness its potential energies in the search for wealth and power. The Buayan were less tempted to spread their influence into new areas, for the belief was that by the beginning of the eighteenth century, profits to be made from within the interior hills and valleys were potentially greater than those to be generated from outside. Most Buayan needs were increasingly satisfied by downriver trade on which they became dependent and which was centralized under Maguindanao state supervision.

Henceforth, it was the English and Dutch traders of Bengal and Makassar, rather than the Maguindanao on the coast or the Iranun sea raiders, who constituted Buayan's greatest military threat. The threat came in the form of periodic European economic assistance on behalf of Maguindanao efforts to conquer parts of the upper valley. Ileto contends that shifts in population and trade patterns in response to the European intrusion in this period saw the rise of the Maguindanao Sultanate of Cotabato.[13] It is also significant that, in the first half of the seventeenth century, the structure and dynamics of statecraft in Cotabato largely worked themselves out at a time when the *presidio* of Zamboanga was abandoned and Spanish administrative activity in the area was almost nil. According to Laarhoven, this was Maguindanao's 'golden age,' which saw the rise of Sultan Kudarat, its most famous historical figure.[14] She notes that, by the beginning of the eighteenth century, the sociopolitical organization of the Maguindanao Sultanate, centered around the 'lords of the great river' and a sultan, a skillful sovereign, who ruled with the consent of his confederation of datus or lords and royal family members.

Given that the ultimate survival of the state relied upon negotiation and compromise, there was little room for tyranny. As Laarhoven observes "all major decisions were made with the consent of the secular and Islamic leadership."[15] She argues that these river lords had established a unified, stratified, agrarian-maritime bureaucracy that rested on principles of utilizing the natural resources of the environment, harnessing the labor of their subjects, and taking full advantage of the strategic geopolitical significance of their singular location for foreign trade. Ecology and demography buttressed a rising Islamic state whose danger zones lay to the north and south, confronting emerging Spanish and Dutch spheres of influence.

One major result of the rise of cross-cultural commerce and wars of rival empires of trade was a systemic shift to maritime raiding and slaving on a more general scale than before by the Maguindanao Sultanate. The accelerated growth of global trade, especially with the Dutch, led to the widespread practice of the acquisition of slaves, by way of purchase or warfare, as a labor force to collect products of the forests and seas as commodities for export. Because much of this activity took place at a time that coincided with the advent of large, standing, maritime populations of sea-faring, trading-raiding peoples throughout the Mindanao-Sulu region, the Maguindanao sovereigns, as Laarhoven and Ileto have shown, often had recourse to these particular people, whose skills and energies were enlisted for the procurement of exotic marine products and who, under the sponsorship of the sultanate and various lords, received encouragement to raid coastal shipping or neighboring shores in the Philippines and the Spice Islands.

Combes attributes the rise of the Maguindanao Sultanate to the aggregation of the seafaring Lutaos who lived on their boats and dressed in moorish robes, replete with turban and marlota. He believed that "their arms and worship were of Arab or Indian origin, but elsewhere points out their links with the King of Ternate."[16] Sopher disputes Combes' suggestion of Ternate-Moluccas origins and the political process of the identification of peoples with particular territories, but Ileto contends that "Dutch tactics were causing migrations of the original inhabitants to other places," thus lending more weight to Combes' argument.[17] The Lutaos were sea raiders and traders and were known to have fostered and maintained strong patterns of mobility and communication throughout the kingdoms of the area. They were highly regarded as being both extremely knowledgeable and versatile in fishing and raiding operations as clients of Malayo-Muslim states in the geopolitical setting of the eastern archipelago, and

> ... their services were sought after in wars, shipbuilding, navigation, and commerce.... The king who had the most Lutao followers was considered the most powerful and the most feared, for the Lutaos have power to invest the seas and coasts, making captives and pillaging, and making themselves masters of the crossings and passages necessary for communication with the other islands.[18]

In this competitive setting, maritime regional powers and cosmopolitan coastal mini-states contended with one another for the services of these Lutao seafarers profiting from their marauding, fishing and slaving to force better conditions of local-regional trade and colonization. Laarhoven, dividing the major ethnic groups into three geographical orbits, notes that at the beginning of the eighteenth century the Iranun and shore Samal occupied coastal areas around the Pulangi and Simaoy rivers, Suguru Bay and further around Ilana Bay. They then moved inland to large Lake Lanao in the southwestern corner of the Tiruray Highlands. She estimates that there would have been perhaps as many as 90 to 100,000 Iranun and Samal in the coastal areas.[19]

Political and economic activities, often initiated by these raiding groups who sought state support, were believed to be the primary reason for the Maguindanao Sultanate becoming so powerful and wresting control from Buayan. The Lutaos and Iranun gave the Maguindanao rulers of Cotabato maritime strength and the conditions for the appropriation of shells, pearls and fishing produce, albeit in the form of a standing state-sponsored fleet, whose endeavors and ultimate goal seem to have been the establishment of a Maguindanao regional order in the area by exacting tribute from local towns and consolidating global-local trade at Cotabato. Similarly, more than a century later, after the volcanic eruption in 1765 in southwestern Mindanao and the subsequent advent and rapid growth of the China trade, whole groups of Iranun and entire Samal populations, dissatisfied with their fate and life under the

Maguindanao Sultanate, moved to the Sulu archipelago where they became subject to the Sultan at Jolo.[20]

A key factor in the eighteenth century Maguindanao expansion was global trade which certainly provides the most convincing explanation of the origins of Iranun expansion and slaving to the north and south. Slave raiding was used to increase Cotabato's population. The mid-eighteenth century was a time of growing political instability and macro-conflict among rival European powers in Asia. The resulting region-wide economic competition led to an increase in trade with the Maguindanao Sultanate, which was an important source of exotic natural commodities for China, such as sea cucumber, bird's nest and cinnamon, as well as more mundane products such as wax and rice. The spread of large scale Iranun raiding by the mid-1750s implies the presence of something worth plundering, so the increased global trade with the Dutch and English also encouraged Maguindanao-sponsored Iranun marauding. By the second half of the eighteenth century, the Iranun had already begun to establish themselves in settlements like Tempasuk and Pandassan, west of the Sulu Sea. These villages were specifically established as forward bases for maritime raiding and the collection of slaves, that the Maguindanao and Tausog could use to procure and process natural commodities to supply western European traders for the China market.

At about the same time, pioneering Bugis merchants and slave dealers were entering the Sulu Sea from the south, skirting the coasts of the Sangir chain of islands and northeast Borneo. As a result, slaves captured by the Iranun also began to be transported by the Bugis and circulated in European colonial ports like Batavia and Makassar, giving the Iranun an added incentive to push their raids further north and west to tap directly into these lucrative colonial slave markets.[21] Ironically, as a substantial number of Bugis worked in the archipelago-wide slave trade and were therefore part of the machinery of enslavement and transportation, when the Iranun took Buginese vessels, as they did near Bugis and Dutch ports in the East Indies, slaves were sometimes part of the captured cargo, and were in turn treated as such, being traded or sold as commodities like any other in Cotabato or Sulu.

However, much of the commerce conducted by Maguindanao lords and merchants, Bugis and Chinese traders was short distance, involving the movement of goods to and from dozens of small ports and towns around the Mindanao and Borneo coasts and in the Sulu archipelago. A smaller number of international regional trade centers in the eastern archipelago also attracted merchants from Mindanao, Sulu, Sulawesi, and often even as far afield as Bengal and the south coast of China. Some of these centers were seasonal meeting places where Maguindanao, Tausog, Bugis and European, and Chinese merchants could trade by barter and procure slaves. These local market towns and smaller regional centers beyond Cotabato acted as outlets for the distribution of textiles, tools, weapons, and other articles of trade, that often were not available in the local communities.

Hence, Maguindanao trade with the rest of Southeast Asia increased in the eighteenth century, and encouraged the Iranun expansion. Maguindanao, on trading and raiding voyages, would have become acutely aware of the unguarded coasts and riches of the Philippines and eastern Indonesia, while the growing China trade, in the latter part of the eighteenth century, provided the incentive for the Iranun to establish themselves in north Borneo and the Sulu archipelago. Some Maguindanao lords made a living exclusively as merchant-traders, but many were part-timers who also engaged in agriculture, crafts and the sponsorship of maritime raiding expeditions. Slaves, the most valuable source of labor-power and goods, were initially acquired as plunder or tribute. Large numbers of slaves, captured in raids, came from the Philippines and the Moluccas. Colonial subjects were primarily seized as slaves from the Spanish and Dutch coastal territories, some of whom were traded for arms, textiles and opium with the Bugis and Chinese. Wealth flooded into Cotabato during the mid-eighteenth century. But in the late 1770s the commercial formation of the Maguindanao State was cut short by the sudden economic ascendancy of the Sulu Sultanate. The Tausog expanded their trade with China and the West and increased their strike force, labor power and population of seafaring peoples. Communities of Iranun, attracted away from the Maguindanao Sultanate, helped to establish a system of maritime raiding and redistributive trade that had very important consequences for the growth of Sulu's power and which, from one season to the next, yielded extraordinary profits to the Tausog.[22]

The sea was always a critical fact of life to the Tausog. Around the forested islands of Jolo and Pata, the Sulu Sultanate had several extensive areas with suitable soils for agricultural settlers, but these were only semi-steeped landscapes of volcanic soil located on medium-sized islands in the center of the archipelago. Agriculture elsewhere was restricted by the scarcity of arable land. A three-level class system, including 'lords' (*datu*), 'commoners,' and slaves (*banyaga, aata*) existed during the latter part of the eighteenth century. Class distinctions then were based more on power (*kawasa*) and wealth (*dayah*), and there was common recognition of the different lifestyles maintained by wealthy and powerful aristocrats who controlled the redistributive trade and sponsored Iranun raiding, as opposed to those who were comparatively poor.[23] The poverty of the land and the geography and ecology of the region's sea-world meant that trading was an essential source of livelihood to the Sulu Sultanate. The Tausog's double island chain straddled the main sea route from the South China coast to the fabled spice islands of the Moluccas, so it is not surprising that they first concentrated the pattern of their expansionist statecraft on the neighboring political rival center of Cotabato.

A key factor in the Tausog's ascendancy was Europe's globalizing trade with China. The West's search for suitable local commodities to exchange for Chinese tea is certainly the most convincing explanation of the origin of the Sulu Sultanate's startling regional expansion to the west and south.[24] The Tausog had a long history of direct contact with Borneo and Eastern Indonesia, and more remotely with China. The Maguindanao had similar kinds of contacts although they were more intense in the first three quarters of the eighteenth century. For the Tausog the singular wind and water geography of their archipelago as well as its ecology and demography enabled them to seize the moment to establish a regional focus and state space: a 'Zone.' Geography became destiny. The physical, cultural and geographical region encompassing the Sulu Sultanate now began to serve a particular interregional role. Its very location, ecology and internal social and political structures becoming an important part of the more general history of capitalist relations between the West and China. Thus, the Sulu Sultanate, as a trading, raiding and slaving state, in 'regional time,' gathered economic, ecological, demographic, technological and social impulses from around it, and retransmitted them in all directions around the region, in this way becoming a globalizing focus for many trends and developments.

In the late eighteenth century, Sulu served as a cross-cultural trading ground for English, Spanish, Portuguese, and American traders and Bugis and Chinese merchants and as a key marauding-outfitting center. The sultanate's strategic geographic position and its exploitable resources played a crucial interregional role. The gradual opening of China to western trade made Sulu's pivotal position in global commerce ever more powerful, both as a regional center of trade and in relation to dominion of surrounding areas—especially the neighboring territories and populations of the sultanates of Maguindanao and Brunei. But in 1768, a direct coercive influence was exercised upon Maguindanao navigation when the British East India Company attempted to intercept the Chinese junk trade with Cotabato and Sulu through the establishment of a competing port at Balambangan. In March 1775, a dawn raid by Tausog and Iranun that resulted in the destruction of this British East India Company factory, led to the onset of the decline of the Maguindanao Sultanate and the subsequent rise of Sulu as a regional emporium.[25] Sulu's salient geographical position and extraordinary military capability, due in no small measure to the windfall of weapons and munitions seized at Balambangan, enabled the sultanate to establish its commercial dominion, and also made the state the pre-eminent center for maritime raiding since the fall of Malacca. As an evolving regional power it now played that pivotal interregional role.

Once the junk trade was cut off—almost entirely diverted to Jolo—the Maguindanao found that a considerable number of Iranun marauders in the town of Cotabato and the ports of Simoay and Sarangani, were unable to find suitable employment and a market for their slaves. Apprehensive about their future prospects, these raiders began to desert the Maguindanao lords and Cotabato in droves and turn to slaving on behalf of the Sulu Sultanate.[26] In times of war in Southeast Asia, the outfitting of private ships to attack the vessels of hostile states was a form of officially sponsored privateering or 'piracy' that was common to the maritime states of the region. But, by the 1780s a rather different form of government sponsored maritime raiding—systematic and long range—was practised by the Iranun and Samal-Balangingi, who, in league with the Tausog, terrorized merchant shipping and coastal communities throughout Southeast Asia. The Iranun raiders operated out of southwestern Mindanao and Sulu ports such as Bual along the north coast of Jolo, and Bait Bait, on Pangutaran Island. Their targets were the passengers, crews and cargoes of the ships of many local states and colonial powers and the innumerable coastal village populations that stretched across the archipelago from New Guinea to Penang.[27]

The Tausog demonstrated even more far reaching power than their Maguindanao rivals by taking primary responsibility for creating a state-making raiding and trading system that became indispensable to the Iranun's way of life and survival. For the Tausog datus who sponsored the confederation of raiders resident in the Sulu Zone, maritime raiding was a form of economic statecraft, characterized by sophisticated financial operations which were linked to advancing war stores and provisions in exchange for captives that fell into the hands of the well armed Iranun. As the Sulu Sultanate expanded its commercial marauding activities, key members of the Iranun confederation and Tausog datus established raiding bases and commercial outposts along neighboring coasts, and even set up raiding bases in Sumatra as staging points for slaving in the straits of Malacca. The arrival of the Iranun and Samal raiders in the Tempasuk-Marudu Bay region of northwest Borneo brought large scale maritime raiding and slaving operations in the South China Sea and along the west coast of Borneo to new levels. The Brunei Sultanate lost control of the region as distant settlements, struggling in isolation and chafing under fear and neglect, joined the seafaring migrants to successfully plunder Brunei trading fleets, fishing boats and fishers off the Borneo coast.[28] However, the overall headquarters of these maritime raiding operations was at Jolo, where Tausog datus supplied the slavers with the most up-to-date weapons, ammunition, textiles, and opium obtained from western traders bound for China.

The Dutch East India Company (Vereeigde Oost-Indische Compagnie or VOC) was obsessed with wringing the maximum amount of profit from the labor of its colonial subjects in the Netherlands Indies, but especially in the spice islands beyond Java and Sulawesi. However, her severely limited naval forces concentrated on such vital ports as Batavia, Gresink, Cheribon, and Makassar, leaving peripheral settlements across the archipelago vulnerable to Iranun attack. Consequently, much of eastern Indonesia was to be scoured clean of labor power. At this critical juncture in the political and economic development of the Sulu Sultanate, Iranun marauding also evolved into large-scale slaving operations and conducted massive raids throughout the Philippines. Ironically, outside Sulu, this rise in maritime raiding was also a consequence of Bugis and Chinese market demand for slave labor in the Netherlands Indies. One British adventurer who visited Jolo, the chief town and seat of the Sultanate on the island of Sulu during this period, described it as, "the greatest slave-mart and thieves market in the whole East Indian Islands. The pirate fleets return here after their long cruises to sell their slaves and booty and buy supplies from the Chinese and Bugis merchants."[29]

The Iranun and Balangingi galley-like *prahus* roamed and plundered much of Southeast Asia without interruption in the opening decades of the nineteenth century. The most notorious feature of their wind-driven raiding operations was the systematic taking of captives who were either ransomed, sold as slaves in colonial cities hungering for labor, or exchanged at Jolo and Sarangani Island off the coast of southern Mindanao. As I showed in *The Sulu Zone*, the Tausog ran a highly organized state-making operation, taking captives from this confederacy of slave raiders in exchange for cargoes of weapons, luxury goods and staples, particularly rice. The division of the plunder was carefully regulated. The ransom or sale of captives was often conducted as a strictly commercial transaction under the auspices of the Sultanate or state, with a certain proportion of the proceeds going to the sultan and to key officials as well as a share to the captain and crew of the raiding prahu.[30]

It must be remembered that slaving and slave ownership were among the principal means of enlarging and consolidating the political influence and wealth of upwardly mobile Tausog, Maguindanao and Samal chiefs. Slave ownership provided labor power, prestige and more importantly, differential access to force and authority in the sociopolitical hierarchy of Tausog and Maguindanao society. High birth only assured social honor. A datu needed wealth to assemble prestige symbols and to attract followers—slaves and freemen—to achieve material well-being and gain political power.[31] The key to the high status of particular datus, who had a great deal of power and authority at this time, was control of global-local trade and the possession of large retinues of slaves and those 'freemen' who were neither datus nor had wealth, prestige or followers, and were not recently captured slaves.[32] Rennell provides some direct evidence from the mid-1760s of the increasingly important place of slaves in the Tausog social system. After a detailed discussion of the currency used by the Tausog, he wrote, "The substance or estates of the chief men consists chiefly in their number of slaves who procure their merchandise for them."[33] In a footnote, he observed that these slaves were "the inhabitants of a part of the Philippine islands that are taken prisoners by the Illanian."[34] A person who managed to acquire a sizeable number of slaves by acting as a leader of a slave raiding or trading expedition could rise into the datu class provided he had the validating symbols and the political power. Nearly half a century later, no person of means could apparently exist in Tausog society without at least a number of slaves to render services with respect to life and property. "There are many slaves in the different islands of the Sulu archipelago, but of their exact numbers no correct estimate can be formed although they are stated to amount to some thousands, a large proportion of whom are Christians. In the town of Sulu alone it is said that there are above 1,000 slaves. Every person who can possibly afford it possessed one or more of these unfortunate creatures, it being reckoned a mark of the most abject poverty and meanness of circumstance not to be provided with them."[35]

Significantly, the economic position of slaves in Sulu was not worse than that of freemen. Wilkes, the American naval commander, who visited Jolo in 1842, remarked, "Some of them (slaves) are quite rich, and what may appear strange, the slaves of Sulu are invariably better off than the untitled freemen."[36] The fact that the institution of slavery played such an important role in Tausog society was signified by the overwhelming slave presence in Jolo and elsewhere throughout the zone. In the celebrated 1838 Singapore trial of 'Illanun' slave raiders, Francisco Thomas, a rescued Tagalog captive, stated, in addition to what he had said in the Recorders Report at the trial, "that at Sooloo where he went on shore he saw many Christian slaves, meaning thereby natives of the island of Luconia (Luzon) and of others in that vicinity, a great portion of whom have been converted to the Roman Catholic faith."[37]

The slaves played an important sociopolitical and economic role in Tausog statecraft, society and culture as they were used for house, field, fishery, trading, raiding, and craftwork. Moreover, as long distance maritime raiding rapidly developed and became far better organized, slave labor supported this form of military organization and specialized communities that were always on a war footing. Those slaves, who were not sold abroad or retained to pull the oar of a prahu, as property of Tausog and Samal masters, did all manner of heavy work, including house and fort construction, boat building, harvesting tripang and pearl beds, fishing, and transporting rice and copra. Physically able men performed this labor. Menial work, the gathering of firewood, light agricultural tasks, and the collecting and processing of certain reef products was performed primarily by women and children.[38]

Many slaves had domestic roles and chores in aristocratic and trading households. They could earn small amounts of money, and arguably, they lived better than many of their kindred in the Philippines and Netherlands Indies, where colonial land and labor policies, and taxation, had created a class of landless, rootless poor. Some enterprising slaves even borrowed capital from their masters and organized trading expeditions in the zone eventually owning slaves themselves and earning enough to buy their freedom.[39] This strong demand for labor power meant captives and slaves were relatively easily assimilated within a remarkably inclusive system of kinship and social organization. The labor and skills of slaves, captured and transported by the Iranun and Balangingi, made possible the complex elaboration of economic, political and social patterns in the Sulu Sultanate, which characterized the way of life and statecraft of the datu class, and ensured their monopoly of trade goods and natural commodities, that became a crucial part of the global system of economic growth and interdependence with China and the West.

CHAPTER THREE

THE IRANUN IN THE SULU WORLD

Maranao was the language spoken by the southwestern Mindanao Muslims. The Iranun were a Maranao-speaking group that was culturally and linguistically related to the Maguindanao.¹ However, the Spanish label 'moro' tended to obscure both the nature and extent of internal ethnic differentiation between Iranun, especially those based in other parts of Southeast Asia, and other ethnic groups of Mindanao and Sulu. Laarhoven notes that the Iranun were linked through kinship and alliances to the Maguindanao.² Early Spanish and Dutch references to the Iranun attest to their encampments in the densely populated Lake Lanao basin, their military prowess and warlike nature, and their willingness to engage in slave raiding for the sultanate of Cotabato.³

The Iranun originally inhabited coastal stretches around the mouth of the Pulangi, polok (*polluc*) harbor, and further round the eastern shore of Illana Bay. By the start of the seventeenth century, thousands had also migrated inland to the lake and plateau region at the southwestern corner of the Tiruray Highlands. The maritime raiders, who, in the nineteenth century were labelled 'Illanun (Illanoons),' were, according to the Spanish, a distinct people, who inhabited the stretch of coast within the great bight of the Bay of Illana, from which they took their name, distinguishing themselves from other ethnic groups. This coast and Bay, whose shorefront constituted a continuous line of impenetrable mangrove and swamps, was readily linked to the great lake behind it, which the Iranun considered their stronghold and home, and hence they were termed by the Spaniards in Zamboanga and Manila a 'distinct race,' '*los Illanos de Laguna,*' or 'the Illanoons of the lake.'⁴ In 1762, Rennell also referred to the Iranun as a separate ethnic group, labelling them "savage peoples who inhabit parts of Mindanao."[5] Capt. Edward Belcher, an Iranun hunter, mentioning the threat posed by the Iranun as 'pirates' and slavers in the mid-1840s, noted they had a much closer relationship to the lake-dwelling Maranao than the coastal Maguindanao and maintained regular communication with the interior. He discussed the 'wild and independent character of the natives of the interior,' arguing that the 'dreaded tribe' of Illanoons are of the same 'stock'—only ethnically, culturally and linguistically 'crossed' to the Malays.[6] Several years later, close to mid-century, the Dominican chronicler and public intellectual Francisco Gainza described the independent maritime raiders living along the eastern side of Illana Bay, who called themselves 'Iranun,' in this manner:

> This large population, designated by some geographers with the name of the Ilana [Iranun] Confederation, in reality does not form a single political body except to defend its independence when it is found threatened . . . They live loaded with weapons; they reside in dwellings carefully encircled by barricades . . . and they maintain their bellicose spirit by continuously engaging in robbery and theft. Through piracy they strive to gather slaves for aggrandizement and to provide their subsistence. . . . In short, this particular society can only be considered a great lair of robbers, or a nursery for destructive and ferocious men.[7]

While the Iranun paid tribute to the Sultan of Cotabato, Laarhoven argues that the Iranun *datus* never submitted to the 'obeisance ceremony' despite recognizing the sultan as the titular head of a super-ordinate state—the sultanate of Cotabato.[8] The Iranun were indispensable allies of the sultanate, but they were generally regarded with some contempt and fear by Maguindanao royalty and portrayed to the Dutch and English, in the context of the politics of ethnic interrelations and state rivalries, as a deceitful, savage people. So poor was the early eighteenth century image of the Iranun that the English captain Silver branded them "murderers and man-eaters."[9] In September of 1775, Thomas Forrest, recounting the cession of Bunwoot Island to the English, confirmed his countryman's near century-old impression of the Iranun as a martial ethnic group—an ethnic community residing within the Cotabato

Sultanate's boundaries, but outside of its laws. He assured the Maguindanao riverine lord, Raja Muda,

> that it would be of greater satisfaction to the English to settle near him than in the Illano districts, where although he had sovereignty of all the islands . . . the Illanos had much power, on which we [the English] could not depend; while we could well depend on his protection.[10]

Forrest's late eighteenth century assessment of the emerging political and maritime strength of the Iranun, as a 'dangerous people,' was certainly correct. In the inland lakes and marshes they built and repaired their raiding prahus, which they conveyed to and from the sea by means of bamboo and rattan platforms and runners built on top of the yielding surface of the mangrove roots and branches–over which the vessels were hauled to and fro by slaves as occasion required. On Lake Lanao too, the Iranun resided on board their prahus with their wives and families, thus living apart from other shore-dwelling ethnic groups, seemingly as a separate and isolated community.[11]

Marauding and maritime slave raiding among the Iranun, from their own cultural-historical perspective, was considered an honorable occupation. Among them, there was no stigma associated with the cultural label 'marauder.' Hence, to be a maritime raider among the Iranun meant that it was the vocation not merely of sea warriors, but of merchants, noblemen, including datus and sherifs, and even sultans. Spanish naval officers familiar with the Iranun world saw them as 'born and bred' to a life of maritime marauding which they simply regarded as a means of living, and not as a notorious criminal occupation.[12] Therefore, no indigenous sailing craft they encountered on the high seas escaped their attack. The Iranun attitude towards marauding and slave raiding as a respectable occupation was perfectly exemplified by the opinion of Datu Laut, an important mid-nineteenth century Iranun lord, residing on the north west coast of Borneo:

> In his own view he was no criminal; his ancestors from generation to generation had followed the same profession. In fact, the Lanuns considered cruising as the most honorable of professions, the only one which a gentleman and a chief could pursue, and would

be deeply offended if told they were but robbers on a larger scale. . . . Notwithstanding his profession, Laut was a gentleman.[13]

Similarly, in January 1841, James Brooke observed a fleet of Iranun 'pirate' ships which, with the white rajah's permission, had gone upriver in Sarawak and remained for several days at anchor. The aspiring merchant adventurer was informed that their goal was to capture the solid gold figurehead from his brig, *Royalist*. Brooke says he did not believe the story, yet took every precaution to see that the ship was safe. He frequently discussed the 'crime of piracy' with these Iranun lords. They always replied that they were following the custom—*adat*—of their ancestors.[14]

Although many European observers, including Raffles and Brooke, referred to the Iranun as hereditary pirates, the 'calling' of marauding and long-range slave raiding had developed only in the eighteenth century. William Dampier, one of the most remarkable mariners of the seventeenth century, lived for seven months during 1686-87, among the Maguindanao and Iranun. Dampier, who crossed three oceans and four continents aboard a British privateering vessel, the *Cygnet*, was a gifted navigator and an exceptional observer and commentator on the unexplored lands he visited.[15] He wrote about Maranao society at the end of the seventeenth century with a certain amount of detachment and in meticulous detail. The term 'Iranun' or 'Illanun' had come to be applied to all Maguindanao—Sulu raiders of the late eighteenth century, but in Dampier's age the term Iranun applied only to someone who was part of the encampment on the great Lake Lanao. In this sense, many seventeenth century Iranun were not 'Illanoon' at all, but Maranao-people of the Lake—vigorous predatory farmers, traders and craftspeople. Slave raiding in this earlier period often extended overland into the interior of the large island of Mindanao. For many Maranao, Iranun and Maguindanao, slaving was a temporary occupation to which they resorted only long enough to acquire captives to work their lands and help them settle down. These hapless people were gained through capture, warfare or by other methods. The Maguindanao raided their tribal neighbors, the Tiruray and B'laans. The Iranun generally conducted raids to the east of the lake region and their victims were most likely the Manobos, Bagobos and Bukidnons.¹⁶ These raids were conducted by small bands of men, rather than by the large numbers and long ships usually deployed in the Iranun maritime raiding of the late eighteenth century.

In his admirable account, Dampier claimed that Iranun-Maranao society was prosperous and stable with a developed commercial life. He noted that they built "good and serviceable ships and barks for the sea." The Iranun traded with the Maguindanao in beeswax and gold from the interior of Mindanao, and received in return "their calicos, muslins and China silk."¹⁷ But, his observations of the Iranun that he visited are a revelation. Dampier wrote that while they were a 'martial race' that had built some 'ships of war,' he made no mention of any marauding propensities or of the terrifying attacks on the coasts of Southeast Asia so characteristic of a century later. Why then, after a century of relative obscurity, did Iranun warrior-aristocrats take to the seas of Southeast Asia to make such a dramatic impact on the population and history of the region? Before the end of the eighteenth century, scant documentation is available regarding the expansion of the Iranun-Maranao from the lake region to the southern coast of Mindanao. Until then, the Maranao remained little known to Spanish invaders, European travellers and traders because of their upcountry agricultural orientation. They were a people just beyond the pale, or out of reach. When Dampier, the English circumnavigator and buccaneer who took part in numerous attacks against the Spanish Manila galleons, visited Cotabato in 1686, he described the insularity of the Iranun-Maranao thus: "The Hilanoones live in the heart of the county; they have little or no commerce by sea, yet they have proe's that row with 12 or 14 oars apiece. They enjoy the benefit of the gold mines; and with their gold buy foreign commodities of the Mindanao people."¹⁸

Ninety years later, Forrest put his finger on one of the reasons for their migration. Natural disaster appears to have caused many Iranun-Maranao to move to the flood plain of the Pulangi River, the coast and beyond. He wrote of an ecological catastrophe in the form of an enormous volcanic eruption (circa 1765), that destroyed entire villages, fields, orchards, and animals. The devastation caused by the Maketering volcano forced groups of Iranun-Maranao to abandon their heartland and flee south and west. Some went short distances into Maguindanao territory.

> About ten years ago, one of the mountains, six or seven miles inland from their part of the coast, broke out into fire and smoke. . . . It ejected such a quantity of stones and black sand, as covered a great part of the circumjacent country, for several feet perpendicular. During the eruption of the volcano, the black sand was driven to Mindanao, the ashes as far as Sooloo which is about forty leagues distant; and the Illanon districts suffered so much, that many colonies went to Sooloo, even to Tampasook and Tawarran, on the west coast of Borneo, in search of a better country, where many of them live at (sic) this day.[19]

The region devastated by the Maketering volcanic eruption simulated a desert made up of thousands of hectares of scorched land rendered infertile by volcanic rubble and ash, or *lahar*. It must have looked just like a grey-black desert. Suddenly, tragically, their world had become smaller. Obviously, from Forrest's account, based on the experiences of eyewitnesses, there was no way to rejuvenate the area and help victims of the disaster to forge new local livelihoods. The consequences of the 1765 eruption for neighboring settlements and the Iranun provinces were enormous. Hundreds, perhaps as many as a thousand people were killed and thousands more were left homeless as volcanic ash and stone covered tens of thousands of hectares of farm land. Innumerable Iranun lost their traditional way of life, occupation and any hope of a future. The wasteland simply could not be rebuilt or rejuvenated in their lifetime. In May 1775, Forrest noted in a journal entry, the impact the dreadful eruption had made on the now 'dry harbor' of Tubug, a principal place for assembling Iranun raiding prahus.

> Large stones loaded many places, even at the sea side; and at Tubug, near Pulo Ebus, I have seen fresh springs burnt out, (at low water) from amongst black stones, of many tons weight, in various parts of that dry harbour. I was told that a river was formerly there, where is not the least appearance of one now. At present there seems to be a good deal of mold intermixt with the black sand, which is favourable

to vegetation; and the country hereabouts is now covered with long grass, called lalang. In some places are reeds eighteen foot high.[20]

Culturally accommodating, the independently-minded Iranun refugees' assimilation into Maguindanao lowland riverine culture proved somewhat difficult according to Forrest's account. Deprived of their former way of life, new fortified villages were built, and the Iranun began to play a far more important role in the unfolding Maguindanao-Tausog commercial world and rivalry–roaming the seas of neighboring coasts and seizing captives. As late as the early 1780s, however, a captive Spaniard who was ransomed at Pasacao, Camarines specifically made the point that the Iranun who were raiding the waters of southern Luzon were not from Sulu but Maguindanao.[21] Cotabato had a new powerful ally in these recently formed migrant Iranun communities and the sultanate's influence was felt straightaway as far west as the Zamboanga peninsula and as far south as the Sangir Islands.

Another possible cause for the out-migration of the Iranun-Maranao was their traditional system of hereditary ranked statuses. Some hereditary aristocrats sought strategic marriage alliances with neighboring Maranao and other communities in order to validate their rank and authority by descent lines. An immigrant Iranun-Maranao (or *I-Lanawen*) raja's claim to rank and privilege established an identity which transcended his own community.[22] His claim to authority was recognized in every community which was defined as Iranun-Maranao. The ties established through such marriages linked Iranun-Maranao speaking communities and other ethnic groups to form a social-political network, based on kinship, group solidarity and common culture, with no clearly defined spatial boundaries. The bond of common dialect, traditions and interlocking marriages tied Iranun communities on Southern Mindanao with those being established by warrior aristocrats on Jolo–and, for purposes of slave raiding, political assistance and war, with still others on the coasts of Borneo, Sulawesi and Sumatra. Other discontented, ambitious Iranun-Maranao sought to escape the pressure of subordination and state-making exerted on them by a highly stratified society and left the lake area to seek wealth, power and good fortune elsewhere.[23] It was these people who were attracted to Sulu's global economic expansion, and to the important potential for personal advancement that existed in maritime raiding.

The dense web of swamp, mangrove and forest between Lake Lanao and the coast acted as a buffer, an illegible nonstate space, in the struggle for power between the sultanates of Cotabato and Sulu.[24] At the end of the eighteenth century, many of the Iranun who were willing to join the slaving expeditions and fight, either for or against the Maguindanao, were recruited from within this impregnable 'wasteland.' Those Iranun who lived near Cotabato were influenced by Maguindanao language and custom.[25] The sources are not explicit, however, on the nature of the jural and political authority exercised by the Cotabato Sultanate over these resettled communities. Marriages were arranged between Maguindanao and Iranun of high social standing to provide the sultanate with political and economic support.[26] Forrest mentions the marriage of the eldest son of an Iranun raja to a daughter of the Raja Muda of Cotabato. He also witnessed many Iranun prahus enter the Pulangi River for a festival sponsored by the sultan of Cotabato on behalf of his granddaughter. It is clear though that many Iranun settlements were never under the sole jurisdiction of the sultan of Cotabato.[27] Iranun oral traditions confirm the more or less autonomous character of these communities whose inhabitants viewed themselves as of the first consequence or allies rather than dependents of the sultan.[28] When, in 1794, Sultan Kibad Sahrijal pledged his support to Spain, whole villages of Iranun had already willingly shifted their allegiance to the Tausog datus at Jolo.

The Iranun established settlements and mooring sites along the river-mouths of the southeast coast of Illana Bay from Punta Flechas to Polloc and along the west coast as far as Sindangan Bay.[29] Their cruisers were fitted out in the vicinity of the Bay of Iligan at Larapan in the north, and at Tubug and Tukurun in the south. Forrest described the harbor of Tubug as the chief point for the assemblage of marauding flotillas.[30] Behind the mangrove-screened wall of Illana Bay and in its innumerable inlets the Iranun lived-in, built, and repaired their prahus with impunity. Unable to return to their devastated plateau-basin, they evaded capture by the Spanish in these new, out-of-reach settlements because of the mangrove swamps and narrow river channels stretching out into the sea. The ingenious construction of bamboo scaffolds and track systems enabled them to rapidly remove their raiding craft from the water. Along the coast of the Bay, the Iranun built a series of camouflaged watchtowers in trees as a further line of defense. From the lake, in their prahus, they also pushed a passage northward via a small river which ran into the sea at Caygam-where there was a Spanish fort permanently inhabited by a company of soldiers. After getting clear, the Iranun, from the platforms of their prahus, often ridiculed the random musketry of the Spaniards, taunting the sentinels with loud shouts and gestures of defiance.[31]

On their passage seaward, when the Iranun had reason to suspect that a special lookout was being kept for them by the Spanish *faluas* stationed at Zamboanga and its neighboring environs, their patience and penetration were incredible. They moved their prahus cautiously along the edge of the mangrove banks at night—no matter how short a distance at a time—and hauled them up into the impenetrable mangrove stands before dawn. By persevering in their slow but steady movement night after night, while unseen lookouts were kept on the edge of the mangrove banks during the day, they finally gained their objective.[32] In the final decades of the eighteenth century, Spanish naval officers often confessed that their attempts to capture these coastal Iranun, who had suddenly been resettled on the local scene, had almost uniformly failed.

The Sulu archipelago also witnessed the dramatic appearance of Iranun communities that specialized in slave raiding. They had primarily left Mindanao to escape from the heavy burden of ecological disaster under the expectation that they were going to something better. These Iranun settled on the north and east coast of Jolo and on Basilan, and established clientage relationships with Tausog datus. In particular, Basilan, which is an island of very considerable size located directly between southern Mindanao, the Balangingi cluster of islets and Jolo, became a place of frequent resort for the Iranun. Some of its Samal Yakan inhabitants likewise became slave raiders from their birth, and it was not unusual for them to identify themselves with the Iranun as maritime marauders. Rennell noted in one of his journal footnote entries that "some of these Illanians [from Mindanao] are now settled at Basseelan of

Sooloo from whence they fit out their privateers."³³ Dalrymple, several years later, around the time of the Maketering eruption, annotating and amending his colleague's journal, added at the foot of the page: "many Illanos are now settled in Sooloo Dominions."³⁴ In the 1780s, many of these Iranun lived in distinct colonies or wards, with their own headman, *nakodahs* and blacksmiths, along with Visayan *renegados*, who had acquired the necessary expertise for successful slave raiding in Southeast Asia.³⁵

The Iranun wards at Jolo were responsible to the Datus Camsa and Anti in the last two decades of the eighteenth century. Almost all of the Sulu-based Iranun craft (upward of one hundred boats, large and small) that carried captives to Jolo were under the command of Camsa, the son-in-law of Sultan Sharaf ud-Din.³⁶ In April 1794, the frigate *Constante*, skippered by the Portuguese master Juan Carvallo, was in the roadstead of Jolo when three large *joanga*, armed with six and eight pound cannon, and each one with a crew of more than a hundred men, dropped anchor. Carvallo was obliged to lodge a complaint with the sultan on behalf of the Manila authorities, as it was public knowledge that the three raiding vessels belonged to his son-in-law, Datu Camsa. The sultan feigned ignorance of the matter and the vessels left for Bual that same night and unloaded their human cargo. Several days later, the cruisers returned to Jolo and were beached and careened outside Datu Camsa's house. One of them had been commanded by Datu Tabuddin, a son of Camsa, and another by a Visayan renegade named Impa.³⁷ Besides Camsa's family, the nephew of the second wife of the sultan and two of his sons also had an interest in outfitting Iranun raiding craft.

The sultan of Sulu exercised a tenuous authority over the Iranun who settled on Jolo through a carefully spun web of marital and political alliances. Incidents of indiscriminate maritime raiding carried out by Iranun–individually and collectively–without the sultan's sanction were widespread throughout the period under consideration. Still it was in his interest to provide them with a market for their captives and booty. More serious problems occasionally arose when the sultan's authority was openly challenged by the independent behaviour of powerful Iranun. In 1772, Mohammad Israel banished a group of raiders from Jolo because they had endangered the interests (presumably trade) of aristocratic

Tausog.[38] Before 1795, Camsa's near total control of Iranun expeditions that used Jolo as a base of operations also led other Tausog datus to conspire against him and expel him from Sulu.[39]

At the end of the eighteenth century, the Iranun population of the Sulu Sultanate experienced rapid economic growth, as Tausog datus, heavily involved in the China trade, became 'silent partners' in maritime raiding expeditions. More interested in the redistributive and exchange aspects of slave raiding, datus advanced the outfits and, equally importantly, provided a market at Jolo for captives and all spoils taken. In 1774, Forrest described many of Jolo's inhabitants as *orang Illano*, "who live in a quarter by themselves."[40] Iranun expansion was in character with the profound social and economic changes then occurring in the global economy of the Sulu Sultanate. Spanish reports covering the period 1774-1795 show the ever-increasing opportunities for the Iranun to settle, trade and equip vessels at Jolo.[41] With the growth of world trade to Sulu, the Cotabato Sultanate continued to decline, and it became a Tausog practice to invite groups of Iranun to settle in the Sulu archipelago for the purpose of slave raiding.

In 1814, Hunt listed the Iranun communities in the Sulu archipelago from which slaving attacks were launched against the Visayas and Sulawesi. By then several thousand resettled Iranun were exclusively engaged in maritime raiding and slaving.

Table 1: The Iranun Communities in the Sulu Archipelago (1814).

Location	Kampong/ Ward	Jurisdiction/ Leadership	Size of Male Population	No. of Raiding Prahus
Jolo Town	Subyon	Datu Molok; Datu Bukon	600	20
Jolo Island	Bual	Raja Muda Buling Panglima Daud	1,500	30
Tulayan Island			300	
Pilas Island			300	10
Pangutaran Island	Bait-Bait	Orang Kaya Malik	Many Iranun	
Basilan			300	
Balangingi Island			Many Iranun	
Tunkil Island		Datu Timbing	500	10
Tawi-Tawi		Maguindanao Datu	300	10
Palawan	Babuyan		600	20

The table is based on information compiled by Hunt for Stamford Raffles. I have listed only those communities designated as Iranun. The other 'piratical establishments' mentioned by Hunt were predominantly Samal-speaking communities, notably the small islands of Balangingi and Tunkil, which clearly also had many Iranun residents.[42] After the 1830s, while the entire Sulu group was still subject to visits from the Iranun from time to time during their extended voyages, they were no longer in the habit of stopping over at any permanent settlements except those at Basilan, Jolo and Balangingi. They generally obtained their supplies of ammunition either at Jolo or by trafficking with other Iranun communities and bases, which were in communication with various small Dutch settlements on the coasts of Borneo and the adjacent islands.

From 1820 to 1848 when global-local trade was firmly controlled by the Tausog, some of the descendants of the late eighteenth century Iranun migrant-settlers shifted their ethnic affiliation as their raiding communities grew and became more ethnically heterogeneous. Daniel, an Iranun warrior, made the following statement in prison shortly before his trial in Singapore in 1838:

> By birth I am an Illanoon and for years have resided at Ballangninghin [Balangingi]. For six years I have been pirating near Macassar, Myungka, Yan Le Lah, Seah-Seah, Tambulan, and other places. Panglima Alip is the chief of Ballangninghin, he is under the Sultan of Sulu. I cannot pretend to say whether the Sultan and Panglima Alip give any directions touching the fitting out of piratical fleets, but the fact is save 'mangoorays (pirating) we have scarcely any other means of getting a livelihood.[43]

By 1838, most of the 29 members of Daniel's ill-fated crew, and many others did not call themselves 'Iranun' but went by the place-name of their village or island, attaching it to their ethonym–*a'a Balangingi*, 'the people of Balangingi' or *a'a Tunkil*, 'the people of Tunkil.' On Jolo, some, by virtue of their raiding exploits, climbed out of their Iranun identity, and adopted Tausog ethnicity. Other Iranun communities remained discrete, unassimilated–so much so that at the beginning of this century they could still be recognized as a separate kind of people in many localities.[44]

CHAPTER FOUR

THE RAIDS, 1754-1838

Introduction

The Iranun burst quite suddenly into Southeast Asian history in the second half of the eighteenth century with a series of terrifying raids and attacks on the coasts and shipping of the Philippines, the straits of Malacca and the islands beyond Sulawesi. Their primary targets were unprotected coastal settlements and sailing boats that travelled throughout Southeast Asia bringing valuable commodities from China and the West back to the most remote parts of the archipelago. Many of these marauders were sponsored by rulers from the trading states of Cotabato, Sulu, Siak, and Sambas. They were soon described as 'Lanun' or 'Illanoon'–'pirates'–by those who suffered their depradations or either travelled with or hunted them and wrote about their widespread impact on the Southeast Asian world.

It is estimated that during the last quarter of this century (1774-1798) of maritime raiding and conflict against the Dutch and Spanish, between 100 and 200 seaworthy raiding *prahus* set out from the Mindanao-Sulu area each year. The sheer size of the vessels–the largest *joanga* measuring upward of 130 feet in length–and the scale of the expeditions dwarfed most previous efforts, marking a significant departure in the naval strategy of Malay maritime raiding as it had been traditionally understood.[1] The Iranun were far more than mere 'pirates' or brigands. The colonial powers and precolonial Malay trading states had to reckon with a dominant force in their own right; a force that was capable of inflicting major defeats on the Spanish and Dutch and toppling local kingdoms. The huge numbers of these skilled sea raiders and slavers that the sultanate of Sulu could mobilize during the heyday of the China trade would henceforth have a profound impact upon Southeast Asia's history.[2]

The geographical range of Iranun-Balangingi slave raiding activity was enormous, spanning all of Southeast Asia and beyond. Until the latter part of the eighteenth century, the *joanga* of the Cotabato and Sulu Sultanates were more or less integrated into fleets belonging to the respective sultanates, but by the end of the century many Iranun vessels were also operating independently. Iranun prahus sponsored by both states had their own target areas but inevitably, there was some overlap. Cotabato and Sulu raiding vessels cruised between the Visayas and Luzon, and out into the South China Sea. Those from Tempasuk, on the northwest coast of Borneo, harassed shipping to the west of the huge island itself. Samal Balangingi, situated midway between the Iranun communities in Mindanao and those on Borneo, operated vessels throughout the Philippines and in the central and eastern parts of the Netherlands Indies.[3]

Iranun maritime raids affected virtually the entire coastline of Southeast Asia, and even stretches of New Guinea and the Bay of Bengal were not secure from slave raids. In the east, the Iranun sailed down the Makassar Strait to cross the Java Sea and South China Sea to attack the north coast ports on Java and the large tin mining island of Banka. Iranun raided extensively in the Sangir Islands, Halmahera and, to a lesser extent, in the Moluccas. They also pushed beyond the defended limits of the Southeast Asian world, crossing the South China Sea to attack undefended stretches of the coastlines of Thailand and Cochin China. At the opposite extremity they also raided, but failed to dominate, the dangerous coasts of New Guinea. In the 1790s, Iranun slave hunters in search of captives extended the limits of their known world even further, sailing far into the waters of the Bay of Bengal, touching at the Andaman Islands and perhaps exploring the southern coast of Burma. There seemed no practical way for the colonial powers to link their respective 'dominions' together in an island-wide network of defense and communication, and consequently the Iranun made the

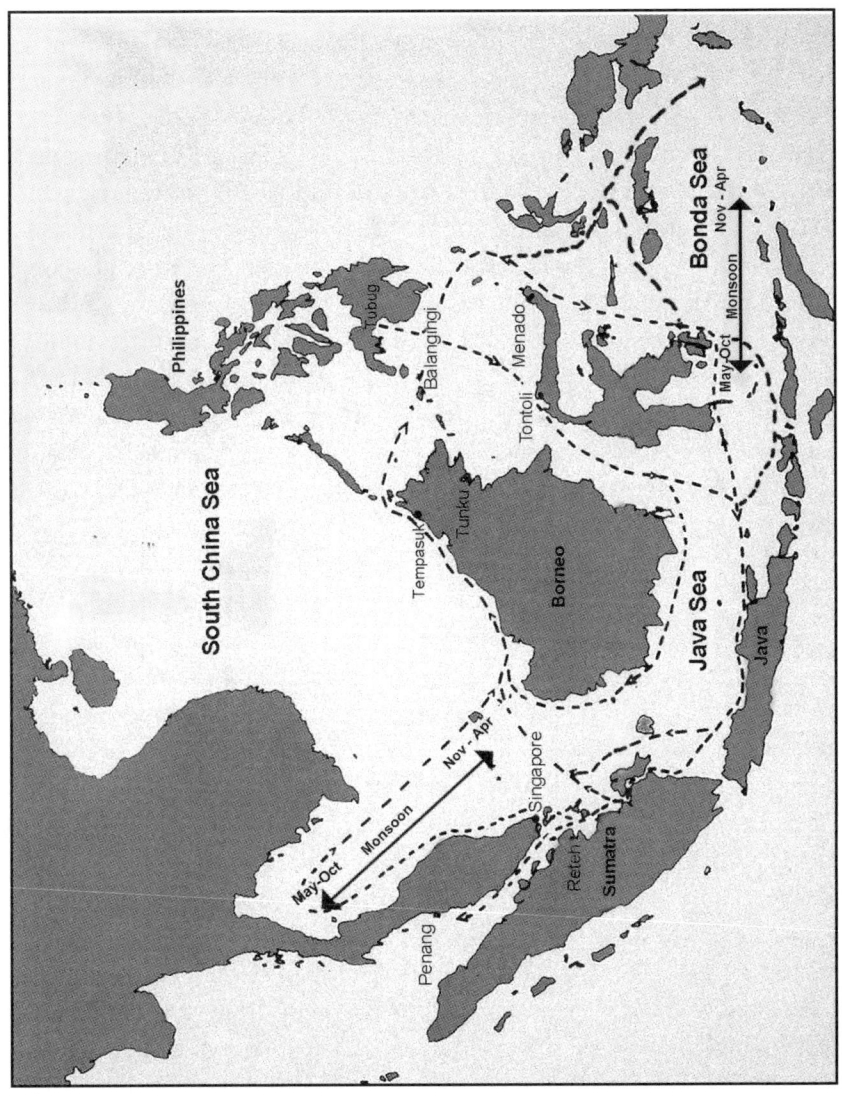

Map 2. Slave raiding outside the Philippines in Southeast Asia.

most of the ill-defined seas and ravaged the coastal populations and commerce. James Brooke was still faced with this far-flung maritime raiding activity in the 1840s. Under his rule, Sarawak also became the scene of increased Iranun slaving and marauding, and he noted that the cruising grounds of these sea raiders were extensive. "They regularly make a circuit of Borneo and travel as far south as the Celebes as well as to Tungana [Trengannu], Callantan, Patani and Jillalo."[4]

In the second half of the eighteenth century many Philippine ports, towns, shipyards, and monasteries were not adequately defended while others were totally defenseless. From the mid-1750s onward, the scale, ferocity and unexpected nature of the initial wave of Iranun attacks were deeply disturbing. Thousands of Filipinos perished or were seized as captives; the more so as the Iranun were Muslims and recognized none of the accepted conventions and taboos that were meant to protect the property and personnel of the Catholic Church in times of war between Christians. The mobility of their huge, well-armed ships made the Iranun attacks doubly terrifying, as they could strike almost without warning anywhere on the coast or on navigable rivers throughout the Philippine archipelago. Francisco Mallari, a Jesuit historian, documents in meticulous detail that the southeastern extremity of Luzon, including the islands of Masbate, Ticao and Burias on its southwestern side and the island of Catanduanes on its eastern flank was, from the mid-1750s to mid-1830s, the site of repeated Iranun slave raiding and plundering.[5] In 1754, Iranun raiders laid waste to coastal communities in Bicol and nearby islands such as Maestra de Campo and Burias, and looted Churches and monasteries to acquire captives for the slave markets or ransom, as well as portable wealth and food. Three years later, the Iranun attacks became even more extensive and, according to church reports, reduced the number of Filipinos paying tribute to the Spanish government by at least 100,000.[6] This terrifying period of Iranun slave raiding activity, which lasted more than 70 years from roughly 1752 to 1832, severely hampered the overall social and material well-being and growth of the Philippine island world and the colonial state.

Having gained considerable confidence and skill during their repeated attacks on the Philippines over several decades, Iranun sea raiders soon began looking beyond the waters of southern Luzon in search of captives. Times were increasingly hard for the Dutch East India Company once the British East India Company had established the country trade at Sulu in the 1770s. The English were now vying to fill the vacuum left by the erosion of VOC power in the straits of Malacca and elsewhere. They turned a blind eye to the raiding activities of the Iranun in the straits of Malacca as long as Britain's geopolitical objectives were furthered. The English wanted to wrest long-standing control of the strait, a major 'choke-point,' with its seaboard prosperity and the monopoly of the tin trade centered on Banka, from Dutch hands. The islands of Banka and Billiton and the regular sailing of coastal trading fleets made the area of the strait of Malacca, rich in mining, shipping and finance, a new lucrative cruising ground for the Iranun. Banka, Billiton and Singkep islands and the coastal states of the Malay Peninsula all beckoned—'countries to west' as the Iranun called them. As the sultanate prospered, in sailing from the Sulu archipelago, the Iranun first touched at Tempasuk, and then proceeded to Karimata, where they dispersed in various directions. Some scoured the coasts of Banka and adjacent ports; some went up the east coast of the Malay Peninsula extending their attacks as far north as the coast of Cochin China; while others proceeded up the straits of Malacca, continuing their hostilities northward of Kedah.[7]

The Iranun were also key protagonists in the global-regional struggle for trade supremacy in the Sulawesi area, and the islands flanking it to the east. As slavers and traders, the Iranun were made welcome in out of the way ports such as Toli Toli, Kylie, Donggala and in small kingdoms, like Tobungku, that were struggling to maintain their independence and 'clandestine' trade against the Dutch East India Company. Cross-cultural commerce, maritime raiding and slaving by the Iranun contributed to the common cause of the English and these local mini-states, to oust the Dutch, not only by capturing cargoes sorely needed by VOC settlements and outposts, but also by forcing the Dutch to disperse their naval forces—thus preventing them from readily attacking the well defended coasts of independent local states and shipping. Forrest and others have produced a vivid record of Iranun maritime raiding exploits directed against Dutch colonial settlements and large numbers of more remote villages with only limited defenses, which stretched from Sangir and the east coast of Sulawesi to the Moluccas and coastal stretches of Timor and the Aru islands.[8]

Iranun Raiding in the Malacca Straits

The direction of early Iranun marauding and maritime expansion was primarily to the west, along the coast of Borneo and the island and delta areas of east Sumatra. It was from Jolo and the satellite communities of Tempasuk and Reteh that the Iranun systematically raided the Malacca Straits at the end of the eighteenth century. The Iranun were initially depicted by the Dutch as maritime raiders when a small fleet was reported attacking Banka in 1783.[9] However, the Malay language history of Riau, the *Tuhfat al-Nafis*, chronicles the real coming of the Iranun to the Malacca Straits, telling of Dutch efforts to wrest control of the valuable tin trade from the Bugis, and of the Malay Sultan Mahmud's decision to summon the Iranun of Tempasuk, in northwest Borneo, to assist in expelling the Dutch from Riau. Mahmud sent a mission, headed by an emissary called Talib, to Tempasuk with a letter for the raja of Tempasuk.[10] In May 1787, led by Raja Ismail, these sea raiders crossed the South China Sea in big heavily armed prahus, 80 to 90 feet long between stem and stern, which indigenous and European observers henceforth called *lanong*, and which successfully assaulted the Dutch garrison.[11]

Seventeen years later, when the British East India Company's economic project against the Dutch in Southeast Asia was being recognized as a major political achievement, castaway and biographer David Woodward decided to write a book about his extraordinary adventures in Sulawesi in the early 1790s. In 1793, sailing as chief mate of the American ship *Enterprise* bound from Batavia to Manila, he was stranded for several years on the west coast of Sulawesi north of Makassar. Woodward profiled the robust, elderly, urbane man living in the west coast village of 'Dungally' (Donggala)–a man who had struggled to save him from enslavement by the coastal chiefs. When Woodward encountered him, Tuan Haji, Thomas Forrest's guide, aged about 60, had travelled far beyond New Guinea to Bengal, Bombay and Mecca, and he was still functioning as a key individual both inside and outside the archipelago-wide web of reigning Iranun lords and cosmopolitan Malayo-Muslim States with trade-based economies–befriending and servicing them, whenever required. However, political and economic success ultimately was to prove Tuan Haji's downfall. The ageing 'great pirate' told Woodward that, in May 1787, he had personally commanded a lanong in the celebrated Iranun–Bugis raid on the Dutch fort at Riau, but the triumph of the project had proved hollow for him, as his vessel was sunk, leaving him impoverished.[12]

The Iranun fleet of warships commanded by Raja Ismail joined forces with Bugis and Malay mariners and spearmen under the command of Mahmud and launched a massive attack on the well-fortified garrison. While the lanongs stood offshore, including Tuan Haji's ill-fated prahu, the Iranun marines laid siege to the fort. According to the Dutch account of the attack, the Iranun deployed their forces in a skillful fashion and surrounded the garrison with their portable cannons. The Dutch command surrendered after securing terms that would permit the remaining troops safe passage to Malacca.[13] Fear of Dutch reprisal led Mahmud to hastily abandon Riau as his residence, but shortly after the surrender, the visiting Iranun ships were able to sail away with impunity, their holds filled with slaves. They did not fear Dutch retaliation and remained to settle in discrete communities on the east coast of Sumatra. These Iranun mercenaries now filled the power vacuum created in that vital part of the archipelago by declining Dutch and Bugis fortunes. Between the Jambi and Indrageri rivers, there sprang up large fortified Iranun communities—Reteh and Saba—as well as a number of small villages. According to the *Tuhfat al-Nafis*, the Inuk River in the Reteh area became the principal base for Iranun maritime raids. By 1790, Iranun bases could also be found in Riau, Jambi, Pulau Berhala, Tungkal, and Air Hitam, while still other Iranun lived in their prahus or were scattered in small clusters of huts along the tributaries of mangrove-lined east coast rivers.[14]

The desire of the Iranun to exploit the numerous vessels and mercantile activity then developing in the South China Sea was a primary reason for the founding of these satellite communities. The burgeoning market in China for exotic commodities—bird's-nest and sea cucumber or *tripang*—was creating new trading opportunities on the coasts and adjacent islands of the Malay Peninsula with the South China Sea acting as the major thoroughfare. For this reason, Reteh was strategically situated across the straits due south of Malacca and Penang, the latter a newly-established British trading station. It was an ideal location for launching attacks upon the nearby islands of Bangka and Billiton with their rich deposits of tin, which the British East India Company was anxious to monopolize for sale in China. This expansion of routes of the global economy with China and the straits, that, in the last quarter of the eighteenth century carried far more valuable shipping than the atrophying prahu lanes between the Moluccas and Sulawesi, was an important factor behind the Iranun raids in the decades that followed.

Frequently, in sailing from Jolo for the straits, the Iranun first visited Tempasuk. The origins of this settlement are not as clear as Reteh. Spanish sources have emphasized that Tempasuk was founded by Tausog, probably towards the middle of the eighteenth century, and heavily settled in the following decades by Iranun from Mindanao.[15] This point of view suggests that among later migrants were those who fled the devastation of the Maketering volcano. Oral traditions, on the other hand, explain the arrival of the Iranun at Tempasuk in a different way, stating that the original leaders of the Iranun settlement were sent to Tempasuk under a political commission from the Sulu Sultanate.[16] But, one thing is certain, the Iranun were strong enough by the 1790s to drive the Tausog out of Tempasuk and establish their own sphere of local influence.[17] Thereafter, the commanders and crew of the Tempasuk raiding vessels were no longer authorized by a commission of the sultan of Sulu to capture the trading vessels of hostile states. The Iranun of Tempasuk, after 1790, were independent mercenaries or privateers because their joangas were private ships in private ownership as opposed to raiding ships belonging to wealthy Tausog sponsors or to the sultan of Sulu. No sovereign or state owned the lanongs of Tempasuk.

From Tempasuk, Iranun prahus made the journey to Karimata from where they sailed in different directions. That the slave raiding activities and marauding of the Iranun in the Malacca Straits threatened the commercial interests and political aspirations of the English and Dutch there is no question. Official despatches from Penang, which was founded in 1786 as an entrepot for the trade of Bengal with China, stressed the necessity for armed cruisers to protect from the Iranun, the hundreds of coasting prahus that frequented its port.[18] These records also show that the Iranun were frequently willing to join forces with, and sell their services to, neighboring Malay rulers to mount politically motivated raids. In 1789, Syed Ali, a noble of Siak, with the aid of an Iranun squadron, attacked Songkhla on the southeast coast of Siam and severed overland communications between the Malacca Strait and the South China Sea. The Iranun raiders burned down the town, seized two junks, and carried off a large number of people.[19] The following year, an Iranun fleet from the Mindanao-Sulu region, consisting of 18 lanongs with heavy artillery and 30 smaller craft and carrying about 1,000 men, attacked the Dutch factory at Perak. The fleet was repulsed.[20] By a curious turn of events, Penang also became the strategic target of this Iranun campaign, which at first had been directed only against Dutch settlements in the Malay Peninsula. Sultan Abdullah of Kedah in his struggle with Francis Light over the territory of Penang used the presence of the Iranun to spread fear and havoc in neighboring areas. The sultan seeking regional security and financial compensation from the East India Company was prepared to forcibly remove Light from the island if demands for adequate compensation, rent and protection were not granted. Wanting to drive the English out of Penang, he sent an emissary to the commander of this fleet when it arrived in Kedah waters. At the sultan's behest, the Iranun raja agreed to attack Penang at night and massacre the English garrison, in return for $20,000 and a guarantee of rapid assistance if they failed in their attempt to take the fort by surprise.[21]

The story of this combined Iranun-Malay raid against the Dutch settlements at Perak with its sequel, the abortive attempt against Penang, was graphically related in Light's dispatch, to Commodore Cornwallis, 11 December 1790:

> Our apparent enemies are called Lanoons and consist of 37 large prows from the island Maguindanao, one of the Philippines and twenty-five others from various places, this fleet sailed from Siak a river on Sumatra opposite Malacca to the attack at Pera.... The enemy, who was hoping for support from the Malays in Pera, finding none departed and returned a few days later to burn the houses at the river mouth.

They were consequently followed for a considerable distance and according to Light,

> The next news I heard . . . the King of Queda has staked the mouth of his river and laid a chain across, at the same time he admitted the Lanoons into Lolar River which is close to Boonting Island and under the pretence of fear has stopped all supplies from coming here. The people in general are of the opinion that he has invited them.[22]

The planned allied raid fell through because the English had learned of their movements beforehand, robbing the 'Lanun' of the element of surprise. Instead, Light struck first against Abdullah, attacking during the night with his own troops. The sultan suffered considerable damage to his force and reputation, but the Iranun emerged from the fiasco unscathed and their constant formidable presence just opposite Penang created fear and confusion in the port for several months.[23]

The Iranun were active in the south as well. Each year some sailed with their kindred at Reteh to the Lampongs and the southern coast of Java to harry villages and gather birds' nest among the coastal rocks.[24] When the east wind began to blow, they cruised their favorite hunting ground in the Gelasa Strait, searching for Javanese trading prahus bound for Malacca, and descended along the coasts of Banka and Billiton in search of slaves and tin. As tin mining spread to Banka there was a noticeable rise in the number of ships plying the waters around the ore-rich, large island. The population estimates of Chinese miners on Banka in the 1780s vary from 6,400 to 13,000.[25] Since the Palembang Sultanate and the immigrant Chinese had risked basing their regional and local economies almost entirely on the mineral wealth of the island, the singular achievement of constant devastating raids dealt a near fatal blow to the miners and the sultanate's already weakened economy. Between 1792 and 1804, Bangka, in particular, was subject to repeated attacks that resulted in the desolation of the eastern part of the island.[26] The 'Lanun' raiders ascended the coastal rivers, attacking interior settlements that hitherto had been considered safe, and crippled the production of the tin mines by carrying away hundreds of Chinese, Malays and Javanese. Settlements could be relocated and stockades constructed to stave them off, otherwise the only alternative was to flee.

The first Iranun attack was directed against Sungailiat in 1792.

Three years later, the attack was repeated but the community had since built a stockade which the raiders could not overpower. In a third effort, they undertook a siege of the stockade but were repulsed by the miners. The Iranun abandoned this part of the east coast and concentrated their activities on the southern extremity of the island where the population was known to be unprotected by forts or stockades. They established themselves in the Kapu River and worked their way around the coast from one river mouth to the next towards Toboali. Settlements along the way offered little resistance and their inhabitants were seized as slaves. Villages along the west coast were deserted before the Iranun would reach them; many families fled inland or to the northern part of the island. From the security of the Banko-Kutto, Selan and Kapu rivers, the Iranun gradually increased their strength and at last attacked and overcame Koba, the nearest settlement on the east coast. They extended their raids further north commanding the mouths of the rivers Koba, Kuru and Pangkul and attacked the important interior settlement at Paku. Nor were Pangkalpinang and Tirah spared as several hundred families were taken into captivity, while others, fleeing ahead of the raids, perished in the interior from malnutrition and disease. The survivors fled to the northern districts where they eked out a precarious living.[27]

The Iranun established themselves in the rivers on the western and southern coasts and their numbers and strength increased over the years. In some parts of Banka as well as Billiton and Singkep, either slaves or cowed local leaders worked tin mines on behalf of absentee Iranun 'overlords,' who had become actively involved in the global-commodity trade. In other cases, they entered directly into the local tin trade forming associations and partnerships with powerful individuals, such as Panglima Raman, who also assisted the Iranun in organizing raids on coastal settlements and shipping and shared the proceeds.[28] Many people fled the islands and a number surrendered themselves to the Makassar-Bugis slave dealers who visited Banka rather than face the famine and pestilence which followed the cycle of repeated raids and plundering.[29] By the time they began to gradually withdraw after 1804, there was little left on Banka for the Iranun, but on their long cruises they continued to visit the island until the 1840s. The *Chronicle of the Netherlands East Indies* for 1820 mentions that during the month of August the Iranun "had made themselves masters of some tin districts in the southeast part of that island, and that they had even erected mud-forts (bentings) upon several points, under the command of Raden Kling of Palembang."[30]

The establishment of the free port of Singapore in 1819 further lured the Iranun to the Straits Settlements and these sea raiders threatened Singapore's early trade with neighboring Malay States. A major concern was the growing number of Iranun interlopers, especially from Sambas, who were battering coastal towns and settlers in the islands near Singapore. Fewer Malay and Bugis prahus sailed, and their captains watched with paralytic rage as numerous Iranun Sambas fleets turned the strait of Malacca into a gauntlet. In the meantime, Singapore itself was left with little protection.[31] East India Company resources, preoccupied with a war in Burma and elsewhere on the subcontinent, were at an all-time low. Iranun slavers were made welcome in out-of-the-way places like Sambas, under the rule of Sultan Annas, and Tempasuk, which fitted out large numbers of straits-bound raiders. Both haunts were still sufficiently far away from Singapore and the east coast of the Malay Peninsula, where large numbers of coasting prahus and Chinese junks exported valuable cargoes of rice, cocoa, timber, textiles, ceramics, and opium. By 1828, when Presgrave compiled his report on the threat of piracy, the fragile nascent economy of Singapore was at its lowest ebb since coastal traders had introduced the convoy system to ward off the mounting tempo of attacks by Iranun from Reteh, Sambas and Tempasuk.[32] Two years later, in 1830, the lack of security on the east coast of Malaya prevented the *nakodah* of trading boats from Patani, Kelantan, Pahang, and Trengganu from making their accustomed voyages to Singapore.[33] Bugis traders, on whose traffic Singapore greatly depended, threatened to desert it altogether and seek other ports. These nakodahs sarcastically criticized English officials for their restraint in dealing with the Iranun and drew their attention to the earnest measures their Dutch counterparts were taking to destroy the 'Maguindanao' and 'Sulu Zeerovers.'[34]

Iranun Raiding in Sulawesi and the Moluccas

The Dutch East India Company monopoly of trade in the lesser Sunda group and the Moluccas restricted the traditional commerce of the

Maguindanao and Tausog with their immediate neighbors to the south and east. The Iranun are of central importance in the second half of the eighteenth century because of their exceptional ability to both disrupt and foster regional trade in an area like eastern Indonesia by attacking Dutch garrisons and preying upon their commerce. Between the late 1770s and early 1820s, large bands of Mindanao and Sulu-based Iranun began operating from islands and ports around Sulawesi. Some of them had initially moved to places like Toli Toli and Tobungku with the tacit encouragement of the British, who silently authorized them to attack the Dutch at sea and on land. Because of their seaborne strength, mobility and an established web of kinship links that extended from the sultanates of Siak and Sambas in the west to Cotabato and Sulu in the east, the Iranun often presented virtually the only challenge and obstacle to Dutch efforts to strangle indigenous seaborne commerce and economic growth. They helped forge and maintain region-wide alliances and networks based on maritime raiding, slaving and trading linked to an emerging global economy that enabled particular Malay states and rulers to challenge the Dutch and, later, the English in Sulawesi and the Moluccas.

In the broader context of macro-contact warfare, Iranun maritime raiding proved strategically valuable in the global struggle between European powers in Sulawesi and the Moluccas. The British East India Company held a duplicitous attitude toward the Iranun. In the straits of Malacca, they publicly deplored the raiding activities of the Iranun and demanded Dutch action to suppress them. Privately, however, in the 1780s and 1790s, they encouraged their marauding activities in Sulawesi and the Moluccas because the Iranun were then acting to their commercial and political advantage by destroying the maritime interests and scattering the population of the Dutch and the smaller states allied with them. Operating 'beyond the line,' the Iranun tended to ignore Dutch trade treaties and found, in Thomas Forrest, a colonial emissary willing to convey letters of friendship and alliance as well as war stores in return for their support.[35] Maguindanao-based Iranun, for example, played a prominent role in attacks on Dutch settlements and shipping in the 1770s and helped several years later to precipitate the 40-year long insurrection of the Tidore Prince Nuku against the Dutch, and in preparing the groundwork for the turn-of-the-century English takeover.[36]

The extensive voyages undertaken by Forrest and his lesser known contemporaries in the outer islands of the Dutch East Indies are quite remarkable. Their range was vast covering the lesser Sunda Islands and the Moluccas as well as the islands in the Timor and Arafura seas. The information these men accumulated in their journals and ship logs about these 'clandestine' voyages contribute to our fragmentary knowledge of the making of the Iranun world and its people. Although not always the first to visit some of these places, their observations and arms' trading activities are nevertheless important because they were undertaken at great risk, and many daunting obstacles were overcome—not least of which was dealing with the notoriously tough Iranun themselves.

The location of Iranun settlements often determined the sphere of their maritime raiding. To the shore-dwellers of Sulawesi, these seaborne raiders became known as 'Maguindanao.' While they were rarely able to distinguish among the several ethnic groups that brought devastation to their coast every year, the people of Sulawesi never forgot from whence came the first Iranun marauders—southern Mindanao, opening like a window on Sulawesi. In the 1850s the label 'Maguindanao' would still be used in that beleaguered area to describe the Balangingi Samal.[37]

Raiding prahus outfitted by Tausog and Maguindanao set out from Ilana Bay, Basilan and Bual on the northwestern monsoon. They frequently sailed along the east coast of Borneo, heading for the satellite port of Tontoli on the northwest tip of Sulawesi.[38] Here the nakodah decided on the expedition's course. When the raiding prahus were numerous, some went through the Makassar Strait while others followed the north coast of the island to reach the gulf of Tomini and the Moluccas. Still other joanga steered directly southeast from Mindanao, down through the Sangir Islands, rounding the northern end of Sulawesi and entering the Moluccan Sea.[39] Forrest gives an account of the passage of a raiding prahu from Cotabato to Sulawesi along the Sangir track. The vessel, which was owned by the brother-in-law of the Raja Muda of Cotabato, touched at the following places after passing Sarangani Island. It sailed in a day to Kawio, another day to Kawalusa near northern Sangir, and one day to Karikita. From there, the craft navigated to Siao in a day where provisions were obtained; then to Tahulandang in half a day, then to Banka and the Sulawesi coast.[40] A fleet that circumnavigated Sulawesi ordinarily concentrated on roving in the Buton group, the gulf of Bone, and the Salayer Strait. These areas were heavily populated and in the direct track of Bugis trading vessels. Availing themselves of the southeast monsoon, the homeward journey via the Banka Strait took less than a week. The bigger prahus that chose to remain longer on the southern coast of Sulawesi had to beat their way up the Makassar Strait, stopping at Pasir for supplies and refitting on Tarakan island on the way north.[41]

It was originally as clients of Maguindanao datus that the Iranun waged war against the Dutch in Sulawesi. In the 1770s, their prahus with renegade guides to direct them made raids on Amurang, on Menado, and on Kema. From Forrest we know that some of these forays involved the family of Sultan Pahar un-Din of Cotabato:

> On the 31st of [July] 1775, came in a large prow belonging to Datoo Malfalla, Raja Moodo's brother-in-law, from a cruise on the coast of Celebes. She had engaged a Dutch sloop, and was about to board her, when the Dutch set fire to their vessel, and took to their boat, notwithstanding the fire, the attackers boarded her, and saved two brass swivel guns ... this vessel brought to Mindanao about seventy slaves.[42]

In Forrest's description of Tuan Haji, a lesser noble of the Molucca Islands, reputedly related to the sultan of Batchian, who navigated a small prahu, the *Tartar Galley*, through the Sangir Islands, the Moluccas and Sulu for him, we see the Cotabato Sultanate fostering alliances that would unite the Maguindanao and their Iranun kindred and allies in Tukurun with Bugis on the Makassar coast, so that they could launch combined raids with more effective force against the Dutch:

> I learnt that Tuan Haji had been at Tukoran, and married Rajah Moodo's wife's sister, daughter to the Sultan then. Before he left Mindanao, and before the coolness arose between him and Raja Moodo, he had ... promised to return to Selangan [Cotabato] by the beginning of the north-east monsoon, and proceed in some vessel of Raja Moodo's against the Dutch in the Molucca islands.[43]

The garrisons of Menado and Gorontalo were stiffened as a consequence of the losses suffered by the Dutch in the northern part of Sulawesi.[44] In their estimation, this area had to be maintained at all cost for two reasons: firstly, it was the granary of Ternate; and secondly, it produced gold. Further, reinforcements, in the form of a sloop of war and six well-armed Ternatan Kora-Kora crewed by a thousand local men (taken into Dutch pay), were sent to Menado when the alarming discovery was made, in 1778, by the governor of Ambon, of a larger political scheme that allied the Iranun of Cotabato with the sultan of Tidore to expel the Dutch from the Moluccas.[45] The dastardly conduct of the old governor had brought upon him and the Dutch East India Company the scorn of the Tidorese, who had begun to hold them in absolute derision. They were wary, however, knowing from past dire experience the treachery of the Dutch. Preparing for the worst, the Tidorese lost no time in forging an alliance, offensive and defensive, with the Maguindanao, with whom they had for some time maintained a secret correspondence. On this occasion, the sultan of Tidore sent Haji Omar, a man worthy of confidence, and whom Forrest relied upon in his voyage to New Guinea, as an ambassador to the sultan of Cotabato.[46] When, in 1779, Sultan Jamul-ud Din was subsequently questioned by the Dutch at Ternate about the intercepted letter, he denied responsibility for its authorship, and alleged that his secretary, a Javanese *ulama*, had abused privilege as he was the only person who had access to his closet and seals and that he, the scribe, was undoubtedly the author of the letter. The *ulama* ably defended himself stating that he had repeatedly warned his sovereign of the consequences of carrying on an 'illicit correspondence' contrary to the tenor of the engagements made with the Dutch.[47]

The newly-appointed governor of Ternate placed too much confidence in his conscripted force and consistently underestimated the Iranun. His arrogance proved advantageous to the marauders. Shortly after his arrival from Batavia in 1778, the outstation of Kema was destroyed by a fleet of 30 'Maguindanao' prahus under the command of Haji Omar (the Tuan Hadji of Forrest's *Voyage to New Guinea*). Significantly, three years later, the Tidorese also appealed to the Tausog for assistance. In 1781, a letter written in Jawi script with the seal of the sultan of Sulu was found on a beach at Pantani, east Halmahera, with the bodies of Tidorese 'rebels.' It stated that the sultan of Sulu had acted upon the instructions of his Tidorese brethren and had sent a Spanish deserter (most likely from Zamboanga) in a Dutch vessel to Bengal to contact Captain Farris (Thomas Forrest), through whom they hoped to secure assistance from the English. While Forrest acted sometimes as a private trader outside the British East India Company's system, he was also an especially favored company servant during the Anglo-Dutch War of 1780–1784, carrying out 'two material and hazardous Employs entrusted to him by the Committee of Secrecy [sic] for the company's advantage.'[48] The colorful sea captain, who treated Aceh and its sultan as his own, with all due respect and consideration, as he had done at Cotabato five years earlier, accomplished much in the early 1780s, including in November 1785, secretly repatriating from Calcutta to the Moluccas a political delegation of ambassadors from the strife-torn sultanate of Tidore.[49] In the next decade the Dutch, who were already hard-pressed to defend their trade and settlements, found it next to impossible to curb Iranun raiding and at the same time suppress the Tidorese rebellion, under Nuku, sweeping the Moluccas.[50] There was a major political explosion in the islands beyond Sulawesi because of Nuku's armed struggle, resulting in a corresponding expansion in maritime raiding populations. Thousands of his followers left their villages moving around the islands, attacking and raiding the Dutch whenever possible. The Iranun who had settled at the forward bases of Toli Toli and Tobungku soon attracted disaffected wandering groups of Nuku's followers who joined them. Sulawesi-based Iranun marauding prospered, as more and more men and women, most of them fugitives, escaped slaves, or former servants and deserters of the company (VOC), gravitated to particular island haunts and Iranun bases, especially at Tobello, Toli Toli and Tobungku. In the 1790s, a group of Nuku's followers settled in the Bay of Tolo, forming a new settlement called Tobello. They were refugees from Ternate, Tidore, Tobello, Ceram, and Bacan who left their homes in the 1780s and 1790s because of the ongoing war between Nuku and the VOC. They joined forces with slave raiding groups already based at Tobungku. Velthoen notes that in the 1780s and 1790s the Tobelo initially clashed with the Iranun, who included eastern Sulawesi on their raiding track, as they began to impinge on the territory of these raiders in the straits of Tiworo. However, by the 1820s, the Tobelo and Tobungku raiders realized it was to their interest to cooperate with these Iranun, fully combining their fleets to raid throughout the eastern archipelago.[51]

Significantly, during these years the roles that the Maguindanao and Tausog played in the raiding patterns, which focused on Sulawesi, changed. The Sulu Sultanate began to take a far more active role in promoting Iranun slave raiding against the southern islands. As the regional trade domain of the Tausog expanded in the 1780s, the basis of Maguindanao raiding strength–the allegiance of the Iranun–waned. The Maguindanao came to recognize in the Tausog a far more dangerous enemy than the Dutch, and one much closer to home. The decision of the sultan of Cotabato to send the Raja of Sarangani to Ternate in 1787 to conclude a treaty of friendship, trade and alliance with the Dutch signalled the curtailment of overt Maguindanao initiatives with respect to large-scale raids against Sulawesi and the Moluccas.[52] It was a sign of the extent to which the regional influence of the Cotabato Sultanate was being eclipsed by the sudden economic and military ascendancy of the Tausog.

Because slavery and the allocation of labor were important facets of the Sulu Sultanate's global economy, the Tausog mounted ever-stronger slave raids against the weaker islands near Sulawesi. The Iranun were extremely active in the Moluccas during the short British occupation of the islands while Europe struggled with Napoleon's genius and tyranny.[53] The new masters, like their Dutch counterparts, lacked the resources to administer the Moluccas properly and concentrated their energies and resources almost exclusively on the affairs of Ambon and Ternate.[54] Indeed, the inhabitants of some of the more distant islands were unaware that the Moluccas had changed hands! The Iranun and their Tobelo allies took full advantage of this apparent weakness to relentlessly attack remote settlements and islands. In 1802, the British commander, Farquhar wrote from Ternate:

> I was repeatedly annoyed...by the... incursions of the Maguindanao ...on the coast of Celebes where they had rendezvoused in great force. These people are a set of rovers of the most daring and desperate kind who have frequently rendered themselves the terror of the small trade vessels in the neighbourhood of Menado and have spread their devastations to a considerable distance in the Molucca seas.[55]

The force of their raids frequently severed, for months on end, all communication between the British outposts and Ambon.[56] The naval force stationed there was wholly inadequate; there were too few warships to patrol the islands and those on station spent most of their time procuring provisions or lying at anchor in the harbor. Not surprisingly, at this time some of the Iranun attacks in Sulawesi and the Moluccas were instigated by Dutch sympathizers and strengthened by Dutch military stores, against their former subjects and the British.[57]

Statements of fugitive captives from Sulawesi show that they were mostly subsistence fishers or local traders. Their tiny settlements were located on exposed coasts rather than island hilltops and those in the imperilled Sangir islands were rendered even more vulnerable to seaborne attack because of their close proximity to Sulu and Mindanao. In 1801, an Iranun squadron of 40 vessels on their way to Sulawesi put in among the Sangir Islands in yet another series of raids which reduced the principal settlement of Sangir to ashes, brought about the death of its raja and the captivity of nearly 200 women.[58] Similarly, just over two decades later, a combined Iranun and Tobelo fleet left a trail of burned villages in their wake as they cruised beyond Sulawesi, culminating in an attack on the settlement of Kalengsusu, located on north Buton. In 1822, a fleet of over 150 prahus, comprising 100 Iranun vessels under 3 headmen and 50 Tobelo vessels, besieged the settlement, which, for several months, woke to a nightmare. When the population was on the verge of starvation, the combined force attacked and overwhelmed the entire populace, carrying them off into slavery.[59] Tontoli, or Toli Toli, served for years as the forward base for such massive Iranun raids around Sulawesi and the Moluccas. In 1812 Hunt wrote:

> Tontoli . . . is a great piratical establishment, governed by Sultan Mohammed Kubu; the town is fortified with 300 guns and 3,000 Illana (Iranun) . . . and 50 or 60 prows. This with the piratical establishments on the island of Maguindanao, are intimately connected with the Sulu government, sharing their spoils, disposing of their booty, refitting and obtaining their supplies from the Sulu datus.[60]

For up to several years at a time, most of the Iranun lived in their prahus in the harbor of Tontoli on a transient basis.

The Dutch recovered their colonial possessions in 1816 after Napoleon's defeat at Waterloo, but outside of Java and the strongholds of Makassar and Menado their authority remained nominal. They continued to maintain a number of small, fortified posts in the Moluccas and the Menado residency in the northeast arm of Sulawesi, but on the majority of the numerous islands east of Sulawesi such as Buton there were no Dutch establishments. Systematic slaving directed against these outer islands from the Sulu archipelago increased between 1816 and 1848 for precisely this reason and the raiders swept up all the captives they could find. The Iranun and Balangingi, not the Dutch, had become the true lords of the eastern seas.

Iranun Raiding in the Philippines

For the Christianized inhabitants of the Philippine archipelago 'Moro piracy' and slave raiding was not a new phenomenon when the Iranun began their incessant forays in the mid-1750s. Muslim raiders from Mindanao had menaced voyagers and villagers in the Visayan Sea as early as the sixteenth century and the Maguindanao had already blockaded ports on southern Luzon a century before the time of Thomas Forrest's visit to Cotabato.[61] Muslim marauders operating from innumerable inconspicuous bays and islands in the southern Visayas harassed the Spanish advance and local shipping lanes to such an extent that, in the seventeenth century, the Spaniards were forced to establish marine patrols and coastal outposts to counter them. However, by the mid-eighteenth century, the hazards of living or sailing along the coasts of the Philippines were totally different—with well-organized Iranun raiders establishing blockades of up to 100 long ships to trap and destroy wealthy towns and friar estates. The biggest Iranun slave raids in Southeast Asia were systematically directed against the Philippine archipelago. In 1754-1755 raiding began in earnest, and for the next hundred years the coastal towns of southern Luzon, the Visayas and northwestern Mindanao were the scenes of persistent, well-organized slave raids, which were on a large scale and almost always launched from the sea. The annual reports of the *alcalde mayores* and friars on these 'moro' attacks, and the crumbling ruins of stone watch towers and fortifications built as far north as Ilocos are fearful reminders of the power of the Iranun and Balangingi slavers in this period. The Spanish rulers and religious in the Philippines had indeed become involved in open warfare with the Iranun, on both land and sea, and on a hitherto unprecedented scale. For more than a century Spain's shipping and colonial subjects would be constantly 'plagued' by Iranun and Balangingi slave raiders, particularly those established along the coasts of southern Luzon, where, in the 1760s, large numbers of them set up forward bases. From these points, in shallow draught, well-armed two and three-masted vessels that the Spanish called *pancos*, they launched hit-and-run expeditions, against the shipyards, churches and landed estates of the greater Manila region and the densely populated areas of southern Luzon that Mallari refers to as 'Bicolandia.' This region consisted of just two provinces; the province of Camarines comprising the districts of Iraya, Riconada, Bicol, and Camarines Norte and the province of Albay comprising the districts of Laganoy, Tabaco, Sorsogon, and Catanduanes.[62] Between 1754 and 1757, the ferocity and sheer destructive nature of the first wave of the new style Iranun maritime raids in the diocese of Nueva Caceres was catalogued in a letter to the King, on 29 June 1758 sent by an angry and frustrated Bishop Manuel de la Concepcion y Matos. He described the raids as "undoubtedly greater than at any other time"; 10 towns and 2 missions completely destroyed; 10 churches looted and reduced to ashes; approximately 8,000 indios captured or killed; 1 priest killed and 2 captured.[63] The Dutch ports were the chief outlets for their Filipino captives who were purchased by the Bugis and transported as slaves. The tragic impact of these initial Iranun raids was a harbinger of the seaborne terror to follow.

The sultanate of Cotabato was the primary springboard for maritime raids against the Philippines between 1755 and 1775.[64] For years, Iranun slaving craft en route to the Visayas, hugged the shore from Zamboanga to Caraga on the north coast of Mindanao.[65] The other route north was extremely hazardous. It was almost impossible to leave southern Mindanao and sail east around Cape St. Augustin into the headwinds and heavy seas. Manila's authority rapidly waned and coastal defenses in many regions were neglected, but the Spanish were determined to prevent the Iranun from using Mindanao as gateway to the north. They slowly closed off this coast to the Iranun of Cotabato, erecting a series of small stone forts with fleets stationed along it. This measure to strengthen coastal fortifications on the north side of Mindanao was another factor that contributed to the migration and resettlement of the Iranun of Cotabato at Jolo, Bual, Basilan, and Balangingi. Denied easy access to Negros Oriental, Cebu and Bohol, by 1765, the track of the Iranun from Illana Bay to the Visayas now lay in the direct path of Tausog and Samal settlements to the southwest. By the early 1770s, the Iranun set a southerly course for the islands midway between Jolo and Zamboanga, Basilan and the Samalese group of which Balangingi was the most important, and steered by them past Jolo towards the northeast coast of Borneo. Upon sighting Balabac Island, to the south of Palawan, they sailed north along its eastern coast, entered the narrow strait between Dumaran island and Palawan, from where they crossed over to the Cuyo islands to obtain food and water before entering the Visayas.[66]

Once in the Sibuyan Sea, raids took place on Romblon Island, on Marinduque Island, and on the western coastal towns of the southern Luzon provinces. Sometimes these assaults were launched from satellite communities on Mindoro, Burias and Masbate. Mamburao was for many years the most important of these Iranun forward bases. Located some distance up a river on the east coast of Mindoro, it was exceptionally well suited for staging maritime raids against the greater Manila region. In 1770, just before its destruction, more than 500 Iranun warriors protected Mamburao's fortified stockade, which was sitting on a sharp bend in the Mamburao River. The community owned ten large vessels, several of which were prizes, including a Canton junk. The fields surrounding the stockade were cultivated by captives who were detained there until they could be sold to Brunei slave traders or transported to Sulu.[67]

While Mamburao and the settlements on Burias were not as large as Reteh, Tempasuk and Tontoli, they were well-established and in close proximity to the Spanish capital. By the mid-1770s, the Iranun raiders had become a real menace; a sinister permanent presence in the Visayan seas, maintaining a string of fortified communities and bases, the most important of which were on Leyte, Masbate and Burias. The struggle with the Iranun had become grim and desperate. The colonial navy,

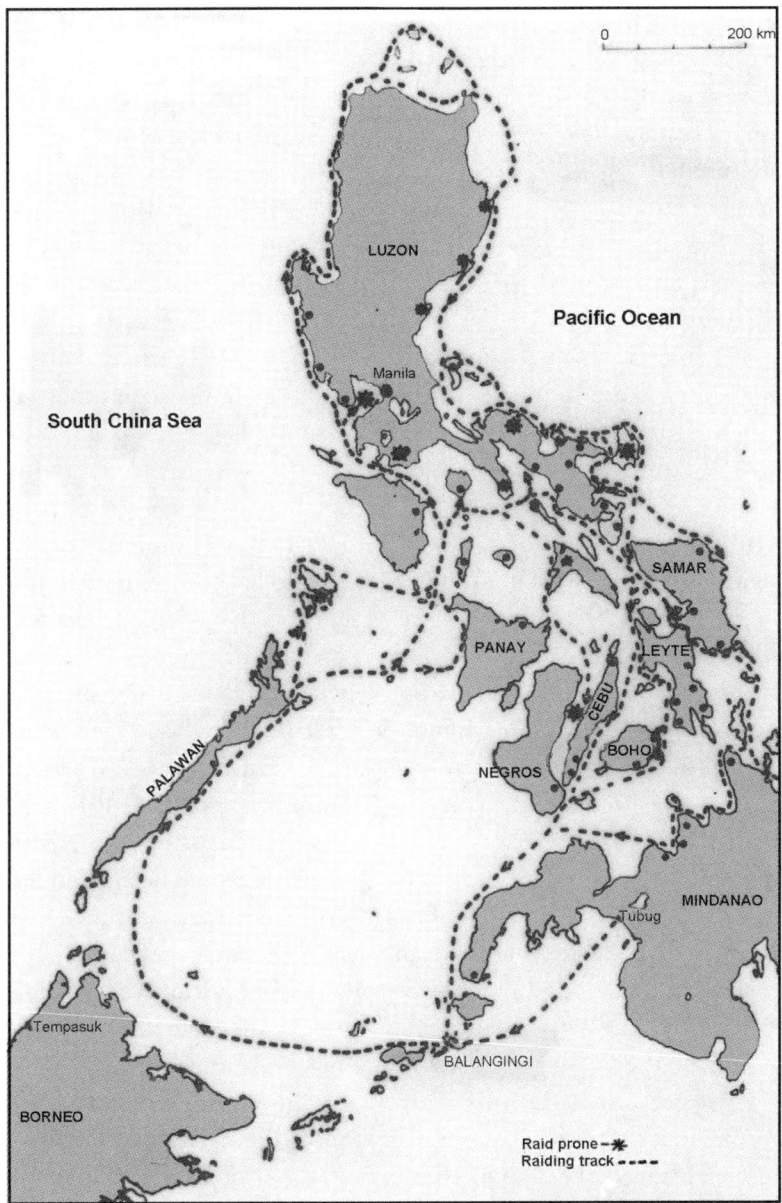

Map 3. Slave Raiding in the Philippines, 1768-1868.

Manila realized, had to have eyes, they had to know where the Iranun were hiding and going. Under such circumstances, escaped captives often became the eyes of Manila, providing valuable information on various Iranun bases and rendezvous points used for attacking nearby islands or coastal towns. In February 1775, Don Juan Miguel de Castillo escaped from the Iranun and listed in uncanny detail the locations of various raiding bases in the Visayas. There was a hamlet of 40 *camarines* (from *camarin*, "a large storehouse") under Datu Dacus in Silanga de Himaguas; various hamlets in Silanga de San Juanico and Rio Bagonlon in Silanga de Leyte, one of which consisted of more than 200 households under a *panglima* and Datus Minuncan, Mangilala and Mathoan; another village of more than 200 houses in the River Payt under Datus Sani, Pari, Matan, Bago, and Aminudin; and still another village located between the River Payt and the town of Palompan, Leyte. The ex-captive also provided startling information about Masbate as a major Iranun base; on the Daraga River there was an Iranun settlement of more than 200 houses where more than 5,000 raiders were based, together with 113 *pancos* and a *galera*. This staging center was a hive of activity, according to the escapee, as expeditions constantly arrived and departed, trading captives for arms and provisions. Don Juan Miguel de Castillo noted too that Malbog, Bagombong, Panamao, Limban-cavayan, Cataingan, and Malbaranon were other sites in Masbate where the Iranun had established their bases. He also stated that there was an Iranun base, consisting of 2 galeras, 8 joanga and 15 pancos, on the southern part of Burias Island under the authority of Datu Amar Casilano.[68] At this time, Thomas Forrest provides some evidence that the Iranun's ambitions now extended beyond mere slave raiding and plunder to regional and political dominance. The mobility of their swift joanga made the Iranun attacks from Burias terrifying, as they could rapidly strike almost without warning anywhere on the west coast of Luzon or up navigable rivers attacking inland communities, monasteries and friar estates. In a January 1776 entry, Forrest mentioned the Iranun who operated out of Burias. He wrote:

> The Ilanos within ten years before 1775 have caused much strife for the Spanish among the islands . . . and, at this time, they possess an island in the very heart of the Philippines, called Burias, where has been a colony of Illanos, for many years, men, women and

children. The Spaniards have often attempted to dislodge them, but in vain, the island which is not very large, being environed with rocks and shoals to a considerable distance.[69]

Slave raiders from Mamburao and Burias concentrated many of their attacks on coastal villages along the outer rim of Manila Bay. By 1772, some of the more defenseless settlements closest to the entrance were deserted.[70] In 1774 and 1780, the village of Mariveles proved particularly vulnerable and failed to mount an effective resistance against attacks. The French navigator de la Perouse described Mariveles' deplorable condition in 1787:

> Toward noon I went on shore to the village, which is composed of about forty houses, built of bamboo. . . . In front of the principal street, there is a large edifice of hewn stone but almost totally in ruins; nevertheless, two brass guns are visible at the windows. . . . They informed us that this partly decayed house was the habitation of the curate, the church, and the fort, but all these titles had not overawed the moors of the islands to the south . . . who seized it in 1780, burned the village, destroyed . . . the parsons house, made slaves of all the Indians who were not able to save themselves by flight, and retired with their captives without meeting with any molestation. The inhabitants of the colony had been so terrified by this event that they are afraid to exercise their industry any longer. The lands are almost overgrown with weeds, and the parish so poor that we could purchase no more than a dozen fowls and a small hog. . . . [The] pastor was a young mulatto Indian. . . . His parish, he told us, consisted of about two hundred persons, of both sexes and every age, ready, at the least warning, to hide themselves in the woods in order to escape the moors who still frequently make their descents upon this coast.[71]

The fear of pursuing one's livelihood was not confined to peasant agriculturalists. The fishers of Manila Bay, and the firewood cutters of Bataan province, who harvested the coastal mangrove, were often seized by Iranun in small vessels rigged like those of the immediate locality.[72] Fear of these sudden forays stopped work, dispersed people and led to periodic shortages of fish and firewood in Manila. Iranun raiders also created havoc with Manila's coasting trade, seizing flotillas of small rice-laden vessels from the provinces of Bataan, Pampanga, Bulacan, Tondo, and Cavite. Traders were forced to travel by the interior rivers to Manila and voyages were far more costly in terms of both time and money.[73] They often ignored the threat of Spanish naval patrols and entered Manila Bay sinking fishing boats and carrying off large numbers of captives. Coasting vessels were boldly pursued right into the harbor under the very muzzles of the shore batteries, before boarding the sailing craft and seizing most of the crew, while other vessels in the harbor were occasionally plundered and burned at anchor in the dark. Disguised as local fishers, Iranun marines even disembarked at the docks of the city on several occasions, capturing unsuspecting individuals off the wharfs. On one occasion, they even went as far as Malate suddenly overwhelming 20 persons returning from a funeral in Pasay.[74] In 1826, a frustrated governor-general, wishing the sea conflict between the Filipinos and '*los duenos de mares*,' (the records occasionally refer to the Iranun and Balangingi as the 'inhabitants of the seas') out of existence, noted that unless the sea raids were contained, Manila and the archipelago would once again experience the cessation and collapse of intercoastal trade and commerce.[75] As late as 1838, the testimonies of rescued captives highlight the continued Spanish frustration in failing to prevent the dazzling success of such lethal forces. The boldness and audacity which the Iranun and Balangingi evinced was exemplified by the fact that, for over 70 years, they had been entering Manila Bay. At these times, they passed the signal station at the island of Corregidor where two gunboats were generally stationed. They captured small vessels or trading boats within the Bay and occasionally massacred the commanders and most of the crew. It was indeed proved at the trial of the 'Lanun' pirates brought into Singapore by the steam gunboat *Diana* in 1838, that six months earlier two Tagalog boys had been taken out of a fishing boat near Cavite, which was only eight miles from Manila.[76]

However, once the Iranun began to develop permanent forward bases and settlements they became more vulnerable to counter attack, and, in 1770, a Spanish expedition destroyed Mamburao.[77] The governor was provoked to take effective action against the Iranun of Mamburao when they seized a large Chinese junk bound for Manila. The unexpected loss of the junk resulted in the Manila galleon *San Joseph* sailing for New Spain with an incomplete cargo. From 1565 to 1815, Spain ran a dangerous shuttle of galleons from the Philippines, where they took on silk, porcelain, spices and other goods sent from China and elsewhere in Asia, to Mexico.[78] The first expedition sent to Mamburao in July failed because of the difficulties it encountered in finding and entering the river. It was not until October that a second expedition of 9 vessels, several Visayan war prahus and 700 troops and artillery arrived at Mamburao. The following morning, after a siege of 12 hours, the Mexican and Filipino troops found the stockade abandoned. When news of the victory reached Manila, a mass was celebrated at the Cathedral. Years later, Iranun continued to resort to the Mamburao river as a temporary haven, but the bases on other islands became more important as their attacks on southern Luzon and the Visayas escalated. The late eighteenth century Philippines was divided into a series of provinces and dioceses by the civil and religious authorities but neither the state nor church had sufficient resources to combat these maritime raiders, and there was no coordinated response to the mounting raids.

During the period 1765-1800, the islands surrounding southern Luzon comprised one massive raiding base. A network of satellite stations stretched around the provinces of Tayabas, Camarines and Albay and Iranun prahus sailed from all of them: Burias, Masbate, Capul, and Catanduanes.[79] The raids became much more frequent and the fleets larger as Sulu's involvement in the China-based world economy increased. Inland areas on Luzon and in the central and southern Visayas became exceptionally vulnerable as Iranun fleets began to seal up navigable rivers, sacking churches and friar estates. Few coastal towns and villages in southern Luzon were spared. Large settlements were the targets of 40 to 50 prahus, or more. These fleets usually contained 2,500 to 3,000 armed slave raiders and carried heavy artillery to erect shore batteries. Large-scale mass attacks took place on towns and villages on both sides of Luzon. In 1755, Virac was destroyed. In 1767, a fleet of 32 prahus overwhelmed Guinyagen. In 1781, Majobac was burned down and in 1793 Obuyon was attacked and levelled by a fleet of 75 prahus. The following year, in 1794, the Spanish finally managed to drive the Iranun off Burias only to have them return with a vengeance several years later. In 1798, many Iranun left Burias to raid the Bontoc peninsula, Catanduanes, Capalonga, and Mambulao in Camarines, and other neighboring islands. In that year alone 25 joanga, rowed by 800 slaves, carrying more than 2,000 Iranun sea warriors descended on the Pacific coast towns of Baler, Casiguran and Palanan reducing them to ashes, and capturing more than 450 Christian inhabitants, including 3 curates who could be ransomed. The following year, 22 joanga raided Bulusan in Sorsogon district burning churches and villages. For the next 30 years, southern Luzon experienced unending waves of Iranun slave raiding activity and marauding.[80]

One of the most damaging aspects of the Iranun's maritime raiding activities were their attacks on the communities and estates run by the various religious orders which were the main fixed centers of the agricultural economy and population. The most devastating raids occurred during Church feasts like Corpus Christi or town fiestas. The immense popularity of these ritual occasions led to large numbers of people gathering at the Church. Absorbed in the revelry, they readily fell prey to the Iranun. Such liturgical moments and festivities in particular communities certainly attracted victims and assailants of the late eighteenth economic development of the Sulu slave trade. Towns and villages built mainly of wood, bamboo and thatch were torched and razed to the ground, while many stone churches and community timber, stone and mortar fortifications (forts, baluarte or watchtowers) were either completely destroyed or abandoned by the terrified friars and townspeople. The Catholic Church was in no sense immune from warfare with the Muslim Iranun and the friars, as a group, arguably suffered a great deal from the Iranun raids. Friars, in beleaguered towns and villages on Luzon, Cebu, Bohol, Leyte, and Samar wrote many accounts of these violent raids. According to these Dominican, Augustinian, Franciscan, and Jesuit sources, the late eighteenth century Iranun raids were often characterized by wanton destruction. The Iranun slave raiders were depicted as appalling savages and plunderers unparalleled in the experience of the writers. It is of course possible that some of these friar accounts of the depredations of the 'moros' may have been exaggerated somewhat by the fear and horror of a Muslim enemy who reduced Churches to ashes and carried women and children off into slavery. But generally their letters and petitions correspond very closely with the destructive accounts of Iranun raids written by people like Thomas Forrest and others in the very different cultural atmosphere of cosmopolitan Jolo and other neighboring Malayo–Muslim states and territories. The friar accounts also agree closely with what the Iranun said about themselves with respect to the level of violence that normally prevailed in Luzon and the Visayas directed against the Church and its personnel.

Some of the old towns were rebuilt on the original site, or a new one nearby, but Iranun maritime raids put a decisive end to many villages. After they experienced the forced harvesting and burning of their fields, the slaughter of their plough animals, and the death of close friends and family, the search for security and the fear of starvation and disease drove Filipinos to abandon villages that had existed for generations. For those who survived the raids, their lives in some essential respects, deep down, were forever after full of inner insecurity. They rarely managed to hide this fact about the dreaded 'Moros' or 'Lanun,' from others, or, to a certain extent from themselves. However, the fate of many lowland Christianized inhabitants was a house of cards existence. If all went well they had nothing to fear. But they knew any strong wind or sudden pealing of the church bell could bring serious danger which could destroy their community and collapse their inner integration as it had failed before as shattered individuals fled in fear and desperation for their lives. Describing the sudden terror the Iranun directly inflicted upon the populace, as well as the religious, the nineteenth century historian Vincente Barrantes, writing out of the concrete economic and political realities of Spain's protracted struggle against Sulu, wrote:

> They waged war not only with bladed weapons but also with muskets which they possessed in large quantity so that at the shout of *Moros* the people fled to the mountains. The religious themselves, so courageous and resigned, came to fear the total destruction of the country notwithstanding the fortifications which they themselves devised and the arms and munitions which they knew how to obtain for themselves. But these Indios were terrified and were hardly useful for anything.[81]

The dilemma facing stricken villagers in the aftermath of a large-scale slave raid was how to resume their original way of life without risking fear of attack and enslavement in the future. Some went to live in larger villages; some looked for new village sites, often on elevated ground; others abandoned the coast altogether for an equally harsh life in the 'illegible, non-state spaces' of the mountain fastness of the interior where sometimes many were reduced to eating tubers and grass to survive.[82] The Spanish labelled as dangerous fugitives these peripheral people who were just out of reach. They called them *cimarrones* and *remontados*. However, on islands like Marinduque, Polillo and Catanduanes, villagers could not readily flee to another area and were forced to stand and fight. The maritime raids closely bound together the inhabitants of the coastal towns of some smaller islands like these for the sole purpose of mutual defense and survival.

The Visayas and the north coast of Mindanao experienced some of the worst slave raids in the last quarter of the eighteenth century. The Visayan Islands were prime Iranun targets with their dense populations and their developed coastal shipping. Through the narrow straits of the Visayan Sea flowed much of the traffic of the Philippines. In terms of seaborne warfare, Spanish naval patrols were unable to take up the cudgels against the raiders. Heavily armed Iranun flotillas wrought havoc on the Philippine coasting trade, and coastal shipping, so essential to the prosperity of the Visayas, all but collapsed. In 1771, over 50 trading vessels were seized from Bohol and the people of Samar and Leyte discontinued trade to Manila for decades at a time. Manila's efforts to ban the construction of coastal 'junks,' which frequently fell into the hands of the Iranun, failed. The governor wrote:

> For the past several years moro raiding has been relentless but it is worse now than ever before, because in the past the raiders only used bladed weapons and lance and were unable to approach and board another vessel, but now they have and use (though not with perfect discipline) cannon and muskets on their vessels. They readily seize small junks and caracaos which the Visayan indios utilise in their trade with this city because the former are slow and unwieldy and the latter are poorly manned and equipped.[83]

Problems of distance and communication posed grave difficulties to the

Spanish, who were powerless to prevent the Iranun from ranging over the poorly defended coasts and straits of the Visayan Sea. The proximity and exposure of the western Visayas, in particular, to Sulu and Mindanao facilitated slave raiding from the south. The Spanish administration was too weak to prevent the inland seas of the central Philippines from becoming a 'Muslim lake.' Control of these waters by the Iranun enabled them to penetrate the hinterlands of Leyte, Panay and Negros by up to 20 miles or more to attack villages.[84] For over half a century, this constant aggression was to be the root cause of the migratory movement of Visayans between Negros, Panay and Cebu. In 1770, 200 raiding vessels were active on the coasts of Leyte and Samar, and it was rumored in the country houses and convents of the Augustinian and Franciscan friars that the sultan of Sulu planned to install his brother-in-law in Leyte to reign over the Visayas. In this transitional period (1754-1775) the infamous reputation that the Tausog developed for promoting slave raiding and marauding was attributable to the activities of the Iranun sponsored by the Maguindanao as well as to themselves. However, as early as 1770 the friars in the Visayas had already perceived a shift in power from Cotabato to Sulu.[85] The remorseless invasion of Leyte between 1768 and 1772 resulted in the captivity of 2,000 Filipinos.[86] In Caraga province, it resulted in the destruction of most of the churches, the death of several friars, and the near total collapse of the trade and agriculture of southeast Mindanao.[87]

Cruickshank argues in his valuable regional study that the Iranun-Balangingi raids were a major theme in the history of Samar during the period 1754-1855 and that the peoples of Samar "suffered severely, but not passively," the attacks against themselves, their homes and their harvests.[88] His analysis deals primarily with the impact of Iranun maritime raiding on Samar and less with the 'moros' in particular. The Iranun led their oar-propelled vessels directly into Samar's key ports on the south and east coasts throughout the 1780s and 1790s, while others circled around to the north probing coastal and inland settlements. With little to stop them at sea, Iranun slave raiders were able to mass their forces for large-scale assaults and blockades on land. Favorite targets were prosperous church centers and coastal fortifications, rich with works of art and craftsmanship in gold and silver, and war stores and provisions.

It was not uncommon for a thousand raiders to come sweeping into a port like Catbalogan using their larger vessels to provide a cover of fire while Iranun storming parties moved in for the direct assault in smaller craft. In time, having established the siege, they plundered nearby villages, markets and rice fields.[89]

The Iranun confronted the frontier villages of the southern Visayas and Mindanao with some of their greatest demonstrations of force. In 1770, the Provincial of the Augustinian Recollects wrote that no part of the Visayan islands had been left unscathed that year. In his province the Iligan *presidio* had staved off an attack by 180 prahus, but the besieged defenders were helpless to prevent the raiders from burning the surrounding villages and church as they withdrew.[90] Few communities on Mindanao could cope with the pace of the onslaught. Since the beginning of the previous decade when the Iranun had first appeared on an annual basis all the villages in Caraga had been burned at least once, and in Iligan province they destroyed the villages of Ipanan, Aliitum, Gompot, Salay, and Sipara. They frequently undertook raids against Camiguin Island.[91] Lingering evidence of these attacks is provided by the name of the principal coastal town, Catarman, which means 'place of fear.'[92] After examining parish documents in 1779, the bishop of Cebu stated that slave raids were the basic reason for declining parish enrollments and the continued poverty of the churches in Caraga, Iligan and Panay.[93] The raids continued and the Visayan's material life grew worse on northeast Mindanao. At the start of the nineteenth century, they could only cultivate their fields, fish and communicate with neighboring villages at great risk.[94] The Iranun now held sway all along the coasts of Luzon, the Visayas and Mindanao. In the year 1800, the Augustinian Zuñiga wrote:

> Until the present day these Moros have not ceased to infest our colonies; innumerable are the Indians they have captured, the towns they have looted, the rancherias they have destroyed, and the vessels they have taken. It seems as if God has perceived them for vengeance on the Spaniards that they have not been able to subject them in two hundred years, in spite of the expeditions sent against them, and the armaments sent almost every year to pursue them. In a very little while we conquered all the islands of the Philippines, but the little

island of Sulu, a part of Mindanao, and the other islands nearby, we have not been able to subjugate to this day.[95]

Though the Iranun expansion of the late eighteenth century was caused, in large measure, by global economic and political developments in Sulu, China and the West, its importance to the history of Southeast Asia can hardly be understated. The effects of the Iranun slave raids and marauding on the economies and societies of island Southeast Asia were immense. The damage to the agricultural economy, coasting trade, demography, and social fabric in many areas was long-term. Despite occasional colonial victories, the inhabitants of many coastal stretches of present-day Malaysia, Indonesia and the Philippines remained too traumatized to return to their devastated dwellings, preferring to resettle inland or found new, larger settlements, far removed from their fields and fisheries and the ever present spectre of Iranun maritime raiders.

CHAPTER FIVE

THE EASTERN ARCHIPELAGO DEFENDED, 1754-1838

The defeat of Napoleon and the decisions taken at the Congress of Vienna led to the Dutch returning to the East Indies with renewed energy and commitment to suppress Iranun maritime raiding and slaving. Over the next quarter of a century there would be considerable public interest expressed in both the Netherlands and Britain about the problem of 'Malay piracy.' In the Netherlands, the journalistic concern was with the extent of the measures taken by the government to combat the 'odious barbarity' of 'pirates' like the Iranun and Tobello. In Britain, however, the journalistic strategy was often to reproach the government for failing to deal with the piracy of such dangerous 'tribes' of the eastern archipelago in an adequate manner.[1]

For the Dutch East India Company, it was apparent that the die was cast much earlier than for the British East India Company in the straits of Malacca, and beyond. By the latter half of the eighteenth century, Bugis, Madurese, Javanese, and other commercial *prahu* shipping suddenly woke up to the fact that Iranun slave raiding and marauding posed a very serious problem. The straits of Malacca, Sunda and Makassar became the primary conduits of regional trading activity, as, during certain times of the year, up to 500 or more ships each week made their way through the various channels. Iranun attacks in these waters were largely violent usually with the sea raiders boarding trading prahus either in broad day light or at night from their swift vessels, before taking possession of the crew, cargo and valuables.

These mounting attacks were considered a real threat to the commercial and political hegemony of the VOC and led the Dutch to increase their antipiracy measures. However, the British East India Company authorities and ship owners, who traded in the waters of the various straits reasoned that the cost of suppression would greatly exceed the cost of the political and economic problems of regional consolidation for their colonial competitors—the Dutch. Hence, antipiracy measures and cooperation with them were given a low priority in Bengal, as the British, in the first quarter of the nineteenth century, attempted to establish their dominion in the Malay Peninsula and throughout the archipelago.

At the start of the nineteenth century the total number of Iranun sea raiders was not known, but, across island Southeast Asia, they must have conservatively numbered between 10 and 15,000. In the eyes of the Dutch there were more than enough of them based in Mindanao, Sulu, Sulawesi, Borneo, and Sumatra, to be the considered the scourge of the seas from Papua to the straits of Malacca forcing the Netherlands East Indies government to take draconian measures to contain them. For example, the Dutch pass system restricted the number of crew and passengers for every registered prahu traversing the archipelago. Local rulers allied with the VOC were also required to provide trading prahus with the passports, declaring the size of the vessel, the armaments and crew. Passengers were to be recorded on departure and arrival. The company also set forth a decree prohibiting the construction of certain types of indigenous sailing vessels. This Act was further reinforced by the edict of 16 May 1806, which stated that, 'no passengers should be granted to the captains, masters or owners of *penjajaps*, *kakaps* or *balloors*, nor to vessels of a like build.'[2] In addition, if such individuals were seen in ports or roadsteads established by the VOC, their ships were to be seized as pirate vessels— with or without a passport.[3]

The credibility of Dutch authority in the region, however, was little improved by an initial series of measures meant to suppress piracy and restore confidence in the political and commercial life of the islands upon their recovery. One of the most important of these dealt with the strengthening of the Colonial Marine. The colonial navy had hastily responded to the first wave of the Iranun onslaught at the dawn of the nineteenth century. Between 1808 and 1811, the administration of G.G. Dandels had made unremitting efforts to oppose the Iranun. The Netherlands East Indies Government commissioned the construction of a large number of inexpensive prahus to be used especially for antipiracy patrol. It was believed that these vessels, ideally suited for riverine and coastal warfare, could police and protect a much greater expanse of water and shoreline than the gunboats of the colonial navy.[4] In 1810, a flotilla of 40 armed prahus was charged with protecting the coasts of Java.[5] This antipiracy squadron captured or destroyed a number of Iranun vessels off Java while several *joanga* were also attacked and driven off among the little islands near Banka. But, the coast guard was too small by itself to properly patrol the archipelago beyond Java and various governors ordered at certain times of the year for the royal navy in concert with the colonial marine to undertake punitive expeditions against the Iranun and their accomplices. The aim was to 'make an example of them' which necessitated using rapid deployment forces and scorched earth tactics: burning their ships, bases and encampments, confiscating their weapons and spreading "terror and confusion" amongst the Iranun and confederate groups like the Tobello.[6]

A necessary first step was to increase the size, strength and strike capacity of the Colonial Marine. In order to intelligently plan, search and destroy missions and countermeasures against the Iranun and Tobello, Dutch Residents and naval officers were instructed to collect detailed information on 'pirate' populations throughout the eastern archipelago. Important information included their size and ethnicity, the location and strength of their principal centers and satellite communities, the nature of their particular economic pursuits and the wealth of the inhabitants.[7] With the assistance of knowledgeable informants (ex-raiders and captives), local villagers and regional traders valuable reports on the subject of Malay piracy were drawn up by Muntinghe in 1818, Tobias in 1821, Kolff in 1831 and Vosmaer in 1833.[8] In order to successfully carry out search-and-destroy missions against the Iranun spread along the coast of east Sumatra, the governor-general also requested M. Praetorious, the resident of Palembang, and M. Du Buy, the resident of Banka, as well as key local informants, to furnish detailed reports and information respecting the Iranun of Reteh, Jambi and other hot spots such as Bali and Baankalen, on the southwest coast of Borneo that they frequented.[9]

Collected together, these valuable reports, by the end of 1833, enabled the Dutch to identify the key 'haunts' of the Iranun and the necessary steps that had to be taken to successfully attack their bases. It was recommended by the antipiracy experts that small copper-bottomed brigs, schooners and sloops, rather than larger warships such as frigates had to be used. The latter drew too much water and had to anchor too far from the coast. Such an expedition would have to be accompanied by special built, light weight attack landing craft which could navigate shallow waters or ascend narrow creeks, yet also hold a sizeable number of soldiers and sailors. These boats were meant to be fast and equipped with oars on both sides and brass swivel guns. Such search-and-destroy expeditions, upon surprising an Iranun base or encampment, would aim to cut off escape routes on all sides. This strategy, it was argued in the various reports, and, by key informants, like Pangeran Syed Hassan Habassy, would cause the Iranun to abandon their raiding boats on the beach, which would be burned.[10]

It was hoped that the news of such wholesale destruction, due to the operations of the Dutch special forces, would travel rapidly to other Iranun communities and cause them to abandon their occupation as maritime raiders. Then, according to the official thinking, the only enemy left to deal with would be those aristocrats and trading states in league with the Iranun who "afforded them every kind of support."[11] The reports on Iranun maritime raiding, compiled between 1818 and 1833, were unanimous in recommending that if local rulers or states knew of Iranun activity but could not prevent it, they had to inform the Dutch Government. If they failed to do so they too would be treated as 'pirates,' and dealt with accordingly.

As early as 1818, Muntinghe had asserted that the only effective means of putting an end to the Iranun threat was to use a "force sufficient to subject and keep under the yoke all the islands and haunts."[12] He added, in order to obtain the desired result, "the object should be, not necessarily to destroy and extirpate, but rather to disarm and subdue these tribes: as to the pirates of Rete however it is difficult to determine their fate beforehand."[13] In order to reduce the number of Iranun, Muntinghe proposed (on the advice of Raja Akil) the construction of 30 to 35 small vessels from 5 to 10 *koyangs* 'constructed according to a model cut in wood' that he had in his possession. The aim was to ensure that these vessels were stronger and as fast as the Iranun raiding ships. They would be supported by a flotilla of five to six gunboats and two to three corvettes.[14] The use of local prahus for patrol work was not new. Years before, it had been proposed that the government build a sizeable fleet of Kora-Kora but no action was taken on the measure. Subsequently, when the Muntinghe plan was approved a different kind of cruising prahu was chosen for the colonial marine—the *Kolek Trengannu*. The boat was light and carried a four-pound cannon and swivel guns. It was crewed by 24 men armed with muskets and pikes who were handpicked from seafaring communities—Bugis, Madurese and Sumbawa fishers. The cruising prahus were placed under the jurisdiction of the residencies.[15]

The Council of the Indies immediately undertook Muntinghe's advice as well as drawing up a new treaty with the sultan of Linga to suppress maritime raiding in the waters of the jurisdiction of his state. He was also forbidden to create an asylum for the Iranun and was expected to seize all individuals suspected of piracy and punish them. At Muntinghe's behest, between 1817 and 1819, a series of similar alliances were also forged against the Iranun with the smaller coastal states of Borneo. In 1817, an alliance was formed with the sultan of Banjarmassin and, in an 1819 treaty with the sultan of Pontianak, it was agreed that the Dutch would maintain a fleet of ships on the coast of Borneo to secure the safety of commerce and shipping. In both cases, the sultans' unqualified support was expected. The Dutch also retaliated against the Iranun by issuing letters of marque of her own to these Malay rulers, hoping that their new found allies might come close to matching the score of property captured. Treaties were also concluded with the sultans of Mampawa and Sambas in the same year and all prahus from both states were to carry Dutch passports.[16]

In the context of this emerging broad strategy against the Iranun, the report of the commissioner of Borneo, M.J.H. Tobias, is of particular importance. The lengthy document, dated October 1821, shows that Tobias' special task required him to examine ways in which to withdraw the populations of Sambas and other parts of Borneo from supporting the Iranun in the future and to turn the slave raiders' way of life in the direction of either commerce or agriculture.[17] Interestingly, Tobias' report specifically mentioned the *Seaflower* incident. The previous year the

Seaflower, a British East India Company vessel of 16 guns, was attacked while conducting trade in the Sulu archipelago. This incident, Tobias believed, highlighted both the audacity and 'cruelty' of the 'Lanouns' and justified the severest measures being taken against them. The sultan of Sambas supplied most of the details of his report. The sultan, according to Tobias, was formerly a principal supporter of the Iranun, but was now "privy to their depradations."[18] In the sultan's opinion it was absolutely necessary to punish all the petty princes and *sherif* who continued either to be directly involved in Iranun maritime raiding or who tacitly encouraged it. The sultan of Sambas, in a fascinating, if not self-serving *volte-face*, now offered his own services to assist such antipiracy expeditions. However, Tobias was wary, arguing that this offer of assistance should be accepted with caution, as the sultan himself had been known to traffic with the Tempasuk Iranun and other 'pirates' such as the Iranun followers of the Prince of Riau.[19]

The information furnished in these early nineteenth century reports enabled the Dutch to form a general understanding of the complex nature of the Iranun-Balangingi slave raiding networks and their critical role in the global-local economy of the Sulu Sultanate. Overall, Dutch efforts to suppress Iranun maritime raiding and slaving and impose a Pax Neerlandica across the archipelago proved unsuccessful. The cruising prahus were only a partial answer at best. Not as swift as the fast sailing, Iranun raiding boats, the importance of the cruising prahus was primarily limited to protecting shipping in the vicinity of the settlements where they were stationed on the coasts of Java, Borneo and Sulawesi.[20] At the same time, by the end of 1829, the colonial navy had been reduced to 'two guard ships, five brigs, nine schooners, and nine gunboats' to police a maritime region encompassing parts of the Malay peninsula and the seas of the Indonesian archipelago dotted with thousands of islands. It was widely recognized that the number of vessels was so low that it was no longer adequate for cruising the archipelago for fixed periods and offering real protection against the Iranun, and it was also inadequate for convoy service. The reasons for the run-down state of the colonial navy were all too obvious. "If in some places it has been unable to put a stop to the attacks and violence of the pirates, its inability is to be attributed solely to the diminution which it has undergone by the financial measures of your

Excellency."²¹ The economic drain of the 1825-1830 Java War and drastic fiscal reform had taken its toll on the colonial navy and the antipiracy campaign. Despite these setbacks, in the early 1830s, a new formidable instrument of empire—steamboats—were placed at the disposal of the Netherlands Indies Government. These warships, in particular the "little iron vessels" were to render important service by constantly cruising along the coasts of Java.²² In May 1830, it had also been decided once again to construct an additional 20 cruising prahus, and later 14 more, to add to the depleted flotilla.²³

In 1834, the Dutch acted decisively against the Iranun settled in straits waters. Three government cruisers, together with 50 prahus fitted out by the Sultan of Riau, attacked Reteh. Eight Iranun *panglima* were taken prisoner to be executed or condemned to hard labor for life.²⁴ Among those still remembered more than a century and a half later as having been beheaded at Lingga were the Iranun rajas Marasan and Markong from the village of Inok situated just north of the Indrageri River.²⁵ Three years later, the Dutch further strengthened the patrol fleet in Riau and reinforced their garrison in that residency to make more marines available for service in the coastguard boats.²⁶ During these same years Singapore's populace, its local authorities, and the Calcutta Chamber of Commerce were calling for Admiralty jurisdiction in Singapore's Supreme Court to try offenses committed upon trading prahus and other vessels in the straits of Malacca.²⁷ The granting of this jurisdiction to its court, and the introduction of armed steam vessels and well-crewed cruisers and skiffs by the British after 1836, also made it more difficult than ever before for the Iranun to raid in the Malacca Straits.

Forcefully pacifying dangerous marauding groups like the Iranun, Tobello and Balangingi was an extremely difficult task in the presteam era. In the 1830s, a financially-strapped Netherlands East Indies Government also experimented with other partially effective measures. The Dutch attempted to turn swords into ploughshares, offering captured Iranun and their Tobello allies the opportunity to abandon the sea, and their profession, in return for clemency and a "more honorable means of existence in agriculture, and the export of their produce."²⁸ It was argued on the Continent and in Singapore that putting an end to piracy between the straits of Malacca and the Saudi Arabian Peninsula was the responsibility of the British. In examining Dutch efforts to suppress Iranun maritime raiding in the seas to the east of the strait of Malacca and in the strait itself, both the *Canton Free Press* and the *Canton Repository* suggested that the Netherlands deserved far more credit as "the pirates show more respect for the Dutch flag than to that of England."[29]

However, the failure of Muntinghe's plan to use flotillas of local sailing vessels in the outer islands to protect coastal communities against Iranun-Tobello slave-raiding was most evident in the Residencies of Menado and Gorontalo which formed the northern peninsula of Sulawesi. This was an extremely fertile and densely populated area, where irrigated rice was grown on a large scale and gold was mined, but it was neither politically well integrated nor administered by the Dutch.[30] The principal targets of the Iranun, Tobello and Balangingi were the fishing villages and riverine agricultural settlements of the Minahassans, the Bolaang Mongondow, and the Gorontalo, dotting the extreme northeastern corner of the peninsula and the gulf of Tomini. Gold miners, fishers and coastal traders–Bugis, Chinese and Arabs–were frequently seized within cannon shot of Dutch outposts at Amurang, Belang and Gorontalo.[31]

By the end of the eighteenth century, the British East India Company had moved to establish trading bases in the straits of Malacca. While the authorities in Bengal began to exert some influence over the commercial affairs of the Straits Settlements, the Royal Navy did not dominate the seas of the area. Iranun maritime raiding and slaving in this region were complex phenomena confronting several global powers, namely Britain, the Netherlands and Spain, and a number of local sultanates, Kedah, Riau-Lingga, Jambi, Siak, and Palembang, all located in the area of highest risk, within a long narrow rectangle drawn to link Banka Island and Billiton to the Riau Archipelago, Singapore and the Malay Peninsula. According to Dutch and British reports, and figures, between 1800 and 1830, Iranun slave raids and marauding accounted for almost half of all the incidents reported in this region. The West's developing involvement in the China trade and the subsequent founding of Singapore contributed to the Malacca Strait and its environs experiencing one of the highest rates of maritime raiding in Southeast

Asia at that time. The annual value of Singapore's entrepot trade in 1833 was estimated at about two million Spanish dollars, but it was in fact worth far more as the settlement acted as the central redistributive point for the circulation of goods throughout Southeast Asia, in every direction. Wong suggests that Iranun marauding in the straits of Malacca seriously damaged English commerce as losses of cargoes and prahus to these sea raiders pushed up local prices and led to an overall decline in Singapore's country trade.[32]

Malay nakodah reported to those campaigning against the 'pirates' that the growth of their commerce with Singapore had attracted fleets of Iranun prahus cruising the straits and the northwest coast of Borneo. The high concentration of prahu shipping sailing the narrow strait of Malacca and the northwest coast of Borneo in both directions, linked to the development of European commerce and the advent of the China trade, provided easy targets for Iranun marauders seeking to supplement their wealth from slave raiding with takings from passing cargo ships. The early 1830s saw attacks in the South China Sea escalate dramatically as the reports flooded into Singapore about trading prahus being boarded, hijacked and burned to the water line by 'Illanoon' raiders, commanded by blood-red uniformed panglima, from large war vessels with evident Iranun markings.

Many nakodah, including the Malay, Dowich, who was chased but not seized in the South China Sea, upon arriving safely at the port, gave information about the size and movements of the 'piratical prows' cruising the sea lanes between Borneo and Singapore. Dowich was the *nakodah* of a 75 ton trading boat which had a crew of 34 and 3 guns. He maintained that in the course of his regular travels to Singapore the coast of Borneo was 'infested with pirates and has been so for years.'[33] These pirates according to this prosperous nakodah were 'Lanoons.' Mah Daut, another Malay nakodah, lived at Muka, situated between Brunei and Sarawak. He often travelled to Singapore to trade raw sago. His boat was about 35 tons burthen and carried 25 men. Mah Daut claimed the slave raiders, in the waters in which he sailed, had never bothered him. He commented however that they were 'said to be many.' He observed, most importantly, that the 'Lanoons' were in fact Banguinnes [Balangingi] from near Sulu.[34]

George Windsor Earl, a private trader and recognized authority on the commerce of the eastern archipelago, was one of the first to issue warnings in print about the damaging repercussions for Singapore's country trade being left defenseless, as the nature of Iranun operations took on a more menacing face. Earl graphically reported the fear expressed in the early 1830s that Iranun maritime raiding could spiral out of control:

> The Dyaks are not the sole occupants of this part of the coast [northwest coast from Point Datu to Borneo proper], for the Lanuns, a piratical people from the island of Magindanao, are established in several of the harbours where they live chiefly in their prahus, which are from twenty to sixty tons burthen. During the south-east monsoon, a proportion of these vessels cruise in the more civilised parts of the Archipelago, chiefly near the entrances of the straits leading to Singapore, where they attack and plunder the prahus of the native traders; and, when about to return to their haunts in Borneo, generally manage to surprise some small town or village, the entire population of which is often carried away into slavery.[35]

He then goes on to note that:

> Piracy and the slave trade were openly carried on within a short distance of three European settlements on a scale and system revolting to humanity; that, within a few days' sail of Singapore, horrors had been for years enacted, which might be suppressed within a few months by vigorous measures; fleets of Lanuns each year waiting for the prahus bound for our great Eastern emporium, capturing them, and often inflicting on their crews miseries equal to those of the middle passage.[36]

Because the key to power in Sulu, Cotabato and elsewhere in Southeast Asia lay in control over labor power, trade goods and war stores, it is not surprising that slavery in the region was bound up with maritime raiding and warfare, or 'piracy.'[37] Captives were a main source of booty for the Iranun and Balangingi; they were also a form of common purpose currency and one of the principal commodities of regional trade. What Earl deliberately failed to acknowledge in his book, *The Eastern*

Seas, was that unprecedented international commercial demands, the development of colonial urbanism and new patterns of consumption across Southeast Asia from the end of the eighteenth century, had created a huge demand for large-scale recruitment of dependent and forced labor. Global-local markets grew, especially those linked with China. Colonial ports like Singapore, Penang and Makassar, and metropolitan cities, such as Batavia and Manila flourished, as did both the necessity and desire to import slaves on a large scale—slaves who were usually exchanged for war stores. Some of the 'Lanun' charged by Earl, often cooperated with local Chinese traders and occasional Europeans, who acted as agents, to meet the demand for slaves in major cities such as Singapore and also in smaller rural communities.[38]

Britain, in the early 1830s, was not prepared to commit war vessels as systematically as the Dutch for the suppression of the Iranun maritime raiding and slave trade—for what was dismissively referred to in English naval circles as 'boat piracy.' While Britain was not prepared to maintain a force of similar strength in their own territories in the straits of Malacca, the Royal Navy extended some protection with the occasional visits of naval warships. The squadron on the East Indies Station, for at least a decade prior to 1840, seldom consisted of less than 10 or more than 18 vessels, and was comprised for the most part of brigs, sloops and small frigates, which were principally employed in the Bay of Bengal, in the Arabian sea, and in the Indian Ocean. Besides cruising in different directions for the protection of mercantile shipping from the shores of northern Australia, and sometimes as far northwestward as the Persian Gulf, it frequently happened that two or possibly three vessels were required to remain on alert among the innumerable islands of the eastern archipelago. Especially off the coasts of Borneo, Singapore and Sumatra, these vessels were involved in the suppression of Iranun-Balangingi slave raiding, and the relief of trading vessels, which, through the stress of weather, or other accidental circumstances, were driven ashore, where they could not remain very long without being visited by the Iranun sailing about from one part of those narrow seas to another.[39]

At the time of the signing of the 1824 Anglo-Dutch treaty, the naval forces placed at the disposal of the straits authorities consisted of a 6-gun brig and a 12-gun cruiser. Hence, in Singapore no effective measures could be taken to suppress Iranun maritime raiding by the British, at the very same time that the Dutch were beginning to experiment with the use of steamers in the generally calm seas of the archipelago to combat the likes of the Iranun and Tobello.[40] The newly formed antipiracy command in Singapore was strapped with a motley collection of leftover vessels and craft; flat bottom boats from the Anglo-Burmese war, government schooners, derelict yachts and several-purpose-built decoy craft disguised as Malay merchant prahus. Besides parsimonious officials in Calcutta, this new law enforcement agency dedicated to defeating piracy also confronted a hostile penny pinching merchant class in Singapore. Consequently, countermeasures taken against the Iranun by the new command in Singapore would be neither easy, nor completely successful. It was almost as if the antipiracy provisions of the 1824 treaty did not exist. The constant inroads of the Iranun and other raiding groups in the immediate environs of the Singapore roadstead eventually forced the hand of the Calcutta Government and gave rise to the suggestion that they support the presence of several ships of war, the expenses for which would be defrayed by a tariff on particular trade items. Interestingly, local British merchants were extremely angry that taxes were to be levied for piracy suppression at their expense, and managed to have the measure quickly rescinded.[41] The various groups concerned with the suppression of piracy in the Malacca Straits–the commercial interests, local authorities and the Supreme Government in Calcutta–wanted the Iranun destroyed, but preferably at little or no cost to themselves. For these English abroad with vested political and economic interests a more active role in piracy suppression by Britain was considered absolutely necessary, since such maritime intervention and colonial expansion would also inevitably bring further commercial success to Singapore.[42] But, their clarion call to focus attention on containing Iranun slave raiding and marauding was to be answered from an altogether different quarter.

In 1838, James Brooke came to Singapore as a young merchant-adventurer and almost immediately became embroiled in the domestic politics of the Brunei Sultanate. He shortly became the self-styled white raja of Sarawak, a province under the nominal control of the sultan of Brunei, and he embarked on a campaign to eradicate Iranun 'piracy' from the northwest coast of Borneo. At the same time, he established his commercial network to Singapore and other markets over which the Dutch, whom he held in contempt, had no formal claim.[43] In 1841, this English interloper, quickly destined to become a romantic visionary in the eyes of the British public, became governor of Sarawak, thus forcing the cession of the territory from the sultan of Brunei, because of his critical role in suppressing an Iranun inspired political coup. This event, the 'rebellion,' which sparked a political revolution in Brunei, focused on a factional feud among the Brunei Malay aristocracy and their Iranun-backed supporters inside the sultanate. Brunei Malays faced their biggest political crisis of the nineteenth century in the wake of James Brooke's audacious intervention, which undermined the support of Pangeran Usop and discredited his most trusted ally and political adviser, Sherif Usman, the powerful Iranun lord of Marudu Bay. Initially, this key turning point in the history of Brunei and the northwest coast of Borneo made Brooke's possible dynastic run all the more intriguing, and serious. To his influential neighbors (the coastal Iranun and riverine Iban of the Skrang basin, who possessed great force), no stretch of coast was big enough to accommodate this conspirator who was working around the clock to bring about their downfall; an individual who was self-consciously shadowy with seemingly more energy than influence.

Brooke's early action packed experiences of courage, tenacity and providential faithfulness in confronting the Iranun and Iban left many of his local supporters and Victorian readership breathless and enthused. His ultimatums on defeating 'Malay piracy' and encouraging free trade lit a fire under the Royal Navy. Brooke, both in word and deed, embarked on a decade-long campaign to eradicate the Iranun and Balangingi with the moral support of his followers in Britain and the indispensable help of several naval captains on station in Singapore waters. Slave raiding and marauding were widespread in Southeast Asia but Brooke conveniently chose to reduce these phenomena in both print and deed to 'Lanun and Dayak piracy.' It would have been impossible for James Brooke and his successors, to have extended the boundaries of his domain, in the years that followed 1841, without the Royal Navy playing an active role in the expansionist affairs of the kingdom of Sarawak.[44] With money from a family inheritance, the young Englishman had purchased and fitted out a small yacht, the *Royalist*, with the avowed intention of destroying 'Iranun piracy' and eliminating the slave trade. But, the tiny yacht and the audacity of the zealous private trader were no match for the score of joanga careened along the coast near Tempasuk or moored safely in Marudu Bay.

The forced opening and capitulation of China to Britain coincided with the course of Brooke's life and political fortunes. In 1840, the duties of the East Indies Squadron underwent a complete change and their principal scene of action, which hitherto had been in western and south Asia, shifted to the eastern coast of the continent. As a consequence of the offensive policy, which Britain then began to adopt toward China, it became necessary to assemble almost the entire force on the command first at Singapore.[45] In the early 1840s, Brooke began an antipiracy campaign, albeit a crusade, against his neighboring political rivals and foes–the Iranun, Ibans and Brunei Malays. He was initially assisted by an English man-of-war, the H.M.S. *Dido*, commanded by Capt. Henry Keppel. Later Brooke also joined forces with other young ambitious naval officers, notably captains Congalton, Mundy, Stanley and Belcher, on punitive expeditions against the Iranun–expeditions which spanned almost a decade.[46] To put a stop to the 'evil' it had to be arrested at its source, according to the thinking now taking hold in English naval circles as a result of Brooke's search-and-destroy forays. For him, serious definitions were not a key in debates over who were 'pirates' in these campaigns. Brooke just told the naval captains to finish them off according to the current tradition. In the midst of purging and killing, Raffles' sense of continually extending the empire and free trade at the expense of the Dutch was always paramount.

It was still clear to Brooke, though, that the Admiralty could not spare enough cruisers to instil sufficient fear of punishment to prevent the Iranun from continuing to slave raid. But the immediate effects of his on-the-spot informal operations helped to force the Iranun and Balangingi out of straits waters and off the northwest coast of Borneo, and to arrest the decline of the prahu trade in the region. In less than a decade, between the years 1838 and 1847, two entire Balangingi squadrons on their extended voyages, mistakenly thought to be 'Ilanoon,' were hunted down and destroyed in the South China Sea by the Royal Navy.[47] In the intervening years several successful Brooke-inspired Royal

Navy backed attacks against the Iranun strongholds of Tempasuk and Marudu forced the surviving slave raiders eastwards. On the other hand, according to an 1846 article in the *Singapore Free Press*, the antipiracy campaigns that were launched by Brooke and Keppel against the Iranun and Iban communities along the northwest coast of Borneo had the ironic effect of disrupting the coasting trade between Borneo and Singapore.[48] But by the mid 1850s, Iranun maritime raiding was no longer a major threat to the Straits Settlements as marauding was increasingly dealt with in a swift cooperative manner by the colonial navies of the British and Dutch.

In the last quarter of the eighteenth century, the scale of the effort that the Spanish devoted to antipiracy operations against the Iranun reflected the inadequate resources at Spain's disposal and the priorities of those in power in both Madrid and Manila. The ideological message was always clear in both the ultimate call for political action to suppress the Iranun and the fervent wish to eradicate 'despotism,' 'piracy' and 'slavery' from Cotabato and Sulu. The agenda was to reform and civilize the 'moro' character in the image of the culture of Catholic Spain. Before 1793, direct Spanish intervention in the affairs of the Sulu Sultanate to ward off the rising wave of slave raids was virtually impossible. The coastal maritime defense had been totally ineffective before 1775 when Gov. Basco y Vargas had established a naval force of light gunboats to pursue the Iranun raiders. Until that time, defense against 'moro' slave raiding and marauding was left to local community effort. During every southwest monsoon, Iranun fleets from Cotabato and Sulu swept up through the Visayas towards southern Luzon. Some struck at islands and towns in the Sibuyan sea while others sailed right through the San Bernardino Strait attacking Catanduanes and the Pacific coast, often as far as Camarines Norte or beyond.[49] The low point of Spanish fortunes against the Iranun in the eighteenth century seems to have been reached by about 1789. The two enemies had come to realize the impossibility of entirely driving the other out of the region. But, the ferocity of the incessant slave raiding and marauding had ushered in a new era, taking on a permanent and sinister character in which the Iranun usually arrived in the Luzon region a month or two after the rice harvest ended and stayed in neighboring waters for up to six months. Nothing struck fear into Tagalog hearts and minds like the sudden, nocturnal descent of the 'moros.' According to the detailed regional studies of Owen, Dery and Mallari the Iranun sunk or captured boats, raided coastal towns, pillaged the villages of southern Luzon, and seized the cattle and people unfortunate enough to be there. However, in cruel irony, they would not harry to death the defenseless survivors who fled to the hills, in order to encourage them to replant crops in time for the next annual raid.[50] At this point, it seems that the Spaniards would have settled merely for a cessation of Iranun marauding in order to reduce the strain on the treasury and the gap, from their standpoint, between civilization and barbarism. The author, for example, of *The State of the Philippines*, published in 1842, wrote the following about the failure of Spain's political program of the 1780s and 1790s with respect to 'moro piracy':

> 'Moros,' with this name we designate the Mahomedans established at Sulu, Mindanao and the other neighbouring islands whose principal occupation is piracy. They have caused us constantly serious injuries and offences without our ever having been able to free the inhabitants of the Colony from such a terrible calamity. Every system has been tried and none has prevented their depradations as may be seen by reading the history of our domination from the discovery of the archipelago to this day.[51]

The success of the slave raiders of the Sulu Sultanate was related directly to the deteriorating financial and military situation in the Philippines in the latter part of the eighteenth century. Iranun marauding placed an enormous burden on the Spanish treasury and the Filipinos for the maintenance of coastguard fleets and the upkeep of forts, troops and a string of community fortifications throughout the Philippines.[52] The government was forced cap in hand to solicit funds from the various religious orders, private institutions and wealthy individuals to meet the persistent expenditures for the defense of the archipelago. In 1773, the governor captain general informed the Crown that the ₱100,000 allotted for defense and mounting expeditions against the Iranun was not enough. As a result of the grave situation, he raised, in Manila alone, more than a quarter of a million pesos by personal donation: ₱170,000 from the Manila Chinese; ₱20,000 from the new Kapitan China for confirmation of his appointment; ₱5,203 from the mestizos of Tondo; and ₱50,000 from a wealthy widow, Doña Maria Israel Gomez de Careaga. The governor described Doña Maria, who donated more money to 'extirpate' the Muslims than anyone else in Manila, as a 'woman of exceptional character and the finest deeds.' She also privately financed the construction of a patrol galley, provided weapons and provisions for the Mamburao expedition, and agreed to supply all rations–food and drink– necessary to support punitive expeditions against the Iranun for a period of five years.[53] Despite such efforts, financial constraints and the advent of regional trade between Manila and Jolo prevented the Spanish from undertaking a large scale campaign against the Sulu Sultanate.[54]

Spain chose instead to wage a defensive 'sea-war' in Philippine waters. The official assumption was that cruising, construction of a coastal defense network, and the building of *vintas* and *barangayanes* deterred raiding. Hence, in this period, there was a demand that the coastguard flotillas be maintained and more vessels and fortifications built. From 1778 to 1793, the Spanish spent over a million and a half pesos to establish fleets of vintas and cannon launches to patrol the seas principally near Manila, but very little was spent on community defense.[55] Village curates and town friars were expected to organize parishioners to build their own coastal defences–*castillo* and *baluarte*–and fortify them from village donations and religious coffers. The most obvious solution to the slave raiding problem would have been a major offensive against the principal centers of Iranun marauding and the occupation of Jolo. This preemptive strategy was apparently not in the best interests of a Manila administration which was in the ironic position of developing a lucrative regional trade with Sulu–a trade that was inadvertently predicated on the 'piracy' it so religiously decried. There was, of course, also the added factor of the extreme difficulty of tracking down the fortified lairs of the Iranun among the hundreds of Philippine and Sulu islands. The Spaniards traditionally possessed a range of light, fast-sailing vessels for antipiracy duty, but it was often difficult for even the fastest patrol craft to come to the aid of a Luzon or Visayan coasting vessel under Iranun attack.

Iranun maritime raiding from 1765 to 1775 highlighted the lack of effective surveillance and patrolling. For the Spanish this meant building ever faster-moving coastguard craft rather than conventional naval vessels.[56] In 1778, recognizing that only shallow draught vessels could pursue the slave raiders, Governor Basco y Vargas organized 'the light navy' [*marina sutil*] to police the 300,000 square miles of seas surrounding the archipelago.[57] A small fleet of vintas, armed outriggered craft, was hastily constructed to patrol the waters from Manila to Panay, and an order was sent to military governors and *alcades mayores* making them responsible for the organization, outfitting and maintenance of vinta squadrons in the provinces.[58] By this measure, Governor Basco hoped, with a stroke of the pen, to establish coastguard flotillas at Cebu, Iligan and Iloilo without undue expenditure by the government. Three years later, a fee in kind, called vinta in Pampanga and Bulacan and *falua* in other provinces, was introduced by the government to further help finance coastguard patrols.[59] Beleaguered provinces could not always raise sufficient funds to support the local vintas, already reeling under the constant pressure of the Iranun onslaught. In 1790, Manila refused to provide the necessary assistance to the alcalde mayor of Iloilo, whose province had incurred an alarming series of raids, and temporary relief–a galley and several vintas–had to be sought from neighboring islands.[60]

Within two decades, the regional based vinta programme collapsed. During the government of Don Felix de Marquina, 1778-1793, 'the moros did much injury.' "Right from the beginning," he wrote in an impassioned letter to the King, the advent of Iranun slave raiding had been an "evil without remedy." From the arrival of Basco y Vargas to the conclusion of Marquina's government, a period of 15 years, ₱1,519,209 had been spent in constructing vintas and other antipiracy vessels to defend the coasts and shipping of the archipelago.[61] Apart from costing the government a minimum of ₱70,000 a year, the vintas had other more serious drawbacks. They cruised only at certain times of the year and then only in good weather. They were stationed in some parts of the archipelago but not in others and, from the beginning, there were never enough vintas to carry out Basco's plan.[62]

In 1793, a special colonial executive was established under the leadership of the new governor, Rafael Maria de Aguilar y Ponce de Leon, to formulate an archipelago wide defense programme and counterattack strategy against Iranun maritime raiding. A special council of experts in naval warfare and Muslim affairs was urgently convened, in response to the steady stream of desperate church reports and village petitions calling for help, to contain Iranun slaving and marauding. At the same time, it was apparent to all present that the actual suppression of 'moro piracy' was no longer strictly a matter for those communities and religious directly affected. The state would now have to take a more direct interest in its suppression.[63] The following year, in 1794, leading military and civilian officials on the council decided to abolish the vintas and replace them with six divisions of *faluas* (cannon boats) and *lanchas* (armed, flat boats).[64] However, the specially built copper-bottomed boats of the antipiracy force, or *marina sutil* were also to prove inadequate to the task of patrolling such a vast expanse of water.[65] In 1803, the Spanish had 30 such boats, 55 to 60 feet in length, each armed with an 18 to 24 pound cannon in the bow and swivel guns at the quarters and capable of speeds up to 6 knots in a favorable wind.[66] However, Iranun raiding vessels made eight to nine knots with sails and oar, and with strong winds might cover several hundred miles in less than a day.[67] As Iranun raiders continued to swarm over Luzon and the Visayas throughout the 1790s, it was apparent to all concerned that the new official policy was in trouble. The successive attempts of several governors-general to confront the Iranun at sea had more or less failed. The cruisers tended to concentrate their activities around key ports when not in the dockyards for repairs. The provincial naval squadrons were rarely a match for the larger Iranun fleets. Patrol boats, not wanting to confront the marauders, spent most of their time at anchor waiting for favorable winds, or cruising well out of range of Iranun guns, when they were sighted.

Further, the falua crews were generally not well-trained while the officers were of poor calibre, some being English and French seamen conscripted off the Manila docks. Officers on the gunboats were also poorly paid:

> They cannot obtain a higher rank than that of Captain, and then they only receive forty dollars which is less pay than an ensign of infantry at Manila. Having no retirement they only think of acquiring if they can some little fortune by trading at the ports to which they are sent for defence. It would be much better to promise them and their crews a sum of money for each prahu or pirate they took.[68]

Nor were the marine grenadiers on the faluas properly equipped:

> The feluccas in which these soldiers embark are very small and the soldiers go on board in coats, knapsacks, shakos and muskets, too much even when not embarked. The people employed in boats of this kind ought to be able to row as well as to fight—no coats, nor helmets, nor muskets, but (rather) short thick blunderbusses, hand grenades, and fireballs.[69]

In 1826, the failure of the marina sutil as a first line of defense against slave raids was pointed out by the Augustinian Provincial, Gregorio Rodriguez, in a candid reply to the governor-general's request as to whether the addition of four faluas and two lanchas would suffice to defend the coasts of Panay and the Calamianes:

> The general opinion in Iloilo [province] ... is that the lanchas ordinarily cause more harm than good. In the nine years of my residence on Panay, I cannot remember ever hearing of the lanchas having been victorious; ... They have not seized a single panco or a single muslim, nor have they been able to prevent them from coming and going with impunity; and, despite all the divisions of lanchas and faluas that presently exist ... the muslims have the audacity to pass right in front of Corregidor, under the Governor's very nose, and it is only after the pancos have gone, that the lanchas set out in pursuit. It is as though you were sending a tortoise to catch a deer.[70]

The frank letter concludes on a desperate note by suggesting that the government reinstate the late eighteenth century practice of offering a bounty to Filipinos for each raiding vessel and Muslim captured—the friars would administer the head money in the victorious villages.[71] The Iranun and Balangingi had so demoralized the provincial naval forces that the Spanish authorities seriously considered reintroducing the reward of head money, which was an accepted practice in the British Royal Navy. The bounty would have been offered to coastguard patrols and coast watchers throughout the coastal defense net of community fortifications, consisting of watchtowers, fortress churches, small forts, and signal towers for each prahu destroyed or 'pirate' they took. However, to offer letters of marque was useless as the Iranun and Balangingi navigated in vessels so "ill-provided" . . . there was little or nothing of value worth taking from them.[72] If letters of marque had been granted they would have been issued with other purposes in mind, namely the slave trade.

Before the Spanish were able to check Iranun slaving and marauding at the source, by establishing key bases for naval operations in the Muslim dominated areas, slave raiding by Filipino Christians was seriously suggested by a leading Manila commentator as a way to both retaliate against and contain Iranun and Balangingi aggression:

> [M]any who know this country particularly las Visayas, point out a sure means, which is at the same time very compatible to the general principle of fighting our enemies with their own weapons. This is to permit the Christians to go to the country of the moros and make any captives they can. They would have to think of defending themselves. We should take many moros and at the same time in exchange for them we should gain Christians whereas the captives we are now in the habit of taking prisoners are so reduced in number. The captives there, Spanish subjects, do not have the influence to get ransomed. On the other hand, should this not succeed the population we lose on one side would be gained on the other. The project does not appear destitute of many probable advantages even though this system has been partially tried and with but little of the desired effect. This may be owing to its short duration or confined limits, since it would be necessary for its success that the Government should authorise or at least tolerate a slave market.[73]

While the Iranun continued to strike at apparent places of local weakness throughout the Visayas and southern Luzon, the turning point in the 'seawar' around Bicolandia occurred in the years between 1796 and 1818.

In desperation, friar-soldiers, popularly called '*el padre capitan*,' in the villages on the wide-open coasts were forced to mobilize the inhabitants of contiguous settlements to build a string of community fortifications and arm their own fleets of *barangayanes* to defend themselves. The barangayanes were similar in certain respects to the Iranun raiding prahus, constructed in the same manner, but they did not exceed 55 feet in length.[74] The most notable example was Fr. Julian Bermejo, the Augustinian friar of Boljoon on southern Cebu from 1804 to 1836. He established a line of *baluartes* or small forts that ran from Tanog to Silbonga. He created an early warning system that used flags to alert villages to the approach of Iranun-Balangingi vessels, and issued instructions on where villagers were to congregate to defend themselves. The *telegrafistas* or signal crew, worked in shifts around the clock and reported the sighting of Iranun-Balangingi raiders using a system of flags, each measuring about 10 meters in length and mounted on 50 foot poles. A white flag signified an impending attack; black was a sign that the 'moros' had turned away; while a red flag signalled the marauder's position—whether north or south. Rene Javellana, the Jesuit historian of Philippine colonial architecture, who has travelled the length and breadth of the archipelago, documenting the defense net that was built to contain the Iranun, graphically describes Fray Julian's signal system in action:

> The rosy fingers of dawn were pushing the dark of night. From his vantage, on top of a baluarte built on the crest of a mountain flanking the town of Boljoon, the bantay greeted dawn with relief. Soon his sentry duties would be over and it would be time to return home and rest. But something on the horizon caught his eye. Were they fisherfolk returning after a whole night at sea or were they warships of the dreaded raiders? He grabbed the spyglass beside him, peered through it, fear creeping up his back. It was what he did not hope for. The outlines of their enemy's prahu were clearly visible through the lenses. He signaled to a companion who sounded the budyong, and then rushed to raise and lower a large white flag, indicating the number of warships that had been sighted. At the foot of the mountain, sentries manning the bastion protecting the church compound saw the signal. The alarm was sounded and again a white flag was raised and lowered. In no time the message of an impending attack was racing through southern Cebu, carried by an ingenious signal system.[75]

The Augustinian friar-soldier also mobilized the inhabitants of Argao, Dalaguite and Sibonga to construct a fleet of ten *barangayan*—a fleet that was ready to put to sea at a moment's notice.[76] Locally crewed and equipped barangayan fleets on antipiracy patrols began organizing themselves better and devising new stratagems to defeat the common enemy–the 'moros.' The squadron that was commanded by D. Pedro Esteban of Tabaco in Albay Province was both respected and feared by the Muslim raiders. In 1796, this remarkable local commander managed to come to the aid of the stricken residents of Bacacay. It was impossible for his fastest vessels to keep up with the Iranun but he caught them by surprise on land, since, at times, many of their shore attacks on villages took at least several hours if not several days. He destroyed 37 joanga, stranding more than 200 raiders who were hunted down or who perished from hunger and starvation.[77] But, the real signal that the tide was perhaps beginning to turn occurred in 1818. That year, at the age of 80, the embattled veteran came out of retirement to capture 9 joanga and sink 18 smaller boats. At dawn on 26 October the elderly Esteban, *ex-gobernadorcillo* of Tabaco and overall commander of the armadillas, saw the first signs of the enemy's strength, intercepting 40 joanga lead by Prince Nune, the son of the sultan of Mindanao. There was no pause, no break from the reconnoitring of the seas as Esteban kept close to the track of the raiders for more than a week. He now joined forces with Don Jose Blanco's squadron (composed of the boats of the towns of Albay Viejo, Gubat, Malinao, and Casiguran) to inflict a major defeat on the Iranun in an extraordinary series of life-and-death struggles at sea, lasting over 13 hours from 5 o'clock in the morning till well after 5 o'clock in the afternoon. The Iranun fleet lost hundreds of marauders in the sea battle itself while a thousand warriors cast ashore fled into the mountains behind Caramoan and Laganoy with only a slim hope of survival. Prince Nune escaped capture, when rescued by one of his commanders, Datu Gampon. Nune and his crew, trapped in the crossfire from both armadillas were virtually sentenced to death. But Datu Gampon, who understood that the sea fight was over, could only save his commander and watch in horror as nearby crews were struck down by grapeshot and musket balls or drown with terrible wounds in a blood red sea. The losses for the Iranun had been staggering. Nearly 2 weeks after the battle, more than 60 corpses of the raiders still washed ashore, most of them in and around Caramoan. Until late December 1818, reports were being written about the starving, sick, confused Iranun fugitives in the mountains of

Caramoan and Laganoy, many of whom eventually came out of the mountains to willingly become prisoners.[78] Nearly a quarter of a century after his famous victory on the shores of Bacacay a now elderly Estaban and the Bicolanos had won a major victory in the battle of Tabogin Bay, that resulted in the active improvement in the defense and administrative policies of the island of Ticao. Although Iranun-Balangingi raids on southern Luzon towns continued for several decades more, they never again had the unparalleled success experienced in the years prior to 1818.[79] To this day the legendary feats of Don Pedro's career of naval conflict with Muslim raiding fleets, lives on in the oral traditions and folktales about a certain Captain Teban, Tibang-tibang, Sargento Juan, and Comisario Juan, from the eastern shores of Camarines Sur to the province of Sorsogon.[80] The barangayanes scheme was so successful that by 1830 the Visayans of southern Cebu and Bohol also employed 70 barangayanes to protect their villages and tripang fisheries.[81]

The consequence of Iranun and Balangingi slave raiding in the Philippine archipelago was often a one-sided perennial struggle for life and property on the part of Filipinos. The *bantay* or castillo, the village watchtower, and the baluarte, which varied from slit trenches on hillcrests to large, stone block houses, were prominent features of most coastal villages. Manila could not afford to assist all coastal settlements in the islands to fortify themselves and, as a rule, built *presidios* only in or near the provincial capitals. Nevertheless, as early as 1769, the government had ordered all villages to use their own resources to build stockades.[82] Once again, the church came to the rescue of weak communities stretching from Ilocos Norte to the coastline of Mindanao. Since Manila had very little to do with community defense, the construction of lookout towers, palisades and forts was managed chiefly by friar-soldiers with local labor. Comyn observed that Filipinos actively defended their villages:

> [B]y opening ditches and planting a breastwork of stakes and palisades, crowned with watch towers, or a wooden or stone castle; precautions which sometimes are not sufficient against the nocturnal irruptions and robberies of the moors, more especially when they come in strength with firearms, in general scarce among the natives.[83]

Friars and priests played a critical role in preventing the Iranun from establishing unconditional dominion over the coasts of southern Luzon and the Visayan Islands. Jean Mallat, in his 1846 history, *The Philippines*, mentions a Recollect-friar missionary stationed at Sibuyan Island near Panay who was called 'Capitan Terror' because of his robust leadership of the local populace in repelling Iranun raids. The friar's memory was still venerated by a brave population, who defended the island from behind the walls of the small fort he helped design and construct, when the Frenchman visited the Philippines in the early 1840s.[84] They were at one and the same time clergy, soldiers and technical advisers, skilled not only in the use of ordinance but also in boat-building, navigation and first aid. Between 1802 and 1848, the Augustinian Julian Bermejo, in his conduct of a 'just war' to defend the mission territories of southern Cebu, trained his flock to take up arms in the bloody, and at times, brutal conflict against the Iranun and Balangingi, earnestly commanding them to "bring me the ears of the Moors you kill in battle."[85] As dominant authority figures, armed with a rosary and Bible in one hand and a sword in the other, they often provided the necessary leadership and organization that knitted Filipinos together to form coast guard flotillas, community militias and sentinel systems:

> In situations of common danger, he [the friar] is their leader by sea and land, and on account of his superior wisdom and courage, he is looked up to as a strong tower against the invasion and inroads of the Mohamedans. It is the prerogative of each missionary in his own parish to issue orders for building or repairing the fort, for providing it with cannon and ammunition, and for the construction of war canoes, which he frequently commands in person. He appoints all subordinate officers, presides over the discipline of the militia, regulates the number of guards, and even directs the sentinel to his proper post.[86]

At the same time, the constant menace and fear engendered by Iranun slave raids enhanced the friar's authority and prestige, enabling him to foster a sense of village dependency.

The implementation of local community defense rested entirely on the Filipinos themselves. They acted as telegrafistas, built and staffed the

Spanish Colonial and Community Coastal Fortifications in the Philippines

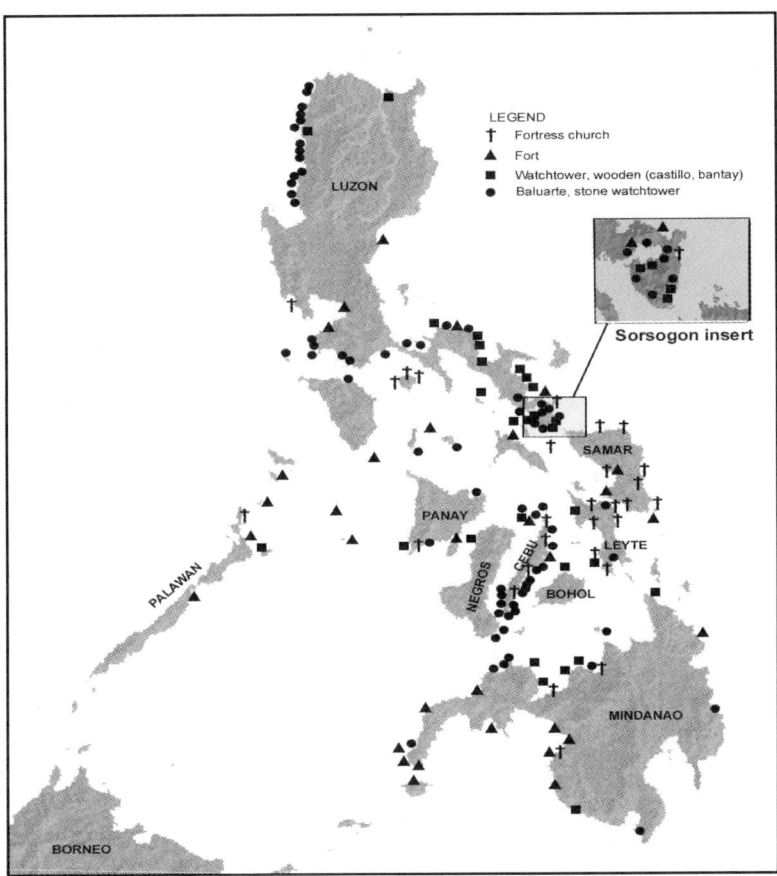

Map 4. This map showing the coastal locations of watchtowers, fortress churches, fortified towns, small forts, and signal towers is based upon the detailed archival research and field work of Rene B. Javellana. Over a decade and a half, he travelled thoughout the Philippines documenting these various lines of defense meant to contain the Iranun and Balangingi. I have set out on the map only the confirmed locations of the most important coastal fortifications. There were a significant number of crown and community fortifications which were either totally ruined or whose status is unconfirmed. See Rene B. Javellana, Fortress of Empire, pp. XVI-XXV.

baluartes, and served on coastguard vessels to defend their coasts against Iranun raiders. Forty-six out of 65 villages in the bishopric of Cebu had a baluarte and/or a stone fort (see Appendix B). Filipinos had built all of them. Once erected, the watchtowers, earthworks, palisades, and small forts had to be maintained and rebuilt when suddenly demolished by seasonal typhoons and earthquakes.[87] Cyclonic storms on southern Luzon not infrequently left a trail of disaster which swept away signal towers and stockades leaving coastal settlements defenseless while torrential rains and flooding rusted cannons and spoiled what little gunpowder villages possessed.[88]

Volunteers took coast-watch roles as the raiding season loomed. Filipino sentinels stood watch day and night during the southwest monsoon.[89] The bantay-bell tower of churches and watchtowers on hilltops furnished some of the best vantage points. In some instances those sentinels who were assigned as telegrafista on neighboring offshore islands, or overlooking key straits, or who served as lookouts over particular rivers or in the highlands brought their families to settle at the distant early warning sites thus forming the nucleus of new settlements. In the local oral traditions, women in one such community on Camiguin island passed their time on the hillsides by skeining abaca fibres for weaving local cloth.[90] But, at the slightest sign of danger a telegrafista rang the church bell or warned the village by signalling with a big flag waved high in the air during the day and with a torch at night. In 1788, Captain Meares wrote of the Mindoro coast: "The inhabitants not only kept numerous and constant fires along the shores, but had even lighted them on the very summits of the mountains."[91] Besides fire there were other commonly used early warning systems to guard against slave raids; women and children scrambled for refuge at the first sound of the sentry blowing on a conch shell horn [budyong], or beating a gong, drum or hollowed-out log, while the militia rapidly assembled to take up their arms in either the baluarte or fortress-church.

The presence of a friar, alleged to be worth more than a hundred bayonets, could exert a strong influence on the security of a village in face of government neglect. Of the eight communities dispersed by Iranun raiding in the bishopric of Cebu in 1779, only one–Cacub in Caraga province–had either a priest or a baluarte. Coastal villages that lacked a friar and a baluarte ran a substantial risk of being attacked. It was in the interest of such exposed settlements to locate near some sort of natural refuge where villagers could flee to safety on first sight of the 'moros.' Mountains or any high ground were an obvious choice, while villages in some instances were encircled with huge groves of impenetrable bamboo or thickets of *pandan*, a plant with a spiny trunk and leaves.[92] On Masbate, cave complexes were fortified and used as temporary dwellings by settlers fearful of returning to the coast.[93]

The appearance of large numbers of slaving prahus with overwhelming firepower was a terrifying experience for Filipinos who lacked adequate arms and patrol boats to defend themselves. One of the most outspoken critics of the government's inadequate assistance for community defense was the bishop of Nueva Caceres whose churches were periodically plundered and burnt. Most of his mission churches with their massive stone walls and high bell towers served as fortresses as well as places of worship, which, in some localities, provided the Filipinos with their sole place of refuge against Iranun maritime raids. In 1770 the bishop accused the government of having forsaken the provinces of Camarines and Albay and urged that revenue from these provinces be made available for their self-defense:

> In conclusion, your Excellency, the truth of the matter is that Camarines and Albay province don't have a king to protect them, let alone a pistol or sword for their own defense. Nevertheless, they pay more in tribute than the combined amount collected from the indios of Bohol, Dapitan and Iligan.[94]

In the 1780s and 1790s, towns and villages throughout the Philippines experienced some of their worst crises, as Basco y Vargas' and Marquina's governorships attempted to turn their attention to the Iranun, who now posed such a dire threat to the overall economy and wellbeing of the Philippines. While, at the behest of the friars, new coastal fortifications were built, town walls restored and cruising prahus constructed all along the coasts of Luzon and the Visayas, the Spanish, and their terrorized colonial subjects, nevertheless, effectively abandoned long stretches of shoreline, the lower reaches of rivers and small coastal islands to the Iranun.

The vexed questions of both the cost and supply of arms and munitions was particularly troublesome for the bishops towards the end of the eighteenth century. Some of their communities had firearms provided by the Church, but were frequently destitute of gunpowder and shot.[95] When communities were fortunate enough to obtain powder it was often not enough and of poor quality. The religious orders had some difficulty purchasing cannon, and were often apprehensive at being unable to obtain gunpowder. The bishops had good reason to be concerned about unsuccessful efforts to purchase arms and powder for their poorly defended parishes. Not only did government officials charge friars and priests exorbitant prices for the hard-to-find gunpowder, but they often rejected out-of-hand petitions for help to purchase war stores from newly founded villages and others that had been raided.[96] The bishop of Nueva Caceres noted in his visits to the seaside towns and settlements of Tayabas, Camarines and Albay that the communities were defenseless having no weapons, cannon or gunpowder, but that these beleaguered villages and towns were ready to purchase the necessary war stores.[97] However, no administrator in Manila wanted to be responsible for the decision of supplying Filipinos with wholesale arms and ammunition. The government objected to such a measure for several reasons:

> The first is arming and instructing a subjugated people, the second is that lacking order, leaders and valour at the least surprise they fly whither they can abandoning their arms and ammunition which fall into the possession of the moros who have in consequence already taken many guns.[98]

Nevertheless, the most effective system of coastal defense gradually developed from the government and Church working closely together with local leaders. Between 1796 and 1818, the Sulu-based Iranun suffered a string of sharp defeats at the hands of well-armed local war leaders, whose provincial forces could respond more quickly than the centralized fleets of light gunboats. By the start of the nineteenth century, the town heads and junta or council, had become an important factor for the Spanish organizing the defense net. In the 1790s, Manila was forced to reconsider its policy towards supplying guns and munitions to coastal settlements because of the extreme harm inflicted on them by the slave raids, especially those conducted by Iranun from Burias. By 1799, the central government felt it absolutely imperative that provincial authorities assume a more direct responsibility for defending the coasts and more remote islands of their provinces. The burden of this task fell to the *alcaldes mayores*, *principales* and *cabeza de barangay* whom the government accordingly entrusted with crown arms and gunpowder.[99] In the following 3 decades (1800-1830), more than 1,500 cannons were distributed among the coastal villages of the Philippines together with other arms, projectiles, equipment, and stores. Undoubtedly, one of the most interesting and provocative alcalde mayor, who taught the indios about coastal defense systems in a profoundly experimental manner, was Jose Marie Peneranda, a Spanish army engineer, who first came to the Philippines in 1829 as a young lieutenant and aide-de-camp of his uncle, Lt. Gen. Pascual Enrile. In May 1834, he was appointed alcalde mayor of Albay, in southern Luzon. Peneranda's appointment at Albay was unusual. He had been personally appointed by his uncle, the governor captain general of the Philippines. Enrile knew Peneranda and was impressed with his practical methodical knowledge and ability, and his interest in the welfare of the people of Albay. It was an unusual appointment, and also an important one, for Albay was known as a difficult province. It was in a poor state, and it was widely recognized that the population was demoralized because of uncaring officials and constant Iranun raids. It would appear that Peneranda was under the impression that he was being sent to Albay by Manila in order to carry out a special mission: that was to put things right, to remove the yoke of fear and oppression from the local Albay population. He arrived in Albay with the feeling of being the chosen protector of these unfortunate people, he felt that action was expected of him, and that if he did not act against the 'moro' threat he would betray his uncle's confidence. Unlike other provincial governors, he avoided abusing his position while systematically strengthening the coastal warning systems, forts and offshore defenses. He transformed the state of the local defenses of Bicol and part of Tayabas using techniques that were profoundly experimental. He created an integrated distant early warning coastal signal system, utilizing signal disks, colored flares and pennants, and sky rockets. He appointed prominent local citizens as heads of the signal stations; and he reorganized the fiscal and material basis of the falua fleets, providing decent salaries for the crews and adequate funds for the maintenance of the boats. In the case of Albay, the establishment of a network of signal or telegraph towers, which were quickly transformed into hamlet sites, staffed around the clock, helped the upgraded *armadilla* maintain vigilance along the coasts in a deadly contest; a protracted struggle that was going on between Iranun and Balangingi slave raiders, partially controlled by those who wielded official power over world commerce and economic growth in Jolo, and the Filipinos of Luzon, a contest nowhere better illustrated than in Bikolandia. In 1832, Peneranda had a fort erected at Burias island and fortified the town of Donsol with a stockade of stout palm trunks. With the assistance of the civil population, he then built a string of wooden observation towers, each with a tall pole on which to hoist a sundisk or flag, that stretched from Putiao to San Bernardino Strait from Matnog to Laganoy Gulf. Within the short space of four years, the young energetic governor vastly improved the defenses of the seaside *visitas* of Bicol and parts of Tayabas. It had been a very uneven conflict for more than half a century, but Peneranda's innovative system of defense progressively helped to repel the large-scale maritime forays.[100]

While this community-based defence policy markedly contributed to warding off Iranun and Balangingi slave raiding in certain provinces, there were limits to its successful devolution however, as alcaldes who were specifically appointed to their office to organize local inhabitants to fight the Iranun, were sometimes convicted for trafficking in arms. Some alcaldes, charged with the defense of provinces, particularly on Negros and Panay, took full advantage of the opportunity to further their personal fortunes, and regularly sold government munitions to the Iranun and Samal.[101] Capt. Edward Belcher recounts having met such a pragmatic individual at the fortified village of Ylin situated on the south coast of Mindanao. The place was surrounded by watchtowers and other fortifications which, "showed that they were not disposed to trust too implicitly to the friendly alliance existing between their neighbors of Mindanao, or Illana."[102] The British naval captain, previously wounded in an engagement with the Iranun off the coast of Sulawesi, implied that the chief spokesperson in the village, the gobernadorcillo, although not an alcalde, was still nevertheless trafficking with the Iranun:

> He was a complete pilot for all the creeks and ports from Manila to Zamboanga, and the pirate haunts as far as Sooloo.... From his intimate knowledge of all the pirate haunts and practices, he must have been in closer contact than the gun-boat crews to which he intimated that he formerly belonged.[103]

In the 1850s, many of these donated guns would be recalled by a government more fearful of awakening nationalist sentiment and the spectre of Filipinos possessing arms than of Muslim slave raids.[104] The Balangingi would appear as far north as Mindoro for another 20 years and the newspaper *La Politica* noted, as late as 1864, that not infrequently remote villages had only sharpened sticks and stones to defend themselves![105]

By the nineteenth century, the Spanish friars and priests had been able to establish over a thousand towns and cities in the island lowlands. The majority of these communities had fewer than 2,000 inhabitants; 200 had a population of over 2,000; 30 over 5,000; 9 over 10,000.[106] The demographic study of the history of population(s) in the Philippines has only recently begun to focus attention on the impact of Iranun and Balangingi maritime raiding on the development of towns and population growth, on the one hand, and migration and the scattering and dispersion of people within regions and provinces and between islands in the late eighteenth and nineteenth centuries, on the other. Obviously, slave raiding concentrated on particular islands, provinces and districts and not others depending on the geographical terrain and other ecological and demographic variables. A diversity of responses and demographic patterns has begun to emerge from regional studies of the impact of Iranun and Balangingi slave raids on the population history of southern Luzon, Cebu and Samar from the mid-eighteenth to nineteenth centuries, undertaken by Owen, Mallari, Dery, Cullinane and Xenos, and Cruikshank.[107]

I would like to examine here, albeit briefly, the impact of Iranun-Balangingi maritime raiding on the population history of one bishopric in Luzon, namely Nueva Caceres, with particular reference to Tayabas,

Camarines and Albay provinces between 1751 and 1815. I have used two types of social statistics—ecclesiastical and civil. The principal demographic data are the censuses compiled at the request of the Spanish Crown by the provincial bishops.[108] I have supplemented the census material with the reports of military officials, parish curates and fragmentary information about community location, presence or absence of a priest, frequency of raids, and enumeration of ordinance, small arms, boats and baluartes to create a community defense profile on 66 communities listed in the 1780 census for Nueva Caceres.[109]

From a systematic comparison of community population fluctuations with community defensive capability and frequency of slave raids, it is possible to reconstruct a more substantial picture of the settlement patterns and migratory movements of the Philippine population of southern Luzon at the end of the eighteenth century. Table 2 lists the location, frequency of raids and/or destruction of communities, and the population variations between 1751 and 1815 of 15 communities that were either destroyed or known to have been raided more than once. There is enough evidence to show that the nature of maritime raiding in Nueva Caceres changed between 1755 and 1800 as the Iranun and Balangingi concentrated their attacks on progressively smaller more isolated targets. There was a shift away from frontal assaults and prolonged sieges of *cabecera* (mission and administrative centers) in Albay and Camarines provinces, to attacks on vulnerable outlying visitas. The visitas of the southern Luzon provinces, more especially Tayabas, were already common targets in the 1790s.[110] In the first half of the nineteenth century, they were to become the principal targets of Balangingi slave raids. This change in strategy by Iranun and Balangingi raiding expeditions was related to the sustained, rapid growth of towns in certain areas, the acquisition of administrative and leadership skills by their civil leaders, and the increased organizational strength and valor of the coastal defense forces.

With better bureaucratic and military organization, the exponential growth of population centers became a key factor in deterring maritime raids (See Appendix E). Settlements that were formerly potential targets increased in size and strength to a point (1,500+) beyond which the risks became too great for the Iranun under most circumstances. The

Table 2. Slave Traiding and Population Variations in Nueva Caceres (1751-1815)

Pueblos	Location	Number of Recorded Raids				Year Community Destroyed by Raiding	Population in 1751 (or 1780)	Population in 1815 (or 1813)	Population Variation between 1751 and 1815 – when Population of 1751 or 1780 = 100
		1755–1779	1780–1790	1791–1800	1801–1815				
Tayabas Province									
Mayobac	Coast	1				1765, 1782	747	0	0
Palanan	Coast			1		1798	1,334	371	27.8
Guinayangen	Coast	3		1		1767, 1791–	1,225	382	31.2
Obuyon	Coast	1		1		1800	850	481	56.6
Baler	Coast			1		1793	977	740	75.7
Casiguran de	Coast			1		1798	796	644	80.9
Baler	Inland	1				1798	1,859	1,624	87.4
Lupi	Coast	2		1		1759–1761	1,585	1,542	97.3
Catanavan	Coast	2	1	1			(1780)	909	125.6
Pagbilao						1759–1761	724		
Camarines Province									
Capalonga	Coast	2	2			1760	492	301	61.2
Indan	Coast	3				1760	2,946	2,446	83.7
Daet	Coast	2	1				3,074	2,903	94.0
Albay Province									
Sorsogon	Coast	2				1755	6,422	4,008	62.4
Virac	Coast	1	1			1761	3,250	4,981	153.3
Caramoan	Inland	2					771 (?)	1,972	255.8

NOTES: The information on the frequency of raids and destruction of pueblos has been compiled from the following sources: Noticias veridicas de los perjuicios, robos, muertes, y cautiveros y otras inhumanidads, que los moros han executado en los anos de 59 y 60 en la Provincia de Tayabas, Camarines, y parages correspondientes a la administracion de los ramos Descalzados de nuestra Santa padre San Francisco y clerigos, pertenezientes a el Obispado de el propio Camarines, AGI, Pilipinas 68I; El Arzobispo de Manila a Vuestra Magestad, 3 June 1761, AGI, Filipinas 603; Alcalde Mayor de Tayabas a Gobernador y Capitan General de las Islas Filipinas, 20 December 1768, PNA, Ereccion de Pueblo de Tayabas III, Testemonio de Provincial de San Francisco, Francisco Xavier Estongo in Numero 46, El Gobernador y Capitan General de las Islas Filipinas a Senor Secretario de Estado y del Despacho Universal de Marina y Indias, 17 Aug. 1770, AGI, Filipinas 490; Alcalde Mayor y Capitan de Guerra a Gobernador y Capitan General de las Islas Filipinas, 18 Sept. 1781, PNA, Ereccion de Pueblo Tayabas 217, bundle 1; Numero 20, El Obispo de Nueva Caceres remite a Vuestra Magestad su ultima visita Diocesana de 1791 y 1792, 1 Dec. 1792, AGI, Duplicados del Obispo de Nueva Caceres 1033; Alcalde Mayor de Tayabas a Gobernador y Capitan General de las Islas Filipinas, 2 Dec. 1793, PNA. Erreccion de Pueblo Tayabas, 1793-1857, pt II, Numero 7, El Gobernador y Capitan General de las Islas Filipinas a Senor Secretario de Estado y del Despacho Universal de la Hacienda y las Indias, 4 June 1806, AGI, Filipinas 510; the letter of Don Matheo de Meza Juez, Provisor y Vicario General Inderado de este Obispo vacante de Nueva Caceres en El Arzobispo de Manila a Vuestra Magestad, 15 July 1814, AGI, Ultramar 683.

population tables for the Province of Albay, 1735-1859, compiled by Dery, show that in spite of the Iranun raids, various towns of Sorsogon, including some on the coast, experienced steady population growth in the first half of the nineteenth century.[111] In 1826, the Provincial of the Augustinians was to write:

> As the population increases in the Philippine islands, the moros cannot cause the devastation they have in the past when they landed, laid waste to towns and carried off many indios into slavery: nowadays there are situated on all coasts sizeable communities that bravely defend themselves, consequently the moros don't attack the large population centres.[112]

In the knowing eyes of celebrated Iranun lords, every town–every village–presented a unique challenge that was different now for every Iranun or Balangingi commander. For some, like the celebrated young Balangingi panglima, Taupan, who had no fear of guns, sails or large populations, and with oar power to burn, the Philippine coastline was a Spanish bastion to be stormed; a hurdle to soar over on the way to personal glory. For others, however, the shoreline was now a minefield in spots, to be navigated with caution and care. The questions increasingly posed by most communities as part of the defense net to the raiders were, who are you today? And, how will you meet our collective challenge? The answers were often simple, and devastating. There was no scaling down of maritime raiding activity after the 1790s–only a change of targets. The new pattern that emerged combined mass attacks with inshore scouring. When mass attacks were successful, results were spectacular, as was the case on the distant northeastern side of Luzon in 1798 (an estimated 450-500 people were seized from Casiguran, Baler and Palanan).[113] But, such successes appear by then to have been the exception rather than the norm. What made the impact of the new raiding pattern so strongly felt was the laser-like Iranun-Balangingi concentration in certain places–mainly the Ragay gulf and Camarines Norte–and more widespread use of shallow draught canoes for surprise attacks either just before dawn or after dusk. Clearly, to pluck unsuspecting fishers and their families, traders and travellers from isolated beaches and coasting boats with heavily armed inshore raiding canoes was easy and safe; and slave raiders, especially the Balangingi, came to rely increasingly on the use of this scouring technique for seizing captives.

It is difficult to estimate the annual number of Filipinos directly lost to maritime raiding through captivity or death in Nueva Caceres. In 1761, the bishop was unable to provide an overall figure for the decline in the population of the provinces but conservatively estimated the loss in Camarines between 1759 and 1760 at 800 people.[114] In 1817, the bishop estimated Iranun marauders captured more than 1,500 people, predominantly boys and girls from the cabeceras and visitas of Albay, Camarines and Tayabas.[115] By 1830, the intensity of Balangingi slave-raiding, closely linked to Sulu's expanding global economy, would tend to support an estimate that on average 750 to 1,500 Filipinos were carried off or killed from Nueva Caceres annually. Further, the cumulative totals rose in the first half of the nineteenth century at an annual rate that was greater than in the last quarter of the eighteenth century. However, throughout the first half of the nineteenth century, southern Luzon was, in demographic terms, a paradox. Despite relentless raids and a pattern of relatively low human densities on the more remote islands, the region's population rose steadily in the first half of the nineteenth century. Direct losses from slave raids varied considerably in different parts of the archipelago. Cruikshank estimates that 100 inhabitants of Samar were either captured or killed each year between 1768 and 1858.[116]

Despite increased government expenditure and cooperation for coastal defense, the continuing high incidence of slave raids on the smaller shore towns that could not be adequately defended was a cause for grave concern. In such settlements, the anxiety of waiting for the slave raiders to strike often became as great as the actual fear of confronting them. Fear itself threatened paralysis of daily life; it disrupted the rhythm of the rice harvest, it prevented fishers from putting out to sea or casting their nets along the shore, and more generally it led to a breakdown in social practices and communication as individuals and communities were separated from one another. People did not visit or travel by sea and newly-born babies and children remained unbaptized for years on end. One of the most obvious results of the incessant slave raiding was the destabilizing effects of local migration and the advent of floating populations dispersed and motivated by fear. The perennial fear of

Iranun and Balangingi slave raids and the need for adequate food and shelter forced terrified Filipinos to abandon their villages and the sea. Throughout this period (1790-1838), large and small scattered groups were constantly on the move seeking resettlement opportunities. They often remained within their province, flocking to larger municipal centers or moving well inland out of reach of the Iranun. Some never settled down again, instead joining the ranks of the *remontados*, or *tulisanes* beyond the pale of Spanish authority.[117]

Spanish recovery would not seriously get under way until almost the middle of the nineteenth century, but then it came rapidly. In the 1820s, Spanish fleets twice attacked various Iranun bases in Mindanao and a Balangingi base on Pilas Island, just off Basilan. While an 1827 expedition landed 500 soldiers on Jolo, holding the sultan of Sulu responsible for sponsoring the raids of the Iranun and Balangingi, but the troops were driven off the island after a pitched battle. The unsuccessful expedition then sailed to Mindanao and destroyed a number of Iranun settlements on the edge of Illana Bay.[118] By mid-century the Spanish had formulated a strategic plan of occupying key positions in the Iranun and Balangingi heartlands. The theory now expressed by Spanish naval experts, knowledgeable about Iranun maritime raiding and the likes of James Brooke, was to control Iranun and Balangingi 'piracy' at the source, or at least check slave raiding by establishing forward bases for naval operations and as places of refuge for victims of Iranun and Balangingi aggression.

However, the most effective blow against Iranun and Balangingi slave raiding and 'piracy' would be struck from another quarter initially, by the able and liberal-minded Narcisco Claveria, the governor-general of the Philippines. In 1848, he secured from Europe prefabricated steam gunboats for the defense of the islands. The arrival of the steamers marked a turning point in the 90 year sea-war (1758-1848) against Iranun and Balangingi slave raiding and marauding. The beginning of the end of their wind-driven way of life was inextricably tied to that moment. Claveria's decision to launch steam warships against Iranun and Balangingi vessels, fortifications and settlements across the archipelago and south of Mindanao was as much a telling message to the Sulu Sultanate as to Spain's colonial competitors, Britain, France and the

Netherlands in Southeast Asia, that Madrid was watching—and that it would not tolerate any interventionism that might have threatened to disrupt the sovereignty that Spain claimed over the region. That is why the Spanish naval strategists settled on steam gunboats in the waters of southern Luzon and the Visayas—and the same reason the governor-general extended their range to Balangingi and Jolo—even though the Iranun and Balangingi's latest transgressions were increasingly far to the south and west. Claveria's decision to discipline and punish them with *kapal api* 'fire ships' marked the start of a new era of conflict with the Iranun and Balangingi; an era which would signal the end of their way of life in less than 25 years. This was the defining moment when the slave hunters became the hunted.

CHAPTER SIX

THE SETTLEMENTS AND BASES

Iranun long distance maritime raiding operations ultimately depended on the land for supply of arms, food and shelter. Hence, island, riverine and interior shore bases were absolutely necessary for the success of the Iranun marauding enterprise. The Iranun did not situate their slave raiding settlements on the margins of the various competing colonial empires at the end of the eighteenth century. On the contrary, they established many of their bases close to the busiest shipping lanes and colonial port cities, namely those centered on Manila, Makassar, Batavia, Penang, and Singapore. At the same time they allocated specific hunting territories to particular fleets, which operated from this chain of settlements, and bases that stretched from Sulawesi in the east to Sumatra in the west. As the last quarter of the eighteenth century advanced, the distance and duration of Iranun voyages made the establishment of these satellite settlements, absolutely critical for the pursuit of their raiding and slaving activities. The sailing distances between Mindanao and Sulu and the edges of the Malay world, as they intersected with the Canton market, were very great. It would have been impossible for the Iranun to have carried on their widespread raiding operations year after year, from their haunts in Illana Bay and the Sulu archipelago, without strategic staging points or forward bases set up within the target areas or at key crossroads and 'choke-points' along the major maritime routes.

Nor by the 1790s were all slave raiders marauding only in the favorable monsoon and returning home annually to Sulu and Mindanao after having joined forces with their colonizing kindred in Borneo, Sulawesi and Sumatra. Cruises could last up to several years or more at a time as the Iranun extended their operations across Southeast Asia, establishing in the process semi-permanent residence in associate settlements on the coasts of Borneo, Sulawesi and Sumatra.[1] A single three-year slave cruise could see Iranun raiders travelling from New Guinea to the Bay of Bengal. James Brooke met an Iranun squadron on one occasion whose rajahs, under a flag of truce, told him that they had been cruising for two years and that their *joanga* had been from the very eastern end of the archipelago to the northwest coast of Borneo.[2] The deposition of Si-Ayer, who had been sailing on board the *prahu* of *nakodah* Uba Koray, a servant of the rajah of Bima, lends credence to what the Iranun commanders told the aspiring white rajah about both the extensive duration of their voyages and the laser-like character of their maritime raids:

> They remained at the island where they had caught us about a month, when they got under weigh and proceeded towards Tanah Bouton. They cruised about for about a year, principally in the Celebes Sea between the various ports of the island and Makassar. They captured during this time many *prahus*.[3]

At around the same time, in 1838, Spanish officers, sharing naval intelligence with their English counterparts in Manila, stressed the fact that Iranun dominion did not rest solely on one major raiding base, which was to prove the Achilles' heel of the Balangingi. Instead, their widespread network of settlements, kin and accomplices did not prevent them from maintaining regular contact and communication with their heartland on the lake in southwestern Mindanao.[4] The distance both in space and time between Sulu and Mindanao and the isolated islands and little frequented corners of Southeast Asia were reduced by this network of associated settlements based on ramified kinship, mobility and alliances for purposes of slave raiding and obtaining plunder. At these outlying fortified bases captives could be put to work temporarily, or transferred as chattel in local markets, raiding vessels safely careened and repaired; and premeditated attacks launched with impunity until the transient Iranun raiders were ready to return to Sulu and Illana Bay.

These Iranun satellite bases that engaged in slave raiding and marauding were established by invasion, founded because of social unrest or natural catastrophe in their homeland, or through support rendered by a local ruler. Although the historical origins of these Iranun settlements differ to a certain extent, they also share much in common with respect to their basic purpose, settlement patterns and ultimate fate. In their heyday (1765-1845), the forward bases maintained a separate Iranun identity but were sometimes aligned with neighboring realms and, at other times, essentially nonaligned. Maritime raiding was the center of their livelihood, but the majority of their inhabitants—women, children and slaves—were either engaged in subsistence agriculture, fishing or local enterprises such as tin or gold mining. Located near the vital straits and rivers that they dominated, these Iranun settlements were comparatively large and prosperous but historically ephemeral. The direction of early Iranun slave raiding and expansion was primarily to the west, along the coast of Borneo and the island and delta world of east Sumatra. It was from Jolo and the satellite settlements of Tempasuk and Reteh that the Iranun systematically raided the Malacca straits at the end of the eighteenth century.

Tempasuk and Marudu

In the mid-1760s, Iranun migrants settled on the Tempasuk and Pandassan rivers and Tuaran plain, situated on the northwest coast of Borneo. The pristine area offered good defensible harbors and anchorages, fresh water and fertile soil, and was an ideal location on the windward passage between Cotabato, Sulu and the strait of Malacca. As early as 1779, Thomas Forrest presented a brief account of the impact of the fiery eruption and seemingly senseless violence that the Maketering volcano unleashed on the interior areas around Lake Lanao. He noted that the Iranun 'suffered greatly' as ashes, rocks, lava, and a huge fast moving cloud of poisonous gas rained down on their doomed villages in the lake region of southwestern Mindanao. In the face of this most devastating eruption that unleashed an awesome fury which erased the traditional Iranun-Maranao way of life (which Dampier had written about a century earlier), thousands of survivors fled for their lives seeking in Forrest's poignant language a 'better country.'[5] As a result of this single violent natural disaster the course of Iranun and Southeast Asian history

THE SETTLEMENTS AND BASES

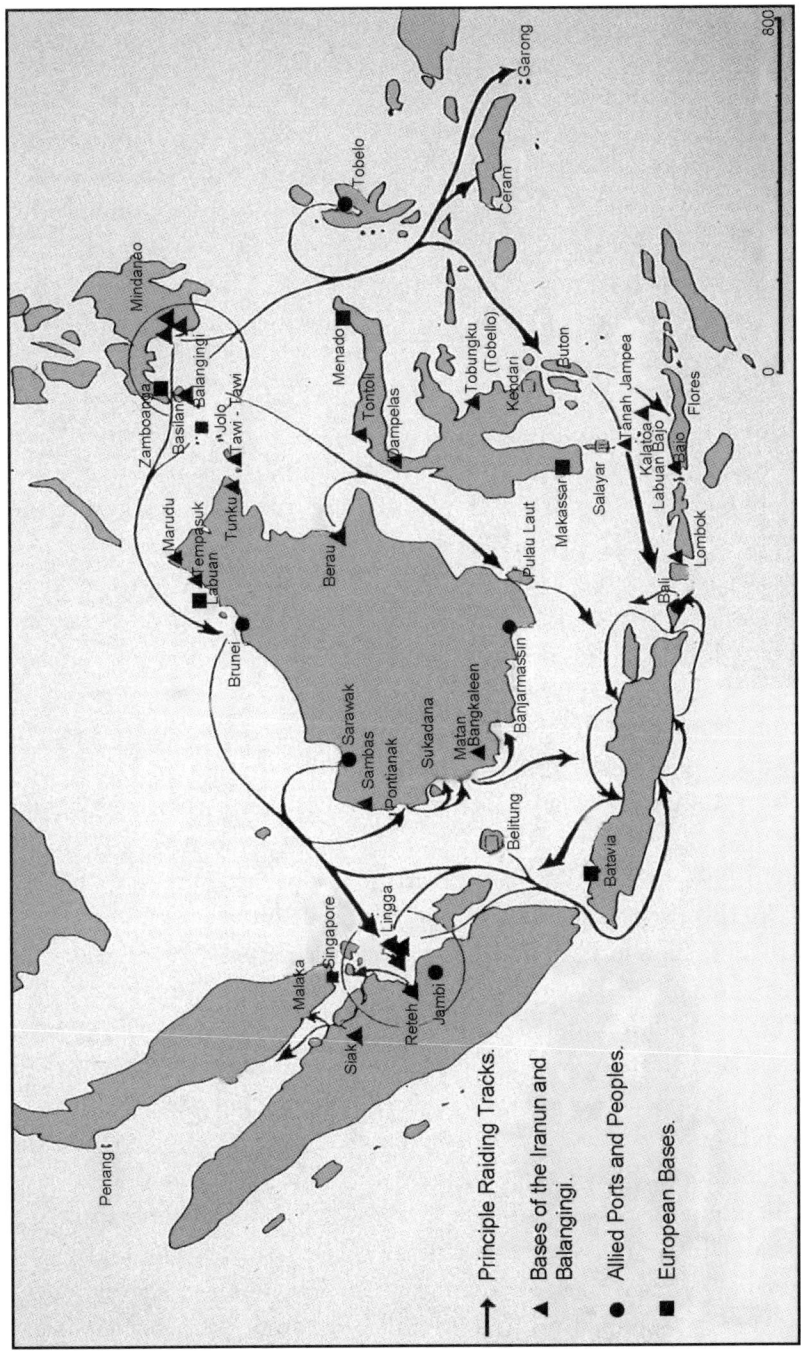

Map 5. Iranun-Balangingi Maritime Raiding and the Malay archipelago in the First half of the Nineteenth Century.

was altered forever. On the same page, in a footnote, Forrest noted the initial consequence of the rugged terrifying results of a stream of scorched and blistered lava that stretched for more than 50 miles. Crowded *prahus* found their way to Jolo's increasingly affluent shore communities, and their cargoes of hundreds of dislocated Iranun-Maranao men, women and children plunged into the surf, waded onto a beach front lined with Tausog trading houses and fanned out in search of a new way of life in Sulu. Forrest's brief comment inserted at the foot of the page noted that, "In the Sooloo capital, called Bowan, is a quarter where some Illanon inhabit."[6]

Forrest, always the astute ethnographer and amateur historian, questioned influential Tausog and Iranun about the recent 'Illano' immigrants. Local informants must have told him that the drama on the Jolo shore had been part of a well-organized operation that had, in recent years, transported thousands of Iranun-Maranao refugees as far as Tempasuk and Tuaran on the west coast of Borneo—many of them to be engaged as slave raiders.[7] At the same time, their Tausog sponsors, utilizing a global trading network which involved western gun running groups of several nationalities, had grown increasingly sophisticated and powerful, shifting slave raiding routes, vessels and communities as swiftly as they discovered new target areas and economic prospects. The Iranun arrivals at Tempasuk quickly attempted to diversify their settlement pattern, marauding methods and range of activity as much as possible. By the early 1790s, they already had the organization, capability and finances to remove their erstwhile Tausog overlords, and shift their raiding routes and activities when local political and economic patterns in the region or enforcements shifted.[8]

The recently founded Iranun migrant settlements of Tempasuk, Pandassan and those in Marudu Bay now resembled mini-states in their political function, as sovereignty increasingly resided with the Iranun rajahs and sherifs on the spot, who rarely were prepared to recognize any political authority higher than their own. In the 1830s, an Iranun lord who called himself Sultan Si-Tabuk led the settlements of Tempasuk and Pandassan. This Iranun chief was allied with one Si-Mirantau of Tuaran, whose name signified their roving way of life. For the future development and prosperity of Tempasuk, Tuaran and Pandassan, the most important of this chain of bases was situated further north at Marudu Bay, where several generations of Iranun sherifs ruled over close to 50,000 upstream inhabitants and collected tribute from them in neighboring areas including the islands of Balabac and Palawan.

Among the sultan of Sulu's riverine chiefs in the Marudu region were several powerful overlords of Iranun descent who possessed religious charisma, physical prowess and a marked degree of political acumen. In the first half of the nineteenth century, the most important of these men to acquire ritualized authority from the sultan was Sherif Usman. His family represented the Sulu Sultanate and the Iranun in the Tempasuk–Marudu area circa 1830-1886. Sherif Usman was married to a sister of the Raja Muda of Sulu.[9] In 1837, a captive, who escaped to a Spanish vessel in the Jolo roadstead, characterized Usman, his former master, as a very powerful sherif residing in Borneo who was married to the sister of Datu Buyo.[10] Described after his untimely death in 1846 as a 'man of character and energy,' Sherif Usman controlled the commodity-procurement trade of the Marudu region, Balabac and southern Palawan.[11] Accustomed to wielding authority, he crushed all resistance on Balabac and reduced the population of the island by nearly half when its Samal inhabitants refused to pay the sultanate tribute any longer.[12] This event occurred in the late 1830s in the midst of a protracted regional struggle between the sultanates of Brunei and Sulu–an event which was further complicated by the sudden intervention of James Brooke and Britain in the political affairs of the northwest coast of Borneo. Usman also promoted slave raiding and marauding against the Brunei Sultanate on a sizeable scale. His town in Marudu Bay was a major staging center for the Iranun and Balangingi, who repaid him in captives for the munitions and rations that he advanced at the onset of each cruise.[13] Usman's following of between 1,500 and 2,000 Iranun and Samal warriors equalled those of Brunei's most prestigious nobles. The *pengiran* of Brunei feared the power and influence he and his family had acquired since the Iranun had first migrated to Tempasuk and Pandassan some 40 years earlier.

Sherif Usman directed a complex slave traffic operation that financed regional wide Iranun maritime raiding. Ironically, he profitably smuggled hundreds of Visayan and straits born captives and other local inhabitants, especially from Brunei, into the neighboring sultanate each year. These captives were then exploited as hostages for ransom or as slaves. Pangeran Usop of Brunei paid up to 500 percent profit per captive, for individuals seized by Usman's Iranun raiders, to the powerful overlord. Principal local dealers in the sultanate cleared around 100 percent when the human cargo was resold in Brunei's slave market or transferred further down the coast. In discussing the 'present politics' of Brunei and the state of his formidable Iranun adversaries to the north, Brooke noted that the sultan of Brunei was 'weak and doubtful; Pangeran Usop, clever, mercantile and adverse . . . [and] Sherif Usman is a pirate, positively and undoubtedly a pirate, direct and indirect.'[14]

On the opposite side, the northeast coast, major Iranun settlements were also established on the Tungku River and the southern part of the Unsang Peninsula. In the 1830s and 1840s they were ruled by the Iranun chief, Raja Laut in alliance with Usman and their kindred at Tempasuk and Pandassan. However, in general it was Sherif Usman at Marudu who was viewed as the overlord of both these Iranun settlements on the opposite sides of north Borneo.[15] The stronghold in Marudu Bay was the nailhead that held together the two parts of the Iranun regional satellite network between the straits of Malacca, north Borneo and Sulu, and Sulawesi, funnelling captives and guns between Tempasuk and Tungku. Captain Belcher contended that the tiny island of Tambesan or, more specifically, the harbor formed by the canal, which separates it from the Unsang Peninsula, was a common place of refuge and headquarters for the Iranun and other raiders of the neighboring seas. It was here that Bugis and contraband Singapore traders furnished arms and ammunition to Iranun and Balangingi raiding vessels as well as those of the Tobello, "which dare not enter a port under European jurisdiction."[16] The most prominent objects of barter were captives, seized by the Iranun and Balangingi on the coasts of the Visayas, Borneo and Sulawesi. They were disposed of amongst neighboring Samal groups, riverine dwellers and tribal peoples of the interior.[17]

The Iranun's good fortune at Tempasuk and Marudu from the 1790s to the late 1830s arose in part from the low level of Spanish and English vigilance. News of their early success in the straits of Malacca and along the west coast of Borneo, precipitated a rush of fresh Iranun to

Tempasuk, Pandassan and Tuaran-Iranun who were eager to emulate the success of the first wave of raiders that had settled there. In the 1790s tin rich Banka was ravaged by Iranun attacks while slave raiders from Tempasuk with their kindred at Reteh were also wreaking havoc on Palembang's shipping–native prahus, Chinese junks as well as Arab and Dutch ships. VOC vessels were being boarded too and some of the 'Europeans,' often mestizo Christian women, who were seized after their boats were attacked in the Malacca Strait, were taken by *joanga* to either Tempasuk or Reteh to become wives of Iranun leaders.[18] During these tempestuous years at the turn of the century, the Iranun of Tempasuk and Marudu engaged in large-scale maritime raiding and slaving operations, and consolidated their control over most coastal areas of north Borneo and amongst neighboring Samal seafaring groups.

There are no extant descriptions of these Iranun settlements and their surrounding environs prior to the early 1840s, when James Brooke and his self-appointed band of naval officers undertook the prime task of stamping out the Iranun on the northwest coast of Borneo. An extract from Belcher's letter of 5 December 1844 described the fortified character of Tempasuk at that time:

> Five of his [Sherif Usman's] piratical *prahus* left the river Tempasook on the 5th of November, the day after we entered Ambong, distant five miles in a direct line; and on our entering the river Tempasook on the 11th, we found five rajahs (Illanou pirates) established on the banks. Our force was too imposing, and they retired, dressed in armour, with shields, swords, spears and highly polished muskets. Tampasook town, the nest of this party, is about ten miles up the river (carrying about five or six feet of water), and protected by 100 pieces of cannon. Our mission was friendly, the recovery of a white female; yet we were there forced to treat civilly a band of the most notorious pirates, and hold communication with them, because they had not committed to our knowledge, any piratical act. The Sultan came down, and was disposed to be very friendly, and will, I am certain, treat our boats with the respect which their force will command.[19]

Two years later, Tempasuk would be destroyed by the royal marines of the

H.M.S. *Daedelus*, while a similar expedition under Captain Mundy's command was sent to Pandassan which "had long been celebrated as one of the notorious haunts of the Illanuns, and was in every respect similar to the town of Tampassuk."[20] Mundy gives an excellent account of the Pandassan settlement shortly before it was put to the torch. The settlement had been evacuated but the crew and landing forces saw . . .

> . . . items of household furniture, detached houses, gardens. While poultry, pigs and goats were everywhere evidencing much personal comfort, and a clear proof that the trade of piracy was at any rate a profitable speculation . . . the soil appeared to be excellent, with sugar cane, bananas and Indian corn growing in great luxuriance, and there were signs of numerous cattle . . . nature had showered her blessings upon these people . . . and had held out inducements to honest industry which nothing but an inborn and deep-rooted love of plunder could have resisted or overcome.[21]

There was ample evidence of an Iranun dual economy embedded in a subsistence agricultural way of life and an orientation towards seafaring. The punitive force also came across many artifacts and souvenirs looted from British and other European ships. They reembarked in their boats, having previously torched every house in Pandassan and destroyed the raiding prahus, which the Iranun were building. Mundy could not help but admire one of the smaller joanga going up in flames. It was about 'fifty feet in length, and beautifully built . . . just completed.'[22]

Rivers were the only major arteries linking the coastal areas and hinterlands of north Borneo. Coastal rivers were difficult to enter even at high tide, because of the shifting sand bars and mangrove switch backs across their mouths; but they provided the only means of access to the rich natural resources of Borneo's interior so highly desired for the China trade. Iranun and Tausog entered the forest valleys and foothills of this heartland from their settlements on the Tuaran, Pandassan, Tempasuk, Paitan, Sugut, and Labuk rivers.

Most of the indigenous inhabitants were Ida'han speakers, living in noncontiguous settlements, practising swidden agriculture or hunting and gathering among the foothills and mountains at the upper reaches of the rivers.[23] The Iranun established a variety of relationships with these ethnically fragmented peoples. Some were the subjects of the sultan of Sulu and paid annual tribute in forest produce. Many others formed part of the following of a particular riverine lord like Sherif Usman. As clients, they labored beside slaves to procure bird's nest, cut rattan and collect wax, when their Iranun and Sulu overlords demanded it. Certain powerful tribal groups at the headwaters of the various rivers were autonomous but developed relatively stable trading and slaving relationships with the Iranun. Particular Iranun river chiefs were key participants in Sulu's global commodity trade. They channelled the flow of natural produce to Sulu to be traded to foreign merchants. A significant number of Iranun lords, attracted by the bird's nest, tripang, camphor, wax, and timber, emigrated with their Iranun-Maranao and Samal clients and slaves and established smaller settlements on or near river mouths along the coasts of north Borneo. Others founded communities further inland at the confluence of several rivers. The sultan's kindred or his representatives, who sometimes were Iranun sherifs, controlled the most valuable river basins. Speculative commercial considerations and slaving opportunities motivated many other Iranun rajahs from Mindanao to establish seasonal residence in this outlying area of the sultanate. From their fortified stockade settlements, these Iranun attempted to coordinate the coast-inland trade, exact tribute from dependent upstream people, and control the settlement and movement of riverine tribal populations.

The Marudu region comprised the north end of the island, as well as the Paitan, Sugut and Labuk Rivers, and extended as far as the west end of Sandakan Bay.[24] The Iranun and Tausog had not always exploited this region. In 1761, Marudu Bay supplied only small quantities of pearls, wax and rice for Sulu's market.[25] The Tausog did not begin to develop trade with this area on a large scale until more than a decade later when the sultanate's global commerce began to grow and, equally importantly, just six years after the Maketering catastrophe. In the last quarter of the eighteenth century, it was the driving ambition to gain control over the rich natural resources of the Marudu region that brought the Sulu Sultanate into direct conflict with the sultanate of Brunei. The Tausog seized the initiative. In 1771, Mohammed Israel led a fleet of 130 large Iranun prahus—joanga—against the Bornean Sultanate.[26] Tausog sponsored Iranun raids directed at the trading boats and settlements of the Brunei *pengirans* in the Marudu region increased with the establishment of the English at Balambangan. The raiding continued unabated. By the early 1780s, immigrant Iranun slave raiders had firmly established themselves at Tempasuk. At the dawn of the new century, they were also entrenched in Marudu Bay. These powerful Iranun settlements, linked to the Sulu Sultanate through commerce and kinship, had all but eliminated Brunei as a competitor in the global economy of the region by 1820.[27] The Iranun settlers and their Samal *bajau* compatriots in the Tempasuk-Marudu Bay region provided commodities from the seabed and forests for the booming interregional trade, and a new form of local market, based on weekly cycles, and reciprocity and exchange—the *tamu* system—rapidly developed amongst neighboring riverine agriculturalists and upland tribes.[28] By popularizing the *tamu* system in northwest Borneo the Iranun of Tempasuk and Pandassan circulated captives and their highly prized locally woven checked cloth with narrow white lines. St. John discusses Iranun weaving, noting that the strong homespun cotton fetched a high price at the weekly *tamu* in the 1850s, varying from one pound five shillings to two pound ten shillings for a piece, 'sufficient for a single petticoat.' He also observed that less Iranun cloth was being woven since the introduction, several decades earlier, of cheap English yarn from Singapore.[29]

Trade with the interior tended to flourish and involved the exchange of nipa, salt, iron, cloth, and numerous types of salted fish for tobacco, rice and forest commodities which were funnelled down the rivers to the Iranun settlements at Tempasuk, Pandassan and Marudu on the west coast of Borneo. But sporadic conflict with tribal people on the coastal plain and in the interior also tended to break out because of the Iranun propensity to slave raid overland. The children of various Ida'han tribes became easy targets for the neighboring slavers hiding in creeks or along paths near their villages. The Tuaran plain of the early 1800s became a hunting ground for the Iranun as the large number of small Ida'han villages provided ample opportunity for them to make lightning-like hit and run attacks. The expansion-bent Iranun settlers in the Tuaran-Papar area proved such a menace to the Ida'han that they combined their forces to place a stranglehold on local Iranun movements on the plain. By way of reprisal, bands of warlike Ida'han kept hovering around the edges of the outlying Iranun settlements to cut off stragglers. Finally, no Iranun could leave their houses even to fetch water, unless accompanied by a heavily-armed party. This began to interfere to such an extent with their maritime raiding activity that they seriously contemplated deserting these pioneering settlements on the Tuaran Plain.[30] Their parents and grandparents had left southwest Mindanao to escape from a heavy burden of natural catastrophe. They too had the expectation that they were going to something better. Sometimes, however, that second generation of Iranun settlers must have looked back from the difficulties and dangers of Ida'han warfare to the more secure life they had in the lake region prior to the volcanic eruption, and wondered whether they had made a mistake in settling on this distant coastal plain. Gradually the slave raiders' settlement at Tuaran was brought to the brink of starvation. The Ida'han's calculated attacks on small groups of Iranun collecting firewood and forest products in the adjacent wilderness led to the ambush and death of so many of them that they eventually abandoned large parts of the Tuaran-Papar region. To guard against further attacks, these pioneers withdrew to Pandassan and Tempasuk; outposts were set up at strategic points near their settlements, and their women, whom St. John noted "frequently mix with the men, and even join in public deliberations," were armed and taught to defend themselves.[31] Earl, writing several decades earlier, just after these events occurred, also observed that Iranun women were warlike and used firearms, and were considered sufficiently powerful to beat off the Dyaks, "from whom alone they are liable to molestation."[32] The neighboring seas were considered a relatively safe haven for these northwest coast Iranun, whom Belcher described as "fierce, proud and well-made men, handsomely clothed and fully armed,"[33] compared to what confronted them in the nearby forests, where their control was always tenuous during the protracted Ida'han campaign. St. John, writing a decade later at mid-century, noted that the Iranun who occupied the mouth of the Tempasuk, had been accused of kidnapping Ida'han children and at Tuaran they were "teazed out."[34] As St. John showed in his best-selling book, *Life in the Forests of the Far East*, the Iranun at Tuaran were considered a very serious threat to the future of the swidden agriculturalists in that part of northwest Borneo. The

Iranun had relied on stealth and terror tactics. The Ida'han responded in the same manner gradually driving out the Iranun at Tuaran. They were considered 'pirates' by the Brunei *pengirans* but also had mistakenly created an 'unappeasable feud' with the Ida'han, by stealing their children. Ida'han farmers led rustic and simple lives, but their natural reality was still all there. If one loses his or her children to Iranun slavers in nearby settlements, it would have been better to fall and die in a ditch or ravine in battle against them with one's spirit and character still intact. The Iranun were arguably among the most courageous of peoples. Therefore, the Ida'han considered it useless to make frontal attacks on them, but instead repeatedly destroyed small parties of Iranun caught beyond the boundaries of their fortified settlements. At last, according to St. John, "the Lanun were forced to leave Tuaran, and joined their country people at Tampasuk."[35]

While the serious conflict with the Ida'han was the result of incessant kidnapping, which had led to mutual reprisals and open warfare, ultimately with the pulling back of the Iranun from Tuaran, the slave raiders faced a new and far more dangerous adversary in James Brooke, "Her Majesty's Vakeel in Borneo."[36] A man of similar temperament and talent cut Sherif Usman's career short. The pengirans of Brunei wanted to wage total war against the Iranun. Hence, they beseeched the young merchant-adventurer to call upon the Royal Navy based at Singapore for assistance in expelling the Iranun from the northwest coast of Borneo, especially those under the command of Usman. The beleaguered Brunei Sultanate brought charges of piracy against the Iranun lord to the ambitious white rajah. Brooke would repeatedly argue in print, in parliament and in public gatherings that to eradicate piracy and slave raiding it was necessary to adopt the tactics of scorched earth warfare, burning and destroying Iranun settlements whenever and wherever possible. Cruising, he argued, would only bring occasional success. Such a stratagem of rampant destruction would have to be inflicted on all 'pirates'–direct and indirect, aiders and abettors; "on Sheriff Osman as well as the Illanuns."[37] The white rajah with the assistance of a strong British naval expedition under Sir Thomas Cochrane attacked Usman's heavily fortified *kota* on the Marudu River in 1845. Sherif Usman was killed and his community dispersed.[38] The destruction of the Iranun settlements at Tempasuk and Pandassan and Usman's fortified stronghold at Marudu led to the end of Iranun rule on the northwest coast.

Ironically, the presence of the Tempasuk and Pandassan Iranun's participation in slave raiding and marauding continued after the defeat of Usman, when, bereft of sponsors in northwest Borneo, the survivors shifted their headquarters and operations to the east coast at Tungku and organized a new confederation with their kindred based there, as well as in Mindanao and Sulawesi. The Brooke-led crackdown on maritime raiding and slaving in northwest Borneo also forced the Iranun to find new ways to reach particular target areas. Long distance journeys, like those that would originate from Tunku in the early 1850s, would still be far more common than the shorter slave raids of their Balangingi brethren. The Iranun would now try a variety of routes, using both large and small vessels, to reach the Moluccas, the Sunda Strait, and the strait of Malacca. Their kinship links and settlements on the east coast of Borneo and elsewhere enabled the former Iranun of Tempasuk and Pandassan to survive under increasingly hostile circumstances, on the edge of one of the most heavily populated commercial regions of the colonial world.

Reteh

In the latter part of the 1780s, Iranun prahus first appeared in the waters of the straits of Malacca in the months of August, September and October.[39] In less than a decade their swift three-masted joanga came to dominate the seas around the islands of Banka and Singkep and east Sumatran coastal waters. The Iranun refugees from southern Mindanao, upon resettling in northwest Borneo, had set up the first forward base for long distance maritime raiding at Tempasuk, whose distance from the straits of Malacca rendered it quite secure as a staging and operational center. From there the slave raiders moved west across the South China Sea to establish a second settlement along the east Sumatra coast near the mouth of the Indrageri River, opposite Singkep Island. Reteh provided easy access to the major shipping lanes of the Malacca Strait and South China Sea. The first wave of Iranun based at Reteh, who extended their operations into the small unfortified rivers along the coast, particularly the Inuk, had been part of the expedition from Tempasuk that forced the Dutch to abandon their garrison on Riau in 1787.[40]

The long range nature and duration of Iranun raiding voyages required satellite communities which served as forward bases close to the confluence of the various trade routes that funnelled through the Malacca Strait—settlements to which the raiders could rendezvous for provisions and refurbish their joanga. Merchant vessels approaching the east Sumatran coast among the offshore islands around Bangka became easy targets for the fast sailing heavily-armed Iranun slavers. Reteh became the earliest stronghold of the Iranun in the western sector of the archipelago, precisely because it was situated upstream on the Sumatran coastal strip alongside the strait of Malacca and close to the entrance of the South China Sea. They began preying upon the prahus of the Bugis from Sulawesi, Chinese vessels from Java and Arab and Malay craft from Palembang.[41] These merchant craft were often at the mercy of the Iranun from Reteh who lurked among the small islands and mangrove infested estuaries of the area. This illegible area of non-state space, became, in less than a decade (1787-1797), an "Iranun coast."[42] The numerous small islands of the Malacca Strait were now home to this first generation of Iranun mercenaries and pioneer settlers whose exploits were graphically recorded by Sultan Mahmud, and also woven into the stories and accounts of the Bugis epic, the *Tufhat al Nafis*. Mahmud bitterly complained that the Iranun were systematically attacking Bangka and had sacked scores of coastal towns and villages. In 1796 alone, the beleaguered ruler noted that more than 1,500 people from that island were held captive at Reteh.[43] The Iranun operating in the straits at this time had more than 80 joanga at their disposal, when joined by kindred from Tempasuk and Illana Bay, who had embarked on a slaving round for several years.

The rulers of Jambi and Siak held sway over the islands and coast, where the Iranun had first careened their joanga and built sizeable stockaded settlements overlooking the Reteh and Inuk Rivers. The recognized rulers of cosmopolitan states, the sultans of Jambi and Siak, frequently traded produce, livestock and provisions with these Iranun for some of their captives and booty. In addition, they provided the raiders with munitions, naval stores and other supplies, which had been brought around the tip of Africa to Java on VOC ships, as, in the 1790s, the sultans had regular access to such war stores. At Reteh, the Iranun were delighted to get their hands on Dutch manufactured pistols, muskets, canisters of shot and other contraband war stores traded at bargain rates. Profiteering local rulers and merchants, some linked by marriage to the Iranun, received looted cargoes at wholesale price from the marauders, and also acquired captive slaves. In November 1831, Captain Kolff, an inveterate Iranun hunter, wrote an important report that dealt in some detail with these so-called 'fugitives' from Mindanao. The specially appointed commander described their vessels as 'formidable', noting that sometimes they did not return to southwestern Mindanao or Sulu for five to six years making their home at Reteh, and establishing themselves on the coastal islands of the river Jambi.[44] Kolff provided a fascinating insight into the nature of the actual relationship between the Iranun, as sinister allies, and the sultan, as a local slave dealer and broker for the raiders of Reteh. The Iranun were well received in Jambi because, "their power is such that the Prince of Djambi finds himself unable to expel them from his States."[45]

At the end of the west monsoon, the relatives of the sultan of Siak and other 'grandees' under the immediate orders of Tungku Long Puti and Tungku Mabamath, who were both subordinate to Said Ali, secretly loaned or rented their vessels to the Iranun at Reteh. When Said Ali would lead a full-scale raiding expedition, usually in the vicinity of Selangor, the number of vessels including the joanga from Reteh could be increased to upward of 80. Ironically, these loaned boats were often provided with Dutch passports. Under the pretext of fishing for agar-agar or tripang, the Iranun of Reteh, Saba and those on the river Indrageri located some of their forces around the islands of Brahalla, Allang Tiga and others in the area. From these sites, they pillaged small merchant and fishing vessels, while some prisoners were taken to the slave market at Jambi and other places along the coast of Sumatra.[46]

M.H.W. Muntinghe, the commissioner at Palembang and Banka, was appointed by the colonial government in 1818 with the prime task of gathering information on the Iranun along the Malacca Strait. His comprehensive report, dated 25 May 1818 and addressed to the Gov.-

Gen. Baron Van der Capellan, contained information regarding piracy committed by the inhabitants of Linga, Riau, the east coast of Sumatra, Billiton, Karimata, and the west coast of Borneo. The commissioner's report showed that on the east coast of Sumatra the Iranun were considered a 'wholly distinct race.' They were universally perceived to be a dangerous threat to their neighbors and to shipping in that part of the region. Iranun from Tempasuk and Mindanao, while cruising in straits waters, met with no countenance or support from the local populace, except that provided by several local rulers and the colony of their kindred at Reteh.[47] Muntinghe, 31 years after the event, accurately recorded the reason for their migration to Reteh; the resettlement was a direct consequence of a war between the VOC and the sultan of Linga. The Iranun at Tempasuk were called to help the sultan and it was "to the forces which they sent him that Reteh owes its origins."[48] Three decades later the descendants of the Reteh force alone stood at 1,000 men with 12 joanga of 16 to 30 tons, each vessel holding 50 to 80 Iranun warriors, and carrying 1 cannon of large caliber and 2 smaller guns.[49] The commissioner also noted in his report that the Iranun of Reteh annually raided the coastal cliffs and rocks of Java and the Lampongs from which the government obtained much of its bird's nest.[50]

In order to assist the Dutch in their efforts to suppress Iranun slave raiding and marauding, local traders willingly supplied detailed information about the east Sumatran coast. What material there is on Reteh in its heyday and its kindred communities is also based on neighboring informants' descriptions compiled between 1818 and 1830. The inhabitants of Reteh were consistently depicted by nearby residents as a community of people completely set apart from neighboring ethnic groups. It was common knowledge that these fierce *orang timor* ('people from the east') were newcomers descended from the Iranun of southern Mindanao who had entered into a war between Sultan Mahmud and the Dutch Trading Company. In less than a generation they had built two large stockaded settlements: Saba was located 6 hours from the mouth of the Jambi river and had an estimated 80 houses; Reteh comprised some 60 houses on another tributary opposite Singkep Island.[51] Opinions on the number of their raiding vessels varied greatly, partly because some of the boats were transients or on lease, while raiding prahus used to convey

THE SETTLEMENTS AND BASES

cargoes of slaves and munitions on trips to Jambi and Singapore were readily converted for trading purposes. In 1831, the Resident of Bangka supplied what he felt was a conservative estimate: Saba, 15 large prahus, 15 small prahus; Reteh, 5 large prahus, 10 small prahus; Toekal, 2 large prahus, 10 small prahus. The larger ordinary Iranun prahus in the Malacca Strait were two-masted and these were employed in pursuit of heavily armed Bugis *paduakans* and Chinese junks. Among their vessels at Reteh were also several lanong or joanga, 'beautiful three-masted prahus with long sweeps that drew 6 feet of water' and were crewed by 80 or more. The smaller prahus ranged between 30 to 40 feet in length. When the prahus were included as domiciles it was believed that the Iranun in the Malacca Strait could muster at least 2,500 men at arms.[52]

Four years after Muntinghe's influential report on piracy was submitted to the government the Dutch mounted an expedition against the Iranun stronghold of Tontoli on the northwest coast of Sulawesi. Several Iranun settlements and many prahus were destroyed during the campaign. Some of the defeated Iranun, fugitives from Tontoli, made their way across the archipelago to Sumatra, and resettled with their kinspeople already established on the Jambi along with other dispersed refugees from Tobello and Gilolo. By the early 1830s, the Iranun at Reteh and Saba had become a heterogeneous ethnic community. In essence, 'Illanun' or 'Lanun' became a commonly accepted regional term for 'pirate' at the end of the eighteenth century. Historically, however, it was an ethnic one too, referring specifically to the Iranun-Maranao-speaking seafarers of the Illana Bay region of southwestern Mindanao. But by this time, at the forward bases and satellite settlements in both the western and eastern sectors of the archipelago, it was no longer possible to regard the Iranun raiders and refugees as a single ethnic, cultural, and linguistic group. The colonial labels 'Illanun' or 'Lanun' obscured both the scope and rate of cultural accommodation and ethnic differentiation that was occurring at Iranun settlements such as Reteh and Tontoli by the 1820s. By then, the Reteh 'pirates' comprised the first generation descendants of Iranun-Maranao-speaking migrants from Tempasuk and Mindanao, and 'Illanoons' of 'alforean origin' that came from the Moluccas, Sulawesi and Saleyer variously labelled as Gilolo and Tobello. The latter comprised individuals originating from Ternate, Tidore, Bacan, and Ceram who had fled their islands after the insurrection of Prince Nuku of Tidore.[53] The Tobello, as an emergent ethnic group, increased in number and strength by combining their maritime raiding activities with the Iranun. Some also took on an ascribed Iranun identity, and other scattered fugitives from Tobungku joined them in the late 1820s. Described in the 1830 report of Pangeran Said Hassan Habassy as "a mass of evil disposed persons" they had worked the seas around Bali from 1824 to 1827 before being driven out of the island and towards their associated haunts on the east coast of Sumatra.[54]

In the 1820s and 1830s, the Dutch colonial navy, armed with the intelligence reports of Muntinghe and others, assembled several cruising fleets and began to sweep the east Indies from one end to the other in search of major Iranun bases. They ratified treaties with the sultans of Indrageri, Riau and Palembang to provide the Dutch forces with men, arms and vessels to suppress Iranun raiding in the straits of Malacca.[55] It was the settlements at Reteh, Riau, Jambi, Pulau Berhala, Tungkal, and Air Hitam–settlements that had a stranglehold on straits trade and were threatening Singapore itself with economic meltdown–which became the prime targets of the 1834 Iranun campaign. In February, the sultan of Linga and the viceroy of Riau equipped 50 vessels which accompanied 3 government cruisers in launching a major attack against the Iranun stationed at the mouth of the Indrageri River. The attack ended with an assault on the fortified base at Reteh and the destruction of settlements and prahus on the Inuk River; eight Iranun commanders, all rajahs and *panglima*, were taken prisoner, three were executed at Linga and the others condemned to penal servitude for life.[56] However, the waters of the Malacca Strait were safe for less than a year. In 1835, despite the burning of scores of Iranun vessels and the destruction of their villages, Javanese slaves were taken on board the cruiser *Ajax* after escaping from Iranun still based at Reteh. These Javanese claimed there were still many of their people held by Iranun on the east coast of Sumatra. This led the Dutch to lodge serious representations against the sultan of Linga who lamely excused himself, pleading his inability to curb continued Iranun slave raiding.[57]

Until 1840, the Reteh descendants of the Tempasuk-based Iranun expedition of 1787 and their archipelago-wide kindred played a vital role in the western sector raiding pattern that originated from the Sulu archipelago. But as the Iranun and Balangingi tended to concentrate their attacks less and less frequently on the Malacca Strait, most of the third generation Iranun at Reteh were culturally accommodated within the local population, and became "Lingganese."[58] The third generation descendants of the first Iranun slave raiders and settlers in east Sumatra were assimilated into the society of their neighboring allies within the space of just 70 years. In Tempasuk, as it was located much closer to southern Mindanao, the maritime raiders were able to preserve their Iranun-Maranao identity far longer, well beyond the end of the Iranun age.

Burias and Balangingi

In the northern sector, the long rivalry at sea between the 'moros' and Spaniards in the Philippines, reached a climax in the mid-1760s, when the Iranun, determined to bring central and southern Luzon to its knees, established a satellite base along the Mamburao River on the island of Mindoro, within easy striking distance of Manila itself. Its strategic success, as a staging platform for slave raids against the surrounding regions, meant that the balance of maritime power in the heart of the Philippines shifted decisively in the Iranun's favor. Spain's control in southern Luzon and the greater Manila area was sharply curtailed as Iranun maritime raiding expanded, enabling both the sea raiders and the Sulu Sultanate to extend their sway into new areas of the Philippines, thereby gaining regional power and strength. But, the Iranun's alarming successes in the far north of the archipelago, amid Manila's vulnerable shipping lanes and harbor facilities, led to Mamburao's sudden downfall. One major attack occurred when the slave raiders seized a huge Manila-bound Amoy junk carrying a cargo for the outward-bound galleon trade with Mexico. This attack proved to be a fatal mistake that was to have almost immediate repercussions for the future of the Mamburao base. In October 1770, the Spanish Governor resorted to a bold calculated measure out of sheer anger and frustration over the sudden loss of the precious cargo of export wares for the Manila galleon, *San Joseph*.

When the Iranun triumphantly sailed their valuable prize into Mamburao, they were to be pursued up that very river several months later by the governor's heavily-armed flotilla and expedition. In a military stroke as ingenious as any the Iranun had ever committed, the governor recaptured a number of local prizes, including the badly damaged junk, while depositing a large landing force to sack Mamburao. The Iranun raiders and settlers, who felt powerless to resist such a large armed force, had already slipped away in the night after the first day of the siege, joining their kindred at other neighboring satellite settlements in the region.[59] Mamburao was abandoned, but over the next several decades maritime raiding continued to flare up in Luzon and the Visayas. The Iranun's intensity of purpose and success compelled the marauders to establish a string of smaller satellite settlements and refitting outposts all around southern Luzon and in the northeastern Visayas, notwithstanding Spain's lack of adequate coastal defenses. Thus by their constant ominous presence on the far side of the Philippines, the Iranun slavers forced the Spanish to adopt a new antipiratical defense system of permanent fortifications built throughout the archipelago, a decision that would have far-reaching consequences for the demographic trends and settlement patterns of the colony.

The late eighteenth century maritime raids on Philippine towns and shipping did not all originate from the mangrove lined inlets of Illana Bay, the coral reefed atolls of the Balangingi cluster, or from Jolo and Basilan. The relentless nature of these raids and their ferocity required a series of permanent bases and refitting centers within the target areas of the northern sector from which heavily-armed Iranun squadrons could stage attacks, year after year. Occasionally, Filipino captives and slaves who were rescued after a badly damaged raiding boat was sunk or deliberately beached on the Luzon coast, gave valuable information to the Spanish authorities about the precise location of these Iranun settlements. Interviews suggested that the Iranun had satellite bases off the coasts of Tayabas, Camarines, Albay, Leyte, and Capul, the latter island being used as a site from which to place a stranglehold on the San Bernardino Strait and stage attacks along the Pacific coast of Luzon.[60] Thomas Forrest had already placed Burias on record as a major Iranun base as early as the mid-1760s. But Spanish coastguard vessels, prowling

THE SETTLEMENTS AND BASES

the seas looking for Iranun ships packed with human cargoes bound for Burias, could not clear the slavers from the island. The exact location of several of these late eighteenth century staging sites could still be remembered by elderly villagers on Burias and Masbate in the first half of this century. On the western coast of a little island called Templo, to the northwest of Burias, is a *sitio* ("small settlement") called 'Ki-moros' which the Iranuns who regularly attacked Tayabas in great force, used as a 'temporary home.'[61] Iranun raiders, according to village-based interviews conducted for the archipelago-wide Historical Data Paper Project in the 1950s, also established fortified settlements on Masbate, such as the sitio of Bagtinyon in the town of Aroray, where they detained captives, refitted their joangas and, leaving their capital ships behind, made lightning-like strikes with smaller auxiliary craft on nearby towns and coastal shipping.[62] Even as late as the second half of the nineteenth century, Balangingi marauders were still established in the Catanduanes and other outlying islets which provided ideal bases from which to raid small isolated villages whose fortifications were often dilapidated or nonexistent.

For the Iranun and later the Balangingi, these northern outposts and refitting bases were the key to their long-term success, especially when they were slave raiding in the off season. These Muslim raiders both preyed upon and lived off the neighboring coasts. The bases had to import or plunder from nearby areas a large proportion of the rice and livestock that their inhabitants needed. Nor were neighboring coastal Filipinos in southern Luzon and the eastern Visayas at all pleased with the sudden presence of their sinister 'landlords.' But, they had no choice in the matter and could do little except harvest their lands and deliver up their crops and cattle to the Iranun who had settled so close to them with impunity.[63] Towards the end of the eighteenth century, these Filipinos, especially those in southern Luzon, eastern Leyte and Samar, suffered terribly during the protracted maritime raids and sieges. However, in the long run the satellite base system itself, holding a *kris* at the throat of Manila, was to prove a turning point, forcing the Spanish government and church to belatedly make a totally new commitment to the coastal defense net of the Philippines.

By the second quarter of the nineteenth century the Spanish, English and Dutch considered Balangingi the most dangerous of all the 'Illanun' bases in Southeast Asia. In the knowing eyes of certain naval officers like Don Jose Maria Halcon and Comm. Edward Blake, who regularly hunted the Iranun and Balangingi, every satellite settlement and every bastion dotted across the archipelago presented a unique challenge–a challenge that was different for each colonial navy. The questions and challenges posed by Balangingi for more than three decades were arguably the most difficult and dangerous for the pirate hunters to confront and resolve. The Samal Balangingi, who, as late as 1838 were often mistakenly confused with the Iranun, were a highly-organized, extremely expert slave raiding group, regional in scope, with significant resources in ships, munitions, capital, especially slaves, and contacts. The Balangingi Samal lived, along with Iranun and other Samal-speaking groups, in a dozen or more villages and fortified settlements scattered along the southern Mindanao coast, the southern shore of Basilan, and on the islands of the Samalese cluster of which Balangingi was dominant.[64] As Sulu's trade with China and the West expanded at the end of the eighteenth century, Tausog datus increasingly retained neighboring groups of Samal seafarers as slave raiders. From Balangingi and related settlements on other islands, Samal-speakers voyaged great distances; they swept the coasts from Luzon to Brunei and from Singapore to Menado, capturing slaves. But, who were the Balangingi? Although Francisco Combes and Thomas Forrest described the warlike activities and trade of the Samal in earlier periods, there are no historical references to the Balangingi as a separate ethnic group before the nineteenth century. In western sources, Muslim maritime raiders are first mentioned as Balangingi, because of their slaving exploits, rather than as Iranun, in the area of Singapore and the east coast of Malaya in the late 1830s. In 1838, several 'Illanun' prahus were destroyed by the steamboat *Diana* off the east coast of Malaya, and some of the badly shaken survivors, when interrogated, called themselves 'Balangingi' after the island which was their major base and home.[65] From that period the ethnic label, 'Balangingi,' began to supersede 'Illanun' in the European literature as synonymous with 'pirate.' The Balangingi Samal seem to have acquired ethnic distinction as 'notorious pirates' only because they specialized in maritime slave raiding and incorporated an incredible number of non-Samal peoples into their society.[66]

THE SETTLEMENTS AND BASES

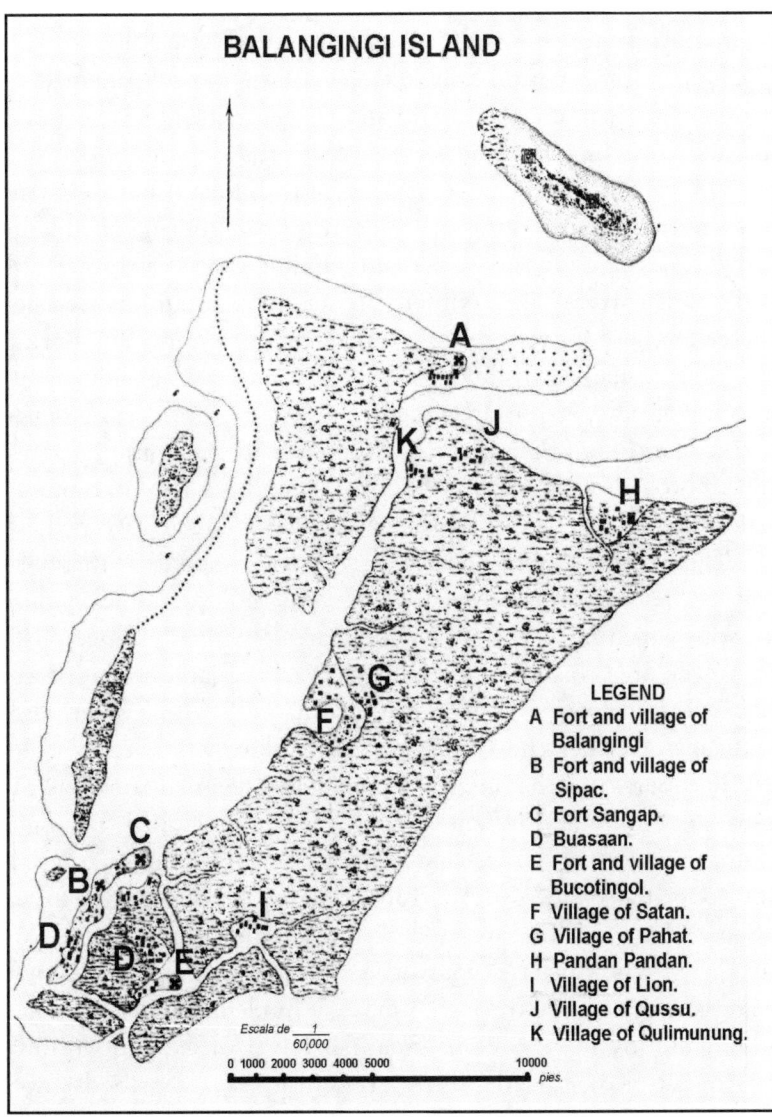

Map 6. A mid-nineteenth century Spanish map of Balangingi, home of the feared Samal slave raiders. The islets in the Samales group were fringed with mangrove swamps awash at high tide but exposed at low tide. Bits of land became separated from one another as the sand barrier inside the encircling reefs changed shape and elevation. Channels into the lagoon opened and closed during the year with tidal movements and shifting currents.

The Samalese group comprised Balangingi island (6 square miles) and Tunkil, a cluster of 4 islets (9.5 square miles) situated in the center of the Sulu archipelago, midway between Borneo and Mindanao. The islets were subject to change in size and shape, with tidal variations and modulations in the wind and weather patterns, separating into small parcels of coral and rock when inundated at high tide. They were fringed with mangrove swamps, and separated from neighboring islands by an extensive series of connected reefs and winding channels through which swirled strong currents and countercurrents. In regard to the treacherous character of these currents, the Spanish military engineer, Bernaldez wrote: "They usually swirl about at six or seven miles an hour [and] we have seen a steam warship dragging both anchors, after letting out more than sixty fathoms of chain on each anchor in Balangingi waters."[67] Balangingi, together with the neighboring islands of Tunkil, Simosa and Bangaloo stretch in a seamless web across the passage between the Sulu and Celebes Seas. Here especially, as Bernaldez noted, swift tidal rips formed by the opposing currents of both seas could periodically develop maelstroms which made the surrounding area potentially dangerous, and therefore the area was often avoided by even the largest European war vessels.[68] But the rocky shoals, waves, wind, and shallow water were not a handicap for either the Balangingi or Iranun, who were absolutely superb mariners. At that critical moment in 'regional time,' as Sulu's slave-based commodity-driven economy rapidly developed, Balangingi's low lying impenetrable seascape constituted a tremendous defensive advantage for these emergent maritime raiders on the brink of forging a new Sama identity. Repeatedly described by the Spanish as a natural "pirates nest," the cluster of four little islands was linked by submerged reefs and accessible only through a maze of hidden channels screened by stands of muddy mangrove. A Spanish naval officer, reconnoitring Balangingi in a disguised sailing craft in 1842, described the Sulu Sultanate's key raiding base, while slowly, but surely improving Manila's naval intelligence about this mysterious bastion:

> The island of Balangingi is one of a number of islands located in the Jolo archipelago, towards the eastern part, some 36 miles from the residence of the Sultan. It runs from north-east to south-west 3 ~ miles wide of which more than a half a mile is covered in mangrove

stands; the island is always partially submerged or inundated which makes it impossible to proceed overland; it is surrounded by reefs which extend in all directions the distance of an 8 calibre cannon shot from the shore, and it cannot be approached from any other point except the channel or canal situated at the southern end, which at its mouth, during high tide is a fathom deep, and has a huge boulder in it, which actually, if removed, the depth of the channel may vary between two, three or four fathoms.

The town and the fortress of Balangingi are situated on the coast near the northern point of the island, an area inundated with shallow sea water; this fortified town consists of very high double thick palisades full of coral rock and it has many eight pound cannon, falconetes (small cannon) and lantancas of small calibre. Balangingi could only be attacked along the shallow strip fronting the fort; in the north-east, a distance of 1° miles, is the channel which leads to Balangingi and the town of Pandongan, these two towns alone on the island have large populations, and annually, 120 to 150 pancos leave this place which for some years now have raided the Moluccas while others devote their attention to the Philippines.[69]

On these islands, the Balangingi Samal constructed wells and four forts (Balangingi, Sipac, Bucotingal, Sangap) to guard their villages and raiding prahus. The forts (*kota*), situated on raised ground and protected by coral reefs on 3 sides, were enormous stockades of 2, 3 and 4 tiers of stout tree trunks, packed with rammed earth and coral to a height of more than 20 feet and defended with heavy cannon.[70] Sali Werble of Isabela, Basilan, at the age of 87, recalled seeing the remains of the Sipac Kota's one meter wide walls when, as a young man, he accompanied Dr. Najeeb Saleely, author of the celebrated *History of Sulu*, to Balangingi on an archaeological dig, in 1924. The fort's posts, according to the former police chief of Jolo, were still intact and made of molave. Hamuluan molave, also used for bulletproof breastworks on the Balangingi prahus, turned rock hard when wet or sunk in muddy places like the foreshore of Balangingi.[71] Remarkably, Hailan Kaligeran de Perez, aged 90, still remembered from her childhood details of what her exiled father recounted to her about his youth on Balangingi. The elderly woman recalled that the banished slave raider spent his life as a young boy inside the large fort on a muddy, coral and mangrove infested raised bank on Balangingi. Most importantly, he explained to her that a remarkable natural asset located at the tip of the island cluster–a hidden channel– protected the forts and a collection of houses. Diego Kaligeran told his young daughter one evening in the sitio of Tigbao, Zamboanga, that the only way of entering Balangingi was through this secret *'butas,'* a blind channel.[72] From a purely strategic and defensive point of view, Balangingi was the best island natural fortification and large-scale maritime raiding base in the Malayo-Muslim world, during the age of sail.

However, Balangingi itself was not an ideal location from the standpoint of subsistence and everyday life for the slave raiders. The island had to import from Jolo or Marudu Bay virtually all the food its inhabitants required–especially rice and sago. Nor was there an adequate supply of fresh water. With no surface water, and with little flora except the ubiquitous coconut palm, the Balangingi Samal were incapable of maintaining the subsistence base required to support a dense population.[73] The islands and seas upon which the Samalan-speaking people of the Balangingi cluster lived placed them in an ecological bind that shaped their demographic origin and relationship to the Sulu Sultanate. The captive Francisco Thomas stated, "The inhabitants of these places [the Samalese cluster] live by piracy and that they have no other means of existence, in fact piracy is the general vocation of the people."[74] The sole orientation of the Samal was, of necessity, towards the sea. As specialists in maritime raiding, boat building and marine procurement, they derived from it their strength, security and wealth. In those areas that fell under direct Tausog dominion the Samal were totally dependent on a marine oriented economy; while in areas just beyond the direct pale of Tausog authority, including Cagayan de Sulu and Basilan, a mixed economy, similar to that practised by the Iranun in northwest Borneo, was dominant. The Balangingi were an emergent strand dwelling people compelled to establish their communities on the small coral and sand islands of northeastern Sulu, and along the eastern shores of Basilan. Lack of self-sufficiency bound the Samal Balangingi to Jolo.

Marcelino Oroa in noting this fact, recognized that the Balangingi had little choice in the matter:

> The inhabitants of the island do not do anything except fishing and piratical raiding. There is no water to drink nor any food to eat on the island. They get water from the nearest island called Faraol (Parol) which is half a mile away from several deep wells there, and food from the market at Jolo.[75]

Balangingi's proximity to Jolo as an outlet for retailing captives; its ecological dependence on larger, neighboring volcanic islands like Jolo and Basilan for rice, fruit and vegetables and trade goods; and the natural barriers surrounding it, help to explain why Balangingi became the natural home of one of the most feared maritime raiding groups of island Southeast Asia.[76]

To understand the important role played by the Balangingi in the slave trade in Southeast Asia, it is necessary to trace their history as an ethnic group. The only historical work which deals with the Balangingi, *Piracy and Politics in the Malay World*, by Nicholas Tarling, does not consider their ethnic origins. Avoidance of this question presents a deceptively static picture of an "outlaw society" with an ethnically homogeneous population. Samal groups in the Sulu archipelago were emergent populations; the success of the Balangingi as slave raiders, as well as that of the Iranun and Tobello, was due in large measure to their ethnic heterogeneity and systems of kinship and social organization that were exceptionally inclusive. Captives' statements present a picture of Samal populations undergoing constant cultural readjustments until 1848, as they established themselves as a different kind of people. At the beginning of the nineteenth century, there was an infusion of ethnically diverse captive people among the Balangingi—mostly through demands for their labor on slave raiding prahus and in the tripang and pearl fisheries—that complicated the identity of Samal populations.[77] The earliest published references to the Balangingi as a separate ethnic group stem from the 1840s, when their activities as slave raiders menaced the areas of northwest Borneo, the Malacca Strait, Sulawesi, and the Moluccas.[78]

Many of the captives brought to Balangingi turned Samal—borrowing language, religion and customs. Insufficient data prevents a precise reconstruction of the overall size and origin of Samal populations at that time.[79] What information there is for the nineteenth century has survived in the statements of fugitive captives. These testimonies show that the incorporation of other ethnic groups took place on a large scale, especially in the second and third generation. In 1836, it was estimated that only one tenth of the male population were actually 'true' Balangingi Samal; the remainder were *renegados* (renegades), more particularly Tagalog and Visayan, and various Malay-speaking captives.[80] In essence, I argue, like the case of the Iranun of Reteh and Tontoli, and the Tobello of Tobungku, that it is a historical fallacy to regard the Balangingi prior to 1848 as a monolithic ethnic, cultural and linguistic group. This homogeneous notion of the Balangingi obscures the extraordinary rate of incorporation and cultural accommodation taking place and the extent of internal ethnic differentiation.

The global economy of Sulu was expanding rapidly enough at that time for Samal populations to absorb ever-larger numbers of captives. A conscious recruitment policy of the Tausog datus, dictated by fluctuations in the trade economy and the hazards of the 'sea-war,' changed the demographic structure and ethnic composition of Samal groupings in less than two generations (1820-1845). Given that Barth considers a ten percent rate of incorporation in a generation drastic,[81] it can be argued that the social and cultural flexibility of the Sulu system was truly remarkable. Village populations in 1836 appear to have ranged from just over 300 people with 10 to 12 prahus (*garay*) at Tunkil to more than a thousand people, with 30 to 40 prahus, at Balangingi.[82] Six years later the size of the fleets at Balangingi were carefully monitored by the Spanish who estimated that up to 150 garay sailed on long range raids each year.[83] In less than a decade, Balangingi's population roughly quadrupled; in 1845, the village had an estimated 4,000 people and 120 to 150 large vessels. The overall Samal population devoted to maritime raiding at Balangingi reached an upper limit, in 1848, with 10,000 people and 200 raiding prahus.[84] The consequence of this extraordinary population growth was the birth of a new Samal identity and an 'emergent' maritime raiding group within the Sulu Sultanate–the Samal Balangingi.

The English and Dutch were handicapped by the fact that they were not sure who constituted the 'Balangingi' Samal and where their long distance maritime raids were coming from. It was not until 1838 that high ranking English naval officers based in Singapore ascertained, from the interrogation statements of prisoners and from personal enquiries, that some of the 'Illanoon' fleets raiding in the straits of Malacca were fitted out at an island called 'Ballanghinin' by the 'Illanoon' survivors—or at other small islets in its immediate vicinity. The psychologically shattered and wounded raiders, held prisoner in Singapore, also repeatedly mentioned the name Sipac. In the charts that the Head of the Straits naval command had in his possession no place precisely answering to those names could be pinpointed. However, an island was found lying "about midway between the islands of Sooloo and Basilun within about six or seven hours sail of either called Bangeengs which from information I have received both from the prisoners and deponents is clearly the same place as Ballinginghin."[85]

Nevertheless, neither the exact location of Balangingi itself nor the nature of the Balangingi's evolving Samal identity were any clearer to Capt. Henry Keppel who was based at Singapore in 1841:

> The Balangingi inhabit a cluster of small islands somewhere in the vicinity of Sooloo; they are of the Badjow or sea-gipsy tribe, a wandering race, whose original country has never been ascertained. At present, as far as I can learn, they are not dependent on Sooloo, though it is probable they may be encouraged by some of the Rajahs of that place, and that they find a slave market there.[86]

In the sea-war against Iranun and Balangingi maritime raiding and slaving, none of the sectors showed much progress until the mid-1830s. On the heels of widespread evidence that 'Illanun' maritime raiding was on the rise, and amid James Brooke's campaign claiming that the Spanish had forfeited the antipiracy crusade particularly with respect to the security of northwest Borneo, a series of disturbing reports and articles in English and Dutch newspapers claimed that Southeast Asia was more awash in 'Illanoon' slave raids than ever before. The questions and challenges posed by Balangingi for the Spanish now became far more real, because the English and Dutch, by the mid-1840s, were seriously contemplating how to destroy this menacing base, as their colonial subjects were paying heavily for their previous neglect and mistakes in curbing the 'Illanoon piracy.' However, the arrival of Narciso Claveria as governor-general and the advent of steam gunboats, a symbol of a new technological and colonial era, severely circumscribed Balangingi power, and changed the course of their history as an ethnic group. Claveria understood that control of Balangingi would cut the Sulu archipelago in two and largely stop slave raiding in the Philippines. When, in 1848, the Spanish, with the aid of steamboats, successfully destroyed the fortified strongholds in the Balangingi cluster and deported hundreds of people—men, women and children—to the distant mountain valleys of north central Luzon to become tobacco and corn farmers, the Balangingi were dealt a major blow from which they would never fully recover.

Tontoli, Tobungku and Tunku

In the 1780s and 90s, the Iranun intensified their slave raiding activities against eastern Sulawesi and the Moluccas. The Dutch assumed that the Iranun wanted Tontoli as a forward base in their undeclared war against the VOC and its allies throughout the Moluccas. While this strategic assessment was correct, it overlooked the fact that the Iranun were expanding rapidly across Southeast Asia and also required staging centers such as Tontoli in the southern sector, in order to fuel their regional drive for slaves. Sulu's statecraft and growing demand for labor had become their first priority, despite the ongoing sea-war with the 'company.' The real threat to the Dutch in eastern Sulawesi was neither the Maguindanao in Cotabato nor the Tausog in Jolo, but rather the fortified bases and refitting outposts that the Iranun had been running for some years. By 1800, migrating maritime raiders from Mindanao and Sulu and their Tobello allies had built their lives and future around Tontoli. The new settlement was the lifeblood of what was fast becoming a formidable 'nation' of people with an extensive series of up-to-date slave raiding routes throughout eastern Sulawesi and the Moluccas. Thomas Forrest, a principal instigator of maritime raids against the Dutch, was aware of how the founding of Tontoli had enabled Iranun and Maguindanao lords like Datu Malfalla, brother-in-law of the Raja Muda of Cotabato, to prosper.[87] He also knew how countless others in

Sangir, Buton, Salayar, Sumbawa, and along the coasts of Borneo felt the wrath of these raiders as the English and Dutch fought over Sulawesi and the Moluccas amidst a great number of regional and ethnic conflicts at the end of the eighteenth century.

The first place the Mindanao and Sulu-based Iranun squadrons visited on their way south were the small islands of Bukit and Binang, situated near Tabukan, on Sangir, and the Pangalasian Islands at the northern entrance to the Makassar Strait, near the coast of Tontoli. Velthoen notes that the Dutch soon identified 'Toli Toli' (Tontoli) in the northwestern corner of Sulawesi as one of the key Iranun centers from which systematic slave raids were taking place as the new century got under way. As early as 1793, the VOC had already established the growing importance of Tontoli as a forward base for Iranun southward expansion, when an official wrote of the "very close alliance" between the 'Maguindanao' and the ruler of Tontoli.[88] In 1812, Hunt identified Tontoli as a "great piratical establishment" with several thousand Iranun regularly domiciled in their joanga for up to several years at a time in the harbor.[89] Tobungku on the opposite coast was the other forward base.[90] Tontoli rapidly developed a multiethnic society based on maritime raiding and slaving, comprising both permanent and transient Iranun and Samal raiders and refugees who had moved south from Cotabato and Jolo. They hunted down the coastal populations of eastern Sulawesi and the fabled Spice Islands and attacked the VOC's shipping, wherever they were found. They also combined their activities with diverse groups of dislocated peasant rebels, freed VOC slaves, and other 'vagabonds' and 'rovers' from several ethnic groups, including those variously labelled 'Tobello,' who had fled to the east coast of Sulawesi and found refuge in Tobungku, where, at times, they both fought against and alongside the Iranun of Tontoli.[91] These ethnically heterogeneous 'Iranun' at Tontoli, who were now being mustered in from the ranks of tribal dissidents, fugitive slaves, indentured servants, and predatory head-hunting people, had either dispersed under duress or been forced into exile by the repressive policies of the Dutch. They were temporarily allied to local rulers, like those of Tobungku and Banggai bent upon economic expansion when asked to fight in local wars, especially against Buton. Evidence from Tontoli and Tobungku suggests that the Iranun there originated from many sources, one of them being deeply rooted in Nuku's popular struggle sweeping the Moluccas. Close ties would be maintained between the revolutionary Prince and his successors, especially his nephew Raja Jailolo, the overlord of Halmahera, and the Iranun warlords of Tontoli until the 1820s, and beyond. This ramifying web of political and economic ties, kinship association and marriages was poignantly signified by the fact that in 1822 when Niru, a son of the raja of Jailolo died in southwest Sulawesi his body was brought back to the Iranun–Tobello stronghold of Tontoli to be buried there alongside his brother Kimelaha Sugi.[92]

By the early 1820s Tobungku, like Marudu on the northwest coast of Borneo, had become a primary staging center for financing and outfitting Iranun slave raiders in east Sulawesi and the Moluccas. Tobungku prospered as large numbers of slaves were put to work in an economy divided between agriculture and marine-based activities–fishing, strand procurement and maritime raiding. A steady stream of captives was supplied to the local rulers from the regional slaving expeditions of the Tobungku-based Iranun and Tobello and those settled at Tontoli. The Iranun of Tobungku and Tontoli actively recruited the Tobello because of their local knowledge of neighboring seas and fearsome reputation as mercenaries. According to Velthoen, local oral traditions mention Tobello settling on Tobungku's coast prior to the 1820s. Notably, Bahunola, in the Bay of Kolondale, and Benteng Ngapi, the ruins of a fort near Lanona, were still remembered in the early 1990s as places where Tobello raiders settled from outside and conducted slave raids both inland and across the seas. In addition Pebatoa, the name of a village on the edge of the Bay of Tolo, means 'place where people were collected' in Tomaiki (a dialect of the Mori language), in other words, the place where the Tobello gathered their captives for transshipment.[93] She also notes these Tobello and Iranun-inspired slave raids had a decisive, albeit devastating impact on the politics, economy and demography of eastern Sulawesi. Iranun maritime raiding in eastern Sulawesi and the Moluccas continued steadily throughout the first two decades of the nineteenth century. Nevertheless, the distinction between Sulu-inspired Iranun marauding and the internecine conflicts of various local spheres of influence centering around Tobungku, Gorontalo and Buton sometimes

THE SETTLEMENTS AND BASES

blurred, as the slave raiders were increasingly drawn into the local-regional arena of interethnic politics and conflict, as the mini-state of Tobungku expanded north into the Banggai archipelago, and to the south.

The slave raiding activities conducted from Tontoli and the protection and finance afforded Iranun raiders by the rulers and merchants of Tobungku, made the port the largest and most prosperous on the east coast, attracting seasonal fleets of Bugis and Makassarese trading prahus. Whole communities of migrants and refugees, fleeing from endemic unrest, settled in relative security along Tobungku's shoreline and became involved in procuring pearls, tortoise shell and tripang or cultivating rice and sago. A substantial majority of the Iranun based around Tobungku, as well as at Tontoli, continued to be recruited from neighboring dispossessed groups who joined them as allies when they realized it was politically in their interest to do so. It was an opportunity not to be lost. The reasons why the 'Tobello' and Gilolo joined the maritime raiders based at Tontoli and Tobungku are not too difficult to understand. The Iranun provided a particular generation, from Tidore, Bacan and Ceram, haunted by the loss of their homes, land and independence, with a distinctive chance to exact revenge against the VOC. Furthermore, their bases also provided social controls on authority as well as social welfare and provision for the injured–benefits lacking in the Dutch settlements. The ethnic heterogeneity of Tobungku in its heyday based largely on Iranun–Tobello maritime raiding and slaving bears witness to the extraordinary linguistic and ethnic fragmentation still present in the area today.

The Tobello were regarded by the Dutch as dangerous as the Iranun. They were scattered and dispersed throughout the Moluccan archipelago, and in the Bay of Tolo on the east coast of Sulawesi, as a consequence of Nuku's protracted regional struggle with the VOC.[94] But, it must also be stressed, that people of 'Tobello' descent in the Bay of Tolo were prominent in the Iranun crews of those settled in Tontoli and Tobungku, by the 1820s. These Iranun and their Tobello allies created a nightmare for the Dutch and their coastal subjects, remorselessly attacking the coasts of east Sulawesi and the Moluccas, carrying off whole populations from small islands to be resettled in Tobungku and Sulu.

From their home base at Tontoli, Iranun fleets rendezvoused at Tobungku, on the east side of Sulawesi, and then split into squadrons that blanketed the whole of the Moluccan archipelago and beyond. Within less than a decade (1820-1830), violent slave raiding attacks seemed like one of those things that people down through the straits of Buton would just have to accommodate. Alternatively, they could move away to more securely controlled areas. It was possible the Dutch would not be able to solve this problem of the expansion and contraction of nonstate space in the outer islands. When, in 1822, an Iranun fleet of over 150 vessels besieged the village of Kalingsusuh on the island of Buton and swept away its population while on the brink of starvation, there was outrage but little surprise.[95] By then, settlements like Kalingsusuh and choke points like the Buton Strait had acquired monikers such as 'graveyard' or 'sea-war zone.' Violence and fear spread almost everywhere from the coasts of Sulawesi and Sangir to Sumbawa and further west towards Batavia. The Iranun maritime raids originating from Tontoli and Tobungku threatened relations between the VOC and local realms, destroyed trade and business, accelerated flight from the coast to the interior and unmercifully trapped pockets of population situated on the margins of the VOC dominion in the Moluccas. Violent Iranun maritime raiding and slaving seemed to affect virtually everything in eastern Sulawesi and it seemed intractable. From 1800 to 1820, the number of deaths and people enslaved climbed dramatically on Sangir, Banggai and Soela as these islands lost the greatest parts of their populations to slave raids or flight from the terrifying countenance of the Iranun and Tobello. During that dark period thousands of displaced people abandoned the coasts of the eastern arm of Sulawesi and Ceram, retreating inland to remote mountainous areas. Contact with the coast and outside world was severed over and over again in many different places. Among those areas worst affected were coastal stretches of southeast Sulawesi, where the islands of Wawoni and Buton were particularly devastated, as large parts were scoured clean and left virtually uninhabited. The collapse of Buton's cotton economy was a matter of simple demographics. Beginning in the decade between 1810 and 1820 most of the population had either been enslaved or moved inland. Consequently, Buton experienced an acute shortage of skilled agricultural labor.[96]

Then something extraordinary happened. Starting in 1822-1823, slave raiding began falling in the Moluccas. Yet, the regional-wide cause of the sudden improvement was not hard to understand. The only thing the Iranun at Tontoli and Tobungku understood and respected was the possible threat, and use of all necessary force. By 1820, both Tontoli and Tobungku were at the top of Batavia's 'get tough' antipiracy agenda. This was a direct result of Muntinghe's important 1818 report regarding 'piracy'—a report that linked their damaging impact to the economy and population of Sulawesi and the Moluccas with the maritime raiding and slaving activities of their kindred stationed at Bali and in the strait of Malacca.[97]

Tontoli did not survive its first real major military test. In 1822, the Dutch drove the Iranun out, temporarily suspending their activity on the northwest coast of Sulawesi. The cruising expedition involved the colonial frigate, *Melampus*, 5 other troop vessels crewed by colonial marines, and 24 Bugis *paduakans*, carrying hundreds of auxiliaries. Several Iranun settlements were burned, 50 raiding prahus were destroyed and 40 Iranun killed.[98] The Iranun attempted to regroup and create new bases at Dampilas and Kylie on the northwest coast. However several years later, after they had been defeated again near Tana Tjampea, they were driven further southwards towards Bankelaan, on the southwest coast of Borneo, Flores and Sumbawa. Among the Iranun 'fugitives' from Tontoli, Kolff noted the dangerous presence of Daing Magassi (also called Passota) who had established himself on the island of Bonerate and was expected 'to assemble before long a considerable force.'[99] In the late 1830s, only Tunku on the northeast coast of Borneo, settled shortly after the loss of Tontoli, and situated on the main raiding route from Sulu to Sulawesi, was still used regularly by the Iranun as a permanent staging base for the southern sector.

Unrepentant fugitive Iranun raiders set themselves up at Tunku on the northeast coast of Borneo, ignoring with impunity the Spanish and Dutch naval authorities. It was a little known location in a place difficult to access where neither colonial government could harass them. After a brief lull of several years, Iranun maritime raiding experienced a renewal in the Sulawesi region, during which Tunku prospered as a principal Iranun base and boasted some of the boldest and most feared maritime raiders. These slavers of Tunku and Sibat maintained an "intimate correspondence" with their brethren in Illana bay, whose fleets they frequently joined.[100] They had settled at three small rivers, Tunku, Sibahat and Mekawa, which were situated within five miles of each other south of Cape Unsang. Tunku, located 8 miles upriver, had a population of over 1,000 Iranun warriors, and could be attacked only by small boats.[101] Captain Belcher described Tunku, in the early 1840s, as a major Iranun 'slave market and pirate den.'[102] Mail, an Iranun merchant, whose name was derived from the chain armor he wore, stated that he touched at Tunku in July 1851 in order to trade. He described the upriver settlement as comprising about 70 houses with a stockade and some large and small prahus, but no fort. According to Mail, all the inhabitants of Tunku were slave raiders. While he was there, the Iranun brought in a Bugis *panchalong* ("large trading boat") that they had captured off Buton. The Iranun imprisoned the crew to sell as slaves and they disposed of the captured goods to various merchants and traders like Mail.[103]

Between the mid-1820s and 1840s, as the villages and prahus of the Iranun at Tontoli, and later at Tempasuk and Pandassan, were being burned and broken up and other smaller strongholds wiped out by the Dutch and English, the population of Tunku grew, becoming a haven in an increasingly dangerous world for displaced Iranun. Sherif Abu, of Kinabatangan, stated to Spencer St. John that many former Iranun raiders of Tempasuk and Pandassan resided at a small river on the east coast of Borneo named Sibahat. Sibahat "is about a day and a night's sailing in a native boat to the southward of the Kinabatangan river. Tunku is a little to the southward, and is also inhabited by Lanuns. The two places together are supposed to be able to muster about 1,000 men. They cruise to the northward among the Philippines, and to the southward in the Celebes and Java seas."[104]

The Iranun had the reputation of attacking everything they met at sea, and the Bugis and most other traditional traders feared encountering them. In this context, by mid-century, Tunku had developed an infamous reputation. William Wyndham, a merchant adventurer residing in Jolo, mentioned the capture of at least three British vessels by the Iranun of Tunku, and the murder of the Europeans aboard at least one of them.[105] The local merchants and village headmen on the coasts of Borneo and

Sulawesi complained bitterly of the insecurity that prevailed on the high seas since the establishment of Tunku, and of being compelled, for purposes of safety, to live well into the interior beyond the reach of sudden strand attacks. Consequently, they could no longer trade with the "great sago producing" areas to the south and east, as the key Iranun raiding settlements closed off the narrow straits between the mainland of Borneo and Sulawesi and the Sulu archipelago.[106]

Raiding eastward and southward, the Iranun based at Tunku caused havoc among Bugis prahus plying back and forth across the archipelago, especially among those journeying from Makassar to Buton. In November of 1851, Sherif Yasin of Bengaya on the northeast coast of Borneo also stated that these Iranun had captured his relation, Sherif Besar, in Sandakan Bay, and had attacked many other local trading prahus. The previous month a large bloodstained, derelict sailing vessel had been found at sea off the northeast coast, completely stripped of its cargo, and without any crew. Yasin also mentioned the ubiquitous fear. "They are kept in such a state of alarm as to be compelled to build their houses far from the sea, and no trader can with safety pass along the coast."[107] However, among the statements from influential local personages, and the depositions of merchants who had suffered at the hands of the Iranun of Tunku, the testimony of Si-Ayer is particularly worthy of attention. It clearly shows the enormous extent of the damage inflicted upon the coasting trade of Sulawesi and the workings of the Iranun slave trade. Si-Ayer, not surprisingly, also noted their cruelty. When he made this remarkable statement in 1851, he was the servant of Mr. Meldrum of Labuan. Five years earlier his extraordinary odyssey had begun when he had been brought initially to Sibahat in rattan handcuffs and halter, and then to Menkawa, two small rivers immediately north of Tunku. Menkawa was the fortified settlement of the Iranun Raja Muda. Two months after his arrival, Si-Ayer was sold to an Iranun from Jolo, named Matalissi, who made him pull an oar in his raiding prahu. Matalissi was about to embark on a slaving expedition in the vicinity of Brunei, when he informed Si-Ayer that the English had settled permanently at Labuan, and that his traditional cruising ground was no longer safe. Matalissi then transferred him to a man named Sindeko, in part exchange for a boat. Nakodah Ursup, a Sambas man, bought Si-Ayer from Sindeko, and

Mr. Meldrum manumitted him. At the time of his sworn declaration, Si-Ayer was working for his new European master 'for wages' at Menggatal on the northwest coast of Borneo.[108]

Six years earlier, in 1845, Si-Ayer had been sailing on board the trading prahu of Nakodah Uba Kuray, a servant of the rajah of Bima, who had sent the nakodah to Mengri, about a day and a night's sail from Bima, to collect a cargo of wax and tripang. He was on his way to the island, having spent a considerable amount of time trading among small settlements, when an Iranun fleet took the prahu. Thus captured, they cruised for about a year, principally in the Celebes Sea between various ports of neighboring islands and Makassar. The slave raiders captured many prahus during this time—upward of thirty according to Si-Ayer—especially near Buton. He also noted that the fleet took many boats that were brave enough to venture out of the Macassar roadstead. Si-Ayer then described his harrowing passage on board the Iranun slaver bound for Tunku:

> The whole Lanun fleet consisted of upwards of twenty boats, large and small; the principal chief was Rajah Muda; his men were about fifty in all, but not many of these were Lanuns; he had very many prisoners on board. I was on board his boat. Altogether the fleet captured, before returning to Tungku, very many boats—I cannot say exactly how many, but I am certain there were more than thirty boats taken. It was the custom of the pirates, on taking a boat, to divide the proceeds at once. The Rajah Muda's share, on our arrival at Tungku, was more than forty slaves. The prisoners were all kept tied, until they showed no symptoms of attempting to escape, we were very sadly treated—water and rice given to us very sparingly. Some died from hunger, some from being handcuffed, some from grief; they untied me after about a month. If prisoners were so sick that they could not pull an oar, they were thrown overboard. I was finally carried to Sibat, then to Makowan.[109]

These Iranun disposed of their plunder and slaves, like Si-Ayer, among the Tausog of Jolo, the Samal peoples living in the vicinity, and to tribes living at the upper reaches of the interior of their rivers.

In 1851, the H.M.S. *Cleopatra* supported by two steamers attacked the Iranun haunt and burned the stockaded village. Many of the raiders were away cruising. The expedition's surprise attack spearheaded by James Brooke cleared the country around the settlement for several miles, and as a Malay auxiliary so graphically expressed the scene, "the whole was reduced to charcoal."[110] However, the devastation was not lasting. The 'invisible' Iranun defenders returned from the sanctuary of neighboring forests and their slave cruises to rebuild Tunku. This Iranun stronghold would not be completely broken up until 1879 when another British steam gunboat, H.M.S. *Kestrel*, was sent to finally finish the project of pacification begun more than 25 years earlier.[111]

CHAPTER SEVEN

THE EXPEDITIONS

An Iranun long-range maritime raiding expedition was an extremely dangerous enterprise. Slave raiders in the course of their way of life faced an astonishing series of life and death struggles, not so much to help the Sulu Sultanate and their overlords win the regional economic and political war but rather to simply return home at the end of each journey to their families and settlements in Mindanao, Borneo, Sumatra, and Sulawesi. To organize and lead the crews of one of the *joanga* expeditions that prowled the seas of Southeast Asia challenging the colonial navies at every turn demanded the best equipment, skill, spiritual strength, and great courage. Some of the joanga and other Iranun boats had crews of 100 to 150 men; the usual complement was from 50 to 100 and they mounted 8 to 10 large swivel guns or *rantanka*.[1]

The sea was their domain. But the Iranun and Samal were forced to abandon Marudu, Tempasuk and Balangingi and other bases and settlements in the years between 1834 and 1848 when the various colonial governments said the slaving expeditions must end and their children would become farmers, at handpicked sites where colonial agents had set up agricultural stations. But in 1815 Tukurun, Tontoli and Balangingi, with their coral and mangrove-infested shorelines on the Sulu and Celebes seas, and, Tempasuk and Reteh with their fortified upriver locations near the South China Sea, were among the most important Iranun and Samal slave-hunting bases. No sites were better situated for launching the large-scale annual expeditions. Since the 1760s, these settlements had been occupied, and defended against competing tribes and states. In the narrow impenetrable margin between the sea and the forest the Iranun flourished. Setting out from Tempasuk and other settlements on the northwestern coast of today's Sabah, they collected sea cucumber and birds' nest, seized the inhabitants of the coasts and rivers everywhere, and took trading prahus on the open sea.

In contrast to the mobile marauding bands of other neighboring sultanates, Iranun and Samal raiding expeditions were strictly predicated on concepts of hierarchy, systems of kinship affiliation and social organization, and processes of interethnic relations and cultural accommodation. At the end of the eighteenth century, the expeditions were initially composed of scores of large fleets. The largest and most important of these, the Illana Bay fleet, was composed of more than 100 joanga and between 10 and 15,000 raiders. It is important to note that the political economy of maritime raiding in the Sulu-Mindanao region operated almost entirely in terms of leaders and personal followings. Authority was exercised over people, rather than in terms of villages per se. Since the key to the accumulation of political and economic power was the manipulation of groupings or combinations of seafaring people rather than villages, it was possible for some men of prowess, charisma and good fortune to exercise political authority with little or no territorial base at all. This depended instead on the number of retainers and followers that could be repeatedly mobilized for raiding expeditions, and slaves who could be acquired in the process of the hunt. However, the sultans of Sulu and Cotabato were the exception to this basic rule of social structure and social organization. In theory, all persons who lived within a particular territory were the sultan's followers or subjects because for him people and territory were coincident.[2]

The sultan of Sulu appointed a *panglima*, the highest-ranking political leader among the Samal slaving communities. Next in the hierarchy was the *maharajah* and *orang kaya*. In the Sulu Sultanate's domain, the political administrative structure of every Iranun and Samal community under its dominion was similar throughout the archipelago. Hence, it was customary for an Iranun ward to also have an Iranun as its maharajah or for a Samal group to have a Samal as its panglima.[3] Maritime raiding expeditions were organized and precisely operated against this social and political backdrop. The social organization of the Iranun and Samal slave raiding system acquired much of its association, flexibility and structure from within its specific cultural-ecological context and wider regional setting. While a hierarchy of delegated power and authority existed, embodied in the sultan and his representatives on the spot, individual boat and fleet alliances nevertheless could rapidly be built up, pyramiding into larger slaving expeditions or political units. As Mednick stresses, however, each individual grouping always retained its singular identity.[4] In the latter part of the eighteenth century, this dynamic system of kinship and social organization was in a constant state of flux and tension. Various *maharajahs, panglimas* and *datus* constantly sought to attract more followers, possess more slaves, place more groupings and settlements under their jurisdiction, and subordinate rivals in order to control markets and labor power in an emerging regional system of global economic interconnections and interdependence. By the late 1830s, the English and Dutch colonial authorities felt that the Sultan of Sulu and his kindred tacitly sanctioned the maritime raiding expeditions of his subjects and gave indirect encouragement to the 'system' by receiving a certain portion of the plunder, including slaves. The impression conveyed in the 1838 statements of rescued captives and 'Illanun' prisoners reveals the shocking realities of a 'system of piracy' and slaving carried on by the Iranun and Samal of the Sulu archipelago. The system was quite beyond the power of being dealt with by an English Admiralty Court in its ordinary jurisdiction in the straits of Malacca and the South China Sea.[5]

The first Iranun bold enough to pursue long distance raiding expeditions became powerful leaders and sometimes created a hereditary rulership. Only a *rajah* or his sons could command expeditions, and these sons often married the daughters of other leading maritime raiders or the rulers of neighboring mini-states. At the beginning of the nineteenth century, their web of marriages created a widespread political and economic kinship net, marked by a struggle to stave off the West with their own economic and political bloc, as China became a vast entrepot for foreign influence and desire over almost every aspect of life. St. John wrote, in his own highly readable account of the years he spent during the middle of the nineteenth century encountering the 'Illanun' around the stronghold of Tempasuk, about the seemingly ad hoc procedures that gave rise to loose associations and groupings of Iranun raiders as being like a confederation. He argued that the 'Lanun' "seldom form regular government, but attach themselves to certain chiefs, who are partial to high-sounding titles, particularly those of sultan or rajah. These chiefs are independent of each other and unite only for defence, or for an extensive expedition."[6]

Maritime raiding, generally in the form of an organized expedition, was conducted by the Iranun and Balangingi on a large scale across Southeast Asia. Participation in organizing and outfitting expeditions, however, was often limited to a handful of wealthy powerful individuals who exercised complete control over such activities. Groups of people and key personnel, such as boat commanders and gunners, as well as items such as raiding boats, munitions and rations were individually owned and regulated by such persons, and all were both saleable or temporarily partible.

In this fluid social system a person who could manage to gain followers and accumulate wealth in the form of slaves, munitions and trade goods could rise into the office of orang kaya (as a local leader) or in rare instances into the rajah or datu class. One obvious way a talented individual could gain such wealth and status was by taking command as a *nakodah*, of a raiding vessel.[7] The personal aid, cooperation and equipment for such a high risk, high gain venture could be obtained from an Iranun rajah or sherif, or from the sultan of Sulu and his representatives, in return for a share of the proceeds. The crews of the nakodahs, who acted as organizers at the local level, were drawn largely from the ranks of those they had grown up within their villages and fought with at sea in different parts of the archipelago. The rajahs, sultans and datus in turn offered security and the nakodahs and crews gained status according to their patron's respective wealth and power. Captives, hunted down and caught by the nakodahs and their crews, along with the *tripang* and pearls harvested by slaves and commoners, were shared among the rajahs' and datus' allied families and networks of followers. Highly skilled commoners could shift their allegiance to another rajah or datu if they felt unappreciated. But no matter how great their talent, commoners could rarely rise into the highest echelons of the trading elite.

The 'pirate wind' or easterly that began to blow in September marked the beginning of a terrifying period for people across the archipelago–a time known as the *musim lanun*, the 'Iranun season.' The datus, rajahs, panglimas, and associated nakodah, and crewmen were prepared.[8] For several months, these seafarers had focused their entire beings on the day when the nakodah making the rounds entered various villages and gave his cry to go to sea. As members of the local elite, the nakodahs and community leaders, usually from neighboring settlements, met to decide in principle where the raiding expedition would go, what to do from an organizational standpoint, and how to deal with possible problems that might be encountered during the dangerous journey ahead. The Iranun and Samal lived either in small compact coastal or riverine settlements often organized as wards within or near large towns or on reef strewn coral and sand islands. A large number of discrete Iranun villages were generally limited to Illana Bay and the coast of northwest Borneo; larger cosmopolitan forward bases contained, in addition to Iranun-Maranao raiders and settlers, Samal speakers, particularly Balangingi, Tobello, Gilolo, captive Christian Filipinos, and members of other ethnic groups. Wards were formed by households affiliating with a particular local leader and mosque. Secondary affiliation was with a smaller group of adjacent households and kin. Membership in these wards and settlements was highly variable as seasonal and long term exoduses occurred in response to slave raiding cycles, changes in maritime economic activity and commodity markets, and the fluctuating incidence of morbidity, mortality and regional conflict.[9]

The Iranun knew that their lives on board a raider depended upon the combined quality of their kinfolk and allies' experience and skills–skills in navigating, seamanship, boat building, fighting, and a shaman's guarded prescription for wounds–that could help them survive and bring a datu wealth. Tobias' 1822 report mentions that Iranun prahus were generally fitted out with an experienced crew, accustomed to a "wandering and hard life."[10] When necessary, as in the case of larger raiding expeditions, nakodahs formed temporary associations, which allied them to a range of kindred families and settlements that were not always geographically contiguous. Permanent fixed crews and steady cooperative organizations were nonexistent. The nakodahs generally prepared to undertake the voyage with their male relatives and their sons or brothers. They were also accompanied by slaves who acted as servants and supplemented the crew.[11]

It was increasingly evident to the colonial naval officers who hunted the Iranun that systematic slaving operations on such a massive scale could not be carried out without the encouragement and instigation of the local rajahs and sultans, acting as state sponsors of the various Iranun and Samal communities. In 1838, this assessment of the complex nature of the economic and political relationship between the social structure, statecraft and raiding ethos of Iranun and Samal communities and the social organization of slaving expeditions, was confirmed by 'Illanoon' prisoners, who stated that the commander of their squadron was a relative of the chiefs of Balangingi with whom the raiding expedition had originated, while they themselves had no alternative but to implicitly obey their nakodah's orders.[12] The statement made by the prisoner Silammkoom is particularly revealing with respect to the line order chain of command that reached right down from the sultan and his kindred to their subjects and followers in the various Samal wards and villages specializing in maritime raiding:

> I am a native of one of the Sooloo Isles called Ballanginghin and usually reside there. The Sultan lives at Sooloo proper. The principal chief at Ballanginghin is Panglima Alip, it is well inhabited and there are large fleets of boats which are employed in collecting seaweed, tortoise shell, tripang and on account of the Sultan who gives the people in return, cloth or any other articles he may think proper. Our fleet consisting of six *prahus* come from Ballanginghin and left that place about three months since. The fleet was commanded and under the sole direction of Orang Kaya Kullul who is a relation of Panglima Alip. Orang Kaya Kullul informed us that the Sultan had desired him to plunder and capture all nations save Europeans. The principal *prahu* was under the immediate command of Orang Kaya Kullul. I have never seen the Sultan of Sooloo. This is my first voyage to the East Coast of the Malayan Peninsula, but for many years I have cruised in the vicinity of the Manillas, Maccasar and other places on which occasion Orang Kaya Kullul took any boats he happened to meet.[13]

At the end of the eighteenth century, all Iranun raiding expeditions and individual slaving vessels were run autocratically. There was a strict hierarchy, chain of command, and code of conduct. The fleet commander and his captains demanded unquestioning loyalty and obedience from all crews under their command. The Iranun generally cruised in squadrons of 30 to 40 joanga with a single fleet commander and a nakodah on board each joanga. There were also many warriors of various ethnic groups and, if required slaves, would also be used to fight to the death in desperate encounters at sea.[14] The overall command of a joanga or garay was the responsibility of the nakodah who, according to the Dutch Resident of Menado's account of Sulu piracy, excelled in "physical force, courage or cunning" and had acquired a certain renown and wealth.[15] He controlled all aspects of the sailing and navigation of the vessel. His crew was often a mixture of Iranun and Samal sailors and captured Filipino and Malayo-Muslim slaves, who had an understanding of the Iranun-Maranao and Samal dialects and whose knowledge of regional languages and navigation routes could prove to be strategically useful. Filipino renegades were highly valued and their martial skills and local knowledge sometimes saved them from the dreadful fate of pulling an oar on the slaves' bench.[16] The Iranun sailors and warriors needed freedom to work the joanga and they substituted as crewmembers individuals who had been seized on earlier expeditions–slaves–some of whom were shackled to an oar only when attack was imminent. As a consequence of compulsory service many innocent people became, as crew, victims of bloody engagements at sea involving the Iranun. On the other hand, it was also true, that many of the slaves, who occasionally outnumbered the Iranun on board, had followed the sea raiders from their youth. They therefore became, although originally against their will, just as proficient marauders as their masters. There are numerous cases in the Spanish and Dutch records where slaves had not taken advantage of the opportunity to escape but rather voluntarily stayed with the Iranun and Balangingi in order to share in the material benefits of an adventurous, if not very dangerous way of life. Apart from the fact that many former captives were married to Iranun and Samal women–and were therefore quickly assimilated into the wider maritime society of their captors, the threat of demotion to the sweeps was usually enough to ensure their complete loyalty at sea.[17]

The activities on board the joanga were divided in the following manner. The nakodahs determined the course and were in command. Once the track was set, these captains rarely left the raiding prahus during the voyage. They had several experienced officers to assist them: the *juru mudi* (*julmuri*), of whom there were two or more on each vessel, were steersmen and were responsible for the crew (*sakay*) and the maintenance of the boat; the *juru batu* (boatswain) tended to anchor and lead line and kept watch for reefs, shoals, rocks, cliffs, trading ships, and the enemy.[18] Accompanying an expedition was at least one *hatib* or *imam*, who read the Qur'an, led prayer recitation, presided over death ritual and acted as legal arbiter and judge (*hakim*) when disputes arose between the commanders and their crew. In this way, strict discipline was maintained in the expedition. Most vessels appear to have carried several robust youth of 12 to 15 years who could provide assistance at the oars if called upon to do so as part of their apprenticeship while learning the finer points of maritime raiding technique and navigation. Often there would be an elderly leader (*orang tua*) on board–a man no longer physically strong enough to be in command, but who placed his rich store of experience at the disposal of the expedition. Women rarely went on raiding expeditions, except occasionally as the consort of a commander.[19]

The crewmembers consisted partly of Iranun or Balangingi warriors whose task was to fight, partly of trusted slaves who had accompanied the sea raiders for years, and ordinary slaves who had been seized on earlier expeditions as well as itinerant tribesmen. The officers and even ordinary crew brought slaves with them to cook, fetch water, and assist with shipboard duties. The slaves were not armed, but were considered an integral part of the crew; it was their job to row, bail, clean, and repair the prahu.[20] The size of the crew depended on the size of the vessel. At the end of the eighteenth century, the largest Iranun raiding boats carried from 80 to 150 sailors and marines and about 100 rowers. But, in the nineteenth century, when maritime slave raiders used smaller craft, the biggest Balangingi Samal prahus were only 70 to 80 feet long and carried a complement of no more than 100 people including slaves. An average sized Balangingi crew numbered about 40. Smaller, less heavily-armed boats carried 25 to 30.[21] For example, Table 3 tabulates the crew sizes of two Balangingi fleets which were destroyed eighteen years apart in 1838 and 1856.

Table 3. Crew size of Balangingi fleets, 1838 and 1856.

1838		1856	
Officers of Vessels	Crew	Officers of Vessels	Crew
Orang Kaya Kullul (Commander)	46	Si Taup (Commander)	32
Si Damah	30	Si Gading	39
Si Tomboh	23	Si Tanusi	28
Si Dunlines	25	Si Udin	32
Si Putlahs	28	Mas Bud	24
Tala Goa	29	Nawan	38

In addition to the rowers and crew, every joanga carried a complement of warriors numbering, on the largest vessels, upward of 100. The Iranun marines, sometimes including tribal headhunters among their numbers, took no part in sailing the ship, and were there simply to fight and engage the enemy vessel. They were expected to do so with unwavering courage and tenacity of purpose, attacking with grappling poles, boarding lances, muskets and the dreaded *kampilan*, a scimitar-like sword. The commander of the marines had no direct say over the sailing of the raiding ship, but he was a superior officer and made decisions in consultation with the nakodah about whether or not to attack a coastal settlement or engage a passing vessel. The chain of command was explicitly set out by the prisoner Tala Goa who, after explaining that he was compelled to do and act as directed by Panglima Alip, the headman of Balangingi, stated from his cell in the Singapore prison in 1838 that: "I am not a panglima. I was placed in charge of one of the boats by Orang Kaya Kullul who had exclusive control of the six *prahus*. The persons in charge of the several *prahus* were besides myself Si Damah, Si Tomboh, Si Dunlines and Si Putlahs.²²

However, on that tense occasion, the rescued Malay trader Amat, singled out his assailants and added the name of Daniel, an Iranun who had lived at Balangingi for years, to the list of prahu commanders:

> I cannot say the precise number of Illanoon in the boat in which I was but I swear that the twenty-two prisoners here present formed part of the crew and that Daniel was considered and acted as Panglima *prahu* besar and Tala Goa, panglima sampan, when I was taken on board the pirate *prahu*.²³

The influence of Visayan renegade captains was most pronounced during the second decade of the nineteenth century, when they commanded up to 70 percent of the Balangingi garays and perhaps 40 percent of Iranun joanga operating out of Mindanao and Sulu. Invariably these renegades leading raiding parties possessed detailed knowledge of the shoals, reefs, coves, and seas of their former provinces, and long standing memories of the liturgical calendar and fiestas of the different Luzon and Visayan towns. The Spanish and Dutch officials came to rue the day that these renegade nakodah, often kidnapped on earlier expeditions, were given authority and responsibility that would not have been possible in their former coastal villages and homelands under colonial rule.²⁴ The Iranun and Balangingi overlords always needed people of courage and conviction to whom they could entrust the day-to-day operation of a maritime raiding prahu and in giving and receiving orders from other nakodahs and the fleet commander. The combination of risk and reward on board slaving ships attracted renegade captives, especially from the Visayas, who were capable of earning the respect, loyalty and cooperation of prospective crew members and, if need be, die young at sea. But talented captives and slaves were not necessarily assured of succession to the position of boat commander. Ultimately, the individual's personal capabilities and physical attributes were the principal determining factors for selection into the elite ranks of the renegade commanders and seafarers. However, there were still moderating factors, which acted as a drag on the upward mobility of such captives irrespective of their innate aptitude for such a way of life.²⁵ The pressure to marry a local woman and embrace Islam was relentless. Of course, only those with ambition and who renounced their Christian faith could hope to command a prahu and live well. Arranged marriages were not uncommon and promising captives were sometimes contracted for a union when a prospective partner was still in childhood or early adolescence.[26] These marriages were frequently used to cement ties of alliance for local families and settlements involved in maritime raiding and they served as a way out of a potentially punishing life of bondage and dependency.

Renegade commanders were among the most feared slave raiders because of their local knowledge of specific target areas which included everything from dialect and dress to subsistence cycles and the liturgical calendar, and when, where and why local inhabitants were apt to be out and about travelling from either one village or region to another. A Spanish naval officer, commenting as to why their rapid descents and slave raids upon the coasts of the Philippines were so successful, stated that "they have many Bisayans (natives of the Visayas) among them, who, are acquainted with the localities, [and] serve them as guides and spies."[27] Numerous eyewitness accounts and descriptions of fugitive captives about the renegades suggest that they lived in Balangingi, Jolo and elsewhere in some comfort with members of their crews under the protection of successive rajahs, panglimas and sultans. A Spanish letter of 1836 details the extent to which the Visayan renegades had become a major thorn in the side of the Manila Government:

> Despite so many Moro-Visayan captives, it is necessary to tell the truth, and the truth with respect to those Visayan captives in Jolo, is that they live in contentment and even freer than those under the rule of some governor of the Visayas. The number of captives is greater than the number of natives who live in Jolo. They get the women they like. They go around freely and at certain times they are allowed to carry arms and it is not difficult for them to escape. Instead many of them join piratical raids.[28]

An Iranun raiding expedition emerged from a combination of support groups drawn from particular wards and villages that came together as occasions arose for the common purpose of maritime raiding. Participation of large support groups in these expeditions was based on ramifying personal kin ties and slaves, and the labor power of both was a critical factor for the in-gathering of allies and supporters in such a major undertaking. The size of the expedition depended not only upon its purpose but also upon complex factors such as the length of time of the cruise, the raiders' familiarity with the target areas and, more importantly, the ability of the organizer to mobilize experienced followers for the venture. Individual communities could manage small expeditions; sometimes whole crews came from a single settlement. However, composite crews were not uncommon in expeditions of less than ten prahus. Iranun and Balangingi vessels frequently left with a skeleton crew of 10 to 15 and travelled to neighboring Iranun and Samal villages and islands to fill out their complements with kindred and slaves.[29] It was common for masters to send unaccompanied slaves on these prahus, but nakodahs were reluctant to take those who objected to their master's wish.[30] Large-scale enterprises entailing 30, 40 or even 50 prahus required the cooperation of many settlements on a regional basis. Organizationally, such expeditions reflected the kinship and alliance networks of powerful datus. For example, of the 26 'Balangingi' vessels that seized Francisco Basilo and 350 other people in 1836, 9 were from Balangingi, 4 from Tunkil, 5 from Basilan, 2 from Pilas and 6 from Iranun settlements on Mindanao.[31] The raiding expedition itself was transitory. These groupings did not have any permanence beyond the immediate voyage. When a slaving expedition was over and many of the patron-client and kinship ties were deactivated, the fleet and crews dispersed to go home to their respective settlements or join another expedition, which was forming somewhere else. Expediency often was paramount; leaders and groups of boats were constantly realigned to conduct slaving forays and independent raiding expeditions patronized by Tausog datus and panglimas.

The establishment of this regional maritime raiding system based on rapid deployment, mutual support and association to wage war at sea was a major accomplishment of the Iranun and Balangingi, whose fleets sometimes combined for the purposes of marauding. The association of the Iranun and Samal into a formidable league of constantly shifting alliances which, by 1820, included some 500 prahus and 30,000 raiders struck terror into the hearts of coastal people, merchants and ship captains all across Southeast Asia. This loosely structured federation was predicated on the principles of hierarchy, kinship alliance and cultural accommodation, and organized around villages in Illana Bay and the Balangingi cluster, with forward bases and settlements strategically situated on the coasts of the Philippines, Sulawesi, Borneo, and Sumatra. This federation enabled the maritime raiders to prosper almost as a state within a series of traditional states, amid one of the fastest growing and heavily populated economic regions of the world.

European sources in Spanish, Dutch and English tended to estimate the strength of the Iranun and Balangingi conventionally in terms of the number of standing warriors in their societies. This form of reckoning caused obvious problems for colonial officials and naval officers when used as a basis for calculating the approximate size of the Iranun complement crewing their fleets as these seafarers moved around in sizeable numbers out of reach of the colonial state. How many men could you get in a joanga or garay? How accurately were they counted? To begin with the last question first, when the numbers mentioned in the sources are comparatively small, as in the interrogation statements of imprisoned slave raiders and the testimony of fugitive captives, such as the statements contained in the trial records of a maritime attack by six 'Illanoon' ships in 1838 that went disastrously wrong, it is reasonable to assume that it is an accurate count. In this rare instance, the surviving boat commanders gave the exact number of crew in the vessels under their command.[32] With larger fleets, for example those swarming around southern Luzon and the southeastern coast of Sulawesi at the end of the eighteenth century, there is a much greater chance that the figures cited in various types of records, including the desperate letters of friars, the frightening journal entries of European ship captains, and the confused accounts of terrified villagers, are at best an approximation. But, at what point can we reasonably begin to assume exaggeration? There is in fact remarkable consistency between various sources from Spain, the Netherlands and Britain as to the size of Iranun and Balangingi fleets.

Before the mid-1760s Iranun fleets of over 50 ships are rarely mentioned, the exception being fleets under royal leadership such as the Maguindanao-inspired expeditions against southern Luzon and the Moluccas with more than a hundred vessels in the previous decade. After the 1780s, however, sources frequently mention Iranun fleets that were 60, 100, 150, or even 200 strong, as well as countless smaller expeditions.[33] For example, the combined fleet that besieged Kalengsusu, north Buton, in 1822 comprised 100 joanga from Tontoli, 50 vessels commanded by Raja Jailolo, and a smaller number led by the Chief Suderama from Tobungku.[34] The tendency has been to accept the larger figures as reasonably reliable. However, in some cases, the only evidence of possible exaggeration is that the figures were large because European authors of the sources could not always readily distinguish among the various ethnic groups accused of maritime raiding who based themselves on the Mindanao and Sulawesi coasts and the string of islands forming the Sulu archipelago, and whose way of life and occupations were similar. But there is widespread agreement between independent, colonial and indigenous sources of the same period in the 1830s that argues in favor of assuming most of the figures, large and small, to be approximately accurate. Only in exceptional circumstances can figures from the primary sources be questioned outright. For example, the repeated assertion of James Brooke, the aspiring white rajah of Sarawak in the 1840s, regarding the number of Iranun ships and crew is almost certainly exaggerated. The figures were dangerously large as part of a circular argument about domestic insecurity and the necessity of forceful intervention, in order to secure royal navy assistance to destroy neighboring Iranun who terrorized the Brunei coast in the 1830s and 1840s.

On the other hand, the British and Spanish knew enough about the 'Illanoon' by 1838 to be able to say how many men their raiding vessels held on average and to account for their approximate fleet size. In the celebrated 1838 trial in Singapore, captives on board the raiding vessels, like Francisco Thomas, told the court recorder that there were a large number of vessels at Balangingi. He had been informed by the slave raiders in the garay in which he was a captive that "there were many boats not less than a 100 which . . . were pirate boats."[35] This was confirmed by the crewmember Mah Roon, alias Mah Sandar, an inhabitant of Macassar, who had been captured in 1836 by a formidable 'Illanoon' fleet of 23 prahus. Mah Roon thought that there were about 200 prahus of the same size as the large one he served aboard that was destroyed by the naval steamer.[36] Four years later a confidential Spanish document describing in detail the topography, population and economy of Balangingi estimated that annually 120 to 150 garay or *pancos* left the place, some to raid in the Moluccas and others in the Philippines.[37] Important further evidence that Iranun and Samal fleets were not small at this time comes from information provided by William Wyndham in the early 1850s. The local merchant-adventurer based at Jolo told Spencer St. John that prior to the Spanish attack on Balangingi in 1848 the Samal slave raiders could muster more than 150 large boats, garay, containing 30 to 50 men each. Besides the big raiding boats, they also possessed many smaller ones used for the capture of trading and fishing boats. Wyndham said that he had seen many large raiding prahus enter the harbor at Jolo over the previous decade.[38]

More numerous than the large ocean-going joanga and garay were the smaller seagoing craft that enabled the Iranun and Balangingi to carry out inshore operations in coastal waters throughout Southeast Asia. Most vessels in this category consisted of single masted prahus and captured trading vessels up to 40 feet in length and 12 feet in width that carried no more than 30 men and between 2 and 4 small cannon. Altogether, the Iranun and Balangingi possessed between three and four hundred of these multipurpose vessels used for scouring the coasts and plying the archipelago's 'inner waters.' We know enough about Iranun and Balangingi raiding ships to be able to say that the larger Iranun fleets of the late eighteenth century carried virtual armies of several thousand warriors while the smaller Balangingi squadrons carried far fewer, usually only several hundred well-armed men. The size of a prahu in relation to its complement was generally in the order of 'five men for each fathom length.' Thus, the larger Samal prahus had 50 to 60 men and the smaller 20 to 30.[39] The literary and visual evidence suggests that the Iranun fleets of the 1790s that attacked the straits of Malacca, southern Luzon and the spice islands, included lanong or joanga, long ships that were much bigger than those used in the second quarter of the nineteenth century, when the superior firepower and maneuverability of steam warships wreaked havoc among raiding fleets trapped on open seas. The larger of these earlier Iranun joanga had a complement of 80 to 100 men. The Balangingi base fleet boasting several hundred vessels was described as follows by a Spanish naval officer in 1838:

> There are about 200 boats in all, of different sizes, engaged in piracy. These boats are beautifully built; are very sharp fore and aft with great beam, and are double banked. The largest carry forty men, the smallest fifteen. If we take an average of 30 men for each boat, this will give six thousand men engaged in piracy, which is the estimate the pirates themselves give of their numbers.[40]

Most Iranun and Balangingi fleets were composed of a number of squadrons of between 6 and 40 vessels each. These squadrons were formed from the various maritime wards and settlements that flourished throughout the area between Mindanao and Borneo and had come to constitute a nursery for the raiding fleets of the Sulu Sultanate by the advent of the nineteenth century. The squadrons were formed into a number of recognized divisions that, if occasion demanded, were capable of combining and operating in a single fleet of up to 400 sail. However, this rarely happened, and generally the divisions were divided into smaller squadrons at their bases and outposts at Illana Bay, Balangingi, Burias, Tontoli, Tempasuk, Reteh, and other less well-known settlements. From these bases, they combined into fleets and split into squadrons that divided the archipelago into quarters. In their heyday the Balangingi could muster at least 150 garay, often double banked and capable of carrying up to 60 warriors, that sailed in fleets of 8, 10, 12, 20, or 30 prahus.[41] The 1838 naval action in the South China Sea, which resulted in the capture of several 'Illanoon' raiding boats and the scattering of the remainder in such a shattered condition that it was assumed that they must have sunk together with all on board, afforded convincing evidence from the statements of the captured raiders that their squadron, consisting of 6 vessels, each carrying from 20 to 50 men, had left Balangingi as part of a larger fleet. It appears from the report of the prisoners captured by the steamer *Diana* that these 6 prahus with 18 more comprising a fleet of 24 sail were fitted out by the sultan of Sulu. They were formed into four squadrons and ordered to cruise in different parts of the South China Sea for the expressed purpose of capturing trading vessels of 'all nations.' This Balangingi flotilla that fell in with the steamship was also directed, in the event of being unsuccessful on the east coast of the Malay Peninsula, to hunt in the straits of Malacca.[42]

There is also a remarkable consistency between sources covering the period 1787 to 1851, as to the relative size of Iranun and Balangingi raiding fleets from the testimony of local observers and captives seized in places as diverse as the Malacca Straits, the coasts of Bali and Lombok, and the sea lanes of eastern Sulawesi. In the late 1780s, the Iranun were particularly successful in closing Riau Lingga to commerce and in preventing the Bugis traders at Riau from getting to sea. Rajah Ali Haji Ibn Ahmad documents in the *Tuhfat Al Nafis* that the Iranun fleets operating in the straits of Malacca consisted of dozens of boats, the largest ranked among the finest in design, carrying up to 80 warriors and over a hundred rowers. Their officers and crew were among the most capable in the region, especially one Raja Merkung who was raiding with . . . "berangai armed with cannon. He preyed on all the bays, river reaches and subject territories of Riau and Lingga, and ruined several traders. . . . Following this, Raja Merkung went to areas in the Riau vicinity, like Ungaran, Buru, Moroh, and Sugi."[43]

In the ensuing 24 years Iranun marauders took thousands of prizes, almost 50 percent of this total was captured by large fleets such as the one encountered on a hazy night by an English warship off the mouth of a bay in south Sulawesi. This incident in February 1811 involving a British brig took place more than 800 miles from Sulu. The Iranun managed to escape during the night, but the previous day the British commander had engaged the fleet and launched a solid attack. During the action in which the Iranun had defended their ships stoutly, the Royal Navy Commander counted 40 prahus, 6 of which mounted an 8 pound cannon besides swivels and small arms operated by 60 to 80 men in each boat. He felt their numbers could not have been less than 1,500.[44] In a similar incident just over a quarter of a century later, but with a rather different outcome, a single schooner, was overwhelmed with heavy casualties by a very superior Iranun opponent. The vessel involved in the Lombok rice trade belonged to George Pockock King who sailed widely throughout the eastern archipelago and, in the mid-1830s, based his operations on Lombok.[45] His trading schooner, purchased the previous year, was seized off a busy port on Lombok's west coast. In October 1837, an Iranun fleet at Ampenan captured the schooner *Maria Fredericka*. The same raiders were later sighted in the Bay of Tambilan numbering some 800 men and 30 vessels. They were reported as heading towards Mindanao.[46] In the deposition of Si-Ayer, taken 9 years later in 1846, the servant of the Rajah of Bima recounted how his sailing boat was seized by a flotilla of more than 10 large Iranun vessels that was part of a fleet consisting of upwards of 20 boats, large and small.[47]

The slave raiding cruises of the Iranun and Balangingi provided a principal means of statecraft for sultans, datus and rajahs who could outfit the expeditions to expand the basis of their regional power and consolidate local authority. Long distance slave raiding and privateering flourished in Sulu during that critical period in 'regional time,' when the markets of Canton were opened to world commerce and the economic growth of the West. This market-driven desire for global commodities—tea, sea cucumber and birds' nest—revealed how Europe's and China's spiralling consumption of those commodities had a profound impact on the cultural-ecological history of the Sulu Sultanate and radically changed the population history of Southeast Asia, shaping tens of thousands of slave destinies. Heavily armed Iranun and Balangingi vessels and their crews were often outfitted and authorized by a commission of the sultan or other leading figures, as his representative, to seize the coastal inhabitants and trading vessels of all nationalities and states. However, these raiding vessels were invariably private ships in private ownership as opposed to prahus belonging to the standing fleet of the sultan of Sulu. This pattern of the nobles of Sulu and neighboring Bornean states, such as Brunei, Sambas and Pontianak, sponsoring privateering in order to seize trading ships and their passengers was increasingly resorted to at the end of the eighteenth century, at a time of the continuing integration of the world capitalist system of ever more areas and specialized territories of Southeast Asia. In the years 1825 to 1826, Captain Kolff noted during the voyage of the Dutch brig of war *Dourga* that the Malay aristocrats of Pontianak, "let out their vessels to pirates, or taking on board some of the shore population, they take to piracy on their own account."[48] The Dutch commander stated that the case of Pontianak was emulated by the example of other nobles authorizing attacks on regional shipping at Linga, Riau and several places opposite Linga, on the south coast of Sumatra, seeking high profit margins and returns from Iranun booty and slaves.[49] Sambas was one of the most powerful of these states, beside Sulu, where Iranun privateering suited the local sovereign, Malay merchants and sherifs who, nevertheless, only partially controlled the activities of the joanga based in their ports. By the 1820s, Iranun raiding expeditions had attained a position of powerful preeminence on the coasts and islands closest to major foreign settlements. From these ports, like Pontianak and Sambas . . . "they issue forth and commit depredations on the native trade, enslave the inhabitants at the entrance of rivers, and attack ill-armed or stranded European vessels, and roving from place to place they find markets for slaves and plunder."[50]

For Tausog and Iranun overlords, like Sherif Usman, who destroyed the coasting trade of the Brunei Sultanate in the 1830s, the outfitting of Iranun and Balangingi fleets enabled them to maintain a forceful competitive advantage over their downstream neighbors and rival states through strict control of international trade and the allocation of dependent labor. It was a comparatively inexpensive way of augmenting their power and statecraft with a lend-lease standing navy and seeking profit by making advances to the raiding expeditions in food, arms and gunpowder to which all nakodahs and ship owners agreed to repay them in slaves at exorbitant rates.[51] Almost every aspect of state formation, life and work in Sulu, Mindanao and elsewhere depended upon rajahs, datus and sherifs acquiring captives in order to build up a loyal following of kindred, commoners and slaves. Prestige and power, their very survival itself, eventually came to depend upon the success of the maritime raiding expeditions. Older aristocrats (principally merchants) and nakodahs who had retired from active business on the sea, and had been prudent enough to amass wealth, added to their fortunes by lending vessels, guns and slaves to younger Iranun and Samal men, as a form of advance. In return, they received a large repayment in captives and goods, but they also ran the risk of losing their property to the enemy or through accident at sea.[52]

As the maritime raiding activities of the Iranun and Balangingi expanded, individual rulers and the governments of various trading states established outposts along the raiding tracks for the exchange of arms and slaves and for purposes of rest and recreation. The overall nerve center of these widespread operations, however, was at Jolo, the capital of the Sulu Sultanate, where the sultan, Tausog datus and their retainers controlled the process of economic growth and engagement with the China trade, supplying the slave raiders with weapons, ammunition, crew, and trade goods. Mr. J. Hunt, an East India Company servant was despatched by Sir Stamford Raffles to the Sulu archipelago shortly after the conquest of Java. Hunt published, at Raffles' request, an account of what he had seen and the information he had collected, in which he particularized 12 different 'piratical establishments' belonging to Sulu, of which the aggregate fleet was estimated at about 200 prahus, and above 8,000 warriors. Hunt stated that in 1812 the share of the booty reverting to the sultan, by virtue of his ritual and symbolic role, was 25 percent, or one-fourth of all captures, while the datus and other nobles advanced guns and powder in exchange for captives. From facts which were elicited during the 1838 trial with respect to the captured 'Illanoon,' it seemed that the same stakeholder system had continued over the past quarter of a century.[53] It was apparent from the evidence of Augustine Santa Maria that this 'Lanun' fleet on its way from Balangingi to the straits of Malacca touched at Madi Mahat or Jolo . . . "where the pirates went ashore and were hospitably received and in no way discountenanced at a time when it is also alleged that the Sultan was present and who, therefore could not but be cognizant of what was going on."[54]

In Hunt's account of Sulu he distinctly charged the sultan with participating in the profits of the 'pirates' of the Mindanao-Sulu region. Some of the Iranun and Balangingi prisoners who, after the trial, were brought again before the Admiralty Court from the hospital prison, corroborated Hunt's statement maintaining that "to this day the sultan still continues to receive a certain portion of the plunder from the boats on their return to Sooloo."[55] When Captain Belcher visited Jolo in the mid 1840s, in command of the frigate HMS *Samarang*, he was repeatedly reassured by leading Tausog datus that they had no connection whatsoever with these maritime raiders who preferred 'self destruction to submitting to capture.'[56] But during his stay in the Jolo roadstead, several Balangingi prahus arrived and the English naval commander was duly informed that slaves captured in the Philippines by these vessels were exchanged in the local market. In Belcher's mind, this 'event' was graphic evidence of the fact that the sultan and datus had created a complex interdependent political and economic system to regulate the slave trade and the activities of raiding ships based in the Sulu archipelago. He was offered sufficient proof of Iranun and Balangingi connections to key Tausog datus at Jolo, and guides to their haunts, if he would act. But as his orders were clear–not to interfere unless an act of piracy on a British vessel was proved–he had no pretense for taking up the cause of the Spanish government against the aristocrats who sponsored the Iranun and Samal raiding expeditions and privateers.[57]

At the end of a slave cruise, the nakodah in the fleet determined the expedition's profit, so that all those who had invested in the enterprise could claim their due in captives and other seizures. As has been noted the sovereign, the sultan, and other high-ranking officials of the state made the first claim. What Belcher observed from on board his warship were various powerful parties in Jolo demanding their stake from a successful raiding expedition. The sultan reputedly took up to one-quarter of the profits. Next in line were powerful datus who had fitted out and supplied the cruisers. These were mostly officials related to the sultan or other leading figures who controlled commerce and allocated labor to harvest the fisheries and forests of Sulu's Bornean dependencies. Firearms hired from their owners in Jolo were recompensed in the form of slaves or bolts of linen cloth. The price paid for borrowing a large *lela* ("portable cannon") was 1 slave, and for a gun, it was 4 to 5 pieces of linen of 20 fathoms length.[58] Sherif Usman of Marudu led one Iranun family that made a huge fortune out of investing in slaving expeditions. A powerful, recently established family, they staked Iranun raiding fleets, which sailed like clockwork to the South China Sea to harry shipping and plunder coastal settlements, at high margins of return. The Iranun and Balangingi on the northwest coast of Borneo, whenever they cruised, obtained their supplies of powder, guns, food, and salt from Sherif Usman and on their return the Sherif's accounts were used to determine his initial investment plus an agreed percentage, paying him at a rate of five slaves for every hundred rupees worth of goods.[59] One of the key Bornean figures besides Sherif Usman, who gave regular encouragement to the Iranun slavers to visit him periodically, was Sherif Sahib of Sadong, further down the west coast. He sponsored many of the Iranun raids on

Dutch shipping and coastal towns further south, even as far as Banjarmassin, by "driving a profitable trade with them."[60] James Brooke believed from reliable intelligence he had gathered about these Iranun incursions into the territory of the Dutch that they were carried out with the material support and blessing of Sherif Sahib of Sadong, "who is a great encourager of the devastating system, and a confederate of the Illanuns."[61]

Once the stakeholders, principally Tausog aristocrats and Iranun merchants, were paid off, the remaining booty, namely captives, or the profit from the transfer or sale of slaves, went to the expedition's crew and their kindred. The participants often came from many wards and settlements dotted around the Sulu chain, so the success or failure of a large raiding expedition of the type that seized Francisco Basilo and more than 300 other people in 1836, affected numerous communities and large numbers of individuals. In general, the division was as follows: the panglima or headman of the village to which the prahu belonged received a slave as tribute. He then offered a part of the remaining slaves on the basis of first claim to the state. The nakodah then claimed at least six slaves, and what was left was divided in half. The juru-mudi and juru-batu received two slaves each, and the balance went to the rest of the crew who received at least a slave each. Those whose task was to fight, would generally, if possible, receive more and most certainly were rewarded with a more highly valued slave, for example one that was younger, stronger or female. On the other hand, if an expedition had not been successful and there were too few slaves then the number that accrued to the captain and higher ranks was reduced.[62] The slaves sent by their masters, who often did the uncomfortable if not dangerous jobs on board the prahus, received nothing, but their masters stood to make a handsome profit. This description of how the profit from the transfer and sale of captives and slaves was divided, based on the statements of imprisoned raiders and fugitive captives, conceals perks in the system that enabled particular crewmembers to supplement their share. Stolen objects were apportioned in the same ratio, but the nakodah and elite warriors, frequently kept objects of enduring value, found in the course of ransacking a vessel or on the body of a fallen defender. Iranun marines often confiscated weapons such as pistols and sabres indispensable to a dangerous occupation based on high risk and reward while Balangingi nakodah in one fleet were known to have divided gold dust—looted from a ship which was raided—between themselves.[63]

Not only was the territorial reach of the Iranun slavers more extensive than any other maritime raiding group in Southeast Asia, but so too were their supply networks for the conduct of war at sea and the organization of military force and action, involving traders, villagers and agents that spanned the vast distance between the strategic ports of Jolo, Singapore and Makassar. Iranun and Balangingi expeditions were fitted out with cannons, ammunition, muskets, and iron at Jolo, Marudu, Tobungku, and Singapore and other less well-known spots such as the settlement of Bali Labogee [Labuan Haji] on the east side of Lombok, Ampenan on the west coast and Kuta, located on an isthmus one to two miles wide and five miles long which connects the southern headlands to the mainland of Bali.[64] Kuta was accessible from either direction no matter which way the monsoon might be blowing. When the Iranun first arrived in numbers in the mid-1820s Kuta had a floating population of several thousand persons including Chinese and Bugis dealers in arms, slaves and opium, and assorted Balinese refugees and renegades from neighboring princely kingdoms. But Singapore was the redistributive hub of much of the arms trade outside Sulu proper.

Sir Stamford Raffles' cavalier patriotic attitude and bitter territorial and trade rivalry with the Dutch, which led to the establishment of Singapore as a free port, was responsible, because of his tolerance, for arms merchants and slave dealers trafficking with the Iranun in the harbor's roadstead, or on the islands offshore. Singapore quickly became an important commercial center for the arms trade despite a ruinous series of passport and navigation acts that the Dutch enacted across the archipelago to exclude all maritime groups, especially the Bugis, from trading with states like Sulu and with the English and Chinese merchants at Singapore. The Bugis smarting under the Dutch system that levied excessive duties on their interisland trade, which was the basis of their prosperity, were ripe for traffic with the Iranun at Singapore, Kuta, Labuan Haji, Tambisan, on the northeast coast of Borneo, and other stapling points. The European and Chinese founders of Singapore wooed the Bugis, welcoming their cargoes of natural commodities and slaves worth hundreds of thousands of pounds a year. Iranun slaves, and Bugis and Chinese munitions were soon readily circulated as common purpose currency in the port. The Dutch Resident of Riau angrily argued that the majority of Iranun in the Malacca Straits found temporary asylum at Singapore and in the surrounding areas. He also claimed that Iranun maritime raiding in the vicinity of Singapore was more ruinous and more frequent than at Riau. The resident bitterly proclaimed that the new influence of the free port, as a regional arms emporium, was both deplorable and dangerous because the Iranun "at these latitudes obtain their powder and ball secretly from Singapore, and the booty captured is taken there privately, and sold at low prices, or exchanged for ammunition."[65] Belcher confirmed the Dutch Resident's claims several years later after touring the shops of Tamil and Malay artisans, located on the east side of the waterfront, stating that, "The eye is naturally attracted to the general fabrication of arms in this region, and to those conversant in the examination of the pirate boats of these seas."[66] He concluded that many of the arms openly displayed in Singapore shopfronts were intended for 'piratical groups' like the Iranun. The royal navy commander argued, much to the chagrin of local manufacturers, dealers and merchants, that it was absolutely necessary to cut off this arms supply if Iranun maritime raiding was to be eradicated. However, Singapore was so dependent in manufacturing, shipping and finance on the arms and opium trade that it not only maintained, but also actively encouraged ties with the Bugis, even at the height of Dutch efforts to detain or seize their shipping. The majority of Bugis trading prahus retained their freedom of movement through evasion, flight or bribery and their 'clandestine' trade in munitions, opium and slaves thrived. In the 1830s, neither Singapore, the Bugis carriers, nor the Iranun slavers stationed at forward bases, could survive without the arms-slave traffic.

During the 1830s and 1840s handpicked naval commanders of various colonial powers, struggling to rid Southeast Asia of maritime raiding, men like Captains Kolff, Belcher and Don Jose Maria Halcon, published warnings across the region about the arms trade and its direct links to Iranun-Balangingi maritime raiding and the slave trade. These detailed reports, which were summarized in newspapers and gazettes, and subsequently published in books provided information and advice to governments and shipping in Southeast Asia about the disproportionate strength of the 'Illanoon' as a consequence of widespread trade in contraband arms. In the decade of the 1830s, they had been placed in charge of surveillance operations, cruising and search and destroy missions. But these commanders had not been able to observe any positive effect such measures had on curbing the arms traffic. Regional wide sightings of heavily-armed 'Illanoon' expeditions and the numbers of reported attacks on prahu shipping and coastal settlements rose steadily in the years between 1826 and 1836.

Beyond Singapore, Balinese lords of various *negara* claimed that the Dutch navigation and passport acts, which banned trade between various princely states in the archipelago did not apply to them, since these rulers had neither negotiated nor signed them. Several rajahs of Karangasem-Lombok and Mataram took full advantage of the heat of the market, providing security and a window of opportunity for European merchant-adventurers like John Burd, Mas Lange and George King, and allowing 'outlawed' activities to flourish in their ports, especially trafficking in arms and slaves.[67] In the 1830s the roadsteads and harbors of the main port villages of Lombok's west and east coasts were crowded with Bugis prahus freighting arms, American whalers from the southern ocean in search of provisions, and British brigs and schooners returning from Australia, hoping to find an outward bound cargo of rice for Singapore or China. It was here that the Bugis of south Sulawesi, the contraband traders of Singapore and the New England whalers furnished arms and ammunition to the Iranun, who made the neighboring seas their cruising grounds. According to an 1835 observer Ampenan, on Lombok's west coast, was one of the busiest ports outside Dutch jurisdiction:

> There are nine ships of three masts, three brigs and three schooners almost all English or belonging to Englishmen while sailing under Dutch flag. There were also three French ships. All ships had a variety of merchandise on board like ammunition and weapons of war, opium from Bengal, textiles and several casks of Balinese keeping.... The ships took in rice which was bought from the bandar in part for tripang and in part for the objects of their cargoes. Six ships had already been loaded, while the others were being loaded.[68]

In provinces in the Philippines corrupt officials, especially the governors and magistrates, did not scruple at selling government issued war stores to the Iranun and Balangingi. At the end of the eighteenth century, it was a lost cause to charge some of the *alcaldes* with the defense of the coasts of their provinces, particularly in the Visayas, because they were solely occupied in promoting their own clandestine commerce and, if such means would personally benefit them, they would issue dubious permits for government vessels to transport munitions and their goods.[69] Many Philippine towns lost their firearms through an alcalde's questionable financial dealings, in welcoming the injection of cash provided by the Iranun for contraband arms. Some villagers also forfeited their government-leased weapons due to their alcalde's alleged misfortune rather than an outright breach of trust. For example, the alcalde trader Domingo Navea's coasting vessel was returning from Manila with a cargo of 100 muskets and other implements for Albay, when 40 Iranun joanga captured the sailing ship in November 1799, after the master of the vessel appeared to offer no resistance. The alcalde viewed the incident at a safe distance from the deck of his escort vessel, a galley, which then simply disappeared over the horizon.[70] While the victorious Iranun greeted such a windfall with jubilation, their primary source of munitions before setting out from Mindanao and Balangingi on a slaving round was, however, Jolo, the capital of the Sulu Sultanate. It is not easy to find out the exact volume of munitions that found their way into Jolo and settlements and islands in the vicinity. Nevertheless, several sources, spanning three-quarters of a century, can be used to illustrate the increased Tausog demand for European weapons and manufactures, and provide an approximate measure of the rapid growth of the trade in munitions from Bengal and elsewhere between 1760 and 1848. These documents also reveal the powerful impact of the arms trade on the material culture and social practise of the Tausog who sponsored the maritime raiding expeditions as well as their growing dependence on the country traders. A comparison of the indent provided by Sultan Bantilan (Muizz un-Din) to Dalrymple in 1761 with Hunt's published figures for Sulu in 1814, and a list of goods for Jolo's market given to an American mariner from Salem by Datu Emir Bahar, circa 1835, provides a useful index of the rate of growth of war stores and other imported articles required at Sulu to outfit and supply Iranun and Balangingi expeditions. The Tausog nobles requested $10,000 worth of arms and ammunition from Dalrymple in 1761. This included heavy ordnance (four six pound cannon) but no other items were specified in detail. Hunt, while fully aware of the clandestine trade in arms and opium from Bengal, provides no figures for war stores and states lamely that they '[would] sell, but these [are] dangerous articles of traffic and ought to be discouraged.'[71] Two decades later, Gamaliel Ward, captain of the Spanish Brig *Leonidas*, revealed the extent to which the arms trade had expanded at Jolo since Dalrymple's time. The Datu Emir Bahar's request included '1,000 15-pound kegs of gunpowder, 6 swivel guns, 6 large cannons preferably brass, 600 muskets, 100 pistols, 4 bags of shot of varying sizes, gun flints, 2 dozen boxes of percussion caps and 8 dozen matchlets.'[72] By 1835, gunpowder and muskets were the principal items desired by Tausog datus. These figures must be considered as only a partial estimate of the overall volume of war stores furnished at Sulu's market, as equally large quantities of gunpowder and firearms reached the Tausog as a consequence of Bugis and Chinese enterprise.

By the second decade of the nineteenth century, a substantial portion of the country trade from India had been taken over by rival Spanish, Portuguese and American traders. Bengal vessels continued to visit Sulu, but without a trading outpost in the region they were at a severe disadvantage and had to leave the full potential of Jolo's commercial development to other merchants who not only brought arms and textiles but sugar, rice, tobacco, and other staples for Sulu's expanding population. This trend was already discernible by 1804: "a great part of ... [this] trade ... [say one half] has of late years been engrossed by the Dutch, the Portuguese, the Spaniards and Americans, in consequence of the English not possessing any commercial depot, or port of exchange in those countries."[73] These competitors did not rearrange the conditions of the country trade at Jolo, but simply increased the tempo of the trade with the sultanate and extended its commercial pattern to Manila, Macao and Singapore.

I would like to examine briefly here American private trade at Jolo which gave further impetus to the importance of Sulu in the interdependent process of world commerce, economic development and state formation. For Sulu, the role of American commerce was analogous to that of the English country trade and should be situated within the framework of the wider pattern of laissez faire trade with the sultanate, which had its origins in Bengal. The munitions traffic to the Sulu Sultanate, pioneered by the free traders of Calcutta, was broadened by Yankee maritime activity after 1820. It was the island-hopping New England vessels, which traded on the edge of the Malay world at Ceram, Ceram Laut and Gorong that later included Sulu on their itinerary to Canton. In 1811, Stamford Raffles described these 'commercial interlopers' who threatened British political influence and economic interests in the outer islands:

> The Americans wherever they go, as they have no object but commercial adventure, are by no means scrupulous how they acquire their profits, and as firearms are in the highest request especially among the more easterly isles these would be considered as the most profitable articles. They have already filled the different clusters of islands in the South seas with firearms, and they would not fail to do the same in the different eastern islands.[74]

It was well-known that Americans had little to offer in Canton except furs, agricultural and domestic implements, articles of coarse cutlery, and dollars. Desperately in need of commodities more attractive on the Chinese market, such as birds' nest, tripang and tortoise shell, the New England traders supplied powder, shot and rifles to the Tausog and Maguindanao. By 1829, firearms had become their stock in trade. According to an article published in the *Singapore Chronicle*, "Almost all the vessels leaving the ports of the U.S. for China, convey muskets, pistols, swords and gunpowder, which they sell on their outward passage to the natives and other inhabitants of Palawan and Maguindanao."[75] The article went on to assert, although there is little direct evidence to support the allegation, that:

> There are Americans living on both these islands who make the necessary arrangements, and who have several small native vessels, constantly sailing about the usual tracks of ships to China in the

proper season, for the sole purpose of meeting American vessels and taking from them their cargoes of warlike stores...."[76]

However, it was not uncommon in this period to find adventurous American and English mariners in the employ of European agency houses, sailing in native craft, small brigs and schooners throughout the archipelago. G.W. Earl mentions one of them as, "a small Spanish brig from Manila, owned and commanded by an American, touched at the Sulus in 1834 and brought a valuable cargo of pearl shell to Singapore. She made the same voyage again the following year."[77] The vessel that Earl was referring to was the Spanish brig *Leonidas* of Manila. In 1836, the *Leonidas* visited Zamboanga and traded at Jolo from the beginning of March to the end of August.[78] Her captain, Gamaliel Ward, was given a letter signed by the Datu Emir Bahar soliciting private trade and a treaty of friendship and commerce with the United States.[79] Ward was still trading privately in Sulu six years later when Commodore Wilkes visited Jolo for several days and managed to negotiate a treaty on behalf of the U.S. Government for trade and protection of American commerce with the Sulu Sultanate. "Besides the trade with China, there is a very considerable one with Manilla in small articles and I found one of our countrymen engaged in this traffic, under the Spanish flag. To him I am indebted for much information that his opportunities for observation had given him."[80]

William Wyndham, an English mariner, firmly established Sulu's trade link with Singapore during these same years. He began his career in the Philippine archipelago as a mate on a Spanish brig trading from Manila to the Moluccas and subsequently sailed as the commander of various vessels which traded throughout the eastern archipelago but particularly to Sulu.[81] By 1842, the shrewd, self-educated trader had settled at Sulu and owned his own schooner, the *Velocipede*.[82] From his commercial establishment in Jolo's Chinese community, he frequented the pearl banks near Tawi-Tawi and navigated as far as the Aru islands to procure tortoise shell and mother of pearl for customers in Singapore. Married to a *mestiza* from Iloilo, Wyndham spoke fluent Tausog and had acquired considerable status and authority in Jolo. In 1848, Spencer St. John described him as being "dressed in Malay costume and from long residence among them, he had assumed much of both the appearance and manner of a native."[83]

After 1820, it was the New England skippers and men like Ward and Wyndham who dealt almost exclusively in firearms, cloth and opium at Sulu. Export manifests rarely disclosed whether their vessels were carrying munitions. It is likely that listings such as 'sundries,' 'ironmongery,' 'ballast' or 'hardware' were conveniently used to mask arms shipments.[84] American captains were adamant in their refusal to provide freight lists to their own consular representatives in the Philippines. The American consul in Manila noted their lack of cooperation in a letter to the State Department in 1823:

> I find it extremely difficult to ascertain the exact amount of the importation and exportation from this island. The commanders and supercargoes of American vessels are very unwilling to give me a list of their cargoes and I have no instructions to compel them to give me the exact amount....[85]

An identical letter was again written towards the end of the following year. In March of 1829, the Salem brig *Quill* called at Manila. Among the articles declared were: 290 barrels of gunpowder, 144 shotguns, 24 large boxes of axes, 150 pounds of shot for the shotguns, 120 dozen axe handles.[86] Although the ship's destination was not stated, the inclusion of these items in the cargo and the fact that March was the beginning of the official trading season at Sulu suggest that the sultanate may well have been included on its itinerary.

For more than a quarter of a century, Wyndham was to be one of the Tausog's most reliable suppliers of munitions, opium, and cotton cloth. He often made several trips to Singapore each year where he traded 'natural produce' of Sulu. In January 1848, the following note appeared under the heading "Tortoise shell" in the weekly market report of the *Straits Times* and *Singapore Journal of Commerce*: "The importation of 4 piculs from Sooloo per *Velocipede* had been taken in barter for Benares Opium; the latter at Duros 550 per chest and the shell at Duros 425 per picul."[87] Spanish captains who traded at Jolo repeatedly accused Wyndham of trafficking in munitions and saltpetre, and the Spanish consul in Singapore was convinced that on more than one occasion he freighted firearms from the port to Sulu.[88]

The country traders from Bengal, the Yankee mariners from the New England seaboard, and a handful of merchant adventurers like Wyndham and Ward played an indispensable role helping to transform Tausog economy and society and altering the course of Southeast Asia's history. The participation of these Europeans and Americans in Sulu's global-regional trade guaranteed the sinews of war for outfitting maritime raiding expeditions and, at the same time, stimulating the economic, demographic and political development of the sultanate. Their trade at Jolo between 1768 and 1848 enabled the Tausog to exercise control over the supply and distribution of firearms to the Iranun and Balangingi as well as opium, textiles and an ever-increasing catalogue of European domestic manufactures and luxury items desired throughout the Mindanao-Sulu region.

The rate of growth of the sultanate's population had not kept pace with its rapidly expanding globalized economy. The West's insatiable desire for natural commodities acceptable in Chinese markets promoted an intensification of Tausog sponsored Iranun-Samal maritime raiding expeditions to seize captives to labor in the fisheries and forests of the sultanate's domain. It was Visayan, Minahassan and Bugis captives as well as flotillas of nomadic Samal Bajau Laut that procured the tripang, mother of pearl and tortoise shell that European traders bartered in China for tea. While the gunpowder and firearms supplied by these merchants allowed the coastal-dwelling Tausog to promote maritime raiding expeditions on a hitherto unprecedented scale and kept the Sulu-Mindanao region free of neighboring competitors and colonial intruders until the late 1840s.

Fig. 2. A "Malay Chief" of Sulu whose wealth and power were based on the careful regulation of global-local trade. He is dressed in high fashion; a head cloth of Bengal manufacture, a brightly colored Chinese silk jacket, satin pants and several splendid kris, which were a reflection of his economic power and social status.
(Courtesy of Frank Marryat, *Borneo and the Indian Archipelago*)

Fig. 3. Entrance to Jolo town in the late 1830s. The trading *prahu,* Tausog or Samal, appears to be crewed by Chinese. (Courtesy of M. Dumont D'Urville, *Voyage au Pole sud et dans L'Oceanie,* vol. 2, 1837-40, pl. 139)

Fig. 4. A street scene in Zamboanga in the late 1830s. The houses were built on posts and ladders taken up at night as security against periodic attacks by Iranun and Samal raiders. The inhabitants occasionally had to seek refuge behind the walls of the *presidio.* (Courtesy of M Dumont D'Urville, *Voyage au Pole sud et dans L'Oceanie,* vol. 2, 1837-40, p. 139)

THE EXPEDITIONS

Fig. 5. A large double-masted, double-outriggered sailing boat of the Philippine coasting trade. The *barangayan,* crewed by seven to ten seafarers, carrying cargo for interisland trade, was a favorite target of the Iranun and Balangingi.

Fig. 6. A heavily-armed trading *prahu* employed in the archipelago-wide coasting trade. The vessel carried two masts and was worked by oars as well as sails. Swivel guns were mounted at the bow, amidship and stern. These traditional work horses of the archipelago were commonly preyed upon by the Iranun and Balangingi raiders.

Fig. 7. A rare portrait of a fiercely independent Iranun warrior by an artist of the Malespina expedition. This skilled seafarer lived on the coast of Basilan in the early 1790s. His shoulder length hair is tied and tucked under a colorful handkerchief probably imported from Bengal.

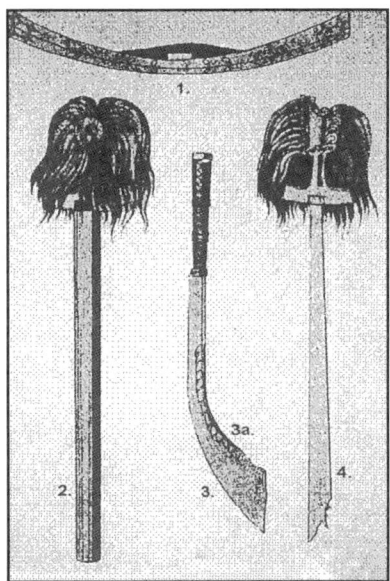

Fig. 8. Iranun weapons, 1840s:
1. Jilolo or Tobello shield;
2. Scabbard of Iranun *kampilan;*
3. Iranun beheading sword;
3a. Holes denoting number of victims;
4. Iranun kampilan, decorated with the hair of victims.

Fig. 9. The *lanong* (joanga) was made for long cruises and flotillas of these ships raided the Straits Settlements under the leadership of the Iranun of Tempasuk and Reteh. The vessel depicted carried 34 oars per side, double banked and steered with 2 rudders. The crew consisted of 150 to 200 men, with seafaring warriors occupying the fighting platform. (Courtesy of Museo Naval, Rafael Mouleon, *Construccion Navales*)

Fig. 10. Much of the inshore raiding on the coastal settlements and beach-heads (rather than on high seas) was done with single-masted canoes. The *salisipan* was a long, low, narrow, oar-propelled craft that was easily hauled ashore. It was open, provided with an oar at the stern for steering, and the crew used either oars or sculls. This craft proved a dangerous enemy for all coastal peoples of Southeast Asia.
(Courtesy of Museo Naval, Rafael Mouleon, *Construccion Navales*)

THE EXPEDITIONS

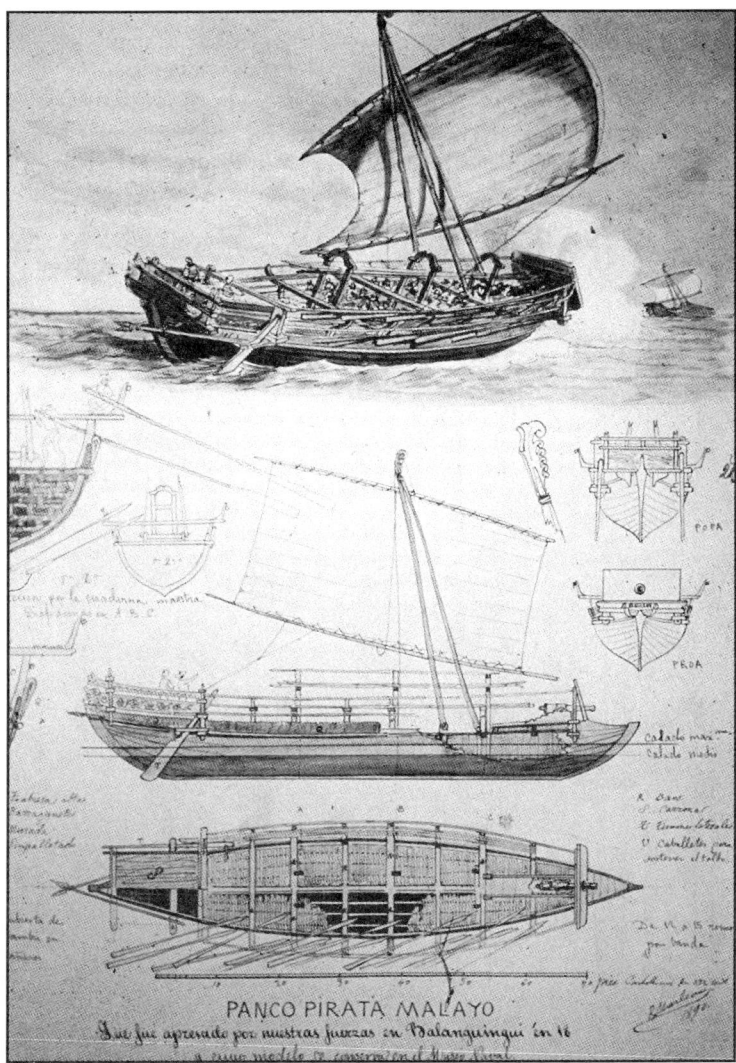

Fig. 11. Drawing of a *garay* under full sail—a Balangingi slave-raiding vessel built for speed, maneuverability and striking power. The garay, very sharp fore and aft with a great beam, drew from only three to five feet of water and moved over reef-studded seas at better than ten knots. The large beam enabled the garay to carry an enormous rectangle sail on the tall collapsible tripod of bamboo.
(Courtesy of Museo Naval, Rafael Mouleon, *Construccion Navales*)

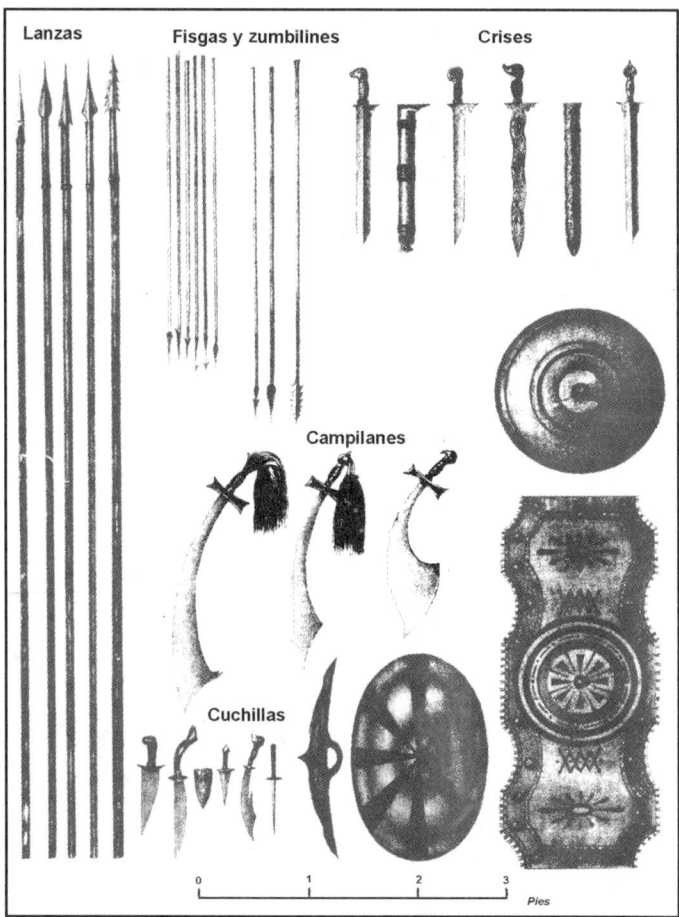

Fig. 12. Iranun-Samal weapons wrought from iron bars and hoops taken off the bales of English textiles, and worked into artistically and technically superior blades and lance heads; the serpentine *kris* regarded as the noblest weapon; the bamboo lance with a variety of spearheads; the *zumbiline* or boarding spear. Shields made of leather and wood were used as protective arms. (Courtesy of Emilio Bernaldez, *Resana Historico de la Guerra a Sur de Filipinas*)

THE EXPEDITIONS

Fig. 13. The Samal Laut, maritime nomadic boat-dwelling fishers of the Sulu zone, performed an invaluable role in the sultanate's globalized economy. They were expert pearl divers and gatherers of sea produce for the China trade.

Fig. 14. A 'negress' slave woman of Jolo in Manila. The woman bears a tattoo on her upper left shoulder. Her Melanesian-like physical features and the fact that this sketch was done by Juan Ravanet in the early 1790s, suggest she was seized from among the islands to the east of Sulawesi.
(Courtesy of Museo Naval)

203

Fig. 15. A Muslim woman from Cotabato captured by Balangingi slave raiders dutifully posed for an unknown Spanish artist circa mid-1860s.

Fig. 16. A *vigia* or *castillo* (village watchtower) at Zamboanga built by local inhabitants for coastal defense. Such watchtowers and small stone and wood fortifications were common features of most coastal villages in the Philippines in the late eighteenth and nineteenth centuries.
(Courtesy of M. Dumont D'Urville, *Voyage au Pole Sud et dans L'Oceanie*, vol. 2, 1837-40, pl. 143)

THE EXPEDITIONS

Fig. 17. The impressive facade of the two storey Jesuit-built church and fort at Boac, Marinduque. The fortress churches of the Philippines were a main line of defense against late eighteenth century Iranun raids. They were often located on top of a hill, with a wall surrounding the Church. The sides of the Church were heavily-buttressed and unequal length walls had openings at each corner for artillery.

Fig. 18. The Boac walls were built at the height of the Iranun raids, in the middle to the latter part of the eighteenth century. The walls, as high as three meters, encircle the top of a hill today called "Mataas Na Bayan" according to the Jesuit art historian, Rene B. Javellana.

Fig. 19. The *Kora-Kora* is a Moluccan *orembai* with outriggers. A large double-ended sailing boat, 15 to 25 meters long from stem to stern, it had a comparatively low freeboard, double outriggers with accommodation for several banks of rowers. The Kora-Kora was especially adapted, unlike the Dutch anti-piracy vessels, to pursue the Iranun and Balangingi in the waters of the Indonesian archipelago.

Fig. 20. The *falua* or sailing gunboat of the Spanish colonial anti-piracy force was equipped with oars and lateen-rigged sails, and crewed by between 15 to 20 men. At the beginning of the nineteenth century such patrols boats, 55 to 60 feet in length, were armed with an 18 to 24 pound cannon in the bow. With oars and sail they were capable of speeds up to 6 knots when patrolling against the Iranun and Balangingi.
(Courtesy of Museo Naval, Rafael Mouleon, *Construccion Navales*)

THE EXPEDITIONS

Fig. 21. The *canonero* was a prefabricated, flat decked, shallow draught (2 meters) steamer that was rigged as a fore and aft schooner. First introduced in 1860, the canonero carried a 24 pound bowgun with swivel guns mounted on the rails. It proved more than a match for Balangingi *garay* in coastal waters and signalled the end of Samal maritime raiding.
(Courtesy of Museo Naval, Rafael Mouleon, *Construccion Navales*)

CHAPTER EIGHT

THE CREW

Who were these 'Illanoon' that crewed the maritime raiding expeditions? Judging from indigenous sources and colonial records, particularly trial records and slave narratives, the majority were fishers and mariners with roots in southern Mindanao and the Sulu archipelago, where life on the sea was in the blood. They were also hapless shore dwellers from the coastal areas of the central Philippines and eastern Indonesia.[1] In the last decades of the eighteenth century when maritime raiding had become a regional wide enterprise, the label 'Illanoon' was applied indiscriminately to all Muslim marauders and those serving as crew. Large-scale maritime raiding involved tens of thousands of 'Illanoon' and their victims, who were seized in the different corners of Southeast Asia, transported and sold as slaves at Sulu and in neighboring ports and settlements. In the Iranun age, the label 'Illanoon' signified a profession that Iranun–Maranao and Samal raiders joined to acquire slaves, prestige symbols and staples in order to live in good fortune at home or abroad. As vehemently independent maritime raiders and seafarers, the Iranun exercised prowess and the use of force all their lives, at a time when Sulu was undergoing dramatic changes in the globalizing context.

The narrow use of the label 'Illanoon' to signify 'pirate' was well established when the Samal prisoner Sabit stated before the Admiralty court that 'the inhabitants of all these places [Balangingi] live by piracy and that they have no other means of existence, in fact that piracy is the general vocation of the people.'[2] More than half of the members of the 'Illanoon' crew put on trial in Singapore in 1838, including Sabit, were either Visayan or Sulawesi men. Nor were many of those who went marauding in previous decades exclusively Iranun-Maranao: Tagalogs, Visayans, Bugis, Tobello, and even the odd Chinese all joined Iranun maritime raids at times. Then, too, there were the Balangingi crews often mistaken as 'Illanoon' by the 1830s. Geographic proximity and group ambitions pitted Muslim Samal raiders against the Catholic Spanish Philippines. Hence, captive Tagalog and Visayan fishers and strand dwellers were drafted in large numbers for Balangingi expeditions rather than being press-ganged into the more motley Iranun crews assembled at the forward bases in Borneo, Sulawesi and Sumatra. On the other hand, vigorous predatory headhunting people, young tribal warriors in search of adventure and soul stuff, particularly the Iban, or Sea Dyaks on *merantau* and the Tobello and Gilolo of the Moluccas often enlisted and served aboard the Iranun raiding ships.

The Iranun and Balangingi took slaves captured from coastal settlements, from fishing and trading boats, and from handpicked volunteers, welding them into their own social order as a crew on shipboard. Some individuals, particularly Visayans, were also 'freemen'; they had switched ethnic and religious affiliation, quickly becoming an Iranun or Balangingi. The rest, slaves, on many of the vessels, comprised Tagalog, Bikolano, Cebuano, and Samareño seamen. In terms of ethnic identity, many early nineteenth century Iranun and Balangingi crewmembers were not 'Illanoon,' but rather ordinary peaceful fishers, traders and farmers who had been seized and traumatically uprooted from their original way of life where the land usually met the sea. It cannot be stressed strongly enough that these captured people of Philippine and eastern Indonesian origin figured prominently in Iranun and Balangingi slave raiding crews. Some of them, like the Iranun, Daniel, who crewed with Orang Kaya Kullul and was tried and sentenced to penal servitude for it in Singapore in 1838, ended up sailing to the four quarters of Southeast Asia. Another formidable member of the same crew, a former resident of Makassar, named Mah Roon claimed he did not volunteer to go. Two of his countrymen (Sukut and Pula Nea) were allegedly in a similar position to himself. Nevertheless, he stood ready to fight to the death rather than submit to the Royal Navy Steamer that had hunted them down in 1838. He, too, was sentenced to transportation and hard labor.[3]

The Iranun and Balangingi preferred captives and slaves, who had been fishers and merchant seamen, to provide the necessary seafaring skills. But when short of crew, for example in times of frenetic global trade and a rising demand for slave labor—a common state of affairs in the first two decades of the nineteenth century—the Iranun impressed as many able-bodied men as they could get their hands on even when they had only limited experience of shipboard conditions. Apart from the island of Basilan, which was a common location from which the Iranun rounded up seaworthy men, the raiders also led off 'vagabond' Tobello, Papuans and Iban to become willing members of their crews.[4] The woolly-haired Papuans often referred to by Europeans as *Alforeans* (a term applied to all people inhabiting the interior of the larger islands in the Molucca Sea), were highly prized.[5] Hence, the Iranun's frequent visits to New Guinea. Wyndham, the Jolo based merchant-adventurer, told St. John in 1852 that the people of New Guinea were piratical and that he had witnessed them looking for fishers to catch. "These are a scourge to the natives, but not dangerous to European vessels, yet in the end equally mischievous to trade."[6] The majority of the Raja Muda's Tungku-based crew that had, six years earlier in the Moluccas, seized a servant of the rajah of Bima, Si-Ayer, were not exclusively Iranun. "The whole fleet consisted upward of 20 boats . . . the principal chief was Raja Muda; his men were about 50 in all, but not many of these were Lanuns; he had many prisoners on board."[7] Tribal warriors regularly made up part of the vanguard of Iranun crews based at Tobungku, Tontoli, Tempasuk, and Reteh. Heads taken from dead or wounded victims served as trophies and ritual 'soul stuff' for Iban and 'Alforean' marines. More than half of some crews, particularly at the start of the nineteenth century when maritime warfare increased with the advent of European rivalry and trade to China, consisted of assimilated Visayans, Tobello and Iban volunteers who had been trained since their youth to equal in ferocity any native-born Iranun or Balangingi. The Iranun and their mercenaries used decapitation and head-taking as instruments of geopolitics. In the interethnic competition over control of maritime raiding and the slave trade, they promised the Iban and 'Alforean' crew members a certain number of heads in relation to the total number of captives they took in hot spots like the straits of Buton and the Malacca Strait. Dark-skinned tribal warriors were among the most feared crewmembers of the vanguard designated to board enemy vessels in search of this gruesome bounty.

The Tobello, followers of the Tidore Prince Nuku, who were dispersed throughout the Moluccan archipelago and in the Bay of Tolo on the east coast of Sulawesi, were regarded as dangerously as the Iranun.[8] The various displaced cross-border ethnic groups constituting the Tobello, from Ternate, Tidore, Tobello, Ceram and Bacan, were, at the end of the eighteenth century, under constant pressure to relocate. In the 1790s they were to be yet another victim of the VOC administration's repressive policy–but with a difference. They, along with their Iranun allies, fought a war against the Dutch. These Tobello and 'Alforeans' were Moluccans who, during the course of the latter part of the eighteenth century, had been forced to move and resettle at the Iranun forward bases in eastern Sulawesi. From the Iranun perspective, and at times by the Dutch, the Tobello and 'Alforeans' were considered 'Illanoon.' There were many who sometimes were also regarded by the English as Tobello, Gilolo or 'Alforean' and at others as Iranun, or more usually vice versa. As a dispersed frontier population, these Tobello and 'Alforean' members of Iranun raiding crews presented a unique set of problems for the Dutch, because of their local knowledge and fierce opposition to Dutch conquest and removal. During the late 1820s, the Iranun and Tobello refugees led some 6,000 warriors and crew on maritime slave raids from their hideouts in the upriver vastness of the southwest coast of Borneo. Bankaalen, according to the interrogation statements of Iranun prisoners, was their principle place of rendezvous and the Iranun crews of these vessels were considered to be largely 'Alforean' in origin–they came principally from Gilolo and others from Sulawesi and Salayer. These same Tobello or people of 'Alforean' descent figured prominently in the crews of a large fleet of 90 joanga described in a report by the Dutch Government in 1827 as a "mass of evil disposed persons."[9]

Although little is known about the conduct of tribal warriors as Iranun crew, we may nonetheless conclude that they invariably attacked prospective prizes and unsuspecting coastal settlements, but did not always necessarily adhere to the strict logic that governed the disposal of booty among many of the Iranun fleets scattered around Southeast Asia. It would seem that many Iban took more heads at sea as 'Iranun' marines than from intertribal warfare after the period of their rapid recruitment, which began in earnest at the beginning of the nineteenth century. The Iranun recognized that Iban warriors traditionally set out to travel, (*merantau*) make warfare and take heads.[10] After striking a ceremonial blow against an enemy, they ritually smoked and hung skulls in their longhouses to break the period of mourning for the soul of a dead person. In this way, they faced their spirit world from the deck of a joanga off the distant coast of Sulawesi, Thailand or Vietnam. One thing is certain though, with respect to Saribas and Skrang headhunting and Iranun maritime marauding in Southeast Asia, its spread was due as much to Europe's desire for Chinese commodities rather than simply the aggressive exuberance of the Iban. Living at the upper reaches of the Bornean rivers in strongly fortified positions, the Iban of the Saribas and Skrang basins had developed an infamous reputation for head hunting on the high seas.[11] It is clear from some accounts that the well-armed warlike Iban were among the most trusted crew and they were given relative freedom aboard the Iranun vessels while cruising in various theatres of operation, particularly the South China Sea and the environs of Sulawesi.

According to the reliably recorded geneological lore of the Iban, *tusut*, in the late 1770s and 1780s the Iban were introduced to long distance maritime raiding by Iranun and Malay river lords and sherifs. Initially, because of their great physical stamina, they doubled as rowers in the Iranun prahus–for which they were rewarded with the heads of the slain captives. But, within the space of a single generation the Saribas and Skrang Iban had become expert seafarers and marines and began to build prahus well suited to their need for stealth and speed.[12] When they joined the Iranun, they sometimes formed large contingents with 20 to 30 prahus travelling distances of over 800 miles. Like their Tobello and 'Alforean' counterparts, the maritime raiding of the Saribas and Skrang Iban was considered to be of a much worse sort than the Iranun, who invariably took prisoners and sold them as slaves. The Saribas and Skrang crewmembers, however, desired only heads and plunder; the Iban's share being the heads and ironmongery, and the Iranun's the human plunder, namely captives. An article, which appeared in the *Singapore Chronicle* as early as 1827, reported that Iban were often Iranun crewmembers. The

Fig. 22. Predatory head-hunting tribal warriors, Dyaks, Ibans, Tobello, and Papuans were frequently led off to become willing members of Iranun raiding crews. Tribesmen, such as the above heavily-armed Dyak from north Borneo, made up part of the vanguard of the Iranun strike force based at Tobungku, Tontoli, Tempasuk, and Reteh.

article stated that some of the Borneo 'Dayas,' "who are found about the ports to the northward of Sambas, at times connect themselves with the pirates, and the condition of the connection is, that the skulls and iron shall be their share–the other plunder that of the pirates."[13] In 1834, George Earl Windsor, who had visited a Chinese settlement near the mouth of the Sambas River just after the departure of the raiders, noted that the Iranun and Iban occasionally joined forces. When they did, the Iban took the heads of their victims and were content with 'iron and trifles' while the Iranun, with a sufficient quantity of slaves, "return to their own country, and their place is supplied by others, who settle for a time on the coast in order to enrich themselves by the same means."[14]

A decade later Captain Keppel in the employ of the Royal Navy relays an account of a visit to an Iban village located in an area of turmoil along the coast. He noted a conversation with an Iban warrior named Luang. The Iban declared he had accompanied Iranun on maritime raiding voyages having been sent by Sherif Sahib of Sadong. Luang said that he had journeyed to the northeast coast of the Malay Peninsula, attacking shipping and settlements along the shoreline of Patani and Trenggannu. The local *orang kaya* then took up the conversation, and detailed many similar acts committed by the Sibuyan Ibans while they were located at Sadong. He concluded by saying that they were sent out and could not refuse. Keppel was certainly struck by the details of the manner in which some of these Saribas and Skrang Iban were gradually recruited and trained to crew the Iranun raiding vessels.[15] Seven years earlier, in 1837, the raja of Pahang had requested assistance from the Singapore authorities to combat Iranun vessels crewed by young 'Dayak' marines that were cruising off the east coast of Malaya. The coastline of Pahang was littered with decapitated bodies that were constantly floating ashore. The following year the celebrated Malay author, Munshi Abdullah, in his account of a voyage to Kelantan, reported the state of fear created by the sinister presence of tattooed warriors and 'Dayak' raiders, Saribas and Skrang Iban, who were crewing on large Iranun prahus and spreading havoc all along the east coast of Malaya in the late 1830s.[16] St. John, a decade later, also tells of a chance meeting he had with another Sibuyan Iban who had sailed on board a joanga with the Iranun to the gulf of Thailand and the coast of Vietnam! When the Iranun sailed along the coast of west Borneo, they regularly stopped at certain places where they were welcomed to pick up Iban crewmembers. "At Sadong, the Sibuyans were employed by them to row their boats under a promise of receiving the heads of all slain, and a very small share of the plunder."[17] The Iban that St. John met had been on Iranun expeditions along the coasts of Cochin China, Cambodia, Siam, and the Malay Peninsula as far as Singapore, but the tables were subsequently turned with the arrival, in the 1840s, of James Brooke and his backers in the Royal Navy. The Iranun working in tandem with the Iban began to be preyed upon relentlessly by the white rajah and his powerful allies.

Benedict Sandin recounts, in his pioneering ethnohistory, *The Sea Dayaks of Borneo before White Rajah Rule*, the turmoil along the coast caused by the arrival of the Iranun and he discusses both aspects and cases of warfare between the Iban and Iranun. Sandin argues that the increased intertribal conflict, documented in the *tusut*, resulted from initial contact and conflict with Iranun rovers that had occurred seven generations previously–about 1770. Specific references in the Iban tradition and folklore of the *Tusut* to the first Iranun maritime raiders, whose crews were notable for their absence of an Iban cohort, comes from the account of Unggang (Lebor Menoa), whose praise name means "ravish the country."[18] He is credited with building the first large Saribas war boat to defend his home country against incursions of the Iranun of Tempasuk and Mindanao. References to the Iranun occur in the account of this famous pioneer-raider's deeds of self-defense just prior to 1800.

> The Ibans first began to meet the Bajau and Illanun sea raiders. Operating from bases in the Philippines, sailing swift and heavy galleys which often mounted cannon, the Illanuns were in the habit of plundering far and wide throughout the archipelago. As in the case of the Brunei tax collectors, contact with the Ibans led to conflict and turmoil. One of the most famous Ibans who fought these pirates was Unggang (Lebor Menoa), the father of Luta. . . . Unggang built a large war boat which he used in his fight against the Illanun and other pirates. He used it to prevent them entering the mouth of the Saribas River and to attack them. Unggang encouraged trade in the area, but only with those who flew a white flag. He killed all others and took their heads.[19]

Iranun and Balangingi crew also included captives because of their apparent seafaring skills and knowledge of target areas and to replace losses. Particularly in the first half of the nineteenth century when the sheer intensity and horror of sea warfare increased with the advent of steam gunboats, more than 50 percent of some maritime raiding crews consisted of renegades and assimilated captives–many of whom had been trained from their youth to crew raiding vessels. There was a sizeable part of a crew who concluded from their slave experience that only a better integration or cultural accommodation would enable them to live as well as they could with the traumatic after-effects of their initial seizure and captivity experience. Their integration into Iranun and Balangingi society as renegades had to permit them to cope with the feelings of guilt and shame, and the often difficult, albeit unanswerable question surrounding bondage and dependency of 'why me?' It had to be a passing-over and integration, which promised to be more resistant to severe trauma than had been the aftermath of the initial captivity and slave experience. Assimilation offered a route to freedom and escape from the harsh experience of being lashed to an oar, which was prevalent in raiding vessels. By renouncing Catholicism, professing Islam and speaking Iranun-Maranao or Samal, Filipino captives and slaves could throw off their rattan bonds and, in theory, become the social equals of their erstwhile Iranun and Samal masters as a consequence of their conversion, sense of kinship and pledge of solidarity and allegiance.

The testimony of fugitive captives often mentions Christian slaves apostatizing–renouncing their Christian religion–and changing sides to serve as crew on a joanga or garay.[20] Many Visayan and Tagalog fishers and mariners suffered exploitation and cruelties at the hands of brutal local officials and friars. The testimonies indicate that when an opportunity arose many able-bodied, captive seamen readily joined the crew of raiding vessels. They protested against the harsh colonial regimes under which they had suffered, when called upon to do so and set up as 'Iranun' or 'Balangingi.' For these men, who could no longer happily return to their homes and families in the Philippines and elsewhere, becoming a renegade offered the possibility of a better way of life, exchanging discomfort and servitude for the opportunity of skilled local work, adventure and social advancement, as a maritime raider. In the

1830s, 40 percent or more of the Balangingi crews were renegades, while some larger vessels boasted as many as 60 among a crew of 80.[21] Renegade commanders were common enough, to move a number of governors-general to report that turncoat-led squadrons of maritime raiders were systematically sweeping Philippine waters, seizing the local populace with laser-like precision. Their names, place of birth or locality were generally unknown, except when a fugitive or ransomed captive described the conditions under which they were forced to sail and, in the process, happened to mention their renegade master by name. The accounts of fugitive captives from the Philippines between 1836 and 1864 document that most of them resided in the Balangingi cluster, especially at Sipac and Tunkil. Domingo Francisco, seized in 1836, reported that his master was a Visayan renegade from Tunkil; Esmerald Francisco, also taken in the same year, reported that his captor was a Visayan renegade from Balangingi while five years earlier Jose German Reales had been sold by his Visayan renegade master from Tunkil to Datu Daniel in Jolo. In a rare case the captive Juan Pedro actually named his renegade master from Balangingi, Tumol.[22] Similarly, 30 statements taken down by the Dutch Resident of Menado, in the mid to late 1840s, show that cultural accommodation and integration of captive seamen were extensive. The statements show, for example, that a sizeable number of Balangingi raiding vessels were commanded by renegades; Marthinos (a Manila man); Malutop (a Makassar man); Sapan (a Manila man); Palain (a Manila man); and Sibangay (a Banggai Islander).

The widespread implementation of this policy of cultural integration of captives (recognized for their nautical and maritime skills) with the Iranun and Balangingi was disastrous for the coastal populace and shipping of the Philippines and eastern Indonesia. Maritime raiding by renegade-led squadrons against economy-minded colonial governments meant widespread corruption, fear and panic, and wholesale slavery and death. Eyewitness descriptions of renegade commanders and crew suggest that they were survivors of the captivity experience who tried to create something positive from their lives–traumatic as they may have been. Safeguarding their newfound freedom and status as a crewmember, often made their lives more dangerous in some respects than their old ones had been under colonial rule and in some ways far more complex because of the historically changing nature of cultural conflict and accommodation. But possibly they were even more meaningful. Such talented captives had for many years selectively intermingled with the native-born populations of Iranun-Maranao and Samal maritime raiders helping to develop the 'Illanoon' and 'Balangingi' labels by which these seafaring marauders first became generally known to the West in the first half of the nineteenth century.

The cultural-ecological setting of the Sulu archipelago was characterized by a dual economic system that prevailed within the Sulu Sea and the relatively shallow waters surrounding Borneo and eastern Indonesia. Individual crewmembers were frequently engaged in this dual economy; as Iranun and Balangingi maritime raiders for part of the year, and for the remaining months as harvesters of exotic marine commodities–tripang, pearl shell, pearls, and agar-agar–for the flourishing export trade with China. Many of the crew doubled as fishers who, apart from possessing the various tools of the trade, such as spears, knives and nets, were invariably skilled divers. In general, the factors influencing the seasonal distribution of the crews for alternative economic pursuits, particularly fishing or the collecting and processing of turtle, shellfish, tripang, and seaweed, were a nakodah's ability to organize and allocate labor power, the proximate location of a given settlement to both fishing and pearling grounds, and market centers, and the relative wealth of its inhabitants, particularly the crewmembers. Once a slave raider returned from a voyage at the end of the period regularly dedicated to maritime raiding, nakodahs and other community leaders increased their wealth through the recruitment of seasonal labor, comprising erstwhile crew and captives. This alternating, interconnected pattern, based totally on marauding and maritime procurement as the principal source of labor and commodities for the China trade, was recognized at the time by the European experts on 'piracy.' In their eyes, and rightly so, the Iranun and Samal fishers were relatively undifferentiated from their maritime raiding brethren. Cornets de Groot, who compiled a lengthy influential overview of historical notices of piracy in Southeast Asia, wrote: "The numerous tribes which are guilty of it [piracy] appeared to be engaged in fishing . . . it is at certain periods only that they repair to a rendezvous agreed upon, invariably for the purpose of preparing fresh enterprises."[23]

The ability of the Iranun and Balangingi to seasonally adjust their labor power and regularize finance within the context of the workings of this dual economic system enabled their transformation and emergence as expert maritime raiders. Seasonal slave raiding and marine procurement conducted under the auspices of the associative network of the Iranun and Balangingi meant full-time employment for many crew, as both followers and slaves. They were often ad hoc groups of seasonal fishers, in the prime of life, who, upon hearing of a given nakodah's decision to slave raid [*mangooray*], joined in sizeable numbers, hoping to seek their fortunes offshore as part of a successful expedition. For these local strand dwellers regularly mustered as crewmembers, such a strategy made sound ecological sense because long distance maritime raiding was wholly compatible with fishing, as a seasonal pursuit occupying only four to five months a year.

The Iranun and Samal employed a variety of marine subsistence and fishing techniques oriented toward the China market and local consumption. Several of the most economically productive strategies involved raiding crew as fishers specializing in procuring *tripang*, oyster shell or manufacturing salt. Spanish naval officers described in their intelligence reports how some of these crewmembers fished the rich pearl banks which spanned nearly the entire Sulu archipelago in an uninterrupted track–in places over 25 miles wide–from the Sangboy Islands in the north to Tawi-Tawi in the south. Dalrymple, in his well-researched "Account of Some Natural Curiosities at Sooloo" noted that the shoals and reefs in the environs of Tawi-Tawi were "extremely intricate and narrow," but invaluable to the commerce of the sultanate, and that "these guts [the intricate and narrow channels] are the most valuable pearl fishery in the world."[24] To this fishery the Balangingi and Tausog from Tunkil, Sipac, Jolo, and elsewhere sent scores of fleets comprising a dozen or more small vessels each, with a joanga or garay for their defense. Every vessel had at least a couple of fishers in it, who were compelled to supplement their income by maritime raiding. There were also several Samal Laut, highly skilled in skin diving, even to the depths of ten fathoms among the reefs, where they readily found an abundance of mother of pearl shell and tripang. Tripang collecting went on year round in the Sulu archipelago, but the most important procurement activity was concentrated in the months of May, June and July.[25]

At the end of the eighteenth century the expansion of western commercial activity to China stimulated the production of tripang and other strand commodities on an unprecedented scale. The statistics in the *estados* for the port of Manila show that the tripang trade developed rapidly after 1768.[26] Perhaps the significance of the figure of 10,000 piculs of processed tripang being marketed from Jolo in 1835 can best be understood in terms of the labor power required to deliver such a prodigious quantity. Tripang procurement and curing was labor intensive work. It was not uncommon for a Tausog datu or Balangingi panglima to employ several hundred fisherfolk (Samal retainers, slaves or Samal Bajau Laut) in flotillas of 50 to 100 small *vintas*, to collect tripang. I have estimated that some 20,000 fishers must have been involved in tripang procurement in any one year at the height of Sulu's trade.[27]

The commercial production of salt was also important in Iranun and Samal settlements dedicated to maritime raiding and tripang fishing. Certain communities in the Balangingi group and on the Cotabato coast were expert in manufacturing salt from seaweed and salt water. The method most commonly practised by strand-dwelling people (Samal, Samal Laut) is described by Forrest who observed it in the 1770s at the salt sheds of Kabug near the mouth of the Pulangi:

> They cut down a quantity of wood always near the sea side, and rear over it a sort of shed, of the leaves of the trees of the palm kind, such as the sago, the nipa, or others. This pile is then set on fire; but as any flame issues, they throw on salt water, to check it. In this manner they continue, till the wood be consumed, there remaining a quantity of ashes strongly impregnated with salt. . . . These ashes they put into conical baskets, point downwards; and pour on fresh water, which carries off the salt into a trough. The lye [residue] is then put into earthen pots, and boiled till it becomes sometimes a lump of salt, [and] sometimes salt in powder. They often burn in this manner seaweed, of which the ashes make a bitter kind of salt.[28]

The ideal conditions for the production of salt by this method were found at Sipac on Balangingi island, Tunkil island and on the north Borneo coast in the vicinity of Marudu Bay. The 1830s statements of the fugitive captives Angel Custodio and Juan Sabala both refer to salt manufacture at Balangingi, Sipac and Tunkil. Interestingly, the latter captive mentioned the founding of the Samal Settlement of Catamar on Balangingi, circa 1832, which had no more than 30 homes and total population of 400 employed exclusively in maritime raiding and salt manufacture.[29] Dalrymple also speaks of the Bolod Islands to the north of Jolo as being "low and flooded, which affords a conveniency for making much salt."[30] In the alternate season, some Iranun and Balangingi crewmembers manufactured salt from the sea and with their women and children walked the strand at low tide gathering seaweed, clams, mussels, limpets, barnacles, and sea urchins.

When the opportunity arose at the end of the procurement season many of these fishers and divers would once again join a crew, that would take shape within hours, or, at most days, of an Iranun or Balangingi vessel bound for the south China Sea or the Moluccas to raid shore communities and attack coasting prahus. These seasonally adjusted crew were an extraordinarily resilient group of men and their alternating way of life on the sea as maritime raiders and on the strand and reefs as fishers of pearl shell and tripang demanded that they be so. Tala Goa, who, in 1838, was placed in charge of one of the raiding boats of a Balangingi squadron, described to the trial judge, who sentenced him to a life of penal servitude, how he was compelled to diversify his employment. He also described the way in which almost every aspect of his life depended on the sea–a sea he was to never see again.

> I live at Ballangninhin with my family. My occupation is diverse, occasionally mangoorap [slave raiding] at other times making salt, planting paddy, collecting tortoise shell etc. I am a follower of Orang Kaya Kullul and I am compelled to do and act as he may direct.[31]

The traditional image of the Iranun and Balangingi as nothing more than spear bearing 'savage' raiders bent on pillage and slaving needs to be balanced against a new understanding of the Iranun-Maranao and Samal as also seasonally engaged in fishing, trade and agricultural enterprises.

However, one should not place undue emphasis on the crewmembers' alternate peaceful economic pursuits and subsistence activities at the expense of the Iranun's warlike actions on the sea and on the land. The special role of the warriors or marines, who were the toughest members of the crew, becomes abundantly clear in an age of imperial trade rivalry and conflict, as does the importance of violence and, from the psychological standpoint of submission, a contagion of fear. The historical sources provide only limited insight into the character, psychological make up, and fate of individual Iranun warriors whose maritime raids caused great destruction in Southeast Asia, especially to Church centers, small island communities and coastal settlements. At the end of the eighteenth century, 'Illanoon' had become a byword for bloodthirsty seaborne raiders–violent marines, recruited from Gilolo to Sumatra and from the Celebes to the Philippines–who inspired terror in the hearts of thousands as they descended in their joanga to plunder defenseless communities that dotted the shoreline from the straits of Malacca to the Birds Head coast of New Guinea. But whether they were really any more wantonly cold-blooded than their colonial adversaries and neighboring rivals was immaterial because by the end of the eighteenth century the traditional image of Iranun warriors, as savagely cruel and destructive had gained widespread acceptance. In colonial depositions and local oral traditions from areas as far apart as the strait of Malacca and the Buton Strait it was clear: "That every native of this vicinity [South China Sea basin] associates the term Illanoon and pirate together which is of itself tolerable proof of the more than dubious character, this class of people now bears and as far as I am aware have for years borne."[32]

In addition to the ordinary crew and oarsmen, every joanga carried a large force of armed fighting men trained to serve on land or sea between 60 and 80 on the larger vessels. These warriors, renowned for their martial skill, discipline and courage, played no part in sailing the long ships and the complement carried on board was there simply to wage war on land and at sea. The exception to this rule were the Iban and Alforean warriors whose extraordinary stamina made them ideal candidates to pull at the sweeps in an emergency.[33] These fighting men were armed with shields, spears, two-handed lanun swords, axes, muskets, and pistols. Standing on the raised upper deck or fighting platform, 40 or 50 of these screaming warriors dressed in bullet-proof, sleeveless scarlet jackets padded with kapok, or wearing various pieces of armor and chain mail, made a terrifying sight as their joanga swept alongside a merchant prahu or descended upon a hapless village. The 'black' Iranun vanguard, comprised of Ibans, Papuans and Alforeans–the most fearless members of the fighting force–armed with spears, machete, kris, and hatchets boarded the vessel or scrambled ashore with lightning speed amidst the din of their frightful battle cry which struck fear into the hearts of their enemies and victims. But, although Southeast Asia was terrorized by the Iranun for more than a century, only a small percentage of their warriors were considered elite enough to stand on the fighting platform as a marine on raiding expeditions to distant shores. Very little is known about these Iranun marines except that they were the dominant members of their joanga. These special warriors were bound together by near total loyalty and strict discipline. Their code of conduct meant that there was no place for shame or dishonor and they would never abandon their commander and companions in battle: an Iranun warrior never expected any quarter particularly from Europeans and hence were prepared to follow their commander to his death if called upon to do so. Tomas de Comyn, general manager of the Compania Real de Filipinas during the first decade of the nineteenth century, published a frank and penetrating appraisal of the commerce and administration of the Philippines and, more particularly, the impact of Iranun and Balangingi maritime raiding on the economy and population of the islands. He described the Iranun warriors as "barbarous infidels," and warned his complacent compatriots, many of them merchants of Manila, 'that these warriors are to be dreaded, and extremely dexterous in the management of the *campilan*, or sword, of which they wear the blades long and well tempered.'[34] Captain Belcher, 25 years later, described the Iranun warriors he met at Tempasuk in early November of 1846 as "fierce, proud and well-made men, handsomely clothed and fully armed."[35] While, according to St. John's account, Wyndham characterized the 'Lanun' six years later as "very fine men, brave, fierce, never giving quarter to Europeans, and cruising in vessels 90 feet long, propelled by from 100 to 120 oar."[36]

Spanish and Dutch naval commanders on cruising voyages often gave orders to take no prisoners when hunting the Iranun. Nevertheless, these expert hunters could not but grudgingly admire the astonishing courage, remarkable fighting qualities and physical stamina of these warriors when faced with absolutely overwhelming odds and near certain death on various occasions. In the desperate actions of particular search and destroy missions that have been recorded they proved absolutely fearless in the face of death. James Brooke helped to preside over the capture of a Brunei pangeran and the killing of his accomplice, an Iranun panglima, at Siru in 1843. They were both well-armed and the Iranun warrior "dressed out with a variety of charms." When eventually cornered and surrounded by Brooke's party their characters were quite different: "The Borneo pangeran remained quiet, silent and motionless; . . . the Maguindanao Illanun lashed himself to desperation, flourishing his spear in one hand, and the other on the handle of his sword, he defied those collected about him."[37]

Despite his quick wit he was soon killed, and the pangeran and his crew captured. In a totally different action two years later–an event that was to be repeated over and over again on the seas across Southeast Asia– an Iranun prahu from Maguindanao was attacked and captured by Major Djacka of Limbotto, north Sulawesi. None of the warriors on board would surrender and thus they were all killed.[38]

The still existing descriptions of the Iranun and Samal warriors suggest that they were as terrifying as they appeared in reliably remembered and recorded oral traditions and locally based historical accounts of the myriad men, women and children who experienced the violence and bloodshed associated with 'Illanoon' maritime raids. Iranun warriors who regularly manned the raiding vessels, the specialist marines who went *magoorap* [raiding] and participated in the slaving expeditions that traumatized the friars and coastal populations of the Philippines, deliberately cultivated a fearsome image and demeanor. They did this to both maintain discipline on board the joanga and to cow their victims into submission, encouraging them to surrender without a fight.[39] However, when this did not happen, Iranun marines were prepared to use extreme violence. The manuscript sources record scores of instances of plundering, burning and beheadings by the Iranun engaged in maritime raids in the Philippines and eastern Indonesia. The Iranun stationed in

Illana Bay developed the reputation from such accounts as being the most bloodthirsty and daring of all those engaged in this violent occupation.[40] According to colonial authorities, the scale of Iranun and Balangingi violence engendered such fear and horror that these 'Illanoon' were imagined on a regional basis to simply be 'savage,' seaborne terrorists. At the same time, mounting evidence suggested that the Iranun and Balangingi were increasingly descended from Filipinos, Indonesians and tribal peoples from across Southeast Asia—not what most colonial officials or victims wanted to hear. Although the notion was unwelcome to many, current intelligence based on captive statements and prisoners' depositions suggested that, far from being an ethnic identity in some original sense, many Iranun and Balangingi warriors were the recent descendants of captives who had arrived in Sulu and Mindanao and had been culturally assimilated into the society not more than 40 or 50 years earlier. Despite such knowledge of the spectacular ethnic and cultural transformation that was occurring, and the associated brutal conflict in various parts of the Philippines, a top secret Spanish naval document of 1842 described the destructiveness and violence of the Samal warriors in these words:

> Balangingi is composed of more merciless, inhuman and cruel people than the rest of the towns, who have no desire to work except piracy; even if they are warned or threatened by the Sultan, these produce no effect on their way of life plundering and capturing either friends or foes.[41]

This traditional view of the barbarous character of Iranun and Samal warriors was also to gain widespread credence with the Tausog when the Balangingi, by virtue of their maritime raiding exploits, were moving towards the brink of freeing themselves from direct Tausog control and influence in the 1850s. Sali Werble of Isabela, Basilan, whose mother was Saadia Aaro of the 'Joloano warrior class,' at the age of 87, recounted the late nineteenth century Tausog point of view of Balangingi marines as being singularly inhuman. He did not not fully understand either who the Balangingi actually were, as an ethnic group, or why they were slave raiding for the Tausog in the first place: "The Balangingis were the robbers of the sea. . . . Balangingis controlled the slave trade, looted and plundered. They were not totally ignorant of religion. They did live by the Koran. The Balangingis were merciless. They were very much feared."[42]

Owen Rutter wrote in a similar vein in his 1930 book, *The Pirate Wind*, about the level of violence that traditionally prevailed among the Iranun and Balangingi warriors. No merchant ship of the colonial powers and no shore village was immune from their attacks which, in their rampant ferocity, made the threat of extreme violence and anarchy an everyday fact of life for the coastal populations of Southeast Asia for long periods of time. Rutter paints a picture of the Iranun and Balangingi marines which portrays them as fierce, dangerous and merciless. In the introductory chapter, he gives a number of graphic accounts of torture and murder of Iranun and Balangingi victims. Rutter also lists numerous examples of ships which had fallen to the raiders' looting and individuals from European, American, Chinese, and native vessels who had been sold into slavery. Rutter called these maritime warriors the "vikings of the eastern seas."[43]

The Iranun warriors, like the Vikings, were worldly raiders who travelled in search of slaves and work, sometimes for years on end, around the great ports of Manila, Makassar, Batavia, Penang, and Singapore. They often spoke a variety of languages, and were familiar with the traditions and religions of all quarters of Southeast Asia. Some were literate, able to negotiate a ransom, or unravel the intricacy of a colonial legal system and they were all knowledgeable in the martial arts, weapons manufacture and seamanship. Some marines doubled on the joangas along with the renegades as translators and gunners. The sea and the opening of China were the key ingredients in all of this. When the region's economy boomed as part of the process of engagement with world commerce, both these factors became catalysts for maritime and tribal people to make new lives for themselves as marines and conscripts aboard Iranun sea raiders. These warriors did the difficult and dangerous work of attacking and boarding traditional sailing boats and colonial merchant ships—from Manila to Malacca, from the Celebes to Singapore—swarming aboard from the raised prow of the joanga or scampering across boarding bridges thrown over to the prize. Few vessels were capable of putting up a real fight against such a calculated onslaught. To break their opponents' will to resist, the Iranun and Balangingi marines made themselves appear as terrifying as possible with their shoulder length, black hair flying, uttering blood curdling trance-like screams at the top of their lungs—sounds that sent shivers down the spine of lightly armed ill-disciplined crews. This stratagem to encourage submission was carefully noted by the Resident of Menado: "A tactic which the pirates often use with great success is to raise a tremendous din by shouting in a strange way. This fills the attacked people with sudden terror to the extent that they do not think of defending themselves and are in fact not capable of doing so."[44]

Iranun marines knew their enemies' capacity for fear. The job of the boarding party, comprised of the most loyal and fearsome warriors, was killing not fighting. These men had to be more fit and talented than ordinary warriors. The vanguard comprised the marines especially selected by the expedition commander. Knowing that attack was everything, they invariably fought in close, hard and fast against any crew that resisted. However, they were not prepared to become cannon fodder for European vessels discharging broadsides at their joanga. These warriors did not exhibit the reckless boldness which distinguished the European buccaneers of the Spanish main. On the contrary, the Iranun warriors were extremely astute:

> They always make an estimate beforehand of the force of those they wish to attack, and if there appears much chance of stout resistance they refrain from operations, or have recourse to stratagem; indeed in general they contrive to approach their prey in such a manner as to avoid suspicion of their real character.[45]

The nakodahs of the raiding vessels were often in their thirties, while the average crewmembers were young men in their late teens or early twenties. The records of fugitive captives and statements of prisoners show that there were few older men on board the joangas and garay with their strict discipline and hazardous way of life. Work at the oar, on the fighting platform and as a deckhand was both physically demanding and dangerous. Few raiding vessels included many men in their forties and fifties. Indeed, the crew needed to be competent at handling the huge mat sails day and night, bailing for days on end, hauling the block and tackle on short notice, coping with the danger of sudden storms and huge swells, as well as dealing with the desperate intensity that surrounded the height of a sea battle. Iranun and Balangingi marauders were regarded as relatively old by the age of 35. The arrest statements of the captured crew of an 1838 'Illanoon' squadron gives some evidence of the average age of key members of a Balangingi raiding squadron. Among the fleet commanders were seasoned able-bodied men like Silammkoon, Si Damah (the son of Orang Kaya Kullul), Si Tombu, Si Dundines, Si Putlah, and Tala Goa who were all in their late twenties and early thirties, while the squadron commander, Orang Kaya Kullul, was in his mid to late forties.[46]

It was common for young captives and adolescent boys, some as young as 10 or 11, to begin to accompany their masters or fathers, brothers and uncles on occasional maritime raiding voyages. Consequently, by the time they had become older teenagers these young men had acquired the necessary nautical and martial skills to enlist regularly as raiders and seafarers with their kin on important slaving and trading expeditions. Forrest noted that Sulu's pearl fishery, so meticulously described by Dalrymple, proved, for the Iranun and Balangingi to be "a nursery for seamen, ready to man a fleet of prows upon an emergency."[47] The 'Illanoon' prisoners brought into Singapore by the steamship *Diana* in 1838 became the reigning object of curiosity in the port settlement. There was certainly nothing either formidable or ferocious about the appearance of these prisoners—some half a dozen of them being mere boys. The story which all of the young boys told their interrogators was that they were carried off by violence from their own homes, and compelled to serve on board the joangas and garay. Indeed, many of the men among them gave the same account of themselves. Some of the prisoners were so young (several not more than 13 or 14 years of age) that to the minds of the English magistrates it was doubtful if they could fairly be considered to have been acting in the free exercise of their own judgement.[48] Hence, the court delayed passing immediate sentence on the prisoners some of whom were deemed to be mere juveniles, "one not more than 13 years of age a circumstance were others wanting affording a strong presumption that some of them might have been acting by compulsion and not in the exercise of their own free will."[49] However, the court failed to realize that by early nineteenth century Iranun standards, sailors and marines were generally able-bodied mariners, already, by the age of 17, hardened to the vicissitudes of fortune at sea.

The crew of the various craft involved in maritime raiding enterprises, which included everything from three-masted joanga to small dugout canoes, were heavily armed with lances, knives, swords, bamboo grappling poles, and shields (See Fig. 12). Muskets and pistols were also part of the standard equipment in the arsenal of most Iranun raiding expeditions. In addition to mounting one or two large cannon and a number of smaller swivel guns on board, the armament of the crew consisted of local and foreign manufactured weapons and implements. Captured Samal raiders were forced to divulge to Dutch officials that their vessels always carried a standard arsenal: "Some guns, pikes, spears (*saga-saga*), long swords, or machetes (*baleng kong*), two pronged barbed iron forks which are attached to long bamboo shafts, round wooden shields with a diameter of approximately four feet, and stones."[50]

When attacking walls the Iranun and Balangingi frequently made use of stones which they threw with great skill and accuracy. The cache of stones was also necessary for making grapeshot canisters. James Brooke corroborates such information about standard armament and equipment on raiding vessels in his short but insightful comparison of Iranun and Balangingi prahus and their cruising grounds. He correctly notes that the Balangingi rarely used large cannon (12-18 pounds) as did the Iranun but shipped their usual store of weapons, including *lelah*, swords, spears, muskets, and munitions as well as long poles with barbed iron points, "with which to hook their prey" and catch a fleeing enemy.[51] St. John grudgingly admired the raiding system of the Balangingi whereby they cruised in large *prahus*–double banked containing from 50 to 60 men– and to each prahu was attached a sampan which could carry 10 to 15 men. They utilized the smaller boat to make the capture of unwary fishers easier. They anchored the large prahu out of sight and sent the small ones in to chase their prey. The Balangingi's most deadly weapon when 'fighting' in this fashion was a "huge double pronged fork, with barbed ends, which they push over the neck of a fleeing enemy, and eventually stop his movements."[52] Another equally lethal weapon in the hands of the Iranun and Balangingi maritime raiders was a long bamboo pike with a pointed barbed steelhead that was used in both boarding operations and hand-to-hand combat. Rennel, as early as 1762, wrote in his journal about the skill of these seafaring warriors as they wielded the lance and pike and hurled the lance like a javelin:

> They are very dexterous in throwing their lances and being commonly poisoned they are very dangerous weapons. The Sooloos report that they have a sort of poison extracted from the bark of a certain tree, that is strong enough to kill any man after a minute's operation.[53]

The Iranun marines also used javelins with short, light shafts of bamboo and wood that were thrown with uncanny accuracy by the boarding vanguard, in the first few moments of forcing their way on board a vessel, to inflict maximum casualties. In addition, the boarders and crew wielded short daggers, machetes and swords of all sorts at which they excelled, and they were well supplied with muskets and pistols. The Balangingi crew on the raiding prahus that were either captured or destroyed off the Kelantan coast by the steamer *Diana* were well-armed with ample muskets, pikes and javelins, while each prahu carried at least one long gun, several swivels and, on average a crew of between 30 to 40 men.[54]

One of the most feared weapons of the Iranun was the *kampilan*, the double-edged scimitar-like broadsword. It was used for hacking rather than thrusting and such weapons were often beautifully finished and owned by hand-picked warriors of high status. The blacksmiths and armorers of Mindanao and Sulu were exceptionally skilled and produced fine long swords and daggers or *kris*, (serpentine daggers) of great strength and flexibility which were beautifully inlaid with silver. The kampilan, kris and short knives, used by Iranun and Samal warriors were exceptional examples of traditional blade work hand forged in Sulu, Lanao and Cotabato. The blademakers within the custom sword-knife making industry who lived in Sulu and Mindanao forged their own kampilan and kris—singular swords and knives that sea warriors held at the back of their shields or carried at their side with pride and which they wielded with an incredible efficiency. After forging the blade in the fire and on the anvil, the sword-maker spent hours filing, fashioning and shaping the blade. The tempered curved kampilan blade was multifullered with exceptional cutting advantages. The final stage in production was carving the intricate decorative handle. The special attention paid to handle craft meant that handle carvers were a different class of artisans from those ironworkers in the blade industry that fashioned only kampilan, kris and barong.[55] The handle of an Iranun kampilan or kris was often made of bone, ivory, ebony or silver and gold, and occasionally encrusted with precious stones and often decorated with human hair. The richly decorated hilts and scabbards of such weapons were an important means of signifying wealth and status among squadron commanders and elite warriors.

The Iranun warriors would use a broadsword or cleaver, either a kampilan or barong, and carry a target or shield on their other arm. The circular target was made of leather covered wood and studded with large-headed brass nails to prevent the wood from splitting under a sword blow. Shields too were often decorated with human hair–and the blond hair of European victims was particularly favored among the Iranun and Tobello. The larger *gilolo* shields, often placed along the gunnels of the joanga to form a protective wall, were rectangular in shape and a full body length. Behind the circular target was a leather or wooden loop to hold it to the warrior's arm or hand. The loop was fastened over the raider's forearm, and his shield hand also held the kris. The kris was about two feet long so it protruded beyond the shield. The vanguard of marines would block a sword blow with the kampilan, then swing the target and dagger into the opponent. Then the warrior would bring down the Kampilan, barong or axe and cut the man in half or decapitate him.

Firearms were traded widely to the Iranun and Balangingi because they had no means of manufacturing them on a large scale. The type of firearms the maritime raiders preferred were those suited for shipboard use that could be concealed, cocked and fired at close range–especially when boarding another vessel. Flintlock pistols and standard issue short firearms such as muskets and musketoons with brass and wood fittings were ideally suited for use by Iranun and Samal sharpshooters on board the joanga and garay. In the waters of Southeast Asia during the first half of the nineteenth century the typical sort of flintlock pistol used on shipboard by the slave raiders had a belt hook, as the warriors needed their hands free when clambering aboard a prize. The butt or wooden stock of both the pistols and muskets were also designed to be used as clubs in hand-to-hand combat. According to Rennel, local artisans faithfully copied Spanish helmets, armor and linked chain "made of strong brass or iron wire, and very pliable." The descendants of these blacksmiths and armorers of Sulu and Mindanao were known, in the first half of the nineteenth century, to be able to repair and reproduce excellent pistols and muskets but only on a very limited scale.[56]

The health and overall safety of the crew were primary responsibilities of the nakodah and the expedition commander. The nakodah usually fed the crew from the beginning to the end of an expedition, that is to say the boat commander provided the crew with rice. They often ate well and looked therefore, in the eyes of their adversaries, to be quite healthy if not robust. Chicken, eggs, dried and fresh fish, salt, and other condiments seem to have been rarely in short supply.[57] There was always an ample supply of rice advanced from Tausog in the interior of Jolo against payment or the promise of slaves. The on board slaves were less well-fed but that depended on the amount of food in stock and the provisions the expedition had been able to loot. The food, which was plundered by the raiders, would be divided equally among them. Before a raiding expedition sailed the nakodahs also decided in council where to obtain provisions in transit and refurbish their vessels during the course of the round.[58] They knew where to obtain beef by raiding specific Filipino agricultural settlements and ranches.[59] They also knew when and where along the route to obtain turtle meat, *kima* or giant clam and tripang, which when eaten fresh with lime was a favorite. Whenever they could the seafarers ate fish, which formed the staple of their diet—the often calm sea providing hundreds of species.

In November 1774, Thomas Forrest wrote of Iranun raiding vessels bound for the Philippines relying almost totally on the bounty of the sea to survive:

> Large ships, navigating those seas, must naturally dread the reefs of rocks, which might produce so much good to them, if in distress for provisions: but to profit from them, they must hit the time of low water spring tides. The vast fleets of Mangaio boats that set out from Soloo and Mindano, to cruise among the Philippine islands, against the Spaniards, trust to the reefs of rocks, which may be said

to surround all those islands, producing them fish for their subsistence; as they only lay in rice, or sago bread.⁶⁰

In the course of such journeys, those captives who had recently been seized received only what was barely required to keep them alive until they were allocated to particular crewmembers. Ebenezer Edwards, an American whaler, who, in 1843, escaped from Balangingi raiders with the help of 'Bajau' fishermen, was able to supply valuable information about his five weeks in captivity. His report notes that after taking the whaling ship *Sarah and Elizabeth,* the Balangingi squadron sailed to Buton where they stayed for a while and undertook fishing. Several times during this period, he was moved from one raiding prahu to another. He was not ill treated, but his ration of rice and water was small and generally spoiled.⁶¹ Similarly, six years earlier, Lieutenant Rauws and a number of European sailors from the stranded launch *William I* were made prisoners of the Iranun and compelled to live in the cramped hull of a prahu, receiving for nourishment only "a little scarcely edible maize, it being so much spoiled."⁶² Twenty years later, in 1857, on the storm swept coast of Samar another European officer underwent a similar ordeal. Lieutenant Colonel Ibanez y Garcia was given the backbreaking task of cleaning the hulls of the Balangingi raiding boats and lashing them to the shore as a tempest brewed. His hands and feet were terribly bruised and swollen. After the storm passed, he had to scour and dig along the coastline for a starchy, fibrous wild tuber (*palao radix radix*), which the captives were forced to eat. The taste, according to the Lieutenant's captivity narrative, was absolutely horrible. Everyone suffered from cramps and diarrhea. Consequently, Ibanez grew weak from dysentery and vomited blood for sometime.⁶³

However, the rest of the crew, especially the warriors, knew it was not their business to be chronically malnourished and they expected to regularly receive their fair share of food and drink. The Samal and Iranun words for fish were almost synonymous in the crew's mind with the word for food. The raiders' fishing grounds were without peer in different seasons across Southeast Asia: there were mackerel, tuna, grouper, cobbler, stingray, and shark. From the beginning to the end of the maritime raiding season, thousands of pounds of fish were caught over a number of months. Large hooks landed shark and grouper; smaller straight-shanked ones with twin barbs caught tuna and mackerel. The Iranun and Samal made their fishing gear from trade commodities, particularly ironmongery and brass and copper wire—their actions linking the land of North America and China and the seas of Southeast Asia; parallel realms that also had profound economic and ecological ties. Much was eaten fresh-boiled in earthenware pots, or steamed in a wrapper of coconut leaves in a wok, a Chinese frying pan. Forrest noted in the course of his voyage to New Guinea that virtually all Muslim seafarers lived off sago bread and fish. He described how slaves would help Iranun prepare the sago, a task no sea warrior would condescend to perform, to be eaten possibly with raw tripang:

> Sometimes they mix a cocoa nut rasped down, with the sago flour; and, putting this into a thin Chinese iron pan, they keep stirring the mixture on the fire, and eat it warm. I have also seen, not only the mahometans, but Papua men, eat ordinary white swallow (Biche de Mer) which is found almost everywhere in the sand at low water. They eat it raw, cut up small, and mixed with salt and lime juice.[64]

But most tripang and fish was filleted, salted and sun-dried to see a raiding expedition through difficult periods when it was unable to take on provisions. Sometimes the Iranun were constantly on the move for long periods of time, as colonial cruisers sent to hunt them down destroyed their haunts and provisions, forcing individual crews to spend weeks occasionally even months at sea. In this harrowing context, of all the sea creatures, the kima or giant clam was one of the most important. Found on submerged reefs throughout Southeast Asia its gifts were an abundance of flesh or meat for food, and shells, large and small, for eating bowls, that could also be burned to make a limestone mixture used to caulk the hulls of the raiding vessels. Thomas Forrest was particularly fond of kima and it helped shape his record breaking voyage and feed the small heterogeneous community that comprised the crew of the *Tartar Galley*. He used to have his crew regularly collect large amounts of kima on the coral reefs at low tide, from which he made a delicious soup or a very good curry by 'stewing it [the kima] with the heart of the *aneebong*, or cabbage tree, which we found abundant in the woods.'[65]

THE CREW

Apart from the sea's bounty, a major source of provisions were the victuals and cargoes looted from trading vessels on a systematic basis. In 1838, the ill-fated 'Illanoon' squadron operating on the east coast of Malaya had, in less than a three-month period, captured three boats laden with rice. One of the victims, Abdullah, recounted how, with his compatriots Sari and Mat Salleh, he had left his village near Patani in a small boat bound for Kuala Buku, about a day's sail from the village, to get paddy. On their return, they fell in with two sampans belonging to the raiding expedition. There were 200 *gantangs* of paddy in Abdullah's boat valued at 2° straits dollars. All of the paddy was confiscated by the 'Illanoon' and Abdullah was separated from his companions and taken aboard one of the raiding prahus.[66] Sometimes, due to evading the relentless attention of colonial warships, maritime raiders were unable to take on provisions, especially rice and sago, and they spent long periods on the open water subject to the vagaries of the sea and sudden changes in the weather, especially storms. Under such circumstances, if the raiders were not able to seize a prize, the crew, suffering from lack of food, were reduced to starvation rations as the scanty stock of provisions dwindled. There are Balangingi Samal stories and statements of captives that recall particularly harrowing voyages when it was impossible to fish, there was no fresh water to be found or collected off the sails, and the food storage baskets were empty. The Spaniards considered it useless to offer letters of Marque against these maritime raiders as they navigated in vessels so "ill-provided that they were frequently without any water to drink" and it was reported that the Balangingi were accustomed in case of emergency to drink their urine or seawater.[67] If they could not hole up in some remote bay or live off the coastal populace, in order to avoid dying of hunger, the eating of faecal matter was not beyond these marauders. The eating of recycled human waste matter at sea by Balangingi desperate to survive was told to Rene Tulawie by his grandfather. One day the young boy asked his grandfather why Tausog children ridiculed his deported descendants by chanting '*Samal Bangingih Mag Kaun Taih.*' The old seafarer told his grandson that during prolonged raiding expeditions, when the Balangingi ran out of food and potable water, they would collect their faecal matter, wash it very carefully and retrieve the hard re-edible grain called *layagan*. At such times, suffering extreme hunger pangs and also, having run out of cigarettes, the slavers would cut up their *boras*, intricately dyed multicolored rattan sleeping mats, and smoke them.[68] According to the oral accounts of elderly Balangingi, as a last resort they were also prepared to drink blood collected from the severed arms and opened veins of captives, in order to muster the strength to survive without food and water for weeks on end, until they managed to reach their island stronghold, and home.[69]

Strict orders of conduct were maintained on board maritime raiding vessels. All members of the crew abided by a customary set of articles–*hukum-hukum laut*–of cooperation, discipline and punishment. Maritime raiding was a difficult and dangerous enterprise and specified rules of conduct were meant to guarantee the safety of the crew and vessel, arbitrate disputes and ensure the correct distribution of the plunder and captives. The codes of conduct could vary somewhat from expedition to expedition depending on the ethnicity of the commander and the composition of the crew. But the codes generally covered a wide range of matters to normalize operating procedures between members of various squadrons, prescribe the character of their ethnic interrelations and conduct at sea, and stipulate how transactions were to be conducted with outsiders, particularly regarding ransom and exchange of captives. The subject matter of the articles, to which all crew members had to agree, included loyalty and obedience, allocation of prizes, safety at sea, property, theft, and assault and murder. Distinctions between civil, penal and private law were not recognized.[70] Some European observers of the maritime raider's way of life noted the hazardous nature of their voyages and commented on the absolute necessity of strict discipline at all times while at sea. Forrest observed that the Iranun had rules and laws to maintain discipline on raiding cruises. While rowing, they also had a song and drumbeat to keep time, and to affirm discipline for those not keeping pace:

> They have particular laws amongst themselves, during those piratical cruises; and keep up a certain order and discipline. In rowing, at which, from habit, they are dexterous, they have always a song as a kind of tactic, and beat on two brass timbrels to keep time.[71]

He also witnessed the absolute necessity of a crew to abide by the customary rules of conduct at the start of a raiding expedition when, just prior to embarkation, all members ritually offered prayers together for a safe and successful voyage. On Monday, 5 June 1775, Forrest went up the Melampy River in a heavily-armed crowded Iranun slave raider:

> She [the Mangaio vessel] road with fifteen oars on a side; and was full of people, the intended crew with their friends. They were going to burn each man a bit of wax candle on a heap of coral rock stones, rudely piled under some spreading trees close by the river. This they declared the tomb of their great ancestor Seriff, who came first from Mecca. In a few days the vessel went a cruising . . . to the island of Tulour, and the coast of Celebes, against the Dutch.[72]

Certain articles pertaining to the safety of the vessel under sail, such as inadvertently starting a fire on board, instances of disobedience between the crew and a superior officer or assault with the intent to do bodily harm or homicide, were considered dangerous offenses and punished swiftly, often with beheading. Theft and rape of female captives were also capital offenses that frequently resulted in the miscreant being executed. The ultimate court of arbitration was presided over by a *hatib* or *Imam*, a judge and religious official for an entire expedition. The boat commanders acted as the council and court of the ship board community, arbitrating disputes, assessing fines and enacting the regulations of the Iranun code, sentencing thieves, deserters, rapists, and murderers to death.[73] To maintain cooperation, law and order among the large numbers of seafarers of different ethnic origins who crewed maritime raiding vessels required strict, albeit violent discipline, replete with the staging of executions on isolated beaches and the exhibiting of severed heads as a form of intentionally macabre theatre. These staged executions, with the offender sometimes buried waist deep in the sand, intended as an efficient demonstration of justice, inspired much fear and also provided an additional source of heads for Iban crew members! The swiftness and severity of the punishment gave rise over time to an intrepid, disciplined and unyielding maritime raiding force, comprising hundreds of battle hardened Iranun and Balangingi crews.

CHAPTER NINE

THE RAIDING SHIPS

The Iranun and Samal way of life was shaped by their marine environment and homelands. The geography of the Mindanao and Sulu region exerted a profound influence on its cultural-ecological development and seafaring traditions. The southern coast of Mindanao and the Sulu archipelago are well-provided with sheltered coastal waters, lakes and navigable rivers with slipways and other protective enclosures for ships, as well as reef girdled islands that were difficult for strangers to approach at low tide unless they had a guide. Hence, from the mid-eighteenth century, Iranun sailing ships and boats became the most important means of waging war, slave raiding and plundering their wealthier colonial neighbors at a time of intense competition between rival states to control regional trade and economic growth. Two hundred years ago, Iranun maritime raiders and seafarers had been voyaging from Mindanao to Sumatra and even as far as Burma. Over the following decades, the relentless Iranun search for slaves—labor power—to satisfy the trade demands and desires of the West and China changed the known frontiers and population history of Southeast Asia. Without seaworthy sailing ships based on a viable tradition of seafaring and shipbuilding, the late eighteenth century Iranun maritime expansion and pattern of federative settlement would have been impossible. There were many different types of purpose-built Iranun and Samal ships that braved the waters of Southeast Asia, from the small, crafted *salisipan* of inshore slavers to the magnificent *lanong* or *joanga* of the early 1800s, that sustained long distance raiding and pioneering settlement across Southeast Asia.

The maritime raiding activities which forged the economic and political might of the Sulu state in the late eighteenth and nineteenth centuries were based upon a series of highly specialized sailing craft. Three basic types of vessels were associated with Iranun and Samal maritime raiding activities: *penjajap* (gubang or panco) a raiding ship used especially by the Iranun and Samal as their principal craft; *kakap* or *salisipan* (vinta or baroto), a sampan or dugout canoe with or without outriggers employed as an auxiliary craft for inshore raiding; and lanong or joanga, the large, heavily-armed Iranun cruiser.[1]

Penjajap were usually boats of light construction, sharp and very long; their size varied; they generally had two masts with square sails. They were quite open, except at the stern there was a small coop, a sort of cabin which served as the nakodah's quarters, and as a magazine for arms. In the bow, it carried one or two guns of larger calibre, the mouths of which were thrust through a wooden bulwark, always set in the direction of the keel of the vessel. The larger vessels also carried many swivels resting upon the ship's side above the deck; the smaller penjajap carried only one or two swivel guns, supported on a post. Twenty or 30 rowers, sitting on benches covered with matting, stroked the oars in rapid unison, either forward or backward. The smaller the penjajap the quicker its progress; for this reason, in those maritime raiding expeditions for which the Iranun had brought together a great number of vessels, the larger lanong were often left behind a neighboring island, and reserved for the purpose of covering a more important attack, while the smaller penjajap and kakap proceeded against their immediate targets.[2] Typical of a small late eighteenth century penjajap was the raiding vessel Thomas Forrest saw at anchor in a harbor on the island of Cagayan de Sulu. This was a sleek vessel that could reach speeds of over nine knots under sail and five knots when rowed by a well-disciplined crew. Even fully loaded it drew several feet of water only and was ideally suited for maritime raiding in the shallow seas of the Philippine archipelago and the southern part of the Celebes Sea. It could also sail inland by tacking up rivers. Forrest wrote in his journal that on the afternoon of 11 November 1774, he discovered in the roadstead at the southwest side of the island a crowded *prahu* with four brass swivel guns (*lantaka*) to which a continuous stream of canoes was ferrying back and forth from the shore. An hour later, he dropped anchor close to the vessel, and recognized her to be:

A Mangaio prow, or armed vessel that goes acruising, generally amongst the Philippine islands, called Bisayan. She was not above four tons burthen, looked very smart, having a gallery fore and aft for the rowers to sit on, as we had; having also the tripod mast and lyre tanjong, and mounting four brass swivel guns, called rantackers, carrying each a four ouce ball. She belonged to the Rajah of the island.[3]

The next morning the talented intrepid captain went ashore to pay his respects to the rajah who owned the vessel. Forrest had a trained eye and could readily tell the difference between a trading prahu, which carried an absolute minimum of armament, and an armed warship which engaged in trade. He was convinced that no great changes had been needed to fit out this prahu to raid, an economical way for the rajah to augment his strike force and harry the Spanish by attacking coastal shipping and launching assaults on seaboard targets. Forrest carried with him his ubiquitous tea kettle and cups, instruments of diplomacy and friendship and some tea and sugar. While the rajah, who 'spoke good malay,' drank tea with him, he discreetly inquired as to the destination of his 'privateer.' A remarkable exchange—more than 225 years old—ensued as the Rajah answered boldly: "Dio Pigy Mangaio, de Nigri Bisaya: 'She is going to cruise amongst the Philippines.' And Forrest, smiling then told him, 'tea was (English punio ciry) English betel, alluding to the betel leaf, which all east Indians chew. He laughed, and said it was very good ciry."[4]

With regard to Forrest's description of early penjajap there is very little conjecture, and likewise much valuable detail regarding certain variants in the design of these raiding vessels. He mentions that some of the prahus that the Iranun fitted out as cruisers were very long and narrow. "Many I have seen fifty feet long, and only three broad; availing themselves, however, of outriggers, without which they would not keep upright. They all use the tripod mast, lyre tanjong, and row with great velocity."[5] Six months later, on 23 May 1775, on the opposite side of the Sulu Sea, Forrest noted that upon entering Tubud Harbor, an Iranun stronghold, he encountered many "Illanoon mangaio prows." His purpose there was to meet with the Rajah Muda. After his meeting and exchange of gifts, Forrest measured a *"magaio* prow" of the penjajap type as the tide had receded and the harbor was dry. He "found her only four foot broad, three and a half feet deep, and forty-two feet long; she had outriggers, mounted six brass rantackers, and had thirty men."[6] Forrest also notes, that, the next day, from the small village of Brass which consisted of about 20 houses, he saw "a very smart mangaio prow, without outriggers; she kept rowing for some little time, as if to exercise the crew, in the smooth harbor made by the island."[7]

The kakap was a small vessel, quite open, provided with a large oar at the stern, in which the raiders used either oars or skulls. They carried only one mast with a single square sail. Like the penjajap they were made of light timber, the planks of which were fastened by wooden pegs, and lashed and tied with hemp rope and reeds; they drew hardly any water, and accompanied the larger penjajap and lanong, like the boats or gig of a large vessel or warship.[8] The Iranun and Balangingi never went to sea in a single kakap; and one could be sure that when a kakap was met, a penjajap or lanong was not far off. The largest were 20 to 25 feet long, and the crew came from the penjajap to which they belonged. For the purpose of inshore scouring eight or ten of the bravest warriors were selected who invariably disguised themselves as local fishers of the area upon which they were about to descend. William Wyndham informed Spencer St. John that prior to the Spanish attack on Balangingi in 1848 the maritime raiders had many kakaps which they used particularly for the capture of fishing boats.[9] During calm weather, Iranun and Samal raiders ran along the seashore in kakaps, or ascended small rivers, trusting to the rapidity of their movements. They knew full well that if taken by surprise, they could always run ashore, and disappear with their craft into the mangrove or tropical forest. The kakap or salisipan proved a dangerous craft for coastal people across Southeast Asia, as it was also an oar propelled boat that was easily hauled ashore. Forrest noted that the Iranun always had a swift kakap or sampan, capable of holding a dozen or more crew, which was used to get close to shore settlements without raising alarm:

> When the boat or prow is large, with her tripod mast struck, they hide among rocks, islands, or in the woods, up some creek. They then detach small sampans, or canoes, to surprise what they can ashore, or afloat, and bring to the capital vessel; which goes home, when she has got a sufficient cargo of slaves and plunder. The

Spaniards not allowing the Bisayans firearms, the latter prove less able to defend themselves.[10]

The lanong or joanga was the largest type of maritime raiding vessel yet known in Southeast Asia. The Iranun were always readily recognizable from the unusual construction of the lanong, which were reminiscent of the corsair galleys of the Mediterranean and for their dexterous management of these frighteningly big craft. They were however less formidable in certain respects, and less numerous than the smaller vessels. They were built at shipyards in Cotabato, Illana Bay and along the Berau River and some other places in that part of east Borneo. They always carried several large guns in the bow, and some swivels on either side. The crew, like those of the other vessels mentioned, were heavily-armed with muskets, a good number of pikes and lances (or bamboos, the point of which was blackened in a fire) kampilans and kris. Most of these vessels averaged 70 to 80 feet long, with 2 or 3 banks of oars or skulls like the Kora-Kora of the Moluccas, but there were also some huge ones constructed towards the end of the eighteenth century that approached a hundred feet or more from stem to stern.[11] The rigging was nearly identical to that of the common penjajap.

The lanong was made for long cruises and, in the 1790s, it was this ship which composed the squadrons that raided the Straits Settlements under the leadership of the Iranun of Tempasuk and Reteh. The largest were upward of 90 feet, and the full breadth of the hull was 20 feet amidships. A dugout keel formed the base of the lower part of the hull, with sides constructed of clinker-built planks. The stern and bow were built up and overhung the keel. The lanong often had one large mainsail forward and two tripod drop sheers that could be raised or lowered on a moment's notice. The detailed Spanish illustration of a late eighteenth century lanong or joanga has a mizzen sail behind the large square lyre *tanjong* ("pointed sail") at the center—a feature not prevalent on all Iranun raiding vessels until the late 1790s. The lateen-rigged square sails helped maneuver well before the wind, but not when the wind was blowing on the side or when the lanong was sailing into the wind. Much of the substantial deck was occupied by a fighting platform and a small poop (a raised section at the stern) containing the captain's cabin.[12] According to

THE RAIDING SHIPS

Fig. 23. A late eighteenth century *joanga* (*lanong*), an Iranun maritime raider, with three banks of oars, under full sail. Upward of 100 feet long, these vessels were provided with large bamboo outriggers, both sides were rowed and paddled by more than 150 men. The biggest Iranun raids were directed against the Philippines, especially southern Luzon.

((Courtesy of Museo Naval, Rafael Mouleon, *Construccion Navales*)

Forrest, the cabin was customarily termed the Koran because the Iranun, who were Muslim, seldom went to sea without their holy book, *alkoran*; which they always kept in the safest place aft–the stern cabin covered with plank boards.[13] Armament consisted of a strong bulwark at the sharp bow, carrying 1 or 2 deck-mounted long guns (6-24 pounders) as well as 8 to 10 swivel guns. Full body *gilolo* style shields were fixed along the undersides of the fighting platform, which was solidly built and many lanong, like the one depicted (Figure 9), carried long bamboo grappling hooks and a boarding bridge. Some of the largest lanong had crews of 100 to 150 men; the usual complement was from 50 to 100, with 40 to 50 elite seafaring warriors dressed in scarlet padded vests, armor and chain mail occupying the upper platform. A large triangular flag or pennant of the commander was affixed to the stern.[14] The battle-ready Iranun would fight for the honor of such a flag and die defending it.

Rolling south on the prevailing monsoon winds particularly around the small islands of the Buton Strait, Makassar Strait and strait of Malacca, trading ships kept a round-the-clock lookout for distant lyre tanjong sails, particularly a three-masted vessel, which might mean a lanong cruising in search of a prize. A European captain and crew would have to work incredibly hard in light wind to out-sail the lanong in order to avoid the fate of being manacled to the oars of a raiding galley before being either held to ransom, or sold in the markets of Sulu or Cotabato. Iranun raiders in their lanong operated efficiently into the first several decades of the nineteenth century, posing a real threat to English and American whalers outward bound for whaling grounds in the southern ocean.

The lanong, however, drew more water than the Balangingi garay, and moved more slowly, either with sails or oars. Captain Kolff in his valuable 1831 report noted that for a number of years the lanong had rarely been encountered to the south of Borneo, and from what he could learn on the spot and from informants, the vessel had become almost unknown to local seafarers. According to his spies, they were being used solely to protect the river strongholds of certain Iranun princes and sherifs who inhabited the northern parts of Borneo and southern Mindanao.[15] Interestingly, it was precisely against some of these Iranun overlords that Captain Keppel fought between the years 1843 and 1844 and against whom his staunch ally James Brooke struggled throughout the 1840s. Keppel, more than a decade later, described one of those rarely sighted lanong mentioned in Kolff's report, sequestered in the Saribas River. It belonged to an Iranun sherif:

> I have known one of these piratical prahus to measure ninety feet in length, with a proportionate beam. The usual armament of such a vessel would be one gun–from a six to a twelve pounder–in the bow; from four to six swivels, or lelas, on each broadside; besides about twenty or thirty rifles or muskets. Such boats would pull from sixty to eighty oars, in two tiers; and her complement of men would be from eighty to one hundred. Over the pullers, and extending the whole length of the vessel, is a light but strong flat roof, made of thin stripes of bamboo, and covered with matting. This protects their ammunition and provisions from the rain, and serves as a platform on which they mount to fight, and from which they fire their muskets or hurl their spears with great precision. The rowers sit cross-legged on a shelf projecting outwards from the bends of the vessel.[16]

The lanong or joanga of the Iranun raiders was similar to the Balangingi garay in some respects but the differences between the two highlighted different stratagems and skills of the neighboring seafarers at two different moments in regional time. The Iranun vessels were larger, more reliant on gunnery, and more heavily-built and -armed than that of the Balangingi. By 1830, the lanong had been all but replaced by the swifter, lightly-armed garay, which meant 'scattered' in Samal, signifying how the Balangingi organized and deployed them.

The earlier systematic large scale maritime raiding and pillaging that was the trademark of the Iranun spearheaded by the lanong gave way to equally devastating coastal raids led by the Balangingi. The Samal marauders favored the smaller, more easily maneuvered garay carrying a single large gun and a crew of up to 60 armed men. Sharp bowed and broad beamed, equipped with oar and sail, it moved easily through shallow water with sailing maneuverability and the garay proved a real nemesis for all unguarded trading vessels.[17] The Balangingi had streamlined their raiding prahu for speed, sacrificing some firepower and tonnage. In proportion to the round hull of the garay, a very large spread of sail was made possible by an unstayed tripod mast. Forrest commented at some length on the advantages of the Samal tripod mast, which consisted of three tall bamboos, the two foremost fitted on a cross beam, the last fixed behind free standing. He felt, as a naval commander, the tripod mast would be an ideal substitute for a mizzenmast on a cruiser; when struck the vessel could appear at a distance like a brig, and deceive an enemy. He also recognized that the tripod configuration was less susceptible to damage from repeated broadsides in a pitched sea battle. But, it was the power and simplicity with which a heavy press of square sail could be dipped around the mast in order to get the best performance, especially on longer tacks, that he most admired. Of this simple dipping lug or square sail, Forrest wrote:

> She had for a mast an artillery triangle (gin or tripod) made of three stout bamboos, which could be struck with the greatest ease by three men. On this was hoisted a large four-cornered sail, called by the Malays, lyre tanjong (pointed sail), because the upper corner appears sharper pointed.... One very great advantage attends the lyre tanjong, which is this; that when the wind freshens, it can, without lowering, be instantly diminished or made smaller, by easing or slacking the sheet, and at the same time winding up the sail, by two men turning the cross bar or winch that is fixed to the inner end of the boom, and which spreads the lower part of the sail. By this means, the sail may be entirely rolled up until the boom touches the yard; the sail always being in this compact manner, as seamen call it, 'taken in.' In the same manner it may be set again instantly, or let out, by turning the winch back the other way; or half set according to the weather.[18]

The Balangingi garay was a beautifully built vessel of lightwood, bamboo, nipa and rattan. The size of the largest garay was 70 to 80 feet in length, but most averaged 50 to 60 feet, while some were even smaller; the normal breadth of the beam was 20 feet, with a projecting stage outside of about 1 foot along which the sailors walked. The hull was ballasted with stones and coral to prevent it from capsizing. Forrest observed that in rolling before a heavy sea, the Iranun and Samal found the projecting

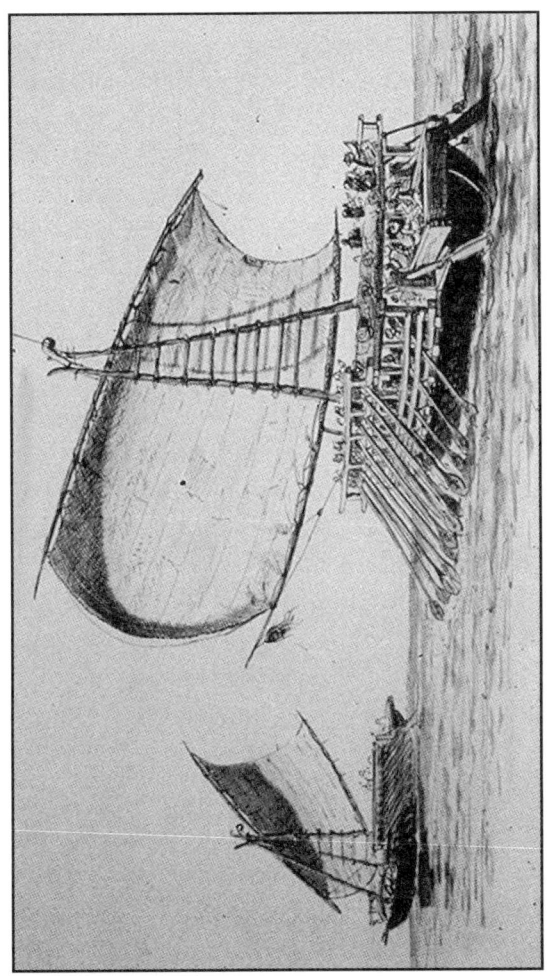

Fig. 24. A Balangingi *garay* or *panco* with two banks of oars under full sail. At the beginning of the nineteenth century Brunei was within easy range of the Balangingi Samal and a squadron of garay hovered about southern Palawan from the middle of March until the end of November to seize Brunei inhabitants and cut off trade to north Borneo. The Balangingi were alleged to have a saying that, "It is difficult to catch fish but easy to catch Borneans."
(Courtesy of Museo Naval, Rafael Mouleon, *Construccion Navales*)

gallery of great practical use because when the garay took water, it buoyed the vessel up "like an outrigger."[19] The garay, very sharp fore and aft with a great beam, still drew only three to five feet of water. The large beam enabled the raiding vessel to carry an enormous square rectangular sail on a tall, stout, collapsible bamboo tripod and move over reef-studded seas at better than ten knots. It was also oar-propelled and 30 to 60 oars were used on the big vessels. The upper tier of rowers sat on the projecting stage. The vessel was either partially open or decked with split cane from stem to stern. Cooking was done on a raised platform over a clay stove while sleeping quarters consisted of the deck and woven mats. The deck of split bamboo and nibong palm was arranged in fixed sections so that any part of it could be removed on a moment's notice. For armament a fixed cannon was carried in the bow in a reinforced bulwark of molave hardwood boards. The crew of the largest garay numbered upward of 80 men with an average complement of 60 while the smallest carried 25 to 30 men. Because it sailed well and was light enough to be rowed swiftly, it possessed the maneuverability and striking power necessary to cope with colonial warships in the second quarter of the nineteenth century.

The two captured 'Illanoon' prahus brought into the Singapore roads in late May 1838 measured between 50 to 60 feet in length. They were well-armed, each mounting a long four-pounder and several swivel guns or *ginjals*, besides carrying a large stock of muskets and spears, and both of them were protected by flat musket proof boards. At the request of the *Singapore Free Press and Mercantile Advertiser* a rare, detailed, on the spot description of a captured garay, the one commanded by the nakodah Daniel, was given to the newspaper by a 'friend':

> The *prahu* captured was 54 feet in length and fifteen feet beam, but their general length was 56 feet, strongly built, with a round stern, and the stern post having a considerable curve, on which the rudder made to fit, was hung on a pintle and gudgeon. The decks, after the same fashion as the Malay prahus, were made of split neebong fastened together with rattan, the neebong being cut into convenient lengths, so that any part of the deck could be rolled up–the depth of the hold about six feet. From the upper edge of the prahu a projection of bamboo nearly two feet broad, was made all around the

vessel from the stockade near the bow to the stern, on the outer edge of which was raised, of the same material, a breast work about three feet high, and outside this their rattan plaited cables were placed around, one coil above another—an excellent protection against shot. These vessels were double banked, pulling 36 oars, 18 on each side, nine of which rested on the edge of the prahu passing through the projecting raised work alluded to, the upper tier of nine oars, being worked over all the lower tier, were pulled by men sitting on the projecting bamboo work, the lower by others sitting on the projecting bamboo work, whose heads could not be seen above it—the oars were worked diagonally in the style, as has been supposed by some authors, of the ancient war galleys, by which contrivance considerable room is saved . . . The rowers among these pirates were of the lower castes, or slaves captured in their cruises; hence a strong Chinese became a valuable acquisition to them, and the oars could admit of two men pulling at each if necessary. Their rigging was of the most simple kind, a large sail forward and a smaller sail aft, made of light mats sewed together—stretched on bamboo above and below, having crosspieces at intervals from top to bottom in the foresail only—which was hoisted on a triangle of stout bamboos forming the foremast—this is done exactly like the Bugis boats, a bamboo lashed close to the outer edge of the vessel on each side, and a third fastened to the deck amidships, immediately behind the stockade, is brought up to meet the two upright pieces, and all lashed together at the top forming a very efficient support to the sail, and excellently adopted for resisting shot.[20]

Each garay had a salisipan attached which could carry up to 15 crew-members. Some sources also suggest that the maritime raiders occasionally put crews on board particular prizes that could be adapted to their needs and sailed to Balangingi to be used alongside the garay in their fleet. For example, Domingo Guzman of Dagupan, Pangasinan, recounted that he was a passenger on a large coasting prahu going to Bolinao when he was captured by the Balangingi. The prahu, according to Guzman, was taken to Balangingi, where he stayed for four months after which he was taken to Jolo and sold to a Tausog datu.[21]

At the height of their strength, in the first quarter of the nineteenth century, all seagoing Iranun and Samal vessels, including everything from the frighteningly large lanong to the small salisipan and canoes, mounted cannon and swivel guns of various sizes and shapes (*lantanka, lella*). Their stock of artillery included superbly cast long 12 pounders and large numbers of smaller 4 and 6 pounders. The cannon were smelted and cast locally from brass and various grades of raw and scrap iron that were imported as ballast and ironmongery from the United States and Bengal. The Iranun also obtained large cannon from captured ships or stole them from colonial outposts and fortifications. By the end of the eighteenth century, there was no shortage of artillery in the Iranun arsenal. Forrest took careful note of the large number of portable cannon and swivel guns in the fort of Rajah Muda of Cotabato; many of which were lying about on a 'stout' floor or mounted on rotten wooden carriages. He felt the seasonally wet climate rather than poor maintenance on the part of the Maguindanao was the culprit:

> The fort is nearly square, and the covered bastion, contiguous to Rajah Moodo's dwelling house, is under the stout floor already mentioned. On the ground are several pieces of heavy cannon [five mounted six and nine pounders], even with the water. All round the fort are mounted many brass swivel guns, the swivel being stuck into posts; also some brass rantackers. The rantacker is a gun sometimes six feet long, and carries a half pound ball.[22]

These cannon and swivel guns could be readily removed at short notice and placed aboard one of Rajah Muda's privately owned or sponsored maritime raiders that would rove the Philippine seas or lurk at likely corners and straits near Buton to pounce on defenceless shipping. Many of the heavily-armed Iranun vessels, with superbly-trained crews, bristled with all sorts of cannon enthusiastically supplied by royal financiers and backers such as Rajah Muda, or neighboring ship-owners and local captains.

The maritime raiders were also well-supplied with gunpowder and shot. Forrest carefully documented the process for the production of salt petre in southwestern Mindanao, and repeatedly stressed the local gunpowder was of poor quality: "To make salt petre, they mix one measure of this stuff (bat excrement) with two of wood ashes; and then filter through it the water of which the salt petre is made. The gunpowder they make here is very coarse grained, and has but little strength."[23]

In January 1776, he observed the fitting out and launch of a 30-ton raiding prahu. The penjajap, destined for Sulawesi waters, was to carry 80 men, and drew about 4 feet 6 inches of water.[24] Forrest watched the shipwrights and crew put the finishing touches on the tall masts, sails, anchors and cables and he also witnessed at first hand ". . . the crew making their powder: about eight men at one time were beating it in a wooden mortar. When made the grains were very coarse. She mounted two four pounders abreast of each other, on her prow or forecastle, and a great many brass rantackers."[25]

It was rare that the Dutch and Spanish were without enemies in Southeast Asia during the eighteenth and nineteenth centuries. England was always a potential foe but with little or no direct military aid forthcoming from the home country to states like Cotabato and Sulu, country traders and merchant-adventurers like Forrest and Wyndham readily freighted manufactured gunpowder to Iranun and Samal raiders. They then sat back to await their indirect bonus from the claims of irate Dutch and Spanish traders under constant threat of attack by well-equipped lanong and garay. Not surprisingly, when Thomas Forrest left the sultanate of Cotabato, after completing his epic journey in the *Tartar Galley*, he chose to give Raja Muda, as a token of his admiration and respect, a farewell present of half a barrel of gunpowder.[26]

The standard armament of the Balangingi prahus usually consisted of two smaller brass cannons, four to six pounders, one in front and one aft, and along the sides were placed some swivels and *rantankers*. The Balangingi usually acquired gunpowder and lead for their arsenal in the capital of the Sulu Sultanate, Jolo, from Chinese, Spanish and English merchants, who were supplied by British and Spanish ships involved in gun running or by sailing prahus from Manila and Singapore. In April 1856, exactly 80 years after Forrest left his parting gift of gunpowder for the young Maguindanao lord, two small barrels of gunpowder were confiscated after a battle with the Balangingi in the forests of an island off the east coast of Sulawesi. Stamped upon them were readily identifiable trademarks betraying their British origin and manufacture.[27] However, the Iranun and Balangingi were never wholly dependent on the outside world for either powder or shot. For example, they used a type of locally manufactured grapeshot, which consisted of a cylindrical rattan plaited canister, about a foot long and six inches in diameter. Both ends converged into conical points and the canister was filled with shattered and sharp pieces of shell and stone. The *rantankers* were charged with this gruesome missile which proved deadly at close range.[28] This homemade grapeshot had such a terrifying effect and caused great damage because it fragmented and flew in all directions on impact cutting through the rigging of an enemy vessel and killing and maiming large numbers of men on board. A British naval commander on patrol testified to the missiles' lethal effectiveness when, in February 1811, he caught part of an Iranun squadron anchored in a secluded bay off the coast of Sulawesi by surprise. When a light breeze sprung up, the captain sent in the heavily-armed gig and came to anchor within pistol shot of the expedition's crew that were quietly encamped on the beach. The Iranun, on suddenly observing the gig's approach, hastily erected a sand battery with eight to ten guns mounted on it. From the commander's report of the incident, we learn what happened to young English sailors and marines straight out of Greenwich, drilled and trained in the rules of Napoleonic warfare, who were plunged from the deck of a schooner into the terror of combat in an Iranun-held bay and jungle in Southeast Asia. Such sudden encounters were brutal, outside time and space, where young English sailors and soldiers, many as conscripts and volunteers, did not have to grow up–they just grew old before their time in the face of an Iranun grapeshot barrage:

> We immediately opened our fire on them; at this they did not appear in the least dismayed but returned it with a very warm and well directed fire with grape, double headed, and round shot and stones, it is however with much regret I have to observe that the . . . soldiers embarked did not perform their duty with the great zeal and alacrity I had reason to expect. The action having now continued for nearly one hour and the vessel much damaged both in her hull and rigging, I found it absolutely necessary to cut the cables to prevent her falling in their hands.[29]

The schooner *Fox* had dared to travel to that remote dangerous place and it came back with the worst imaginable news. The Iranun squadron of 40 prahus had survived, managing to silently slip away in the dead of night! The night time always belonged to the Iranun navigators who could sail in the pitch darkness, relying solely on the sound of the currents and a tell tale star to guide them to safety. Unlike their adversaries, they had no inexperienced boys, only veteran gunners and seafarers.

As they raided the coasts of Southeast Asia, between the eighteenth and nineteenth centuries, all Iranun long-ships had flags or pennants attached to them which blew out in the wind. The sighting in the distance of such a pennant on the stern of a rapidly approaching lanong was often a sign that little quarter would be given and sent a shiver of paralysis down the spine of the ship's crew. In 1846, Capt. Rodney Mundy of the British Royal Navy fell in with three large Iranun lanong belonging to the Tempasuk and Pandassan rivers towards which they were steering when first sighted by the English commander. The warships *Ringdove* and *Royalist* gave chase. The Iranun prahus raised a 'black flag' and attempted to attack the two vessels.[30] Black–sinister and threatening, symbolizing death and evil–was generally used as a battle flag in the late eighteenth century and its use spread rapidly among the Iranun across Southeast Asia, signifying that no mercy would be given to those who resisted. However, on pennants and flags, most raiding prahus also employed the individual insignias of their commanders to inspire both confidence and terror on the high seas. The symbols of death used by these nakodahs were designed to terrify their victims and the raven flag, with a picture of a black raven at its center, was a favorite design flown on Iranun and Balangingi ships. In 1838 Silammkoon stated at his trial before the recorder of Singapore, Sir W. Norris, that none of the Balangingi vessels in the squadron flew the flag of the sultan of Sulu, which Thomas Forrest had described some 60 years earlier as "the gates of Mecca, red, on a white background."[31] The flag his boat flew was not "the national flag of Sooloo it was made by Tala Goa. The other boats had flags of diverse colors according to the fancy of the commanders."[32] However, the celebrated Balangingi maritime raider and war leader, Panglima Taupan, was not above adopting the Sulu colors to suit his own purposes.[33] Iranun and Balangingi raiding vessels, not only carried a suit of sails for various localities, but a range of flags to match and it was a common practice to fly a friendly colonial flag or a local or neutral one when approaching a larger well-armed vessel, and to replace the original flag with a black one or the commander's trademark pennant at the last moment, if it was felt that the vessel could be seized. In 1803, for example, 8 Ternaten Kora-Kora were dispatched to Menado to chase and disperse a fleet of 'Maguindanao junks' that consisted of 12 sail, all displaying English colors which had attacked and taken a Dutch *panchallong*. The Dutch crew of 18 men escaped in their long boat when the vessel was upon the point of being boarded and barely reached the safety of the Gorontalo roadstead.[34] Not surprisingly, when a British naval task force destroyed the Iranun stronghold of Pandassan in 1846 they came across many looted souvenirs from British ships, including flags and pennants.[35]

Almost every aspect of seafaring life in Sulu and Mindanao depended on wood and bamboo, which the Iranun and Samal worked skillfully. An Iranun or Samal boat builder needed special tools like an axe, adze, mallet, saw, and chisel to fashion maritime raiding vessels of great beauty and strength. A young Iranun boy would start out carving model prahus, play canoes, paddles, and spears. If he showed aptitude, he began an apprenticeship carving small salisipan and fishing canoes, only later in his adolescence being given task work on a penjajap. Then, as a man and as an accomplished boat builder, he was prepared to fashion the keel of 50 to 60 foot raiding vessels and large lanong from a single teak or ebony log. Boat building, as a key industry, was both an art and science in the Mindanao-Sulu region. The shell of Iranun and Samal vessels was built up from the keel (a hollowed out log) without nails. Fibre lashings and wooden dowels were used to bind clinkered planks and ribs together to form the hull. Certain communities specialized in building raiding prahus and shipwrights transmitted their knowledge and skills from one generation to the next. Thomas Forrest observed the construction of numerous penjajap and several lanong at Cotabato along the banks of the Pulangi River in south Mindanao:

> In that part of the town of Cota Intang . . . live a few Chinese; but many Maguindanao mechanics, vessel builders and merchants. They build their vessels of various dimensions, and employ them in trading from one part of the coast to the other; often in cruising amongst the

(Bisayan) Philippine islands, for slaves and plunder. They cruise also as far as the coast of Java, and the islands of Celebes and Borneo, seizing whatever prows they can muster. These vessels are always very long for the breadth, and very broad for their draft of water.[36]

The Maguindanao and Iranun also constructed raiding vessels on the forested coast of Sibuguey Bay in 1775: 'Here [Sibuguey Bay] are built many stout vessels, good timber being in great plenty.'[37]

By 1790, the center of boat building activity in the Mindanao-Sulu region had shifted away from Cotabato to the Sulu archipelago. Basilan and nearby islands were especially rich in hardwood timbers and other shipbuilding materials, and the Iranun and Samal of Maluso became celebrated boat builders.[38] Jolo Island itself was well-supplied with good timber and Parang was the most well-known place on the island for building garay or penjajap.[39] Forrest noted that, in the 1770s, the interior of the island was dotted with stands of teak trees which were as numerous as on Java, from which the Chinese gathered the leaves to line the cane baskets used to pack the birds' nest which was exported in huge quantities, from Jolo.[40] Wooden wedges hammered with wooden mauls split planks cleanly from the soaring straight grained hardwood timber that had been cleared and felled from stands on Basilan, Jolo and the east coast of Borneo during this period of rapid development and windfall capital. The Iranun and Samal were superb craftsmen and these boat builders could bend small planks into shape by grooving them with an adze and steaming the corners. Forrest considered boat building to be a singular art among the Iranun and Samal, and he then described how this most critical of material possessions was generally built:

> Their most useful art is vessel building, which they perform by doweling the planks one upon the other, so as to never require calking. They then fit the timbers, the beams going without, and, as it were, clasping the planks, like vessels called Burrs in Bengal river. This has one bad consequence, as, at those beam ends, the vessels are always leaky.[41]

While he was at Cotabato in January 1776, shortly before his departure for Bengal, Forrest participated in the launch of a 30-ton maritime raider:

> She was quite new . . . had a great deal of room on her deck, and galleries around her; but so little room below, that she was continually swagging from side to side; which is the case with all their vessels, more or less, and was with mine. I observed that they launched her without anything on her bottom. They said they would bream and pay her bottom in ten days.[42]

This vessel, and hundreds of others like her, had the singular advantage of being doweled and lashed together with rattan rather than nailed. Hence, if damaged they could, under hot pursuit, be beached, rapidly dismantled, with the sections and parts carried into the safety of the forest, to be reassembled on the opposite coast when the danger had passed. According to Forrest's expert eye, the late eighteenth century raiding prahus of Sulu were generally better constructed than those at Cotabato.[43]

Learning about the specific qualities of these maritime raiding vessels was a daunting task for colonial navies. It was all too easy, when writing in a broad manner about the general physical characteristics of the raiding prahus, to leave out the bits of important detail where naval commanders or ship captains either were not sure, or there was just no information. With regard to the published written descriptions and illustrations in early and mid-nineteenth century travel accounts and other comparable literature there is a great deal of conjecture. Complete accuracy was impossible as many of the authors rarely had direct experience of the sailing vessels of that grim commerce, the slave trade. However, those commanders, who made it their life work to hunt the Iranun and Balangingi, had no shortage of ideas. The officers of the Spanish and Dutch navies built a reputation in the 1830s and 1840s as men who pioneered the science of making maritime raiding as difficult–and often as extremely dangerous–as possible. They had captured prisoners and shipwrights build, sometimes on the spot, exact replicas of their raiding vessels and provide sketches of their raiding tracks and places of rendezvous. The naval museums of Spain and the Netherlands became well-known, at the turn of the century, for these repatriated scale models. The Museo Naval or Naval Museum in Madrid,[44] was noted for a beautiful, three foot copy of a Balangingi garay, the vessel in which Samal maritime raiders sailed thousands of miles around Southeast Asia in search of slaves so that the English and continentals could drink tea and the Chinese consume birds' nest and tripang at their leisure.

In the Museo Naval, Monleon's extraordinary 1890s aquarelle sketches of the Iranun and Samal vessels of the Mindanao-Sulu region were based on the small-scale models built by indigenous craftsmen that were brought back to Spain by members of naval and scientific expeditions throughout the nineteenth century. These sketches and paintings present a wealth of technical, nautical and ethnographic detail that is lacking in much of the historical literature and research to date. They describe ship construction, general layout, rig and sailing practice, the mechanics of these sailing vessels, and the seafarers employed according to their respective ethnic groups.

The Spanish and Dutch commanders were particularly concerned to look at the rig and hull construction of the raiding vessels and speculate about how the whole complex was handled with respect to speed, maneuverability and navigation. It is not easy from the surviving literature to ascertain exactly how fast the galley slaves or monsoon winds could propel these raiding vessels forward. Forrest estimates between four and five miles during the first hours of rowing, but some Spanish naval officers suggested speeds as high as nine knots for long periods, and perhaps faster in short bursts.[45] Forrest was aboard a newly-launched maritime raider of 30 tons when it rowed 3 miles up the Pulangi River. He wrote that the crew rowed at the rate of four miles an hour:

> The number of oars was sixteen of a side; but, as they were all fixed by rattans at the edge of the gallery, as many more might have been fixed within those: for the oars led (if I may so say) much up and down, making a great angle with the horizon. She had a very high tripod mast.[46]

He also presents the journal of another southward bound cruiser in January of 1776, a "Mangaio prow belonging to Datoo Malfalla, brother-in-law to Rajah Moodo, from Maguindanao, to the coast of Celebes."[47] The rare journal contains information on the daily movements of the slave raider, places where the prahu stopped to get provisions (Karikita, Siao), and maritime raiding. It took the vessel just under six days to reach the north coast of Sulawesi under oar and sail. Slaves and handpicked crew either stood or sat on the deck or sat cross-legged on the projecting gallery, each one of them manacled and pulling on an oar at various levels. They were encouraged to row in unison to the sound of drum beat and brass cymbals. The rowers were also urged by the crew to sing both night and day as sometimes slaves were compelled to row for long stretches without a break–10, 12 or even 14 hours at a time. Forrest, a consummate musician, who played both flute and violin, was particularly fascinated by a rowing song, which was sung by the galley slaves and crew of these maritime raiding vessels. This Muslim 'chearing song' was introduced by Tuan Haji on Forrest's *Tartar Galley* with beneficial results:

> I found Tuan Hadjee in high spirits chearing (sic) up the rowers with a certain tactic song, to which a man beat time with two brass timbrels. This song was in the Mindano tongue, and is much used by the Mangaio boats, not only to amuse and chear up the mind, but to give vigor to their motion in rowing.[48]

He even provides an English translation of the three stanzas of the song sung in alternate voices with a chorus.

MAGUINDANAO MANGAIO SONG

Chorus	Chear up - hurrah!
	Chear up - hurrah!
	Let's gain the ocean far away:
	Let's gain the ocean far away:
First Man	Behold yon island afar,
	What fishes abound in its main;
	Behold yon island afar,
	Haste, haste, and the fishes obtain.
Chorus Repeated	
Second Man	Fast by the Capezine land,
	Castilian dames you will find:
	My lads, for Capezine land,
	Pull, pull, with the whole of your mind.

Under sail the shallow-draught, light, single-masted garay that the Europeans called penjajap or panco proved impossible to contain, as it silently glided out of protected coves and inlets at night on the slightest breeze or moved at breakneck speed across the open sea behind a strong prevailing wind. The colonial vessels that chased the garay rarely overtook them due to their swiftness. During their high level meeting in Manila in 1838, Don Jose Maria Halcon informed Commander Blake about 'Illanoon piracy' and that he had witnessed on one occasion upward of 200 Iranun sail, large and small, off Luzon. On attempting to pursue them with his *falua* squadrons, they literally sailed out of sight, disappearing in a most extraordinary fashion before his very eyes, dousing mast and sails, and gliding into a safe haven among the almost impenetrable stands of coastal mangrove.[49] Fifteen years later, the head of the falua command in the Visayas, still expressed frustration at the poorly designed and badly built ships at his disposal that were unable to cope with the swiftness of the garay and the local elements, for which these raiding boats were so ideally suited.

> The head of the light naval fleet answered on the 16th of the said month, expressing difficulty in pursuing the Samal pirates and the kind of vessels they use; hence, it was necessary to let the season of typhoons and strong breezes pass first so that the tenders (faluas) could be able to navigate at night, and it would be favourable to the tender to be able to surprise some vessel. This is the only means to punish severely the pirates, because in the day time the tenders could be seen in the far distance by the pirates who could hide themselves in the mangroves where it is difficult for the tender to pursue them.[50]

Nor were English naval commanders spared the embarrassment of lacking the appropriate equipment and seafaring skills to consistently trap such raiding vessels. In 1846, Capt. Edward Belcher, upon landing at Dumuran, south Mindanao, saw "several suspicious looking characters" among the trees. He also saw a vessel which he claimed was "too large and rakish for fishing pursuits." Belcher insisted that he had not expected any Iranun to be present there and simply ordered his crew to be armed as a precautionary step. He then recounts an experience of extraordinary seamanship of an era that the Iranun and Balangingi Samal would shortly never know again:

> We had scarcely quitted the ship when the boat from the island, which was now discerned to be pulling a number of oars, made an attempt to escape to windward, but the fleetness of our boats rendering such a manoeuvre in that direction impossible, he with great rapidity raised his tripod, and set an enormous sail, steering directly across our course. We noticed their huge Illanoon swords, which glittered in the sun.[51]

Belcher's crew gave chase but like his Spanish counterparts soon lost sight of the Iranun vessel.

Until almost the middle of the nineteenth century, many of the raiding vessels of the Iranun and Balangingi were more or less integrated into the fleets of the Sulu Sultanate. However, by the late 1830s, both Iranun and Balangingi vessels were also operating independently, particularly some of those crewed by raiders residing at forward bases who were not prepared to return to Mindanao and Sulu at regular intervals. Ships of both ethnic groups had their own cruising grounds, but inevitably, there was some overlap determined in large measure by the direction and distribution of the monsoon winds which had such a profound influence on the history of trade, settlement and maritime raiding. Iranun galleys cruised between Mindanao and New Guinea–and beyond, as well as back toward Penang and Vietnam. The Samal and their Christian renegades from Balangingi harassed coastal settlements to the west of Borneo and regularly circumnavigated the Philippines tormenting shipping and coastal communities before heading south to operate garay in the west and central Moluccas.[52] Shortly before the maritime raiding vessels sailed from Mindanao and Balangingi to reach the cruising grounds, the raiders prayed together to Allah the Merciful. They knew their lives depended on his great spirit, and they undoubtedly also prayed alone at sunrise shortly before departure for a divine wind and a safe journey. The nocturnal departure of a Balangingi squadron from among the low islets clustered between Basilan and Jolo is described by Javellana in the following manner:

> A stiff southwesterly filled the sails of the garay, the Samal Balangingi warship. Sixty oars hit the water in rhythm, manned by Visayan slaves bound by ropes to projecting platforms built on either

side of the vessel. On board, warriors were armed to the teeth. The vessel was cutting ten knots, heading in a bee line for the Visayan coasts. Behind were smaller and lighter crafts, the salisipan. The flotilla was cruising in the pre-dawn darkness, ready to pounce on unsuspecting fishing communities along the rugged shores. This scene was no nightmare spawned at the dead of night but a real danger that threatened the Visayan towns growing under a hispanic sun.[53]

The monsoon winds bore the Iranun across the South China Sea between the months of August and October; by the middle of October the winds were too strong in the Malacca Strait for maritime raiding, but ideal for the return voyage via Sulawesi and the Moluccas. The warm humid southwest monsoon (*habagat*) the 'pirate wind,' usually appeared in the Philippines in early May, attained maximum intensity in August, and gradually disappeared in October and November, while the same region is affected by the *amihan* or northeast monsoon during the months between December and March. The Iranun split their fleets into divisions and squadrons that quartered the whole archipelago. Taking full advantage of the prevailing winds of the amihan and habagat, they circumnavigated Borneo and went as far afield as New Guinea. Their wind-driven and oar-powered galleys appeared like clockwork in the gulf of Siam and beyond, out into the Bay of Bengal as far as Burma. They annually raided the central and northern sections of the Philippines and the regularity of these sweeps led the local populace of Trengannu, Kelantan, Patani and elsewhere to refer to particular months of the year, notably August, September and October, as the '*musim lanun*' ("Lanun season") and the monsoon itself as the "pirate wind."[54]

The Iranun and Balangingi used three different tracks or routes for raiding expeditions mounted against different parts of the Philippines. The main route of attack was along the western edge of the archipelago, sailing north from Jolo along the northern part of Borneo, then to the southeastern and eastern part of Palawan and the south Calamianes. Along this track, they ravaged small settlements and captured slaves. They then crossed over to the Bicol Peninsula and the central Visayas, gathered captives, before returning to their bases via the outward-bound route. Alternatively, they proceeded to the coast of southern Negros, then to Palawan, and then to their point of departure by November. Between December and March, when the north wind prevailed, they then set out for Sulawesi and the Moluccas. This southerly route originated from Sarangani, then to the island of Sangir and from there, they sailed to Sulawesi and seized slaves and whatever they could loot from their coastal raids. They returned via the same route. From Balangingi and Tubug, the slave raiders navigated the southern and eastern parts of Mindanao and then proceeded to the Visayas, returning via the same route.[55] Mallari notes that when the southwesterlies or 'pirate wind' blew from April until the end of October, those Filipinos living close to the San Bernardino Strait or along coastal stretches of the Samar or Sibuyan seas constantly scanned the horizons for the first signs of massed sails.[56]

At the beginning of the nineteenth century both sides of Borneo were within easy range of the Balangingi Samal and, from the middle of March to the end of November, squadrons of garay hovered about southern Palawan to seize the inhabitants of Brunei and cut off its trade with the rest of the island. Many people from Brunei were taken into slavery. The Balangingi had a saying: 'it is difficult to catch fish, but easy to catch Borneans.' On the opposite side of the huge island its inhabitants called the easterly wind 'the pirate wind' as the Balangingi cruised the northwest coast from the middle of March and returned to the east side of the island in late November.[57] Iranun prahus that extended their depredations as far north as Siam or proceeded up the strait of Malacca, returned to north Borneo and Mindanao by mid-October when the monsoon became too strong to slave raid successfully, but was favorable for making the long return journey to their homeland. Some sense of the vast extent and direction of the Iranun-Samal maritime raiding routes was understood for the first time on board the 'Illanoon' prahu taken as a prize by the war steamer *Diana*. No less than seven individuals, who had shortly before been captured in separate boats and seized in distinct places extending from Cavite, which is situated in Manila Bay to the immediate vicinity of Singapore and the northeast coast of Malaya, were rescued.[58]

On their southward journey the Iranun and Balangingi, if they were not taking the Sangir track mentioned in the journal of an Iranun prahu belonging to the brother-in-law of Rajah Muda of Cotabato, usually sailed along the coast of Borneo heading for the northeast corner of Sulawesi. In early 1776, Forrest detailed her swift passage down the Sangir track:

> The prow, which left Maguindanao, during the N.E. monsoon, after passing Serangani, went to the following islands before she reached Celebes. First Kalingal, three hours from Serangani; it is inhabited and resembles English Bunwoot. Then, in one day to Kabio: it is inhabited. In another day to the island Kabalusu, near the north part of Sangir. Hence in one day to Karikita, which afforded some provision. Hence in one day to Siao, near which she got plenty of provisions on a small island, behind which is a fine harbour. Thence to Tagulanda in half a day, thence to Banka, and thence to Tellusyang, which is near the coast of Celebes.[59]

For those prahus taking the opposite route down the east Bornean coast, the Pangalisian islands were a usual place of rendezvous. Here the nakodahs convened a council to discuss the cruising tracks to be taken. When the prahus were numerous a squadron of them would steer through the Makassar Strait, intercepting trade to that entrepot, then separating to scour the Java Sea, while another squadron followed the north coast of Sulawesi in order to reach the Banka Strait and the Moluccas. Still other prahus proceeded immediately south eastwards and, passing along the Sangir group, entered the Moluccan Sea. Those in the western sector of the archipelago joined together southwest of the Bangka Strait, then visited the Tambelan and Natuna islands, proceeding up the west coast of Borneo, calling at Marudu before passing through the Balabac Strait on the homeward run.[60] Those operating around Sulawesi undertook the homeward bound journey through the other, equally important Banca Strait, at the opposite end of the archipelago, availing themselves of the southwesterly winds.[61] Forrest noted that the island of Banca, with its high hill, was a significant landmark and that the neighboring islands were much frequented by "mangaio cruisers, not only from Maguindano, but from Sooloo."[62] From there, the maritime raiders would reach Illana Bay and Balangingi in three to five days depending on the prevailing winds and currents.[63]

The Iranun and Balangingi relied on the prevailing winds in navigating their prahus across Southeast Asia. The raiders were rarely out of sight of land for long because the islands lay so thickly on the sea. Essential to their navigation was a thorough knowledge of the shores, headlands, coves, deltas, and mangrove swamps. Some Iranun acquired this deep ecological knowledge by long experience. The British East India Company master mariners like Dalrymple and Forrest, as key protagonists in the Anglo–Dutch struggle for Asian supremacy, produced a vivid record of the Iranun's navigational skills and seamanship. Dalrymple described the remarkable ability of one such navigator, Bahatol, who was alleged to be older than 90 years. Dalrymple dismissed as inaccurate the large variety of printed and manuscript charts for the Sulu archipelago and the northern part of Borneo, except for the one drafted for him by Bahatol. Of Bahatol's mental sketch of the islands, coastlines and rivers Dalrymple wrote:

> Amongst the authorities of this kind, I cannot omit mentioning a very extraordinary chart, of the Sooloo Isles, and northern part of Borneo; it was formed by the description of Bahatol, . . . from the reflected experience of almost a century: particular observation was made some use of, in limiting the islands adjacent to Sooloo, and mistakes in these, were the source of some confusion: but, though it cannot be supposed a draught, made from memory, and delineated by the hands of another, should be free from very material errors and omissions; I need not be afraid of exceeding, in my applause of so remarkable a work of natural, genius![64]

Frequently the navigators were assimilated captives or slaves who had an intimate knowledge of local dialects, creeks, ports, and navigation tracks of the area from which they had been previously uprooted and were now returning as assailants. To assist navigators, most raiding prahus were equipped with a compass, and many carried a good brass telescope to enable them to make out shoreline features, craft and communities in detail.[65] Brass gilt compasses made by the finest English instrument makers of the day were regularly given as gifts to leading rajahs and their boat commanders by Forrest and his compatriots. Forrest gave a pocket compass to the Iranun brother of the rajah of Balabagon at Teytan harbor, a well-known roadstead for mooring maritime raiding vessels. The previous year he had also presented a compass to a rajah of Cagayan de Sulu who, when interviewed, had also admitted that his boat was about to set out on a slave raiding cruise in the Philippines.[66] Compasses were also plundered from European vessels or purchased in colonial ports. Sailing directions of other kinds were used when the Iranun struck off across expanses of open sea: bearings were taken from the direction of the winds, the currents, and the position of the sun. At night they were guided by the stars, the moon and weather signs. Even in the sky, the Iranun and Samal raiders saw the sea; every type of star, wave and current, every rock and navigational landmark had been given a name. There were at least a dozen words to describe the color of the sea and the varying tides. In deep haze and fog the Iranun and Samal navigated by reading the currents, swells and sounds as if hunting a living creature. A veteran navigator informed Dalrymple that proven weather signs were passed on from one generation to the next. The most important signs were principally from lightning. When lightning flashes upward there will soon be wind; high, tremulous lightning is a sign of rain; low, tremulous lightning indicates a hill; when the lightning is red, it indicates a rocky formation; when yellow, the hill is earth; low flashes upon the surface of the water denote a shoal beneath it; a shoal above water has an atmosphere hanging over it, which appears like an island; low, long lightning, upon the surface, shows an island with trees: when an island is high at one end, the lightning will be in a slanting line that corresponds to the hill.[67]

Fertile, uninhabited, remote islets furnished the Iranun and Balangingi with food, water and firewood and served as careening places, where their prahus could be hauled up on a beach and turned above ground on logs to be cleaned and repaired. To maintain the overall optimum condition of the vessels when away was of vital concern to the raiders, and at these concealed spots their hulls were examined and overhauled every few months during the course of their voyages. The marauders had their own names for the islands in this network so as not to betray their exact location. Dutch knowledge of these places was largely based on testimonies of escaped captives: the small islands on the northwest coast of Borneo north of Tanjung Datu; the islands to the south of Celebes–Kalatoa, Tana Jampea and Bonerate; on the northeast coast of Celebes, the islets of Banca and Talisse, and small bays and coastal sites on Sumbawa, Komodo and Flores.[68] The island of Lembah near Kema was sometimes used by the maritime raiders as a provisioning spot but especially by those raiding vessels, which, crossing over from the east coast of Sulawesi to the Banca Strait, moored there, having been guided to the spot by the high mountain, Klabat.[69] Similarly, in the Philippines, carefully selected spots were chosen for replenishing provisions, and maintaining and careening their prahus. The most important sites, before the nineteenth century, were located in the Sibuyan Sea on the islands of Mindoro, Masbate and Burias.

When the Iranun and Samal navigators actually drew detailed maps of their numerous interconnected worlds of forward bases, rendezvous points, slave markets, places for careening vessels and replenishing stocks, an indigenous representation of space and human settlement emerges from the perspective of privileged powerful regional maritime raiding groups. The mapping of Southeast Asia according to Iranun and Samal patterns of space and representation, depict communicentric regional visions of an expansionist history and cross-border territories based on a common sense of kinship, group solidarity and maritime raiding. However, this interdependent federative vision, so often closely associated with regional conflict, came to an end when the Iranun and Balangingi warrior elite lost the power at sea to protect the raiding communities and bases so clearly delineated on their maps. After the mid-nineteenth century, the leather charts, protected in bamboo containers across the generations, were invariably confiscated from vanquished settlements and captured raiding prahus as part of a regional-wide colonial pacification project.

CHAPTER TEN

BLOOD UPON THE SEA AND SAND

The Iranun relied on surprise, terror and overwhelming force when attacking traditional sailing boats and European vessels on the high seas and when sacking coastal towns and villages. They operated out of bays and islands situated near major straits across the archipelago through which funnelled a constant procession of merchant *prahus* ("trading vessel") from all quarters of Southeast Asia, and beyond–vessels that were bound for Batavia, Penang, Singapore, Manila, and Makassar. From England, the United States and continental Europe, other larger sailing ships, laden with arms, opium and textiles for the China market repeatedly ran the gauntlet of these narrow straits which were the hunting grounds of the Iranun and Balangingi. At the end of the eighteenth century, as Western traders started to appear in Canton and began exporting tea along with other goods, the expansionist Iranun set up forward bases across Southeast Asia, ignoring Dutch, Spanish and British authority with impunity. The trading operations of European corporate enterprises, particularly the British East India Company and the VOC, as well as those of private Western traders led, within the short span of three decades (1770-1800), to an unprecedented growth of Iranun society and population-based on long distance maritime raiding and its integration into modern world commerce. Some Iranun raiders, as both pioneers and mercenaries, established themselves in Reteh on Sumatra's east coast. Others sought a safe haven in Tempasuk, northwest Borneo, as well as further south fronting the South China Sea, while a number of the boldest of these marauders prowled the coasts of southern Vietnam,

Thailand and even Burma, where no governments seemed capable of stopping them.

The local shipping figures published in colonial gazettes and reports at the start of the nineteenth century showed an inexorable rise in the incidence of sailing boats attacked at sea, scuttled or lost in the waters of the major straits and islands of the archipelago. Here, the Iranun mostly targeted merchant traders operating out of major local and regional ports, stealing their cargoes, equipment, occasionally, the prahus themselves, and, enslaving the crews. Most worrisome in relation to the rising level of attacks on shipping that were taking place in different regions of Southeast Asia, was the increased use of heavy ordnance and muskets against sailing prahus and their crews while still in port, when navigating the open sea, or hugging a coastline invariably dotted with small islands, coral reefs and sandbanks. James Brooke noted that such vulnerable spots were precisely where the Iranun tended to concentrate. The seasonal pattern of using offshore islands and nearby bays to attack trading ships plying certain routes as they approached land, led to such dangerous places being commonly referred to as 'rats' nests.' The Iranun had, in the white rajah's words,

> . . . attained an importance on the coasts and islands most removed from foreign native settlements. Thence they issue forth and commit depredations on the native trade, enslave the inhabitants at the entrance of rivers, and attack ill-armed or stranded European vessels, and roving from place to place they find markets for slaves and plunder.[1]

In the vast open tracts of sea, the Iranun generally attacked traditional trading vessels, particularly sailing boats such as *mayangs*, *lamba*, *janggolan* and *padawakan*, and small Chinese junks.[2] The raiders kept a vigilant lookout and, provided with good telescopes, they often kept out of the way of dangerous vessels, namely European warships. But they indiscriminately attacked every prahu or ship for which they thought that they were more than a match, without any distinction of nationality or neutrality, or having much regard as to the value of the prize. However, the Iranun rarely picked targets like the big East Indiamen merchant frigates, well-armed fast ships, carrying 24 to 28 guns on a single deck, that were freighting opium to China. The speed and fighting capacity of these vessels often scared away the Iranun and other such raiders, unless the frigate ran aground, struck a reef or was becalmed. On the other hand they frequently struck at smaller two-masted square-rigged European vessels like brigs and fore and aft rigged interisland schooners and trading ketches.

For decades on end Iranun maritime raiding became the most serious problem confronting interisland shipping in the waters around the straits of Malacca, Java, the Philippines, and Sulawesi. The Iranun marauders hid in the innumerable bays, creeks and waterways of the key straits and adjacent islands and employed hit and run tactics against slower moving merchant prahus, which, with smaller less well-armed crews, were favorite targets. The speed of Iranun vessels meant that attack was inevitable once the merchant sailing boat was sighted. However, the maritime raiders were not above the use of subterfuge to aid their engagement and capture of prizes. The Iranun always made an estimate beforehand–based on local knowledge and what they saw through the lens of their spyglass–of the speed and fighting capability of the vessel they wished to attack. If there appeared much chance of stout resistance, they either refrained from operations and broke off the pursuit, or had recourse to the effective ruse of utilising false colors, sails and rig. Indeed, the Iranun usually contrived to approach their prey in such a manner so as to avoid suspicion of their real intention and character. Each *lanong* and *penjajap* carried several suits of sails of the form and material of the traditional boats of the various nationalities whose coasts and sea routes they visited, and in each particular locality targeted, they hoisted the appropriate rig with their raiding boats divested of all warlike appearances. Sailing in the guise of a peaceful trader or large fishing boat, their guns were carefully concealed under mats.[3] As the Iranun closed upon a targeted vessel, deceiving its Javanese, Buginese, Macassarese, or Visayan crew into thinking they were from the same locality, most of the marines hid from sight, while renegade crew, in local garb, stood on the deck in full view, gesturing in dialect to make both the disguise and deception complete. The renegade seafarers would establish some pretense for getting close to the craft that the Iranun wished to surprise, such as pretending that their fire had gone out and begging for a fresh supply or wanting to replenish provisions through barter trade.[4] The early nineteenth century seafarer Si-Ayer described how a seemingly ordinary trading parley east of Sulawesi turned to horror when disguised Iranun closed in suddenly, seizing him and several of his fellow crewmembers.

> We were on our way to the island [of Mengarie] having spent a good deal of time amongst small islands, when we were taken by a fleet of Lanuns. Being near a small island, named Turunguoi, two small boats came out to us and told us to come to the island, as they wished to trade with us for food in exchange for birds' nests. We went, and found upwards of ten large Lanun boats there, and were all seized to the number of twelve, and handcuffed.[5]

Across the archipelago, the Iranun at Reteh were often provided with passports by local 'grandees' and under the pretext of fishing for *agar-agar* (seaweed) or *tripang* they approached and pillaged small trading and fishing vessels.[6] Once alongside, they threw off their disguise and leapt on board their prize, generally taking the crew completely unawares. In this way they had them at their mercy. The similarities between the disguised Iranun and Balangingi, and Malay and Filipino sailing boats were so great that the real identity of the assailants did not often become apparent until the very last moment as the raiders pulled alongside. The extraordinary account, written in 1857 by Lieutenant Colonel Ibanez y Garcia, describes the age-old skill of this Samal subterfuge which outwitted his Visayan crew—much to his horror on a fateful June morning:

> The sea was calm, except for the silvery ripples created by the boats keel as it knifed effortlessly through the dark-blue waters of Bohol. The vast expanse that lay ahead was peppered with seagulls performing their daily aerial acrobatics, now and then diving into the brine for a delicious catch. On board the boat was a Spaniard, Infantry Lt. Col. Don Luis Ibanez y Garcia, the Governor, Politico of Surigao. He had been sailing from Surigao via Cebu and Leyte. When they weighed anchor at Mausim [Maasin] (Leyte) that fateful dawn, they feared the possible boredom and mental fatigue of their long trip to Manila. Suddenly it happened. As if from nowhere two boats appeared, approaching fast. 'Fishermen to hawk their catch,' so

they thought. But such complacency was shattered. In lightning fashion, two big wooden planks went over their boat's parapets, as nimbled, *kris* and sword-brandishing dark-skinned men climbed over. I and my companions were held at bay. At the same time some set fire to the boat's hull.[7]

Ibanez, his entourage and crew had become captives of one of the most feared Balangingi bands led by the *Panglima* Taupan and the chief, Tumugsuc.

The tactics of seamanship and sea warfare of the Iranun and Balangingi varied with time, locality and circumstance. But, at the end of the eighteenth century, in the age of deep water sailing ships, there was a consistent approach to pursuing and engaging larger heavily-armed coasting vessels. The close pursuit began with several lanongs firing their large bow cannons as they attacked from both sides and the rear in a pincer-like movement, hoping the balls would dismast the victim and destroy the rudder. Strong noisy rowing in a light breeze brought the 80-foot lanongs abreast of the outstripped Malay, Chinese or Bugis vessel, enabling Iranun sharpshooters to take careful aim with their muskets. As the lanongs swept alongside the large vessel, raking the deck of the merchant ship with well-directed musket fire, iron grappling hooks and long bamboo forked poles were thrown across and embedded. As the prey tried in vain to sail away, grappling hooks and poles drew it against the side of the attacking lanong. Finally, exhausted after several hours of running battle, the merchant crew faced the vanguard of Iranun warriors that poured across boarding bridges brandishing kris, kampilan and lance. In hand to hand close fighting members of the merchant crew were overpowered and killed swiftly with a blow of the kampilan or the thrust of a lance. The ship was now stopped and more Iranun warriors nimbly leapt on board to kill the gunners. Then other members of the vanguard jumped from the rigging to the poop deck to cut down the first mate and captain so the chain of command and discipline collapsed. As more raiders boarded the merchant vessel, shinnying up bamboo poles or throwing over boarding bridges, they raised a tremendous din, shouting and screaming at the top of their lungs in a terrifying trance-like state. The high-pitched wailing sound in the midst of the engagement often filled ill-disciplined, poorly-trained and paid merchant crews with such terror that they were unable to defend either themselves or the vessel.[8] In such desperate life-and-death situations everything depended on the valor, conduct and intelligence of the crew and the skipper. However, in many instances the unnerved crew surrendered out of fear and surprise, choosing the path of least resistance. As an 'Illanoon' squadron approached a trading sampan off the Patani coast in 1838, the slave raiders threatened some of the beleaguered ill-armed crew with guns, others with lances, and they surrendered without a struggle. Some of the captured crew were so terrified on seeing the raiders approach with their Iban complement that they leapt into the sea, and it was all the nakodah could do to restrain himself and others from following their example. The skipper begged the raiders for mercy, and the 'Illanoon' did not harm them, but tied their arms and put them in the hold down under the bow of the garay. They confiscated the vessel's cargo of rice, the nakodah's property (consisting of several articles of silk and cotton clothing) and the sampan which belonged to him. She was then set adrift by the raiders, an ominous sign for anybody else planning to go to sea in sailing ships in that locality.[9]

The Iranun spread despair throughout the eastern archipelago among owners of merchant vessels. In the straits of Salayer and elsewhere, 70, 80 or even more prahus were often seen attacking convoys of more than 20 well-armed Bugis *paduakens*, invading Salayer and devastating entire coastal provinces on Buton.[10] The Iranun prahus, with a lighter build and rigging could, either in calm weather or with the wind, set more hands to the oars, and thereby attack more swiftly and readily escape pursuit. The necessity of constantly employing cruisers to protect the archipelago's coasts and sealanes to prevent vessels being carried off was highlighted by the number of attacks on merchant sailing ships in the straits of Banka in 1829. In May, a prahu-sloop, coming from Sumanap, and carrying 15 men, was sunk by the Iranun, above Billiton. Between Muntok and Jebus another merchant vessel also became their prey, while a large Iranun galley, with double banks of oars, well-armed and carrying 150 men gave chase to a sloop coming from Singapore, which, however, managed to escape by taking refuge at Banka. In October, 4 lanongs were reported cruising near Gusung Assam, and 15 more large vessels, of a similar character, had, it was said, gone up the Banju Assim River, off Palembang, from which place they set out to devastate the coasts of Banka. Toward the end of that month, a large *paduaken*, coming from Makassar, fell in with two lanongs in the straits of Banka; half of her crew were already disabled when she was rescued by the Dutch schooner of war *Zephyr*.[11] Just under four decades later, Alfred Wallace, the great Victorian naturalist and little known codiscoverer of the theory of evolution, mentioned, in *The Malay Archipelago*, his own highly readable account of the nine years of biological exploration he carried out during the middle of the nineteenth century, a similar harrowing incident. In a traditional sailing boat constructed for him by a master boatwright on the tiny island of Kei in the Moluccas, Wallace meandered around the Spice Islands—the Bandas, Sulawesi, Ceram, the Aruls, and Irian Jaya. During this time he was nearly killed by the Balangingi and, in 1858, narrowly escaped from an attack by 'Sulu pirates' off the Arul islands, southwest of New Guinea. He recalled how, when not struggling with one of his numerous bouts of malarial fever or pondering the problems of evolution, it was graphically brought home to him that only the 'fittest would survive' as his fast sailing prahu was chased on several occasions by Balangingi squadrons slave hunting in the area.[12]

Although the Iranun and Samal occasionally kept prize vessels to augment their fleets, they seldom lumbered themselves with anything from the cargo of a prize, except rice or gold dust or other extremely precious commodities. The seizing and sale of captives was the principal purpose of Iranun and Balangingi cruises and once a vessel was ransacked it was often set ablaze or left to drift without sail or rudder as a ghost ship. The sighting of such a derelict by a passing merchant ship served notice that the Iranun had journeyed that way, unsettling even the most disciplined crew.

Squadrons of Iranun and Balangingi would lurk at key points along the major trading routes where regions of calm or light winds occurred. These regions of variable winds, situated between the prevailing monsoon systems, often brought calm or light sea breezes and were avoided at all cost by trading ships. At certain times of the year slave raiders waited patiently for larger European merchant men and big trading prahus to get becalmed in these still spots, and then they descended upon them like locusts in multiple squadrons of eight to ten oar-powered lanong or garay. In the period under consideration hundreds, if not thousands, of ships were wrecked in Southeast Asia's busy sea lanes, which lay in the middle of the bustling shipping route that stretched from Europe through India to China. Many crashed on groups of submerged rocks; others fell victim to the Iranun's sea wars or to rough seas and heavy gales. Off the coasts of Borneo, Malacca, Sumatra, Java and Sulawesi, trading vessels, because of stressful weather or other accidental circumstance, were becalmed, stranded or driven ashore on reefs and sandbanks. At these times they could not long remain without being visited by plundering bands of Iranun and Samal, who rowed out in swift prahus from secluded bays, creeks and rivers. Until the pacification and annexation of the outer islands of the Indonesian archipelago by the Dutch in the first part of this century, it had been the *adat* of Southeast Asian, Muslim seafaring groups–Iranun, Samal, Bugis, Makassarese, and Mandar–that any vessel that stranded or wrecked on a reef or close to shore could be legally plundered. Their customary point of view was that if such a mishap took place it was a gift or reward from the sea itself. It was also a deliverance of material wealth and a blessing to a people who dutifully prayed to Allah. The Secretary of Lloyd's Returns or list of British vessels that had, throughout the first half of the nineteenth century, either been captured, attacked or plundered by the Iranun and Balangingi, is replete with the names of ships that sailed from Manila, Batavia, Semarang, and from Canton to London, Liverpool, Sydney or elsewhere, and were never seen or heard of again. The entry of 19 March 1841 from Macao reads "a sharp-built vessel, of about 400 tons, newly coppered, with P.M. on the stern, and burned to the water's edge, was passed in the Palawan passage."[13] In 1845, ships that met a similar fate included the *Wetherall* and *Gulnare* that were last sighted passing through the Sunda Strait. The American brigs *Logan* and *Hannah* that sailed from Manila were also boarded and plundered by the Balangingi.[14] The crews of such ill-fated vessels–missing, stranded or becalmed–were rarely heard of again. They were killed, drowned or sold as slaves at Sulu and other markets by the Iranun and Balangingi. St. John recalls the case of the *Fiery Cross* which was shipwrecked on the coast of north Borneo. The Balangingi searched reefs far and wide in vain in order to share in the wealth and spoils, which in this case was not forthcoming because they were unable to locate the wreck.[15]

But in many other recorded instances of shipwreck and stranding the Balangingi and their Iranun brethren were far more successful. When, in May 1837, the Dutch launch *William I* was stranded on the rocks of Lucipara in the Timor Sea it was attacked by several Iranun prahus and plundered of most of its possessions. The crew were "ill-treated and made prisoners."[16] Seven years later, in June 1844, the crew of the English barque, *Premier*, bound for the island of Bali from Hong Kong, suffered a similar fate. The stranded sailors were made prisoners of the sultans of Berau and Bulungun after their ship was wrecked on Pulau Panjang. The former ruler looted the stranded vessel and divided the crew between himself and the rajah of Bulungun. The sultan of Gunung Tabor at Berau intended to sell the European members of the crew to the Segai, predatory swidden agriculturalists living in the central dividing range of Borneo. Capt. Edward Belcher, while in Manila, received a letter from one Captain 'Brownrigg' claiming that the British barque, *Premier*, and its crew had been taken by the Iranun after they became wrecked off the east coast of Borneo. Upon interviewing some lascars who had been bought by Wyndham, the British merchant-adventurer based at Jolo, the naval commander received further information of the events. The lascars had given Brownrigg's letter to Wyndham, who then conveyed it to the British consul. Interestingly, the lascars knew Brownrigg, their captain, as Milne. Belcher set out from Manila to assist Brownrigg and on arrival at Gunung Tabor, Berau, was greeted with 'genuine cordiality' and much formality. The astute sultan had kept a detailed journal of the events surrounding the stay of the *Premier's* crew in his region. (The sultan also knew Brownrigg as Milne.) He showed Belcher that the crew had been freed and taken away by the Dutch schooner of war, *Egmond* two months earlier. Evidently, Milne had been difficult and disagreeable and displayed no interest in the fate of the lascars who were part of his crew. With Captain Belcher's assistance, Milne also managed to reclaim all the goods looted from his ship– although the sultan's people managed to retain a few odd possessions which they had 'salvaged.' Belcher proceeded to draw up a treaty of friendship and commerce with the sultan of Gunung Tabor and then sailed to Bulungan where he recovered the 12 remaining lascars.[17] Four years later, on 8 December 1848, Captain Keppel, who was making a career for himself hunting Iranun, found the stranded wreck of the *Minerva* on the northwest coast of Borneo. He was, however, too late to assist the crew, who had just been carried off by Iranun, to be sold on the opposite coast. The vessel had been gutted and all the copper and iron bolts and brass fittings removed. As the wreck smouldered behind them, the frustrated naval captain, with James Brooke by his side, could see the Iranun prahus in the distance, making off with captives and plunder.[18]

The bigger sailing ships of Holland, England and the United States were conspicuously present in documents, journals and newspaper accounts describing Iranun attacks and warfare at sea from the late 1780s to the mid-1860s. None of these nations' vessels, crews, cargoes, or passengers were safe from the depredations of the marauders of Illana Bay, Tempasuk, Reteh, and Tontoli. Not even the heavily-armed English East India Men bound for China, who had negotiated treaties of friendship and commerce with the sultanates of Sulu and Mindanao and the gun running American whalers, were necessarily immune from the marauders' calculated attacks in the open waters of Southeast Asia,. Ironically, at the end of the eighteenth century, the British relied on the Iranun to harry and destroy the shipping of their Dutch competitors, but they also were not always able to secure immunity from attack by their sinister ally. The sea journey east and south, from India to China, or west to east, across the Pacific Ocean via the straits and waters of Southeast Asia was a terrifying prospect for many early nineteenth century seafarers and passengers. The expectation of enslavement or death on the high sea at the hands of the Iranun sent terror into the minds of many a crew bound for China. The voyage itself was imaginatively rather like a trip into interstellar space today. It was a dangerous journey on a medium to small scale sailing vessel into uncharted waters for three to five months or more; a stressful passage through still unmapped rocks, shoals and reef-strewn seas to trade with states dotted across the archipelago and China. For some seafarers there was no prospect of return. The fear engendered by such a harrowing passage is evident in the journals and logbooks of captains like John Meares who made a voyage from China to the northwest coast of America in the years 1788 and 1789. He knew his vessel might not be spared while passing through the Visayas:

> We took the opportunity of favourable weather we now enjoyed to put the ship in a state of defense. The guns were accordingly mounted, a sufficient quantity of powder and ammunition was fitted, and every other necessary preparation made, as those seas are infested with numerous bands of pirates. Two very fine ships had lately been taken by them. One of them was the *May*, of 300 tons, and mounting twenty guns, and had been on a trading voyage from Bengal to the coast of Borneo . . . the proas of Magindunao and Sooloo issue forth in such swarms, that it becomes dangerous for a weak ship to sail those seas. These proas are manned with a hundred, and sometimes a hundred and fifty men, well armed, and generally mounting pieces of cannon of 6 or 12 pounders. . . . These people cruise in fleets of 30 or 40 . . . proas . . . and though we did not very much apprehend that they would venture to attack two ships, it would have been unpardonable negligence if we had not prepared ourselves. . . .[19]

The journal kept by William Haswell of his voyage on the Salem barque, *Lydia*, under Moses Barnard, reveals the extent of the pessimism on board as they worked their way southward from Manila to Zamboanga. Entering the Visayan Sea the crew began to make boarding nettings, and to get their arms in the best order. But Haswell, in his entry of 22 October 1801, held out little hope for the barque, if attacked by the Iranun:

> . . . had we been attacked we should have been taken with ease, they are so numerous in their prows, and we but eleven in number exclusive of our passengers: total on board–viz the captain, two officers, cook, steward and six men before the mast: passengers, the Governor of the Marianna Islands, his lady, three children and two servant girls and twelve men servants, a fryar and his servant, a judge and two servants: total twenty four and . . . to my certain knowledge they would not have fought had we been attacked.[20]

Three days later the suddenly becalmed passengers aboard the *Lydia* feared for their lives as night set upon them. The young Yankee sailor wrote of the terror of the Spanish entourage:

> We were often becalmed close to land, and all our passengers in the greatest consternation for fear of being taken and put to death in the dark and not have time to say their prayers, but to our great satisfaction we saw the lookout fort of Sambongue and . . . the next morning was abreast of the town.[21]

Haswell soon learned that the *presidio* was a poor place to get a ship supplied. In the words of the Spanish governor's wife, there were "plenty of coconuts, water and girls but nothing else."[22]

The marvellously detailed journal kept by Mrs. Alonzo Follansbee, a passenger on board the 400-ton *Logan* (one of the largest ships built at that time), of a voyage from Boston to Canton in 1837-1838 describes her quarters which doubled as the ship's armory. When the young bride arrived on board the vessel, she found the captain, her husband, had a large room nicely fitted up for her with white drapery curtains, a bureau, washstand across one corner, chairs and Brussel carpets. However, the space had formerly been used as a storeroom and one side of it was lined with a formidable array of muskets, pistols, sabres, cutlasses, and boarding pikes. In a closet, under the stairs, the door of which opened out of her room, large canisters of ammunition were stored. At first sight of her otherwise comfortable quarters, Mrs. Follansbee was horror-struck and . . .

> . . . could compare it to nothing else than one of Bluebeard's secret chambers. The captain soon convinced me that it was the only convenient place on board for them, and that they were necessary articles in those piratical times, and that no ship was safe without being well-armed, in case of emergency. And besides these we had two cannons, and two swivels aboard.[23]

All the way out from the Atlantic Ocean to the Sunda Strait, Mrs. Follansbee had practised loading and firing muskets and pistols at targets so that in case of an emergency she could defend herself. But her young energetic husband, in whom the owners of the *Logan* had placed great confidence, said her practice would be "of little use, if pirates got on board the ship, and that my fate would be worse than death, and it worried him more than anything else."[24]

In the early hours of the morning, three days before December of 1805, John Carlton, master of the *Putnam*, standing on a patch of mosquito-ridden swamp and beach in Southeast Sumatra, witnessed in dismay the loss of his ship. For Carlton, Iranun homicide had become a real-life horror story. The motive, the Yankee skipper said, was the same as for numerous other attacks he had heard about in the bazaars in Batavia–pepper and prizes. But in one way, Carlton's loss was unlike the others. His was the first case where the Iranun had captured a Salem ship and cargo and got away with it. Between 1799 and 1846 ships and merchants from Salem, Massachusetts, carried on an almost exclusive trade in pepper on the coasts of Sumatra. The barter trade opened between America and the Malay coastal states of Sumatra during the volatile times following the Revolutionary war. The first cargo of the valuable pepper, sometimes referred to as 'black gold,' arrived at Salem from the Sumatra coast on 15 October 1799, in the schooner, *Rajah*. However, the enormous profits that the Salem pepper trade made in the various ports of the Mediterranean and the Baltic, and the fate of her pepper ships, were challenged by the Iranun during that half century period–most particularly along the unchartered, east coast of Sumatra between the years 1800 and 1832.[25] Hence, it was not uncommon at this time, in this trade, for Salem vessels to cruise in company along the coast of Sumatra, offering mutual protection against attacks by these feared marauders.

In late December 1805 one pepper ship did not come into Salem that year. Nathaniel Bowditch had previously made a successful voyage in command of the *Putnam* and was a part owner of her on her subsequent voyage when she was actually captured. Several of the crew were killed by the Iranun and the vessel was never recovered.[26] Most Salem vessels sailed directly to the northwest coast of Sumatra and then explored along the south coast in search of a cargo. If, however, the season was nearly over or the harvest had been poor, these intrepid mariners who were engaged in the pepper trade would drop down to the straits of Sunda, pass through and cruise up the east coast of Sumatra via the Banka Strait in search of pepper that might be obtained in the low, swampy deltas of the large rivers. That was what the *Putnam* did and what Captain White was to do 14 years later when Iranun fleets, like that which attacked the ship *Putnam* in November 1805, cruised the Banka Strait. An account of the *Putnam's* capture, by Iranun off Bintan Island on 18 November 1805, is contained in a series of hand-written copies of letters and documents kept by John Carlton, the master of the ill-fated Salem pepper trader. The *Putnam* had sailed from Batavia to Palembang where Carlton tried to procure a cargo of tin and pepper through the Dutch Governor. However, only the governor's wife, a local woman of some standing, could secure the cargo from the Malays, but she would not do it because of a domestic altercation with her husband! After six weeks at Palembang, on 15 August, Carlton agreed to sail to Bania with a Malay prince who promised to get him a cargo of tin there. After 40 days at Bania only half of the tin had been loaded. They then proceeded to Lingga Island and to Bintan Island where Carlton loaded pepper. While there, on 28 November, the *Putnam* was boarded by disguised Iranun raiders under the pretext of bartering for pepper. They proceeded to kill six crewmembers and take the ship. The remaining crewmembers escaped by boat. Carlton was on shore during the incident. The stranded captain then went to Malacca aboard the ship *Malcolm*, where he filed a protest and "performed other things for the recovery of the wounded and provided for the well-being of the remainder of the ship's company."[27]

Another episode on the southeast coast, that again pitted the Iranun against the Salem merchants, occurred in January 1819 when Capt. John White took the brig *Franklin* out on a voyage to Cochin China to seek new lines of trade. Several days after leaving Batavia the *Franklin* was heading up the Banka Strait with vast swamplands that form the delta of the Palembang river on the port side and the beaches backed by the broken ridges of the highlands of Banka island to starboard. Ever since the 1790s, the Banka Strait had claimed the grim distinction of being the site where scores of attacks on shipping and hundreds of homicides had occurred annually, keeping it among the region's most dangerous spots even though the number of violent crimes, and notably maritime attacks and murders, was dramatically rising region wide. In this notorious spot, White sighted three large *lanongs* through his looking glass. Each had two banks of oars and on the largest vessel he counted 37 oars down one side. He estimated that the raiders had at least a 185 oars in total, which implied well over 450 in the 3 vessels. Each prahu had a heavy bulwark across the bow with the muzzle of an 18-pounder projecting through it, but either the Iranun did not have enough powder or they were afraid to use a big enough charge to make the artillery effective.[28] But White realized that in hand-to-hand fighting with spear, kampilan and kris the Iranun would be fearless and very difficult to overcome.

The Iranun galleys had a tremendous advantage in a calm or light airs because they could attack from any direction while a ship without wind lay helpless. Unfortunately, on this occasion there was hardly enough wind to keep the *Franklin* moving. With the brig drifting perilously close to the raiders the captain fired repeated broadsides from the *Franklin's* six pounders, but the Iranun maintained a menacing position just out of range of the barrage of grapeshot and canister falling near them like hail. Fortuitously, just when the Salem Captain found his locally built gun carriages giving way under the strain of battle, a breeze sprung up and he ran for the protection of the small Dutch port of Minton near the northwest corner of the island, where he reported the attack and the collapse of his artillery. Wisely, Captain White did not sail for Singapore until his battery was thoroughly overhauled and even then he only went out on a favorable wind under sail accompanied by a British brig for mutual protection.[29] It is interesting that Captain White noted that these Iranun came from the same locality in the Palembang delta region as those who had brazenly captured *Putnam* 14 years before.

The tradition of European mariners, especially the Dutch, saving the last bullet for themselves or detonating the powder magazine to avoid a horrible death at the hands of their Iranun captors was considered a necessary precaution. Herman Melville, himself, in his youth, an ordinary seaman in the Pacific basin, wrote in his classic *Moby Dick*, which appeared in 1851, of one of the most dangerous places on earth–the Malacca Straits:

> Time out of mind, the piratical proas of the Malays, lurking among the low shaded coves and islets of Sumatra, have sallied out upon the vessels sailing through the straits, fiercely demanding tribute at the point of their spears. Though by the repeated bloody chastisements they have received at the hands of European cruisers, the audacity of these corsairs has of late been somewhat repressed; yet, even at the present day, we occasionally hear of English and American vessels,

which, in those waters, have been remorselessly boarded and pillaged.[30]

Captain Ahab's whaling ship, the *Pequod*, was pursued by the Iranun while passing through the equally perilous Sunda Straits, but by wetting the sails to gain speed, he escaped them.[31] Melville's fictional account of the obsessive skipper's narrow escape was actually played out live aboard the *Logan* on 22 April 1838 when the large merchantman was temporarily becalmed in the Sunda Strait. An Iranun vessel was in sight, and fast gaining on the *Logan*, and there was not enough wind for the Yankee trader to get out of the lanong's reach. Time stood still as Alonzo Follansbee, spyglass in hand, realized that, over the course of the day, everything might change in his life forever. The journal entry of that frightening encounter, as the capricious weather became a sinister ally of the Iranun raiders, reads as follows:

> It was a fearfully anxious day for all hands. Our cannon, swivel guns and pistols were soon got in readiness. Swords, cutlasses, boarding pikes and ammunition hustled on deck, ready for them, still there seemed little chance for us, as they were gaining on us every moment, up to 5 p.m. ... They had the advantage of us in having plenty of men to row their vessel, but these were all that could be seen. At 5 p.m. they were less than a mile from us, and no wind, and we were powerless, and they fast coming upon us. Fortunately about half past five p.m. a good breeze sprang up, and we were soon out of their reach. I have never seen such an anxious time since we came so near going on to the Goodwin Sands, on the coast of England, or cause for greater thankfulness to our heavenly Father for again saving us from a worse fate.[32]

An openly declared Dutch or British engagement with Iranun raiders began with the distant ominous sound of drums beating, cymbals clashing and a cacophony of war cries and chants reaching a fever pitch, as more than a thousand men were aboard the eight to ten vessels appearing over the horizon. The brigantine or barque continued to make good speed–lying many miles off the coast of Java, Borneo or Sulawesi and running at around nine to ten knots. The weather began to worsen. The sea built in height as the sharper winds bit. Swapping the watch every half-hour, the crew remained calm and confident. It still wasn't time to worry. But by early afternoon, the captain and his mates were reassessing the situation, as the size of the advancing fleet appeared to have almost doubled. Turning back to port seemed as dangerous as heading for the haven of the southern ocean. But as the wind rose, the Iranun sails—which towered above the prevailing swells, came more often. Then came the onslaught the European mariners were dreading. Iranun boarding parties piled into salisipan and pulled for the bow and stern of the merchantman. The seafarers and deckhands were all talking to each other and helping each other as best they could. They were scared. They had to be scared but it was no panic situation. The captains of such sailing ships tried not to get involved with people who panicked. They did not need that sort of seafarer on board. The disciplined albeit fear-stricken crew on the brigantine or barque cleared the decks for action, put on as much canvas as possible and sailed for their lives. Although the armed merchantman might eventually be surrounded by oared salisipan and lanong, the high sides of the boat and heavy seas often combined to make it difficult for slave raiders to row and sail their long, narrow attack craft alongside the larger European vessel, without smacking against the hull on the prevailing swells. While the merchantman was firing broadsides to port and starboard the Iranun warriors attempted to board the ship from the bow and stern, disabling the rudder in the process.

Once on board, the raiding parties set about securing control of the ship as quickly as possible. The kampilan, in the minds of hapless European sailors, was a weapon that represented the ferocity of the Iranun warrior himself. The blade was razor sharp and resilient. In the hands of an Iranun warrior launching a boarding raid on a European ship it had only one purpose—to kill the enemy. In the confined space of the ship's deck it was an ideal weapon. The vanguard of warriors with kampilan and kris went eye to eye at the crew of a merchantman prone to fight back. They slit their throats to frighten them into submission. But crews were known to resist to the bitter end. In February 1803, for example, a sloop of war was dispatched from Ternate with a cargo of rice. She had proceeded no further than the straits of Banca when a large Iranun fleet made its appearance and after a short resistance with swivels only, (since the commander had very imprudently stowed away his guns in the hold under his cargo of rice) the sloop was captured. However, the master and his mates together with the surgeon, fought desperately on this occasion, but were all killed even before the Iranun boarded. The crew fought on with handpikes—the only weapon left for them—until overpowered by the multitudes that rushed on board the vessel. They all fell victim to the slavers who carried the ship off in triumph.[33] Other crews confronted with the same situation either deliberately set their vessels alight scuttling them or blowing them up causing a rain of shattered timbers and mangled corpses when the ship's powder magazine was detonated as a last defiant gesture of resistance. The Dutch in particular were prone to take such drastic measures. Thomas Forrest, in the process of explaining how he came to be in the possession of several Malay sermons printed in Roman characters, described, albeit briefly, one such furious battle that took place in early 1776 off the coast of Sulawesi between a Dutch sloop and several lanongs:

> They [the sermons] were got with other plunder on board the Dutch sloop that was burnt, when attacked by Malfalla's Mangaio prow, as mentioned in the journal. The crew having fired her, took to their boat, while some bold Mindanao men jumped on board and saved many things; among the rest, two Dutch brass swivel guns, two pounders.[34]

In a memorable incident, 30 years later, a merchant ship, belonging to Phefferkorn and Wensing—2 Dutchmen who were residents of Sumanap from the island of Madura—were attacked by 40 Iranun prahus in the straits of Banka. The Dutchmen on board the vessel, realizing there was no chance to resist or escape, permitted the Iranun to board in great numbers and then blew her up, killing every soul on board. Such was the fear that the Iranun had created in European minds, that suicide was preferable to falling into their hands. One M. von Brankhorst, then an official at Sumanap, had a monument erected to commemorate the memory of such an intrepid act.[35]

The same ill fortune was the experience of small government and privately owned sloops, ketches and brigs in the first half of the nineteenth century. From the waters of the Philippines to Bali—and beyond—vessel after vessel was taken. In 1836, the year that George King moved his trading operation from Kuta to Ampenan and sought the protection of the raja of Mataram, he expanded his fleet of the barque, *Pleidus*, and two smaller vessels, the schooners *Ladjoe* and *Monkey*, which all flew the Dutch flag, buying a third schooner, the *Maria Fredericka*.[36] The following year, when the new schooner, commanded by Capt. Andrew Gregory, was lying becalmed off Ampenan on the west coast of Lombok, two Iranun prahus attacked in flank approaching on the pretext of obtaining some provisions. It was cleverly done. The captain lay ill in his cabin, and one of the crew, whom he had recently disciplined, bore a grudge against him and encouraged the Iranun to come aboard. Immediately, more than 40 of the vanguard from both prahus swarmed over the side onto the schooner's deck and, in a matter of minutes, forced the compliant crew below, seized the bewildered captain and mate, and then steered the vessel to Tungku, their base on the northeast coast of Borneo.[37] In June 1838, a similar fate befell the Dutch cutter *Petronella*, with a cargo of merchandise valued at 6,000 guilders, on an island huckstering round from Kema to Gorontalo. The captain, C.Z. Pieters, penned a graphic account of a journey that suddenly became a desperate fight for survival when he faced the 'savagery' of the Balangingi deep in the heart of the Celebes Sea. He first realized something was amiss on the evening of 14 June about nine o'clock on the eighth day of his voyage to Gorontalo, when he observed the shape of a prahu on the starboard quarter. Pieters hailed her three times, asking from where she came. When he repeated the inquiry a fourth time the garay was so close upon the *Petronella* that he could plainly see that the vessel was a Balangingi raider in full pursuit of him. Shortly afterwards the Balangingi fired upon the cutter with a four-pounder and at the same time hoisted a light as a signal to other prahus which immediately replied in the same manner. Pieters realized from the lights winking in the dark that there appeared to be ten prahus in his vicinity. All these vessels now collected in his wake and followed the ill-fated cutter from the late evening till morning. On the dawn of the 15 June the Balangingi prahus, numbering ten in all, five large ones and five small, ranged close up and a life and death engagement ensued which lasted till ten o'clock. One of the *Petronella*'s crew was killed by a cannon ball and the sailor who generally served the long gun also lost his life to a Balangingi marksman. Two of Pieters' rowers were also so severely wounded that they were rendered incapable of pulling an oar. Two or three times the Balangingi tried to board his vessel, but Pieters succeeded in keeping them off until he was so badly wounded in the left arm that he was no longer able to defend himself. The defiant captain then described what happened when he received another wound, in the chest, which prevented him from keeping his place on the stern of the ship:

> When I found that I could no longer fight, I threw the weapons which were within my reach into the sea and had the keg of gunpowder placed beside me with the full determination to blow us all up rather than fall into the hands of the pirates. The pirates, armed with spears or tridents, then climbed into my prahu, and one of their leaders approached me with his drawn sword and ordered me to surrender. When he observed that I was covered with blood from my wounds, he sheathed his sword, but seized me so tightly by the throat that I could scarcely breathe. . . . What further occurred I know not as I fainted from the pain . . . when I came again to my senses I found that I was stripped naked and bound in a prahu, and that all my clothes and the goods which I had in my boat were plundered.[38]

Two years later, the *Mary*, a fishing vessel under the command of Captain Blosse, which had also been taken by the Iranun near Lombok, arrived at Timor. The crew recovered their liberty only by paying a heavy ransom. Captain Blosse stated that the Iranun in whose hands he had been prisoner had also captured three American fishing vessels and had taken them to Sulu. To the best of his knowledge, the crews of these vessels continued to remain prisoners. When the French vessels, *Astrolobe* and *Zelee* arrived at Jolo in 1839 during their voyage of discovery, the Tausog, thinking that they were Dutch vessels seeking vengeance for the earlier capture of the *Maria Fredericka* while she was riding at anchor in the roadstead, prepared to make a vigorous defense—which proved unnecessary on that occasion.[39]

Experience proved the Iranun and Balangingi were extremely quick to discern and instantly avoid any large vessel of European appearance. They tried to steer clear of direct confrontation with European warships, particularly three masted frigates and fast sailing brigantines. The Iranun had quickly learned to distinguish between heavily-armed and well-manned warships and merchantmen, by the colors of their hulls and canvas, giving the former a wide berth–men-of-war were generally painted black while merchant vessels were often painted brown-grey.[40] Unless becalmed, stranded or deceived by stratagem, a well-armed and manned European warship usually had the advantage in terms of firepower and devastating gunnery as long as the Iranun could be prevented from boarding the vessel. Once on deck, however, the Iranun relied on martial skill, courage and overwhelming numbers to seize such a rare prize by force.

William Wyndham, before he permanently settled in Jolo to supply the sultan and key datus with munitions, opium and textiles, had, in the 1830s, sailed as a mate on a Spanish brig trading between Manila and the Moluccas. The merchant adventurer reported a narrow escape from the Iranun that he had experienced while sailing on the Spanish vessel. When navigating near Wette in the Timor Sea the lookout at the masthead had spotted a number of large prahus. The lookout frantically sung out, 'A prahu in sight . . . two . . . three . . . four. I cannot count them, sir!' From the crow's nest with his glass, Wyndham shortly made out no less than 38 vessels. There was only a light breeze blowing, and no chance of running before them; nor was there much hope of defending the ship, as most of the crew were sick. Wyndham and the captain then decided to risk all by dressing in Wyndham's old British uniforms from his Royal Navy days and masquerade as British naval officers. Bluffing, they decided to gamble on a high-risk approach and bore down between the lead Iranun prahus. Striding confidently up and down the poop, Wyndham could see the two largest lanongs were the size of the brig herself, their guns were on deck but carefully concealed with mats. The few Iranun crew on deck were also cunningly disguised as traders. In this desperate cat-and-mouse game, hoping to deceive the Iranun squadron as they drew abreast, Wyndham, put on a brave face, and began questioning the slave raiders, who declared they were merchant traders. Trying to convince them that the brig was a warship, he claimed that they were hunting an Iranun fleet: "We have heard of some pirates down here, and are come to look for them." The Iranun feigned ignorance claiming that they had seen none and offered to accompany the brig to Makassar for protection. A breeze sprang up; the beleaguered brig made headway and by nightfall was clear of the fleet. During the night, however, the wind had all but disappeared, and the brig was becalmed. As dawn broke Wyndham and the captain nervously wondered whether their stratagem had succeeded in outwitting the Iranun. Years later he recounted how they felt as he heard the man on lookout duty shout that the Iranun were out of sight, "In the morning the traders were no longer near, they could be seen in the distance pulling away as hard as they could. The ruse had succeeded, and they all felt more comfortable, for they could not have defended their vessel ten minutes."[41]

To provide an example of the extent of the damage the Balangingi had caused to commerce year after year, Wyndham, some 15 years after his hair-raising escape, cited the fate of the English whaler *Sarah and Elizabeth* to St. John when he visited Jolo. Here ecological factors are clearly important: the deep waters and narrow channels of the Timor Straits area caused whales to concentrate and come in close to shore. Hence, the Timor Sea was an important operational area for European and American whalers entering from either the Indian or Pacific Oceans. In November 1818, Rose Freycinet, disguised in men's clothing, was smuggled on board the corvette *Uranie*. While becalmed for 24 days in the narrow straits of Ombai, she experienced at first hand '. . . the devilish waters where we had been as it were enclosed in an oven,' as well as the occasional companionship of English whalers, also contending with difficulties of all kinds. She and her husband, the captain, welcomed their gossip of whales and whaling. The whalers over dinner on board the *Uranie* also talked to them about the Iranun and of their own experiences cruising on the Timor Sea and in the fishing grounds of Sulawesi. Wyndham, Melville and others showed conclusively that both the Iranun and Balangingi with a rather different 'hunting' culture born from the sea, were able to prove their daring and skill, stalking the Anglo-American whalers in the 1830s and 1840s in an area where whales frequently surfaced.

In 1843, the whaler, *Sarah and Elizabeth*, was anchored in a bay near Kupang off the island of Timor. The captain, needing wood and water, sent three boats ashore, with the second and third mates and 14 men, armed only with axes. Significantly Captain Bellinghurst had refused them firearms. It proved a fatal error of judgement on his part but he barely had time to rue the decision. Five Balangingi prahus followed by some salisipan suddenly appeared in the entrance to the bay. The raiders witnessed the whaler's landing party stranded on the beach and quickly landed some of their warriors and captured the men. The captain of the *Sarah and Elizabeth* had watched the events unfold from the deck of his ship in disbelief and dismay. The garay began to close in on the anchored whaler under oar and sail and Captain Bellinghurst broke out the muskets but no cartridges could be found. Panic then ensued and the rest of the crew pulled away in the two remaining whaleboats leaving the majestic vessel to her fate. The captain, in his fear and haste to desert the ship, accidentally left his personal pocket watch behind. When the Balangingi stepped onto the deck of the whaler there was total silence, except for the whimpering of the Captain's dog, which Bellinghurst had unceremoniously abandoned. It was the only living thing on board. Two other whaling ships being in company at a distance, sent rescue boats from all directions towards the *Sarah and Elizabeth* about 16 miles away. But, according to the captivity narrative of the rescued third mate, Ebenezer Edwards, she was observed to be on fire fuelled by the barrels of whale oil in her hold. As her sister ships came within sight of the *Sarah and Elizabeth* she blew up and sank. As it happened, when St. John had visited Wyndham at Jolo, the captain's watch was in Datu Daniel's possession.[42]

The need to replenish the supply of stores and provisions in the course of a long trading voyage exposed many European vessels to the risk of being boarded and destroyed by the Iranun. Forrest warned his readers and would-be traders both of the ruse and of the often dangerous circumstances surrounding the provisioning of large merchant vessels in the eastern archipelago. He detailed aspects of the alarming history of the 'trading' stratagem:

> In a large vessel, I must have carried with me a stock of provisions, which the settlement we fitted out from, could not well afford; besides, when at places that afforded provisions, in a vessel of any size at anchor, I must have sent ashore my boat, which would have been liable to insult. I have known many such things befall ships' boats in Malay countries, where designing people, by a show of

civility, entice the crew or commanding officer to be off their guard. Commodore Watson, in the *Revenge*, lost his boat going through some straits, by the island of Salwatty. Many voyages have failed, many trading country vessels have been cut off, and some wrecked from unexpected accidents of this kind.[43]

During the English administration of 1811-1816 the coast of Java was 'ever infested' with Iranun raiders. There were constant reports of such approaches and attacks on large British sailing vessels, including the *Wellington*, *Modest*, *Coromandel*, *Matilda*, *Helen*, and *Nautilus*.[44] Since provisions and cargoes could not always be furnished at Jolo, country traders had to be prepared to risk accompanying Tausog datus and their Iranun followers to their districts in other parts of the Sulu archipelago. In 1821, Lt. William Spiers, an officer of the Royal Navy on leave of absence, conducted a trading voyage in the *Seaflower* from Bengal to Sulu. On 2 August, several weeks after his arrival at Jolo, he left, for the Tawi-Tawi group with one of the datus 'for a large quantity of eastern produce [tortoise shell, pearl shell, wax, and brass guns] which he said he had collected at the islands of which he was rajah.'[45] During the ten days the vessel was at Jolo, Lieutenant Spiers formed the opinion that the atmosphere was relaxed and calm. He was repeatedly told by Tausog that his "countrymen who had visited that place, had in every instance behaved with the strictest good faith in all their dealings there."[46] When Spiers left for Tawi-Tawi to procure a cargo that he had contracted for with a datu in Jolo, and which was to be paid for by him upon delivery in the islands, he was anxious about his possible reception there. Sultan Ali ud-Din allayed his fear and provided him with a letter addressed to his subjects, which directed them to "treat us as friends wherever we went and render us all the assistance in their power if we stood in need of it."[47] The datu who accompanied the vessel remained on board the *Seaflower* for nearly two weeks, and Spiers developed considerable confidence in him. Ten days after leaving Jolo, the country trader reached the environs of Tawi-Tawi. The Datu Molok arrived from Jolo shortly afterwards with several large Iranun prahus. The *Seaflower* was anchored near Buna-Buna, where brass cannon and other cargo were being brought to the vessel. Spiers then described what ensued when the Tausog and Iranun boarded the ship under the ruse of 'trading':

> Datto Mollok the Raja Bander of Sooloo . . . was most lavish in his protestation of friendship embracing me. . . . He even called for the Sultan's letter and shewd it all around. He purchased a number of articles, etc. and drank at my table in the most friendly way; all appeared to be best of friends; our people had just sat down to dinner when at a signal by Datto Mollok, those on board drew their cresses, those alongside jumped on board . . . after a short but very desperate conflict, it pleased the almighty God to give us victory, . . . their loss could not have been less than 40 to 50 killed among whom was the Datto Mollok. . . .[48]

Four of the crew were killed and several wounded. The captain, Lieutenant Spiers, received 12 wounds, and lost the use of his right arm. The *Seaflower* although a small vessel of 16 guns, was fitted out and crewed by 60 sailors, chiefly Europeans, and the captain, an officer of the Royal Navy.

Three decades later, in 1851, it was the same trading ruse, signifying their audacity and power, that was more skillfully employed by the Iranun to end the career of Captain Burns, the grandson of Robert Burns, on the northeast coast of Borneo. Under the guise of peaceful traders, Iranun came on board Burn's ship, the *Dolphin*. They quickly killed Burns, who had a terrible reputation for ill-treatment of local women, for greed, and for insulting people of all nationalities and statuses. The Iranun who cut off the *Dolphin* near the western end of Marudu Bay went on board the schooner ostensibly to trade camphor and other goods, including turtle shell and pearls. With a kris hidden in a mat, and while pretending to hand the mat to Mr. Burns, Memaden, an Iranun, thrust the weapon through him. The Iranun then killed three sailors and Burn's *njai* or mistress. Kreemon, one of the *Dolphin*'s crew, gave a graphic account of what happened when, at seven o'clock in the morning, the Iranun came aboard from their *prahus* to 'do business.'

> Eight or nine men came on board, armed as before, when suddenly the Captain ran forward; he had a wound on his face, and bleeding;

at this time we were all working forward, so that I, and I believe others, did not see the commencement of the amuck: the Captain called out, 'Jangan lawan, jangan lawan, lagee'; he ran out on the jib-boom, three or four of the pirates, followed him, and I saw him no more. On this the pirates turned to attack us, when we all jumped overboard; one juru moodee was murdered on the deck; he had run to the place where the lascars slept. Mr. Burn's servant was killed near the foremast; one lascar was killed in the water, with a spear; at this time we were swimming about, when the pirates called us up: 'Marcela atas keeta trabulee bunee lagee keeta man burlayer'; on this we came on board. As we came up they tied each of our hands; they said to each of us; 'Will you sail the ship and live, or refuse and die?' They held aloft their *Krisses* till we answered; we said we wished to live; the anchor was then weighed and the vessel got under weigh. The pirates said, 'These dead bodies throw overboard'; we lifted Mr. Burns; he had one wound across the forehead, one on the neck, one on the side; he must have been struck from behind, as all the wounds were on the right side; we threw the corpse overboard; the Captain's woman (Nar) had one wound on the right side of the neck; we found her body in the cabin; we threw over four corpses . . . we then sailed away.[49]

The Iranun also threw overboard nearly all the clothes, books and papers they came across. Memaden then ordered the surviving crew to sail the schooner to Tunku. On the way south, they anchored at Bengaya in Labuk Bay where the local river lord, Serif Yassin, became suspicious of their motives. Yassin recognized the ship as Burns' and, fearing possible reprisal from the British, seized the schooner and those on board. Memadan managed to escape to the forest with two of Burn's sailors—a Portuguese and a Javanese. But, on the beach at Labuk, two Iranun warriors were held down and unceremoniously beheaded by Yassin for killing the crewmembers of a ship flying British colors. Their heads were preserved and taken as trophies to the British naval station at Labuan as proof of the assistance rendered by Yassin against the Iranun raiders based at Tunku.[50]

On the coast of north Borneo, another Scotsman with a very different reputation did manage to survive the trading ruse, escaping an

Iranun squadron and the severe punishment that was meted out to many European masters. Capt. John Dill Ross, a successful and respected trader, was considered by the coastal populace of northeast Borneo as "first in the earthly classifications of powers, followed by Captain Alejo [Spain] second, and the Sultan of Sulu."[51] The carrying trade between Singapore and Labuan was dominated by Captain Ross. Arriving at the settlement of Labuan in 1860 as the master and part owner of a small, heavily-mortgaged schooner, *Wild Irish Girl*, Ross began to carry the mail, Tausog and Chinese passengers and their cargoes between Labuan and Singapore.[52] Through industry, seamanship and the support of the Labuan traders, he built up commerce and firmly established the Sulu Sultanate's vital trade link with Singapore via Labuan. His voyages were especially important to the Tausog because, shipping from Singapore to Sulu declined somewhat after Wyndham's death in 1856, and Makassar had been declared a free port.[53] Ross, whose seafaring ability and courage as a master earned the respect of Tausog nakodahs, made an average of seven voyages a year between Singapore and the Borneo coast freighting arms and opium.[54] As Sulu's trade with Labuan grew, his circumstances improved. He managed to save enough money to purchase the schooner outright and then replace it with a brig, *Lizzie Webber*. Subsequently he replaced this brig with a barque; he built a number of brick shops at Labuan and lent money, a few hundred dollars at a time at high rates of interest, to the Chinese merchants in the settlement.

On his last run in 1863 on his second vessel the *Lizzie Webber*, a fine brig with a battery of 6 12-pounders, he came across trouble when leaving Labuan and heading towards the Brunei coast. While at Labuan, Ross had confidently allowed local traders aboard. One was a man called Si Rahman. He traded nothing, but appeared very interested in the cargo of money and arms on board. Ross' chief Malay officer, Kassim, was suspicious and eventually discovered that Si Rahman was an Iranun lord. The next day, after leaving Labuan, Ross noticed an Iranun squadron of eight vessels had settled in his wake, chasing the *Lizzie Webber*. The brig had little choice but to heave to and fight as the wind began to subside. Si Rahman, poised on a raised platform and dressed in scarlet, led the maritime raiders. He stated that all he wanted to do was to trade for some tobacco, but Ross refused him permission to board. Kassim then fired on Si Rahman and so the desperate battle began. The *Lizzie Webber's* decks were cleared for action, muskets and cutlasses issued, the guns rolled out, and loaded with canister and shot, while Si Rahman boldly exhorted his followers from the fighting platform of the lanong. He claimed to be invulnerable and indeed many shots aimed at him appeared to miss altogether. As time passed without a quick resolution to the conflict, Ross was at a clear disadvantage with wounded crew and a dwindling supply of ammunition. He resorted to using bags of straits dollars as shot, while his disciplined seamen fought courageously against the Iranun barely managing to hold them at bay. After three hours the Iranun broke off the engagement and seemed to pull away, but only to return on the starboard side of the *Lizzie Webber*. It was then that Ross thought he was finished, but, at very close range and with a single carefully aimed canister of shot from one of the 12-pounders, the captain himself killed Si Rahman and the vanguard of a boarding party. It was the decisive moment–the turning point in the sea battle. Si Rahman's sudden death shocked the remaining Iranun crews and the squadron withdrew. However, later in the afternoon they returned with revenge on their minds. The battle recommenced but this time Ross was far more successful. He destroyed several Iranun vessels with a continuous discharge of his cannons and he rammed several others before sailing away. Fortunately, the wind had returned.[55]

In contrast to the battles on the high seas, much of the inshore raiding against coastal settlements was done with single masted sailing vessels that carried up to 20 men. Before a descent was made on a village or stretch of sandy beach, the large prahus were hidden in a creek among the mangrove on an uninhabited part of the coast, or alternatively they remained offshore and out of sight. The raiding canoes (salisipan, kakap, baroto) were used at dawn and dusk, with most of the crew lying concealed on the bottom of the craft, leaving only two or three men disguised as Visayan, Malay or Chinese fishers to navigate. They picked off fishers at river mouths, surprised sampans leaving for religious festivals in neighboring villages, and rushed ashore to carry off unsuspecting individuals who may have been involved in strand procurement, salt manufacture or cutting mangrove. Tibercio Juan stated that in 1834, in less than three months, four Balangingi garay seized more than a hundred fishers and tripang gatherers from the coasts of Masbate, Panay, Negros, and Cebu.[56] In 25-feet canoes the 'people-fishers' searched for early morning strand dwellers combing the beach with their backs bent to the sea. In summer men, women and children combed the beach at low tide gathering clams, mussels and sea urchin. They also walked the tidal flats gathering limpets and barnacles and picking agar-agar. From the canoes, whoever spotted the villagers would nod his head slightly in their direction. To point was dangerous and would have alerted the victims. The canoe paddles parted the sea so quietly and quickly that the raiders were nearly on the villagers before they started. The bowman fired his pistol, fatally wounding the father with a strike in the heart or lungs. Women and children were taken in preference to men because they fetched higher prices at Sulu. Those who attempted to flee were struck down with wooden cudgels and if they resisted strenuously were killed on the spot. During the second month of Ibanez's captivity with Taupan's expedition some of the most tragic moments occurred. It was in July 1857 when the Balangingi raiders sailed the coast of Leyte, foraging for food and water. On one occasion Taupan returned, his kris covered with blood. He had just killed a local woman he had accidentally chanced upon on the beach, who had attempted to escape. Shortly afterwards, the Balangingi proceeded in the direction of the village of Guinonocan. They encountered a man, his wife and child and two other boys in a sailing boat. They killed the man swiftly and made captives of the rest.[57] This hit-and-run mode of attack that destroyed the harmony of villages and families was used to terrible advantage by the Balangingi throughout Southeast Asia. In the mid-1960s, the Balangingi storyteller, Haji Abdurahim, recounted for the anthropologist, William Geohegan, how, more than a century earlier, this systematic low level inshore raiding had worked:

> So [they] leave the day after tomorrow, early in the morning, away toward the Bisayas. When they get to the Bisayas, they make a circuit, going around like this. They make a circuit of the tidal reef flats. Now if they sight some people gathering food [in the shallow

water], they get down. When they get down [from the boat], they capture some people there. They stay there . . . [until] about three, or four at one place. [Then you know] to another place, also. So it's just like that, what they did. Just capturing people. Now when its time to return home, they might take five, ten, twenty people. When they arrive, they're taken to many places, to be sold. So then, they're made into slaves, 'servants' . . . Around a hundred years ago. Even more than a hundred, around a hundred and fifty years back.[58]

In 1838, statements were taken from the survivors of a Balangingi squadron part of which had been destroyed off the Trengganu coast. Their sinister presence had become all too apparent to the coastal Malays. Villagers kept stumbling upon decapitated bodies washed ashore. Up and down the long stretches of coastline there had never been such a sight–men, women and children, entire families, all floating in on the tide. Hundreds of headless bodies, signifying the presence of Iban crewmembers on board the raiders were hitting the beaches. For more than seven months, the Balangingi had been away raiding in Philippine waters and on the east coast of Malaya. They had used the long canoes repeatedly in their seizures. Francisco Thomas stated:

> I reside at Cavite about two hours sail from . . . Manilla, and about seven months since, myself, my father Juan Mateo, Nicholas, Marselo and my younger brother Augustino St Maria . . . went out to fish in a sampan, and when after a considerable distance from the land we were attacked and captured by four Illanoun pirates. My father was shot through the head and killed by . . . Succum.[59]

Others reported similar experiences. Essee, a Siamese woman: "I live at Patani and about half a month since myself, eight other women and a man named Boh Kay How were collecting shellfish on the beach when a number of pirates landed from three sampans and seized the whole party. Boh Kay How was killed by the pirates [and] the females were put on board six large . . . prahus." Omar, about seven years old: "I am a native of Calantan [Kelantan] and sometime ago . . . myself and my father named Lebby Ahmad were fishing close to the beach when we were seized . . . my father resisted and attempted to escape and in the struggle was killed by the pirates." Yusof: "I am a native of . . . Calantan. About 15 days since, myself, father and another man called Pak Tigal went out to fish in a sampan when we were captured by the pirates." Ahmat: "I reside at Calantan on the east coast of the Malayan Peninsula. That about the third of May instant myself, Alli, Mohammed, and Moonien went out to fish. On reaching the mouth of the river Gunging which is situated a few hours from Calantan, I and my companions were seized by a number of Illanoon who were in a sampan."[60]

Coastal scouring accounted for the vast majority of seizures after 1800. One unfortunate Filipino was taken captive twice in this manner:

> I was fishing for tripang with nine others in a small canoe near Masbate Island when we were pursued by four Balangingi *baroto*. . . . One of my companions was killed when he resisted seizure . . . I was taken along with 150 other captives to Pilas Island and allotted. I fell to Candayo, one of the *nakodahs*. After two months Candayo sold me at Jolo to the Muslim Siangu with whom I remained for eight years. Last year [1844] I accompanied my master to Palawan on a trading expedition, and while I was fishing two Balangingi *pancos* passed and seized me. I was taken immediately to Pilas and sold.[61]

Although such seizures were considered demographically insignificant at the province level by colonial authorities by the 1830s, inshore raiding with shallow draught canoes made a tragic difference in the lives of individual families in isolated small settlements. The family-oriented nature of subsistence activity provided ample opportunities to seize children, and mothers who could not bear the pain of separation were known to have run to the seashore and begged to be taken with their children as *banyaga*.[62]

Silent capture and swift retreat marked Iranun and Balangingi inshore raids from the south, as they lay in wait along a path to the beach or to a creek for unsuspecting Tagalog and Visayan women and children. Despite the momentary terror and violence of such abductions, victims—especially women and young boys—were generally welcomed as possible new members of the Iranun and Samal communities to which they were taken, sometimes many hundreds of miles away. Many of these captives accepted their new role and fate, as they replaced members of slave raiding communities lost to battle, storm and illness on the high seas.

The Iranun and Balangingi assimilated many of the captive men and adopted some of the boys to replace their own losses, while attempting to meet the ferocious labor demands of commodity-driven global markets. Consequently, the identities of their own communities were always in flux. More than two-thirds of some Samal Balangingi settlements, particularly in the 1840s when sea warfare increased with the large scale advent of steam gunboats, consisted of adopted Visayan and Malay captives who had been assimilated into the society to replace village based crews and entire squadrons lost at sea. Those Iranun and Samal who joined raiding expeditions knew by definition that their way of life was a violent, albeit hazardous occupation. There is little doubt that in naval engagements the slave raiders suffered greatly from violence inflicted upon them by both rival colonial navies and the sea itself. The Iranun and Samal seafarers who went maritime raiding were a hard class. In the seas of Southeast Asia they suffered gale force storms, sweltering heat, exposure to illness, shipwreck and deadly encounters with the hunter-killer cruisers of Europe's colonial navies. On sparse rations and in cramped conditions, they sailed their prahus across Southeast Asia and more often than not arrived home safely, with their holds crammed with captives. The development and expansion of the Sulu Sultanate could not have occurred without the Iranun and Balangingi fleets of deep sea raiding ships and the remarkable courage and skill of those who crewed them. But many of them did not return from the voyages. Because slave raiders were vulnerable to the elements as well as the depradations of colonial cruisers and steam warships that prowled the seas hunting them at every turn, most Iranun and Samal viewed the death of some crew on raiding voyages as inevitable.

Mid-February 1838 was as close as you could come to the perfect Balangingi panorama. An unusually deep blue sky and beneath it the settlements and mangrove harbor, a shade deeper in color, were streaked by the neat sails and hulls of Orang Kaya Kullul's modern well-equipped squadron of six garay. Aboard the second largest slaver, Si Damah, son of Orang Kaya Kullul, was euphoric–a new adventure in his life had just begun as the tiny armada set sail for the coast of east Malaya and Cochin

China. Even older hands like Silammkoon, who had taken part in many slaving voyages to Manila and Makassar, and Daniel, a Balangingi-based Iranun with almost as many expeditions under his belt, still revelled in being part of their first raiding expedition to the east coast of the Malay Peninsula. Their garay under the command of Tala Goa was a beauty, one of Balangingi's newest prahus. The third largest sailing in the inaugural raid, with a crew of 29 and armed with 2 long guns, she had already been slave raiding more than half a dozen times. Built of light timbers, the 55-feet craft had been carefully refitted and armed at the village marine yard owned by the fleet commander, Orang Kaya Kullul. Maritime raiding was the most dangerous of endeavors, and it is not surprising that at sunrise just before embarking the skippers and their seafarers committed their lives and safety to Allah, and prayed for help and courage. But while the skies were comparatively clear and the winds pushed them north and west, Tala Goa and his crew did not know they were bound for disaster.[63]

Mortality rates on raiding vessels varied greatly depending on the crew's age, health, nutrition, sanitary standards on board, and sudden variations in weather and climate, particularly storms at sea, which all contributed to a mortality rate of at least five percent during a three month journey. With this in mind, adult male Iranun and Balangingi warriors and seafarers had the highest survival rates. Young boys and older men in poor health were twice as likely to die as their companions, while the highest mortality rates were from tempests and pitched battles at sea. Violent storms at sea and colonial cruisers on search-and-destroy missions swept away entire crews–the trapped populations on board battered, sinking raiding boats. In a very real sense, these maritime raiding expeditions were at the heart of a deadly contest between the Iranun and the west, to dominate the seas and maintain control over the coastal populace, involving very experienced mariners, warriors and their craft. But the ocean occasionally served a sobering reminder that it was the dominant immutable factor in these events. Forrest wrote about how Iranun sailors refused to die in a struggle with a cruel sea by casting themselves overboard in an effort to avoid tragedy:

> In bad weather they throw out a wooden anchor, and veer away a long ratan cable, which keeps their head to the sea. Sometimes in an extremity, the crew will jump overboard, and, with their bodies

under water, hold by the outriggers for hours together, to ease the vessels weight: and certainly the crew is most of the loading, for the vessels carry no ballast, and draw little water, in their passage from island to island.[64]

The mid-1750 survivors of one sea tragedy detailed how their large squadron struggled to make headway going south on the Pacific coast of Camarines. Maritime raiding was a rich man's occupation but not even the wealthiest joanga commanders were always spared the worst of the weather: their size, speed and head start did not permit Datu Pariden's giant lanong-class boats to escape the impending storm's full fury. The expedition's nakodahs knew they were bound for weeks of bad weather as violent northerlies lashed the Pacific side of Luzon with winds of more than 30 knots and seas of 5 to 7 meters swell. Aboard the large command vessel of Datu Pariden's fleet that had plundered the Catanduanes and other places, the crew took the signs of the severe storm warning in their stride. The fleet of 72 lanong continued to make some progress—lying about 20 nautical miles off the coast of Mambulao and running at around 3 knots. The weather continued to worsen. The ferocity of the gale now exceeded all expectations. Under the circumstances, taking big seas on the bow was more dangerous in the high winds than trying to turn and run for the shelter of the coast, but none was able to make for the nearest landfall. The datu firmly believed his fleet could not weather the storm much longer. The wind continued to rise, the great waves came more often. Then came the series of waves the Iranun seafarers had dreaded all along. It was the third week in November when they were hit by the storm's breaking fury. Some of the 60-, 70- and 80-feet lanong were lifted and thrown through the air at a 45 degree angle, smashing against the next giant prevailing swell. The impact destroyed the oars along the side of the galleys, a huge crash, a heap of noise, as water poured in and ships began to sink. Below floorboards, food, equipment and manacled captives floated in the rising bilge. The crews defiantly tried to hand bail but, exhausted, soon realized the futility of their task. With the vessels dismasted, rudderless and partially submerged, there were no life boats or life vests to be handed out as prahus were driven apart and began to fill with water. They sank or were abandoned one after the other all along the coast. Above the sound and fury of the wind and giant waves, what could not be heard up and down the Catanduanes coast was the terrified cry of doomed and dying men, hanging in the masts and rigging of their ships or adrift, among the towering swells. Experienced crewmembers knew they would have to grab onto a piece of flotsam, as the big prahus broke apart in the eye of the tempest. It did not take long–just over a week, from 20 to 28 November, for the entire fleet to be battered beyond recognition by wave after wave–giant waves that flipped prahus over when they were hit. Many never righted themselves. Wind and waves defeated efforts to reach the stricken vessels. Within days Datu Pariden's joanga was gone–one of six dozen lanong that were presumed sunk in the week-long calamitous storm during which time the vessels were flung about in the rolling waters by 90 miles per hour winds and 35-feet swells. Mallari documents how, further along the shoreline coast-watchers found the wrecked hulls of some of these lanongs strewn on the beaches, along with shredded church vestments and a sacred statue. That was all that remained of the fleet of 72 lanongs that foundered and sank with the loss of more than 4,000 lives. There were eight bedraggled survivors whose extraordinary tenacity saved their lives in the storm tossed sea. These men had hung onto wreckage, floating for hours on end before being washed ashore onto the exposed sands and captured by personnel of the fort of San Fernando. These Iranun raiders had more than enough. They had learned that there are conditions on the sea that are beyond the capability of seafarers to withstand. They were the sole survivors of an extraordinary tragedy and, as prisoners of the Spanish, they would never sail again.[65] Clearly, before the era of steam, typhoons or the perfect storm posed a greater menace to the Iranun and Balangingi than any single western nation's naval forces.

Despite sizeable numbers of Iranun and Balangingi perishing from time to time in storms and shipwrecks at sea, for which the historian has little or no details, more slave raiders were ultimately killed in battle, such as at Tabogon Bay in 1818; run through with a cutlass, cut down by grapeshot, drowned or injured and left floating on the sea for the sharks. The statements of the eighteen 'Illanoon' captured by the steam warship *Diana* and brought to trial before the Recorder of Singapore, at a special criminal session held on 7 June 1838, gives new insights into the lives of, and relationships between, the slave raiders on a garay and the terror of sea warfare, as their vessel slowly began to sink to the floor of the South China Sea, and they had only slim hope of survival. Clad mostly in tattered, bloodstained tight cotton shorts and a few scarlet, padded vests, the men of Tala Goa's crew were manacled at the wrists as they waited to be interviewed in the prison hospital near the harbor. They were given some rice and vegetables and they ate voraciously. Some of the more seriously wounded were ministered to where they lay on the ground of the cell. None spoke English, officials said, but in Samal the prisoners spoke quietly among themselves about the sudden nature of the unprecedented disaster that had befallen them—starkly revealing the shocking realities of life on board a Balangingi slave raider, and the human experience of a new kind of sea warfare. News of the slave raider's landing and defeat was the talk of Singapore, which was at that time a sizeable free port community and British colony with over 30,000 residents. It was rapidly becoming one of the most affluent emporiums in Southeast Asia. Singapore's roadstead was broad and its ocean front, that overlooked the straits of Malacca, was lined with large trading houses and godowns sheathed in bright-weathered tiles—many of them with wrap-around verandahs and flagpoles fluttering the Union Jack.

The prisoners brought in by the warships *Diana* and *Wolf* were reigning objects of curiosity and fear in the settlement; so much so that a reporter of the *Singapore Free Press and Mercantile Advertiser* among others of the public went to have a look, to gaze at the 'faer lion': "There is certainly nothing either formidable or very ferocious in the appearance of these savages; and with one or two exceptions, they are about as miserable a looking crew as we ever beheld—some half dozen of them being mere boys."[66]

At the newspaper office, curious patrons chatted like seabirds over the excitement. It was the most extraordinary thing some of them had ever seen. Everyone seemed to know something about what had happened—even those who saw nothing but Tala Goa's damaged raiding boat, which had been towed into its station in the harbor. The craft, a mid-1830s garay 54 feet in length with a single mast, had a battle scarred look about it—a low profile with a small stern cabin, ruined rudders, a hull coated with chipped lime paint and a broken and dangling mast at its center. The boat originated from a distant island called 'Bangingi' in the Sulu archipelago, officials said, but naval investigators declined to say more. On the other hand Tala Goa, the garay commander, said he sailed the slave raider from Balangingi in mid-February as part of a squadron under the command of Orang Kaya Kullul.[67]

Captain Congalton of the steamer *Diana* had captured the prisoners off Trengannu. Their garay was one of a squadron of six chasing a Chinese junk when the *Diana* fell in with them. He observed, from the masthead, the well-armed junk return a spirited fire. The 'Illanoon' were preparing to renew the attack when sighted by the steamer, but the warship was not then visible from the deck of the garay. As the steamer approached, with smoke billowing from her funnels, the raiders bore down upon her, thinking her to be a vessel on fire, but finding themselves mistaken, as they could not close the range, they turned away and endeavored to escape. The *Diana* gave chase and steered right for the middle of the fleet, taking Tala Goa's prahu in tow after totally disabling her. The others, badly damaged and favored by nightfall and squally weather, effected their escape. Belching steam and smoke, the paddle wheels of the *Diana* seemingly defied the wind and current. Nobody had ever seen anything like it. Chugging downwind and upwind, deafening broadsides roared from cannons on the black monster's deck, as the steamer poured a fire of grapeshot and ball into the wounded and dying men. Tala Goa, manacled in his prison cell, and some other commanders, lucky enough to escape with their lives, would never forget the haunting sound of the steamboat whistle–a precursor of change and symbol of a new era. In the initial attack of the steamer, the nakodahs lost, by their own account, nearly all their best fighting men. The surviving prisoners were those usually reserved for pulling an oar, bailing or cooking and this decimation perhaps accounted for the 'inferior display of physical vigor presented by the survivors,' in the public's mind.[68]

The remaining four garay which had broken off the engagement were chased in a southeasterly direction until night fell which enabled them to evade the warships in a squall. However, the prahus were so disabled that the surviving members of their decimated crews were obliged to abandon several of the boats. So many had been killed or wounded that it was observed, when they pulled away, that they were baling out nothing but blood, and scarcely showing a man at the oars. They could not pull more than two or three oars on either side, and the prisoners felt that there must have been twice as many killed on board each of the garay that escaped, as there had been on board Tala Goa's captured prahu. The crippled condition of the prahus forced the nakodahs to seek the temporary haven of the Rendang islands to refit the damaged boats. Near these islands the pursuing British cruisers boarded a sampan with three men in her belonging to Trengannu, and were informed by them that, on the morning of 20 May, they had seen four 'Illanoon prahus' in the vicinity, from one of which a number of dead bodies had been thrown overboard. That same garay had sunk a few minutes after having transferred her crew to the other three prahus, which also appeared in a very disabled state. They pulled away to the southward, navigating the South China Sea at night from memory as if walking through the rooms of one's house in the pitch dark.[69] The ships did not touch land for nearly two weeks as dysentery and fever took its toll on the maimed crews who, before sighting the islands and calm shallow waters of the northwest coast of Borneo near Tempasuk, were reduced to drinking seawater and their urine. Many of the first Balangingi to die in Orang Kaya Kullul's expedition to the east coast of the Malay Peninsula did not even make it back to the shores of north Borneo, and Balangingi. They died at sea, buried, not in a community cemetery, but in a watery grave–hastily cast overboard as casualties while the fleet fled the approaching enemy.

A similar loss occurred 9 years later when the steam warship *Nemesis* with James Brooke on board intercepted a Balangingi fleet of 11 garay just beyond Cherimon island off the coast of Brunei. The Balangingi hove to and opened fire along the 'whole extent of the line' of the *Nemesis* and one British sailor was killed. The barrage was answered and 'after a most gallant defence made by the Balanini's, the men fighting hand to hand in the water,' two of the raiding prahus were seized. Three of the garay broke off the engagement and set sail to escape, while six others were beached–the crews having fled into the forest. When the *Nemesis* turned to pursue the three prahus, the Balangingi on the beach remanned their vessels and attempted to set sail. In the end, six garay escaped, four were destroyed and one seized.

The largest prahu mounted six guns, one of which was a brass nine pounder, and carried by a crew of fifty men. The prahus were protected by ampilans, or flat musket proof boards fitted to the gunnel. The total force of the Balaninis on board was about three hundred and fifty men . . . of the pirates [there were] between forty and fifty dead.[70]

Almost exactly eight years after Orang Kaya Kullul's shipwrecked fleet dumped nearly 150 battle weary and wounded Balangingi into the calm sea off Tempasuk, came the startling news that half of a badly disabled fleet had foundered in a stretch of sea along the Brunei coast, spilling nearly 4 dozen desperate Balangingi raiders ashore. After the crippled fleet of 1838 had been towed away from the beach, the residents and warriors of Tempasuk had stayed behind and did their best to comfort the sick and wounded. In 1847, however, the fate of the stranded survivors of the defeated shipwrecked Balangingi fleet was very different. Many local Bornean residents had witnessed the raiders' landing in scattered disarray, and news of the foundering swept through villages faster than word travelled by sea. The forces of the sultan of Brunei hunted down the Balangingi stragglers and had these impersonal, implacable prisoners, who had loomed like a terrifying presence for decades, publicly punished–cutting them down in a production line execution.

But, in the largely unwritten history of the tragedy surrounding death and dying on the raiding boats, individual nakodahs or the fleet commander often tried to bring the corpse of a ranking crew member home with them, whenever possible. According to Islamic belief and funerary practice the spirits of the dead demanded that their descendants honor their memory and tend their graves.[71] In late July 1846, Captain Mundy headed towards the Iranun base at Tempasuk in the war steamer *Phlegethon*. He spotted an Iranun prahu, with 50 oars, attempting to reach the entrance of the Tempasuk River. The *Phlegethon*, however, soon overhauled the prahu and the British boarding party took possession of the vessel without a fight. There were only 20 men and the nakodah on board–and a large teak coffin, swords, spears, and krises. When questioned, the commander admitted immediately that he was an Iranun and a 'pirate chief.' He said that he had been on a cruise when one of his officers had died of natural causes and they were bringing him home for burial. The boarding party insisted that the coffin be opened. Mundy found that the person who had been killed in battle was 'desperately maimed.' The Iranun commander was enraged by this act, but admitted that his crew had been in an engagement, recently. Then a Filipino crewmember on the lanong plucked up his courage and identified one of the Iranun as the man who had taken him captive and sold him into slavery the year before. Shortly afterwards, while inspecting the raiding prahu, two other Tagalogs came forward, declaring that they had been taken from the coast of Manila, and had since been compelled to labor as slaves on board the lanong. Orders were immediately given to put the crew and the rajah in irons. A fight ensued around the coffin of the dead warrior, but eventually all were cuffed.[72] Eleven years later, Lieutenant Colonel Ibanez y Garcia, under quite different circumstances, when he himself had been held as a captive for ransom, had witnessed a mortuary ceremony where Panglima Taupan presided over the ritual. He had read Arabic from a small book while his crewmembers had recited verses from the Koran. Once the ceremony ended half a plucked and gutted chicken had been boiled in water and salt. After the ceremonial meal the slave raiders had prepared a coffin and lay the dead seafarer's body in it to be brought home to his place of origin at Balangingi. On their way back to the boats it was high tide and Ibanez y Garcia had to wade through the chest high rushing water. That night after the mortuary ceremony for the deceased Samal mariner, he himself lay near death with fever.[73]

Disastrous incidents, such as the loss of half of the 1838 Balangingi squadron, occurred repeatedly in various parts of Southeast Asia, with devastating consequences for the slave raiders' settlements and families. Their vessels and crews were relentlessly hunted down in the ensuing decade, never to return. In 1843, off the Southeast coast of Saleyer, a squadron of Dutch ships of war destroyed and burnt 36 Iranun and Tobello prahus, several were from 65- to 80-feet long. Two years later, the war brig *Haai* overtook 8 Iranun prahus anchoring near the island of Kalatoa, and destroyed them all, while in May 1847, 9 years after the destruction of Tala Goa's fleet, the steamer *Nemesis*, with James Brooke on board, encountered a Balangingi squadron of 11 prahus. Ultimately eight were destroyed in a desperate seven-hour battle.[74] Upon a maritime raiding expedition's return, and particularly after a tragic voyage, such as the ill-fated expedition led by Orang Kaya Kullul, prayers of thanksgiving and condolence were offered in conjunction with a *selamatan*, [ritual meal]–for the safe return of the survivors and to farewell crewmembers who had died in fatal encounters at sea. The summer weather and setting in Balangingi could not have been more different from the tumultuous battle and seas that brought havoc and death to the raiding squadron. Many of the unscathed slaving garay were tied up at makeshift docks and platforms or careened on the tidal flats. Close family members of Tala Goa and other friends and families from his village, whose kin had died or were missing in action–like Daniel–broke down and wept as the battered squadron, with gaps in the sailing formation, arrived. The 'harbor' at Balangingi was a good place to say goodbye before the few corpses brought back were covered with sand and crushed coral. It was still the safe haven at the end of every maritime expedition where, for more than 50 years, expeditions and alliances had been formed and friendships forged. The Iranun and Balangingi operated a welfare system based on a portion of captives and plunder being set aside to help compensate disabled seafarers and families who had lost fathers and sons during a raiding expedition. The process of a cultural accommodation began as captives, prepared to convert to Islam, were readily adopted into families by widows, who were unable to adequately care for their children, because of the fatal circumstance of their husbands' deaths at sea. In other instances, a fatherless child was taken in by his close kin, usually by a married sister, an aunt or grandparents.[75]

The grief-stricken families of Tala Goa's village gained some comfort from knowing their husbands and sons had died doing something that defined their 'culture' and identity and its rugged maritime orientation and way of life. Panglima Alip, the headman of Balangingi, knew that the bond of the sea and the profession of maritime raiding was so strong that all Samal sailors, warriors and fishers keenly felt the loss of those who did not return from the fateful voyage–more than 90 killed, 150 wounded and 18 taken prisoner, including Tala Goa. He knew too that they would learn from the tragic circumstance of their deaths. They already had some respect for British warships and they had always had it, but this ill-fated 1838 voyage meant that the survivors now increasingly viewed the steam warships with dread in their hearts. The Balangingi families who had lost kin on this occasion, as well as in 1847 at the hands of James Brooke, immediately sought revenge, beseeching the sultan of Sulu to organize an expedition to avenge their defeat. The deaths were deeply felt by the entire Samal raiding community, but especially by those who had sailed with the deceased. The Balangingi learned from the disastrous circumstances of the lost raiders of 1838 and 1847. They knew that on both occasions the situation would have been far worse if not for the remarkable courage and skill of their crews under fire. But they also now knew that on open seas, away from the security of the coastline and shallow waters, war steamers had captured the future. Two of Orang Kaya Kullul's oldest and closest commanders were dead. But the expedition leader knew that all 360 men on the 6 garay went into the raiding voyage with their eyes open to danger. More than 100 men had been lost but maritime raiding and the sea were in Orang Kaya Kullul's blood. When he and his men were fit again, Orang Kaya Kullul would replace the casualties with assimilated captives and sail again with the fearless Panglima Taupan–a commander wiser for the experience.

CHAPTER ELEVEN

THE CAPTIVES

It is the main purpose of this chapter to combine the testimonies and narratives of former captives with manuscript sources and travel accounts to describe the life of individuals on board the slave *prahus*. The experience of captives from the moment of seizure, and their passage in the slave prahus, to their transfer and settlement in Sulu emerges from anonymity in the slaves' testimonies. I want to employ these statements to portray life on board and the captivity experience as it was known from the inside not just 'by documenting important conditions, changes or relations which are hard to detect in the experience of any particular individual but by accumulating the experiences of many individuals.'[1] My concern here is to use the technique of collective biography to answer some of the questions regarding what it was like to be a captive of the Iranun and Balangingi. As a historical source, the testimonies of the fugitive captives of the Sulu Sultanate are both invaluable and neglected. They provide fresh evidence about the captivity experience under the Iranun and Balangingi that cannot be found in more traditional sources.

These captive statements, recorded during the period between 1790 and 1860, make us acutely aware of the profound cultural-ecological and economic transformations of Southeast Asian history. They also present local-regional history and topics such as agency and ethnicity that are both extraordinary and everyday on a larger scale that is challenging historiographically. The testimony of the fugitive captives raises basic issues about intentionality and identity: the way the slave raiders used and abused captives; how the reconstructed identities and roles on board the raiding vessels were different from European perceptions and images of the 'Lanun' and their 'culture'; and how the process of captivity and slave raiding made many of those taken aboard uniquely, if not ambiguously, Iranun or Balangingi. In 1838, prisoners, interrogated by colonial officials, claimed they were in fact former captives who, as slaves, were forced to take part in numerous attacks. But, in the eyes of the court and public at large, these slaves were nevertheless still considered 'Illanoon'– at a time when the dreaded 'Lanun' was considered an overarching category by Britain and other European nations.[2] These ex-captives and slaves were an intrepid bunch of men who represented an important class of people on the raiding vessels. Among them was Mah Roon, a Mandarese, who with two of his compatriots named Sindrah and Pannisil were "treated as slaves and compelled to perform all kinds of work," on board the raiding prahus. Sukut and Pula Nea, two other Mandarese, were also in a similar position to Mah Roon and compelled to go in search of slaves and plunder.[3] What emerges from these unpublished statements is that the crew of the lanong and garay were not simply 'Iranun' or 'Balangingi,' with respect to the problem of ethnic self-definition, but they also included many men violently carried off from their own homes in the Philippines and Indonesia, and forced to serve on board the raiding prahus.

The slave trade proved a highly lucrative business for the Iranun and Balangingi in the eighteenth and nineteenth centuries. Thousands of prisoners were forced to endure great hardship in their passage on the slave prahus–a passage in cramped and inhuman conditions which could last from several weeks to several months. The captive statements, especially those of men like Mah Roon, have led to important changes in our historical understanding of the Iranun and Balangingi as ethnic groups. The dominant image of terrifying slave raiders from the Sulu Sea has been balanced by a new appreciation of the wide ranging incorporation of captives in the economic and political life of these groups, extending from the straits of Malacca to eastern Sulawesi.[4]

Most captive statements were taken when *banyaga* or slaves escaped to European ships. They contain data on the social status of banyaga, their occupations and roles on board the slaving vessels. Spanish and Dutch strategic interests required information on the social organization of maritime raiding and ethnic interrelations in the Sulu-Mindanao region, and consequently evidence given in interrogations revolved around these issues. Virtually all the statements concern the experiences of banyaga who fled from Jolo island, with the exception of a small number furnished by those rescued either by cruising expeditions or who managed to escape from Tempasuk, Marudu Bay or Gunung Tabor. While banyaga from Jolo were disproportionately represented, many of them had spent a period of their captivity elsewhere and provided information on their servitude in other parts of the Sulu archipelago, especially Balangingi. The age of the banyaga at the time of their interrogation ranged from 9 to 60 years, and the captivity experience overwhelmingly represented was that of adults–the period between 20 and 50 years of age. Out of 180 banyaga listed in Appendix F, only 4 were women.

Carlo Ginsburg, a gifted Italian historian, whose classic works have challenged us to retrieve social worlds that more conventional history does not record, describes particular types of legal-juridical documentation, as "written records of oral speech."[5] For instance, according to Ginsburg's methodology, the written proceedings and statements of the fugitive captives of the Sulu Sultanate could be considered comparable in certain respects to the notebooks of an anthropologist who studied a cultural system where maritime raiding, violence and slavery were an everyday occurrence. Or, to put it another way, centuries ago the Spanish or Dutch naval officer as anthropologist, went to war, performing a type of 'fieldwork' in the Sulu and Mindanao region. The intricate details about material life and social activities, recorded in the confidential proceedings and documents of these officers, were incidental to the central purpose of gathering naval intelligence on the strength and social organization of the fiercely independent slave raiders, their societies, and the nature of maritime raiding, material life and market transactions. Hence, tangential information was not likely to have been distorted. It is precisely because this historical evidence could be used to tease out hidden information to recapture the broader patterns, while also developing a sense of the lives of captives on board the prahus, that these testimonies have proved so valuable. Sifting through the broad body of official statements of fugitive captives, generated between 1836 and 1862 by Spanish and Dutch naval officers and merchant traders–documents most historians considered to have been among the neglected archival 'curiosities' of a pirate principality and a 'clash of civilizations'–it has proved possible to construct a history of the captives from below; a stunningly different type of social history based on documents of seemingly little consequence.[6]

The Spanish frequently carried several interpreters who were fluent in Tagalog and Visayan on their warships. All Filipino captives who sought refuge on board Spanish vessels were interrogated immediately. In the rare instance when a Malay speaker escaped to a Spanish ship, the statement was usually deferred and taken in Malay at Zamboanga. On the other hand, Tagalog or Visayan slaves who fled to Menado were generally unable to understand the specific questions put to them in either Malay or Dutch nor make themselves understood. As a rule, the Spanish 'experts' sought answers to the following series of questions about maritime raiding: What is your name? What is your age? What province and village in the Philippines did you come from? What activity were you engaged in when seized? Where and when were you seized? Who were the slave raiders? How many vessels were in the squadron? How many persons had they captured? Were the slave raiders pursued at any time during the course of their cruise by one of the coast guard flotillas? How were you employed and treated? What role do slaves play in maritime raiding? Do vessels leave from Jolo to go on slave raiding forays? And, is there any other information that you can provide us with in respect to maritime raiding and slaving?[7] The Dutch officers asked fugitive captives more than 30 questions that focussed principally on slave raiding.[8] The Spanish and Dutch sources complement one another, and together contain detailed analytical information that portrays the captivity experience and maritime raiding from the deck of a lanong. What is fascinating about the captive statements is that they provide insight into the hardships and perils suffered by captives, revealing the shocking realities of life on a slave raiding prahu–the way it felt, the way it affected people so profoundly. These statements are one of the most important sources produced for the recent history of maritime Southeast Asia, and they continue to provide one of the most comprehensive depictions of the human experience of maritime raiding and captivity. Researchers can really sense the fear, desires, hopes, and the incredible tragedy of some of these captive people on board the Iranun and Balangingi slaving boats.

In the proper atmosphere, a single question from a sensitive interrogator to a captive, for example, 'Why did you escape?' could spur the respondent to pour out their life story in a lengthy response. Some of these extraordinary accounts, sometime related by Europeans, were later published as articles in period journals or as small books in the 'Malay pirate' genre, and proved extremely popular in England and on the continent. Among these texts is the narrative of the English whaler Ebenezer Edwards who described his captivity among the Balangingi and a whaling voyage gone wrong in the Timor Sea in the *Sarah and Elizabeth*, as well as Lieutenant Colonel Ibanez y Garcia's little known account of his experience of travelling as a captive in the Visayas with Panglima Taupan. Taupan achieved lasting fame, as one of the most remarkable of all Balangingi leaders, by defiantly resisting the Spaniards after the destruction of Balangingi in 1848. Edwards wrote a report that contains useful information about his five weeks in captivity on the raiding prahus, the activities of the Balangingi slavers, conditions on board the garay and trading goods and transactions.[9] Ibanez y Garcia was a complex man and a soldier and it is from his account that we learn about some of the horrific acts that the Balangingi performed to instil fear and terror–if only to weaken the captives' will to resist, once they had been taken on board. After nearly two months of harrowing captivity, witnessing Christian Filipinos repeatedly hunted down with long trident poles, Ibanez wrote:

> I have seen a seriously injured father whose wife and children were captured, while the pirates laughed at the father. I have seen them beat the children while saying, 'You must be happy,' they were told 'because with us you do not have to pay taxes or perform personal services!' I have seen an emaciated woman, denied food for two days, while her baby cried because she had no milk to squeeze from her breasts. I have seen people eat filth and garbage, just as I have seen pirates kill men as though they were lambs because they enjoyed the sight of blood.[10]

Banyaga were captured by attacking sailing boats–prahus, schooners, junks–and coastal villages. According to Ibanez y Garcia, Balangingi and

Iranun vessels disguised as local trading and fishing boats pounced 'like vultures' upon coastal vessels commanded by Chinese, Tagalog, Arab, Bugis, and Europeans.[11] The Iranun and Balangingi treated their captives harshly at times but rarely killed any who did not resist capture. The raiders often singled out wealthy passengers and important crewmembers for special treatment, forcing them to strip naked as they were searched for concealed valuables. Ibanez y Garcia observed that, at certain times of the year, only the most courageous or foolhardy of individuals would be willing to undertake the entire journey through the Visayas by sea. He knew that many reprehensible stories about the practices and conditions on board the Iranun and Balangingi slave ships were rife. The Spanish officer, the governor militar of Surigao, found out in June 1857 that such shocking shipboard conditions were customary, especially among some of the most experienced slave raiders. While there were strict rules regarding ransacking of a captured vessel's equipment and cargo, the possessions of passengers and crew could be looted with impunity. Ibanez y Garcia watched helplessly as the Balangingi grabbed everything they could lay their hands on. In a frenzy, the slave raiders broke everything in sight, looting all they could carry away from the prize. Ibanez y Garcia's captor, Tumugsuc, ordered him and his companions to be bound and, with their baggage, were transferred to his garay. Dazed, Ibanez y Garcia watched Tumugsuc brazenly hide his money, jewelry and powdered gold. Tumugsuc, looked up and threatened the officer, saying, "I will kill you if you reveal this to my headchief"[12]–the celebrated Panglima Taupan.

Interestingly, the treatment of Muslims as captives of the Iranun and Balangingi has been misrepresented in some books and documents, particularly by those campaigning for the suppression of maritime raiding. Muslims, especially those of other seafaring groups like the Bugis, Mandarese and Macassarese, did not expect to be spared rough treatment. However, *hajis* and *imams* travelling on captured sailing boats were often set at liberty as soon as possible. When Orang Kaya Kullul's squadron of six prahus intercepted the large Pontianak-based merchant prahu of the trader Sabit, which was proceeding from Pulau Laut to Tanjong Datu, (off the southwest tip of Borneo) all Sabit's property was seized, the boat sunk, and the trader himself and others were made prisoners. However, five of the passengers were hajis and thus considered religious leaders by the Balangingi. They were released the same night, after the raiders had taken everything out of Sabit's prahu and sunk her, but the rest of the captives were bound with rattans to prevent escape.[13]

Capture at sea or along the seaboard was only the first of many traumatic experiences Asians and Europeans would suffer on their journey to Sulu. The second would be the hardships of the sea voyage and life on board a maritime raider. In the 1830s and 1840s, prisoners who made the trip crammed into the hold of slaving ships with their arms bound, endured poor food, bad sanitation and extreme overcrowding—sometimes spending long periods of time at sea. The captivity experience of a new prisoner taken on board a raider consisted of two closely related, but separate, matters. First, there was the initial trauma of being imprisoned on an Iranun or Balangingi vessel which completely destroyed the individual's previous social and cultural existence—cutting them off from family, friends and role and status in life. At the same time, the prisoners were subjected to constant intimidation, terror and violence, including the very real threat to their lives. Second, there were the social and psychological after-effects of the trauma of capture—effects which not all individuals could control. Under extreme stress and deprivation, many succumbed to the personality-disintegrating fear, humiliation, hatred, self-loathing and shame. For example, in May 1807 the Dutch cruiser *De Vrede*, under the command of Captain Beckman, was attacked by 7 Iranun vessels, each with a complement of 100 men. After a desperate fight the crew of the cruiser escaped by abandoning their vessel, boarding the long boat and heading for shore. Left on the cruiser, Beckman and his lieutenant, Stokbroo, jumped into the sea when the Iranun scrambled on deck. The former drowned, the latter was taken captive by the Iranun, "who shaved his head, stripped him of his clothes, and carried him with them to the lampongs, where he had to undergo every kind of ill treatment, and was even threatened with death."[14]

Trussed up in the hold of a lanong or garay, many of those seized by the Iranun and Balangingi would eventually find their way to Sulu and Mindanao facing, at worst, indefinite slavery, or, at best, a relatively quick incorporation into Balangingi or Iranun society. The main concern of many new captives was to maintain intact their personality, ethnic identity and culture of origin. They hoped, at some point in the foreseeable future, to escape, and return to their former world as the same person who had left it. At first, all their emotional efforts were usually directed towards this goal, but the raiders could not allow captives to maintain a semblance of such attitudes and behavior on board the slave prahus. Therefore, initially, the Iranun and Balangingi were concerned with the disturbing process of radically changing the attitudes of their captives, by means of discipline and punishment so they could no longer be considered the same as they used to be before captivity. New captives, including professional soldiers like Ibanez y Garcia, could not survive on board a raiding prahu longer than a month or two without being very concerned with the central problem of staying alive. Unfit captives, in particular, presented the raiders, crew and seasoned prisoners with potentially difficult problems. Complaints about the initially unbearable existence in the prahus added an additional strain to life on board, as did the inability of some individuals to adjust to captivity. Malingering behavior among the slave rowers or bailers could endanger the whole crew. Hence, a new captive put to the oars, who could not endure the combination of a poor diet and backbreaking labor, became a liability to the crew and other prisoners. These individuals usually died during the first weeks of captivity in the slave boats, and from the raiders point of view it seemed just as well to dispose of them as soon as possible. Experienced captives were sometimes forced to assist in getting rid of the 'unfit,' in this way incorporating into their own behavior the Iranun-Balangingi ideology and culture of violence that was associated with slave raiding. Si-Ayer demonstrated mental toughness, but he vividly remembered how the attrition of 'unfit' captives occurred over several months on board the Iranun boat in which he was held captive. The vessel had a large human cargo on board:

> The prisoners were all kept tied, until they showed no symptoms of attempting to escape; we were very sadly treated–water and rice given to us very sparingly. Some died from hunger, some from being handcuffed, some from grief; they untied me after about a month. If

prisoners were sick so they could not pull an oar, they were thrown overboard.[15]

At the outset of their passage to the Sulu archipelago, captives were subject to the harshest treatment. The Balangingi raiders of Tala Goa's captured garay confessed to having taken, during the three months they were out, three Malay boats laden with rice, several Chinese sampan, and one Thai trading prahu. One Chinese, a Siamese, and three or four Malays, were found on board Tala Goa's battered prahu. These captures were made on the east coast of Malaya, and each of the captives wore a rattan twisted collar, with which to make them secure at night. This halter was to be used repeatedly in ensuing decades, as a sign to signify Iranun and Balangingi cruelty under slavery.[16] When raiders plundered and sunk a prahu or seized people from the shore, the captured persons were separated from one another and taken aboard different vessels. Nah Soo Hong: "Lim Kiat was put on one boat and myself on another." Francisco Thomas: ". . . myself and brother were put on board one boat and Nicholas and Marselo in others." Yusof: "my father and I were put into one boat. . . . Pak Tigal was on board a different one." Abdullah: "I was separated from my companions and taken onto one of the prahus. . . ." Amat: "on reaching the piratical fleet, myself and companions were put in different boats. . . ." Once on board, they were stripped naked, a rattan ring was put around their necks, and some were tied down to the side of the prahu with their hands and feet bound with sharp rattan manacles. A Kelantan Malay stated that "on reaching the piratical [prahu] . . . my hands were put into a kind of stocks and a rattan collar around my neck. . . ."[17] C. Z. Pieters recalled:

> . . . when I came again to my senses I found that I was stripped naked and bound in a *prahu* . . . The commander of the *prahu* in which I was caused me to be tied up by the hands, feet, and neck. The rope at which captives are tied by the neck is taken off in the day-time. At six o'clock in the evening, whether they are inclined to sleep or not, they must lie down and are bound by the feet, hands and neck to the deck of the *prahu*, and the rope by which their necks are confined remains within reach of the pirates who are keeping watch.[18]

In the first stages of the passage captives, particularly robust ones remained tied up for weeks, even months. They were deliberately caned with a flat piece of bamboo on the elbows, knees and the muscles of the arms and legs so that they could not swim or run away.[19] Younger children were not fettered but they were caned. In his personal narrative, Ibanez y Garcia described how the Balangingi compared the exploitation of the Spanish Government with their own social system, when punishing children: "I have seen them cane some boys for recollecting the memory of their parents, telling them at the same time, 'you should be content to be with us, since you will not have to pay the *tributo*, nor perform personal services.'"[20] Captives were also ill-fed at this stage of the journey to further weaken their will to resist. Ideally, they were given barely enough rice, sago and water to survive. Ebenezer Edwards, a third mate from the whaler *Sarah and Elizabeth*, said, "Our food consisted only of a little rice and water and the rice was generally spoiled and the rations so small that we never had enough of it."[21] After C. Z. Pieters had been six days in the Balangingi prahu, he bravely asked one of the raiders, who appeared to be the 'mate,' and who was eating at the time, for some food, and to be permitted to return to his country. The Balangingi seafarer immediately got up and gave the audacious captive, "a blow in the eyes which completely blinded me and left me insensible for more than an hour."[22] For the survivors of a Balangingi squadron destroyed off the Sarawak coast in 1862, nothing was as unpalatable as the salt water they were forced to drink: ". . . they never gave us fresh, but mixed three parts of fresh water with four of salt, and all they gave us to eat was a handful of rice or sago twice a day."[23] One part of Ibanez y Garcia's captivity narrative recalls his desperate struggle to survive, when, in his pathetic state, it was impossible to get enough to eat on a daily basis. There was not a great deal of food to be had, and the Spaniard was constantly taunted:

> To further my agony, often during meal times, Taynan, Panglima Taupan's woman, would snatch the rice and fish right from my hands giving it to her friends and leaving me nothing to eat. She would look wickedly at me, waiting for me to drop dead in hunger.[24]

When sufficiently cowed, captives were put to the oars in gangs, where they rowed in relays night and day.[25] The oar-powered galleys of the Iranun and Balangingi were crewed by 80 to 160 male captives and slaves who provided the necessary acceleration and speed in light winds or calm periods. The captives and galley slaves sat in tiers; the lower tier sweeps were pulled by men sitting inside the prahu itself; the upper by others sitting on a projecting bamboo stage. Most cruises were long and the captives were expected to row for days on end. Not all men could survive the strenuous ordeal of pulling an oar even when a slave voyage was short. For captives who had to endure this harrowing role for months, or perhaps even years, a favoring strong wind was a godsend. A lanong or garay could then set one, two or three sails and be propelled along at a considerable speed without the oars, but it was still the rowers who always provided additional power in a chase and who drove the vessel forward when sailing into the wind. Most galley slaves were Tagalogs, Visayans and 'Malays,' but an occasional strong Chinese and European took their place on the deck or bench. There was also a sizeable number of Iban and other tribal oarsmen on the lanong who were either nominally free (their debt obligations having been assigned by the creditor to one or more Iranun on board), or who joined as volunteers on a *merantau*. They received a different treatment from that of the captives, and had extra privileges. They could, for example, wear tattoos and feathered headdresses and were not manacled by rattan shackles.

The Iranun used to stop at different places along the Sarawak coast to muster in strong young Iban males to row the lanong–under a promise of receiving the heads of the slain.[26] The captive rowers and galley slaves had the lowest status among crewmembers. Their conditions and treatment on board were not good and they slept fastened together in a jumbled assemblage on the deck, in the hold or on the bamboo scaffolding. The nakodah, officers and warriors, however, were scarcely better off, lodging on the fighting platform or the stern of the vessel. The nocturnal groaning of bound captives in the hold and the relentless smells rising from the bilge were hard to endure for those recently captured and put to the oar who lay exhausted on the deck at night.

The captives sat cross-legged, naked from the waist up, with one or two of them pulling on each oar. They were driven by the rhythmic sound of a drum and cymbals while crewmembers would not hesitate to crack a cane across their backs to ensure that all oars struck the water in rapid unison. Forrest noted that while rowing on cruises the Iranun had a special song and drum beat to keep time without the slightest break in order to revive the flagging spirits of those lagging or about to faint.[27] As valuable as a nakodah's drum and rattan cane–real instruments of discipline–to propel an oar-powered galley, was his boat's rowing song. The verses of most songs were brief, woven in and out of a chanting melody as a box drum kept beat and the captives pulled their weight. An exhausted captive, who collapsed at the oar, ran the risk of being unceremoniously thrown overboard to drown. Ibanez y Garcia, who, while naked and near delirious, had felt the rattan on his back several times, noted the even more excessive hardship suffered by captives forced to pull the oars:

> I will never forget what I saw. Christian captives with rattan halters around their necks tied to the bench on which they sat. Their feet and wrists bound by ropes. They sat there in that position on the deck of the boat under the scorching heat of the sun, the rain, and in the wind's eye. Some simply collapsed over their oar, dying. Others were untied just on the verge of passing out, in order to regain consciousness, only to be tied up once again to the oar.[28]

The memories were equally singular, if not haunting, for 12-year-old Francisco Thomas, who had experienced the worst fate that could befall a young boy captured by the Balangingi. He witnessed his father's death at the hands of Tala Goa's crew and, less than a month later, was made to work the oars in a garay sent to raid Malay shipping:

> The stout man named Tala Goa was captain or Panglima of the prahu. The prisoners Succum and Sunok were in the piratical boat which captured us off Cavite and it was the former that killed my father. While on board the prahu I was compelled to pull at the oars and to do anything I was desired.[29]

Once having embarked on a cruise, the Iranun and Balangingi increased their manpower through the forced labor of fresh captives like Francisco Thomas and his younger brother. It is difficult to imagine how hard the conditions were for these captives aboard Iranun and Balangingi vessels. Shackled day and night, disabled by sickness and fear, the prisoners were pressed into service for the crewmembers—fetching water, cooking for them, bailing at sea, collecting firewood, crushing coral rocks, to make *chenam* (lime mixed with oil) to put on the vessel's bottom and, periodically, caulking the hull. The slave raiders preferred fishers and mariners who came off the regional sailing boats and who had seafaring skills and good physical constitution. But, when hard-pressed for manpower on an extended cruise, or in the aftermath of a costly sea battle, the raiders forced all captives they could get their hands on to work the often crowded sometimes disease-ridden slaving ships. When Iranun and Balangingi visited uninhabited islets to clean, repair and provision the vessels, there was no respite from the backbreaking ordeal and horrible conditions for captives. Ibanez y Garcia recounted how he was forced with a storm brewing to lash the boats securely to the shore despite the fact that his hands and feet were terribly bruised and swollen. After the tempest subsided the vessels were refloated and anchored off a nearby island where, for two days, the Spaniard and other captives . . . "were forced to gather firewood and haul water; as a consequence of this arduous work . . . my hands bled and were affected by inflammation and sores; there was no remedy except to bear the pain in silence."[30]

The Iranun and Balangingi treated female captives on board reasonably well; women were considered of much greater value, with one woman being worth three men as objects of trade and exchange. Providing the women did not offer resistance, the captors did not display wanton cruelty towards them.[31] Female captives usually received some protection, although slave raiders, who lead a wandering and hard life, did not display much delicacy in their treatment of women and particular men were not always constrained in their amorous advances. But they did not, as far as is known, have recourse to violence and the criminal act of rape with women.[32] Indeed, before the vessels' arrival in port and a division of the spoils had taken place, the general interest which all crewmembers shared in the booty of human cargo expressly forbade the sexual abuse of female captives. Furthermore, within the first generation, those captives most likely to be assimilated into Tausog and Balangingi culture were females, because of the singular importance of their productive and reproductive capacities. However, there are some records of captive women on board slaving vessels suffering a 'little gentle compulsion,' with one unfortunate female being immersed in water up to the neck for a day or two.[33]

Despite lack of information on the marital status of female captives prior to capture and purchase, it is clear that many marriages and families were destroyed by the Iranun and Balangingi slave trade in Southeast Asia. Many men were also slaughtered in the course of the capture of the women—particularly during numerous festivals of the Catholic Church in the Philippines, which drew the female population abroad in visits to different churches and shrines.[34] But any occasion served the raiders' needs, and whether it was a christening, wedding, funeral, or dance they made use of it. Male captives, often in a state of shock and disbelief, did not like to be reminded of their families and friends from whom they had been so recently and traumatically separated. But for many female captives on board, the violent uprooting was somewhat different—partly because they had already lost their husbands. It is mentioned by women in the captive statements that they had some realization of the futility of an escape and an attempt to find their way back, since they knew that death would await their failure. But there was another contributing factor. They soon realized that female captives were generally not subjected to harsh labor and, in fact, that there was the possibility they might enjoy a more reasonable life than their female kindred and friends so suddenly left behind in a terror-stricken Philippine or Indonesian village.

Not surprisingly, little, or nothing, is known about the experiences of captured European women or women of 'light skin' who eventually became Iranun or Samal. Perhaps, free in spirit, at one with the sea and driven by fate and captivity to live with their captors, they became adept at adopting their ways, eventually marrying one of their seafarers. Except perhaps for their blue eyes and golden mane some of these kidnapped women, who had sailed the Makassar and Sunda Straits as passengers on an ill-fated schooner or stranded brig, had in every way become like an Iranun or Samal woman. When the occasional European woman was snatched in an arrogant Iranun attack on a European sailing ship, she was usually ransomed—a technique the raiders had developed for other important personages like Spanish friars and colonial officials. But for some reason the captors kept certain of these nameless captive women–to possibly become wives to important warriors and leaders, at some later date. Their unknown accounts add another dimension altogether to the captivity experience at sea. It is the story of a possible way of life that is subversive because the European captive woman never returned and picked up the threads of her former life. Her European existence and way of life were gone forever–swept away in a maritime raid. Capt. Edward Belcher, whose exploits against the Iranun and Balangingi are announced in the chapter headings of his book, *Narrative of the Voyage of H.M.S. Samarang, during the years 1843-1846*, recounts his futile search for one such English woman living beyond the 'civilized' reach of the powers of the traditional English state and family. His mission was to locate and rescue this kidnapped English woman who was assumed to be living in an Iranun village in the Bay of Ambong on the northwest coast of Borneo. Belcher did not find the woman in the squalid village which had about 50 houses and 'a few . . . leprous Badjaws, or Sea Gypsies, for inhabitants.'[35] In the 1930s, Owen Rutter, a former district officer of Tempasuk, writing about Belcher's vain search for an European female slave, envisaged his quest ending on the sandy beach of the small bay in this manner: "She might have told him roundly that she had never asked the British Navy to come and look for her; that she did very well where she was and that she preferred to remain the wife of a prince rather than end her days in an English country town."[36]

The Iranun and Balangingi sometimes permitted people they seized to redeem themselves by ransom. Often this was done soon after their seizure, but banyaga were also ransomed in the Sulu archipelago by the Tausog, after having spent a considerable period of time in captivity. When on long cruises, slave raiders went out of their way to take captives for whom ransoms might be obtained. A banyaga was always entrusted to fetch the ransom. Zuñiga observed that only certain types of persons could be ransomed:

> The only captives suitable for this kind of barter are wealthy chiefs and religious missionaries; these can be ransomed since their relatives or religious brethren have the ready cash which the Moros require. Because of this the price of a captive has risen enormously.

> A religious cannot be ransomed for less than 1,000 pesos, nor an Indian chief for less than 300 pesos in silver, rice, or other articles. . . . They are particularly fond of card games, and playing cards constitute one of the items which they accept for the ransom of captives.[37]

In 1785, Iranun vessels arrived at Pasacao, in the Ragay Gulf, in the hope of obtaining a ransom for a captured Spaniard and a mestizo. The bishop of Nueva Caceres freed the former but not the latter.[38] Given the magnitude of slavery, it was inconceivable for the Church to ransom Filipino slaves, generally. Nevertheless, their villages were sometimes expected to raise money for the ransom of friars, and were left impoverished as a result.[39]

Ransom negotiations were often fraught with unanticipated difficulties and dangers as became all too evident at Masbate in 1757. Unlike some coastal settlements, the town of Ticao, on Ticao island, presented unique problems because of its geographical isolation and a sparse frontier population who were fiercely opposed to removal, despite the island's weak defenses. In October 1757, the Iranun stormed the town, burning and looting the church and *convento*, forcing the terrified populace and the local friar to flee to the interior. However, after the failure of Fray Manuel de Sta. Catalina's initial attempt to escape with his flock, as the barking of his pet dog betrayed him, he persuaded his captors to ransom him at Masbate as they sailed southward. But before reaching the fort at Masbate the friar fell victim to duplicity although a ransom for ₱500 had been negotiated. The Spaniard had been assured safe conduct by the Iranun, for the purpose of ransom negotiations, but the ten men who left the fort with the ransom were seized, despite advancing under a flag of truce. For the stunned Spaniards in the fort, who followed the train of events from the parapets, the ransom negotiation was too laissez faire. The entire episode had left the Christian Filipinos at the mercy of the Iranun. The Spaniards, fearing for the padre's life, refrained from action and watched helplessly as the raiders herded their fresh captives aboard the vessels and weighed anchor with impunity. The flagrant violation of ideas of justice and personal property at stake in this case, with respect to the conduct of ransom negotiations, led the Spanish to send a merchant captain, Pedro Maztambide, to Lanao to ransom the deceived friar for ₱800.[40] The testimony of Tagalogs and Visayans and local officials as set forth so fully in some accounts of captivity, make it clear that the hopes and aspirations of the indios at the start of the nineteenth century differed little from those of the local elite with respect to ransom and redemption. Both hoped to be freed before being spirited away to Sulu or Mindanao. But the hopes of indios being ransomed were invariably dashed as their families and communities frequently faced an impossible scale of fees or demands. In that sense, the difference in their value regarding wealth and social status was at the root of the markedly different fates experienced in the ransom process. The records seem to suggest that some people of social standing were able to sustain greater changes in wealth-holding than others in order to be ransomed. For example, in November 1805, a fleet of 20 *pancos* under the command of Datus Capasa, Tabor, Tumbao, Tiroden, and Catansa attacked Mambulao, Camarines Sur and captured 15 fishers, including the son of a Ragay *principalia*. They then parlayed for the boy's ransom while maintaining a blockade of all trade and communication between Ragay and Mauban. Fifteen years later, in May 1820, Don Pedro Estevan, '*el terror de los moros*,' while patrolling the Albay coast, successfully ransomed, for the sum of ₱730, Albay Province's collector of Tobacco Revenue, [*Cobrador del Tabaco*], Don Bernardino de los Santos and three ex-*gobernadorcillos* captured by the Iranun.[41]

Nor was it a widespread practice for Malay royalty to obtain the release of their kindred by negotiation and ransom. Efforts were rarely made by *kerajaan* that were dotted across the archipelago, to liberate captives by force, negotiation or ransom, although their aristocratic kin sometimes managed to independently gain their own release by ransom.[42] This was often done on the spot through intermediaries who conveyed messages between the captives and their families, made credit arrangements, ensured that the ransom took place as planned as well as securing a passage home for the ransomed captives. After seizing large sailing vessels, the Iranun, occupying a position of strength, often called for a parlay to ransom the nakodah for booty—which was usually quite substantial. Frequently, most of the ransom came from the fortunes of the prisoner's family or business interests and could include pieces of gold and silver, gold dust, jewellery, opium, silk, and other textiles. On 27 April 1843, the Chinese nakodah, Tay Song Que, sailing out of Pontianak, stated before the Resident Council of Singapore that 9 days earlier he had sighted a fleet of 120 Iranun prahus off the coast of Borneo near Tanjung Datu. The raiders had captured one *tope*, a three masted freighter, belonging to Pontianak, and two other trading boats. The Chinese captain then described why the use of ransom as a form of 'forced trade' proved so popular with the Iranun:

> The nocquedah of the tope was an Arab, who was detained until redeemed for 200 dollars by his relations at Pontreanak; the pirates released the crews, and allowed them to return on shore. The tope which was captured was bound to Singapore with a cargo, consisting of yams, rattans, and some gold.[43]

Eighteen years later, in July 1861, Spencer St. John, on board a Sulu prahu, was a fellow passenger with a group of former captives that were being repatriated at the behest of the sultan of Sulu.[44] On board was a 'respectable native named Inchi Ngah' who had been taken off Pontianak by a Balangingi prahu. On the Tausog prahu, he recognized some of his compatriots who had been missing for over a year. They had been captured by the Balangingi and taken to Sulu. The sultan took an interest in their case, because they were of high rank, and sent them back to Borneo as ransomed passengers on board the Sulu trader.[45]

By 1800, there was a standard scale of ransom fees: a friar was valued at about ₱2,000, a European at ₱300, and a male Filipino slave at ₱30 to ₱50. Lascars taken from English ships were ransomed at ₱100 each.[46] The heavy ransoms offered for friars meant that they were especially coveted.[47] In 1769, the governor of Zamboanga paid 2,200 *kangans* (bolts of cotton cloth) to ransom 3 Augustinian friars;[48] a priest from Mariveles was ransomed for ₱1,000 in 1770;[49] the *cura* ("curate") of Casiguran, Tayabas, was captured in 1798 and ransomed for ₱2,500; and in 1823 the Provincial of the Recollects, Pedro de Santa Eulalia, was seized with another friar while making his annual *visita* and the Order had to pay a ransom of ₱10,000 for the two of them![50] The ransoming of priests and other Europeans at Jolo was a common practice in the eighteenth century, and the sultan took an active part in such negotiations, especially in cases that involved the governor of Zamboanga.[51]

The incessant attacks by Iranun and Balangingi on Southeast Asian shipping resulted in increasing numbers of European and Chinese hostages being taken for ransom. European captives were either held on board until a ransom was paid for their release or were transferred and sold, to become slaves of the Tausog or Iranun. Those European captives who surrendered to the Iranun often prevailed on them to call at a particular port to collect a ransom for their release. For example, in 1837, Iranun prahus captured and plundered the stranded colonial launch *William I* off the coast of Timor. The lives of the crew were spared, but they were forced to survive in the crammed hold of a slaving prahu. The Dutch prisoners, however, succeeded in discussing terms to supply the raiders with '1,000 piastres, some bales of opium, a certain quantity of cloth, and some trifling articles.' During this period of their captivity, two other lanong arrived, and a new consultation upon the fate of the prisoners followed. Some Iranun wished to put them to death immediately, or suggested that at least they should be transported and sold at Manila or Jolo, but the desire for a heavy ransom persuaded them to keep to the original agreement. Lieutenant Rauws and an European sailor were put on shore at the entrance to the Bay of Bima. They were charged with finding the ransom and goods within the term of three days and bringing them to a specified place. Meanwhile the other Dutch officers Muller and Schrooejestiyn remained as hostages. Lieutenant Rauws was successful in collecting the sum necessary for the ransom of his fellow prisoners, with the aid of the Dutch official at Bima and the sultan. The exchange took place on 19 July 1837.[52] In July 1840, the fishing vessel the *Mary* was taken by Iranun raiders off Lombok. The crew also managed to recover their liberty after paying a heavy ransom.[53]

By 1840, however, the sultan of Sulu no longer publicly condoned the seizure or ransom of Europeans. He did not consider it advantageous from the standpoint of trade and politics to permit Europeans, particularly English and Dutch mariners and Spanish priests, to be brought to Jolo where their presence could become a *cause celebre*, thereby jeopardizing relations with western powers. The ransom issue became an increasingly important problem in the context of the antipiracy campaigns mounted by the English and Spanish against the Sulu Sultanate in the 1840s. James Brooke and various Catholic religious orders in the Philippines argued that Iranun and Balangingi maritime raiding needed to be eradicated in order to liberate, rather than ransom, European captives in Jolo and elsewhere. This colonial policy position became a source of increasing resentment and conflict between the Tausog and Balangingi after 1835. The Balangingi refused to yield the religious and Europeans among their captives to the sultan, to be dutifully turned over to the Zamboanga authorities. Instead, they continued to defiantly press for a ransom. However, when a ransom could not be found, and European captives became *persona non grata* to the Tausog, they were increasingly put to death by the Balangingi.

> A renegado from Cebu, who was one of the pirates, came in secrecy to verify my worst fears. He assured me that he had overheard the chiefs discussing whether it would be more sensible to kill me to avoid the problem of bringing a 'white face' to Jolo, since the Sultan would be obliged to surrender me to the governor of Zamboanga, and he might, perhaps turn my captors over to further ingratiate himself with the governor. On the other hand, they could ransom me for a high price to be delivered to a trusted person and I could be set free.[54]

Trying to make the best of a rapidly deteriorating situation, Panglima Taupan summoned Ibanez y Garcia:

> You will die if you fail to accept my two proposals. First, you must pay me one thousand duros (a duro was equivalent to 50 centavos), a barge, and four cannons as ransom for your freedom. Second, we will allow you to go back to Maasin but you must capture a thousand fishermen and deliver them to me as slaves!

Ibanez y Garcia was furious. He had no money; neither would he commit treachery. "You might as well dispose of me as you wish," he desperately shouted.[55] Taupan was expected to rise to an occasion like this and that he had to do so was the obligation of a *panglima*. Ibanez y Garcia might have been slain then and there as the psychology of the moment demanded he be killed. The death of Ibanez y Garcia would have been the preordained conclusion of a ritual that satisfied Balangingi expectations, and reaffirmed Taupan in his role as the crusading warrior against Spanish Imperialism. The Balangingi behaved as their leader expected them to behave on this occasion; so in his fashion did Ibanez y Garcia. Taupan, however, altered the ritual and spared the Spaniard's life but from then on he was physically abused and constantly threatened with death. Days turned into weeks. Before dawn on 10 July 1857, as Taupan's fleet skirted the coast of Leyte, the Balangingi lookout vessel sighted three *barangayen* approaching. On board one of them was the Spaniard Don Jose Bergel and his men. Taupan and his companions prepared for a sea battle. Once again, Filipino captives were lined up on the parapets to serve as human shields. Heavy bursts of shellfire came from the oncoming boats followed by silence. Then a voice boomed across the still dark sea, asking if Luis Ibanez y Garcia was being held captive on board. The Balangingi answered affirmatively and at the same time raised a white flag while they continuously repeated '*pagary!,*' meaning friend in Arabic. At the stroke of dawn, one of the Balangingi boats proceeded to the small island designated for the possible negotiated release and ransom of Ibanez y Garcia. Don Jose Bergel was there, waiting. Taupan demanded 1,000 *duros*. Ibanez y Garcia objected to the exorbitant price. He made Taupan understand that he could never repay the people who would raise the money. All his personal possessions were gone—stolen by the Balangingi. Nor could he be presented to the sultan of Sulu in his present emaciated condition. Ibanez y Garcia had previously learned that the sultan had given strict orders not to harm any Spaniard captured in Visayan waters. Panglima Taupan thereupon launched at Ibanez y Garcia with his kris. But for the timely intervention of Tamtum, the Samal pilot of the prahu, he would have been struck dead. In the end, Taupan settled for 500 duros. Together with a Spanish boy, Jose Costas, and three servants, Ibanez y Garcia was to be released the following day. His clothes and other belongings of lesser value would be returned, but not the gold, silver and jewelry.

Ibanez y Garcia woke the next morning, 11 July 1857, too weak to stand. He had to be carried to the beach. The seashore was now filled with unsuspecting curiosity seekers, some of whom had brought the Balangingi tobacco, fruit and wine. Taupan received them graciously, calling them friends, and assuring them he never harmed locals who came bearing a white flag. On the beach Don Jose Bergel handed over the ransom money to Panglima Taupan. Having received the ransom, Taupan ambled over to Ibanez y Garcia, embraced him and heaped praises on him, calling him brother. He then told Ibanez y Garcia to go and that the Spanish boy and the servants would follow shortly. Then, reminiscent of the subterfuge surrounding the transfer of Fr. Manuel de Santa Catalina at Masbate a century earlier, suddenly, as if on cue, the Balangingi seized the 15 men who had conveyed the ransom money. The raiders opened fire indiscriminately on the crowd of spectators as they swiftly propelled their garay toward deeper water and out into the open sea.[56] Now in the safe company of Bergel, Ibanez y Garcia pleaded with the *gobernadorcillo* to lend him a ship to pursue Taupan. None was available.

Before 1850, European slaves in Jolo were regularly redeemed by ship captains who traded there:[57]

> I was taken for sale on board the Spanish brig *Leonidas* the captain of which was called Escrebano. As they could only speak Spanish there, we went to the American barque *Minerva*. The master of this vessel was named M.A. Somes. After Unkud and I had saluted the captain, the latter asked me where I came from and what my name was. I replied that I was from Menado and that my name was Cornelius Zacharias Pieters. As soon as I had said this . . . he told me you must not take it ill that I have not shaken hands with you, for if I did that they would ask a large price for you. You had better now go forward and I will speak with this man about your purchase. . . . After I had remained about half an hour forward Unkud called me to return home with him, because, as he said, this unbelieving captain would not purchase me. The latter however told me in the English language that Unkud had asked a very high price, and would not take a cent less than a thousand dollars. As I agreed with the captain that the amount was too great and I knew that I would never be able to repay him such a sum, I said that I would return in a couple of days to inform him of my wishes regarding the matter.[58]

Pieters refused to eat during the next several days and his worsening health and depression was a cause of real concern to his master. Three days after he had begun the hunger strike, Unkud sold him to Captain Somes for ₱300.[59] In 1834, Somes had been described by an American seafarer as the captain of the brig *Luzon*: "Captain S. is a fat and jolly Yankee, but as he has a wife and child at Manilla, he calls himself a Spaniard and sails under Spanish colours. The supercargo of the *Luzon*, I believe, is an Irishman. His name was Windham."[60]

William Wyndham, who lived for at least 15 years in Jolo where he possessed great influence with the Tausog, who made him a *datu*, also had a mestiza wife and daughter.[61] He ransomed dozens of captives from his trading base at Jolo and acted as an intermediary on any number of occasions. Ebenezer Edwards did not know the fate of the second mate of the *Sarah and Elizabeth*, John Adams, or the apprentice, Thomas Gale, who had been captured with him, but they were taken to Sulu by the Balangingi where they were ransomed and then sent home by Mr. Wyndham.[62] Captain Belcher first learned of the appointed lot of the crew of the *Premier* upon interviewing some lascars who had also been ransomed by the merchant-adventurer Wyndham.[63] Ship captains plying their wares in the Jolo roadstead also frequently took advantage of the fact that they held out the sole opportunity of redemption for Filipino captives. Spanish merchant-traders considered them a cheap, dependent source of labor, and redeemed Tagalog and Visayan captives had to work their ransom price off in passage. Their indenture, as crewmembers on a trading vessel, was apt to last up to a year and take them further and further away from their villages.[64]

Violence was inherent in the maritime raiding culture of the Iranun and Balangingi. It was both systematic and endemic on the sea and in the settlements and bases populated by slave raiders armed with guns, swords, boarding axes, and kris. The Iranun were the most feared maritime raiders on the high seas and, while they might show mercy to an indigenous crew, they rarely gave quarter to Europeans because of the atrocities and bad treatment they had suffered at the hands of the Spanish and the Dutch. The European colonizers instructed their subjects to exterminate those Iranun who resisted capture–decapitating them or cutting off their ears as proof.[65] European captives who were not ransomed by the Iranun often ran out of luck. Eventually, the wheel of fortune turned and their torture and death sprang out of a basic attitude in the Iranun and Samal towards such captives, their colonial governments and trading partners. In the 1830s and 1840s, a vicious cycle, involving atrocities committed by Iranun against European captives and the suppression, hanging and beheading of slave raiders as 'criminals' by colonial authorities, escalated. Ibanez y Garcia promptly recognized that all his Balangingi captors brought slaves with them on board–to work for them and also to be counted as crew. The Spaniard also quickly learned that some of these individuals had been enslaved for so long that when they took part in maritime raids they exceeded their masters in mistreating captives.[66] During the two-month period of his captivity, his captors would amuse themselves by forming a circle and have Ibanez y Garcia stand half naked in the center. Fierce-looking Balangingi armed with krises and delivering blood-curdling shouts, would rush at him as if bent on killing him. The Spaniard constantly dodged their parry and thrust in order to avoid a serious wound. The warriors then hit him over and over again with their tough carabao-hide shields. Exhausted and trembling from the calculated blows, Ibanez y Garcia would drop to the ground, half-dead. At this point, Panglima Taupan would shout: "Igo na, igo na, ugma na sa buntag! [Enough for today. We shall continue tomorrow!]"[67]

The Iranun often singled out European merchant captains and mates, particularly those considered abusive and cruel by indigenous crewmembers, to be tortured and executed. This arbitrary form of 'justice' was usually dispensed by one of the more fierce commanders who in the testimonies of fugitive captives excelled in 'physical force, courage or cunning.'[68] The fate of the master and the first mate of the Dutch schooner, *Maria Fredericka*, epitomized how the Iranun invariably tortured and killed some European captives. With the assistance of a crewmember who bore the captain a grudge, the becalmed vessel was quickly boarded and taken to Tungku where the Europeans were landed, buried up to their waists in sand and hacked to death by Iranun kampilan. Some 15 years later, an Iranun warrior said that this execution had occurred at the behest of the aggrieved 'traitor.' In such moments, nobility was no birthright. Rather it was defined by one's actions. Hence, the captain, Andrew Gregory, was killed by an elderly Iranun chief, Raja Muda, who "walked up to him, and with one blow cleft him from the shoulder to the side with his kampilan."[69]

The decapitated bodies were sometimes left at the site of the gruesome ordeal. When Ibanez y Garcia was finally allowed off the raiding prahu for the first time he recalled that it would have been better had he not gone ashore: 'For there I saw four skeletons, human bodies unburied, the flesh devoured by birds of prey. From the clothes they wore, they were Christians.'[70] In the 1830s and 40s, handbills appealing for donations, that had been printed by crippled and maimed victims of the Iranun, Balangingi and other maritime raiding groups, regularly circulated on the waterfronts of Liverpool, Bristol, Portsmouth and Boston. The texts vividly describe the tragic fate of some China-bound western seafarers who fell into the hands of the Iranun and other 'Malay' raiders. For example, William Edwards sailed from Liverpool at the end of May 1844 on board the *Jane Ann* and returned a shattered, silent man, after he was landed on the Merseyside via Boston on 10 December 1845. The Liverpudlian seaman's handbill distributed in dockside district taverns among drunken seafarers, prostitutes and malcontents reads as follows:[71]

TO A GENEROUS PUBLIC

I am a poor young man who have had the misfortune of having my Tongue cut out of my mouth on my passage home from the Coast of China, to Liverpool, in 1845, by the Malay Pirates, on the Coast of Malacca. There were Fourteen of our Crew taken prisoners and kept on shore four months; some of whom had their eyes put out, some their legs cut off, for myself I had my Tongue cut out.

We were taken about 120 miles to sea; we were then given a raft and let go, and were three days and three nights on the raft, and ten out of fourteen were lost. We were picked up by the ship *James*, bound to Boston, in America, and after our arrival we were sent home to Liverpool, in the ship *Sarah James*.

Two of my companions had trades before they went to sea, but unfortunately for me having no Father or Mother living, I went to sea quite young. I am now obliged to appeal to a Generous Public for support, and any small donation you please to give will be thankfully received by

> Your obedient servant,
> WILLIAM EDWARDS

There was a very real possibility of dying from the harsh treatment and poor diet suffered routinely, during a period of captivity on board a raiding prahu. Whether a captive's health deteriorated, depended on a number of factors: the captive's physical condition before seizure; the size of the vessel on which the captive was placed, and the number incarcerated on it; the length of time spent manacled and lashed to the side of the vessel; and whether the prahu was able to touch at islands or isolated stretches of coast for any length of time where captives might rest and recuperate. A 60-feet Balangingi garay would carry between 20 and 40 crew and occasionally as many as 70 captives. Those restrained were packed together, for weeks and even months on end, among the provisions stowed in a cramped hold or on deck with no shelter from tropical heat and the deluge of squalls and storms. There was a terrible stench below deck; the captives suffered from extremes of damp, heat or cold; the hold was usually awash and filthy; there was no silence and no privacy; the work at the oars was monotonous and exhausting. Their strength ebbed away.[72] Sizeable numbers died on voyages from the combined assaults of malnutrition, rough treatment, hard labor at the sweeps and faecal-borne diseases. Juan Apolonio, who was seized by the Balangingi when very young, remembered that many captives had died at sea. Si-Ayer also related a similarly chilling account of his passage in an Iranun prahu in 1847. Diomicio Francisco was among the 475 captives in 36 prahus who survived a voyage to Sulu; others had died from hunger, hardship or were drowned in passage.[73] On the other hand, the lot of Felix Feliciano was more fortunate than his captive companions on board, when he was unexpectedly dumped over the side of a garay into the Sulu Sea. The Tacloban fisherman recounted his fate at the hands of the Balangingi to his rescuers at dockside in Zamboanga. He was captured in 1847 and placed on one of three garays returning to Sipac. However, as they approached their stronghold the Balangingi were intercepted by four Spanish *faluas*. In order to escape the slave raiders immediately threw

Feliciano and several other captives overboard as bait, and the Spaniards were forced to alter course to rescue them. They were taken to Zamboanga.[74] The attrition on board slave raiders was highest among Europeans who were far less inured to such hardship than Filipinos and Malays; the work at the oar, the continual struggle with the elements, infectious diseases, the very real fear of torture and death, and a diet of seawater, unwashed sago and burnt rice was too much for most of them.[75]

After 1830, grave dangers faced the newly captured and came from both sides on board a lanong or garay. Mortality among captive ranks in passage rose sharply because of more frequent encounters between colonial war vessels and the Iranun and Balangingi. In such engagements, no quarter was expected. The slave raiders, driven to the brink of death, usually forced their captives to come up from below and sit side-by-side on the deck as human shields, forming *la muralla de sangre* ("wall of blood"). For Spanish, English and Dutch naval officers, torn between duty and compassion, the captives now became cannon fodder in the ruthless spectacle and morality (or lack of it) of sea warfare. Under these circumstances, Spanish naval officers confronted by this terrible stratagem calculated that to redeem four captives, they had to kill ten.[76] This macabre calculation was borne out at the expense of captives as early as 1838. Steam gunboats and colonial cruisers often kept firing barrage after barrage at raiding prahus caught on the open sea, and captives were invariably the first casualties. Those forced above as human shields, and others, helplessly tied up in the hold, were decimated as their blood washed across the splintered deck and their mangled bodies flooded the hold. In the fateful 1838 encounter between Orang Kaya Kullul's squadron and the steam warship, *Diana*, the steamer kept up an incessant fire on the six raiding boats, killing and wounding a great many Balangingi as well as the captives.[77] Tala Goa's disabled prahu was captured and another smaller vessel boarded, but it was abandoned in a sinking condition, after Amat, along with other terrified captives and 22 of the battle-weary Balangingi raiders on board had been safely removed to the steamer. Amat later recalled how, after his capture off Patani, Tala Goa's garay returned down the coast during which time the Balangingi commander captured two fishing sampans containing four men all of whom were subsequently killed by shelling from the steamer. Yusuf, a 12-year-old Kelantan Malay, also tragically recounted how he and his father went out to fish and were captured by the Balangingi but were put on board the same garay that was sunk by the *Diana*. Yusuf's father was killed by cannon fire from the steamship and the boy himself was wounded with shrapnel in the left shoulder.[78] Similarly, Nah Soo Hong, a Patani fisher who had intended to go to Pahang, was seized and secured at the bottom of Tala Goa's prahu, while Amat had also been taken that same day. Nah Soo Hong noted that the steamer had fired its cannon for a 'considerable time' killing and maiming a great many, including himself: "I was wounded on the head."[79] In the aftermath of a similarly bloody 1845 sea battle, in which the entire Iranun crew refused to surrender and fought to the death, the 20 surviving captives found on board the sinking lanong were described as being in a "most deplorable state."[80]

On the inward-bound voyage, out of necessity captives were sometimes bartered between flotillas or to coastal communities for foodstuffs. A seaman from Catanduanes related how:

> ... on the following day the Iranun continued sailing towards Polillo where they seized several people, afterwards they rendezvoused at Daet with fourteen Balangingi *panco*, which accompanied them to an island at the edge of the Visayas where the captives were allotted. I was bartered to a Balangingi for a half a cavan of rice.[81]

A Cebuano silversmith stated:

> The Balangingi flotilla sailed towards Dumaguete and then crossed over to the Mindanao coast passing close to the port of Santa Maria, from there they sailed to Boalan where they exchanged some of the captives for rice before the vessels in the squadron separated for Balangingi and Tunkil.[82]

Soesa, a trader from Buntung, stated: ". . . the fleet belonged to Balangingi and left for that place after the prahus were overhauled in Buntung where I was bartered to a Buginese trader."[83] The Balangingi prahu, which carried Ebenezer Edwards as part of its human cargo, had 36 crew on board and 20 prisoners. Edwards' report noted that nine of the Balangingi, who appeared to have some authority, spent entire days smoking opium. Several times he was transferred from one garay to another as a pawn in gambling matches among the nakodahs; Edwards mistakenly thought he was being sold to different commanders.[84]

Occasionally, captives managed to escape by jumping overboard. In 1868, Albert Bickmore, a professor of natural history, wrote in his journal:

> While I was at Kema two Malays appeared at the house of the officer with whom I was residing, and said they were natives of a small village on the Bay of Gorontalo; and that while they were fishing, they were captured by a fleet of [Balangingi] pirates, who soon after set out on their homeward voyage; . . . while the fleet was passing Sangir . . . they succeeded in escaping by jumping overboard and swimming a long distance to the shore.[85]

Stories of captivity and escape from the 'Lanun' abound in local oral traditions. According to one account, the name of a town in the Cuyo Islands, off the northeast coast of Palawan, originated in this way: "Lucbuan comes from the Cuyono word 'Lucbo' meaning 'jump.' Once, a moro . . . boat came to that place and captured indios to be carried away as slaves. At the point where the old fort now stands, a captive jumped off the boat and escaped. The name Lucbuan was derived from that incident."[86] To deter captives from leaping overboard, the Balangingi had a supply of long bamboo trident ready to throw at an instant's notice. They were capable of throwing one of these pronged spears accurately up to 30 yards, and captives ensnared by one of them were easily recaptured.

It was far more common for captives to escape when a squadron touched at an island for some time. Dino: "When the pirates obtained water on Siloeang island, I ran away. . . ." Sodo: "I was always bound and made to row, but I managed to escape while drawing water on Siloeang island." Salama: "I ran away while hauling water on Siloeang island."[87] Antonio Juan:

> . . . the Balangingi set a course for Quinluban island to approach the Calamian group. But heavy seas and strong winds forced them to put in at Cabra island for shelter where they seized two people. After having been there for two days I fled to the mountainous part of the island and remained in hiding for a week until hunger forced me to return to the coast. I began to build a raft to sail to

> Quinluban. Several people accidentally stumbled upon me while I was at work on it but fled, fearing I was a Moro. After much persuasion they realized I was not a Muslim and returned to help me finish the raft. These four people had been chased by the Moros and had to abandon their *baroto*, but reached the shore before the pirates could overtake them.[88]

Escape often meant leaving members of one's family behind. Maria Damiani, a 14-year-old, recalled with candor:

> I don't remember the year I was captured because I was still young. I had been travelling with my parents in a small sailboat when we were seized by pirates from several Moro *pancos*; my father had the good fortune to escape on an island the flotilla touched at, but we were taken to Tunkil.[89]

The small, uninhabited islands of Banka and Talisse at the northwestern tip of Celebes, which, with the mainland, form the strait of Banca, were the final place of call for all Balangingi fleets operating in the eastern archipelago, before they began the last leg of the journey to Sulu. Here they took on water, repaired the prahus, and frequently divided their captives: "We were taken on board one of the prahus and bound to one another. At Banka island my companions were allotted among the pirates and only I was retained to be taken to Balangingi."[90] Pieters, the Menado based captain, stated:

> ... I had been bound for eighteen days and nights when we reached the island of Banka. Off Likupang, the captives who were on board the ten prahus and who amounted to one hundred in number, were divided amongst the pirates. Amongst these captives were natives of Ternate, Tidore, Bouton, Banggai, Sangir, Makassar, and Gorontalo.[91]

Sometimes the distribution of the captives did not take place until after the fleet returned home. In 1833, Francisco Sacarias was seized between Cebu and Bohol by a fleet of 18 Balangingi prahus under the command of Languyang. "On their return to Balangingi they divided the 180 captives who stood beside the men who seized them. An equal number were apportioned to each prahu, after which Languyang chose eight captives for himself."[92] Juan Pedro was seized two years later. "The squadron crossed to Balangingi . . . the distribution of the captives was as follows: 10 captives for the commander Tamsi; 5 captives to each prahu; 3 captives for each fighting man; and 2 captives for each 4-pound cannon loaned."[93]

The rules governing the division of captives were complicated, and information regarding this matter is not altogether clear. The value of captives varied greatly according to their sex, age and personal condition. The mid-1830s price of a male was $30 more or less; a female depending on age and physical condition was worth $50, $80 or, perhaps, even $100 straits dollars. The price of children without parents or guardians was determined by similar criterion while infants were estimated to be worth half the price of a man.[94] The information given to Spanish and Dutch officials by the Tausog concerning the rules observed to determine profits and paying out of shares of the booty, namely captives, was inconsistent. On this matter, the sultan and the datus were not altogether honest or at least they were reticent. Nevertheless, colonial officers in Zamboanga and Menado, over several decades, managed to piece together a sufficiently clear picture of the accounting process by questioning hundreds of fugitive captives. According to Jansen, the Dutch resident of Menado in the mid-1850s, the normal procedure was for the captives to be divided among the raiders according to their rank and role. In the initial division of the captives on behalf of the members of the expedition, the commander received the largest number—as many as eight or ten. The nakodah of each prahu kept at least six of the best captives for himself. The *jurumudi* and *jurubatu* each received two captives. Each crewmember received a captive, but distinctions were made between those whose principal task it was to fight and those who sailed the prahu. The former were entitled to a larger number of captives than the latter, and they had to be of superior quality—younger, stronger or women. *Banyaga* who accompanied their masters on expeditions or who were lent or hired out did not receive captives. As crewmembers, their share in the captives reverted to their masters. If the number of captives was so small that after the panglima and nakodah had taken their share, there was not a sufficient number left to be divided among the jurumudi, jurubatu, and the crew, the ranking officers' shares were decreased. The panglima and nakodah received one captive each or three captives together, and the remainder were divided among the members of the expedition; one captive becoming the property of two or three crewmembers.[95]

The distribution of captives, which often took place on the islands of Banca and Talisse, frequently gave rise to violent and sometimes bloody altercations among the raiders, especially when more than one person claimed rights to a particular captive. Islamic law also reserved a portion of the captives seized for the sultan as the embodiment of the State. Payments to local officials and investors had to be made in captives too. The heads of villages from which the prahus originated received a captive for each prahu sent by their community.[96] When the Balangingi panglima visited Jolo he was obliged to give the sultan and datus who fitted out the vessels a proportion of the captives. Languyang gave his patron, Datu Dacula, a minimum of eight captives every year, in addition to repaying him in captives for his advance support in war-stores, and formal consent to make the slave raid.[97]

There were also strict provisions pertaining to the distribution of confiscated property which was apportioned in the same ratio as captives, but objects of enduring value were frequently kept by the nakodahs themselves. The captain claimed the largest percent of gold and other partible wealth and what remained was sometimes divided with the senior crewmembers. Hence, nakodahs were able to supplement the pay of their officers from the share of any loose precious metals or money looted in ransacking vessels. Jansen was able to confirm this practice as a consequence of the destruction of part of a Balangingi squadron in April 1856, off Minahassa. On their return journey to Sulu, the raider's six prahus had surprised a large Bugis *paduwakan* and killed the commander and two crewmembers. Two sons of the Bugis nakodah were taken alive by the Balangingi raiders. One of them, subsequently rescued from a sinking garay in the straits of Banca, related to the Dutch resident that there were 60 reals of gold dust on board his father's ill-fated vessel. Upon questioning Balangingi prisoners and other captives who had been freed about the missing gold dust, Jansen learned that the nakodahs of the six garay had divided it among themselves. This was corroborated by a rescued Ternaten boy who added the following detail:

> When the pirates, while stranded on the beach, were attacked by the local populace and civil guard of Menado, they fled into the forest.

His master, *Nakodah* Taup, took him along and forced him to carry a little box filled with gold which he subsequently, when he became separated from his master, threw away in the forest because of its weight.[98]

Any man found stealing or concealing such valuable plunder from the nakodah and the rest of the crew risked death. Tumugsuc, who captured Ibanez y Garcia and brazenly hid his jewelry and powdered gold, threatened to kill the Spaniard if he revealed the transgression to the fleet commander, Panglima Taupan. Immediately after his capture, Tumugsuc asked Taupan's permission to take Ibanez y Garcia aboard his garay. There he was forced to lie silently beside Tumugsuc in an extremely narrow space, his knees against his chest, his pillow a rock wrapped in filthy rags. While he lay in agony, the Spanish soldier watched the Balangingi raider bring out his booty—a watch, a variety of golden crosses and the jewel he had taken earlier that day from Ibanez y Garcia. Tumugsuc asked the Spaniard the meaning that Christians attached to such objects. Then, to quote Ibanez y Garcia, "with a wry smile and apparent gentleness, he searched my body. He forced me to open my mouth to verify that nothing was hidden in it."[99]

The condition of captives who survived the lengthy passage to Bangka materially improved once they had been allotted.[100] It was in the master's interest to see that they were cared for and watched over in the final stage of the voyage:

> As long as a new captive has no fixed master, he must each day serve a different person, by whom he is fed. As soon as he is appropriated by one of the pirates he is allowed to eat with the slave of his master, and if his owner is well disposed towards him he received a short baju and a small sarong.[101]

At the time of their disposal captives were apt to be given a new name: ". . . My master asked me what my name was and I told him it was Jumaat, on which he gave me that of Kantores."[102] While many took Samal names, others were given names associated with the place of their seizure or birth: a fisherman from Buntung, Makoboe, ". . . while fishing . . . I was attacked near Makoboe."[103] A Chinese fisherman seized by the Iranun near

Banjermasin was called Banjer;[104] and a Filipino from southern Luzon was named Albay. Pieters described the end of his passage as a captive with a slave raiding expedition, and entry into the Sulu world:

> From Bangka we proceeded to Balangingi. During the voyage we had to struggle with strong contrary winds and high seas for eight days. When we reached Balangingi our flag was hoisted and the relations of the pirates hastened on board. They asked us what country and place we belonged to. I answered that I was a native of Murang; they asked where that was and I replied that it lay between Kwandang and Gorontalo. As they seemed to think that Murang and Amurang were the same place, I explained to them that this was not the case, adding that Amurang was inhabited by subjects of the Company. They then asked if these people were Dutchmen, to which I answered that there was properly no distinction between subjects of the Company and Dutchmen.[105]

For captives like Pieters and for his captors, in the course of their rugged life, the division of the spoils and change of the monsoon heralded the end of the maritime raiding season. This period either marked a time of rejoicing or grief and mourning, depending on the fortune and fate of particular raiding expeditions. This most influential maritime world in transition, in which the vast majority of captives and raiders lived in the early nineteenth century, can only be understood in terms of the interdependent and interconnected forces of global capital– namely the commodification of markets and cultures in China and the west, and the large scale reallocation of labor to satisfy both demand and desire. The days were now passed in careening and repairing the garay, trading at Jolo, gambling and cockfighting and the nights in smoking opium. All the while powerful regional incentives lay close at hand to plan new slaving and raiding expeditions at the start of the next monsoon.

CHAPTER TWELVE

DISPOSSESSION, DEFEAT AND DIASPORA

The Balangingi visited the Philippines twice annually, once in March and again in October.[1] From 1830 to 1848, *alcades mayores* made repeated reports to the government of sightings on their coasts, of villages being attacked, and of their inhabitants and fishers being killed or carried off by the Balangingi. These were published in Manila. A government circular of 17 February 1847 called for provincial leaders to supply the following information: movements of slave raiders on the coasts of their province; activities of the *fuerza sutil*; the number of captives seized by the slavers per month; and the state of the coastal defenses. It was the small settlements far from the *cabeceras* with little or no outside communication or defense, and those situated on offshore islands which could not be protected from the mainland, that were exposed to the greatest danger. On Luzon these settlements were found principally on the Pacific coast. In favorable weather the Balangingi came up from the south or circumnavigated the island in a clockwise direction, to attack the weaker settlements, especially Palanan, Polillo, Capalonga, Indan, Daet, and Caramoan.[2] On their way north to the Pacific the Balangingi made rapid attacks on west coast villages, and they appeared on the Zambales coast every year from 1836 to 1841. In this period, villages in the Calamian group, Cuyo and other adjacent islands, particularly Dumaran and Linapacan were frequently subject to Samal slave raids by combined fleets of up to a hundred *prahus*.[3] In the central and southern Visayas, the Balangingi continued to attack coastal villages on Panay, Negros, Cebu, Samar, and Mindanao.[4]

In another direction, Brunei was within easy range of the Balangingi

343

and, from the middle of March to the end of November, a squadron hovered about southern Palawan to seize Brunei inhabitants and cut off trade to north Borneo.[5] The calculated attacks were an important contributing factor to Brunei's overall decline. The Balangingi were alleged to have a saying 'It is difficult to catch fish but easy to catch Borneans.'[6] In the same manner, the Maluso Samal of Basilan harried settlers of Zamboanga who attempted to trade with Cotabato.[7] Houses beyond the *presidio* walls were scattered and the Samal often attacked them at night. Fishers and other inhabitants sometimes had to leave their huts after dark and seek refuge behind the walls of the presidio. In 1842 Wilkes wrote:

> One or two huts which were seen in the neighbourhood of the bay, are built on posts twenty feet from the ground, and into them they ascend by ladders, which are hauled up after the occupants have entered. These, it is said, are the sleeping huts, and are so built for the purpose of preventing surprise [attacks] at night.[8]

The raids made it impossible for townspeople to fish and, ironically, Zamboanga became dependent on its assailants, the Samal of Maluso, for fresh supplies. In the south, the Balangingi disputed Bugis rights to subject peoples and to control over marine produce. The Tausog needed slaves to replace divers in the pearl and tripang fisheries, and Balangingi maritime raids forced large numbers of Samal Bajau Laut, who were clients of Bugis chiefs in the Berau area, to migrate to Tontoli and Makassar.[9]

The beginning of the end for the Balangingi came in 1848, when a Spanish fleet, including three steam gunboats, bombarded Balangingi, forcing the raiders to abandon their stronghold and disperse across the archipelago. Then, in the 1860s, a Spanish fleet of steamers remained on station in key straits throughout the Philippines, putting a decisive stop to the seasonal raiding activities of the Balangingi slavers. Prior to 1848, Spanish policy against the Balangingi was based on principles of containment; periodic naval expeditions were sent to destroy the shipping of the slave raiders and their Tausog patrons. However, by mid-nineteenth century, the Spanish authorities had decided to annex a number of the Muslim Sultanates in the south, including Sulu. This major shift in strategic thinking and foreign policy was primarily meant to prevent the British and Dutch from expanding their colonial positions and territorial interests in the Philippine archipelago and adjacent areas. The maritime raiding activities of the Balangingi would be severely curtailed by the advent of steam gunboats but, in 1848, the Spanish also used slaving and the destruction of the raiders' forts on Balangingi as a pretext to declare war on the Tausog and force the sultan of Sulu to sign a treaty acknowledging Spanish sovereignty.[10]

By the first quarter of the nineteenth century, the sea war in the Philippines between Spain and the Iranun and Balangingi had taken on a permanent and normal character of a stalemate in which each party recognized the other as an equal with authority generally limited to the territory each controlled. But in 1848 the combined forces of the Spanish navy and army laid waste to the Samal forts at Balangingi, dispersed the survivors, and forcefully relocated the prisoners of war. This was the decisive moment, the turning point in the history of the century-long conflict between Spain and the slave raiders. The Balangingi were on the brink of climbing out of their Samal identity after nearly half a century of constant upheaval, and, according to Frake, "establishing themselves as a different kind of people."[11] But, in the aftermath of the Spanish devastation of their island stronghold in 1848, they did not succeed. After that event the Balangingi, as 'notorious pirates' and a construed single ethnic group, disappeared from the pages of the historical literature and geographical reports. Balangingi fortunes changed in the 1840s and with them the pattern of maritime raiding in Southeast Asia. The destruction of Tempasuk and Marudu by the English in 1845 also forced Iranun groups to relocate on the east coast at Tunku. The loss of these confederate communities made it more difficult for the Balangingi to conduct slave raids in the western sector of the archipelago. This event, coupled with the founding of Labuan by James Brooke and the appearance of steam gunboats on the northwest coast of Borneo, forced them to gradually withdraw from that area and increasingly concentrate their activities on the Dutch possessions.[12]

At the same time, the Spanish adopted a far more aggressive policy in the south. The new governor of the Philippines, Narciso Claveria, understood the strategic importance of the control of Balangingi which became the focal point of a new Spanish strategy. A daring naval attack aimed at the throat of Sulu, namely Balangingi, was the key to cutting the sultanate in two and stopping slave raiding in the Philippines. Governor Claveria, both to protect Spain's claim to sovereignty over the Sulu archipelago and prevent political interference by other European powers, initially authorized an expedition against Balangingi in 1845, and established a small fort and naval base on Basilan in the heartland of the Balangingi.[13] Although the expedition had been ill-prepared—lacking sufficient troops, artillery and scaling ladders—and ultimately failed, the Spanish managed for the first time to fully reconnoitre the Samalese group at close range, and thus form a detailed picture of the topography, defenses and population of Balangingi.[14] Armed with this information, Claveria devoted the next several years to systematically organize a formidable task force comprised of the best-trained and equipped colonial troops—an expedition that his personal honor and patriotism demanded he command himself. As part of his programme to strengthen the military in the Philippines, he ordered several steam warships from the British which were to prove indispensable in the upcoming campaign against the Balangingi.[15] The belching smoke and lively tone of the steamer's whistle would both captivate the Balangingi and stricken their hearts and minds with terror. By 1848, the Balangingi and Iranun maritime raiding culture was already on the wane as the 'manifest destiny' of a vigorous Spanish governor to push southward was about to shove them aside. The fate of the Balangingi had already been sealed with the arrival of the new governor and the first war steamers. Claveria would write his battle speeches, for example, with deep-seated political intentions and dreams of Spanish conquest, colonial rivalry and ambition. He would dedicate his naval invasion to his Queen, projecting disparaging images of the Balangingi as 'savages' and 'barbarians' and Jolo, their principal entrepot, as a place where Spanish subjects were enslaved and in danger of apostasy.[16]

In 1847, two years after the initial unsuccessful attack, the governor of Zamboanga informed Manila that the Balangingi were busily fortifying their island, which was divided into four distinct parts by a labyrinth of small, narrow channels. According to Spanish spies, hundreds of captives were employed in gathering rocks and coral to reinforce the four forts that

DISPOSSESSION, DEFEAT AND DIASPORA

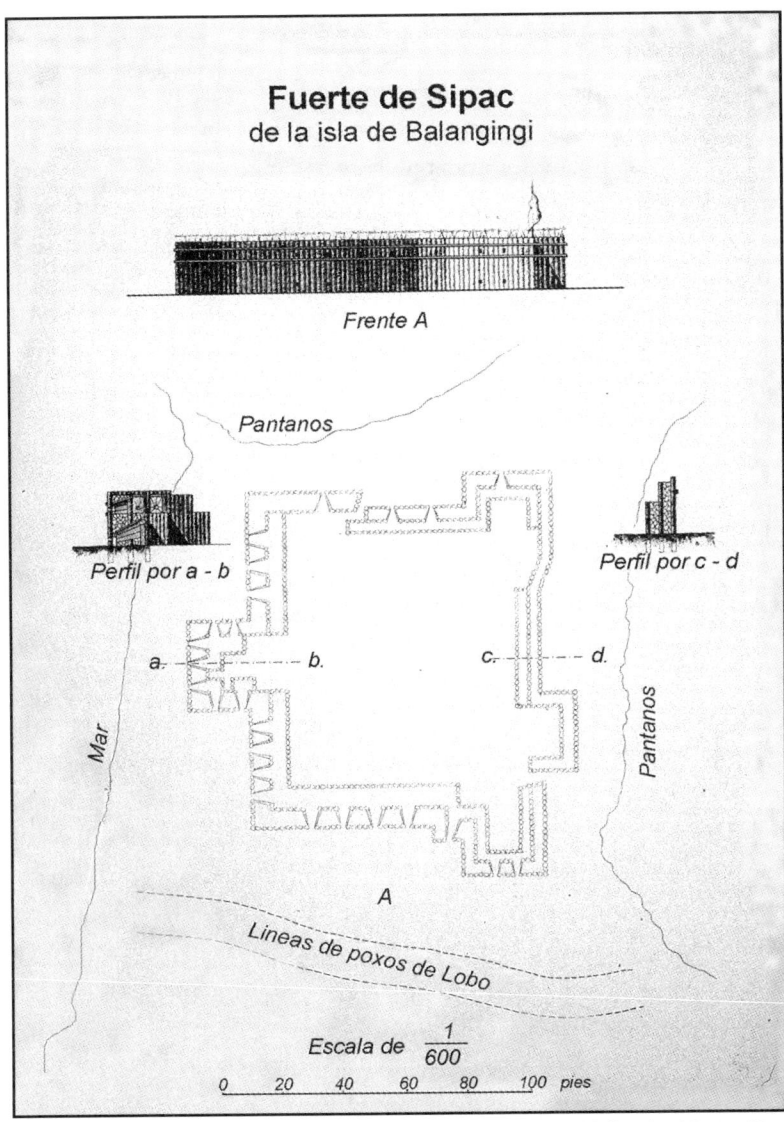

Fig. 25. Spanish plans of the heavily fortified Samal stronghold (*kota*) of Sipac. The kota was situated on raised ground, protected by reefs, rocks, mangove and a defense moat, and defended by heavy cannon.
(Courtesy of Emilio Bernaldez, *Resana Historico de la Guerra a Sur la Filipinas*)

were constructed of stout palisades set close to each other in three rows of varying heights. The artillery was set in ideal positions, some of which was situated in covered enclosures commanding the principal channel leading to the fort. The walls of these forts, which were located at difficult points of access, surrounded by swamps, were over 20 feet high and could not be readily scaled without purpose-built ladders—as the 1845 landing force discovered belatedly and much to their dismay. The immediate vicinity of each of the forts was booby trapped with sharpened bamboo stakes and concealed pits were dug to trap and maim the vanguard of an assault force. The fort at Sipac, the largest of the four, was provided with additional redoubts and towers that the Spanish army engineers subsequently acknowledged showed exceptional skill in design and construction. The Balangingi also attempted to block the mouth of the key channels, though that kind of work progressed slowly. Even so, by June 1847 the foundations of rock and coral were already three fathoms deep.[17] Claveria knew the sea war against the Balangingi and Iranun would never be brought to a close until the key, this island stronghold, was in his pocket. The governor's expedition, headed by Claveria himself, consisted of 3 war steamers, schooners, 3 transport brigs, brigantines, a detachment of the marina sutil and 500 crack troops. It was secretly fitted out and left Manila for Zamboanga on 27 January 1848.[18] Before the attack, a large auxiliary force of Zamboangueños joined the expedition at Caldera Bay, facing the presidio. The governor ordered that no quarter be given as the steamers and task force approached Balangingi island in the early hours of 16 February 1848. The three black ships belching smoke as they came over the horizon just before dawn, announced the arrival of Claveria's invasion force, and must have posed a terrifying sight to the stunned Samal sentinels on duty—and this in an age when most Balangingi would have still deemed their island impregnable and virtually 'closed' off to the outside world.

The 1848 defeat of the Balangingi by Claveria and his sizeable task force is one of the most important military feats in the nineteenth century history of colonial warfare in Southeast Asia. Almost a decade after the turmoil, tragedy and dislocation that surrounded the event, Emilio Bernaldez, who served under Claveria as an army engineer, wrote an important account of the journey to the south. His was the story of one maritime community's tragedy in the face of war set against the wrenching backdrop of social and political change in the Philippines. He told of the courageous defense and massacre of the Balangingi at the level of the individual response, the bloody battles that followed, and the capture and eventual destruction of the various forts. How realistic was *Resana Historica de la Guerra al Sur de Filipinas*? Only those like Bernaldez who had experienced the hell of this small war could know. But there was no doubt his book effectively created a sense of the death, the bloodshed, the noise, the pain. In the minds of longstanding local observers like Wyndham, in the campaign correspondence of Claveria and his officers, as well as in the oral traditions of the Balangingi, the desperate heroic battles of extermination between the slave raiders, especially at Sipac fort, and the combined forces of the Spanish army and navy, represented to both sides their own great epic–their crusade or their Masada. But this epic proved no more true (or false) than any other. In the end, the largest diaspora of Samal people in recent history, effected through invasion and war, and forced removal and relocation was accomplished.

The Balangingi were caught unprepared for the devastating attack. More than half of their men were away on slave cruises or collecting provisions, and those remaining were terrified by the *kapal api*, 'fire ships,' with their superior armament and paddle wheels, chugging downwind and upwind. The Spanish troops, however, consisting of three regular companies of infantry, two companies of militia, and detachments of artillery, pikemen, engineers, and laborers, experienced difficulty in landing in the shallow water, mud flats and mangrove swamps. They therefore attacked the most accessible fort, Balangingi, first. The Balangingi, according to the Spanish, fought like fiends but to no avail. They were overwhelmed by sheer strength of numbers and firepower and more than a hundred Samal men perished in the defense. Claveria's victory speech, delivered inside Balangingi fort on 17 February 1848 amidst the acrid smell of sulphur and the stench of the dead and dying, highlighted the ferocity and valor of the encounter. He acknowledged the courageous resistance of the Balangingi but stressed that the bravery of his own Filipino troops was greater, as during the attack they were in the front line, while the Spaniards were held behind in reserve. To these troops he stated, "Climbing that celebrated wall you showed how courageous you are and what we can expect from you [tomorrow]."[19] Once the Spanish troops managed to get inside the fort, many Balangingi defenders were killed by Spanish bayonets, a weapon unfamiliar to them, by shrapnel or, when they tried to escape, by desperately leaping from the walls. On 18 February military funerals with full honors were conducted for the Spanish officers and rank and file who died at the fort of Balangingi. After the ceremony, the respite for Claveria's blooded troops was abruptly ended by his clarion call to attack the fort at Sipac. It was an even more dangerous mission. Governor Claveria was a brave, ambitious and intelligent officer. Bravely, ambitiously and intelligently he attacked Sipac, the greatest fortress the Balangingi had ever built in Southeast Asia, from several sides simultaneously, with the three steam warships, while he mustered nearly a thousand troops for the landing. He and his assault force wiped out the Balangingi at Sipac in an unbelievable, crazed, murderous battle. Shortly before the titanic struggle started Claveria exhorted his troops: "Soldiers, be prepared for another victory. The fort at Sipac, which is as large as that at Balangingi, or even larger, is waiting for us. I hope that the flag of 'Castilla,' thanks to your courage, will soon fly over that fort. I will reward you all, I certainly will."[20]

According to Balangingi oral tradition the battle of Sipac Fort was about courage, betrayal and the morality of war and faith because it would have been impossible for the Spanish to enter the principal secret channel to gain access to the heart of the island and the fort at low tide unless they had a guide. In the folk memory of the Balangingi it was presumed that a traitor, a renegade, secretly led the forces of Claveria into this hidden channel—a channel through which certain boats could enter even when the tide was out.[21] From a distance, the advancing Spanish troops could see a large red flag with a raven that was unfurled by the Sipac defenders—red symbolizing courage, the black raven signifying death.[22] The Balangingi flag was a stirring sight as it flew in the wind. It symbolized a fiercely independent people's aspirations and ideals, and their history. The simple sight of the raven flag in the breeze would stir the Balangingi to great feats of courage and sacrifice and bring a lump to the throats of their assailants. For the Spanish forces the message was all too clear: the Balangingi were prepared to fight to the death. The Samal warriors fought ferociously despite possible betrayal and at Sipac drove the attackers from the walls of the fort, situated in the ravine of an isthmus, three times, before the Spanish were able to penetrate the outer defenses under the cover of artillery fire from the steamers. After the battle on 20 February, Claveria's speech, delivered inside the smouldering ruins of Sipac Fort, acknowledged the brutal character of the hand-to-hand combat between the soldiers, marines and militia of Zamboanga, who scaled the walls of the fortress, and its stalwart defenders. Under a constant hail of bullets, stones and spears the vanguard resolutely deployed the ladders against the walls of the 850 square yard *kota*. After a few minutes of preparation, the shock troops went up the ladders that were firmly placed and defended at all cost, despite being shot at from almost point blank range by Balangingi sharpshooters. However, the covering fire from Spanish soldiers and marines also found their mark. Wounded and dying Samal warriors on the breastwork fought on amid the smoke and uproar, but they were gradually forced off the top of the outer wall. Once over the top, the scaling force faced another obstacle, as they had to hack their way through stands of bamboo picket fences with axes and swords. The Balangingi warriors then attacked the invaders in close with kris, spears and kampilan. Their blades clashed and clanged with the bayonets and cutlass as crazed Spanish soldiers and Samal warriors, drenched in blood, closed in on one another, slashing, hacking–providing graphic scenes of brutality, horror and death from Spain's war with the 'savage' Balangingi. The carnage was extraordinary as men were blown apart or collapsed and fell from the walls–cut to pieces by the swords, bayonets, grenades, and shrapnel.

But the Balangingi, despite their heroism in the midst of one of the nineteenth century's fiercest colonial battles, had made a fatal mistake–a strategic mistake based on years of successful sea warfare and the power of arrogance that would bring enough suffering and pain to last the Balangingi several life times. The Balangingi had not fortified all sides of the Sipac fortress. The defenders had not imagined the possibility of a naval bombardment by steam warships, mounting either large cannon or mortars launched against the seemingly impregnable seaward wall of the kota. They believed the reef-strewn seaward approach could not be taken by force. Consequently, the women and children were mistakenly hidden by the warriors inside the center of the inner stockade of the fortress. Hence, these noncombatants suffered the most brutal bombardment by seaborne cannon, mortars and land batteries—fire support—as the Spanish attack reached its horrific climax. Once inside the stockade, the Spanish troops found the anguished Balangingi warriors, who expected no quarter, killing their women and children out of sheer desperation, and then impaling themselves on the phalanx of Spanish bayonets. Claveria's report noted that his troops: ". . . destroyed everything and I witnessed some of those 'barbarians' killing their own women and children, so that we would not get them, and after that they threw themselves to their own death rather than surrender. It was terrible."[23]

In the immediate aftermath of the mass ritual killings, more than two-thirds of the defenders were dead or dying. The fort was littered with piles of corpses; dismembered bodies lined the beaches and floated in the mangrove channels. The battle-hardened governor described the backdrop of this hard won victory as a 'terrible sight.' Others, attempting to escape, leapt to their death or were picked off by well-positioned Spanish snipers. The slaying stopped, amid the cursing and weeping, only after the Spanish commander promised clemency to the warriors. The Samal men then submitted, put down their blood soaked arms and surrendered. They, along with Samal women and children who survived the carnage, were immediately marched out of their devastated bastion as prisoners of war to the waiting Spanish ships.[24] The horror of the attack at Sipac and the terror and haunting nightmare inspired by the steam warships, *Elcano*, *Magallenes* and *Reina de Castilla*, which were built by the English, was recorded in a remarkable *jawi* document found on one of the survivors. But amid such awesome firepower, a lesser-known wounded Balangingi woman named Camarang addressed a letter to her lord, the sultan of Sulu:

> It is a vassal of thine who sends this letter along with Dayda, in the name of the six persons, men and women, who have here been taken captive by the Christians. . . .
>
> The black ship fired its guns at us many times until noonday, and we could no longer bear it.

Then they stayed six days, until they had finished destroying our stonghold.

We have great sorrow, even unto death.

Hear us, who are vassals of the Sultan, and doubt not that from the time of our forbears nothing so fateful ever befell.

The chief Olancaya therefore said: Let us all bear witness together by our deaths, for now is the appointed end of our faithful observance.

And Oto, his son, said: There is no help. O Imam Baidola, let us meet death together, you and I!

And Dina said: Be not afraid, my uncle; let us die bearing witness, and so depart from this world.

And Donoto made answer: By the life of our grandsires, we must hang back no longer.

And Binto replied: My father, there is nothing to hold us back; let us die fighting, and not part company ever again.

To the Sultan of Sulu from the vassal Camarang. [25]

In the Balangingi oral tradition there is a story that has been handed down over the generations about why a sizeable number of women and children at Sipac survived the conflagration only to become political pawns in the hands of the Spanish. They were to be held as hostages at Zamboanga to force their absent husbands and other seafarers, especially Panglima Taupan, Palawan Dando and Tumugsuc, to reluctantly seek a truce and surrender. The story was recounted in the mid-1980s by Rene Tulawie, who had heard it from his grandfather, Tulawie–a Balangingi warrior. When the Spanish forces attacked Sipac Fort, the key Samal commanders were away on a trip to obtain provisions, namely rice, for the people on the island. Hence only a small number of warriors as well as the indigent, elderly, women and children were left behind which makes the valiant defense of the fort all the more extraordinary. During the battle, according to the elderly Tulawie's account, the surviving women and children were hidden in several camouflaged bunkers–large makeshift pits covered with boards, mats and earth. When the bitter fighting subsided, a Spanish sergeant accidentally stumbled upon their hiding place. Exhausted, he was about to sit down in the middle of the destroyed stockade. He put his gun down and, as the rifle butt struck the blood-soaked ground, he heard a hollow sound come from just beneath his feet. Immediately, he called his companions and several engineers to open the site. When the boards and mats were pulled away, they discovered, much to their amazement, nearly 200 cowering women and children–some wounded, nearly all naked–who had been deliberately hidden at the height of the attack in the underground shelters and hence were spared from the great, destructive crossfire or the mass ritual killings.

The Balangingi who died in the battle totalled 450 and another 350 men, women and children were taken prisoner. The Spanish liberated nearly 300 captives from the Philippine provinces and the Dutch islands.[26] In the 4 to 5 days following the assault on Sipac Fort, where the bloodshed was so terrible, the Spanish soldiers burned the already decomposing bodies of their foes in pits and trenches, razed to the ground the 4 forts, destroyed 7 villages, and 150 vessels, as well as 7,000-8,000 coconut trees. Their scorched earth policy left Balangingi desolate and unfit for habitation.[27] Claveria spoke about the mopping up operations with his usual sense of candor and patriotism suffused with a mixture of violence and action. The speech also contained positive imperatives for the eyes of the region, acknowledging a sense of great accomplishment with no remorse for the sorrow of war:

> The nations in the area should acknowledge and thank you for this very important service, and the many people who were rescued owe you their freedom. Very soon we shall occupy the rest of the island. We shall destroy their resources, their defenses, the ships and boats they use for piracy. Then we shall rest, feeling proud of the fact that we accomplished a great service on behalf of mankind, especially in the Philippines. We shall leave these islands in a state of proof that no one can ever insult us without being punished.[28]

The Carthage-style conquest of Balangingi was complete and the expedition returned to a triumphant welcome in Zamboanga and Manila. There were parades and festivities held in honor of the remarkable victory, and news of it was officially broadcast across the provinces on broadsheets in a variety of dialects. A 'Te Deum' or thanksgiving mass was held in the capital's cathedral and Claveria was decorated and promoted to Viscount by the Spanish Queen, while many of the officers and men received citations for valor and were variously rewarded.[29]

Although many Balangingi were killed, others transported, and their vessels burnt, the Spanish victory was not decisive since more than half the male population had been either absent raiding or collecting provisions when the attack occurred, while hundreds of others had managed to elude their assailants and escape to Sulu.[30] In December 1848, some Samal attempted to reestablish themselves on Balangingi and Tunkil under Julano Taupan, who had been away purchasing rice to provision the strongholds when the Spanish attacked. He had taken refuge on Sulu, but had failed to convince the sultan and the *ruma bichara* to assist him in getting back the prisoners, especially the women and children being held at Zamboanga. The sultan realized he could no longer oppose the Spaniards to the degree that his predecessors had done—not if Tausog trade and regional relationships were to survive. Taupan, however, did not share the sultan's sentiments and he defied the sultan and began to resettle his following on Balangingi and Tunkil. But they were quickly dispersed by a second Spanish expedition, which also destroyed Bual several months later.[31] In the years 1848-1851, there were few slave raids reported in the Philippine archipelago, as Samal groupings were generally disorganized and leaderless.[32] Owing to the successive Spanish campaigns, the Samals, more than ever before, were thrown onto their own economic, social and political resources. They still had a considerable number of prahus in 1850, but the action of the Spanish cruisers tended to scatter the Balangingi throughout the Sulu archipelago, and on to the coasts of southern Palawan, north Borneo and beyond.[33]

Key Tausog datus, who had used the Balangingi for their own ends in the global-regional trade network, were not all easily persuaded to stop supplying them, once the sultanate's interests demanded a change in policy and tactics with respect to maritime raiding. Some datus cared little for the newly-forged alliance between Spain and Sulu and even less for the commercial opportunities that were made possible with Manila and the Philippine archipelago. From 1852, Balangingi-Spanish hostilities in Luzon and the Visayas led to renewed maritime raiding, especially once a sea war was informally declared by Panglima Taupan, around that time. The destruction of Balangingi in 1848, and the bombardment of Jolo in

1851, denied the slave raiders their best northern bases in the Sulu archipelago but did not prevent their inflicting depredations on neighboring regions from newly-established strongholds. Initially, more than 500 survivors of the attack on Balangingi had fled to the island of Ygan, near Jolo. Some of them, mostly women and children, subsequently relocated at Bulansa on Basilan.[34] On a visit to Sulu in 1851, St. John and his crew noticed some 'suspicious' individuals who were 'watching them at every point.' In his account he stated that these individuals were insolent and inclined to pilfer. They later found out that they were some of the refugees who had survived the mass destruction at Sipac and 'they had no time to forget what they had suffered from the well-deserved attacks of the Spanish.'[35] In order to protect themselves from the Spanish steamers the Balangingi now always chose places to live which, like Ygan, were far too shallow to approach with such war vessels. Hence, the newly-established Balangingi settlements of Dundong and Kabungkul had to be reached via intricate channels and mangrove swamps and their houses, like those of late eighteenth century Iranun, were also completely covered by trees.[36]

These Balangingi who had come face to face with mass death inside the Sipac Fort and survived, having come so close to being one of the statistics of Claveria's campaign of extermination, were relatively unique, both psychologically and morally. It followed that a new social integration for these survivors was more difficult than anything that they had experienced before. And this was especially so for their leaders particularly Panglima Taupan, Palawan Dando and Tumugsuc who had been absent during the onslaught. The Spanish would soon learn that, for these people, the experience of devastation and relocation was far more meaningful than that of other Samal and Iranun who had been spared such an horrific experience. The Samal survivors of 1848, and in particular Taupan, no longer regarded themselves as indestructible, but proved to be capable of integrating into their personality and character as a single ethnic group, one of the most trying experiences to which a Southeast Asian could be subjected—namely the horrors of confronting a common cast of colonial mind and set of attitudes and policies, a genocidal mentality, and, a dazzling array of weapons of mass destruction. Here we must concentrate on the changing emotions of these warriors and the intense bond that developed between these survivors under terrible stress. And how the horror of Claveria's war meant they were no longer only fighting for patriotic reasons against Spain, but for their very survival as an ethnic group—and for the survival of each other and their families. The Samal slave raiders had suffered heavy losses with the introduction of war steamers to the Philippines and had been driven from their strongholds on Balangingi. They would never be able to regain their former strength in the face of the major defeat and entrapment that had already taken place. But the Balangingi were not yet prepared to succumb to the threat the steamship posed to their future, and the colonial frame of mind that created and maintained that threat, portraying them as 'savages' and 'wildmen,' who stood in the way of Christianity, progress and free trade.

The Balangingi now tended to operate in waters closer to home and did not limit their operations to hunting down the shipping and goods of foreigners. What emerged in the Mindanao-Sulu region now were Balangingi raiders preying on Tausog and other local shipping, in a sustained way. But having turned on their former overlords and neighbors because of internecine competition for resources further contributed to their demise. In an atmosphere of increased colonial naval pressure and local conflict, mobile Samal and Iranun bands, that had once been loosely associated or allied, now began to come apart as they turned against one another and their Tausog sponsors in a free-for-all that would last into the mid-1860s. By the early 1850s, the traditional role of the Balangingi in the Sulu Sultanate had changed quite dramatically. As maritime raiders, living on their own fortified island, the Balangingi had enjoyed a certain degree of independence. This process of gaining relative autonomy accelerated after the destruction of Balangingi as some of their new outposts grew into self-governing Samal raiding communities, beyond the pale of Tausog authority. In the earlier years of the sultanate's rule an *orang kaya*, who had been appointed by the sultan, controlled Balangingi. His moral and political authority was sanctioned by the State. But throughout the 1840s the balance of power began to shift away from the sultan, and toward leading Balangingi *panglimas* and commanders. Then in the turbulent political years of the early 1850s, the Balangingi, despite their major defeat and the loss of their homeland, re-emerged as a maritime force still capable of preying on Philippine and Indonesian shipping over wide areas of Southeast Asia. Iranun-Samal maritime raiding had long served the needs of the sultanate and the datu merchant community. But in the 1850s there was a tendency for the control of maritime raiding to devolve from the top of Tausog society to the upper and middle echelons of Samal society, from the functionaries of the sultanate (late eighteenth century) to powerful coastal datus (early nineteenth century), and finally to Samal functionaries and warriors (mid-nineteenth century). When this political devolution reached the upper and middle strata of Samal and Iranun society, seafarers like Panglima Taupan and Palawan Dando–as true warrior chiefs–began to organize a new social world for the vanquished Balangingi independent from the dictates of Tausog commerce and Spanish imperial authority. The new society and organization was then used to attack the sultanate's shipping and property. In response, those Tausog who controlled the flow of the sultanate's global trade resorted to extreme violence, calling upon the assistance of the Spanish navy to eradicate the Balangingi. Taupan's ascendancy, leadership and slave raiding campaigns came to symbolize the process through which the Balangingi Samal had taken total control of maritime raiding in the aftermath of their defeat in 1848. Their hard-won separation was in many ways a response to the sultanate's campaign to collaborate with Spain against this development. Claveria's letter of 19 February 1849, addressed to the sultan of Sulu, reflected the extent of the political anarchy and intrigue that had become commonplace after the fall of Balangingi. The Spanish Governor realized that the sultan, his 'brother,' no longer actually controlled the Balangingi still at large, and his response was both swift and decisive–a campaign of terror:

> My dear brother: It has been drawn to my attention that Panglima Taupan with many followers, who had the opportunity to escape last year's attack on Balangingi, has returned to the island. I know that Taupan is one of the leading pirates who never respects the authority of the Sultan, as he has attacked several vessels of the Sultan's and used the flag of the Sultan for his own purposes. He cannot live except by piracy. He returned to Balangingi simply to renew his piratical life, a detestable practice. I have sent forces to destroy them

as everyone knows I want to protect innocent people and at the same time persecute the pirates without let up. At the same time, I appreciate your offer to help me punish these pirates.[37]

The Balangingi were now forced to sever in most instances the reciprocal relations with Tausog overlords central to the process of capital accumulation and maritime raiding. Rather than slave raid for advances in kind using the weapons and vessels owned or loaned by Tausog merchant capitalists, Samal Balangingi now increasingly commanded ships as their own property, and the crew shared equally in the risks of their common fortune and fate. After being driven out of their original island stronghold by the Spanish, many of the Balangingi survivors settled on islands in the Tawi-Tawi cluster, which became a major Balangingi base for attacks on Dutch and English shipping. Others subsequently moved to Tunku or resided on the streams flowing to the southern shore of Cape Unsang just across the channel from Tawi-Tawi on Borneo's east coast.[38] These Balangingi Samal and their Iranun allies were still well-organized, regional in scope, with sizeable resources in ships, weapons, slaves and contacts. As the Spanish and other colonial authorities cracked down on the old South China Sea and Moluccan slaving routes, the dispersed Balangingi responded by exploiting somewhat different routes–through the Philippines, around Borneo and the lesser Sunda islands, and they used new as well as old tactics. Repeated, long journeys, like those undertaken by the Iranun in the early 1800s, were far less common as the Balangingi tried a variety of routes through the Philippines and the Moluccas, using fewer ships in large numbers of smaller squadrons. By the time colonial naval forces reached the scene the Balangingi had usually vanished. They now typically remained at sea only a few days at a time before returning to their temporary bases to dispose of booty.[39]

Though the Spanish held many Balangingi women and children prisoners, Taupan refused to accept a truce and they soon managed to return to their maritime raiding activities. Establishing a base on Tawi-Tawi and flying the flags of various rival 'nations' of Spain, they preyed upon Spanish commerce in the Philippines. In Labuan and Singapore the rumor had taken hold that the Spaniards had slaughtered virtually all the

Balangingi. But in 1851 St. John's on-the-spot report from Jolo put the rumor to rest, as he noted that hundreds had escaped and were now hiding in places all over the Sulu archipelago—particularly at "Tawee Tawee and nearby islands such as Binadan."[40] Taupan, accompanied by Panglima Alip, established a base on the small island of Boan in Tawi-Tawi. This island was described by the governor of Zamboanga as:

> another strategic point for Samal pirates because this place is very shallow and big ships cannot get close to the island. Only small vintas can gain entry to the island. Similarly, the Samals of Simasa joined by the Samals of Dong-Dong have again returned to piracy and have joined Taupan's group at the island Boan, Tawy Tawy.[41]

After the initial failure to compel the Balangingi to surrender at Zamboanga and relocate under a flag of truce, the Spanish resorted to the use of overwhelming force against Taupan's faction that continued to resist. After 1852, Taupan's actions triggered a general sea war that lasted until 1858. For the entire duration of this war, Taupan led hundreds of Balangingi warriors on maritime raids from their hideouts in the vast reefs of the Tawi-Tawi chain. The second Balangingi campaign dragged on for six years, costing the Spanish colonial government hundreds of thousands of dollars, and countless more Balangingi and Filipino lives. Lieutenant Colonel Ibanez y Garcia's captivity narrative, *Mi Cautiverio: Carta que con motivo del que Sufrio entre los Piratas Joloanos y Samales en 1857*, proved that between 1848 and 1852, despite the Samal defeat and diaspora, Panglima Taupan was able to exert considerable leadership and authority over the dispersed Balangingi, temporarily reuniting them as a 'people.' At the same time, he used a regional web of kinship and association that often involved maritime raiding groups of several nationalities—notably Iranun based at Tunku—as well as shifting routes, vessels and bases as swiftly as they were discovered by Spanish naval commanders. Nevertheless, according to Ibanez y Garcia's harrowing account, traffic in Filipino captives was not being stopped, as some colonial officials had believed. The Samal raiders now disposed of their goods and plunder among Iranun and Bajau in their vicinity, and among tribal people of the interior of Bornean rivers, which harbored their newly-established fortified villages.[42] Ibanez y Garcia's narrative contained many anecdotes about the frightening conditions he witnessed on the coasts of Leyte and Samar as Panglima Taupan stepped up intelligence and the tempo of Balangingi raiding efforts. The audacious panglima seized passenger and trading boats, put coconut and banana plantations to the torch and landed on the coast of Samar at Lauaan to kill men, women and children, obviously haunted by the memory of the horror of Sipac Fort and the tragic circumstance of his imprisoned family. For Taupan, this sea war produced no winners.[43]

The Balangingi resistance of the 1850s, masterminded by an extraordinary warrior-chief, or pirate, depending on one's perspective, was led by Julano Taupan. He was one of the most remarkable figures of one of the most influential maritime ethnic groups of mid-nineteenth century Southeast Asia. By the early 1840s Panglima Taupan had become one of the principal leaders of the Samal slave raiders operating from Balangingi. Taupan, considered by the Spaniards to be the last of the great Muslim raiding chiefs, was also, in the eyes of his own people, one of the greatest. He was feared by his enemies and revered by his own society and followers. Taupan was fearless and a superb seafarer, but he had to chart a new course for his own life and for that of his followers after the destruction of Balangingi. He and his survivors now lived in a complex fast moving world of steam warships, new naval strategies and regional security pacts. However, Taupan realized that through brilliant strategy and cut throat courage the dispersed Balangingi would cope with that world and do the Spanish considerable harm. In the fateful years between 1848 and 1851, Panglima Taupan was forced to pause and reassess where he was in the world and what was truly important to him. It was because of a catastrophic event, the wholesale destruction and dispossession of his homeland, and the death of many friends that he reflected on what was really important in the lives of the Balangingi as an ethnic group. Following his completion of a provisioning voyage, Taupan had returned home to a seemingly annihilated society and was overwhelmed and haunted by the alienation of the site of the horrific battle at Sipac, where so many members of his community died or were deported. Standing there, Taupan knew that warriors like himself, who were away when it all happened, would never be normal again. They would not be able to speak in their normal voice, in a normal way. But he was not over-burdened by the historical baggage he brought with him as a Samal panglima visiting the desolate ruins of Balangingi for the first time. In the light of such defeat, some lesser men would have been unable to see through the past to the present. It is understandable that Taupan's first visit was likely to have occasioned a painful meditation on past and present. What was at issue was the balance between the two for his people's future. It required real commitment to take stock and take some positive steps from their Sipac experience–horrible as it had been– to first assess then do something about their autonomy and future as an ethnic group. It was something that Taupan owed not only to himself but to his imprisoned family in Zamboanga, as well. It is against this background of the scars of war that Panglima Taupan's maritime raiding exploits were to become the subject of so much conversation, consternation and controversy from the drawing rooms of Manila to the *conventos* of every province in the Visayas.

There is no photograph or engraved portrait of Julano Taupan, war leader of the Balangingi at Tawi-Tawi, who resisted the domination of both Jolo and Manila, and who became a renowned Samal hero. Taupan, as a panglima, did not rise from negligible social origins to become the principal headman of the Balangingi after 1848. Nobility was his birthright but his character and legend were already partially defined by his actions under Panglima Alip from the mid-1830s, during his early slave raiding days. He was a warrior, he was a leader and he was prepared to sacrifice everything for his people. Taupan became the scourge of the Philippine coasting trade and his own squadron raided the northeast coast of Luzon. The expedition commanders were drawn from a pool of the sultan's local appointees and other talented members of the Balangingi elite. In the early 1840s, with the escalation of the sea war that pitted Spain against Sulu, Taupan's fame spread. By 1845, it led to his being recognized by the sultan and the Spanish authorities in Zamboanga as one of the most powerful and important headmen on Balangingi, alongside Panglimas Alip and Gaub.[44] He was a man who was tied deep within himself to a globalizing situation–a market-driven situation that bred slave raiding, violence, new ethnic identities, and communal ways for Taupan's diverse seafaring people. Nevertheless, he increasingly wanted to make a go of life, in the mid-nineteenth century colonial world unfolding around him, separated from the machinations of the Sulu Sultanate. We watch after 1848 how he was defeated again and again in his aspirations by the combined forces and intrigues of the Spanish navy and the sultanate. Yet Taupan was kept going, driving himself and his followers beyond endurance, by the desire to see at least the Balangingi Samal hostages and his wife and children released in that interconnected world which was so complex and alluring but now dangerous for the Balangingi at every turn. In the end, bewildering frustration over the initial hostage crisis and the fact that Taupan could see no other way out, led both him and his followers to extreme acts of violence and slave raiding, simply because they knew no other solution, except shame and submission. The Spanish terms were unconditional surrender. By 1852, Panglima Taupan and his followers shared the feeling that no alternatives existed. Revenge was in the wind.

The dispossessed Balangingi of the 1850s were under constant pressure from the Spanish to surrender and relocate, and they were to be another victim of the Spanish administration's mid-century removal policy, but with a difference—Taupan initiated an undeclared sea war against Spain in the Philippines. Disruption caused by Taupan's systematic campaign of maritime raiding and the staggering cost in lost lives and trade provided a measure of how serious a challenge it was to Spanish authority. He proceeded to wage a hit-and-run style of war from the islands around the Visayas, with an inferior force and little popular support, facing a technologically superior enemy. But the final result of Taupan's efforts was his treacherous seizure, under a flag of truce, by the Spanish after he had agreed to meet with them to discuss an end to the six year long struggle and an exchange of hostages at Simisa, including some members of his family.[45] After the destruction of Balangingi in 1848, the Spanish first used the Samal women and children as hostages to force their husbands and kindred to surrender and make peace. The political ploy did not work. So after a short time, the Spanish assembled their steamers and regularly swept the Visayas and the Sulu archipelago from one end to the other. Repeated punitive campaigns ended with a series of major sea battles off the coasts of Samar and Mindanao and attacks on Taupan's bases to the south. Hundreds of Balangingi were killed during the six year long war, many of their ships captured, and others destroyed.⁴⁶ Taupan sent his raiders to prey on shipping in less troubled waters in the Moluccas, the Banda Sea, the Java Sea, and along the Bornean coasts. But their activities were short-lived. The British and Dutch dealt with the Balangingi menace by joining forces across the region, stationing steamers in all the key straits of the archipelago at certain times of the year when the slave raiders traditionally appeared in those waters. The Dutch navy concentrated on Taupan's Balangingi operations around Sulawesi and Bonerate, and the British, with James Brooke's full support, stationed ships at Labuan to protect the Borneo coasting fleets in the South China Sea.⁴⁷

As there was no indication that the Spanish, or the world at large, were deeply concerned about the fate of the Balangingi prisoners held hostage in the presidio at Zamboanga (especially members of his family), Taupan's ability to give positive meaning to the sea war he was waging against the outside world eventually began to vanish. Panglima Taupan had provided much of the 'life drive' for his people and their future. Everybody and everything in the fragmented world of the dispersed Balangingi, of necessity, depended on his great courage and inner security. But, in 1858, when the circumstances of his life were extremely harrowing and destructive, in the face of constant desolation, pain and living death the battle-weary Taupan was ready to strike a truce. The previous year, in 1857, the 'light fleet' based at Basilan had launched a surprise attack on Simisa, a major Balangingi settlement, where they rescued 76 captives, and took 116 prisoners, including many current members of the families of Balangingi leaders. After the ultimate removal of those Balangingi prisoners who survived the Simisa raid through to their incarceration in the presidio at Zamboanga, Taupan was very convincing as a man torn apart by his love for his wives and children held captive back in Zamboanga. He lived with a parallel fear that they may leave him, deported at any moment by the Spanish authorities, to another more distant destination, possibly Manila or even the Marianas Islands. Later, on 7 July 1858, Panglima Taupan, Palawan Dando and Tumugsuc, against whom the lightning-like assault at Simisa had been specifically directed, voluntarily presented themselves to the governor of Zamboanga to seek peace and exchange Samal prisoners–especially women and children–for 60 Christian captives, 1 priest and 1 European woman.⁴⁸

However, these men were betrayed by the Spaniards. Their families were not returned to them and the celebrated Balangingi leaders were seized as prisoners of war. The governor-general described why the Spanish at Zamboanga broke the truce, imprisoning Taupan and his immediate followers:

> Three moros being the leaders because of their audacity and energy enjoy universal notoriety among the moros. They have been the perennial scourge of our towns. Victims of their perfidious and covert acts, have related bitter accounts of the pirates ferocity for many years. The names of Panglima Taupan, Palawan Dando and Commander Tumugsuc are all well known for the crimes they have left in their wake. They cannot inspire trust so despite their protests they remain in prison. These are precisely the pirates whom Your Excellency perceived with foresight whose presence aboard the ship destined to transport them would have been dangerous.

He then continued his justification to the Crown for their imprisonment under a flag of truce,stating that:

> The Samal pirates live free recognising no authority but force. They are men who have no law nor faith, not genuinely accepting that they have surrendered their slaves, arms and vessels under a solemn pact. But at any moment without hesitation they would violate the terms with complete disregard simply to satisfy their vengeance.[49]

Even at the time of Panglima Taupan's surprise arrest and removal from his principal followers, during the meeting convened to discuss the possible terms of surrender, he remained defiant to the end. Taupan delivered the following exhortation to his captive people: "You who are resigned to this suffering I offer you hope and sufficient confidence that together with our families who today make this sacrifice with us that we will be able to rebel and seize Zamboanga. We will regain our lost freedom."[50]

The Spanish realized the best stratagem to end this extraordinary man's career, short of life imprisonment or execution, was to banish him to Cagayan, north central Luzon, simultaneously with Palawan Dando and Tumugsuc who were to be sent to Nueva Vizcaya and Isabela respectively. The Spanish proponents of deportation and forced resettlement argued that Spanish progress in the Philippines and their 'manifest destiny' were dependent upon the removal of the Balangingi as 'savages' from the pathway of Spanish civilization. The governor-general, in his letters to Spain, justified his actions in removing the Balangingi by portraying himself as a humanitarian in an army uniform. The military orders issued in both Zamboanga and Manila made it apparent that there was a conscious effort to minimize the chances of hostility by the imprisoned Balangingi and to complete the task of deportation as quickly and efficiently as possible with little regard for the well-being of the Balangingi.[51] Taupan's ill-fated attempt to bring peace between the Balangingi and the Spanish by surrendering for the final time through an arranged exchange of hostages had failed. The worst fears of the Balangingi leaders were realized only weeks after Taupan had delivered his memorable address in Zamboanga. The panglima and his warriors had difficulty accepting the fact of removal because of the social ties and bonds of friendship with their people that were about to be broken. Forced to face the reality of abandoning the sea, the symbol of their traditional life and current misery, Taupan and his commanders steadfastly refused to admit to the Spanish naval interrogators their purported crimes. The Balangingi warriors of Simisa, particularly the 26 who belonged to the elite group composed of panglimas and other principal leaders (over half of whom were born at the height of the China trade), were brought by express steamship to Manila, where they were first confined at the Cavite Arsenal. They were later transferred to Fort Santiago and placed under heavy guard. Initially the Balangingi prisoners sent to the fort numbered 38 but they were later joined by 52 women and young children who had remained in detention at Zamboanga after their men had been sent to the capital in chains.[52] Their fate had already been sealed. It had been decided that Taupan's group would be exiled to the interior of north central Luzon. A large number of Samal still confined in the prison of the plaza presidio in the south, slated for deportation, at local expense, to other places outside the archipelago, including the Marianas, were instead to be settled at Zamboanga.[53]

In early April 1859, the governor of Zamboanga expressed grave concern that the Balangingi deportees held in the presidio prison should be sent to Manila with all due haste, particularly members of the families of the leaders already incarcerated in Fort Santiago. He considered the transport of the Balangingi prisoners to be an urgent matter and expressed fear that some of the more resolute followers of Taupan and Palawan Dando who were imprisoned in the presidio might escape.[54] The Balangingi women and children along with some warriors, held prisoner in Zamboanga, were brought to Manila by the merchant ship, *Jesusa*. Before their deportation, a decision had been made by the presidio authorities to conscript able-bodied Samal prisoners, with the exception of several young children, to labor in chain gangs on public works. During their confinement in the presidio, the Balangingi prisoners earned some ₱17.14 for various public work that they rendered. The governor of Zamboanga forwarded this money to the governor of Tondo in Manila, in order to buy clothing for the Samal women who had lost nearly all their apparel in the Simisa assault and were almost naked and dishevelled in appearance.[55] Nor did the Spanish authorities spare the renegades. They too shared the fate of the women and children sent on the long journey north–deportation. The Spaniards were particularly harsh on those who: "feigned ignorance, of the cruelty they had inflicted upon the Visayas which was far worse than the crimes committed by the moros whom they imitated."[56]

Of the 26 Balangingi women who accompanied their children, all minors, only 2 were deported from Zamboanga with their husbands. Among the others, there were the two wives of Panglima Taupan; the two wives of Palawan Dando and the wife of Tumugsuc, the famous Balangingi nakodah. All their husbands were incarcerated in the dungeon of Fort Santiago.[57] Nuyla, the youngest wife of Taupan, with her small child, expressed the wish to join her husband in the prison.[58] Despite her infirmity and old age, the mother of Palawan Dando was also among those brought from Zamboanga. Martin Santo Domingo, a fluent speaker of Tagalog, Visayan and Samal dialects, was facing a life sentence as a renegade, but he was handpicked from among the Balangingi prisoners to act as an interpreter on behalf of certain deportees. He agreed on the condition that he, along with his Balangingi-Christian wife, who like him was born in Camarines province, and their son, might be given their freedom. Martin Santo Domingo's time among the Balangingi had thoroughly acquainted him with their customs and way of life.[59] When the Balangingi women and children arrived in Manila in June 1859 Martin Santo Domingo was summoned to question them so they could be reunited with their families. He identified women who were wives of those Balangingi warriors who had been sent from Zamboanga to Manila ahead of the rest of the group. There were several female prisoners who, as displaced wives of Balangingi leaders, immediately caught the interpreter's attention. One was Aleja Valentina a wife of Palawan Dando. This woman had been seized by Palawan Dando in one of his raids in the Calamianes. Rather than be reunited with him, she preferred to return to her family there to raise her infant son by the celebrated slave raider. On the other hand, the prisoner Maria Silveria, wife of the renegade interpreter, Martin Santo Domingo, did not want to be isolated from her husband, knowing that he had been separated by Spanish decree from the rest of the imprisoned raiders for the purpose of using his knowledge of Samal culture and dialects to collaborate.[60]

While the four principal Balangingi leaders remained shut up in the dungeon of the fort, their families were in the same locality occupying space in the public prison, the *corregimiento* of Tondo. The personal fate and courage of these Balangingi women, who must have felt so uncomfortable in Manila, bearing the harrowing scars of the sea war, almost defies translation. Sabi, another of the wives of Palawan Dando from the island of Simisa, petitioned the government, from the cell of the public prison of Tondo, to join her elderly mother Painon and her daughter Ymbag who were both sent to the Hospicio de San Jose. The former, to live there until the end of her life at the Asilo de Beneficencia; the latter to receive Christian religious instruction which the foundation gave to orphaned children who stayed there. Because of her mother's extreme age, Sabi was torn between her role and duty as a wife and that of daughter and mother. With her child, she chose to join Painon, her mother, despite the fact that her husband, who had lost his right arm in the battle of Simisa, needed her badly.[61] It was Tainun, Palawan Dando's mother, who, despite her infirmity, had followed her captive wounded son from Zamboanga to Manila, and who ministered to him in his hour of greatest need. In a brief communique, dated 25 February 1860, the administrative Head of the Hospicio de San Jose announced that the *mora*

Sabi, wife of the Balangingi leader Palawan Dando, who was incarcerated in Fort Santiago, had died on 27 December 1859. Sabi's badly injured husband, Palawan Dando, died grief-stricken and lonely in Fort Santiago the following April.⁶² The petitions of women like Sabi, Nuyla and others help us to hear the unheard voices of the Sulu world in conflict–in this case, the voices of Balangingi women–who were imprisoned and even exiled for their powerful political and religious beliefs and family ties. There is a very strong sense here of the silence being broken with respect to the underside of the Samal-Spanish conflict. These are petitions, fragmentary narratives, in which Balangingi women emerge as central protagonists in the culmination of over a century of political and cultural conflict, challenging the dominant political rhetoric of Spanish success and the stereotypes and myths of cultural submission that they so effectively perpetuated. Similarly, the Balangingi women Si-Galali and G. Ejusmu also sent a strongly worded message to the Tribunal stating that they wished to join their mother and mother-in-law respectively, in the Hospicio de San Jose.⁶³

The governor-general and delegate of Finance ordered that of the 49 prisoners held in Fort Santiago, 44 should be transported by the brigantine *Paz* to the tobacco plantations in Isabela province.⁶⁴ Panglima Taupan and Palawan Dando and their immediate followers implored the clemency of the Spanish authorities in Manila, claiming that by virtue of the Royal pardon granted to them by the Spanish Crown they should not be exiled to Cagayan. The Balangingi Samal, as prisoners of war, were declared to be direct vassals of the Crown–like the Spanish colonists and Filipino subjects themselves. The Balangingi prisoners' appeal to the Crown for clemency was accepted by Spain on the grounds that the influence of Islam, and not global-capitalism, had left its barbaric mark. In the Spanish mind, it was the link between Islam and 'piracy' that was essential to the Balangingi's development and evolution as slave raiders. This belief partly explains both the basis of the pardon and Spanish attempts to resettle the Balangingi in northern villages, thus freeing the Samal from enslavement to Islam and also from the influence of their celebrated chieftains like Taupan and Palawan Dando. The pardon was granted to guard against the future use of combinations of Samal power that could rival the authority of the Spanish, and on the condition that they were banished from the sea and their homeland, forever. The key phrase in the Royal order of 19 April 1859 rationalizing the deportation of the Balangingi and the damning of Islam stated: "Piracy was an occupation that found religious basis and was viewed not as a criminal act arising from moral degradation but rather, lack of civilisation."[65]

For the forcibly displaced Samal slave raiders, the trauma of the conquest of Balangingi was immense, but it was not adequately understood by them until 1858. The primary message of the deportation sought to invalidate the totality of Balangingi life and replace it with Spanish-Christian values–largely by forced means. They were to practise the agriculture and arts of civilized 'man' and learn the worship of the true God. Islam, which, sanctioned slavery, was to be replaced by Catholicism. At the same time, traffic in men, women and children, the basis of the wealth of Sulu's market, was to be replaced by the lucrative profits derived from the surplus value of the *deportados*' labor for the tobacco monopoly in the Philippines. The distant tobacco plantation in Cagayan would serve not only as an economic outpost of empire, it was also meant to be an agent of change among the banished seafarers. Farming was to be encouraged and Christianity taught in order to acculturate and assimilate the Balangingi mariners. The Spanish were determined to break down the social structure, culture and religion of the Samal slave raiders, thus transforming them into 'Filipino' farmers and colonial subjects indistinguishable from their Yoggad neighbors, the original inhabitants of Isabela.[66] United with like-minded reformers and officials in Madrid, the Spanish group in Manila quickly pushed through the removal policy designed to educate the Balangingi in Christian and civilized ways, and erase any memory of 'their bloody occupation . . . [so they would] become docile Christian and peaceful subjects.'[67] These events surrounding the surrender and removal of the Balangingi provide deep insight into Spanish attitudes and policy and clearly display their ethnocentric approach to the Balangingi and strong antagonism toward Islam.

The Balangingi men deported to Cagayan petitioned for their families, deliberately held behind in Manila and Zamboanga, to also be relocated with them in the mountain fastness of Isabela, so that they could live there permanently. These Samal women and children were eventually placed in the corrigimiento of Tondo while the transfer to Isabela was arranged.[68] It took some time due to lack of proper transport, but on 19 March 1860 the outnumbered Samal women and children began the final leg of their long bewildering journey northward—a journey that was directed towards getting rid of them as an independent seafaring people and depriving them by violent means of their island lands.[69] The general removal of the Balangingi from the Mindanao-Sulu region under the provisions of Taupan's surrender, was without a doubt the most consequential event in recent Samal history. That afternoon in March the deportees boarded a small ship called the *Josefita*, bound for the Spanish-owned tobacco plantations in the Cagayan Valley. There were around 40 women on board whose vanquished husbands had been sent there ahead of them. These Balangingi women on the *Josefita* were sailing for the town of Camarag and other nearby towns of the province. Three months later, on 25 June 1860, Tumugsuc and Abubacal, the son of Palawan Dando, and their families were sent to Cagayan aboard the boat *Bella Carmen*.[70] The former, Tumugsuc, was deported to Nueva Vizcaya and the latter, Abubacal, to the interior town of Lepanto. The Spanish had decided to separate the respective leaders and their families to prevent the possibility of a mass outbreak in the small towns of the Cagayan Valley.[71] The Spanish authorities on the spot made it very clear to the Balangingi that any attempted flight to freedom was hopeless from the beginning, and could only end with deportees dead, and with the remainder being soon rounded up from the rolling hills and high mountains surrounding the Cagayan Valley.

The final events in the heart-breaking story of bloody fighting, fierce determination and, ultimately, tragic defeat and removal occurred when the navy delivered to the Manila authorities the renegade prisoner, Martin Santo Domingo, interpreter of Samal dialects and Spanish collaborator. He was placed under the supervision of the Superior of the Jesuits for re-education in Catholicism. He was Balangingi, known to the Spanish as Martin Santo Domingo. To his Samal brethren he was a warrior and a master of languages. But in a different time and place, the memory of his spirit, albeit 'Filipino,' lived on in a village in Calamianes. With his wife and son, he was sent by the Spaniards, to Bulosan, Albay. This place was decided on because he could no longer return safely to his village having acted as a guide for Taupan's group when they were on slave raiding expeditions in areas within the radius of his own hometown. The Spanish realized that the ethnic origins of the Balangingi Samal were not shrouded in the distant past. The close identification and cultural accommodation of Martin Santo Domingo with the Balangingi, especially with Panglima Taupan, would only make many in his village even more uncomfortable–this, despite Martin Santo Domingo having assisted navy interrogators to seal Taupan's fate over the *Soterana* incident.

While the Tribunal had decided to deport all Balangingi leaders to their respective destinations, the government reserved final judgement on Panglima Taupan who remained in chains at Fort Santiago. He was placed under the jurisdiction of the Commander of the Navy and found guilty of piracy for the capture of the Spanish schooner *Soterana*. Instead of sending Taupan to Bontoc in the Cagayan Valley, he was transferred to the Cavite Arsenal where he died in a cholera epidemic that swept the area in 1861.[72] Three years later, in October 1864, still deeply disturbed by the circumstances of the remarkable panglima's death, 39-year-old Maria Manobo, a Balangingi, testified in Zamboanga, that while in Manila, she had heard that Panglima Taupan had died as a prisoner, shackled and alone in the Cavite Arsenal. She used words that she had undoubtedly spoken many times to other Samal who possessed no such memories, and the Spanish were concerned if not disturbed, realizing that even in death their removal policy had failed to erase the memories of Panglima Taupan.[73]

Margarita Cojuangco in, *Kris of Valor*, has sympathetically recounted the odyssey of the Balangingi who were resettled in the Cagayan Valley to work on the Tabacalera plantations. She has reconstructed the history of the Samal Balangingi diaspora spanning four generations of exiles, offering new materials, insights and an ethnohistorical perspective based on several periods of fieldwork in Cagayan as well as in the Mindanao-Sulu region.[74] The first generation of exiled survivors who were forced to live and work in a hostile alien environment never quite gave up the belief and age-old practises of their seafaring life ways.

As soon as the *deportados* arrived, the governor of Isabela sent the first group to the town of Camarag (Echague) to forced-labor on public works. Meantime, the season for planting tobacco and corn had begun. The exiles were given two days every week in which they were free to cultivate their fields and subsistence gardens and construct their houses. Balangingi warriors, who were formerly under the leadership of Panglima Taupan, Palawan Dando and Tumugsuc were distributed throughout the provinces of Nueva Vizcaya, Cagayan and Isabela. These exiled seafarers, along with their families, were designated land to cultivate and where they could reside–land that was within sight of the sentries or the tribunals of the towns in order to discourage them from escaping. Once free, on bonds of good behavior, the exiles were allowed to devote themselves entirely to working in the tobacco and cornfields and to practise age-old handicrafts compatible with their previous way of life. Eventually they were exempt from forced labor.[75] Although some of the first generation exiles and many of their descendants became Christians, I could find nothing in the Dominican archives (Isabela Province was under Dominican jurisdiction) concerning the deported Samal populations except a brief statement written by Fr. Buenaventura Campa in 1890:

> There is in this town Echague . . . a group of moros, the remnant of the prisoners exiled from Balangingi and Jolo after the expeditions of 1848 and 1851 which were commanded by the Governors Claveria and Urbiztondo, those transported a number of years later, and the descendants of the first exiles most of whom have already died.[76]

Hailan Kaligaran de Perez, aged 90, whose father was among the 350 Samal Balangingi exiled by the Spaniards, remembered him planting tobacco under the strict supervision of the Spanish planter and administrator 'Bohel' (Vogel): "There were no soldiers in the hacienda. When my father did not plant tobacco he did not get money. Otherwise Bohel gave him money."[77]

Interestingly, on the night of 4 April 1860, because of the low wages and hard labor imposed by Vogel, a handful of Balangingi escaped, taking a big *banca* ("sailing canoe") out of the settlement of Tumauini. They followed the Cagayan River until they reached Echague, Isabela, a natural confluence and stapling point for all sorts of trade and water transport. These Balangingi fugitives whose names were listed on an official wanted circular–Suti, Balangbingan, Bunang, Sadia, Caul, Ydding, Balanbulan, Misul, and his wife Matappiz–decided to settle as unobtrusively as possible on the other side of the *embarcadero* at a place called 'Dammang' which means 'across.'[78] As frontier pioneers, the fugitives opened up nearby lands, planting rice, corn, and vegetables which they traded with local merchants and farmers. As experienced tobacco farmers, they produced a fine grade of leaf for wrappers. There was a *sitio* in Dammang called 'Sinagan' where the Tabacalera collected high quality wrappers for cigars, especially cultivated by the fugitive exiles and their descendants. According to Cojuangco's elderly informants in Dammang, these first Balangingi arrivals, who were fleeing the regimen of the tobacco plantations, used a self-made banca and 'introduced the boat building skills to construct bancas to the local fishermen.'[79]

What meaning could the exiled Balangingi find in their forced removal and their social response to it? Each generation of exiles had to cope with their own history. The most difficult part of this was coming to terms with the traumatic events surrounding the destruction of Balangingi in 1848, the assault on Simisa a decade later, and the removal process itself. For the first generation, these events were all part of the protracted Samal-Spanish sea war, and the fall of Balangingi and the alien universe of the tobacco plantations. But in some fashion the members of the second and third generations had to also comprehend and deal with the crucial social and psychological problems in the lives of their parents and grandparents; and for the older generation of exiles the traumatic events were the fall of the Balangingi and the alien universe of the tobacco plantations. The problem of loss and restor(y)ing in Cagayan was to rewrite both the past and present, and that initial process of the excavation of 'family' sites and histories in turn impacted on issues of ethnicity, language and distance (geographical, historical and social). Clearly, some second and third generation exiles found the easiest way to try and cope with the world taking shape around them was to adopt the attitude in part that one must live one's own life and not be bothered by what both revolutionized and traumatized the lives of their former seafaring parents. Within a generation, some of these Balangingi, who had been baptized into Catholicism, had intermarried with neighboring Yoggad, Ilocano and Tagalog migrants, in Camarag and elsewhere.[80]

However, Haji Datu Nuno, alias Antonio de la Cruz, the Jesuit-educated youngest son of Panglima Taupan, established the importance of the places in which they had lived, and how much they grieved when they lost them. According to the oral traditions of the Nuno family, Noyla, his pregnant mother had been deported to Tumauini after the fall of Balangingi. In Tumauini she gave birth to a son, Haji Datu Nuno, who was baptized Antonio de la Cruz. Throughout the mid-1850s, Panglima Taupan is alleged to have made six or seven excursions throughout the Visayas and as far north as Mindoro and Ilocos searching for his wife and child, all in vain. But in the family history carefully handed down across the generations, Taupan is supposed to have eventually met his son, by then a ten-year-old Christian orphan residing in Echague, in Vigan. The oral account states he made his son promise to relocate the exiled Balangingi scattered throughout the north, as one people in their original homeland in the south. Panglima Taupan also stressed to the young man that his true identity was Balangingi and his true faith was Islam.[81] In fact, it is likely that Antonio de la Cruz was born in 1849, the year after the attack on Balangingi, to Noyla, Taupan's second wife. In 1858, several of the Panglima's wives were captured at Simisa, including Noyla, and her young son. It is highly likely that this was Taupan's son by Noyla, who in 1858 was nine years old. In 1866, at the age of 17, he was deported to Isabela. In the intervening years, he stayed in Manila and was given some formal instruction by the Spanish. He petitioned the government to return to Mindanao in 1881, to utilize his services as a culture broker, in a manner deemed most useful by the Zamboanga authorities. He could speak and write Spanish fluently. The local officials on the spot sought his assistance to facilitate the settlement of Taluksangay which was being populated by Samals.[82]

Many Balangingi who had lost a place of profound importance found it unforgettable. Feelings about lost or destroyed places, namely Balangingi and Simisa, roused their deepest emotions. As Panglima Taupan tragically learned from the Spanish strategy of removal and the meaning of lost places, losing a home or a village or being forced to leave a homeland was also meant to be like losing a loved one. Panglima Taupan and his orphaned exiled son, each in their own way, had to confront and examine what it meant to lose a place forever and why some of the first and second generation exiles kept on returning to those places so large in their memories. Both men, the father, a warrior, and the son, a man of letters, must have considered the meaning of the many lost homes, villages and the seafaring way of life. Hadji Datu Nuno's return to Jolo and Zamboanga in 1881 tells a human story of grieving and loss that is also inspiring. He was not returning to nothing. Hadji Nuno perceptively saw the beginning and the end of things for the exiled Balangingi in the sea. The most drastic demonstration of this simple but profound realization was provided when some Balangingi exiles who had lived in the Cagayan valley for more than 40 years, who had not changed their attitudes and beliefs so radically, chose to return to their 'real life' in the south. For those Balangingi their choice suggested a (re)viewing of Balangingi and what it meant to be Balangingi or 'moro' people from a far away outside (Cagayan) on the edge of remembering, forgetting and imagining. In the end, the forced removal and banishment of the Balangingi from their homeland did not lead to a condition of permanent exile for everybody. At the beginning of this century, Haji Datu Nuno, the son of one of the most revered and feared Balangingi chiefs, arranged with the American colonial authorities to repatriate some exiled Samal to Mindanao and Sulu. Francisco Vogel, the Spanish tobacco planter in Isabela, agreed to send those settlers who wished to go, providing they turned their land and plough animals over to him. In 1905, a hundred men, women and children returned to Zamboanga on the S.S. *Mauban*, and Haji Nuno settled them at Taluksangay, Tigboa and Tupalic.[83] Among those Balangingi deportados banished to the Cagayan valley and repatriated to Zamboanga by Haji Nuno were Hailan Kaligeran's father, Diego Kaligeran, and his mother. In the ensuing years, they would recount to their son, Hailan, who was born in Zamboanga shortly after their return from exile, the eyewitness stories and anecdotes of the ferocious defense of Sipac Fort, and the forced removal from their island homeland and relocation in the north.[84]

In 1941, R. Wendover, an American in charge of the 'cutch' camps in Zamboanga province, overheard several bark-peelers speaking Ilocano. When he asked them how they came to speak this central Luzon dialect, one of the men, Kising, stated that,

> he was born at Tumauini, in Isabella, and that his father's name was Damsig and his grandfather's name Insani. Both his father and grandfather, he said, had been taken to Manila aboard a Spanish ship. . . . Later, along with some two hundred other men,

women, and children they were taken to Tumauini and Echague on the Cagayan river. Many of them were christianized and Damsig married ... a Tumauini girl, Kising ... being the first born son.[85]

While none of the original exiles was still alive then, at Taluksangay an old woman, who was a second-generation exile, told her story.

She said her name was No-Jula, the daughter of Kasan, widow of Zalim. She was born in the Echague district about fifty-five years ago. She said her father, Kasan, had been captured by the Spaniards on Balangingi and had been taken along with the others, first to Zamboanga and then to Cagayan. Some of her relatives had escaped from Balangingi and had settled at Taluksangay, which was the reason why she had come here. Those of her group taken to Cagayan were settled near Echague, among the Ibanogs. They were at first put to work on the *haciendas* and kept under the surveillance of the government. The children were apprenticed to various planters to learn tobacco and corn cultivation. After some years they were given parcels of land and left free to sell their tobacco to buyers. As they lived in their own communities they were allowed to retain their own religion.[86]

The Spanish had been quite successful in turning these maritime people into tobacco cultivators, and from No-Jula's account, they appear to have known nothing about the sea upon their return to Mindanao. Her memories of Cagayan were fond ones. "One could always raise tobacco there and we had money and made a good living. Here [Taluksangay] many of us are landless and living is very hard."[87] In 1941, there were about 200 families of the second, third and fourth generation of Balangingi Samal exiles living around Zamboanga.[88]

Thirty years later, Majul noted that the Christian descendants of the exiles in the Cagayan valley were still recognizable, and the older ones could remember the *Kalimah* as recited by their grandparents. This tended to corroborate information given to me in 1974 that small isolated pockets of these people, Muslim Yoggads, who were located at some distance from Echague, still practised the Qur'an and traced their original settlement in the area to the removal and transportation of the Balangingi in 1848.[89] Some of those third and fourth generation Balangingi exiles who did not return to Zamboanga maintained some semblance of cultural roots that resisted the process of political incorporation and cultural assimilation promoted by Spanish policies and the increasing integration of local, regional and global economies. Margarita Cojuangco has highlighted the persistence of a Muslim cultural identity in Yoggad society, which takes common Balangingi ancestry, as the basis for membership, and promotes a collective trans-local or trans-regional identity, in a modern multiethnic state, the Philippines.[90] The rise and fall of the Balangingi in the nineteenth century demonstrates that there was no fixed 'Balangingi identity' before this century, but that it was always in flux. Conversely, as a consequence of the emergence of the Balangingi slave raiders as a distinctive ethnic group, any 'Filipino identity,' actual or imaginary, was also in flux and equally precarious. Hence, one has to take into account the political, economic and sociocultural aspects of these identities directly affected by colonialism, global commerce and slavery in order to understand how the Balangingi identity and ethnic community evolved and was maintained and reconstructed over time as a single ethnic group.

CHAPTER THIRTEEN

COLONIALISM'S PIRATES: THE 'SAVAGE' MYTH, ETHNIC IDENTITY AND HISTORY

Abandoning the Sea

Despite the destruction of Balangingi and the Samal Balangingi diaspora of 1848-1858, maritime raiding continued in the Philippine archipelago for three more decades. These dispersed Balangingi, who were known in the European records as 'Tawi-Tawi pirates,' were able to assemble between 60 and 100 prahus by joining forces with kindred groups in Jolo, and the Iranun of Tunku.[1] As in the past, Samal raiders attacked smaller poorly-equipped and poorly-defended villages in Tayabas and Albay provinces, but the greatest number of captives were taken from the coasts of Panay and Negros.[2] Since many Balangingi coastal attacks and abductions took no longer than 60 minutes, it was impossible for even the fastest Spanish vessels to come to the aid of the individuals or sailing ships under attack. There was, of course, the additional problem of hunting down the Balangingi lairs among the hundreds of islands in the central and southern part of the Philippine archipelago. However, in terms of sheer numbers of boats and firepower, the Spanish were now superior to the Samal, especially after 1860 when steamers were introduced on a large scale in the Philippines. This forced the Samal to reduce drastically the size of their flotillas. Of the new stratagem a Spanish naval officer wrote: 'Whereas in the past four expeditions of one hundred sail set out, now one hundred expeditions of four sail leave [the Sulu archipelago] and the problem is not destroying them, but finding them.'[3] The Balangingi's near total reliance on this mode of evasion was also noted by the English consul in Manila:

> Piracy still exists and large numbers are still carried . . . from these coasts into slavery but piracy is now carried on in small bodies of light boats and directed against the coasts and small craft of contiguous parts of these possessions, and no longer appears, as formerly, in combined operations of large fleets of proas. . . .[4]

At the same time, the suppression of Balangingi maritime raiding was now principally a matter for Spain and the colonial government in the Philippines, and Claveria's successors had a real interest in putting an end to its existence. The scale of the effort that Spain now devoted to antipiracy operations against the dispersed Balangingi largely reflected the imposing resources at its disposal and the new priorities of those in power in Manila in the aftermath of the destruction of Balangingi in 1848. The southerly shift of Samal marauding activity was intensified by the advent of flotillas of war steamers in Philippine waters. In 1860, under Governor-General Norzagaray, 18 prefabricated steam gunboats, (*canonero*) were sent from England (around Cape Horn) and assembled at the Cavite shipyard en masse. With the arrival of the steamers the Spanish navy abandoned cruising among the islands, deploying instead the vessels in key straits in the archipelago through which the Balangingi passed, and at several stations in the Sulu Sea. The English vice consul at Iloilo reported:

> Of the steam gunboats which are replacing throughout the Archipelago the heavy sailing boats (*faluas*) previously employed, Yloilo has been supplied with two. These have in some measure promoted . . . communication with neighbouring islands and provinces, and occasionally with Manila, and are likely to prove much more effectual in repressing piracy than the former gunboats. Recently they have had several encounters with the pirates of the Sooloo sea, in the immediate neighbourhood of Yloilo, and have brought in five pirate *pancos* and other smaller boats, making away with between two hundred and fifty to three hundred of these habitual depredators of the Philippine coasts.[5]

The speed, firepower and maneuverability of the canonero stemmed Samal-Balangingi maritime raiding. Many observers, including St. John, stressed that the sudden appearance of these steam warships were 'beginning to disgust them with the life,' of maritime raiding.[6] After 1860 garay no longer prowled unchallenged and Samal losses mounted as fleets were defeated and swept away. In less than three years, four squadrons were destroyed by the steamers in the Visayas alone. When the canonero were encountered in open sea, the Balangingi were annihilated:

> In the channel between Tawi-Tawi and Borneo fifteen *pancos* were sighted. Their numbers, movements, and course appeared suspicious, and the Tausog on board, who were experienced in such matters, felt they were Balangingi. The *canonero Samar* began pursuit. The chase lasted two hours during which time the pirates made strenuous efforts to reach the security of the Tawi-Tawi coast. When unable to do so, because we had placed ourselves between them and the shoreline, the *pancos* hove to as a group to fight. I then gave the order to sink them; a half an hour was all that was necessary to accomplish it, during which time the ram and cannon worked in unison to destroy them. . . . I continued steaming on course towards Borneo amidst the debris and bodies that covered the sea.[7]

The port of Isabela on Basilan was fortified by the Spanish and became their principal steamship post in the south. From there and from Balabac, nine or more gunboats regularly patrolled the Sulu Sea. The appearance of steam gunboats in the Visayas and the Sulu Sea, and a series of expeditions conducted by the Spanish navy against Samal settlements on Tawi-Tawi, from 1860 to 1864,[8] forced the Balangingi to shift their marauding activities away from Philippine waters into the Sulu Sea. Nevertheless, Negros Oriental and Surigao suffered attacks along their coasts until 1875, and desultory slave raiding was still experienced in various parts of the Philippines on the eve of the twentieth century.[9]

The English and Dutch undertook similar measures in a joint venture to protect the coasts of Borneo, Java and Sumatra in the early 1860s. During the appropriate season, they placed steam gunboats at fixed stations all along the raiding track of the Samal and Iranun. The British, who in the last quarter of the eighteenth century had set the Iranun loose on the populations of the Netherlands Indies and allied realms of the VOC, were now more than prepared to assist the Dutch in shortening the lives of the Iranun and Balangingi—fostering hell on high water. In the second half of the nineteenth century, Britain, the imperial power that had once encouraged Iranun maritime raiding as a strategic weapon against the Dutch, having now established her own colonial claims, destroyed the remaining Iranun and Balangingi bases with Batavia's assistance, hunting down the defiant predators all over the region, from east Java to east Borneo. Britain and her former global rival discovered common colonial interests in an orderly South China Sea system of regional capitalism, through which trade and commodities would flow and capital accumulate without attack by the Iranun and Balangingi who continued to haunt the sea lanes of Southeast Asia.

The British and Dutch colonial governments and navies reached a maritime cooperation agreement following the devastating work of the Spanish antipiracy campaigns of 1848-1858 aided by steam warships and naval experts in Muslim affairs based at Manila and Zamboanga. The British and Dutch authorities drew up a plan which would help the Straits Settlements and the Netherlands Indies tackle major problems, including Iranun and Balangingi maritime raiding, arms and drug smuggling and distant search and rescue operations. This was the first time since the mid-1830s that these two colonial powers had more or less agreed on a course of action that would seriously constrain Iranun and Balangingi maritime operations. Rarely had these nations agreed to limits on activities affecting the national security of their colonies. The antipiracy cooperation plan, which covered maritime boundaries, piracy, slave trafficking, and illegal arms, also sought to improve communication and cooperation between the British and Dutch maritime monitoring services, including their navies, coastguards and policing operations. Under the plan, both countries would share knowledge about the movements of Iranun and Balangingi at sea, assist in the identification of maritime raiding ships and work together on antipiracy and emergency rescue operations. Naval memorandum on the proposed plan described the guidelines for the maritime agreement as a comprehensive approach and major contribution to regional security and the development of colonial capitalism. The importance of these early 1860s guidelines stemmed from the unfolding complexity of the regional economic-geographic setting, the significance of maritime issues in the region, and the ongoing propensity for 'illegal' Iranun and Balangingi activities to occur at sea.[10] However, not all the recommendations in the plan were supported by Spain. Manila had reservations about a number of issues including naval cooperation, maritime surveillance and ongoing claims over territory in north Borneo.

By shifting attention away from colonial relationships now and the tension between integrative and 'disintegrative' forces thought to be shaping Southeast Asian lives economically, culturally and technologically, and in terms of changing ethnic and political identities, the historian is able to treat the quarter of a century after 1860 as a critical period worthy of consideration in its own right. I have traced in detail in *The Sulu Zone* the fateful relationship between Sulu's trading aristocracy, the Iranun and Balangingi maritime raiders and the British, Dutch and Spanish naval forces based in Singapore, Batavia and Manila, examining the impact of global-regional development and strategic initiatives after 1860 on the fortunes of the Tausog political system. After the maritime raiding fleets were swept aside in the mid-1860s, local western observers said the Sulu Sultanate was now all about drug money, gun running, debt slavery, and high risk. Debt bondage as an economic institution was most fully developed in Southeast Asia in the second half of the nineteenth century, as global trade and monetization affected local social systems and regional trade networks. At the same time, the very survival of slavery in different parts of Southeast Asia, as elsewhere in the world, was being called into question. The main slave-raiding areas in the South China Sea and the waters of eastern Indonesia and the Philippines had, for more than a quarter of a century, attracted the intense naval pressure of Britain, the Netherlands and Spain. Hence, by the 1880s, the number of newly captured slaves moving across the region had been reduced to a trickle.[11] During the boom years of high colonialism, slave life in Sulu was both transformed and degraded, as the number of imported Tagalog, Visayan and Malay captives as a percentage of the overall slave population of the sultanate declined. Slaves still brought directly from the Philippines and eastern Indonesia experienced more difficult if not shorter lives.[12] However, while many Balangingi, notably Panglima Taupan and his followers were driven into exile and forced labor, pockets of Samal maritime culture remained surprisingly resilient in the shadow of the burgeoning colonial plantation and mining economies. The post 1860s force and trajectories of the various Iranun–Samal diaspora still remained very much alive even as the modern plantation and colonial capital tried to seal the doors to the seas of Southeast Asia.

But the eventual abolition of slave traffic in Southeast Asia was a mortal blow to the economy of a state like the Sulu Sultanate. When aristocratic Tausog, in Sulu, and others could no longer rely on maritime slave raids to supply sufficient numbers of captives for their needs, the amount of tribute ordinarily collected from dependents increased dramatically, and the fines in the various legal codes also increased. In the 1870s and 1880s, Tausog datus could no longer depend on traditional institutionalized sources of wealth accumulation, namely, the acquisition of imported slaves, because of concerted colonial efforts to eliminate maritime raiding. The political importance of maritime raiding and slaving in Sulu statecraft as a means of gaining material support, prestige and prowess declined. There was no longer a sufficient social incentive to go slave raiding and the Iranun-Balangingi age had all but faded away by 1898. The presence of the British at Labuan, of the Spanish in the Sulu Sea, and the Dutch on the east coast of Borneo made the Sulu-Mindanao region itself the final theater of Balangingi operations. The elephants cruised and the mosquitoes, as was anticipated, began to disappear. By 1875, the Iranun and Balangingi were confined to capturing riverine shore dwellers and Samal Bajau Laut on the north Borneo coast. A combined fleet of Iranun and Samal prahus from Tunku and Tawi-Tawi were alleged to have captured 600 people in 1877, and the following year straits officials heard numerous reports of Tawi-Tawi slave raiders scouring north Bornean waters with impunity.[13] The future prosperity of the northeast coast under the North Borneo Chartered Company was made secure only after the H.M.S. *Kestrel* bombarded Tunku in 1878, and Dutch steamers took active measures in the Berau region.[14] Tunku's destruction and the presence of Dutch warships on the southern periphery of the Sulu Sea were responsible for a drastic decline in the size and number of Samal forays down the northeast coast. Raids, however, continued to be made against north Bornean territory until the 1890s.[15] The North Borneo Chartered Company–administratively weak, plagued by a host of financial problems, and concerned about the territorial designs of its Dutch neighbor—was unable to prevent maritime slave-raiding, especially by the Samal in Darvel Bay, or the continued movement of captives from Tawi-Tawi to Bulungan.[16] Small-scale Samal marauding and slavery were abolished only when the Americans closed the slave markets on Sulu and Tawi-Tawi in the first decade of the twentieth century.

The Merciless Savage and Empire Building

Spanish colonization of Mindanao and Sulu began with the concerted naval campaigns against the Balangingi after 1848 and culminated in the late 1880s with the occupation and conquest of the old ruling families that confronted the Spanish forward movement in mainland Mindanao. During that time, a period which witnessed the eventual economic and political collapse of the Sulu trading sphere and the consolidation of high colonialism, both the Spanish and English systematically created, in official documents and pronouncements, novels and short stories and theatrical productions, a composite image of Iranun and Balangingi 'character,' as an ideological prelude and intellectual justification for the mid to late nineteenth century conquest and colonization. One of the most enduring characteristics of three centuries of Muslim-Christian relations and conflict in the Philippines was the susceptibility of non-Muslims to think about the Iranun and Samal in stereotypes evoked by the Spanish policy of *Divide et Impera*, giving the Muslim and Christian Filipinos disparate identities.[17] Over the previous three centuries, most Spanish and Filipinos cast all Muslims, particularly the Iranun and Balangingi, in stereotypical images that changed somewhat from time to time to suit new colonial needs and conditions but which were invariably denigrating. They were collectively labelled 'moros'—an appellation carrying the burden of foreign connotations from the time when Islam challenged the Holy Roman Empire for the domination of Europe. By the 1850s, the Iranun and Balangingi, infamously labelled as 'moros,' were regarded simultaneously as depraved, uncivilized, subhuman savage warriors and shiftless, untrustworthy foreigners, who were unable to handle their own affairs and liable to annexation and conquest. Hence, in the aftermath of the Spanish conquest of late nineteenth century Mindanao and Sulu, the Iranun and Balangingi, were still branded 'moro' which remained synonymous in Christian Filipino minds with pirate, savage and bandit. Such preconceived ideas and notions about the stereotypical meaning of 'moro' and a contested sense of time and space, had already been amplified in the metaphysics of Muslim-hating and empire building in the Philippines when the earlier tide of Iranun and Balangingi maritime raiding and the heresy and 'menace of Islam' swept over the archipelago in the latter half of the eighteenth century.

The Iranun and Balangingi were considered in the minds of ordinary Filipinos and Malays to be well-organized, numerous and ruthless. Their massive fleets and small-scale operations were hallmarks of the Iranun and Balangingi. Flotillas of lanong attacked large trading ships and regional centers, while Balangingi slave raiders, hundreds strong, harried small settlements along the coasts of the Philippines and Sulawesi and left such a feeling of dread among the local populace that anything threatening or evil became synonymous in the minds of mothers and children with the 'Illanoon' and 'moros'–the notorious 'pirate tribes of Mindanao and Sulu.' The lesson to be learned everywhere across Southeast Asia was deep and powerful, especially for ordinary Christian converts whose belief system was essentially animist but whose world under colonial rule was rapidly becoming 'modern.' On Luzon or Sulawesi, a Tagalog or Menadonese might see clearly what they might become if they did not live according to their highest evangelized nature. The Iranun warrior and Samal seafarer became important for the Spanish and Dutch colonial mind, not for who they were in and of themselves, but rather for what they showed 'civilized' colonized men and women they were not and must not be. Every year, for decades on end, formidable expedition commanders had rampaged throughout Southeast Asia, spreading terror and bloodshed. While a residue of great fear remained for those left behind, mourning the absence of their lost kin, the captives did not always feel the same way once they had been forcefully moved to Sulu and Balangingi and assimilated to their new way of life.

Stemming from profound differences between the cultures of Spain and England and the cultures of the Iranun and Balangingi, as well as from Spanish and English colonial self-interest, convictions of superiority, and a chronic disinclination to view Iranun and Balangingi motives and actions from any perspective but their own, these myopic imperial images and beliefs signified by the signs 'Moro' and 'Illanun' defamed and dehumanized the Muslim inhabitants of Sulu and Mindanao, reducing them in the European mind and imagination to something sinister and faceless, akin to the barbarians who resisted Roman rule and Christianity–barbarians who had to be cleared from the seas of Southeast Asia rather than the lands of Caesar's empire. Not only did the pejorative images associated with the labels 'Moro' and 'Illanun,' as ethnic pseudonyms, contribute to further misinformation, misunderstanding and hostility, but they justified and made more acceptable–as their lasting legacy does to this day–the final aggression and injustice. Over the course of the nineteenth century 'Moro' and 'Illanun' emerged as terms of 'character,' in colonial policy and practice and public discourse, wrongly implying a single group of people with a common language, territory and set of beliefs that carried the burden of savagism. Frake has stressed that the label 'Moro,' in the context of the Spanish *reconquista*, inquisition and colonization by Spain of the Philippines, became not only a religious label but an ethnic one as well; a label for a social identity and character to which defamatory behaviors and traits were ascribed.[18] By the repeated use of the appellation and the accusation, Spanish administrators and friars and English colonizers and intellectuals, established the Islamized inhabitants of Sulu and Mindanao, as dangerous fanatical 'rovers'–Muslim pirates– who transgressed local-regional borders and boundaries; boundaries only recently forcibly imposed and maintained by the colonial powers. Hence, they were framed and represented as uncivilized and outside the law. The Spanish and British used the labels 'Moro,' 'Moor' and 'Illanun' to obscure the nature and extent of internal ethnic differentiation that existed in the Sulu-Mindanao region. The Muslim maritime raiders were never characterized in an individual manner; the Iranun and Balangingi were meant to drown in an anonymous collectivity under what Alfred Memmi called the 'mark of the plural.' "They are this." "They are all the same."[19] Thus by the turn of this century the 'Moros,' in the eyes of Filipinos, had become the 'pirate tribes of Sulu and Mindanao.'

The memory of the Iranun and Balangingi maritime raiders lingered well into the first half of this century long after they had ceased to pose an imminent menace. For example, Cullinane and Xenos stress, in their reconstruction of the regional demographic history of Cebu, that the memory and fear of 'Moro depradations' is embedded in the legends and folk histories of many municipalities and parishes of Cebu to this day.[20] 'Moro' came to symbolize all that was dangerous, dark and cruel about the tragic confrontation, and the Iranun and Balangingi's adherence to Islam. For the Spanish the colonial enterprise in the Philippines was in many ways a religious enterprise. For the British sea tenure and empire were also finally to be demonstrated from a different sort of theology– capitalism and industrial technology. But the fundamental characteristic and central focus of the centuries-long mutual conflict and tension had always been the fact that almost everything that mattered to the Iranun and Balangingi had come to be defined and measured by the sea–the seas which in so many ways were invented, 'discovered,' and eventually conquered by the Spanish and English. The central fact of domination and empire was the fundamental attitude and belief that the Iranun and Balangingi possessed their seas only as a natural right, since that possession, in the minds of the Spanish and English, existed prior to and outside of a properly civilized state. What followed then, was that the sea was technically *vacuum domicilum*, and that the Spanish and English, who would control the sea and make it productive for Christ and world commerce, who would give it order and regulate interregional trade, were obliged to take over and exterminate the 'moros' and 'Illanun' of the 'eastern seas' in order that laissez faire trade and colonial Christian enterprise could be carried out successfully. This extreme posture and situation had always been incomprehensible to the maritime Muslim people of Sulu and Mindanao, and it was also clear that the central focus of these cultures in conflict had always been in the sea–the sea which, in more ways than one, was 'discovered' by Spain and Britain and functioned as a political instrument, a commodity, a national prerogative and aspiration. The Iranun and Balangingi were defined by it, measured by their domination and use of it, and were to be dispossessed of it. But, in the latter half of the nineteenth century, even as the Balangingi Samal were deported and the last Iranun villages and raiding prahus were burned or broken up, the denigrating image of the 'Moro' and 'Illanun,' as 'slave raider and savage pirate,' now began to hold new moral meaning for both the European and Christian Filipino imagination. The myth of the 'savage' now both evoked and guaranteed the final success of the larger sacred-secular drama of colonialism, conquest and annexation and the vision of the Filipino people's own place in it, just before the dawn of the twentieth century.

In nineteenth century Spanish literature on the *guerras piraticas de Filipinas* and English accounts about the 'Illanoon' and 'Malay piracy' there is an association of the male Muslim physical and psychical self with the raw environment and nature which uses the sea–littoral ethnoscapes– as a canvas against which 'moro' and 'Illanun' identity and place might be interrogated and problematized as a precursor to the cant of conquest. These images that were carved out of language systematically by the Spanish and British were also imposed on the seas and islands of the Iranun and Balangingi, as a geographical sign of their dangerous, uncivilized, albeit contaminated character, and labelled as ominous, 'vile' sites, unclean sites beyond the pale. These sites of noncolonial space were important, as were the maritime people who lived in them, precisely because they were areas out of reach of colonial and state control. The networks of atolls, rocks, shoals, and submerged reefs were described as natural 'nests' and 'webs,' implying a breeding ground for rats, other vermin and spiders–frightening dirty creatures in peoples minds that always caused fear and harm. Hence, the best means of eliminating the danger of such sites of contamination and pollution, cunningly perceived to be 'infested' with rodents and insects and, carefully masked by linguistic images of filth and disease, was to 'eradicate' them, meaning the extermination of the Iranun and Balangingi. This reading of the sea and the maritime world of the Sulu zone in mid-nineteenth century European texts was not uncommon. The use of such pejorative language to describe the presence of these formidable seafarers from land-based representations associated with filth, pollution and danger does not, however, undermine a potent 'other' political-historical reality. Rather, it demonstrates the suspect nature of certain European histories, as their authors attempt to reinforce western-centered myths, identities and traditions. Reconstructing and reinterpreting the ethnohistory of the Iranun and Balangingi in this way discloses the nineteenth century reading positions made available by the hundred year-long crisis in Spanish-Philippine history and identity politics. The dialogue of difference, when reinforced, invokes violence and breaks down the cultural stubbornness and resistance declared within specific historical landscapes. Eradication actually meant the systematic attempt by the Spanish government to wipe out the entire culture and maritime way of life of the Iranun and Balangingi. Three years before the wholesale destruction of Balangingi, Claveria had already used the chilling discourse of purity and danger and ethnic cleansing,[21] in a letter written to the Minister of War dated 12 April 1845, as an intellectual justification and symbolic statement to wage total war against the 'moros,' thus demonizing the Balangingi in the process:

> It would be in vain to listen to their promises nor pay any attention to their guarantees in order to persuade them to renounce such an infamous trade [in slaves], because this traffic constitutes the sole means of their livelihood. It is identified, to say the least with their very existence; and they are like animals who always cause destruction ... the only means of dealing with them is to exterminate them.[22]

In his penetrating analysis of the state of the Philippines published three years earlier, Sinibaldo Mas used vermin and illness as metaphors to reinforce pejorative social attitudes towards various 'moro' groups, namely the Iranun and Balangingi, the scourge of the nineteenth century Philippines. In his probing 1842 book, *Estados de las Islas Filipinas*, Mas demonstrated that 'moro' was a metaphor for a 'vile horde,' the terror of their own time, a mark of doom, but the writer, who was socially and politically concerned, felt from the microbiological standpoint that the illness could be treated and 'cured.' Mas argued that establishing a flotilla of steamers would be an extremely useful first step, but it was still not a radical enough remedy: "It would be easier to destroy a squadron of 40 or 50 large vessels than these ['moro'] launches. So it is with bugs, fleas and other insects of a bad breed."[23]

However, in the face of the relentless political and social upheavals caused by the 'moro' raiders, the interest in Manila, in Mas' epidemiological common sense, lay in his willingness to cut to the heart of previous interpretations of the serious danger and illness implicit in the medical metaphor with which friars and earlier administrators had described the enemy of all humankind. He advocated instead radical surgery–total war and banishment. In other words, urging a wholesale policy of ethnic cleansing. Sinibaldo Mas' discourse on 'moors and piracy' carried with it a ring of truth for Claveria with its emphasis on rampant Muslim piracy, ideas of pollution, the multiplication of paranoia and the creation of terror sapping the human and economic foundations of the colony. To justify their violence, Mas portrayed the 'moros' as being vile and savage–just as Claveria's expeditionary force portrayed the 'moros' of Balangingi as being fierce, malevolent slave raiders, in order to vindicate the ferocity of their crackdown and the eventual fate of the Samal.

Stamford Raffles and James Brooke and Dutch officials, like Muntinghe and Tobias, had also repeatedly maintained in their writings and public pronouncements, especially Brooke, that the 'Illanun' were 'fierce, numerous and warlike; without question the worst pirates in the archipelago.' Brooke's essentially racist portrait of the Iranun based on a deep-seated animosity and mistrust would be echoed half a century later in Joseph Conrad's influential fiction. It was now over 40 years since the Spanish exiled the Balangingi from their island homeland, and a bit less since the Iranun gave up, no less willingly, their stronghold at Tungku. Though some of the racist and imperial writings of individuals like Sinibaldo Mas and James Brooke had lost none of their sting in the intervening years, Conrad was more inclined to portray what it was about the Iranun background and their way of life which led them to act as they did in their relationships with Europeans. Conrad began writing his 'Eastern tales' in an age when the rhetorical aspect of the New Imperialism played an important role in a linguistic, albeit cultural, reappropriation of the Malayo-Muslim world of Southeast Asia. Besides the visible alteration of that world by colonial conquest and annexation, imperial writers, wielding their pens as instruments of empire, were fictionalizing the environment, creating powerful literary structures that would frame and reinforce the patterns of dominance over particular geographical areas and conquered subject peoples.[25] The 'Illanun,' as indomitable other, differentiated both racially and by creed, challenged this hegemonic imperial process and rhetoric and the narrative strategies of Conrad as he explored the encounter between Europeans and 'Illanun' in his novels with an Indonesian setting. Conrad's fictional 'histories' of contact and colonialism focus uneasily on the cultural encounters between Europeans—merchant-adventurers, vagabonds and colonial officials—and, non-European people, particularly the 'Illanun,' reconstructing the experience of both sides between various extremes, and collision, leading to the eventual destruction of previously autonomous groups like the Iranun and weaker Europeans.

Relying primarily on Raffles, Brooke, Belcher, and Keppel as his principal ethnographic and historical sources on the 'Illanun,' Conrad has shown in his fiction how many European men, all non-English, suffered from a deep malaise in the presence of the dreaded 'Illanun.' Many Dutch, German and Eurasian traders lived in fear that these Muslim maritime raiders would sweep them and their fledgling enterprises and daredevil schemes into oblivion; and several relied on opium to comfort themselves and assuage their anxiety in the face of 'the terror.'[26] In Conrad's fiction, 'Illanun,' both noble and savage, had their destined place in the unfolding order of Anglo-Saxon imperial history according to the dictates of time. Both kinds would be eliminated through superior British moral values, technology and legal-juridical processes and the passage of time to make way for the presumed sovereign British way of life. The noble 'Illanun' deserved Conrad's pity for his late nineteenth century condition and his passing, but his roving maritime way of life no less than that of the ignoble 'savage' raiders, demanded strict censure according to Darwin's evolutionary scale of progress and the passage of Anglo-Saxon history. Conrad's texts exemplify the position that fiercely independent seafarers—'Illanun'—of Malayo-Muslim states such as Sulu were inscribed with shared values and shared norms through the structure of that state; a state framed and represented as a 'pirate' state and slave state. In the end, his fiction demonstrates there is legitimation of the interests (economic, racial, class, religious) of the dominant Anglo-Saxon group. This kind of legitimation is evident in his writings with his protagonist Tom Lingard's desire to 'clean up the pirates' because their values differ from and do not conform to the

Anglo-Saxon ideas that are embodied in the dominant social order and with the legitimation of imperial and colonial practice. What Conrad preached in his novels with an east Indonesian setting, about the inevitability of Anglo-Saxon civilization and imperialism dominating the oceans and superseding Malayo-Muslim savagery, regardless of courage or nobility, the children of his English and continental readers learned also from textbooks that were replete with similar images of Asia, about travel, adventure, color prejudice, and the forging of empire.[27] An important legacy of the politically conscious literary output of Joseph Conrad in the years of high colonialism was his (un)masking of the ideological biases or wills to power that lay behind the pretensions to universality and impartiality of particular moral views. In other words, early twentieth century readers were reminded of the way in which conceptions of 'reason' or of 'goodness' were the historical and contingent constructions of particular societies and cultures, and the links between such constructions and power.

Conrad's novels helped shape the vocabulary and the imagery that turn-of-the-century colonial administrators and settlers used to describe their actual experiences in maritime Southeast Asia and the lifestyles they observed among its seafaring peoples, like the 'Illanun,' Samal and Bugis. In turn, the accounts of explorers, naval officers, missionaries, and other travellers and adventurers provided the 'factual' basis, and therefore a validation, for the ethnographic image and imagining about other people and places rendered by Conrad. This dark, refracted, albeit somewhat tempered version of the 'Illanun,' as a symbol of the naturally free savage, persisted into the twentieth century, sometimes grudgingly advanced by a seemingly impartial Conrad. In the mid-1880s, he had briefly sailed in the Sulu and Celebes seas as first mate on a Singapore-based Arab-owned steamer, the S.S. *Vidar*, and, as a fellow seafarer, had found something to admire in the Iranun maritime way of life. But having had no actual first-hand contact with them Conrad generally conceived of them as bloodthirsty raiders, intent on murder, pillage and slave taking. G.J. Resink, a professor of Indonesian legal history, used the writings of Joseph Conrad to show that there were still numerous independent Malayo-Muslim realms beyond Dutch Java at the end of the last century. According to Resink, a mixture of Iranun, itinerant European-merchant adventurers, Bugis and Arab traders were the most important *dramatis persona* visible on the horizon of the eastern archipelago under Joseph Conrad's western eyes.[28] But Conrad actually believed that in the judicial and administrative control of other peoples like the 'Illanun,' the British had no ethical equals in the West. The English trait of 'simplicity of motive and honesty of aim' was not found in the business methods of most of the protagonists of Conrad's Indonesian fiction.[29] The reader does not have to be told their nationality, one only has to look at their names—Willems, Schomberg, Almeyer, and Hudig.[30] Conrad's novels and short stories set in the eastern archipelago, explore the ambiguous self and that 'in between' space, for their moral thinking and their moral lives, arguing that the Anglo-Saxon imagination and technological superiority both resists and shows up the inadequacies of that larger dichotomy between the West and the non-West as well as a host of other ones, including such philosophical distinctions among the English and continental Europeans between reason and emotion, fact and value, thought and experience. It is against this background of the reader being constantly reminded of Conrad's belief in the superior quality of Anglo-Saxon patterns of governance, judicial administration and trade that the historian must determine how the celebrated author has framed and re-presented the 'Illanun character' in his novels.

The almost mythical Capt. William Lingard—the model for Tom Lingard in Conrad's novels with an Indonesian setting—known as the Rajah Laut, or Lord of the Seas, all over Southeast Asia from Singapore to the Torres Straits, and from Timor to Mindanao, had made his fortune in the 1860s and 1870s by discovering a secret passage to sail up the Berau River in East Borneo. Tom Lingard, the celebrated Rajah Laut, in *The Rescue*, is also depicted as a man of 'high mind and pure heart' in accord with Conrad's conception of Anglo-Saxon superiority in administering the lives of Asian peoples. The author is able to forcibly demonstrate the English merchant-adventurer's innate Anglo-Saxon virtues of courage, objective justice, assumption of responsibility and trust, while attempting to effect control over the 'Illanun,' a Muslim seafaring people with a philosophy totally alien to that of Lingard. In *The Rescue* the 'Illanun' and their lord, Daman, a man of prowess, with his fleet of between 30 and 40 raiding prahus, play a central role in the novel. They had come to help

Hassim, the Wajo prince, reclaim his territory from which he had been expelled by civil war and Dutch intrigues. They were simultaneously on the lookout for gunpowder, arms and plunder during the course of their special mission. Daman proudly tells his followers, "The Illanun seek booty on the sea. Their fathers and the fathers of their fathers have done the same, being fearless like those who embrace death slowly."[31] Conrad subtly portrays the 'Illanun' carrying out the dictates of their destiny and the not so subtle oppression and betrayal that such an autonomous destiny demands. Daman hates Europeans because of the treatment of his ancestors at their hands but Conrad adds tragic stature to Daman's view of life to keep the novel from becoming simply another romantic tale of Malay pirates and far-flung empire: "His father and grandfather . . . (having been hanged as an example twelve years before) had been friends of Sultans, advisers of rulers, wealthy financiers of the great raiding expeditions of the past. It was hatred that had turned Daman into a self-made outcast."[32]

When the Illanun lord and his chief captured two European men and held them for ransom, Daman's aim was to obtain sorely needed arms and gunpowder from both Lingard and a stranded European yacht, which was under the Rajah Laut's protection. Forced by circumstance, and the drive of his own instinct, Daman entered into negotiations with Lingard:

> It was perhaps a great folly to trust any white man, no matter how much he seemed estranged from his own people. . . . Lingard's brig appeared to him a formidable engine of war. He did not know what to think and the motive for getting hold of the two white men was really the wish to secure hostages.[33]

Lingard himself was extremely wary of the Iranun lord, despite his own charismatic reputation as a great warrior, a Rajah Laut–the king of the sea, which had secured his safety at the parley up until then. He knew that 'not one of them but has a heavy score to settle with the whites.'[33] Wasub, a loyal friend, had also warned Lingard to exercise extreme caution in approaching Daman at the meeting: "Daman is crafty and the Illanuns are very blood-thirsty. Night is nothing to them. They are certainly valorous. . . . Tuan should take a follower with him . . . one who has a steady heart . . . and quick eyes like mine—perhaps with a weapon—I know how to strike."[35]

Lingard eventually secured the release of the hostages—he and Daman being sworn to keep their word.

The character Babalatchi, the skillful one-eyed 'prime minister' and *shahbandar*, who features in *Almayers Folly* and *An Outcast of the Islands* was also an 'Illanun' and had been a 'pirate.' Joseph Conrad did meet a Dongala trader called Babalatchi when he was on the *Vidar* but it is not certain that aspects of the life of the historical and fictional characters match.[36] Conrad's character could also have been partially based on a seaman called Jadee. Jadee's life cycle and background fits with Babalatchi's remarkably well—having been sold as a slave to 'Sulu pirates' when he was very young. Both had similar careers as maritime raiders and *serangs*.[37] In *An Outcast of the Islands* the reader is given an insight into Babalatchi's 'Illanun' past:

> Babalatchi had blundered upon the river while in search of a safe refuge for his disreputable head. He was a vagabond of the seas, a true Orang-Laut, living by rapine and plunder of coasts and ships in his prosperous days; earning his living by honest and irksome toil when the days of adversity were upon him. So, although at times leading the Sulu rovers, he had also served as Serang of country ships.... He gathered experience and wisdom in many lands, and after attaching himself to Omar el Badavi, he affected great piety.... He was brave and bloodthirsty without any affection, and he hated the white men who interfered with the manly pursuits of throat-cutting, kidnapping, slave-dealing, and fire-raising, that were the only possible occupation for a true man of the sea. He found favour in the eyes of his chief, the fearless Omar el Badavi, the leader of Brunei rovers, whom he followed with unquestioning loyalty through the long years of successful depredation. And when that long career of murder, robbery and violence received its first serious check at the hands of white men, he stood fearlessly by his chief.[38]

In Conrad's panoramic examination of history, the 'Illanun' were neither devoted to nor inspired by the Anglo-Saxon idea of 'simplicity of motive and honesty of aim.'[39] In the English writer's representation,

COLONIALISM'S PIRATES

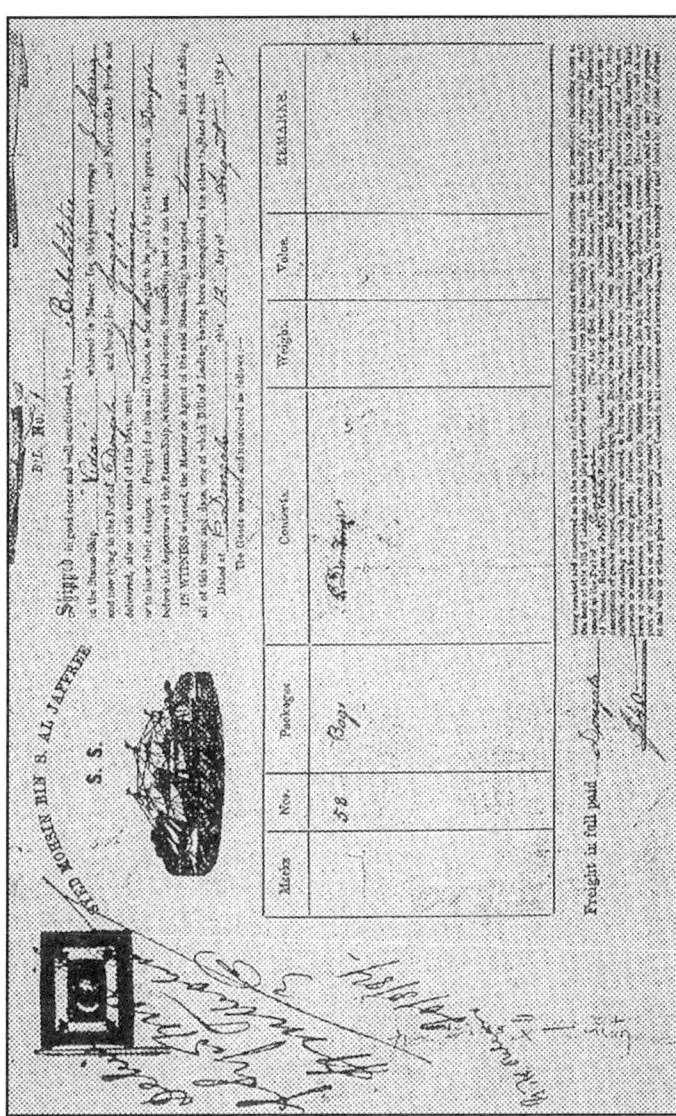

Courtesy of Stirling Memorial Library, Yale University.

Fig. 26. The character Babalatchi, the skillful one eyed 'prime minister' and Shahbandar, who features in *Almayer's Folly* and *An Outcast of the Islands* was also an 'Illanun' and had been a 'pirate.' Joseph Conrad met a Dongala trader called Babalatchi when he was on the S.S. *Vidar* but it is not certain that aspects of the life of the historical and fictional characters match.

where the Illanun raided they intended to be masters and suffered no rivals. While Conrad admired the sea being the home of the Iranun more so than the land he still considered them, like the Arab traders, both unscrupulous and resolute.[40] Conrad, when writing about 'Illanun' character traits and reasons for 'Sulu piracy,' drew upon the West's deep seeded distrust of the Islamic world. Despite the passage of more than a century, the echoes of religious wars fought by Muslims against infidels on Java and Sumatra reverberate through his fiction. Conrad, in *The Rescue*, depicts Daman and the 'Illanun' as Muslim pirates descended from nomad, camel-riding ancestors, notwithstanding their inspired bold leader. The Europeans, whose yacht was perilously stranded repeatedly, use as synonyms 'moors,' 'savages' and 'barbarians,' when mentioning the Iranun. Conrad, through this not so subtle process of negation, which unduly stresses Muslim religious zeal and fanaticism, makes the 'Illanun' seem even more dangerous—as militant Islam served to prolong and nurture mutual hostility in the face of western progress:

> Daman ... advanced alone. The plain hilt of a sword protruded from the open edges of his cloak. The parted edges disclosed also the butts of two flintlock pistols. The Koran in a velvet case hung on his breast by a red chord of silk. He was pious, magnificent and warlike.[41]

In *An Outcast of the Islands*, Conrad also dwells on Islam, war and men of prowess, introducing the blind, dispossessed leader of Brunei Rovers, Omar il Badavi, Babalatchi's ex 'pirate' chief, in a similar vein:

> I knew him well when he had many slaves, and many wives, and much merchandise, and trading prahus and prahus for fighting. Hai-ya! He was a great fighter in the days before the breath of the Merciful put out the light in his eyes. He was a pilgrim, and had many virtues: he was brave, his hand was open, and he was a great robber. For many years he led the men that drank blood on the sea: first in prayer and first in fight! Have I not stood behind him when his face was turned to the West? Have I not watched by his side ships with high masts burning in a straight flame on the calm water? Have I not followed him on dark nights amongst sleeping men that

woke up only to die? His sword was swifter than fire from heaven and struck and flashed. Hai! . . . Those were the days and that was a leader, and I myself was younger; and in those days there were not so many fireships with guns that deal fiery death from afar.[42]

Conrad thus perpetuated in the English-speaking world the reconquista 'moro' image of the Iranun–bloodthirsty thieving Muslims–as a legacy of the Spanish friars and other European colonizers. However, when considering maritime raiding activity in Southeast Asia, it must be remembered that the Iranun were often defending their religion as well as their political system and right to trade, along with the hypocrisy that allied the English with the Iranun against the Dutch in the sea war of the late eighteenth century. Old Jorgenson, the former captain of the *Wild Rose* and Lingard's fellow adventurer in *The Rescue* could remember the *Padri* war, and the name of Sentot, who fought by the side of Prince Diponegoro and who, as a *Ratu adil*, earned the title 'King of the South shores of Java.' It is Sentot's grandson who is one of Daman's lieutenants. Conrad therefore links the anticolonial religious wars and jihad at the start of the century and the eventual elimination of 'Illanun piracy' at the end of the century to the final formation of one state, the Netherland East Indies, embracing the Indonesian archipelago.

Despite the celebrated author's literary efforts to dissect the social and psychological impact of European colonialism along the margins of a Malayo-Muslim maritime frontier, his attempts to embroider certain aspects of 'Illanun' character and traits fails. Conrad's portrayal in literature of the 'Illanun,' Bugis and Arabs as 'Muslim souls,' individuals with inner lives capable of depth or superficiality, whose capacities for moral understanding and growth were intrinsically bound up with their loves and grief, their imaginations, their preparedness to be surprised by and to wonder at each other and their Islamic world in conflict with the West, intentionally fostered a legacy of animosity and mistrust. In Conrad's case, moral understanding was inseparable from emotional response, and that to recognize a fact about the 'Illanun' was to be able to judge or value it, and that the capacity for serious and authentic thought about the 'big' facts of human life in the maritime world of the Islamic Iranun was conditioned by his experience as a 'Polish nobleman, cased in

British tar' and his reader's response to it. Conrad helped western societies to remember the close of a traumatic period in Southeast Asia's history after nearly a century of upheaval from state-sanctioned maritime raiding by the Iranun and Balangingi that had directly affected hundreds of thousands of people and fostered a culture of fear and violence. His literature helped both citizens and institutions to forge individual and collective perspectives and memories of the 'Illanun,' consideration of whose actions were still especially painful on personal grounds to many, and establish boundaries between the 'Illanun' and 'the reader.' The real strength of this orphaned Slavic seafarer, who even later as a famous author among the British, but always British with a difference, was that he addressed some of the deepest moral and philosophical implications of the West's rise to world domination, in a manner which took seriously literature's distinctive way of thinking about language, self and the creation of a new Anglo-Saxon world under colonialism and the destruction of old societies and cultures within Asia, Africa and Latin America. Conrad's moral imagination and literary ethics were consciously Anglo-Saxon, deliberately privileging a particular sort of English conception of autonomous rationality and class-biased conceptions of social order that both framed and constructed negative images of maritime Islamic peoples and 'far eastern' landscapes. Images of the 'Illanun' were fixed in Euro-American imaginations by the linguistic reappropriation and rhetorical processes of negation in his dramatic novels and short stories of the clash between East and West.

Commodities, Ethnicity and History

In *Iranun and Balangingi*, I wanted to resolve an apparent paradox in Southeast Asian history about 'piracy' and politics in the Malayo-Muslim world and European imperial policy and expansion in the region. The paradox is that the rise of the Sulu Sultanate, increased maritime raiding and the opening and imminent decline of China at the hands of Europe took place at much the same time, (the end of the eighteenth and first half of the nineteenth centuries) as the introduction of tea, an important commercial plant from China, in Europe.[43] By the end of the eighteenth century, Britain's insatiable desire for this commodity was to change the face of Asian history and shape the future destinies of both Sulu and China. The capitalist world economy came to dominate the Sulu Sultanate and its environs. Chinese demand for exotic commodities, suddenly of great interest to Europeans, encouraged both the establishment and 'take off' of subregional trade networks and the production of goods. New entrepots emerged, especially in the area of the Sulu Sea and Borneo. The island of Jolo became a major center for cross-cultural trade in the recent history of Eastern Asia and the Sulu Sultanate flourished. The Tausog became locked into a vast web of trade and exchange involving the exploitation of the rich tropical resources of the area, with producers, distributors and controllers involved in a complex set of relationships and structural dependency. For the sultan, with his capital located on the seacoast, the entrepot and neighboring areas incorporated a set of cultural-institutional practices typical of centralized trading states based on redistribution for the production and acquisition of goods, on the one hand, and kinship, warfare, slavery, and other forms of organization and culture on the other.

Certain lessons and examples from history about global economic-cultural interconnections and interdependencies tend to explain patterns and events which have formally been glossed over. For example, sugar 'demanded' slaves and the Atlantic slave trade. Similarly, tea, inextricably bound to sugar as product and fate, would also inadvertently 'demand' slaves in the Sulu-Mindanao region and thus lead to the advent of Iranun-Balangingi maritime slave raiding. Since the British primarily wanted sea cucumber, sharks fin, pearls, and birds' nest for the trade in China tea, the issue of the nature of productive relations in Sulu–slavery–suddenly became primary. The demand for certain local commodities in return for imports affected the allocation of labor power and the demand for fresh people throughout the Sulu zone. In this globalizing context, tea was more than simply the crucial commodity in the development of trade between China and Britain. It was also a plant that was instrumental in the stunning systematic development of commerce, power and population in the Sulu zone which changed the regional face and history of insular Southeast Asia.[44]

Within the Sulu zone centers of distribution and exchange developed and, in association with the development of larger interregional markets, capital flows and technology transfers international trade increased and the sultanate established itself as a major entrepot. The steady influx of captives to collect and process commodities for the thriving China trade made the Sulu Sultanate a strategic location to do business. When Englishmen like Dalrymple, Rennel, Forrest and others first came to Sulu in the 1760s they recognized that the 'zone' was a potentially inexhaustible source of natural commodities for the China trade. They soon learned too that Tausog datus and other leading inhabitants of this region would exchange these products for manufactured industrial goods. Eager to extract natural resources from this virtually unchartered area, European merchants extended their international trade network and knowledge of the world to the 'zone,' after 1768. The speed of historical change is important here. The reverberations from the shock waves of Braudel's time of 'economic systems and states' emanating from events on the southeast coast of China, because of the intersections of the world capitalist economy, were felt especially early in the Sulu archipelago.[45] The English, to protect their financial interests in China, distributed firearms and gunpowder on a large scale to the coastal chiefs, who controlled the redistributive trade of the Sulu zone. The early acquisition of cannon, gunpowder, flintlock rifles and shot from the European-China traders in return for exotic commodities led to increased traffic in slaves, warfare and, at the same time, ever rising levels of arms imports into Sulu in the last quarter of the eighteenth century. Inexpensive British manufactured muzzle loading flintlock rifles and other arms imports led to the reframing of Southeast Asian political boundaries, especially in the area of the Sulu archipelago and eastern Indonesia. The Tausog managed to maintain organized maritime military power on a large scale and consolidate control over trade for an extended period of time because of the strength and discipline derived in part from the improved guns and industrial technology of Europe—firearms that would threaten the social order and stability of much of Southeast Asia when placed in the capable hands of the Iranun and Balangingi.

The British were fully aware of the importance of Sulu in their efforts to open China to trade and dominate world commerce and economic growth. The primary vehicle for British colonization of Southeast Asia was the British East India Company, one of the world's largest trading and shipping companies in the eighteenth and early nineteenth centuries. Country trade activity in Sulu was an integral part of its struggle against the Dutch and its trade rivalry with Spain. Like the British East India Company, the VOC, the Dutch East India Company, was a chartered monopoly representing both public and private interests with mercantile establishments in Indonesia, South Africa, Sri Lanka and Japan. The VOC attempted to dominate the trade and shipping of Indonesia until its abolition in 1798, when it went bankrupt and faced mounting British instigated Iranun raids and naval competition. The plight of the VOC in the 1790s forced a reluctant Netherlands Indies onto the regional stage before a rapt audience of British 'piracy' watchers who believed the Iranun could help destroy the already tarnished image of the mercantile chartered company and provide conclusive evidence that the Dutch were incompetent to deal with the maritime raiders. While the broad contours of Sulu's colonial experience are familiar, they also reflect the enduring legacy of the late eighteenth-century precolonial period, the specific policies and practices of the British East India Company and the Dutch and Spanish, and the crucial timing of the sultanate's incorporation into the world of global commodity production, which in turn set the stage for the Iranun and Balangingi maritime raids of the late eighteenth and nineteenth centuries.

The unceasing demands of both Europeans and Chinese for exotic commodities like sea cucumber and birds' nest increased slaving activity among certain groups in the Mindanao-Sulu region, who were lords of the sea and skilful warriors. To obtain more guns and ammunition, metal tools, textiles and opium for the Tausog and for themselves, these maritime raiders had to obtain increasing numbers of slaves to collect and process particular commodities to sell to the China tea traders. Thus, there was a rising demand for tea in Europe with a concomitant increase in regional-wide slave raiding activity in Southeast Asia. Tausog datus partially repatterned the social organization and ethnic identity of particular maritime groups to meet the soaring European and Chinese demand, and to gain direct access to western technology and Chinese trade goods. In this way the exchange of Chinese tea and European firearms as entangled commodities, embedded within the framework of expanding economic growth and improved military organization, set the stage for the explosive emergence of particular maritime marauding populations in the space of just several decades. Moreover these highly mobile raiding populations took it upon themselves to 'modernize' and acquire foreign technology, including gunpowder weapons, to rapidly strengthen their strike force and social organization, and to enhance their ship building techniques and nautical skills. Indeed the post 1780 era saw maritime slave raiding more widespread and intense than at any earlier time as the Iranun and Balangingi borrowed both knowledge and technology from European and Chinese traders. Chinese compasses, European charts and brass telescopes were all widely used to significant advantage as 'weapons of war' by these intrepid sea raiders. The Iranun and Samal Balangingi, armed with the latest navigation aids and firearms, struck fear into the hearts of coastal and riverine people throughout Southeast Asia. The local populace was soon afraid to live along unprotected stretches of the seacoast or come down to the ocean front from the interior. Until quite recently, villages in many parts of eastern Indonesian, particularly on Buton, were either situated well inland, or, if on the coast, on steep cliffs with extremely difficult access, the historical legacy of defense against the threat of Iranun and Balangingi marauders and slave raiders.[46] Barnes in his classic study of Lamalera, a remote community on the South Coast of the island of Lembata, near the eastern end of Flores notes the village is really a 'twin settlement,' with a lower one (Lamalera Bawah) on the beach and an upper one (Lamalera Atas) on a nearby clifftop for protection from earlier maritime slave raids. Such villages in eyrie-like settings were usually palisaded, but in this case (as at tira, the site of Southon's fieldwork in Buton) the main defense was inaccessibility. An early missionary told his superiors that the Iranun and Balangingi would never, 'in an eternity,' climb up to the upper village, and if they did somehow manage it, they would never get down again from the cliff top location to the shore except by falling. Heersink also notes that on Salayer most of the nineteenth century settlements were situated in the interior. Here the northern and southern extremities of the island were the least safe, and suffered most from Iranun 'piracy,' while the alluvial westcoast became the prominent zone of security and trade.[47] New evidence has also emerged supporting the widespread fear and dread of the Iranun in the Java Sea. Stenross, researching the traditional sailing boats of Madura, recently accidentally stumbled upon people with terrifying memories of the Iranun still intact on the north coast, in a small isolated village. In Tamberu he found—while discussing photographs of Bajau grave markers shaped like miniature boats—evidence of centuries old oral traditions about the 'Lanun' that are indicative of cultural confrontations and conflicts. These confrontations originated in the violent intimacies of the encounter between expansive Iranun and their desire for *sirih* (betel nut), and struggling, oppressed coastal people. Obviously, the fear of the Iranun went a long way since their maritime raiding tracks crossed regional and ethnic boundaries like no other before, not bypassing even a tiny village like Tamberu, reaching extremes of pain and alienation among the Madurese coastal inhabitants there. This is a lingering image and memory of the 'Lanun' immersed in impending danger rather than one of noble seafarers and warriors on a path of glory in a sea war against the Dutch.[48]

The regularity of these raiding sweeps were as predictable as the winds which carried the Iranun and Samal Balangingi boats to their target areas. Each year on the approach of the 'pirate wind' in August, September and October that brought these lords of the eastern seas and people fishers to the southern Visayas, Borneo and the straits of Malacca, the Dutch, Spanish and English issued customary warnings to coastal towns and small craft. Scattered along the coastline of the Philippine archipelago one is still able to find, sometimes with some difficulty, the remnants of the century-long terrifying presence of these raiders—an old stone watchtower, a crumbling church-cum fortress, or the ruins of a Spanish fort and cemetery—decaying monuments to the export of tripang and birds' nest and a host of other commodities and the import of firearms from Europe and the United States along with many Chinese goods. The remains of such neglected sites and fortifications, primarily concentrated along the coasts of Ilocos, Catanduanes, Albay, Cebu, Leyte, and Samar, bear silent witness to the advent of sudden affluence in the Sulu Sultanate and deep despair, displacement and dispersion of people throughout the Philippines.[49]

Indeed, the rapid development of maritime slave raiding was to keep pace with Sulu's global trade by providing the essential requisite for the continued growth of commodity production and processing in the Sulu-

Mindanao region–labor power. One extraordinary feature of the global interconnections between Sulu slavery and the advent of the capitalist-world economy, was the rapid movement of systematic maritime slave raiding across the entire region as one Southeast Asian coastal population after another was hunted down. From the end of the eighteenth century to the middle of the nineteenth, Southeast Asia felt the full force of the slave raiders of the Sulu Sultanate. Captive people, from right across Southeast Asia in their tens of thousands, seized by these sea raiders were put to work in the sultanate's fisheries, in the birds' nest caves, or in the cultivation of rice and transport of goods to local markets in the regional redistributive network. Thus the Sulu state created and reproduced the material and social conditions for the recruitment and exploitation of slaves in the zone. More than anything else it was this source and use of labor power that was to give Sulu its distinctive predatory character, as a 'pirate and slave state,' in the minds of Europeans in the nineteenth century. China's tea trade and the global economy changed the pattern of maritime warfare and economic and social relationships among particular seafaring populations in the Sulu and Mindanao region, increasing its intensity and scope across the region. It led to widespread decimation and displacement of entire populations throughout the lowland Christian Philippines and much of the rest of Southeast Asia. Sulu was primarily an ascendant trading state, standing at the center of a widely spread redistributive network and economy. But it was under Tausog sponsorship and in the service of that interdependent globalizing economy that others raided throughout the Southeast Asian world. It is worth emphasizing again the powerful economic forces that were pushing the Tausog aristocracy in the direction of acquiring more and more slaves. In the first place, their desire for various kinds of commercial products coming in from world commerce had to be satisfied–demands that were constantly increasing. These demands were both a consequence and cause of slavery. In order to trade, it was necessary for the Tausog to have something to give in exchange. Hence the collection and exchange of natural commodities was dominated by those datus with the largest number of slaves–that is, by the sultan and certain datus on the coast who were directly involved in Sulu's global trade. Secondly, the more dependent Sulu's economy was on the labor power of slaves, the larger loomed the question of its supply of slaves. The only way for the Tausog to obtain the commodities which formed the basis of their cross-cultural trade was to secure more slaves, by means of long-distance maritime raiding.

It began some 235 years ago, first mentioned in a short paragraph on the pages of Thomas Forrest's history of reconnaissance and travel—the initial migration of several thousand distraught people from the lake region of southwestern Mindanao across a strait to the neighboring island of Borneo, landing at Tempasuk.[50] There was no simple solution to the problem of the Iranun-Maranao refugees from the Lake Lanao region, as there would be no simple solution for the problems of the refugees of Prince Nuku's war against the VOC over the next several decades. Many were farmers who needed land, but parts of southern Mindanao had become a devastated rocky volcanic landscape with no empty arable land. Fishers were better off, but they needed boats and nets. At first the Maranao or 'Iranun' newcomers had negligible impact on the traditional societies who had lived on the northwest coast of the large island for centuries. But within the short space of just several decades a major transformation occurred. More Iranun-Maranao speaking migrants arrived. They took control over much of northwest Borneo, using European arms and the seafaring technology of large scale maritime raiding developed in southern Mindanao and the Sulu archipelago, as a direct consequence of the impact of the China trade on Tausog economy and society. Fortified Iranun-Maranao communities and bases with an aristocracy linked by kinship and long distance maritime raiding soon emerged and spread to the straits of Malacca around present-day Palembang. By the early nineteenth century, the once small band of Iranun refugees and adventurers that Forrest had chronicled in passing, had developed into a loosely unified confederation with a new culture centered around maritime raiding and slaving triggered by the rise of the Sulu Sultanate and its ferocious desire for captives and slaves.[51] The migratory maritime raiders spread to the rest of Southeast Asia, establishing major bases in the Philippines, Sumatra, Lombok, Flores, and Sulawesi. Forrest noted that some of the Iranun-Maranao migrants and warriors, who had formerly held a lowly rank within the traditional hierarchy of the Maguindanao and Tausog involved in the China trade, became men of power and prowess, both a master and a lord, when they became 'Illanun.'

The latter part of the eighteenth century marked the opening of China to trade with the West, but the second half of the century had also been a century for raiders, refugees and recalcitrants in the eastern archipelago. By the 1780s and 1790s VOC officials were becoming numb to the seemingly endless campaigns of ethnic conflict and rivalry in Sulawesi and the Moluccas, and the subsequent repression and collapse of Prince Nuku's anticolonial struggle, particularly the streams of traumatized poverty-stricken people who fled from the VOC sanctioned violence. But the Dutch could not afford to ignore the problem of these disaffected refugees living in fear of repression from Ceram, Batchan, Tidore, Sangir, and elsewhere. However, these homeless, stateless groups were neither contained nor helped to start life anew and became ideal fodder for the invading Iranun whose cause they served. Without land on which to grow food and without a job, these 'Tobello' opted for the food and rewards that the Iranun offered. They were angry and powerless. The Iranun gave them power and the chance for revenge. Their emotions against the VOC were easily manipulated so they could strike back. And the plight of these refugee groups became the excuse for a whole series of violent episodes and Iranun-inspired raids that lead to another exodus of pro-Dutch refugees and allies in the early decades of the nineteenth century. By the late 1830s, islands in the Banggai archipelago were completely deserted because of the overwhelming intensity of these slave raids.

Iranun-Tobello maritime raiding increased in Southeast Asia at the start of the nineteenth century as did the cost to the world economy in Asia and economic growth, which then topped hundreds of millions of pounds. Estimates of losses from maritime raiding reached as high as several million pounds a year. Most cargo insurers like Lloyds were helpless in the face of the onslaught. If challenged on the open sea, the Iranun did not hesitate to kill their victims, take over their ship and sell both the ship and its cargo in Sulu or on the black markets regionwide. Theoretically, a ship stolen in the straits of Malacca or the Java Sea could simply turn up as far away as Jolo or Tunku, with a different sail and rig, name and flag. Most attacks occurred in the narrow parts of the major straits of the region. At certain times of the year, in these bottlenecks and chokepoints the trading prahus generally had to slow down in the crowded sealanes. The Iranun usually approached and boarded when the sea was calm, the air still and, with most crewmembers exhausted after a long chase panic set in. The raiders, using swift oar-and-sail driven boats, skillfully synchronized the speed of the prize and threw grappling hooks and boarding bridges on to the deck. They lost no time in taking over the captain's quarters, disarming and manacling the crew and breaking open the ship's armory. The British and Dutch realized that if they just ignored the Iranun they would become bigger, more dangerous and equipped with ever more sophisticated raiding technology. And that is exactly what happened in the first half of the nineteenth century with Indonesian waters having the highest risk of maritime attacks, and the number of cases increasing every year. The Iranun sea warrior habitually armed with a *kampilan*, lance or gun struck terror into the hearts of Christian Filipinos and 'Malay' Muslims alike. Captives interrogated by colonial officials had often been traumatized by the violence they had witnessed during the sea attacks and settlement raids along the coastline. The oral traditions of their descendants still speak of 'the terror.' Oral informants traditionally recount how their families had lived along the coasts of the Catanduanes, eastern Visayas, eastern Palawan, Buton, Sangir, or west Borneo for generations. It had been their homeland. Then suddenly one day many sails massed on the horizon–'Illanun' or 'moro' sails. They tell of the terrifying landing on the beach and of the way that the slave raiders ended years, perhaps several decades of anonymity and a quiet life, that hid their ancestors from the war at sea and the machinations of the world economy. In some instances the kin who were absent at the time of the raid could not readily comprehend what had happened. Occasionally, a young boy who had been away fishing returned to find the body of his father on the beach while his mother and all his brothers and sisters had simply disappeared–swept away as captives. Beyond the collective memory of such a traumatic time, the very landscape itself in much of the region constitutes a persistent feature of this officially sponsored violence, bearing silent witness to the suffering of its victims. For example, the Iranun coming from Sulu in the 1790s raided and settled in Berau, where a low green hill, Gunung Illanun, still bears their name.[52]

By arguing for a broader global economic perspective in order to understand the significance of Iranun and Balangingi maritime raiding and slaving interesting complex questions are raised about what constitutes our conception of 'culture' and ethnicity. In the period under consideration, thousands of captive people were allocated throughout the Sulu-Mindanao region each year as slaves, and the borderlines of 'culture' and ethnicity were increasingly blurred by the inclusive practices of cultural accommodation and assimilation. I maintain that the Iranun and Balangingi not only lived in an increasingly interdependent world but that they also lived within the sphere of an emergent multiethnic state–the multicultural inhabitants of which came from many parts of Eastern Asia and elsewhere in the world. How are identities–single or multiple–forged? What symbols, rituals and perceptions create a strong sense of collective identity? The traditional assumption of a 'culture' as enduring over time despite outward changes in people's lives and value orientations is both 'empirically misleading and deeply essentialist.'[53] As Roger Keesing noted, there is no part of eastern Asia where both the production and reproduction of 'culture' and cultural meaning can be characterized as unproblematic, without glossing over or disguising radical changes in relation to ethnicity, power and hierarchy that have differentially affected states like Sulu and maritime frontier ethnoscapes like the zone.[54] In terms of not exaggerating the boundedness, discreteness and homogeneity of life taking shape in the Sulu zone at the end of the eighteenth century, the power of language, religion, memory, and commodities as both signs and symbols in the construction of new identities and communities is perceived as central. This aspect of *Iranun and Balangingi* defines the formation of ethnic identity in the light of tightening ties to the capitalist world economy and the wider world of darul Islam. I have stressed the inextricable relationship between maritime raiding, slavery, forced migration, 'homeland' and cultural identity as being critical factors that led to the emergence of new ethnicities and diasporas. Captives and slaves were encouraged to adopt Islam and marry. Some slaves who thoroughly accepted the dominant culture were permitted to purchase their freedom. Manumission was commonly practised and freed slaves were assimilated into the general population, assuming a new ethnicity and status. For slaves of the Iranun, Balangingi and Tausog conversion and marriage were prerequisites to manumission. This expedient reconstructing of ethnicity and identities, resulting from the interconnected complex influences generated by the China trade, compels us to think about related notions of society and 'culture' in more processual ways.[55] Historians of the region need to locate the emergence, maintenance and abrogation of populations, and the 'cultures' and ethnic self-definitions they encompass, within the framework of a series of historically changing, imperfectly bounded, multiple and branching integrated sets of local, regional and global social and economic alignments.

In the Philippines today, it seems history is still being used and abused to shape the future. The Philippine past is ideologically crucial, and the stakes in the struggle to control it are high indeed, especially with respect to the ethnohistory of the Iranun and Balangingi. How does possible contestation over the nature and relevance of explaining the birth of Iranun and Balangingi ethnicity itself give meaning to identities and broadly held societal views in the Philippine present? Some Balangingi and Maranao would rather not hear too much about their ethnic origins with Luzon and the Visayas—regions they annually raided and ruled from the sea in bygone days. I have argued in this book and elsewhere that today's Balangingi are principally descended from Christian captives arriving from the Philippines between 1800 and 1848. Fresh insights and undeniable evidence from the statements of the fugitive captives of the Sulu Sultanate backs up this view that wave after wave of captives transported from Luzon, Cebu, Negros, Leyte, Panay, and Samar came to dominate the local Samal populations in Balangingi. The existing culture transmitted religion, language and certain maritime technologies and nautical skills and the arriving peoples greatly affected the existing population and their history. Ethnohistorians like the Comaroffs, Leach, Keesing, Wolf, and myself have stressed that the genesis, persistence and transformation of ethnicities must be understood within a set of fluid self-defining systems, embedded in economic and political relations and contingent upon specific historical forces and events. We are now acutely aware of the 'origins' of Balangingi and Iranun ethnicity to their present configuration, and of the dynamic and ecological aspects of 'culture' and place as well as how ethnic identities have been constructed and reconstructed in local-regional history on a large scale.

By tracing the history of the Iranun across Southeast Asia the base system emerges as a major social innovation. But it appears that the transient colonizing Iranun invested far more in indigenous aspects of local regions and their inhabitants than has been thought to be the case. Under concerted colonial pressure, the Iranun federative network that transcend political boundaries, composed of peoples with distinct languages and different forms of social organization, based on a string of satellite communities, ultimately proved fragile, because if one base collapsed the whole maritime raiding network was more vulnerable. By the mid-1850s, as the Iranun lost more distant places of importance to them in the straits of Malacca, Sulawesi and elsewhere they struggled in search of a new ethnic identity abroad and the concomitant reconstruction of a new subjectivity as, for example, 'Linganese' around the cultural landscape of Reteh. The case of the Balangingi both prior to and after losing their homeland also shows that maintaining and managing ethnic self-identification and the writing of its history in the Philippines, has been both a dynamic process, and a contested domain and that cultural difference as signified and articulated by ethnicity is both problematic and precarious. This is the historical process recounted by myself and a growing number of anthropologists and historians attempting to understand extraordinarily diverse peoples and ethnic origins in the history of Asia east by south—in my own case, by attempting to address here one of the most politically sensitive issues in Philippine society and history. The evidence, mostly written testimonials, as well as oral traditions, is very strong, if not overwhelming. Yet, perhaps, the most striking part of the untidy history of the Iranun and Balangingi since the late eighteenth century, which argues against bounded homogeneous ethnic groups, is how little attention it has received among most Filipinos both Muslim and Christian alike. Its forces and characteristics are both historical and mythical, global and local, and Islamic and Christian. The relationship is a dialogic one between varying periods of Southeast Asian and Philippine history. The historical representations, certain phases and traditions are inseparable from one another and flow through each other. As they are brought to life in *Iranun and Balangingi*, these 'dead men and women' speak to each other and the world, and in so doing disquiet notions of Philippine identity, unsettling the dominant visions of history like *Kasaysayan*, the handsomely produced ten-volume *History of the Filipino People*, in which the Iranun and Balangingi are historically omitted, culturally silenced and never visible. In an echo of eighteenth century beliefs, many intellectuals and ordinary citizens still prefer to suppose that the origins of the Balangingi and Iranun are neatly shrouded in the distant past as 'moros,' denying the fluid nature of ethnic identity and a more precise historical method for tracing the process of ethnic self-identification. If today's Balangingi and today's Cebuano, Ilocano, Tagalog, Visayans, and Yoggads share the same ancestral roots, what does that reveal for understanding what it means to be 'Filipino' and for political relations between Christians and Muslims? Again, the questions posed about the birth and accomplishment of ethnicity in *Iranun and Balangingi* for understanding both the recent and distant past in Southeast Asia are far-reaching, if one considers the complex and contemporary theoretical cultural implications of the nature of 'ethnicity,' (often associated with economic and political conflict in developing societies) as a key concept for unravelling the development and history of the terms 'Indonesian,' 'Malay,' 'Thai,' 'Burmese,' and 'Vietnamese.' These labels have been successfully created by modern states in the interest of national unity and to mythologize history.

The formation and prosperity of the Sulu Sultanate, as this study of the intersections between maritime raiding, entangled commodities and the economic and cultural history of the state indicates, was based above all on the labor of captives and slaves. It was the role of the Sulu state, within its large trading zone, to maintain the material and social conditions for the recruitment and exploitation of slaves. The enormous increase in global trade which affected state formation, statecraft and economic integration made it absolutely imperative to import captives from outside the zone to meet labor power requirements. As commodities from China, Europe and north America flowed to Jolo, the Tausog aristocrats thrived, and there emerged the Iranun–strong, skilled maritime people who were the scourge of Southeast Asia, as they raided and slaved in 90-feet long prahu. The sea and tropical forests were the life force of the sultanate, where tens of thousands of captives and slaves labored annually to collect and process exotic commodities for the China trade. The arrival of captives on a hitherto unprecedented scale, because of lack of labor power, and their gradual 'disappearance' through inclusive systems of kinship and social organization into the lower levels of Tausog and Samal society was central to the political development and expansion of the Sulu Sultanate and its redistributive trading system. The rising demand for captives and slaves from across Southeast Asia reshaped the character of the political economies of Sulu and China and, as part of the same process, gave birth to the advent of highly specialized mobile communities of maritime raiders. Thus the history of slaving and the slave trade and the rise of the Iranun and Balangingi must be framed as part of a unitary historical process, which explains the major factors contributing to the formation and maintenance of their ethnic identity, namely the intrusive roles played in their sudden development and expansion by the global economy and singular entangled commodities, particularly tea, sea cucumber, birds' nest, and firearms. Maritime raiding, or what the Spanish, Dutch and British labelled piracy, was not a manifestation of decay and dependence but rather it was the result of phenomenal economic growth and strength. The state-sanctioned system of maritime raiding and slaving in Sulu was part of a vital effort to partake in and control a rapidly increasing volume of global commerce caused by the advent of Europeans in the China trade in the late eighteenth century. Accusations of cultural decadence and barbarism that were repeatedly directed against the Sulu Sultanate by the leading European participants in that trade are both ironic and incorrect when approached from the perspective of a unitary historical process. The Sulu Sultanate was able to channel its resources for statecraft and for social structure in the direction of maritime slave raiding when the new circumstances of the China trade suddenly made collecting and processing of exotic commodities so profitable in the zone.

The large-scale progressive intake of captive peoples from various parts of Southeast Asia and elsewhere also reflected the Sulu Sultanate moving closer to Europe and China, both economically and culturally. In the pages of this study the Southeast Asian world has changed through the intersections of the global economy centered around the Sulu and Celebes seas, as well as the sultanate's, China's and the West's complicated place within it. Here, Southeast Asian farmers and fishers are traumatically uprooted and forced to live in a distant economic region—a world comprised of winners responding to new economic opportunities of 'globalization' and losers, those experiencing fragmentation and being forced to live in ways unanticipated before that moment of capture and enslavement. Trade debts in Jolo are paid off by captives and slaves serving Tausog masters in the fisheries and forests of the zone. The point is that tens of thousands of ordinary Southeast Asians lived among Muslim maritime peoples–raiders and fishers–completely removed from those with whom they had been born and grew up. They found themselves abroad in the mangrove coasts, sand beaches and coral reefs of the zone, first because advanced technologies and new social alignments made long distance maritime slave raiding easier and, second because revolutionary economic historical developments forcefully landed them in an unintended place–the Sulu zone. European traders joined Tausog datus to spark off one of the largest population movements in recent Southeast Asian history with hundreds of thousands of individuals sent into slavery across the Sulu-Mindanao region. By the start of the nineteenth century, slave identities in the zone were being shaped and changed by the forces of the capitalist world economy as distinctions of ethnicity and culture blurred and broke down; thousands of 'outsiders' were being assimilated into the lower stratum of a rapidly expanding trading state and society. The China trade from the standpoint of these individuals made the populating and demographic origins of the zone yellow, black and white rather than just brown. All this ethnic edging up against one another and establishing ongoing relations involving conditions of slavery had been for the sake of a widely consumed, mildly addictive commodity which had become a necessity in the European diet and way of life–tea. I have placed more emphasis on demography than Braudel did in his classic study of the Mediterranean basin because the 'real motor of social change' was population. Slavery and maritime raiding were not solely economic institutions which enabled the late eighteenth century expansion of the Sulu state and domination of the regional trade network. Slavery and the management of ethnic self-identification had virtually become the very basis of social organization and statecraft in the sultanate. Sulu provides an exceptional case study of *how* collective identities were established, made real, and took on a particular ethnic and cultural content.[56]

In this volume, which is a blend of social history with solid ethnography, I have argued that there was no fixed 'Iranun' or 'Balangingi' identity prior to the imposition of colonial rule at the end of the nineteenth century. The formation and maintenance of their ethnicity was continually in flux because of competing forms of social organization and discontinuities in space and time, caused by their integration into the capitalist world economy and fearful rise to regional prominence. As a consequence, the shifting political, economic, social, cultural, linguistic, and religious aspects of their identities have been taken into account, in order to understand the birth of the 'ethnicity' and history of the Iranun and Balangingi—a history which spans several centuries and encompasses a past that still evokes feelings of anguish, conflict and hatred. This manner of historically conceptualizing the 'ethnicity' and 'culture' of these now two quite separate and distinct maritime communities leads us to a new way of framing and representing a sense of kinship, group solidarity, common culture and conflict, particularly political struggles, in the ethnohistory of Southeast Asia. By stressing the problem of self-definition and the reconstruction of identities and the meaning of homeland and lost places, as a revealing social and psychological process in its own right, *Iranun and Balangingi* challenges the lineal notions of history and bounded static conceptions of 'culture' and ethnic groups that were imposed, imagined and maintained by Europeans both before and after colonization. The labels 'moro' and 'Illanun' provided a major intellectual justification for Spanish, British and Dutch retaliation and religious incursion against Sulu and Mindanao in the nineteenth century. Until quite recently, the appellation 'moro' was synonymous with a specific social disposition, 'cultural' attitude and behavior and associated with ignorance, depravity and treachery. The label, by turning history into myth and stereotype, signified an Islamic people in the Sulu archipelago and Mindanao who were still considered to be 'savages,' 'pirates' and 'slavers.' This view of the history of the Iranun and the Balangingi was once orthodoxy; it is now under challenge as factually inaccurate, unjust and actively destructive. I have documented, through their own and other accounts of their lives and activities, the formation of their ethnicities, their participation in a regional search for slaves, their struggle for freedom against European powers, their key role for statecraft in the capitalist world dominated economy of Sulu and the tragic fate of their maritime raiding organizations and networks. I have attempted, based on intensive analysis of archival sources, fieldwork notes and oral traditions, to reconstruct an accessible history of the ecological, economic and political achievements of the Iranun and Balangingi over a century and a half; a history which also provides a firm ethnohistorical basis for understanding their past and future between the myths.

APPENDICES

Appendix A

A Letter Soliciting Trade between the United States and Sulu

To Capt. G.E. Ward
    Navigator of the Spanish Brig Leonidas

[Seal]

Sir,
I herewith inform you that having consulted with the Sultan and chief Datoos, I find it is the wish of all as well as your humble servant to establish a commercial intercourse Between [Sulu] and the United States of America which I believe will be equally Beneficiall to both parties and as you cannot enter into any contract without the consent of your Gov.^{mt} am requested to inform you that it is the General wish of all the chief men of Soloo that you return here with a cargo of American produce according to the enclosed list which I am authorized to State will meet with a ready Sale to the extent of fourty or fifty Thousand dollars. Further that you shall have every privelege and protection while in our Port That the most favoured enjoy. Also that if your Govern.^{t} will give you power to form a treaty with us on equitable terms that we Should be much pleased thereat. For we are well acquainted with the Glory that the Americans have gained in their Struggles with other Nations.

Wishing you a safe and speedy return to the Land of the Brave and the home and embraces of your friends.

I remain your H^{bl} Servant
D'Amilbahar

[Seal]

Soloo —
P.S. We Trust to see you again in eight or nine months with a Cargo that will pay you a handsome Profit.

Yours
D'Amilbahar

[Seal]

Source: Papers of William D. Waters, Peabody Museum, Salem.

APPENDICES

Appendix B – The Coastal Defenses of the Bishopric of Cebu, 1799

COMMUNITY	LOCATION	PRESENCE OF PRIEST	CHURCH AS FORTI-FICATION	BALUARTE (Stone towers, block houses, Palisades) CONSTRUCTED BY INDIOS	FORT CONS-TRUCTED BY INDIOS	GARRISON OF BALUARTE/FORT	PRESIDIO AND COMPLE-MENT	NATURAL DEFENCE	COMMUNITIES DISPERSED BY RAIDING
CEBU PROVINCE									
Talibon	Coast	Priest	Wood Church	Wood Baluarte	Stone Fort	—			
Loon	—	Priest	Wood Church	Stone Baluarte	Stone Fort	—			
Malabohoe	Coast	Priest	Stone Church		Stone Fort	Indios and priest			
Tagbilaran	Coast	Priest	Stone Church	Stone Baluarte	Stone Fort	Indios and priest			
Baclayon	Coast		Wood Church	Stone Baluarte	Stone Fort	Indios and priest			
Loay	Coast	Priest	Wood Church	Wood Paisade		Indios			
Dimiao	Coast	Priest	Wood Church	Stone Baluarte	Stone Fort	Indios and priest			
Hagna	Coast		Stone Church	Stone Baluarte	Stone Fort	Indios and priest			
Davis	Coast	Priest	Stone Church	Wood Paisade	Stone Fort	Indios			
Danao	Coast		Wood Church		Wood Fort	Indios and priest			
Catmon			Wood Church	Wood Baluarte		Indios			
Dinabongan	Inland	Priest	Stone Church	Stone Baluarte	Stone Fort	—			
Loboc	Inland		Wood Church		Stone Fort	Indios and priest			
Malabago						Indios			

421

Appendix B (cont.)

COMMUNITY	LOCATION	PRESENCE OF PRIEST	CHURCH AS FORTI-FICATION	BALUARTE (Stone towers, block houses, Palisades) CONSTRUCTED BY INDIOS	FORT CONS-TRUCTED BY INDIOS	GARRISON OF BALUARTE/ FORT	PRESIDIO AND COMPLE-MENT	NATURAL DEFENCE	COMMUNITIES DISPERSED BY RAIDING
CALAMIANES PROVINCE									
Tatay	Coast	Priest	Wood Church		Stone Fort	Indios and priest			
Dumaran	Coast		Wood Church	Wood Baluarte		—			
Silanga	Coast	Priest	Wood Church		Wood Fort	Indios and priest			
Culion	Coast	Priest	Wood Church	Stone Baluarte	Stone Fort	Indios and priest			
Linapacan	Coast		Wood Church	Wood Baluarte		Indios			
Bintoan	Coast		Wood Church						
Carong	Coast	Priest	Stone Church	Stone Baluarte	Stone Fort	Indios and priest		Mountains	Dispersed
Agutaya	Coast	Priest	Stone Church	Stone Baluarte	Stone Fort			Mountains	
Cuyo									
PANAY PROVINCE									
Romblon	Coast	Priest	—	Stone Baluarte		Indios and priest			
Sibuyan	Coast		Wood Church	Stone Baluarte		Indios			
Tablas	Coast		Wood Church	Stone Baluarte		Indios			
Banton	Coast	Priest	Wood Church		Wood Fort	Indios and priest			
Mambusao	Inland	Priest	Stone Church	Wood Palisade					
Batang	Inland		Wood Church						

Appendix B (cont.)

COMMUNITY	LOCATION	PRESENCE OF PRIEST	CHURCH AS FORTI-FICATION	BALUARTE (Stone towers, block houses, Palisades) CONSTRUCTED BY INDIOS	FORT CONS-TRUCTED BY INDIOS	GARRISON OF BALUARTE/ FORT	PRESIDIO AND COMPLE-MENT	NATURAL DEFENCE	COMMUNITIES DISPERSED BY RAIDING
CARAGA PROVINCE									
Tandag	Coast	Priest	Stone Church		Stone Fort		73		
Marihatog	Coast		Wood Church					Mountains	Dispersed
Liangan	Coast								Dispersed
Paniquian	Coast		Wood Church	Wood Baluarte		Indios			
Bayuyo	Coast		Wood Church						Dispersed
Catel	Coast	Priest	Wood Church	Stone Baluarte			No. unknown		Dispersed
Bagangoa	Coast								Dispersed
Bisilig	Coast		Wood Church						
Hinatuan	Coast								
Surigao	Coast	Priest	Wood Church	Wood Baluarte		Indios & soldiers			
Cabungbungan	Coast		Wood church	Wood Baluarte		Indios			
Hiraquet	Coast		Wood Church	Wood Baluarte		Indios			
Cacub	Coast			Wood Baluarte		Indios			Dispersed
Butuan	Inland	Priest	Stone Church	Wood Baluarte	Wood Fort	Indios and priest			
Hinago	Inland					Indios			
Tubay	Inland		Wood Church					Mountains	
Habongan	Inland							Mountains	
Mainit	Inland							Mountains	
Talacoban	Inland		Wood Church						
Linao	Inland			Wood Palisade		Indios	No. unknown		

Appendix B (cont.)

ILIGAN PROVINCE

COMMUNITY	LOCATION	PRESENCE OF PRIEST	CHURCH AS FORTIFICATION	BALUARTE (Stone towers, block houses, Palisades) CONSTRUCTED BY INDIOS	FORT CONSTRUCTED BY INDIOS	GARRISON OF BALUARTE/ FORT	PRESIDIO AND COMPLEMENT	NATURAL DEFENCE	COMMUNITIES DISPERSED BY RAIDING
Iligan	Coast	Priest	Wood Church	Stone Baluarte		—	78		
Dapitan	Coast	Priest	Wood Church	Wood Baluarte	Stone Fort	Indios and soldiers	20		
Misamis	Coast	Priest	Wood Church				68		
Cagayan	Coast		Stone Church	Stone Baluarte		Indios	20		
Tagoloan	Coast		Wood Church		Wood Fort				
Alitutum	Coast		Wood Church						
Salay	Coast	Priest	Wood Church			Indios and priest		Mountains	Dispersed
Cugman	Coast		Wood Church			Indios		Mountains	
Manbahao	Coast		Wood Church	Wood Baluarte					
Guinsiliban	Coast	Priest	Wood Church	Wood Baluarte					
Zamboanga	Coast		Wood Church	Stone Baluarte	Stone Fort	Indios and priest	370		
Ilaga	Inland	Priest	Wood Church			Indios and priest			
Lubungan	Inland	Priest	—	Stone Baluarte		Indios			
Bagug	Inland		Wood Church	Wood Baluarte					
Hiponan	Inland		Wood Church	Wood Baluarte					

Notes: Blank – implies that characteristic not present in the community
Dash – No information

Source: This table was compiled from the following source: *Pasa reveremente los testemonios que refiere sobre el estado de los Yglesias y Bienes de la administracion de los religiosos Franciscanos Y Augustinanos Descalzos: co lo demas que expone en orden a las otras respectivos de su jurisdiccion, El Obispo de Zebu, Don Matheo Joachim Rubio de Arevelo a vuestre Magestad, December 21, 1779*, AGI, Filipinas 1027.

APPENDICES

Appendix C – An Inventory of the Land and Sea Defenses of Albay Province, 1799

PUEBLOS	LANCHAS and VINTAS	PANCOS	CANNON						RIFLES
			8 POUND	6 POUND	4 POUND	2 POUND	1 POUND	½ POUND	
Albay	1						1(?)		12
Palanas		1				3	2		18
Virac		1			2	6	2		6
Bato-Bato					1	3	2		4
Caramoan		1				2	1		12
Payo		1			1		3		4
Tambongan		1			1	1	1		12
Biga		1			1		3	2	4
Pandan		1			1	1	1	2	6
Bagamonac					1		3	2	6
Tagbon					1		3	2	3
Caramoan							3	2	6
Laganoy		1				3			12
Tiui	1				5	8	4		18
Malinao	1				1	4	1		12
Tabaco	1		1			1	1		12
Bagacat					2	1	2		6
Libac		1				4	2		6
Bulysan	2					2	2		6
Gubat	2				5	7			24
Casiguran						4			18
Luban		1			10	6	2		34
Bacon	1		2		3	4			24
Sorsogon			2	1		2			40
Quipia		1		1	2	4	2		12
Donzol	1				2	2	2		6
San Jacinto	1					2			8
Mobo	1				5	6	6	4	14
Bakeno		1			2	2	2	2	6
	15	12	5	2	47	78	50	18	345

Source: In several instances the number of cannon do not correspond to the sum total because of damage to parts of the document. See *Numero 8, Junta celebrades por los gobernadorcillos y principales de la provincia de Albay sobre la necesidad de vintas, lancas, canones, polvara, y balas para perseguir los morosy, contener sus hostilidades*, 15 May 1799, PNA, Ereccion del Pueblo Albay, 1799-1864.

Appendix D
Population Variation in Nueva Caceres between 1751-1780 and 1815.

	1751	1780	1782	1786	1790	1794	1798	1801	1815
CAMARINES PROVINCE									
Tabuco		100.0	65.5	81.8	86.1	82.7	*	10.6	143.2
Santa Cruz		100.0	63.1	75.9	90.6	77.0	*	4.4	68.6
Daet		100.0	112.2	150.9	106.4	114.9	*	105.3	*
Indan	100.0	24.9	*	60.4	90.4	*	70.2	*	83.7
Paracale		100.0	184.8	250.5	388.9	*	127.0	*	133.3
Mambulao		100.0	*	*	*	*	*	260.0	281.3
Capalonga	100.0	97.2	64.8	67.9	49.4	54.0	*	45.1	61.2
Naga		100.0	115.5	107.8	94.2	111.6	110.9	163.3	201.3
Camaligan		100.0	101.4	84.8	99.0	125.4	116.4	134.8	150.4
Canaman		100.0	78.3	131.4	112.7	113.2	127.0	132.9	154.6
Magarao		100.0	174.5	200.4	218.2	246.5	272.1	291.8	258.7
Gupao		100.0	99.2	105.2	92.3	92.2	214.5	79.2	105.3
Bombon		100.0	103.7	112.7	99.2	105.9	*	114.8	123.3
Calabanga		100.0	101.8	135.3	144.9	115.1	183.1	154.5	161.2
Libmanan		100.0	101.6	117.8	127.2	122.7	134.7	138.5	163.3
Milanor		100.0	104.5	119.8	118.0	114.8	122.7	129.8	120.2
Bada		100.0	113.6	117.2	99.7	102.7	136.1	140.2	140.6
Bula		100.0	97.2	120.2	124.7	182.5	133.6	127.9	183.2
Nabula		100.0	114.3	147.1	159.3	147.4	148.4	155.9	204.4
Batto		100.0	101.6	101.6	106.1	113.3	121.8	113.6	180.3
Iraga		100.0	95.2	109.9	120.7	106.1	135.8	144.2	204.9
Buxi		100.0	113.7	118.6	117.4	132.6	116.9	155.9	225.2
Polangi		100.0	101.7	102.9	104.4	104.3	117.2	123.5	106.2
Libon		100.0	104.1	80.7	109.8	101.5	96.6	122.8	204.1
Das		100.0	101.9	102.4	112.3	108.8	106.8	112.4	157.8
Ligao		100.0	99.8	102.7	115.6	99.8	102.5	108.0	113.1
Guinobatan		100.0	74.1	91.0	108.7	108.7	104.3	106.5	83.7
Camarines		100.0	80.3	78.4	78.8	72.0	78.9	82.0	87.8
Cagsava		100.0	79.1	82.5	71.4	63.1	56.2	53.1	58.1

Appendix D (cont.)

ALBAY PROVINCE							
Albay		100.0	50.5	92.6	125.5	126.4	110.5	*	100.1
Ligbog		100.0	184.2	90.6	*	75.8	*	90.5	165.5
Bagacay		100.0	92.9	97.5	105.3	95.4	*	105.9	123.6
Tabaco		100.0	204.6	188.5	179.3	179.0	*	217.0	210.3
Malinao		100.0	101.2	89.5	92.0	119.7	*	134.1	132.9
Tivi		100.0	111.1	118.5	143.8	110.6	*	188.8	166.1
Lagonoy		100.0	11.4	114.0	97.3	*	*	209.6	262.9
Caramoan	100.0	125.2	197.1	197.9	179.4	189.2	*	*	255.8
Biga		100.0	76.6	*	88.5	87.2	*	97.2	71.3
Birac	100.0	103.6	80.6	101.4	143.4	135.8	*	126.7	153.3
Bulusan		100.0	96.8	79.4	108.8	111.3	*	104.5	127.3
Gubat		100.0	102.1	110.9	130.8	118.2	*	137.5	195.4
Galte		100.0	79.9	451.4	106.8	*	*	132.8	*
Casiguran		100.0	96.3	112.6	113.1	112.1	*	131.2	172.5
Luban		100.0	85.0	79.6	74.4	63.0	*	56.1	65.3
Sorsogon	100.0	20.6	29.7	31.1	30.1	33.0	*	33.8	62.4
Bacon		100.0	104.9	101.5	125.4	120.9	*	137.4	202.2

Appendix D (cont.)

TAYABAS PROVINCE								
Cayabas		100.0	104.7	108.7	112.4	107.7	116.6	138.2	203.1
Mauban		100.0	97.6	104.8	109.0	119.9	125.6	137.2	158.5
Lucban		100.0	98.3	89.0	86.3	94.3	99.7	96.3	113.3
Pagbilao	100.0	79.1	85.8	71.8	85.1	90.2	109.3	128.2	125.6
Sadjaja		100.0	*	106.0	109.2	133.1	150.0	151.2	207.0
Polillo		100.0	94.9	108.1	118.0	102.6	122.9	130.0	144.5
Lampon (Binangonan)		100.0	102.6	130.4	117.8	124.6	153.0	164.9	199.0
Casiguran (De Baler)	100.0	142.3	70.7	76.9	77.3	92.2	107.7	70.1	80.9
Atimonan		100.0	192.4	209.9	201.8	218.2	220.0	252.1	349.1
Gumaca		100.0	101.5	120.9	130.2	128.2	129.8	148.7	186.0
Maobac	100.0	54.1	*	*	*	*	*	*	*
Guinayangan	100.0	21.9	*	*	*	*	*	*	31.2
Catanavan		100.0	87.6	84.0	55.1	76.2	*	60.8	97.3
Obuyon	100.0	29.4	24.4	26.1	*	*	*	31.8	56.6
Baler	100.0	70.7	49.1	64.0	69.8	76.9	78.0	88.1	75.7
Palanan	100.0	93.6	61.3	*	38.8	38.8	44.9	26.1	27.8
Lupi	100.0	126.5	*	*	*	*	*	42.2	87.4
Manguirin		100.0	27.4	32.4	32.4	45.6	35.8	*	49.5
Goa		100.0	62.5	55.5	77.1	1-5.3	*	134.6	133.7
Tigaon		100.0	120.9	123.5	*	160.4	*	134.0	211.2

Notes: Formula Used Variation = $\frac{\text{(Population} - \text{base} \times 100)}{\text{Base}} + 100$

Where 'Base' is the population for either 1751 or 1780
No data is shown by asterisk.

Appendix E

Statements of Balangingi Prisoners, 1838

1. Statement of Silammkoom

I am a native of one of the Sooloo Isles called Ballongningkin [Balanguingui] and I usually reside there. I sometimes trade in a small way such as selling Padi at Basilon and Mindanao. The sultan lives at Sooloo proper. The principal chief at Ballongningkin is Panglima Alip, it is well inhabited and there are large fleets of boats which are employed in collecting sea weed, tortoiseshell, [and] trepang, . . . on account of the Sultan who gives the people in return, cloth or any other article he may think proper. Our fleet consisting of six prahus came from Ballongningkin and left that place about three months since. The fleet was commanded and under the sole direction of Orang Kaja Kullul, who is a relation of Panglima Alip. Orang Kaja Kullul informed us that the sultan had desired him to plunder and capture all nations save Europeans. I have never seen the sultan of Sulu, this is my first voyage to the east coast of the Malayan Peninsula, but for many years I have cruised in the vicinity of Manilas, Makassar and other places on which occasion Orang Kaja Kullul took any boats he happened to meet.

2. Statement – Prisoner Mah roon alias Mah sandar

I am a native of Ujang Pandan, Makassar—I was captured about two years since by a forminable Illanoon fleet consisting of 23 prahus—When I was taken I was proceeding to Mandas in company with two of my countrymen named Sindrah and Pannsil. After cruising about for some time the piratical fleet went to Ballongningkin where I was treated as a slave and compelled to perform all kinds of work. Panglima Alip is the chief of Ballongningkin and Orang Kaja Kullul is considered the second person in authority. The sultan lives at Sooloo proper—We left Ballongningkin about three months since. The fleet consisted of six prahus–the whole under the command of Orang Kaja Kullul. I did not voluntarily join the pirates. I was compelled to go, two other of my countrymen (Sookut and Pula Nea) are in a similar position as myself.

Ballongningkin is well peopled and I think there are about 200 prahus of the same size as the one destroyed by the steamer.

3. *Statement made by Daniel*

By birth I am an Illanun and for years have resided at Ballongningkin–for six years I have been pirating near Makassar, Myungka, Yan Le Lah, Seah-Seah, Tambulan, and other places. Panglima Alip is the chief of Ballongningkin, he is under the sultan of Sulu. I cannot pretend to say whether the sultan and Panglima Alip give any directions touching the fitting out of piratical fleets, but the fact is save 'Mangoorays' (pirating) we have scarcely any other means of getting a livelihood. Six boats left Ballongningkin under the command of Orang Kaja Kullul . . . Talagoa was panglima of our boat . . . we had a crew of 29 men, 6 of whom were killed and several wounded.

4. *Statement of Tala Goa*

I live at Ballongningkin with my family. I occasionally magoorap (pirating) [and] at other times [I am] making salt, planting Paddy, [or] collecting tortoiseshell. I am a follower of Orang Kaja Kullul and I am compelled to do and act as he may direct. Panglima Alip is the chief of Ballongningkin, he of course, was aware of the subject of the cruise and Orang Kaja Kullul received instructions not to molest trading boats to and from the ports of Singapore and Tringanoo. I can say nothing positively relative to the sultan of Sooloo. I am not a panglima, I was placed in charge of one of the boats by Orang Kaja Kullul who had exclusive control of the six prahus–the persons in charge of the several prahus were besides myself, See Deman, See Tambie, See Dundine, and See Puttah. Ballongningkin was destroyed by a force from Manila when I was quite a youth.

Source: Bonham to Maitland, 28 June 1838, PRO, Admiralty 125/133.

Appendix F

The Statements of the Fugitive Captives of the Sulu Sultanate, 1836-1864

The statements have been compiled and ordered as a series from the following sources:

XVIII. 1 Declaraciones de todos los cautivos fugados de Jolo y acogidos a los buques de la expresada divicion, con objeto de averiguar los puntos de donde salen los pancos piratas, la clase de gente que los tripulan, la forma en que se hacen los armamentos y otros particulares que arrojan las mismas declaraciones, Expediente 12, 4 October 1836, PNA, Mindanao/Sulu 1803-1890.

XVIII. 2 Relacion jurada de los cuarenta y cinco cautivos venidos de Jolo sobre el bergantin Espanol *Cometa*, 19 March 1847, PNA, Piratas 3.

XVIII. 3 Relacion jurada de los cuarenta y cuatro cautivos venidos de Jolo sobre el bergantin Espanol *Cometa*, 8 February 1848 (statements 1-10); Relacion jurada de los individuos cautivos venidos en la Fragata de guerra Inglesa *Samarang*, procedente de Jolo, 15 March 1845 (statements 1-14); Relacion jurada de los cuatro cautivos venidos en el navio Ingles de guerra *Agincourt*, procedente de la Isla de Borneo, 11 December 1845 (statements 15-18); Relacion jurada de los dos individuos cautivos venidos en la corbeta de guerra Francesa *Salina*, 17 September 1845 (statements 19-20); Relacion jurada de los cinco cautivos venidos en la Falua de la division de la isla del corregidor, 23 August 1845 (statements 21-24); Relacion jurada de los seis cautivos venidos de Jolo sobre el bergantin Espanol *San Vincenre*, 14 January 1850 (statements 25-30). The remaining captives were brought to Manila on the following vessels: the steamer, *Elcano* (31); Brigantine, *San Ramos* (32-33); Frigate, *Magnolia* (34); Brigantine, *Cometa* (35-39); steamer, *Reyno de Castilla* (40-41), PNA, Piratas 3.

XVIII. 4 Relacion de los cautivos rescatados y evadidos del poder de los mores dentro del presente ano que se embarcan con esta fecha en la goleta de S.M. *Animosa*, 22 July 1864, PNA, Piratas 3.

XVIII. 5   Verklaringen van ontvlugten personen uit den handen der zeeroovers van 1845-1849, ANRI, Menado 37.

XVIII. 6   Verklaringen van ontvlugten personen uit den handen der zeeroovers van 1845-1849, ANRI, Menado 37.

Appendix F (cont.)

Statements of the Fugitive Captives of the Sulu Sultanate, 1836-1834

	CAPTIVE	MASTER	PERSON SOLD TO	PLACE	PRICE	YEAR OF CAPTIVITY	AGE
1	Mariano de la Cruz	Tusan (Tunkil)	Datu Mhd. Buyo	Jolo	5 bundles of Ilocos cloth	1836	21
2	Francisco Feliz	–	Amanang	Jolo	3 bundles of cotton cloth, 2 glass water bottles, 2 plates, 2 cups	1834	45
3	Domingo Francisco	Visayan Renegade (Tunkil)	Chinese Mistizo Merchant	Jolo		1836	35
4	Juan Salvador	Balangingi Samal	A Taosug	Jolo	5 pieces of cotton cloth	1836	–
5	Manuel de los Santos	Balangingi Samal	A Taosug Merchant	Jolo	Assorted goods to the value of 60 pesos	1836	27
6	Esmerald Francisco	Visayan Renegade (Balangingi)	Tiboral	Jolo		1836	50
7	Maria Gertrudiz	Balangingi Samal	Tiglam	Jolo	Bronze Lantanca (cannon)	1834	35
8	Marcelo Teofilo	Maluso man			25 pieces of cotton cloth		43
9	Tibarcio Juan	Balangingi Samal	Datu Mende	Parang	–	1834	41
10	Juan Monico	Balangingi Samal	A Taosug	Jolo	6 lengths of gauze (cotton or silk) and a Visayan belt	1836	14
11	Maria Damiana	Tunkil Samal	Chinese-Intiao	Jolo		1833	14
12	Domingo Candelario	Balangingi Samal	Man from Laminosa – resold in Jolo 6 months later	Jolo (Basilan)			28
13	Francisco Mariano	Balangingi Samal	Sold at Parian Batang – escaped then sold at Tapul island – escaped, seized and sold to a Muslim trader (Jolo)	Jolo		1826	40
14	Juan de los Santos	Tunkil Samal	Suynan – retainer of Datu Sadula	Jolo		1829	21
15	Juan Florentino	Pilas man	A Taosug	Zamboanga		1835	35
16	Pewdro Santiago	Basilan-Bagbagon (village)	A Visayan Renegade	Jolo		1835	16
17	Agapito de la Cruz	Balangingi Samal	Escaped – seized by a Taosug from Guimba	Interior of Jolo		1831	29
18	Juan de la Cruz	Balangingi Samal	Sold at Jolo, then at Siassi	Jolo		1826	25
19	Manuel Feliz	Balangingi Samal	A Taosug	Interior of Jolo		1831	26
20	Vizcente Remigio	Balangingi Samal	Datu Tael	Jolo		1833	31
21	Juan Santiago	Balangingi Samal	–	–			
22	Juan Sabala	Balangingi Samal	Datu Molo	Jolo	Bronze lantanca	1834	40
23	Augustin Juan	Balangingi Samal	Datu Tael	Jolo	10 lagas of unhusked rice	1826	35

Appendix F (cont.)

	CAPTIVE	MASTER	PERSON SOLD TO	PLACE	PRICE	YEAR OF CAPTIVITY	AGE
24	Pedro Antonio	Balangingi Samal	Samal Fishermen	Babaon Village		1828	24
25	Jose German Reales	Visayan Renegade	Datu Daniel	Jolo	A bundle of cloth and 3 balls of opium	1831	30
26	Angel Custodio	Balangingi Samal	A village headman (Balangingi)	Jolo		1835	19
27	Anastacio Caullo	Balangingi Samal	A Muslim from Sandacan Muslim Trader			1826	36
28	Francisco Agustin	Iranun				1832	23
29	Alexo Quijano	Balangingi Samal	Datu Bendahara	Jolo		1828	33
30	Matias de la Cruz	Balangingi Samal	Datu Mhd. Buyo	Jolo	30 pieces of cotton cloth	1825	33
31	Juan Teodoro	Balangingi Samal	A Chinese	Jolo	70 pieces of cotton cloth	1834	56
32	Evaresto Pinto	Balangingi Samal	Antonio – Visayan renegade Pata	Jolo		1835	25
33	Santiago Manuel de Tuna	Balangingi Samal	Datu Bendahara	Jolo		1828	50
34	Francisco Gregorio	Balangingi Samal	A Muslim – Sagio	Jolo		1829	28
35	Francisco Sereno	Sipac Samal		Jolo		1834	28
36	Mariano de la Cruz	Balangingi Samal	Datu Salipasan	Jolo		1836	28
37	Juan de la Cruz	Balangingi Samal		Jolo		1830	57
38	Francisco Sacarias	Balangingi Samal	Datu Molo	Jolo		1833	25
39	Juan Apolonio	Balangingi Samal	Datu Mhd. Buyo	Jolo		1831	25
40	Matias Domingo	Balangingi Samal	Datu Daniel	Jolo		1834	18
21	Francisco Basilio	Balangingi Samal	Aamiang	Jolo		1836	30
42	Juan Pedro	Renegade – tumol (Balangingi)	Salane	Jolo		1835	26
43	Diomicio Francisco	Balangingi	Amanan				
44	Francisco Augustino	Binuong Balangingi	Ande				
45	Francisco Xaiver	Tunkil Samal	A Chinese	Jolo		1836	28
46	Eusebio de la Cruz	Balangingi Samal	A Chinese merchant	Jolo	5 bundles of cotton cloth	1836	35
				Jolo	2 red boxes, 3 pieces of cotton cloth, 1 glass water bottle	1836	28
47	Pedro Francisco	Balangingi Samal	A Chinese merchant – Sa Hua A Muslim merchant	Jolo		1832	
48	Vizcente Santiago	Balangingi Samal	A Taosug merchant	Pangutaran Island		1832	38
49	Gabriel Francisco	Tukil Samal	Ransomed by the Spanish captain of the schooner Soledad			1833	45
50	Marino Sevilla	Balangingi Samal				1835	40

Appendix F (cont.)

	NAME	PROVINCE	AGE	STATUS	ACTIVITY WHEN SEIZED	NO. OF RAIDING VESSELS	RETAILING POINT	PERIOD OF RESIDENCE AT RETAILING POINT	PERSON SOLD TO AT JOLO	MEANS OF MANUMISSION	YEAR OF CAPTIVITY
1	Lorenzo Sixto	Surigao	33	Married	Fishing – 4 others	8 Pancos	Balangingi	2 weeks	Sinden	Ransomed for 40 pesos	1845
2	Alejandro Valuenzuela	Tondo	47	Single	Trading	3 Pancos	Balangingi	1 week	William Wyndham	Ransomed	1844
3	Pedro Flores	Capiz	30	Married	Trading	5 Pancos	Balangingi	3 days	Simindo	Baroto – to *Cometa*	1844
4	Pedro Ysadoro	Capiz	40	Married	Fishing	4 Pancos	Balangingi	3 weeks	Sumaran	Baroto – to *Cometa*	1844
5	Simon Ylario	Cebu	19	Married	Fishing – 7 others	8 Pancos	Balangingi	1 month	Utu	Escaped	1846
6	Angel Manuel	Leyte	45	Widow	Fishing – 1 other	3 Pancos	Balangingi	3 days	Vay-Chinese	– Came with his master to Manila	1841
7	Alejandro Juan	Leyte	18	Single	Fishing	5 Pancos	Balangingi	1½ years	William Wyndham	Escaped to the *Cometa*	1845
8	Damaso Soledad	Cuyo	23	Married	Trading	3 Pancos	Balangingi	1 week	Sandiasan	Escaped	1846
9	Angustin Bernardo	Cebu	35	Married	Trading	3 Pancos	Balangingi	4 days	Datu Mirasan	Ransomed by W. Wyndham	1845
10	Manuel Valdez	Samar	30	Single	Fishing – 1 other	8 Pancos	Balangingi	1 week	Camunug	Escaped to *Cometa*	1846
11	Alberto de la Cruz	Negros	30	Single	Trading – 19 others	?	Balangingi	1 month	Datu Sisi	Escaped to *Cometa*	1846
12	Juan Pedro	Cebu	40	Married	Fishing – 5 others	3 Pancos	Balangingi	4 days	Alm'ain	Escaped to *Cometa*	1846
13	Vincente Remigio	Cebu	28	Married	Fishing – 5 others	3 Pancos	Balangingi	4 days	Datu Abdula	Escaped to *Cometa*	1846
14	Totibio de la Cruz	Mindoro	26	Single	Fishing – 2 others	2 Baroto	Balangingi	8 days	Barit	Escaped to *Cometa*	1845
15	Jose de la Cruz	Cebu	42	Married	Fishing – 3 others	8 Pancos	Balangingi	5 days	Sacan	Escaped to *Cometa*	1844
16	Manuel Francisco	Leyte	28	Single	Cutting Nipa – 3 others	4 Pancos	Balangingi	1 week	Undin	Escaped to *Cometa*	1846
17	Pedro Apolinario	Negros	30	Married	Delivering a church despatch	3 Salisipan	Balangingi	1 month	Panguindayan	Escaped to *Cometa*	1844
18	Ygnacio Francisco	Leyte	19	Single	Fishing – 1 other	2 Pancos	Balangingi	2 months	Ymban	Escaped to *Cometa*	1842

Appendix F (cont.)

	NAME	PROVINCE	AGE	STATUS	ACTIVITY WHEN SEIZED	NO. OF RAIDING VESSELS	RETAILING POINT	PERIOD OF RESIDENCE AT RETAILING POINT	PERSON SOLD TO AT JOLO	MEANS OF MANUMISSION	YEAR OF CAPTIVITY
19	Gregoria de la Conception	Albay	48	Widow	Travelling	6 Pancos	Balangingi	2 years	Machadi	Escaped to Cometa	1838
20	Pliesto de la Cruz	Zambales	20	Single	Trading	3 Pancos	Balangingi	2 weeks	Datu Ayut	Escaped to Cometa	1842
21	Juan Francisco	Cebu	30	Married	Trading	9 Pancos	Balangingi	2 weeks	Vincent Chinese	Came with his master to Manila	1846
22	Ambrosio Magno	Ilocos Sur	25	Married	Fishing – 2 others	7 Pancos	Balangingi	1 month	Balatjan	Escaped to Cometa	1844
23	Antonio Francisco	Albay	30	Single	Travelling	8 Pancos	Tunkil	1 month	A Muslim	Ransomed for 40 pesos	1846
24	Carlos de los Santos	Cebu	30	Married	Fishing – 2 others	8 Pancos	Balangingi	2 nights	Damblod	Ransomed for 25 pesos	1846
25	Fernando Francisco	Cebu	36	Single	Trading	9 Pancos	(Sipac)	11 days	Bala	Ransomed for 60 pesos	1846
26	Francisco Eusebio	Cebu	25	Married	Fishing – 1 other	8 Pancos	Balangingi	1 month	William Wyndham	W. Wyndham sent to Manila	1845
27	Eulalio Composano	Albay	23	Single	Trading	5 Pancos	Balangingi	2 days	Daut and then to W. Wyndham	W. Wyndham sent to Manila	1844
28	Gelacio Gabriel	Ilocos Sur	55	Married	Trading	3 Pancos	Balangingi	5 days	Datu Maasi	Ransomed for 15 pesos	1846
28	Pedro Sabado	Ilocos Sur	45	Married	Trading	3 Pancos	Balangingi	5 days	Datu Maasi	Ransomed for 15 pesos	1846
30	Gabriela Santiago	Ilocos Sur	44	Married	Fishing – 5 others	3 Pancos	Balangingi	2 weeks	Ynban	Escaped to Cometa	1842
31	Juan Velano	Iloilo	35	Married	Fishing	4 Pancos	Tunkil	month	–	Ransomed to Cometa	1846
32	Celedonio Justo	Iloilo	36	Married	Fishing – 2 others	3 Pancos	Tunkil	month	Bairo	Ransomed to Cometa	1846
33	Francisco Salvador	Leyte	17	Single	Travelling – 19 others	5 Pancos	Balangingi	week	Abdumanl	Escaped to Cometa	1844
34	Franscisco de Leon	Cebu	36	Married	Trading	9 Pancos	Balangingi	2 weeks	–	Ransomed Capt. Cometa	1846
35	Geronimo Ibanez	Samar	21	Single	Trading	8 Pancos	Balangingi	2 months	–	Ransomed to Capt. Cometa	1846
36	Juan Jose	Iloilo	21	Single	Travelling – 6 others	4 Pancos	Tunkil	6 days	Uray then to W. Wyndham	W. Wyndham sent to Manila	1845

Appendix F (cont.)

	NAME	PROVINCE	AGE	STATUS	ACTIVITY WHEN SEIZED	NO. OF RAIDING VESSELS	RETAILING POINT	PERIOD OF RESIDENCE AT RETAILING POINT	PERSON SOLD TO AT JOLO	MEANS OF MANUMISSION	YEAR OF CAPTIVITY
37	Jacinto Dioneso	Iloilo	37	Married	Seized in Camarines	5 Barotos	Tunkil	week	Majumat	Ransomed by Capt. *Cometa*	1846
38	Vincente Ferrer	Iloilo	40	Married	Travelling – 14 others	1 Panco	Amian Island	2 months	W. Wyndham	W. Wyndham sent to Manila	1845
39	Jose Bruno	Iloilo	25	Single	Travelling	3 Pancos	Balangingi	–	W. Wyndham	W. Wyndham sent to Manila	1846
40	Juan Gregorio	Iloilo	43	Married	Fishing – 3 others	3 Pancos	Tunkil	week	Datu Camalic	Freed by Capt. *Cometa*	1846
41	Clemente Tranquilino	Albay	32	Married	Travelling	8 Pancos	Sipac	3 months	Sibotoc	Freed by Capt. *Cometa*	1846
42	Jose Manacio	Camarines Sur	19	Single	Trading	8 Pancos	Balangingi	2 months	Capt. of *Cometa*	–	1846
43	Martino Antonio	Iloilo	22	Single	Fishing	1 Panco	Balangingi	3 days	Sold on Basilan	Escaped from Basilan to Zamboanga	1846
44	Fausto Francisco	Negros	9	Single	Fishing – 6 others	3 Pancos	Tunkil	2 months	Capt. of *Cometa*	–	1846
45	Juan Miguel	Negros	10	Single	Fishing – 6 others	3 Pancos	Tunkil	2 months	Capt. of *Cometa*	–	1846

Appendix F (cont.)

	Name	Province	Age	Status	Activity When Seized	No. of Raiding Vessels	Retailing Point	Period of Residence at Retailing Point	Person Sold To	Place	Price of Sale	Means of Manumission	Year of Captivity
1	Martin de la Cruz	Mindoro	55	Widow	Fishing	5 Pancos	Balangingi	3 days	Buto	Jolo	–	Escaped 1846	1844
2	Francisco Santiago	Misamis	20	Single	Travelling	2 Pancos	Sipac	6 days	–	–	–	Escaped to Zamboanga	1847
3	Manuel Molo	Leyte	55	Married	Travelling	6 Pancos	Balangingi	5 days	–	Catifan Island	–	Escaped to Cometa – 1847	1842
4	Pedro Armero	Cebu	25	Single	Fishing – one other	8 Pancos	Balangingi	3 days	–	Tapiantana	–	Escaped to Pasanhan & Zamboanga	1846
5	Ambrosio Mision	Bohol	28	Married	Fishing – 5 others	8 Pancos	Balangingi	3 days	–	Jolo	–	Escaped to Zamboanga	1847
6	Pedro Francisco	Bohol	18	Single	Trading	8 Pancos	Balangingi	1 day	Sapdula	Jolo	–	Escaped to Cometa	1847
7	Cerapio Parenas	Ilocos Sur	40	Married	Fishing	7 Pancos	Balangingi	month	–	Jolo	–	Escaped to Cometa	1846
8	Mateo Francisco	Cebu	19	Single	Fishing – one other	2 Salisipan	Tunkil	–	–	Jolo	–	Escaped to Cometa	1847
9	Juan Francisco	Cebu	22	Married	Trading – 7 others	2 Pancos	Balangingi	2 days	Datu Abu	Jolo	–	Escaped by baroto to Cometa	1847
10	Saturnino Martin	Capiz	18	Single	Fishing – 2 others	8 Pancos	Balangingi	4 days	Sipay	Jolo	–	Escaped to Cometa	1846
11	Francisco Anostacio	Iloilo	18		Fishing	Salisipan	Balangingi	1 year	Ahmat-trader	Jolo	–	Escaped by baroto to Samarang	1843
12	Jacinto Pedro	Iloilo	50	Married	Fishing	Salisipan baroto	Tunkil	–	Bua	Jolo	–	Escaped by Baroto to Samarang	1843
13	Fragido San Juan	Zamboanga	23	Married	Constructing a lime kiln		Tapiantana	7 days		Gunong Tabur	–	Capt. Belcher negotiates freedom	1842
14	Mateo San Francisco	Camarines Sur	20	–	Fishing	9 Pancos	Tunkil	–	Chinese	Jolo	–	Escaped to Samarang	1842

438

Appendix F (cont.)

	Name	Province	Age	Status	Activity When Seized	No. of Raiding Vessels	Retailing Point	Period of Residence at Retailing Point	Person Sold To	Place	Price of Sale	Means of Manumission	Year of Captivity
15	Juan Benedicto	Iloilo	27	–	Trading	10 Pancos	Balangingi	1 month	–	Malludu	–	Escaped to English expedition	1883
16	Mariano Domingo	Iloilo	25	Single	Fishing	15 Pancos	Balangingi	1 year	–	Malludu	–	Escaped to English expedition	1821
17	Francisco Vincente	Cebu	40	Married	Fishing	10 Pancos	Balangingi	3 months	–	Malludu	–	Escaped to English expedition	1843
18	Juan de la Cruz	Iloilo	31	Single	Cutting wood	12 Pancos	Tampasuk	–	–	Malludu	–	Escaped to English expedition	1840
19	Felix Torres	Albay	23	Married	Travelling	9 Barotos	Balangingi	3 years	–	–	–	Escaped to French vessel	1842
20	Juan Florentino	Iloilo	40	Married	Fishing	4 Pancos	Pilas	2 months	Siangui	–	–	Recaptured by Balangingi	1835
21	Antonio Juan	Calamianes	–	Single	Fishing	2 Barotos	Balangingi	1 year	–	–	–	Escaped from marauding expedition	1844
22	Domingo Apolinario	Mindoro	–	–	Travelling	2 Barotos	Balangingi	6 years	–	–	–	Escaped from marauding expedition	1841
23	Nazario de la Cruz	Albay	–	–	Travelling	7 Pancos	Visayan Is.	–	–	Balangingi	–	Escaped from marauding expedition	1840
24	Severino Santiago	Zamboanga	–	–	Fishing	2 Pancos	Basilan	–	Datu Molok	Jolo	–	Escaped from marauding expedition	1845
25	Casimiro Santiago	Capiz	27	Single	Trading – 18 others	12 Pancos	Balangingi	1 day	Adul Jaman	Jolo	1000 pieces of Chinese coin, 1 piece of cotton cloth.	Baroto to San Vincente	1838
26	Pedro Gregorio	Capiz	26	Married	Trading – 4 others	3 Pancos	Tunkil	2 weeks	Datu Maribajal	Jolo	50 cavanes unhusked rice	Escaped to San Vincente	1846

IRANUN AND BALANGINGI

Appendix F (cont.)

	Name	Province	Age	Status	Activity When Seized	No. of Raiding Vessels	Retailing Point	Period of Residence at Retailing Point	Person Sold To	Place	Price of Sale	Means of Manumission	Year of Captivity
27	Domingo de la Cruz	Iloilo	30	Married	Fishing	3 Pancos	Tunkil	1 month	Majaradia	Jolo	5 pieces white cotton cloth	Escaped by baroto to *San Vincente*	1840
28	Juan Feliz	Leyte	24	Single	Travelling	5 Pancos	Sipac	2 months	Guichay	Jolo	90 cavanes unhusked rice	Ransomed by Capt. *San Vincente*	1847
29	Eleverio de Juan	Iloilo	15	Single	Fishing	2 Pancos	Tunkil	2 days	Datu Buyog	Jolo	5 large pieces black cotton cloth	Escaped to *San Vincente*	1845
30	Lucas Barcarcel	Pangasinan	25	Single	Trading	6 Pancos	Balangingi	month	Eman Said	Jolo	6 pieces white cotton cloth	Escaped to *San Vincente*	1838
31	Pedro del Remedio	Cebu	36	Single	Trading	20 Pancos	Balangingi	2 years	Datu Labuan	Jolo	20 cavanes unhusked rice	Escaped by baroto to *Elcano*	1823
32	Francisco Mariano	Samar	45	Married	Trading	5 Pancos	Balangingi	–	Gaya	–	–	Escaped to Pasanhan	1847
33	Francisco Aquino	Samar	31	Married	Trading	9 Pancos	Balangingi	2 weeks	Lacha	–	109 cavanes unhusked rice	Escaped to Pasanhan	1846
34	Ignasio Ambrocio	Bohol	25	–	Trading	8 Pancos	Sipac	6 months	Chambit	–	–	Escaped to Wyndham's vessel	1848
35	Nicolas Antonio	Albay	30	–	Trading	12 Pancos	Balangingi	3 months	Datu Salabansajasin Olo	–	–	Escaped to *Cometa*	1844
36	Lucas Felis	Iloilo	27	Single	Fishing	2 Pancos	Tunkil	1 month	Digno	–	–	Escaped to *Cometa*	1843
37	Esteban Escribano	Iloilo	60	Married	Trading	4 Pancos	Balangingi	2 weeks	Tampin	–	–	Escaped to *Cometa*	1846
38	Gaspar Regulacion	Samar	20	Single	Fishing	2 Barotos	Balangingi	1 month	Anti	–	–	Escaped to *Cometa*	1846
39	Juan Tubis	Samar	40	Married	Trading	–	Balangingi	1 night	Buso	–	–	Escaped to *Cometa*	1845
40	Juan Fernando	Capiz	28	–	Travelling	4 Pancos	Balangingi	1 week	Esmo	–	–	Escaped by *banca* to Zamboanga	1845
41	Dionieso Fernando	Capiz	15	–	Travelling	4 Pancos	Balangingi	1 week				Escaped by *banca* to Zamboanga	

APPENDICES

Appendix F (cont.)

	Name	Province	Community	Age	Status	Activity When Seized	No. of Raiding Vessels	Retailing Point	Period of Residence at Retailing Point	Person Sold To	Place	Means of Manumission	Year of Captivity
1	Andres Reyes	Iloilo	Molo	12	Single	–	–	–	–	–	Tunkil	Rescued by Navy expedition to Tunkil	1860
2	Maria Hermigia	Iloilo	Iloilo	30	Married	–	–	Tawi-Tawi – 1860	–	–	Patian Is. - Jolo	Escaped to Zamboanga	1864
3	Paduman, Malay	Moluccas	Macassar	30	Single	–	–	Tawi-Tawi	–	–	–	Escaped to Zamboanga	1860
4	Tuyo, Malay	Moluccas	Macassar	28	Single	–	–	Tawi-Tawi	–	–	Tawi-Tawi	Escaped	1862
5	Vincente Andunday	Samar	Bobon	40	Married	–	–	Carondong	–	–	Patian Is. - Jolo	Escaped to Zamboanga	1860
6	Gregorio Arawa	Tayabas	Gumaca	40	Married	–	–	Punuan	–	–	Punuan – Jolo	Escaped to Zamboanga	1859-1860
7	Anastielo Francisco	Iloilo	Iloilo	19	Single	–	–	Balangingi	–	–	Jolo	Escaped to Zamboanga	1862
8	Tomas Meiguelleno	Cebu	San Nicolas	30	Single	–	–	Balangingi	–	Taupan	Jolo	Escaped to Zamboanga	1844
9	Eulogio Dano	Cebu	San Nicolas	23	Single	–	–	Balangingi	–	–	Jolo	Escaped to Zamboanga	1847
10	Sebero Munez	Cebu	San Nicolas	43	Married	–	–	Balangingi	–	–	Jolo	Escaped to Zamboanga	–
11	Julian Domingo	Capiz	Capiz	30	Married	–	–	Lom Lom Island near Jolo	–	Datu Asivi	Jolo	Escaped to Zamboanga	1860
12	Teodora de los Santos	Romblon	Capidiocan	32	Married	–	–	Balangingi	–	Datu Asivi	Jolo	Escaped to Zamboanga	1861
13	Marcos de la Cruz	Cebu	Talisay	20	Single	–	–	Tunkil	–	Yting	Tawi-Tawi	Escaped to Zamboanga	–
14	Lorenzo Debulgando	Iloilo	Dumangas	13	Single	–	–	–	–	–	Caboncol	–	–

441

Appendix F (cont.)

	Name	Place of Residence	Age	Activity When Seized	No. of Raiding Vessels	Retailing Point	Person Sold To	Place	Employment in Captivity	Means of Manumission	Year of Captivity	No. of Years in Captivity
1	Tongua	–	–	Travelling	8 large Pancos, 4 Salisipan, 4 Vintas	Balangingi	A woman	Jolo	Trader in cloth with Chinese	Escaped in a small sailing craft	1838	7
2	Omia	–	–	Travelling	8 large Pancos, 4 Salisipan, 4 Vintas	Balangingi	Retained by Samal master – Mintas	Pilas	Domestic work	Escaped in a small sailing craft	1838	7
3	Hajati	Gorontalo	–	Travelling	24 Pancos 24 Salisipan	Balangingi	Agas	Gunong Bara	Agricultural work	Escaped in a small sailing craft	1835	10
4	Paulino Josebeo	Batangas	–	Fishing	6 large Pancos 3 large Pancos	–	Retained by master	Balangingi	Restored vessels	–	1845	1
5	Diaminie	Tontoli	–	Fishing	3 small Vintas	Balangingi	Retained by master	Balangingi	–	Escaped from marauding fleet at night in small baroto to shore	1845	1
6	Rapar	Tombaririe	30		4 large Pancos 4 small Vintas	Balangingi	Salie	Jolo	Domestic work – porter	Escaped in a small sailing craft with a Sangir captive	1843	3
7	Sadai	Makassar	–	Trading	3 Pancos	Balangingi	Yakie	Bual	Agricultural work for Yakie's mother	Escaped with 3 other Makassarese captives to Chiauw by small sailing craft	1842	4
8	Sarenko	Boeton	–	Fishing	3 large Pancos	Balangingi	Saha	Jolo	Agricultural and domestic work	Escaped with 3 other Makassarese captives to Chiauw by small sailing craft	1843	3

Appendix F (cont.)

	Name	Province	Age	Activity When Seized	No. of Raiding Vessels	Retailing Point	Person Sold To	Place	Employment in Captivity	Means of Manumission	Year of Captivity	No. of Years in Captivity
9	Lasado	Boni	–	Fishing	5 Vintas	Balangingi	Yakie	Bual	Agricultural work	Escaped with 3 other Makassarese captives to Chiauw by small sailing craft	1834	12
10	Hatibi Soleman	Bangai	–	Travelling	6 large Pancos 6 small Vintas	Balangingi	Yakie	Bual	Agricultural work	Escaped with 3 other Makassarese captives to Chiauw by small sailing craft	1843	3
11	Kilapon	Amoerang	20	–	4 small Pancos	Balangingi	–	Balangingi	–	Escaped with another in a small sailing craft to an island near Tontoli	1843	3
12	Mootalo	Kwandang	–	Travelling	4 large Pancos 2 small Vintas	Balangingi	Retained by master	Balangingi	Domestic work	Escaped while collecting fire-wood & water for marauding fleet	1846	1
13	Tabarong	Sangir Island	30	Travelling	4 large Pancos	Balangingi	–	Balangingi	Domestic work	Escaped from marauding fleet at Lembe Island - near Kema	1843	3
14	Kadasa	Hila Island	15	Fishing	1 small Panco	Sipac	Ganadoan Iranun	Patian	Agricultural & Domestic work	Escaped with 3 others from Patian Island by small sailing craft	1843	3
15	Abdul	Gonong	25	Fishing	6 large & 5 small Pancos	Sipac	Gondorico - a blacksmith	Patian	Agricultural & Domestic work	Escaped with 3 others from Patian Island by small sailing craft	1845	1

Appendix F (cont.)

	Name	Place of Residence	Age	Activity When Seized	No. of Raiding Vessels	Retailing Point	Person Sold To	Place	Employment in Captivity	Means of Manumission	Year of Captivity	No. of Years in Captivity
16	Njow	Kilbat	30	Travelling	4 large Pancos	Balangingi	Sakajang	Patian	Fishing and domestic work	Escaped with 3 others from Patian Island by small sailing craft	1845	1
17	Francis Mariano	Manila	45	Collecting tripang and nests	3 large Pancos	Sipac	Uming	Parang	Fishing and domestic work	Escaped with 5 others in a small sailing craft to Menado	1837	10
18	Francisco Basilio	Cebu	28	Trading	7 Pancos	Sipac	Uming	Parang	Agricultural work	Escaped with 5 others in a small sailing craft to Menado	1842	5
19	Siado	Bolang	25	Fishing	3 large Pancos 3 small Vintas	Balangingi	Sawadi	Sulu	Agricultural work	Escaped with 5 others in a small sailing craft to Menado	1844	3
20	Jacob Estephanus	Taboekan	50	Fishing	1 large Panco 1 small Vinta	Balangingi	Uming	Parang	Agricultural work	Escaped with 5 others in a small sailing craft to Menado	1827	20
21	Pedro Francisco	Leyte	30	Travelling	5 large Pancos	Basilan	Uming	Sulu	Agricultural work	Escaped with 5 others in a small sailing craft to Menado	1843	4
22	Kawase	Goron	45	Travelling	6 large Pancos	Balangingi	Bajang	Balangingi	Agricultural work	Escaped with 3 others in sailing craft	1846	1
23	Madi	Tumbuka	30	Collecting sago	3 large Pancos	Balangingi	Ybie	Balangingi	Agricultural work	Escaped with 3 others in sailing craft	1844	3

Appendix F (cont.)

	Name	Place of Residence	Age	Activity When Seized	No. of Raiding Vessels	Retailing Point	Person Sold To	Place	Employment in Captivity	Means of Manumission	Year of Captivity	No. of Years in Captivity
24	Ramaka	Ratahan	40	Fishing	3 large Pancos	Balangingi	Arik	Ubian	Agricultural work	Escaped with Madja to Gorontalo in small sailing craft	1846	1
25	Abdul	Djupandang	30	Fishing	1 large Panco 1 small	Balangingi	Tallaga	Tapiantana	Fishing and domestic work	Escaped to Zamboanga in small sailing craft then sailed on a Sulu brig to Menado	1841	6
26	Sendie	Dongala	30	Trading	3 large Pancos 2 small Vintas	Sipac	–	Pangalmata	Agricultural work	–	1844	3
27	Sirua	Kalumpang	40	Fishing	3 large & 3 small Pancos	Basilan then Sipac	Idris	Pangalmata	Agricultural work	Escaped in small sailing craft to Taboekan with Sendie	1841	6
28	Benonko	Lacasan Is.	50	Trading	4 large & 4 small Pancos	Tunkil	Hassan	Tunkil	Agricultural work – salt manufacture	Escaped with 2 others in small sailing craft	1847	1
29	Abdulla	Pontianak	40	Trading	9 large & 1 small Pancos	Tunkil	Suiding	Tunkil	Agricultural work – salt manufacture	Escaped with 2 others in small sailing craft	–	–
30	Pedro Juan	Iloilo	50	Trading	3 large Pancos	Balangingi	Suiding	Tunkil	Domestic work – salt manufacture	Escaped with 2 others in small sailing craft	1813	35

Appendix F (cont.)

	Name	Place of Residence	Age	No. of Persons Seized	Fleet Size	Armaments of Each Vessel	Commander of Vessel	Crew per Vessel	Where Marauding Flotilla Originated	Who Fitted and Equipped the Flotilla	Islands Used for Obtaining Water	Islands Used for Careening, Caulking, etc.	Time of Year When Vessel Put to Sea	Year of Captivity
1	Tongua	–	–	–	8 Pancos 4 Salisipan 4 Vintas	–	–	50	Balangingi	Datus of Sulu	Kassaputang River near Kaydipang	Unknown island near Kottaboona	–	1838
2	Omai	–	–	2	8 Pancos 4 Salisipan 4 Vintas	–	–	10*	Balangingi	Datus of Sulu	Kadoga-Sulu Islands		–	1838
3	Hajati	Gorontalo	–	2 Voyage	24 Pancos 24 Salisipan	8 Brass cannon	–	30*	Balangingi	Inhabitants of Balangingi	Cham-Sangir Islands	During voyage vessels brought ashore	–	1835
4	Paulino Josebo	Batangas (Philippines)	–	3 Fishing	6 large Pancos	3 Leila (brass cannon)	Marthinos (a Manila man)	–	Balangingi	Inhabitants of Balangingi	Talissie		Nov.	1845
5	Diaminie	Tontoli	–	1 Fishing	3 large Pancos 3 small Vintas	3-1 pound cannon	–	40	Balangingi	Panglimas at Balangingi	Banka Island & 3 Brothers Islands	On one of the 3 Brothers Islands	–	1845
6	Rapar	Tombaririe	30	6	4 Pancos 4 small Vintas	Rantanka (brass cannon)	–	40 10*	Balangingi	Inhabitants of Balangingi	Banka & Menado Tua	Banks Island	West monsoon	1843
7	Sadai	Makassar	–	2 Voyage	3 Pancos	5 Rantanka	–	20*	Balangingi	–	Small Islands south & west Celebes	Places where water is obtained	–	1842
8	Sarenko	Boeton	–	2 Fishing	3 large Pancos 5 Vintas	1 Rantanka	Samau'uh	50	Balangingi	–	Monde Island	–	–	1843
9	Lasado	Boni	–	4 Fishing	–	–	–	–	Balangingi	–	–	Balangingi on their return	–	1834
10	Hatibi Soleman	Bangai	–	4 Voyage	6 large Pancos 6 small Vintas	1 Leila	–	–	Balangingi	–	–	–	–	1843
11	Kilapon	Amoerang	20	3	4 small Pancos	2 Brass cannon	–	6*	Balangingi	Inhabitants of Balangingi	–	–	–	1843

* = number of crew on a small craft.

Appendix F (cont.)

	Name	Place of Residence	Age	No. of Persons Seized	Fleet Size	Armaments of Each Vessel	Commander of Vessel	Crew per Vessel	Where Marauding Flotilla Originated	Who Fitted and Equipped the Flotilla	Islands Used for Obtaining Water	Islands Used for Careening, Caulking, etc.	Time of Year when Vessel put to Sea	Year of Captivity
12	Moetala	Kwandang	—	2 Voyage	4 large Pancos 2 small Vintas	Lella	Dangie and Manalompo	30 10*	Balangingi	Inhabitants of Balangingi	Telisa and Lembe – near Kema	Salua-Buaya Island near Gorontalo	—	1846
13	Taborong	Sangir Island	30	19 Voyage	4 large Pancos	Lella	Padawi and Sabitong	30 50	Balangingi	Inhabitants of Balangingi	Talise Island	—	—	1843
14	Kadasa	Hila Island (Ambon)	15	8 Fishing	1 small Panco	Rantanka & Lella	—	6*	Sipac	Inhabitants of Sipac	Pulsu Tudju	Batu Kapul – near Lembu Island	West Monsoon	1843
15	Abdul	Gonong (under Banda)	25	1 Fishing	6 large & 5 small Pancos	2 Lella	Malutop (a Makassar man)	30 6*	Balangingi	Inhabitants of Balangingi	—	—	—	1845
16	Njow	Kilbat	30	3 Voyage	4 large Pancos	5 Brass cannons	—	50-60	Balangingi	On Mindanao by those who trade with Balangingi	Obie Island	—	West Monsoon	1845
17	Francis Mariano	Manila	45	3 Tripang nests	3 large Pancos	3 – 1 pound Cannons	Inam Tarawie	50	Sipac	Inam Tarawie & Kapitan Rajah	Sugut Island	Binur Bulan Island	West Monsoon	1837
18	Francisco Basilio	Cebu	28	6 Voyage	7 Pancos	6 Cannons in large Prahu, 2 cannons in small Prahu	Sapan (a Manila – man)	50 30*	Balangingi	Inhabitants of Balangingi	Tinunajan Island	Birik Island	—	1842
19	Siado	Bolang (Simoi)	25	1 Fishing	3 large Pancos 3 small Vintas	5 Cannons in large Prahu, 3 cannons in small Prahu	Lumujul	—	Balangingi	—	Banka Island	—	—	1844

* = number of crew on a small craft.

Appendix F (cont.)

	Name	Place of Residence	Age	No. of Persons Seized	Fleet Size	Armaments of Each Vessel	Commander of Vessel	Crew per Vessel	Where Marauding Flotilla Originated	Who Fitted and Equipped the Flotilla	Islands Used for Obtaining Water	Islands Used for Careening, Caulking, etc.	Time of Year When Vessel Put to Sea	Year of Captivity
20	Jacob Estephanus	Taboekan	50	2 Fishing	1 large Panco, 1 small Vinta	4 cannons in large Prahu, 1 cannon in small Prahu	Sarip Mie	30 10*	Balangingi	Sherifs on Balangingi	Kawao Is. near Mindanao	–	West Monsoon	1827
21	Pedro Francisco	Leyte	30	2 Voyage	5 large Pancos	5 Rantanka	Palain (a Manila-man)	50	Sipac	–	Kaibirang Is. near Manila	Kalanbaman small islands	West Monsoon	1843
22	Kawase	Goron (under Ceram)	45	11 Voyage	6 large Pancos	2 Lella	Sangie	30	Balangingi	–	An island near Gorontalo	Balangingi on their return	–	1846
23	Madi	Tumbuka (under Ternate)	30	5 Sago collecting	3 large Pancos	1 Lella	Leso	20	Balangingi	Inhabitants of Balangingi	The Bugis Coast	Kabina Island	West Monsoon	1844
24	Ramaka	Ratahan (Menado)	40	Alone fishing	3 large Pancos	1 Brass cannon		50	Balangingi	Inhabitants of Balangingi	Tandjongtola near Gorontalo	–	–	1846
25	Abdul	Djupandang (Makassar)	30	6 Fishing	1 large Panco, 1 small Vinta	3 Rantanka	Lasama	30	Balangingi	Maguindanao people	–	At Balangingi on their return	–	1841
26	Sendie	Dongala (Bugis)	30	2 Voyage	3 large Pancos, 2 small Vintas	1 large Rantanka	Sibaugay (a Bangai islander)	40 10*	Sipac	Inhabitants of Balangingi	–	Dongala	–	1844
27	Sirua	Kalumpang (Tontoli)	40	7 Fishing	3 large & 3 small Pancos	1 large Cannon, 2 Rantanka	Utap	–	Sipac	Inhabitants of Balangingi	–	–	West Monsoon	1841
28	Benonko	Lacasan Island	50	9 Voyage	4 large & 4 small Pancos	4 Rantanka 4 Lella	Hassan	40 10*	Tunkil	Panglima Hassan	–	–	–	1847
29	Abdulla	Pontianak	40	4 Voyage	9 large & 1 small Pancos	4 Lella	Hassan	40	Tunkil	Panglima Hassan	–	–	–	–
30	Pedro Juan	Iloilo	50	10 Voyage	3 large Pancos	1 large Cannon	Hassan	40	Tunkil	Panglima Hassan	–	Balangingi	–	1813

* = number of crew on a small craft.

NOTES

Chapter 1

[1] See Charles Frake, "Abu Sayyaf Displays of Violence and the Proliferation of Contested Identities Among Philippine Muslims," *American Anthropologist* 100, no. 1 (1998), 41-54; Benedict Sandin, *The Sea Dayaks of Borneo Before White Rajah Rule* (London: Macmillan, 1967), 63-65, 127; Esther Velthoen, "Wanderers, Robbers and Bad Folk: The Politics of Violence, Protection and Trade in Eastern Sulawesi 1750-1850," in Anthony Reid (ed.), *The Last Stand of Autonomous States, 1750-1870 Responses to Modernity in the Diverse Worlds of Southeast Asia and Korea* (London: Macmillan 1997); James F. Warren, *The Sulu Zone, The World Capitalist Economy and the Historical Imagination* (Amsterdam: VU University Press/CASA, 1998).

[2] Raja Ali Haji ibn Ahmad, *The Precious Gift of Tuhfat Al-Nafis* (Kuala Lumpur: Oxford University Press, 1982).

[3] James F. Warren, *The Sulu Zone 1768-1898 The Dynamics of External Trade, Slavery and Ethnicity in the Transformation of a Southeast Asian Maritime State* (Singapore: Singapore University Press, 1981), 147-156, 165-181.

[4] Ibid., 152-53.

[5] Warren, *The Sulu Zone, 1768-1898*, 154; Owen Rutter, *The Pirate Wind Tales of the Sea-Robbers of Malaya* (Singapore: Oxford University Press, 1986).

[6] The United Nations Conventions on the High Seas and Convention on the Law of the Sea (1982) both define piracy in the same

manner. Article 101 of the UN Convention of the Law of the Sea defines piracy as:

> a. any illegal acts of violence or detention, or any act of depredation committed for private ends by the crew or passengers of a private ship or a private aircraft and directed
> 1. on the high seas, against another ship or aircraft, or against persons or property on board such a ship or aircraft.
> 2. against a ship, aircraft, persons or property in a place outside the jurisdiction of any state;
>
> b. any act of voluntary participation in the operation of a ship or of an aircraft with knowledge of facts making it a pirate ship or aircraft;
>
> c. any act of inciting or intentionally facilitating an act described in para (a) or (b).

[7] Sir James Brooke to Lord Stanley, 4 October 1852, Parliamentary Papers, House of Commons, 1852, vol. XXXI [1538], Borneo Piracy.

[8] This is a slightly modified version of the pragmatic definition provided by the International Chamber of Commerce (ICC) and its International Maritime Bureau (IBM).

[9] For a study of how Southeast Asia became a crucial part of a global commercial system between the fifteenth and the mid-seventeenth centuries see, Anthony Reid, *Southeast Asia in the Age of Commerce 1450-1680: Volume Two: Expansion and Crisis* (New Haven: Yale University Press, 1993).

[10] George Windsor Earl, *The Eastern Seas* (Singapore: Oxford University Press, 1971), 384.

[11] Blake to Maitland, 13 August 1838. East India Company and India Board Records, Board's Collection, B.C. 86974, 4.

[12] E. Presgrave to K. Murchison, Resident Councillor at Singapore, Report on Piracy in the Straits Settlement, 5 December 1828. India Office Records, Board's Collections, (IOR), IOR/F/4/1724 (69433).

[13] See, Warren, *The Sulu Zone, the World Capitalist Economy and the Historical Imagination*, 9-12, 39-49, 58-64.

[14] See James F. Warren, "Who were the Balangingi Samal? Slave Raiding and Ethnogenesis in Nineteenth Century Sulu," *Journal of Asian Studies* 37, no. 3 (1978), 477-90.

[15] Warren, *The Sulu Zone, 1768-1898*, 162.

[16] Virginia Matheson, "Tuhfat Al Nafis" (Ph.D. diss. Monash University, 1973), 583-87; Stukken Betreffende Riouw, 1787-1788, Arsip Nasional Republik Indonesia, Riouw 20/3.

[17] Warren, *The Sulu Zone, 1768-1898*, 150-51; Melvin Mednick, "Encampment of the Lake: the Social Organization of a Moslem Philippine (Moro) People" (Ph.D. diss. University of Chicago, 1965), 47.

[18] Sir James Brooke to Lord Stanley, 4 October 1832, Parliamentary Papers, House of Commons, 1852, vol. XXXI [1538], Borneo Piracy.

[19] In these Euro-centered histories, which dwell on the activity of the Iranun and the Balangingi at length, the term 'piracy' is conspicuously present in the titles: Vicente Barrantes, *Guerras Piraticas de Filipinas contra Mindanaos y Joloanos* (Madrid, 1878); Emilio Bernaldez, *Resana Historica de la Guerra a Sur de Filipinas, sostenida por las armas Españoles contra los piratas de aquel Archipielago, desde la conquista hasta nuestras dias* (Madrid, 1857); Jose Montero y Vidal, *Historia de la Pirateria Malayo Mahometana en Mindanao, Jolo y Borneo*, (Madrid, 1888); Nicholas Tarling, *Piracy and Politics in the Malay World*, (Melbourne: F. W. Cheshire, 1963). See also, A. J. F. Jansen, 'Aantekeningen omtrent Sollek en de Solloksche Zeeroovers,' *Tijdschrift voor Indische Taal-, Landen Volkenkunde, uitegeven door het (Koninklyk) Bataviaasch Genootschap van Kunsten en Wetenschappen* (hereafter *TBG*), VII (1858), 212-43; "Berigten omtrent den Zeeroof in den Nederlandsch-Indischen Archipel, 1857," *TBG*, XVIII (1868-1872), 435-457; "Berigten . . . 1858" *TBG*, XX (1873), 302-26; W. R. Van Hoevell, "De Zeerooverijen der Soloerezen," *Tijdschrift voor Nederlandsche Indies* II (1850), 99-105.

[20] Charles Boxer, *The Dutch Seaborne Empire 1600-1800* (London: Penguin Books, 1973); Kristof Glamman, *Dutch Asiatic Trade, 1620-1740* (The Hague: Nijhoff, 1958); Leonard Blusse, *Strange Company: Chinese Settlers, Mestizo Women and the Dutch in VOC Batavia*, (Dordrecht: KITLV, 1986).

[21] See Holden Furber, *John Company at Work: A Study of European Expansion in India in the Late Eighteenth Century* (Cambridge: Harvard University Press, 1951), 160; C. Northcote Parkinson, *Trade in the Eastern Seas, 1793-1813* (London: Cambridge University Press, 1937), 141; Michael Greenberg, *British Trade and the Opening of China, 1800-*

1842 (London: Cambridge University Press, 1951), 16; S. B. Singh, *European Agency Houses In Bengal, 1783-1833* (Calcutta: K. L. Mukhopadhyay, 1966), 1-3.

[22] Thomas Forrest, *A Voyage to New Guinea and the Moluccas 1774-1776* (Kuala Lumpur: Oxford University Press, 1969), 20-21; D. K. Bassett, 'British Commercial and Strategic Interest in the Malayan Peninsula during the late Eighteenth Century,' in J. Bastin and R. Roolvink (eds), *Malayan and Indonesian Studies* (Oxford: Oxford University Press, 1964), 134-35; 'Thomas Forrest, and Eighteenth-Century Mariner,' *Journal Malaysian Branch Royal Asiatic Society* 34, no. 2 (1961), 113-14.

[23] East India Company Board Minutes. Add. 75. 29,169, F.118.

[24] John Herbert to Capt. Thomas Forrest, 5 February 1799; Thomas Forrest's Mission on the *Fly* Ketch, East India Company Records, Bengal Secret Consultations, 28 February 1782.

[25] Thomas Forrest's mission on the *Fly* Ketch, East India Company Records, Bengal Secret Consultations, 28 February 1782.

[26] Light to G. G., 22 December 1790, Straits Settlement Factory Records (FWCP, 12 January 1791); H. H. Clodd, *Malaya's First British Pioneer: The Life of Francis Light* (London: 1948), 75; R. Bonney, *Kedah 1771-1821 The Search for Security and Independence* (Kuala Lumpur: Oxford University Press, 1971), 90-92.

[27] See James Francis Warren, "Moro," in Ainslie T. Embree (Editor in Chief), *Encyclopedia of Asian History*, vol. 3 (New York: Charles Scribner's Sons, 1988), 39; Charles O. Frake, "The Genesis of Kinds of People in the Sulu Archipelago," in *Language and Cultural Description* (Stanford: Stanford University Press, 1980), 314-18; Francisco Mallari, S.J. "Muslim Raids in Bicol, 1580-1792," *Philippine Studies*, 34 (1986), 257.

[28] Norman G. Owen, *Prosperity Without Progress Manila Hemp and Material Life in the Colonial Philippines* (Berkeley: University of California Press, 1984), 27.

[29] Warren, *The Sulu Zone, the World Capitalist Economy and the Historical Imagination*, 9-19; *The Sulu Zone 1768-1898*, 252-55.

[30] Pablo Fernandez O.P., *History of the Church in the Philippines, 1521-1898* (Manila: National Book Store, 1979), 203.

[31] On sources and methodology see Warren, *The Sulu Zone, the World Capitalist Economy and the Historical Imagination*, 51-58.

[32] See Peter Burke, *The French Historical Revolution: The Annales School 1929-89* (Stanford: Stanford University Press, 1990); Paul Baran, *The Political Economy of Growth* (London, 1957); Andre Gunder Frank, *World Accumulation, 1492-1789* (London: MacMillan Press, 1978); Immanuel Wallerstein, *The Modern World-System: Capitalist Agriculture and the Origins of the European World Economy in the Sixteenth Century*, (New York: Academic Press, 1979).

[33] Eric Wolf, *Europe and the People Without History* (Berkeley: University of California Press, 1982).

[34] J. C. Van Leur, *Indonesian Trade and Society* (The Hague: Van Hoeve, 1967).

[35] Ibid., 153, 261.

[36] Warren, *The Sulu Zone 1768-1898*, 147.

[37] Barrantes, *Guerras Piraticas de Filipinas contra Mindanaos y Joloanos*; Bernaldez, *Resana Historica de la Guerra a Sur de Filipinas*; Jose Montero y Vidal, *Historia de la Pirateria Malayo Mahometana en Mindanao, Jolo y Borneo*; Tarling, *Piracy and Politics in the Malay World*.

[38] Alexander Dalrymple (1737-1808) joined the East India Company in 1752. He was active in the Sulu archipelago between 1759 and 1764, putting forward the ill-fated Balambangan project, but lost the command of Balambangan to John Herbert in 1771. He was later hydrographer to the company (1779), and first hydrographer to the Admiralty (1795-1808). James Rennell (1742-1830) served in the Royal Navy and East India Company Marine, when he was commissioned the surveyor general of the company's possessions in Bengal. In the latter part of his life he was the celebrated geographer of his day. See Alexander Dalrymple, *Oriental Repertory*, 2 vols. (London: 1808); "Account of Some Natural Curiosities at Sooloo," in *An Historical Collection of the Several Voyages and Discoveries in the South Pacific Ocean*, vol. 1 (London: 1770); Howard Fry, *Alexander Dalrymple and the Expansion of British Trade* (London: Cass, 1970); James Francis Warren, "Balambangan and the Rise of the Sulu Sultanate, 1772-1775," *Journal of the Malaysian Branch Royal Asiatic Society* 50, no. 1 (1977), 73-93; on James Rennell see Ann L. Reber, "The Sulu World in the Eighteenth and Nineteenth Centuries: A

Historiographical Problem in British Writings on Malay Piracy," (M.A. diss., Cornell University, 1966); James Rennell, *Journal of a Voyage to the Sooloo Islands and the Northwest Coast of Borneo, from and to Madras with descriptions of the islands, 1762-1763,* British Museum.

[39] The Memorial of Thomas Forest to the Court Directors of the East India Company, 29 June 1779; East India Company Court Minutes, 21 July 1779, vol. 88, F.188.

[40] Forrest, *A Voyage to New Guinea and the Moluccas, 1774-1776,* 174-337.

[41] E. Presgrave to K. Murchison, resident councillor at Singapore, Report on Piracy in the Straits Settlements, 5 December 1828, India Office Records, Board's Collections, (IOR), IOR/F/4/1724(69433).

[42] J. Hunt, "Some Particulars Relating to Sulo in the Archipelago of Felicia," in J. H. Moor (ed.), *Notices of the Indian Archipelago and Adjacent Countries* (London: Cass, 1967), 31-60.

[43] Parliamentary Papers, 112-13; Owen Rutter, *The Pirate Wind Tales of the Sea Robbers of Malaya* (Singapore: Oxford University Press, 1986), 45-48; Luiz de Ibanez y Garcia, *Mi Cautiverio; Carta que con motivo del que sufrio entro los Moros piratas Joloanos y Samales en 1857* (Madrid: G. Alhambra, 1859); Warren, *The Sulu Zone 1768-1898,* Appendix E, Statement of Balangingi Prisoners, 1838, 429-30; Appendix F, The Statements of the Fugative Captives of the Sulu Sultanate, 1836-1864, 299-315.

[44] A particularly valuable biographical sketch of Panglima Taupan is provided by Margarita de los Reyes Cojuangco in her history of the Samal diaspora spanning four generations of exiles. See Margarita de los Reyes Cojuangco, *Kris of Valor: The Samal Balangingi's Defiance and Diaspora* (Manila: Manisan, 1993).

[45] Warren, *The Sulu Zone, the World Capitalist Economy and the Historical Imagination,* 53-55.

[46] Donna Haraway, "Situated Knowledges: The Science Question in Feminism and the Privilege of Partial Perspective," *Simians, Cyborgs and Women: The Reinvention of Nature* (New York: Routledge, 1991), 191.

[47] On methodology see Warren, *The Sulu Zone, the World Capitalist Economy and the Historical Imagination,* 51-58; "Explorings and Reflections on Southeast Asian History," *Our Cultural Heritage,*

edited by John Bigelow (Canberra: The Australian Academy of Humanities, 1998), 183-99.

⁴⁸ Warren, *The Sulu Zone 1768-1898*, 237-51; 298-315.

⁴⁹ Governor of the Straits Settlements to Rear Admiral Maitland, Commander in Chief in the East Indies, 28 June 1838, Admiralty 125/133.

⁵⁰ Parliamentary Papers, 112-13; Rutter, *The Pirate Wind*, 45-48; Ibanez y Garcia, *Mi Cautiverio*, 1-29; "Adventures of C. Z. Pieters among the Pirates of Maguindanao," *Journal of the Indian Archipelago and Eastern Asia* (1858), 301-12.

⁵¹ Governor of the Straits Settlements to Rear Admiral Maitland, commander in chief in the East Indies, 28 June 1838, Admiralty 125/133.

⁵² Tarling, *Piracy and Politics in the Malay World*, 8.

⁵³ Ibid.

⁵⁴ Cesar Majul, *Muslims in the Philippines* (Quezon City: University of the Philippines Press, 1973).

⁵⁵ Reber, "The Sulu World in the Eighteenth and Nineteenth Centuries" (M.A. diss., Cornnell University, 1966).

⁵⁶ Tarling, *Piracy and Politics in the Malay World*, 9.

⁵⁷ Warren, *The Sulu Zone1768-1898*, xi-xvi, 252-55; *The Sulu Zone, the World Capitalist Economy and the Historical Imagination*, 9-24; 58-64.

⁵⁸ Frake, *The Genesis of Kinds of People in the Sulu Archipelago*, 314-318; "Abu Sayyaf Displays of Violence and the Proliferation of Contested Identities Among Philippine Muslims," 42-43.

⁵⁹ Luis Camara Dery, *From Ibalon to Sorsogon: A Historical Survey of Sorsogon Province to 1905* (Quezon City: New Day Publishers, 1991), 59.

⁶⁰ Warren, "Moro," 38.

⁶¹ Lofti Ben Rejek, "Barbary's 'Character' in European Letters, 1514-1830: An Ideological Prelude to Colonization," *Dialectical Anthropology* 6, (1982), 346.

⁶² Majul, *The Muslims in the Philippines*, 107-316.

Chapter 2

¹ Warren, *The Sulu Zone, 1768-1898*, xix-xxii, 67-74.

² Sue Mednick, "Encampment of the Lake: the Social Organization of a Moslem Philippine (Moro) People" (Ph.D. diss. University of Chicago,

1965); Reynaldo C. Ileto, *Magindanao, 1860-1888: The Career of Datu Uto of Buayan*, (Ithaca: Cornell University, 1971), 1-2. Thomas H. McKenna, *Muslim Rulers and Rebels Everday Politics and Armed Separation in the Southern Philippines* (Berkeley: University of California, 1998), 27.

[3] Ruurdje Laarhoven, *Triumph of Moro Diplomacy, The Maguindanao Sultanate in the 17th Century* (Quezon City: New Day Publishers, 1989), 99.

[4] See Ileto, *Maguindanao, 1860-1888*, 1-12.

[5] Melvin Mednick, "Some Problems of Moro History and Political Organization," *Philippines Sociological Review* 5, (1957), 42; Forrest, *A Voyage to New Guinea and the. Moluccas 1774-1776*, 276.

[6] Forrest, *A Voyage to New Guinea and the Moluccas, 1774-1776*, 301.

[7] Thomas Kiefer, *The Tausog: Violence and Law in a Philippine Moslem Society* (New York: Holt Rhinehart and Winston, 1972), 22-24; Clifford Sather, *The Bajau Laut Adaptation, History and Fate in a Maritime Fishing Society of South Eastern Sabah* (Kuala Lumpur: Oxford University Press, 1997), 35-43; "Sulu's Political Jurisdiction over the Bajau Laut," *Borneo Research Bulletin* 3, no. 2 (1771), 58-62; Harry A. Nimmo, "Reflections on Badjau History," *Philippine Studies* 17 (1968), 32-59; J Wulf, "Features of Yakan Culture," *Folk* 6 (1964), 52-72.

[8] Ileto, *Maguindanao, 1860-1888*, 1-2.

[9] Mednick, "Source Problems of Moro History and Political Organization," 39.

[10] Ibid., 49.

[11] Ileto, *Maguindanao, 1860-1888*, 2.

[12] Ibid., 3.

[13] Ibid., 4-5.

[14] Laarhoven, *The Maguindanao Sultanate in the 17th Century*, 99.

[15] Ibid.

[16] Francisco Combes, *Historia de las Islas de Mindanao, Iolo, y sus Adyacentes* (Madrid: 1667, ed. W. Retana, 1887), 28-29.

[17] David Sopher, *The Sea Nomads: A Study Based on the Literature of the Maritime Boat People of Southeast Asia* (Singapore: Memoir of the National Museum, no. 5, 1965), 307-14; Ileto, *Maguindanao, 1860-1888*, 5.

[18] Ileto, *Maguindanao, 1860-1888*, 5.

[19] Laarhoven, *The Maguindanao Sultanate in the 17th Century*, 109-10.

[20] Forrest, *A Voyage to New Guinea and the Muloccas, 1774-1776*, 192-93; Mednick, "Some Problems of Moro History and Political Organization," 43; Warren, *The Sulu Zone, 1768-1898*, 150-52.

[21] No. 2, May 1767, AGI Filipinas 669; No. 4, 5 July 1814, AGI, Filipinas 810; AR, Kolonien Archief 2922, 667; Felix Renouard, *Voyage Commercial et Politique aux Indes Orientales*, vol. 2, 275; Barrantes, *Guerras Piraticas*, 160-61; Montero y Vidal, *Historia General de Filipinas*, vol. 2, 369. In 1773, two Filipino women were taken off a Portuguese packetboat en route from Batavia to Macao that was forced to put into Manila for provisions. The women (who were the concubines of two Chinese passengers) had been captured by Maguindanao in 1761. One had been sold in Batavia for the equivalent of ₱90 and the other, ₱112. They testified that there was a thriving trade in Filipino slaves at Batavia and that there were a large number of them in the city. No. 9, 19 December 1775, AGI, Filipinas 359.

For a copy of the decree of 16 June 1762 forbidding the retailing of Spanish subjects in the Netherlands Indies, see AR Kolonien Archief 2922, 667; no. 2, 9 May 1767, AGI, Filipinas 669. Part of the decree reads:

> No slaves are permitted to be brought from the eastward above the age of 14 years, and the names and number of all slaves that may be brought from the eastward must be inserted in the pass. The importation of slaves belonging to the King of Spain is prohibited under penalty of 500 Rix dollars, and the annulment of the purpose.

Mr. Raffles to 1st Earl of Minto, governor-general of India, 18 February 1811, IOL, EUR. F. 148/5, 114.

[22] Warren, *The Sulu Zone, 1768-1898*, 150-53.

[23] Thomas Kiefer, "The Tausug Polity and the Sultanate of Sulu: A Segmentary State in the Southern Philippines," *Sulu Studies*, 1 (1972), 30; Cesar Majul "Political and Historical Notes on the Old Sulu Sultanate," *Journal of the Malaysian Branch, Royal Asiatic Society* 38, pt. 1 (1965), 28; Warren, *The Sulu Zone, 1768-1898*, xxii-xxv.

[24] Warren, *The Sulu Zone, The World Capitalist Economy and the Historical Imagination*, 9-10.

[25] James Warren, "Balambangan and the Rise of the Sulu Sultanate,

1772-1775," *Journal of the Malaysian Branch, Royal Asiatic Society* 50, pt. 1 (1977), 73-93; Warren, *The Sulu Zone, 1768-1898*, 17-37.

[26] Warren, *The Sulu Zone, 1768-1898*, 151-53.

[27] Ibid., 153.

[28] Ibid., 157, 190.

[29] J. Hunt, "Some Particulars Relating to Sulo in the Archipelago of Felicia," 50.

[30] Ibid., 50-51; Warren, *The Sulu Zone, 1768-1898*, 229-31, 244-45.

[31] Warren, *The Sulu Zone, 1768-1898*, xxiv.

[32] Kiefer, "The Tausug Polity and the Sultanate of Sulu," 30.

[33] James Rennell, *Journal of a Voyage to the Sooloo Islands and the Northwest Coast of Borneo, from and to Madras with descriptions of the islands 1762-1763*, 38.

[34] Ibid., 38.

[35] "The Illanoon or Sulo Pirates," extract from the *Singapore Free Press*, 6 April 1847, Admiralty 125/133-Sulu Piracy.

[36] Wilkes, "Jolo and the Sulus," 166.

[37] Governor of the Straits Settlements to Rear Admiral Maitland, commander in chief in the East Indies, 28 June 1838, Admiralty 125/133.

[38] Warren, *The Sulu Zone, 1768-1898*, 219-28.

[39] Ibid., 223.

Chapter 3

[1] Mednick, "Encampment of the Lake: the Social Organization of a Moslem Philippine People," 18; personal communication, David Barradas, 7 February 1974.

[2] Ruurdje Laarhoven, "Lords of the Great River: The Maguindanao Port and Polity During the Seventeenth Century," *The South Asian Port and Polity Rise and Demise* edited by J. Kathirithamby-Wells and John Villiers (Singapore: Singapore University Press, 1990), 166. The word Maguindanao is derived from the root *danao* which means inundation by sea, river or lake. Maguindanao means "That which has been inundated." It is the most appropriate term that could have been designated to describe the broad lowland of the Rio Grande de Cotabato because of the often flooded condition in which this intermontane basin and

neighboring river valleys are found. It was the Maguindanao, people of the flood plain, who lent their name to the vast island which the Spaniards shortened and corrupted to Mindanao. Najeeb M. Saleeby, *Studies in Moro History, Law and Religion* (Manila: Bureau of Public Printing, 1905), 13.

[3] Laarhoven, "Lords of the Great River: The Maguindanao Port and Polity During the Seventeenth Century," 166; Ileto, *Maguindanao, 1860-1888*, 4-6.

[4] Commander Blake to Rear Admiral F. Maitland, 13 August 1838, Admiralty 125.133-Sulu Piracy.

[5] Rennell, *Journal of a Voyage to the Sooloo Islands and the Northwest Coast of Borneo, from and to Madras with Descriptions of the Islands, 1762-1763*, 38.

[6] Edward Belcher, *Narrative Voyage of the HMS Samarang, During the Years 1843-1846*, vol. I (London: Reeve, Benham and Reeve, 1848), 106.

[7] Bernaldez, *Resana historico de la Guerra a Sur de Filipinas, sostenada por las armas Espanoles contra los pirates de aguel achhipielago, desde la conquista hasta nuestras dias*, 46-47.

[8] Laarhoven, *The Maguindanao Sultanate in the 17th Century*, 111.

[9] Ibid., 112.

[10] Forrest, *A Voyage to New Guinea and the Moluccas 1774-1776*, 250.

[11] Commander Blake to Rear Admiral F. Maitland, 13 August 1838, Admiralty 125/133-Sulu Piracy; "The Illanoons," *Singapore Free Press and Mercantile Advertiser*, 13 December 1838.

[12] Commander Blake to Rear Admiral F. Maitland, 13 August 1838, Admiralty 125/133-Sulu Piracy.

[13] Capt. Charles Hunter, R.N., *The Adventures of a Naval Officer*, ed. Spencer St. John, (London, 1905), 83.

[14] Roger Mundy, *Narrative of Events in Borneo and Celebes down to the Occupation of Labuan, from the Journals of Jemaes Brooke, esq., Together with a Narrative of the Operations of H.M.S. Iris by Capt. Rodney Mundy* (London: John Murray, 1848), 240-41.

[15] William Dampier, *A New Voyage Round the World* (London: 1697. Reprint with an Introduction by Sir Albert Fray, 1937).

[16] Laarhoven, *The Maguindanao Sultanate in the 17th Century*, 110;

Stuart Schlegel, "Tiruray-Maguindanaon Ethnic Relations: An Ethnohistorical Puzzle," *Solidarity* 7, no. 4 (1972), 25-30.

[17] Dampier, *A New Voyage Round the World*, 227-28.

[18] Ibid., 333.

[19] Forrest, *A Voyage to New Guinea and the Moluccas 1774-1776*, 192-93; See also Mednick, "Some Problems of Moro History and Political Organization," 43.

[20] Forrest, *A Voyage to New Guinea and the Moluccas 1774-1776*, 192-93.

[21] PNA, Ereccion Pueblo, Camarines Sur 1785-1837, fol. 14.

[22] Mednick, "Encampment of the Lake: the Social Organization of a Moslem Philippine People," 47.

[23] Personal communication, David Barradas, 7 February 1974; W.R. Van Hoevell, "De Zeerooverijen der Soeloerezen," *Tijdschrift voor Nederlandsche Indie* 2 (1850), 100.

[24] On the efforts of states to concentrate and regulate their populations see James Scott, "The State and People who Move Around," *IIAS Newsletter* 19, no. 3 (1999), 45.

[25] Mednick, "Encampment of the Lake: the Social Organization of a Moslem Philippine People," 30-31.

[26] Majul, *Muslims in the Philippines*, 365.

[27] Forrest, *A Voyage to New Guinea and the Moluccas 1774-1776*, 193, 237-38.

[28] Jeremy Beckett, 17 January 1975.

[29] Tomas de Comyn, *State of the Philippines in 1810, Being a Historical, Statistical and Descriptive Account of the Interesting Portion on the Indian Archipelago* (Manila: Filipiniana Book Guild, 1969), 132; Saleeby, *Studies in Moro History, Law and Religion*, 15.

[30] No. 7 GCG a Señor Secretario de Estado, 4 June 1806, AGI, Filipinas 510; Forrest, *A Voyage to New Guinea and the Moluccas 1774-1776*, 193.

[31] Commander Blake to Rear Admiral F. Maitland, 13 August 1838, Admiralty 125/133-Sulu Piracy; "The Illanoons," *Singapore Free Press and Mercantile Advertiser*, 13 December 1838.

[32] Ibid.

[33] Rennell, *Journal of a Voyage to the Sooloo Islands and the Northwest*

Coast of Borneo, from and to Madras with descriptions of the Islands, 1762-1763, 38.

[34] Ibid.

[35] Iranun blacksmiths had developed their industrial art to a degree unparalleled by their Tausog or Maguindanao neighbors. At the beginning of the nineteenth century, they introduced important changes in the smithing industry and brass manufacture at Jolo. Arturo Garin y Sociats, "Memoria sobre el Archipielago de Jolo," *Boletin de la Sociedad Geografica de Madrid* 10, (1881), 193.

[36] No. 7 GCG a Señor Secretario de Estado, 4 June 1806, AGI, Filipinas 510; Barrantes, *Guerras Piraticas*, 159-161; Montero y Vidal, *Historia General de Filipinas*, vol. 2, 372.

[37] Montero y Vidal, *Historia General de Filipinas*, vol. 2, 372.

[38] GCG a Señor Secretario de Estado, 12 January 1773, AGI, Filipinas, 493.

[39] Barrantes, *Guerras Piraticas*, 181.

[40] Forrest, *A Voyage to New Guinea and the Moluccas 1774-1776*, 322.

[41] Juan Cencelli a Señor Conde de Aranda, 16 April 1774, AHN, Estado 2845, caja 2; No. 7, GCG a Señor Secretario de Estado, 4 June 1806, AGI, Filipinas 510; Montero y Vidal, *Historia General de Filipinas*, vol. 2, 311.

[42] Hunt, "Some Particulars Relating to Sulo in the Archipelago of Felicia," 50-51, 57-60.

[43] Bonham to Maitland, 28 June 1838, Admiralty 125/133-Sulu Piracy.

[44] Byer-Hollerman-Philippine Customary Law, vol. 6, paper 162, no. 23, Christie "The Moros of Sulu and Mindanao," 43.

Chapter 4

[1] Warren, *The Sulu Zone 1768-1898*, 147-48, 256-58.

[2] Warren, *The Sulu Zone, The World Capitalist Economy and the Historical Imagination*, 39-49.

[3] Warren, *The Sulu Zone 1768-1898*, 156-71, 189-90.

[4] Mundy, *Narrative Events in Borneo and Celebes Down to the*

Occupation of Labuan, from the Journal of James Brooke, esq., together with a Narrative of the Operations of HMS Iris, 17.

[5] Francisco Mallari, S.J., "Muslim Raids in Bicol, 1580-1792," *Philippine Studies* 34 (1986), 257.

[6] Majul, *Muslims in the Philippines*, 248.

[7] Warren, *The Sulu Zone 1768-1898*, 154, 157.

[8] Forrest, *A Voyage to New Guinea and the Moluccas, 1774-1776*, 228-29, 303, 319; Parliamentary Papers, House of Commons, 1851, vol. LVI, pt. I [1390], "Historical Notices upon the Piracies committed in the East Indies, and upon the measures taken for suppressing them, by the Government of the Netherlands, within the last thirty years." Abstracted from articles by Cornets de Groot in the *Moniteur des Indies*.

[9] Barbara Watson Andaya, *To Live as Brothers Southeast Sumatra in the Seventeenth and Eighteenth Centuries* (Honolulu: University of Hawaii Press, 1993), 224.

[10] Stukken Betuffende Riouw, 1787-1788, ANRI, Riouw 20/3; Matheson, "Tahfat Al Nafis" (Ph. D. diss. Monash University, 1973), 583-87.

[11] Matheson, "Tahfat Al Nafis," 1051.

[12] David Woodward, *The Narrative of Captain David Woodward and Four Seamen* (London: Dawson, 1969), 17.

[13] Stukken Betuffende Riouw, 1787-1788, ANRI, Riouw 20/3; Matheson, "Tahfat Al Nafis," 583-87, 1051.

[14] Kommisar se Palembang, aan den Gouvenuer General van Nederlandsch Indien, 25 May 1818; No. 115, De Resident van Banka, aan den Gouvenuer General over Nederlandsch Indien, 29 January 1831, AR, Archief Kolonien 4168.

[15] Extract from Mr. Presgrave's Report on the subject of piracy, 5 December 1828, PRO Admiralty 125/133; No. 7, GCG a Señor Secretario de Estado, 4 June 1806, AGI Filipinas 510; Barrantes, *Guerras Piraticas*, 159-60.

[16] Personal communication, Clifford Sather, 6 April 1972.

[17] Barrantes, *Guerras Piraticas*, 160.

[18] Francis Light to Consul at Fort William, 13 December 1786, IOL, Straits Settlement Factory Records 11355; Major Kyd to John Thornhill, 26 December 1795, IOL, P/4/39, 302; Mr Graham to Mr. Dundas, 29 May 1795, IOL, H/Misc/437/6, 153.

[19] Light to Consul at Fort William, 16 July 1789, IOL, Straits Settlement Factory Records/2.

[20] Light to Consul at Fort William, 5 December 1790, IOL, Straits Settlement Factory Records/2.

[21] Light to Consul at Fort William, 5 January 1791, IOL, Straits Settlement Factory Records/2; R. Bonney, *Kedah 1771-1821 The Search for Security and Independence* (Kuala Lumpur: Oxford University Press, 1971), 90-93.

[22] Light to governor-general of India, 11 December 1790, IOL, Straits Settlement Factory Records/4.

[23] Bonney, *Kedah 1771-1821 The Search for Security and Independence*, 91-94.

[24] Kommisar te Palembang, aan den Gouveneur-General von Nederlandsch Indien, 25 May 1818, AR, Archief Kolonien, 4168.

[25] Watson-Andaya, *To Live as Brothers Southeast Sumatra in the Seventeenth and Eighteenth Centuries*, 219; See also Mary Heidhues Somers, *Banka Tin and Mentok Pepper: Chinese Settlement on an Indonesian Island* (Singapore: Institute Southeast Asian Studies, 1992).

[26] Thomas Horsfield, "Report on the Island of Banka," *Journal of the Indian Archipelago and Eastern Asia* 2 (1848), 318-24.

[27] Horsfield, "Report on the Islands of Banka," 315-17; Testimony of Pangeran Syed Hassan Habassy, 15 October 1830, AR, Archief, Kolonien 4168.

[28] Watson-Andaya, *To Live as Brothers Southeast Sumatra in the Seventeenth and Eighteenth Centuries*, 225.

[29] "The Piracy and Slave Trade of the Indian Archipelago," *Journal of the Indian Archipelago and Eastern Asia* 3 (1849), 587.

[30] Parliamentary Papers, 72.

[31] Report by Councillor of the Indies M. Muntinghe, 31 August 1821 and Report of Commissioner of Borneo M.J.H. Tobias, October 1821 in Parliamentary Papers, 71, 76-77; Mundy, *Narrative Events in Borneo and Celebes Down to the Occupation of Labuan*, 12-13.

[32] E. Presgrave to K. Murchison, resident councillor at Singapore. Report on Piracy in the Straits Settlements, 5 December 1828. India Office Records, Boards Collections, (IOR) IOR/F/4/1724(69433).

[33] *Singapore Chronicle*, 18 April 1833; T. J. Newbold, "Outline of

Political Relations with the Native States on the Eastern and Western Coasts, Malayan Peninsula," in Moor (ed.), *Notices of the Indian Archipelago*, 90.

[34] *Singapore Chronicle*, 25 August 1831.

[35] Warren, *The Sulu Zone 1768-1898*, 161-162; Farquhar to Colonel Oliver, 1 June 1802, IOL, P/2-5/18; Forrest, *A Voyage to New Guinea and the Moluccas, 1774-1776*, 228-29.

[36] Warren, *The Sulu Zone 1768-1898*, 161-162; Farquhar to Colonel Oliver, 1 June 1802, IOL, P/2-5/18.

[37] N.839, 8 June 1855, AR, Schaarsbergen, Kolonien 5873.

[38] Vosmaer aan den Gouveneur-General van Nederlandsch Indien, 25 November 1833, AR, Kolonien Archief 7168.

[39] Jansen, "Aanteekeningen omtrent Sollok en de Solloksche Zeerovers," 232.

[40] Forrest, *A Voyage to New Guinea and the Moluccas, 1774-1776*, 303, 319.

[41] H. Van Dewall, "Aanteekeningen omtrent de Noordoostkust van Borneo," *Tijdschift voor Indische Taal Land-en Volkenkunden, uitgegeven door het (Koninklijk) Bataviaasch Kunsten en Wetenschappen* 4 (1885), 442.

[42] Forrest, *A Voyage to New Guinea and the Moluccas, 1774-1776*, 228.

[43] Ibid., 229.

[44] Account of Celebes by Alexander Dalrymple, April 1763, IOL, H/Misc/795/11, 43; Farquhar to Colonel Oliver, 1 June 1802, IOL, P/255/18.

[45] Farquhar to Colonel Oliver, 1 June 1802, IOL, P/2-5/18.

[46] Warren, *The Sulu Zone 1768-1898*, 162.

[47] Farquhar to Colonel Oliver, 1 June 1802, IOL, P/2-5/18.

[48] Court Minutes, 9 February 1780, IOL, vol. 88, F. 485.

[49] Forrest's memorandum to Warren Hastings, 1784, BM. Add. 29, 169, F.118.

[50] Farquhar to Colonel Oliver, 1 June 1802, IOL, P/2-5/18.

[51] Esther Velthoen, "Armed Bands and Protection Rackets: 'Gangster' Politics in Eastern Sulawesi 1700-1850," paper presented at the conference "The Last Stand of Autonomous States in Southeast Asia and Korea, 1750-1870," Bali, 19-21 August 1994, 16-19; Parliamentary

Papers, 75 contains information on the 'pirates' of Tobello originating from Ternate, Tidore, Bacan, and Ceram.

[52] IOL, G/21/1, 367; F.W. Stapel (ed.) *Corpus Diplomaticum Neerlands-Indicum*, Vol. 6 (Hague:Martinus Nijhoff, 1955), 437.

[53] Farquhar to Lord Clive, 1 June 1802, IOL, P/242/42, 2551.

[54] Colonel Oliver to Lord Clive, 6 March 1802, IOL, P/242/42, 2612.

[55] Farquhar to Lord Clive, 1 January 1802, IOL, P/242/42/2551.

[56] Charles Court to Marquis Wellsley, 30 June 1801, IOL, P/165/76.

[57] Farquhar to Lord Clive, 1 January 1802, IOL, P/242/42, 2612

[58] John Hayes, commander of the Company ship *Swift* to the Resident at the Molucca Islands, 21 August 1801, IOL, P/242/42.

[59] Velthoen, "Armed Bands and Protection Rackets: 'Gangster' Politics in Eastern Sulawesi 1700-1850," 15-16.

[60] Hunt, "Some Particulars Relating to Sulo in the Archipelago of Felicia," 51.

[61] Majul, *Muslims in the Philippines*, 107-68; Mallari, S.J., "Muslim Raids in Bicol, 1580-1792," 257-72.

[62] Mallari, S.J., "Muslim Raids," 258.

[63] PNL MF Ramo: Filipinas, Reel 3, Tomo 5, Exp. 3, fols. 197B-98; Mallari, S.J., "Muslim Raids," 276.

[64] No. 46, GCG a Secretario de Estado, 17 August 1770, AGI Filipinas 790; Alexander Dalrymple to Secret Committee, 7 February 1764, IOL, G/4/1, 402-403.

[65] No. 28, GCG a su Magestad, 1 August 1765, AGI Filipinas 611, 4.

[66] Ibid.

[67] No. 99, GCG a Secretario de Estado, 10 July 1771, AGI Filipinas 491, 1-3.

[68] Ereccion de Pueblos-Samar, 1796-1798, tomo 1, Razon de lo todo lo acontecido a Don Juan Miguel del Castillo en el tiempo que estuvo cautivo entre los moros, Manila, 17 February 1775.

[69] Forrest, *A Voyage to New Guinea and the Moluccas, 1774-1776*, 302.

[70] No. 165, GCG a Secretario de Estado, 16 January 1772, AGI Filipinas 491; No. 226, AGI, Filipinas 492, 4.

[71] J. F. de la Perouse, *A Voyage Round the World in the Years 1785*,

1787 and 1788, 3 vols. (London: *1798*) in *Travel Accounts of the Islands, 1513-1787* (Manila: Filipiniana Book Guild, 1971), 365-66.

[72] No. 7, GCG a Señor Secretario de Estado, 4 June 1806, AGI Filipinas 510, 51; no. 226, AGI Filipinas 492, 4; Joachim Martinez de Zuniga, *Estadismo de las Filipinas: o mis viajez por este Pais*, 495.

[73] No. 70, GCG a Secretario de Estado, AGI Filipinas 491; no. 1, 10 October 1772, AGI Filipinas 626.

[74] Miguel Angel Espina, *Apuntos para Hacer un libro sobre Jolo, entresacados de los escritos por Barrantes, Bernaldez, Escosura, Francia, Girandier, Gonzales, Parrados, Pagos y otros varios* (Manila: Imprenta de M. Perez, hijo, 1889), 118; Montero y Vidal, *Historia de la Pirateria Malayo Mahometano en Mindanao, Jolo y Borneo*, vol. 1, 336.

[75] Cartas 1825-1826, folio 206, Gobernador-General de Filipinas to Señor Secretario del despacho de Marina, comercio y Gobernacion de Ultramar, 4 February 1826.

[76] Bonham to F.K. Maitland, 28 June 1838, Admirality 125/133-Sulu Piracy.

[77] No. 70, GCG a Secretario de Estado, 26 December 1770, AGI Filipinas 491; No. 105, GCG a Secretario de Estado, 12 July 1771, AGI Filipinas 491; No. 1, Consejo de las Indias, 10 October 1772, AGI Filipinas 626.

[78] See William Lytle Schurz, *The Manila Galleon* (New York: E. P. Dutton, 1959).

[79] No. 482, GCG a Señor Secretario de Estado, 31 March 1775, AGI, Filipinas 360; No. 7, GCG a Señor Secretario de Estado, 4 June 1806, Filipinas 510, 61, 95; No 46, GCG a Señor Secretario de Estado, 17 August 1770, AGI, Filipinas 490; Comyn, *State of the Philippines in 1810*, 119.

[80] Alcalde Mayor de Tayabas a GCG, 20 December 1768, PNA, Ereccion de Pueblo, Tayabas 111; Alcalde Mayor de Tayabas a GCG, 18 September 1781, PNA, Ereccion de Pueblo, Tayabas 217; Alcalde Mayor de Tayabas a GCG, 2 December 1793, PNA, Ereccion de Pueblo, Tayabas 99 (1793-1857 pt. II); No. 7, GCG a Señor Secretario de Estado, 4 June 1806, AGI, Filipinas 510; Montero y Vidal, *Historia de Filipinas*, 377; Mallari, S.J., "Muslim Raids," 277-79; Owen, *Prosperity Without Progress Manila Hemp and Material Life in the Colonial Philippines*, 25-26.

⁸¹ Barrantes, *Guerras Piraticas de Filipinas contra Mindanaos y Joloanos*, 54.

⁸² Scott, "The State and the People who Move Around," 45.

⁸³ El Provincial de Recolectos de Filipinas informa a Nuestra Magestad de el estado de las Islas, 15 June 1771, AGI, Filipinas 685; see also, Expediente sobre la falta de trafico y comercio con aquellas capital de los naturales de las Provincias de Catbolonga, Leyte y Samar, en las Visayas, Consejo de las Indias, 1 August 1780, AGI, Filipinas 645; No. 248, GCG a Señor Secretario de Estado, 8 June 1773, AGI, Filipinas 493; No. 165, GCG a Señor Secretario de Estado, 16 January 1772, AGI, Filipinas 491.

⁸⁴ No. 46, GCG a Señor Secretario de Estado, AGI, Filipinas, 490, 32.

⁸⁵ El Provincial de Recolectos de Filipinas, a Vuestra Magestad, 5 June 1771, AGI, Filipinas 685.

⁸⁶ Expediente de Fray Bernardo Suarez Provincial de Augustinos Calzados de las Islas Filipinas, 18 May 1772, AGI, Filipinas 627.

⁸⁷ No. 226, II, AGI Filipinas 492, 10; No. 28, Expediente del Provincial de Augustinos Recolectos, 10 October 1772, AGI, Filipinas 627.

⁸⁸ Bruce Cruikshank, *Samar: 1768-1898* (Manila: Historical Conservation Society, 1985), 99.

⁸⁹ Ibid., 84-100.

⁹⁰ El Provincial de Recolectos de Filipinas informa a Nuestra Magestad, 5 June 1771, AGI, Filipinas 685.

⁹¹ No. 226, II, AGI Filipinas 492, 10.

⁹² Historical Data on Catarman, HDP Misamis Oriental, 45.

⁹³ El Obispo de Zebu, a su Magestad, 21 December 1779, AGI, Filipinas 1027.

⁹⁴ No. 4, 5 July 1814, AGI, Filipinas 510.

⁹⁵ Zuñiga, *Estadismo de las Filipinas: a mis viajez por este Pais*.

Chapter 5

¹ Parliamentary Papers, House of Commons, 1851, vol. LVI, pt. I. [1390], "Historical notices upon the piracies committed in the East Indies, and upon the measures taken for suppressing them, by the Government

of the Netherlands, within the last thirty years." Abstracted from articles by Cornets de Groot in *Moniteur des Indies*, 63.

[2] Ibid., 65-66.

[3] Ibid., 66.

[4] Testimony of Pangeran Syed Hassan Habassy, 15 October 1830, AR, Archief Kolonien H68; Horace St. John, *The Indian Archipelago: The History and Present state*, vol. 2 (London: Longman, Brown, Green and Longman, 1853), 192-93.

[5] Parliamentary Papers, 67.

[6] Ibid., 84. M. D. H. Kolff was placed in command of this force to undertake expeditions against 'pirates.'

[7] Kommisar de Palembang, aan Gouvenuer-General van Nederlandsch Indien, 25 May 1818, AR, Archief Kolonien 4168.

[8] Ibid., Vosmaer aan der Gouvenuer-General van Nederlandsch Indien, 25 November 1833, AR, Archief Kolonien 4168.

[9] Parliamentary Papers, 85.

[10] Ibid., 88.

[11] Ibid., 84.

[12] Ibid., 70.

[13] Ibid.

[14] Ibid.

[15] Testimony of Pangeran Syed Hassan Habassy, 15 October 1830, AR, Archief Kolonien 4168.

[16] Parliamentary Papers, 71.

[17] Ibid., 76-77.

[18] Ibid., 77.

[19] Ibid.

[20] Testimony of Pangeran Syed Hassan Habassy, 1830, AR, Archief Kolonien, 4168.

[21] Parliamentary Papers, 83.

[22] Ibid., 105 on the steam gunboat and Technological Imperialism see Daniel R. Hendrick, *The Tools of Empire Technology and European Imperialism in the Nineteenth Century* (New York: Oxford University Press, 1981); Michael Adas, *Machines as the Measure of Men: Science, Technology, and Ideologies of Western Dominance* (Ithaca: Cornell University Press, 1989).

[23] Ibid., 84.

24 Ibid., 94-95.

25 Personal Communication, Virginia Matheson, 1 April 1975.

26 "Piracy and Slave Trade of the Indian Archipelago," *Journal of Indian Archipelago and Eastern Asia*, 4, (1850), 619.

27 G. Buckley to W. Macnaghten, 24 July 1835, IOL, P/13/13.

28 Parliamentary Papers, 81.

29 Ibid., 107.

30 "Aantekeningen nopens den staat en tegenwoordige gestelheid der Moluksche Eilanden," AR, Kolonien Archief 2954.

31 Resident van Manado, aan Den Gouvenuer der Moluksche eilanden, no. 11, 6 January 1846; no. 135, 14 March 1846; no. 565, 10 August 1846, ANRI, Manado 50.

32 Wong Lin Ken, "The Trade of Singapore, 1819-1969," *Journal Malaysian Branch Royal Asiatic Society*, vol. 33, pt. 4 (1960), 82-83.

33 Parliamentary Papers, House of Commons, 1851, vol. LVI. pt. II, "Operations Against the Pirates on the Northwest Coast of Borneo," 131.

34 Ibid., 131.

35 A. Keppel, *A Visit to the Indian Archipelago in HMS Maender, with portions of the Private Journal of Sir James Brooke*, KCB, vol. 1 (London: Richard Bentley, 1853), 203-204.

36 Ibid., 206.

37 Warren, *The Sulu Zone, The World Capitalist Economy and the Historical Imagination*, 39-52.

38 James Warren, "Looking Back on 'The Sulu Zone': State Formation, Slave Raiding and Ethnic Diversity in Southeast Asia," *Journal of the Malaysian Branch of the Royal Asiatic Society*, vol. LXIX, pt. I (1996), 28-30; "Slavery in Southeast Asia," in Seymour Drescher and Stanley L. Engerman, *A Historical Guide to World Slavery* (New York: Oxford University Press, 1998), 83.

39 Parliamentary Papers, House of Commons, 3 March 1853, "Rear Admiral Sir Thomas Cochrane's Dispatches to the Lords of the Admiralty, with their enclosures"; "East India Station," 1.

40 "Piracy and Slave Trading of the Indian Archipelago," *Journal of the Indian Archipelago and Eastern Asia*, 4 (1850), 47.

41 Governor Ibbetson to Fort William, Calcutta, 4 May 1833. IOR/F/4/1474(57847).

[42] C.M. Turnbull, *A History of Singapore 1819-1975* (Singapore: Oxford University Press, 1977), 41-42.

[43] See Nicholas Tarling, *Piracy and Politics in the Malay World*, 112-46; *Britain, the Brookes and Brunei* (Kuala Lumpur: Oxford University Press, 1971); *The Burthen, the Risk, and the Glory: A Biography of Sir James Brooke* (Kuala Lumpur: Oxford University Press, 1982).

[44] Parliamentary Papers, 137-140; see Henry Keppel, *The Expedition to Borneo of H.M.S. Dido for the Suppression of Piracy, with Extracts from the Journal of James Brooke, esq., of Sarawak*, 2 vols. (London: Chapman and Hall, 1847); Mundy, *Narrative of Events in Borneo and Celebes down to the Occupation of Labuan, from the Journals of James Brooke, esq., Together with a Narrative of the Operations of H.M.S. Iris by Capt. Rodney Mundy, R. N.*

[45] Parliamentary Papers, 3 March 1853, 'Rear Admiral Sir Thomas Cochrane's Dispatches to the Lords of the Admiralty, with their enclosures,' 'East India Station,' 1.

[46] See Keppel, *The Expedition to Borneo of H.M.S. Dido for the Suppression of Piracy*; Belcher, *Narrative of the Voyage of H.M.S. Samarang, during the years 1843-1846*; and Mundy, *Narrative of Events in Borneo and Celebes down to the occupation of Labuan, from the Journals of James Brooke, esq., Together with a Narrative of the Operations of H.M.S. Iris by Capt. Rodney Mundy, R. N.*

[47] Bonham to Maitland, 28 June 1838, PRO, Admiralty 125/133.

[48] *Singapore Free Press*, 4 August 1846.

[49] Mallari, S.J., "Muslim Raids in Bicol, 1580-1792," 257-86; Owen, *Prosperity without Progress Manila Hemp and Material Life in the Philippines*, 26.

[50] Owen, *Prosperity without Progress Manila Hemp and Material Life in the Philippines*, 26.

[51] Extracts from *Estados de las Islas Filipinas*, PRO, Admiralty 125/133.

[52] No. 234, GCG a Señor Secretario de Estado, 12 December 1772, AGI Filipinas 493; no. 265, GCG a Señor Secretario de Estado y del Despacho Universal de Marina y Indias, 12 January 1773, AGI Filipinas 493.

[53] No. 276, GCG a Señor Secretario de Estado, 16 January 1773, AGI, Filipinas 493.

54 No. 7, GCG a Señor Secretario de Estado, 4 June 1806, AGI, Filipinas 510.

55 Notes translated from the Spanish relative to the pirates on Mindanao, PRO, Admiralty 125/133.

56 No. 31, GCG a Señor Secretario de Estado, 11 January 1770, AGI Flipinas 489; no. 226, I, AGI Filipinas 492, 25.

57 GCG a Señor Secretario de Estado, 20 December 1778, AGI, Filipinas 687; no. 7, GCG a Señor Secretario de Estado, 4 June 1806, AGI Filipinas 510.

58 No. 125, GCG a Señor Secretario de Estado, 22 May 1779, AGI, Filipinas 494, MN, Coleccion Guillen, Tomo V, Documento 33; no. 7, GCG a Señor Secretario de Estado, 4 June 1806, AGI Filipinas 510.

59 Eliodoro Robles, *The Philippines in the Nineteenth Century* (Quezon City: Malaya Books, 1969), 73; in 1829, the *vinta* was replaced with a tax on the coasting trade called *cabotaje*, but the *vinta* was revived shortly afterwards and was in force until 1851. Montero y Vidal, *Historia de Filpinas*, vol. 3, 154.

60 No. 7, GCG a Señor Secretario de Estado, 4 June 1806, AGI, Filipinas 510.

61 Notes translated from the Spanish relative to the pirates on Mindanao, PRO, Admiralty 125/133.

62 No. 7, GCG a Señor Secretario de Estado, 4 June 1806, AGI, Filipinas 510; no. 4, Ventura de los Reyes a Señor Secretario de Estado, 5 July 1814, AGI Filipinas 510.

63 Francisco Gainza, *Memoria y Antecedentes sobre las expediciones de Balanguingui y Jolo* (Manila: Establecimento del Colegio de Santo Tomas, 1851), 32-33.

64 No. 7, GCG a Señor Secretario de Estado, 4 June 1806, AGI Filpinas 510.

65 Notes translated from the Spanish relative to the pirates on the island of Mindanao, PRO, Admiralty 125/133.

66 R. Farquhar to the Marquis Wellesley, 6 January 1804, IOL, 166; Bernaldez, *Resana historico de la guerra a Sur de Filpinas, sostenida por las armas Espanoles contra los piratas de aquel archipielago, desde la conquista hasta nuestros dias*, 36-143.

67 MN, Coleccion Guillen, Tomo V, Documento 33; Bernaldez,

Resana historico de la guerra a Sur de Filpinas, 143.

[68] Notes translated from the Spanish relative to the pirates on the island of Mindanao, PRO, Admiralty 125/133.

[69] Ibid.

[70] Montero y Vidal, *Historia de Filipinas,* vol. 2, 500.

[71] Ibid., 505; for other suggestions on the offering of head money and issuing letters of marque, *ordenanzo de corso,* see no. 10, 15 July 1777, AGI Filipinas 636; no. 13, Consejo de las Indias, 31 July 1777, AGI Filipinas 360.

[72] Notes translated from the Spanish relative to the pirates on the island of Mindanao, PRO, Admiralty 125/133.

[73] Ibid.

[74] Bernaldez, *Resana historico de la guerra a Sur de Filipinas,* 44.

[75] See Rene Javellana's superbly produced book, in which he has measured, drawn and documented the colonial era fortifications of the Philippine Archipelago, *Fortress of Empire Spanish Colonial Fortifications of the Philippines 1565-1898* (Manila: Bookmark, 1997), 143.

[76] Montero y Vidal, *Historia de Filipinas,* vol. 2, 501-04.

[77] PNA. Ereccion del Pueblo Albay, 1772-1836, fols. 279b, 283b.

[78] Ereccion Pueblo Albay, 1772-1836, Tomo, fol. 292-93, Circular del Alcalde Mayor de Albay, 1 November 1818 to Señor Gobernadorcillos de la Cordillera y Tabaco; fol. 311, Francesco Alarco, Substituto Gobernadorcillo de Caramoan to Alcalde Mayor de Albay, Caramoan, 8 November 1818; folio 262-63, Extracts de lo contenido en las diligencias remitadas por el administracion de Albay con consulta de 13 de Noviembre ultimo, relatives el choque que tuvieron con los Moros Dan Pedro Estavan y demas que abajo expresan, Manila, 22 December 1818; see also, Luis Camara Dery, *From Ibalon to Sorsogon: A Historical Survey of Sorsogon Province to 1905* (Quezon City: New Day Publishers, 1991), 71-72.

[79] PNA, Ereccion del Pueblo Albay, 1772-1831, no. 8; Owen, *Prosperity without Progress Manila Hemp and Material Life in the Colonial Philippines,* 28.

[80] Luis Camara Dery, "Bikol History in Bikol Folklore: Documentary evidence of five Bikol Oral Traditions," in *Tracing: From Solsogon to Sorsogon* (ed.) Reynaldo T. Jamoralin (Sorsogon: Sorsogon Arts Council, Inc. 1994), 53-55.

[81] MN, Coleccion Enrile, Tomo XVII, documento 16; Francisco Osario a GCG, 3 August 1834, MN, Coleccion Guillen, Tomo XIII, MS. 1740, 132.

[82] No. 46, GCG a Señor Secretario de Estado, 7 August 1770, AGI Filipinas 490.

[83] Comyn, *State of the Philippines in 1810*, 120.

[84] Jean Mallat, *The Philippines; History, Geography, Customs, Agriculture, Industry and Commerce of the Spanish Colonies in Oceania*, Fr. Pura Santillan Castrence (Manila: National Historical Institute, 1983), 193.

[85] Javellana, *Fortress of Empire Spanish Colonial Fortifications of the Philippines 1565-1898*, 181.

[86] Pierre Viscomte de Pages, *Travels Round the World in the Years 1767, 1768, 1769, 1770, 1771*, 148.

[87] There are ample references to the destruction of coastal fortifications by natural forces. For earthquakes see Historical Data on Oslob, HDP, Cebu; Historical Data on Pasacao, HDP, Camarines Sur, 4; by volcanic eruption, Historical Data on Libog, HDP, Albay; by typhoon and hurricane, no. 27, GCG a Señor Secretario de Estado, 5 December 1844, AHN, Ultramar 5157; no. 11, GCG a Presidente del Consejo de Ministros, 11 February 1852, AHN, Ultramar 5163. Notices of the rebuilding of watchtowers and *baluarte* were sometimes placed in the Manila newspapers: 'A *telegrafo* has been built in the pueblo of Lingayen, Pangasinan province to relace the one destroyed in a storm.' *Estrella de Manila*, 15 July 1848.

[88] MN, Coleccion Enrile XIII, Documento 9.

[89] No. 7, GCG a Señor Secretario de Estado, 4 June 1806, AGI Filipinas 510.

[90] See historical data on San Pascual, HDP, Masbate; historical data on Catarman, HDP, Misamis Oriental; historical data on Bacacay, HDP, Albay.

[91] John Meares, *Voyage Made in the Years 1788 and 1789 from China to the North-West Coast of America* (New York: N. Israel/Amsterdam Da Capo Press, 1967), 21.

[92] Historical Data on Numancia, HDP, Surigao; Historical Data on Libon, HDP, Albay; Historical Data on Bugao, Catanduanes; Historical

Data on Mamperao (Camarines Sur), HDP, Zamboanga del Sur; Historical Data on Tarangoran, HDP, Samar, vol. 8, 10; Historical Data on on Culasi, HDP, Antique; Historical Data on on Bato, HDP, Catanduanes; Historical Data on on Pandan, HDP, Catanduanes.

[93] Historical Data on Unson, HDP, Masbate.

[94] No. 46, GCG a Señor Secretario de Estado, 17 August 1770, AGI Filipinas 490.

[95] El Provincial de Recolectos de Filipinas informa a Nuestra Magestad, 15 June 1771, AGI Filipinas 685; no. 43, 16 October 1785, PNA, Ereccion de Pueblo Camarines Sur, 1768-1837, VII; no. 7, 4 June 1806, AGI, Filipinas 510.

[96] No. 14, Alcalde Mayor de Tayabas a GCG, 23 December 1794, PNA, Ereccion de Pueblo Tayabas, 1793-1857, pt. II; see also no. 7, GCG a Señor Secretario de Estado 1806, AGI Filipinas 510.

[97] Barrantes, *Guerras Piraticas de Filipinas contra Mindanao y Joloanos*, 148-49.

[98] Notes translated from the Spanish relative to Pirates on the island of Mindanao, PRO, Admiralty 125/133.

[99] No. 8, 15 May 1799, PNA, Ereccion del Pueblo Albay, 1799-1864.

[100] For a fine discussion of Jose Marie Peneranda's defense system see Francisco Mallari, *Vignettes of Bicol History*, (Quezon City: New Day Publishers, 1999), 39-52; see also Dery, *From Ibalon to Sorsogon*, 97-100. Dery outlines in detail Peneranda's official measures for all local officials in coastal towns and his orders for the establishment of signal towers.

[101] Notes translated from the Spanish relative to Pirates on the island of Mindanao, PRO, Admiralty 125/133; no. 7, GCG a Señor Secretario de Estado, 4 June 1806, AGI Filipinas 510; MN, Coleccon Enrile, Tomo XIII, Documento 9.

[102] Belcher, *Narrative Voyage of theHMS Samarang, During the Years 1843-1846*, 86.

[103] Ibid.

[104] No. 2042, 31 December 1851, PNA, Ereccion de Pueblo Albay, 1834-1864.

[105] No. 1035, 7 November 1864, AHN, Ultramar 5197; Fedor Jagor, *Travels in the Philippines*, (Manila: Filipiniana Book Guild, 1965), 164.

[106] Robert Reed, "The Primate City in Southeast Asia: Conceptual Definitions and Colonial Origins," *Asian Studies*, vol. 10, no. 3 (1972), 310-11.

[107] For detailed discussion of the impact of Iranun-Samal raiding on Samar, Albay and Cebu see Cruikshank, *Samar: 1768-1898*, 84-105; Owen, *Prosperity without Progress Manila Hemp and Material Life in the Colonial Philippines*, 24-30; Mallari, "Muslim Raids in Bicol, 1580-1792," 257-286; Dery, *From Ibalon to Sorsogon A Historical Survey of Sorsogon Province to 1905*, 75-87; Michael Cullinane and Peter Xenos, "The Growth of Population in Cebu During the Spanish Era: Constructing a Regional Demography from Local Sources," in Daniel F. Doeppers and Peter Xenos (eds), *Population and History: The Demographic Origins of the Modern Philippines* (Madison: Center for Southeast Asian Studies, University of Wisconsin, 1998), 71-138.

[108] There are considerable problems in using the censuses. Their accuracy is suspect, particularly for analysis of population growth rates, and they must be used with utmost caution by historians. A number of factors are responsible for inaccuracies in the records on which censuses are based. Friar error is one of the most important factors that must be taken into account when considering the reliability of religious records. Population counts in censuses were difficult to tally and reflect the care, neglect and eccentricities of parish priests who kept them. Some friars with meticulous attention for detail sometimes made errors when copying records for transmission to Manila. Other friars were prevented from reporting current populations of distant villages by illness, poor communication–unnavigable rivers and impassable roads–and fear of the Muslims. Another consideration has been partial destruction or loss of key censuses, or parts thereof, to ravages of war, climate and to negligence by record-keepers and governments in the past. Comyn, *State of the Philippines in 1810*, 1-3; Nicholas P. Cushner, *Spain in the Philippines* (Quezon City: Ateneo de Manila University, 1971), 108-112.

[109] For demographic data, see AGI Filipinas 323; the first census for Nueva Caceres known to have survived is for 1780: see AGI, for 1782, 1783, 1785, 1786, 1787, AGI, Indiferente General 1527; 1789, 1790, AGI, Ultramar 661; 1794, AGI, Duplicados del Obispo de Nueva Caceres 1033; 1795, AGI Ultramar 682; 1800, 1801, 1803, AGI, Duplicados del

Obispo de Nueva Caceres 1033; 1813, AGI Ultramar 683; for 1815, AGI, Ultramar 684. See also the Franciscan returns for 1793, AGI, Ultramar, 666; 1796, AGI, Ultramar 699. Much of the information on community location and defense has been assembled from a number of key sources; no. 20, 1 December 1792, AGI, Duplicados del Obispo de Nueva Caceres; no. 8, 15 May 1799, PNA, Ereccion del Pueblo Albay 1799-1864; and a map, Plano Geografico y Ydrografico de la Provincia de Camarines ano de 1823, AGI, M. y P. Filpinas 134. See Appendix D.

[110] No. 57, 14 November 1793; 2 December 1793, PNA Ereccion de Pueblo Tayabas 1793-1857, pt. 2; no. 7, 4 June 1806, AGI Filipinas 510.

[111] Dery, *From Ibalon to Sorsogon*, 76-78.

[112] Montero y Vidal, *Historia de Filipinas*, vol. 2, 501; see also MN, Coleccion Enrile, Documento 9.

[113] No. 7, 4 June 1806, AGI Filipinas, 510.

[114] AGI Filipinas 681; El Arzobispo de Manila a Nuestra Magestad, 31 June 1761, AGI Filipinas 603; no. 46, 17 August 1770, AGI Filipinas 490, II.

[115] El Obispo de Nueva Caceres a Nuestra Magestad, 14 May 1817, AGI, Ultramar 684.

[116] Cruikshank, *Samar 1768-1898*, 99-100.

[117] See Greg Bankoff, *Crime, Society, and the State in the Nineteenth Century Philippines*, (Quezon City; Ateneo de Manila Press, 1996).

[118] Majul, *Muslims in the Philippines*, 267-68.

Chapter 6

[1] AR, Archief Kolonien 4168.

[2] Parliamentary Papers, House of Commons, 1851, vol. LVI, pt. II "Operations Against the Pirates on the Northwest Coast of Borneo," 136-37.

[3] Parliamentary Papers, House of Commons, 1852, vol. XXXI [1538] "Borneo Piracy."

[4] Blake to Maitland, 13 August 1838, PRO, Admiralty 125/133.

[5] Forrest, *A Voyage to New Guinea and the Moluccas, 1774-1776*, 192-193.

[6] Ibid., 193.

[7] Ibid.

[8] Barrantes, *Guerras Piraticas de Filipinas contra Mindanaos y Joloanos*, 160.

[9] St. John, *Life in the Forests of the Far East*, vol. 2, 192.

[10] No. 8, 9 November 1837, PNA, Mindanao/Sulu 1816-1898.

[11] Bulwer to the Earl of Granville, 28 May 1872, CO 144/36.

[12] Carlos Cuarteron, prefecto apostolico, a GCG, 27 October 1857, PNA, Isla de Borneo (1).

[13] Relacion jurada de las cuatro cautivos benidos en al navio Yngles de Guerra Agincort, 11 December 1845.

[14] Mundy, *Narrative Events in Borneo and Celebes Down to the Occupation of Labuan, from the Journals of James Brooke, esq. together with a Narrative of the Operations of H.M.S. Iris*, 11-12.

[15] Leigh Wright, "The Lanun Pirate States of Borneo: Their Relevance to Southeast Asian History," Conference on Southeast Asian Studies, Kota Kinbalu, 22-26 November 1977, 7.

[16] Belcher, *Narrative Voyage of the H.M.S. Samarang, During the years 1843-1846*, vol. 2, 123-24.

[17] Warren, *The Sulu Zone 1768-1898*, 198-200.

[18] Andaya, *To Live as Brothers: Southeast Sumatra in the Seventeenth and Eighteenth Centuries*, 225.

[19] Parliamentary Papers, House of Commons, vol. LXI, 'Extract no. 1 from Captain Sir Edward Belcher's Letters,' dated at Manila, 5 December 1844, 4-5.

[20] Mundy, *Narrative Events in Borneo and Celebes Down to the Occupation of Labuan*, 192-193.

[21] Ibid., 194-95.

[22] Ibid., 196.

[23] The ethnic nomenclature traditionally applied to populations on the east coast of north Borneo is particularly unreliable. Observers and writers frequently failed to recognize the ethnolinguistic distinctions perceived by the various indigenous populations. D. J. Prentice cites several reasons for the current confusion: (1) indiscriminate use of a foreign label (i.e., 'Murut' or 'Dusun') applied to widely divergent groups; (2) a local genuine name for a particular ethnic group is wrongly used and applied outside its original referent; an ethnic group is referred to by several different names by neighboring people, none of which necessarily

need coincide with the antonym; (4) the group has no name for itself other than that of the village where they reside, a toponym, which can change if the community moves to another site; (5) a people have accustomed themselves to being labelled in a particular fashion, in response to government and other authorities, who have ignored ethnolinguistc distinctions and expect populations to place themselves in one of the official categories. However, all the indigenous languages of north Borneo seem to be members of the Ida'han family (the language family Ida'han is not to be confused with the coastal dwelling ethnic group Ida'an situated near Lahad Datu). For an excellent discussion of the present state of linguistic analysis in north Borneo and the related problems of ascription and ethnic nomenclatures, see D. J. Prentice, 'The Linguistc Situation in Northern Borneo,' 369-407; also see G.N. Appell, 'Social and Medical Anthropology of Sabah: Retrospect and Prospect,' 246-86; Frank M. LeBar, ed. and comp. *Ethnic Groups of Insular Southeast Asia*, vol. 1, 147-48.

[24] Hunt 'Some Particulars relating to Sulo in the Archipelago of Felicia,' 53.

[25] 'Memoir of the Sooloogannan Dominion and Commerce,' 26 February 1761, PRO, Egremont Papers, 30/47/20/1.

[26] No. 276, GCG a Señor Secretario de Estado, 9 July 1771, AGI Filipinas 492.

[27] Jose Marie Halcon a GCG, 31 December 1837, AUST, seccion Folletos, Tomo 117, 45.

[28] D.S. Ranjit Singh, "Brunei and the Hinterland of Sabah: Commercial and Economic Relations with Special Reference to the Second Half of the Nineteenth Century," in Kathirithamby-Wells and Villiers (eds), *The Southeast Asian Port and Polity*, 240.

[29] St. John, *Life in the Forests of the Far East*, vol. I, 382.

[30] Ibid., 238-40.

[31] Ibid., 370.

[32] Keppel, *A Visit to the Indian Archipelago in H.M.S. Maender, with Portions of the Private Journal of Sir James Brooke, KCB*, 203.

[33] Belcher, *Narrative Voyage of the H.M.S. Samarang, During the Years 1843-1846*, vol. 2, 406-407.

[34] St. John, *Life in the Forests of the Far East*, vol. I, 238-40.

35 Ibid., 370.

36 Mundy, *Narrative Events in Borneo and Celebes Down to the Occupation of Labuan*, 14-15.

37 Ibid., 12-23.

38 Warren, *The Sulu Zone 1768-1898*, 79.

39 Ibid., 154.

40 M.W.H. Muntinghe to G.G. Baron Van der Capellen, 15 May 1818, in Parliamentary Papers, House of Commons, 1851, vol. LVI, pt. I [1390], 'Historical Notices upon the Piracies committed in the East Indies and upon measures taken for suppressing them, by the Government of the Netherlands within the last thirty years,' abstracted from articles by Cornet de Groot in the *Moniteur des Indies*, 68-70.

41 Andaya, *To Live as Brothers*, 225.

42 On the goals of statecraft and legible and illegible space see, James Scott, "The State and People who Move Around," *IIAS Newsletter*, no. 19 (1999), 3, 45.

43 Andaya, *To Live as Brothers*, 225; Warren, *The Sulu Zone 1768-1898*, 158-59.

44 Report to Captain Kolff, 1 November 1813, in Parliamentary Papers, 89.

45 Ibid.

46 Parliamentary Papers, 69-70, 91.

47 M.W.H. Muntinghe to GG Baron Van der Capellen, 15 May 1818, in Parliamentary Papers, 68-70.

48 Ibid.

49 Ibid.

50 Ibid., 71.

51 Testimony of Raja Akil in Kommisar de Palembang, aan de Gouveneur-General van Nederlandsch Indien, 25 May 1818, AR, Archief Kolonien 4168; no. 115, De Resident van Banka, aan de Gouveneur-General over Nederlandsch Indien, 29 January 1831, AR, Archief Kolonien 4168.

52 De Resident van Bantam aan der Gouveneur-General de Nederlandsch Indien, 16 October 1831, AR, Archief Kolonien 4168.

53 Report of M Practorious de Resident van Palembang 17 January 1831 and M Du Buy de Resident van Banka, 29 January 1831, aan de

Gouveneur-General van Nederlandsch Indien in Parliamentary Papers, 84.

[54] Testimony of Pangeran Syed Hassan Habassy, 15 October 1830, AR, Archief Kolonien 4168.

[55] Parliamentary Papers, 107.

[56] Ibid., 94-96, 97.

[57] Ibid., 99.

[58] "Piracy and the Slave Trade of the Indian Archipelago," *Journal of the Indian Archipelago and Eastern Asia*, 3 (1849), 586; "Berigten omtrent den Zeeroof in den Nederlandsch-Indischen Archipel, 1858," 322.

[59] No. 70, GCG a Señor Secretario de Estado, 26 December 1770, AGI Filipinas 491; no. 105, GCG a Señor Secretario de Estado, 12 July 1771, AGI Filipinas 491; no. 1, Consejo de las Indias, 10 October 1772, AGI Filipinas 626.

[60] PNA Mindanao/Sulu, 1770-1897, fol. 26.

[61] PNL Historical Data Papers Masbate, no. 60, 2.

[62] Mallari, S.J., "Muslim Raids in Bicol, 1580-1792," 279; see PNA Mindanao/Sulu, 1770-1897, fols. 56–56b; PNL HDP Masbate, no. 58, 1.

[63] Owen, *Prosperity Without Progress Manila Hemp and Material Life in the Colonial Philippines*, 26; Warren, *The Sulu Zone 1768-1898*, 297-98.

[64] Warren, *The Sulu Zone 1768-1898*, 182-83.

[65] Statements of Balangingi prisoners, 1838, in Bonham to Maitland, 28 June 1838, PRO Admiralty 125/133; Warren, *The Sulu Zone 1768-1898*, 297-98.

[66] Warren, *The Sulu Zone 1768-1898*, 184.

[67] Bernaldez, *Resana historico de la guerra a sur Filipinas, sostenida por las armas Espanoles contra los piratas de aquel archipielago, desde la conquista hasta nuestros dias*, 15, 153.

[68] R.F. Wendover, "The Balangingi Pirates," *Philippine Magazine*, vol. 38, no. 8 (1841), 324.

[69] Report of Marcelino Oroa to the Governor-General of the Philippines, 9 August 1842, PNA, Mindanao/Sulu, 1838-1885.

[70] Bernaldez, *Resana historico de la guerra a sur Filipinas*, 153.

[71] Margarita de los Reyes-Cojuangco, "The Samal Balangingi: An Experiment in Colonial Diaspora," MA Thesis, University of Santo Tomas, 1986, 378.

[72] Ibid., 382.

[73] Warren, *The Sulu Zone 1768-1898*, 183.

[74] Bonham to Maitland, 28 June 1838, PRO Admiralty 125/133.

[75] Report of Marcelino Oroa to the Governor-General of the Philippines, 9 August 1842, PNA, Mindanao/Sulu, 1838-1885.

[76] Warren, *The Sulu Zone 1768-1898*, 183.

[77] Ibid., 184.

[78] Statements of Balangingi prisoners, 1838, in Bonham to Maitland, 28 June 1838, PRO Admiralty 125/133.

[79] Rennell and Forrest make only passing references to the Samal Islands. Rennell, *Journal of a Voyage to the Sooloo Islands and the Northwest Coast of Borneo*, 54; Forrest, *A Voyage to New Guinea and the Moluccas, 1774-1776*, 21-22.

[80] Statements of Angel Custodio, Juan Salvador, Domingo Candelario, and Juan Santiago in Exp. 12, 4 October 1836, PNA, Mindanao/Sulu 1803-1890; Diary of William Pryer, 9 March 1879, 874/68.

[81] Frederick Barth, *Ethnic Groups and Boundaries* (Boston: 1969), 22.

[82] Statements of Jose Ruedas, Gabriel Francisco and Matias de la Cruz in Exp. 12, 4 October 1836, PNA, Mindanao/Sulu 1803-1890.

[83] El Gobierno Politico y Militar de Zamboanga a GCG, 30 May 1842, PNA, Mindanao/Sulu 1838-1885; Exp. 12, 17 February 1845, PNA, Mindanao/Sulu 1803-1890.

[84] Information obtained by Charles Grey at Singapore from William Wyndham relating to Sulo, 24 February 1847, PRO, Admiralty 125/133; Van Hoevell, 'De Zeerooverijen der Soeloerezen,' 102.

[85] Bonham to Maitland, 28 June 1838, PRO, Admiralty 125/133.

[86] Henry Keppel, *The Expedition to Borneo of H.M.S. Dido for the Suppression of Piracy, with Extracts from the Journals of James Brooke, esq. of Sarawak*, 2 vols. (London: Chapman and Hall, 1847).

[87] Forrest, *A Voyage to New Guinea and the Moluccas, 1774-1776*, 228.

[88] ARA, Comite Oost-Indische Handel en Bezettingen 1791-1800, 1793 paragraphs 53, 103 in Velthoen, "Of Chiefs and Warriors, A Historical Study of Precolonial Eastern Sulawesi 1650-1905," Ph.D. diss., Murdoch University, forthcoming 2001.

[89] Hunt "Some Particulars Relating to Sulo in the Archipelago of

Felicia," 51.

[90] Velthoen, "Armed Bands and Protection Rackets: 'Gangster' Politics in Eastern Sulawesi, 1700-1850," 18-19.

[91] Parliamentary Papers, 72, 75; Velthoen, "Armed Bands and Protection Rackets," 19.

[92] ANRI, Beshuit 31 October 1824, no. 1, 4b, 4c, in Velthoen, "Of Chiefs and Warriors, A Historical Study of Precolonial Eastern Sulawesi 1650-1905," Ph.D. diss. Murdoch University, forthcoming 2001.

[93] Esther Velthoen, "Of Chiefs and Warriors, A Historical Study of Precolonial Eastern Sulawesi 1650-1905," Ph.D. diss., Murdoch University, forthcoming 2001.

[94] Parliamentary Papers, 64.

[95] Velthoen, "Armed Bands and Protection Rackets," 19.

[96] Velthoen, "Of Chiefs and Warriors, A Historical Study of Precolonial Eastern Sulawesi 1650-1905," Ph.D. diss., Murdoch University, forthcoming 2001.

[97] M.W.H. Muntinghe, Parliamentary Papers, 68-70.

[98] Ibid., 72.

[99] Ibid., 85, 89.

[100] Deposition of Sherif Abu, 22 August 1851, in Parliamentary Papers, House of Commons, 1851, vol. XXXI [1538] "Borneo Piracy."

[101] Captain Massie to Rear-Admiral Austen, 16 March 1852, in Parliamentary Papers, House of Commons, 1852-1853, vol. LXI [55], "Burns Schooner Dolphin."

[102] Belcher, *Narrative Voyage of the H.M.S. Samarang, during the years 1843-1846*, vol. 2, 123-124.

[103] Deposition of Mail, 24 October 1851, in Parliamentary Papers, House of Commons, 1851, Vol. XXXIm [1538] "Borneo Piracy."

[104] Deposition of Sherif Abu, 22 August 1851, in Parliamentary Papers, House of Commons, 1851, vol. XXXI [1538] "Borneo Piracy."

[105] Spencer St. John to Rear-Admiral Austen, 25 November 1851, in Parliamentary Papers, House of Commons, 1852-1853, vol. LXI [55], "Burns Schooner Dolphin."

[106] Ibid.

[107] Deposition of Sherif Yasin, 1 November 1851, in Parliamentary

Papers, House of Commons, 1852-1853, vol. LXI [55], "Burns Schooner Dolphin."

[108] Deposition of Si-Ayer, 7 November 1851, in Parliamentary Papers, House of Commons, 1852, vol. XXXI [1538] "Borneo Piracy."

[109] Ibid.

[110] Captain Massie to Rear-Admiral Austen, 19 February 1852, in Parliamentary Papers, House of Commons, 1852-1853, vol. LXI [55], "Burns Schooner Dolphin."

[111] Warren, *The Sulu Zone 1768-1898*, 197.

Chapter 7

[1] Extracts from Mr. Presgrave's Report on the Subject of Piracy, 5 December 1828, PRO Admiralty 125/133.

[2] Mednick, "Some Problems of Moro History and Political Organization," 44.

[3] Warren, *The Sulu Zone 1768-1898*, 185-86.

[4] Mednick, 49.

[5] Bonham to Maitland, 28 June 1838, PRO Admiralty 125/133.

[6] St. John, *Life in the Forests of the Far East*, vol. I, 370.

[7] Warren, *The Sulu Zone*, 186-87.

[8] Rutter, *The Pirate Wind Tales of the Sea Robbers of Malaysia*, 28.

[9] Geoghegan, "Balangingi Journal," 5.

[10] Parliamentary Papers, 76.

[11] Jansen, "Aanteekeningen omtrent Sollok en de Solloksche Zeeroovers," 222; Warren, *The Sulu Zone 1768-1898*, 188-89.

[12] Secretary to the government of India to the Admiralty, 21 January 1841, PRO, Admiralty 125/133.

[13] Statement of Silammkoon, in Bonham to Maitland, 28 June 1838, PRO Admiralty 125/133.

[14] Warren, *The Sulu Zone*, 187-88.

[15] Jansen, "Aanteekeningen," 221.

[16] Warren, *The Sulu Zone*, 151-52, 187, 210.

[17] Ibid., 222-23.

[18] Jansen, "Aanteekeningen," 223-24; Warren, *The Sulu Zone*, 187-88.

[19] Ibid.

[20] Ibid., 222; Bonham to Maitland, 28 June 1838, PRO Admiralty 125/133.

[21] Statement of Angel Custodio, Alex Quijano and Mariano Sevilla on Exp. 12, 4 October 1836, PNA, Mindanao/Sulu 1803-1890.

[22] Statement of Silammkoon in Bonham to Maitland, 28 June 1838, PRO Admiralty 125/133.

[23] Statement of Amat in Bonham to Maitland, 28 June 1838, PRO Admiralty 125/133.

[24] Jansen, "Aanteekeningen," 222.

[25] Mednick, "Some Problems," 51.

[26] Warren, *The Sulu Zone*, 247.

[27] "The Illanoon," extracts from the *Singapore Free Press*, 6 April 1847, PRO, Admiralty 125/133.

[28] Governor Salazar a Señor Secretario de Estado, 17 December 1836, PNA, no. 46, libro 66, Cartas 1836-1837.

[29] Statements from Mariano Sevilla and Juan Santiago in Exp. 12, 4 October 1836, PNA, Mindanao/Sulu 1803-1890.

[30] Statements of Alex Quijano, Domingo Candelario and Mariano Sevilla in Exp. 12, 4 October 1836, PNA, Mindanao/Sulu 1803-1890; Statement of Mah Roon, 2 June 1838, in Bonham to Maitland, 28 June 1838, PRO Admiralty 125/133.

[31] Statement of Francisco Basilo and Mariano Sevilla in Exp. 12, 4 October 1836, PNA, Mindanao/Sulu 1803-1890.

[32] See the statements of the Illanoon prisoners, in 2 June 1838, in Bonham to Maitland, 1838, PNA, Mindanao/Sulu 1803-1890.

[33] Warren, *The Sulu Zone*, 189.

[34] ANRI, Besluit 31 October 1824, no. 1, 2, in Velthoen, "Of Chiefs and Warriors, A Historical Study of Precolonial Eastern Sulawesi," Ph.D. diss., Murdoch University, forthcoming 2001.

[35] Statement of Francisco Thomas, 2 June 1838, in Bonham to Maitland, 28 June 1838, PRO Admiralty 125/133.

[36] Statement of Mah Roon, 2 June 1838, in Bonham to Maitland, 21 June 1838, PRO Admiralty 125/133.

[37] Marcelino Araa to the governor-general of the Philippines, no. 9, 9 August 1842, PNA, Mindanao/Sulu, 1838-1885.

[38] St. John, *Life in the Forests of the Far East*, vol. I, 209.

[39] Jansen, "Aanteekeningen," 222.

[40] 'The Illanoon,' extracts from the *Singapore Free Press*, 6 April 1847, PRO, Admiralty 125/133.

[41] Ibid.

[42] Secretary to the government of India to the Admiralty, 21 January 1841, PRO, Admiralty 125/133; Rear Admiral Maitland to Lord Auckland, 30 May 1838, PRO Admiralty 125/133.

[43] Raja Ali Haji Ibn Ahmad, *The Precious Gift: The Tu-hfat Al Nafis* (Kuala Lumpur: Oxford University Press, 1982), 262.

[44] Captain Court to the chief secretary, Fort William, 16 February 1811, IOL.

[45] On King's career see Alfons van der Kraan, *George Pockock King: Merchant Adventurer and Catalyst of the Bali War, 1846-1849* (Clayton: Monash University, no date).

[46] Parliamentary Papers, 106.

[47] Deposition of Si-Ayer, 7 November 1851, in Parliamentary Papers, House of Commons, 1852-1853, vol. LXI [55], "Burns Schooner Dolphin."

[48] Parliamentary Papers, 89.

[49] Ibid.

[50] Statement of James Brooke in Parliamentary Papers, House of Commons, 1851, vol. LVI, pt. II "Operations against the Pirates on the Northwest Coast of Borneo."

[51] Ibid.

[52] "The Illanoon," extracts from the *Singapore Free Press*, 6 April 1847, PRO, Admiralty 125/133.

[53] *Singapore Free Press*, 28 June 1838.

[54] Bonham to Maitland, 28 June 1838, PRO Admiralty 125/133.

[55] Ibid.

[56] Belcher, *Narrative Voyage of the H.M.S. Samarang, During the years 1843-1846*, vol. 2, 208-209.

[57] Ibid.

[58] Jansen, "Aanteekeningen," 227.

[59] Mundy, *Narrative Events in Borneo and Celebes Down to the Occupation of Labuan, from the Journals of James Brooke, esq. together with a Narrative of the Operations of H.M.S. Iris by Capt. Rodney Mundy*, 18.

60 Ibid., 375.
61 Ibid., 239-40.
62 Jansen, "Aanteekeningen," 229-30.
63 Ibid., 230.
64 Van der Kraan, George Pockock King: Merchant Adventurer and Catalyst of the Bali War, 1846-1849, 229-30.
65 Keppel, A Visit to the Indian Archipelago in H.M.S. Maender, with Portions of the Private Journal of Sir James Brooke, Vol. 1, 279.
66 Belcher, Narrative Voyage of the H.M.S. Samarang, During the years 1843-1846, 184.
67 See Van der Kraan, George Pockock King: Merchant Adventurer and Catalyst of the Bali War, 1846-1849; Aage Krarup Nielson, Mads Lange Til Bali (Kobenhaven: Gyldenalske Boghandel, Nordisk Forlag, 1941); Henke Schulte Nordholt, 'The Mads Lange Connection,' Indonesia, no. 32 (1981), 16-48.
68 Van der Kraan, "George Pockock King," 6.
69 Notes translated from the Spanish relative to the pirates on the island of Mindanao, PRO, Admiralty 125/133.
70 Ereccion Pueblo Albay, 1799-1864, PNA, vol. 2, fols. 107-107b, 114.
71 Warren, The Sulu Zone, 49.
72 "Goods for Sooloo Market," MS Peabody Museum, Salem. Figures are lacking for the earlier period, but the value for gunpowder alone which exceeds the total worth of Dalrymple's order, shows remarkable expansion.
73 Farquhar to Lord Wellesley, 16 February 1804, IOL, p/166.
74 Thomas Raffles to Lord Minto, governor-general of India, 20 September 1811, IOL, EVR. F. 148/7, par. 67.
75 J. Dalton, "On the Present State of Piracy, Amongst these Islands, and the best method of its Suppression," in Moor, Notices of the Indian Archipelago, 26.
76 Ibid.
77 Earl, The Eastern Seas, or Voyages and Adventures in the Indian Archipelago in 1832, 1833, 1834, 444.
78 Log kept aboard the brig Leonidas (8 February 1836-25 September 1836), 656/1835A, Peabody Museum, Salem. No entries are

listed in the log between 5 March and 31 August when the vessel was conducting trade at Sulu.

[79] Letter soliciting trade between the United States and Sooloo, Papers of William D. Waters, Peabody Museum.

[80] Wilkes, 'Jolo and the Sulus,' 171.

[81] No. 293, Gobierno Militar de la plaza de Zamboanga a GCG, 23 August 1847, PNA, unclassified Mindanao/Sulu bundle.

[82] St. John, *Life in the Forests of the Far East*, vol. 2, 203.

[83] Keppel, *A Visit to the Indian Archipelago in H.M.S. Maender*, 59.

[84] Dorothy Shineberg, 'The Sandalwood Trade in Melanesia Economies, 1841-1865,' *Journal of Pacific History*, vol. 1 (1966), 132.

[85] G.W. Hubbell to John Quincy Adams, Secretary of State, 31 December 1823, U.S. National Archives, Consular Despatches, Manila 1817-1840.

[86] No. 234, 12 April 1829, AGI, Ultramar, 664, 818.

[87] The Straits Times and Singapore Journal of Commerce, 19 January 1848, vol. 4, no. 242.

[88] No. 293, Gobierno Militar de la plaza de Zamboanga a GCG, 23 August 1847, PNA, unclassified Mindanao/Sulu bundle; no. 30, 5 November 1847, AHN Ultramar 5159.

Chapter 8

[1] Warren, *The Sulu Zone 1768-1898*, 297-315.

[2] Bonham to Maitland, 28 June 1838, PRO Admiralty 125/133.

[3] Ibid.

[4] Parliamentary Papers, House of Commons, 1851, vol. LVI, pt. I [1390], "Historical Notices upon the Piracies committed in the East Indies and upon measures taken for suppressing them, by the Government of the Netherlands within the last thirty years," abstracted from articles by Cornets de Groot in the *Moniteur des Indies*, 75.

[5] This term, which has been variously corrupted Alforias, Alfores, Alfours, Alforen, Arafuras and Harafuras, is a Portuguese word, apparently derived from the Arabic article al, and the preposition fora, 'without.' The Portuguese applied it to all people beyond the reach of their authority, or who were not pacified by them, and consequently the

label was applied to hill and upstream people of the Moluccas. See John Crawford, A Descriptive Dictionary of the Indian Islands and Adjacent Countries (Kuala Lumpur: Oxford University Press, 1971), 10.

[6] St. John, Life in the Forests of the Far East, vol. 2, 214.

[7] Deposition of Si-Ayer, 7 November 1851, in Parliamentary Papers, House of Commons, 1852-1853, vol. LXI [55], "Burns Schooner Dolphin."

[8] Parliamentary Papers, 64.

[9] Ibid., 85.

[10] On headhunting and heads as trophies see Derek Freeman, Report on the Iban (London: The Athlone Press, 1970), 6, 36, 73, 100, 113, 150; W.R. Geddes, Nine Dayak Nights (London: Oxford University Press, 1973).

[11] Copies of extracts of despatches from Sir James Brooke respecting Military operations against illegal pirates on the River Moratatias in March and April 1849, in Parliamentary Papers, House of Commons, 1852, vol. XXXI [1538], "Borneo Piracy."

[12] See Benedict Sandin, The Sea Dayaks of Borneo Before White Rajah Rule (London: MacMillan, 1967), 59-89.

[13] 'Memoir on the Residency of the Northwest Coast of Borneo,' in Moor, Notices of the Indian archipelago, 9.

[14] Earl, The Eastern Seas, 214, 269-70.

[15] Keppel, A Visit to the Indian Archipelago in H.M.S. Maender, with Portions of the Private Journal of Sir James Brooke, vol. 2, 65.

[16] Kisah Pelayaran Abdullah, ed. Kassim Ahmad (Kuala Lumpur, 1960), 40, 61.

[17] St. John, Life in the Forests, 239.

[18] Sandin, The Sea Dayaks, 62-64. Pringle, Rajahs and Rebels The Ibans of Sarawak under Brooke Rule 1841-1941, 48.

[19] Sandin, The Sea Dayaks, 62-64.

[20] Statements of Juan Florentino, Manuel Feliz, Diomicio Francisco, and Mariano Sevilla, in Exp. 4 October 1836, PNA, Mindanao/Sulu 1803-1890; Extracts from Singapore Free Press, 6 April 1847, PRO, Admiralty 125/133; No. 137, Carlos Cuarteron, prefecto apostolico, a GCG, 12 August 1878, PNA, Isla de Borneo (2); Comyn, State of the Philippines in 1810, 124; Barrantes, Guerras Piraticas, 108, 161, 265-66.

[21] Warren, *The Sulu Zone 1768-1898*, 184, 187.

[22] Ibid., 299-309.

[23] Parliamentary Papers, 64.

[24] Dalrymple, *Oriental Repertory*, 525.

[25] On the skill of these divers see Warren, *The Sulu Zone*, 72-73.

[26] Warren, *The Sulu Zone*, 265-80.

[27] This estimate has been arrived at by using the few examples in the literature, archival documents and private manuscripts to provide ratios between the number of people involved in marine procurement and their annual output at small collecting centers in the Sulu zone. I have used these figures in conjunction with the statistic for the estimated volume of tripang (10,000 piculs) and mother of pearl (12,000 piculs) exported from Jolo in the 1830s to establish the relative size of the labor force. For example, Hunt wrote that at Towson Duyon in Sandakan Bay, 'A *hundred bajow or fishermen* [are] employed in catching and curing tripang; they obtain about *fifty piculs* annually,' and at Loo-Loo 'there are . . . *thirty to forty Bajow fishermen* employed in catching tripang; *twenty or thirty piculs* are cured here annually.' On Tawi-Tawi there were '*eight hundred Islams*, chiefly the slaves [clients?] of Datu Mulut Mondarasa and Datu Adanan. They produce annually for the Sulo market *three hundred piculs of Kulit tepoy [mother of pearl], forty piculs of beche de mer* . . . and some very valuable pearls. . . .' At Basilan, '*fifteen hundred Islams* produced *twenty piculs of black birds' nest, three hundred piculs of Kulit tepoy*, a few pearls, some tortoise shell, and 20 or 30 prows of paddy for annual export.' Hunt, 'Some Particulars relating to Sulo,' 54-55, 59 (emphasis added). These figures tend to support the conclusion that the collecting and curing of a picul of *tripang* or a picul of mother of pearl shell required the average annual labor of two men for *tripang* and four men for mother of pearl. This means that in the first half of the nineteenth century an estimated 68,000 men labored in Sulu's fisheries.

[28] Forrest, *A Voyage to New Guinea and the Moluccas, 1774-1776*, 221; Hunt, "Some Particulars relating to Sulo in the Archipelago of Felicia," 44; Garin, "Memoria sobre el Archipielago de Jolo," 198.

[29] Statement of Angel Custodio and Juan Sabala in Expediente 12, 4 October 1836, PNA, Mindanao/Sulu 1803-1890; see also the statements of Benoko, Abdulla and Pedro Juan in Verklaringen van ontulugten

personen uit den handen der Zeeroovers van 1845-1849, ANRI, Manado 37; Forrest, *A Voyage to New Guinea and the Moluccas, 1774-1776*, 369.

[30] Dalrymple, *Oriental Repertory*, 520.

[31] Statement of Tala Goa in Bonham to Maitland, 28 June 1838, PRO Admiralty 125/133.

[32] Bonham to Maitland, 28 June 1838, PRO Admiralty 125/133.

[33] St. John, *Life in the Forests*, 239.

[34] Comyn, *State of the Philippines in 1810, Being a Historical Statistical and Descriptive Account of the Interesting Portion on the Indian Archipelago*, 119-20.

[35] Belcher, *Narrative Voyage of the H.M.S. Samarang, During the Years 1843-1846*, vol. 2, 406-07.

[36] St. John, *Life in the Forests*, 211.

[37] Mundy, *Narrative Events in Borneo and Celebes Down to the Occupation of Labuan, from the Journals of James Brooke, esq. together with a Narrative of the Operations of H.M.S. Iris by Capt. Rodney Mundy*, 308-09.

[38] Parliamentary Papers, 119-20.

[39] Jansen, "Aanteekeningen omtrent Sollok en de Solloksche Zeeroovers," 226.

[40] Statement of James Brooke in Parliamentary Papers, House of Commons, 1851, vol. LVI, pt. II, "Operations against the Pirates on the Northwest Coast of Borneo."

[41] Marcelino Oraa to the governor-general of the Philippines, 9 August 1842, PNA, Mindanao/Sulu, 1838-1885.

[42] Interview of Charlie Werble alias Sali Werble in Cojuangco, "The Samal Balangingi: An Experiment in Colonial Diaspora," 380.

[43] Rutter, *The Pirate Wind Tales of the Sea Robbers of Malaya*, 19.

[44] Jansen, "Aanteekeningen," 43.

[45] "The Illanoon," extract from the *Singapore Free Press*, 6 April 1847, PRO, Admiralty 125/133.

[46] Statements of Balangingi Prisoners in Bonham to Maitland, 28 June 1838, PRO Admiralty 125/133; Warren, *The Sulu Zone*, 297-98.

[47] Forrest, *A Voyage to New Guinea and the Moluccas, 1774-1776*, 328.

[48] 24 May 1838, *Singapore Free Press and Mercantile Advertiser*.

[49] No. 21, Bonham to Prinsep, 15 June 1838, IOL.

[50] Jansen, "Aanteekeningen," 27.

[51] Statement of James Brooke in Parliamentary Papers, House of Commons, 1851, vol. LVI, pt. II, "Operations against the Pirates on the Northwest Coast of Borneo."

[52] St. John, *Life in the Forests*, 238.

[53] Rennell, *Journal of a Voyage to the Sooloo Islands and the Northwest Coast of Borneo*, 37.

[54] Bonham to Maitland, 28 June 1838, PRO Admiralty 125/133.

[55] Garin, "Memoria sobre el Archipielago de Jolo," 193.

[56] Rennell, *Journal of a Voyage to the Sooloo Islands and the Northwest Coast of Borneo*, 37.

[57] Jansen, "Aanteekeningen," 228.

[58] Ibid.

[59] Owen, *Prosperity Without Progress Manila Hemp and Material Life in the Colonial Philippines*, 28.

[60] Forrest, *A Voyage to New Guinea, 1774-1776*, 43-44.

[61] Parliamentary Papers, 112-23.

[62] Ibid., 105-06.

[63] Ibanez y Garcia, *Mi Cautiverio Carta con motivo del que sufrio entre Los Moros Piratas Joloanos y Samalos en 1857*, 14; Palaw is a large, vigorous growing aroid, the tubers and leaves of which are eaten especially in times of scarcity.

[64] Forrest, *A Voyage to New Guinea*, 74.

[65] Ibid., 64.

[66] Statement of Abdullah in Bonham to Maitland, 28 June 1838, PRO Admiralty 125/133.

[67] Notes translated from the Spanish relative to the pirates on the island of Mindanao, PRO, Admiralty 125/133.

[68] Santanina Rasul, 'The Samal Bangingih,' in Cojuangco, "The Samal Balangingi: An Experiment in Colonial Diaspora," 410.

[69] Statement of Haji Abdurahim in "Balangingi Piracy," Notes of William Geoghegan, 7.

[70] Mednick, 'Some Problems of Moro History and Political Organization,' 45.

[71] Forrest, *A Voyage to New Guinea*, 303.

[72] Ibid., 219.

[73] Jansen, "Aanteekeningen," 222; Warren, *The Sulu Zone*, 187.

Chapter 9

1 Warren, *The Sulu Zone 1768-1898*, 256-58.

2 Parliamentary Papers, House of Commons, 1851, vol. LVI, pt. I [1390], "Historical Notices upon the Piracies committed in the East Indies and upon measures taken for suppressing them, by the Government of the Netherlands within the last thirty years," abstracted from articles by Cornets de Groot in the *Moniteur des Indies*, 90.

3 Forrest, *A Voyage to New Guinea and the Moluccas, 1774-1776*, 13-14.

4 Ibid., 14.

5 Ibid., 302.

6 Ibid., 217.

7 Ibid.

8 Parliamentary Papers, 90.

9 St. John, *Life in the Forests of the Far East*, vol. 2, 209.

10 Forrest, *A Voyage to New Guinea*, 302.

11 Parliamentary Papers, 90.

12 Warren, *The Sulu Zone*, 257.

13 Forrest, *A Voyage to New Guinea*, 10.

14 Warren, *The Sulu Zone*, 257.

15 Parliamentary Papers, 90.

16 Keppel, *A Visit to the Indian Archipelago in H.M.S. Maender, with Portions of the Private Journal of Sir James Brooke*, vol. 1, 132.

17 Warren, *The Sulu Zone*, 257.

18 Forrest, *A Voyage to New Guinea*, 9-10; Sailors may be interested in the following technical description of the fitting of these sheers, from Belcher's *Voyage of the Samarang* i. 265: 'On the fore part of the fighting deck is a small pair of bitts, each bitt-head being placed about three feet on each side of the center line; through the heads of these bitts a piece runs, windlass fashion, its outer ends being rounded, which pass through the lower ends of the sheers in holes, this arrangement completes a triangle, having this windlass base of six feet. The heads of the sheers are joined by a solid piece of wood, perforated as a sheave-hole for the halliards, by which the sail is hoisted; a third spar is attached, which, taken aft as prop, instantly turns this mast, upon its windlass motion, to its vertical, and almost, as by magic, we find the sail expanded or reduced instantaneously.'

[19] Forrest, A *Voyage to New Guinea*, 94.

[20] "The Illanoon," extracts from *Singapore Free Press*, 6 April 1847, PRO, Admiralty 125/133.

[21] Statement of Domingo Guzman, PNA, Ereccion del Pueblos, Cebu, 1818-1877.

[22] Forrest, A *Voyage to New Guinea*, 183.

[23] Ibid., 188.

[24] Ibid., 134.

[25] Ibid., 313.

[26] Ibid., 289.

[27] Jansen, "Aanteekeningen omtrent Sollok en de Solloksche Zeeroovers," 227.

[28] Ibid.

[29] J. Brown to Chief Secretary Fort William, 16 February 1811, IOL.

[30] Mundy, *Narrative Events in Borneo and Celebes Down to the Occupation of Labuan, from the Journals of James Brooke, esq. together with a Narrative of the Operations of H.M.S. Iris by Capt. Rodney Mundy*, vol. 2, 199.

[31] Forrest, A *Voyage to New Guinea*, 328.

[32] Statement of Silammkoon in Bonham to Maitland, 28 June 1838, PRO, Admiralty 125/133.

[33] Captain General a Sultan de Jolo, 19 February 1849, PNA, Mindanao/Sulu, 1803-1890.

[34] Farquhar to Chief Secretary Fort St. George, 18 February 1803, IOL.

[35] Mundy, *Narrative Events in Borneo*, 194-95.

[36] Forrest, A *Voyage to New Guinea*, 184.

[37] Ibid., 196.

[38] Statement of Mariano Sevilla in Exp. 12, 4 October 1836, PNA, Mindanao/Sulu, 1803-1890; Apuntes sobre la Isla de Basilan 1892, SJA, XIV-9, 32; BH-PCL, vol. 1, paper 160, no. 1, Livingston, "Constabulary Monograph of the Province of Sulu," 5.

[39] Statement of Marcelo Teafilo in Exp. 12, 4 October 1836, Mindanao/Sulu, 1803-1890; van Hoevall, "De Zeerooverijen der Soeloerezen," 102; BP-PCL, vol. 6, paper 162, no. 23, Christie, "The Moros of Sulu and Mindanao," 38.

[40] Forrest, A *Voyage to New Guinea*, 324.

[41] Ibid., 298.
[42] Ibid., 312-13.
[43] Ibid., 330.
[44] See the detailed plans and illustration based on this model of a *garay*, Figure 20 in Warren, *The Sulu Zone*, 178.
[45] Forrest, *A Voyage to New Guinea*, 217; Commander Blake to Rear Admiral Maitland, 13 August 1838, PRO, Admiralty 125/133.
[46] Forrest, *A Voyage to New Guinea*, 313.
[47] Ibid., 302.
[48] Ibid., 27, 304.
[49] Commander Blake to Rear Admiral Maitland, 13 August 1838, PRO, Admiralty 125/133.
[50] No. 106, The Governor Politico Militar Zamboanga to governor captain general of the Philippines, 15 September 1853, PNA, Mindanao, Sulu, 1803-1890.
[51] Belcher, *Narrative Voyage of the H.M.S. Samarang, During the Years 1843-1846*, vol. 1, 198-99.
[52] Warren, *The Sulu Zone*, 153-54.
[53] Javellana, *Fortress of Empire Spanish Colonial Fortifications of the Philippines 1565-1898*, 63.
[54] Warren, *The Sulu Zone*, 154; Rutter, *The Pirate Wind Tales of the Sea-Robbers of Malaya*, 28.
[55] Guillermo Casanova to the governor-general of Zamboanga, 9 November 1868, PNA, unclassified Mindanao/Sulu.
[56] Mallari, *Muslim Raids in Bicol, 1580-1792*, 271.
[57] No. 100, Major Eades to the sultan of Sooloo, 16 January 1804, IOL, p/154; Enclosure 2, James Brooke to the Earl of Aberdeen, 31 March 1845, in Parliamentary Papers, 136-37.
[58] Bonham to Maitland, 28 June 1838, PRO, Admiralty 125/133.
[59] Forrest, *A Voyage to New Guinea*, 303.
[60] Jansen, "Aanteekeningen," 231; "The Illanoon," extracts from *Singapore Free Press*, 6 April 1847, PRO, Admiralty 125/133.
[61] Jansen, "Aanteekeningen," 231.
[62] Forrest, *A Voyage to New Guinea*, 319.
[63] Jansen, "Aanteekeningen," 232.
[64] Dalrymple, *Oriental Repertory*, 500-501; Rennell, "Journal of a

Voyage to the Sooloo Islands and the Northwest Coast of Borneo," 21-22.

65 Dalrymple, *Oriental Repertory*, 553.

66 Forrest, *A Voyage to New Guinea*, 15.

67 Dalrymple, *Oriental Repertory*, 507.

68 Gregori, "Aanteekengingen en Beshouwingen betrekkelijk de Zeeroovers en hunne rooverijen in den Indischen Archipel, alsmede aagaande Maguindanao en de Sooloo-Archiipel," 305-06.

69 Jansen, "Aanteekeningen," 234.

Chapter 10

1 Statement of James Brooke in Parliamentary Papers, House of Commons, 1851, vol. LVI, pt. II, "Operations against the Pirates on the Northwest Coast of Borneo," 134.

2 See Adrian Horridge, *The Prahu Traditional Sailing Boat of Indonesia*, Singapore: Oxford University Press, 1985.

3 "The Illanoon," extract from the *Singapore Free Press*, 6 April 1847, PRO, Admiralty 125/133.

4 Ibid.

5 Deposition of Si-Ayer, 7 November 1851, in Parliamentary Papers, House of Commons, 1852-1853, vol. LXI [55], "Burns Schooner Dolphin."

6 Parliamentary Papers, House of Commons, 1851, vol. LVI, pt. I [1390], "Historical Notices upon the Piracies committed in the East Indies and upon measures taken for suppressing them, by the Government of the Netherlands within the last thirty years," abstracted from articles by Cornets de Groot in the *Moniteur des Indies*, 91.

7 Ibanez y Garcia, *Mi Cautiverio Carta con motivo del que sufrio entre Los Moros Piratas Joloanos y Samalos en 1857*, 7.

8 St. John, *Life in the Forests of the Far East*, vol. 2, 239; Jansen, "Aanteekeningen omtrent Sollok en de Solloksche Zeeroovers," 226.

9 Statement of Abdulla in Bonham to Maitland, 28 June 1838, PRO, Admiralty 125/133.

10 Parliamentary Papers, 96, 111-12.

11 Ibid., 82.

[12] Alfred Russel Wallace, *The Malay Archipelago: The Land of the Orang-Utan, and the Bird of Paradise: A Narrative of Travel with Studies of Man and Nature* (London: MacMillan, 1869), 261, 333-34.

[13] Parliamentary Papers, House of Commons, 1850, vol. LV (23), "Papers Relative to Piracy in East India and the China Seas," 2.

[14] Ibid., 3.

[15] St. John, *Life in the Forests of the Far East*, vol. 1, 291-95.

[16] Parliamentary Papers, 105-06.

[17] Belcher, *Narrative Voyage of the H.M.S. Samarang, During the Years 1843-1846*, vol. 2, 216-246; Rutter, *The Pirate Wind Tales of the Sea Robbers of Malaya*, 159-68.

[18] Keppel, *A Visit to the Indian Archipelago in H.M.S. Maender, with Portions of the Private Journal of Sir James Brooke*, vol. 1, 44-45.

[19] John Meares, *Voyage Made in the Years 1788 and 1789 from China to the North West Coast of America*, 19-20.

[20] Journal of the *Lydia* from Manila to Zamboanga and Guam from 20 October 1801 to February 1804, kept by William Haswell, East India Marine Society, Salem, Peabody Museum.

[21] Ibid., (entry for 25 October 1801).

[22] Ibid., (entry for 6 November 1801).

[23] Journal of the *Logan* from Boston to Canton via London and St. Petersburg, 1837-1838, kept by Mrs. Alonzo Follansbee, East India Marine Society, Salem, Peabody Museum (Vol. 1, entry for 7 May 1837).

[24] Ibid., (Vol. 1, entry for 22 April 1838).

[25] Capt. John F. Campbell, "Pepper, Pirates and Grapeshot," *American Neptune*, vol. 21, no. 4 (1961), 292.

[26] James Duncan Phillips, "The Attack on the Marquis," *American Neptune*, vol. 9, no. 4 (1949), 239.

[27] Letter copy book, December 1805-March 1806 kept by John Carlton, the Master of the Ship *Putnam*, VFM 1512, Manuscripts Collection, G. W. Blunt White Library, Mystic Seaport Museum.

[28] Phillips, "The Attack on the Marquis," 245-46.

[29] Ibid., 246-47.

[30] Herman Melville, *Moby Dick or the Whale*, The Franklin Library: Franklin Center, 1979, 357.

[31] Ibid., 359-60.

[32] Journal of the *Logan*, (Vol. II, entry for 22 April 1838).

[33] Farquhar to Chief Secretary Fort St. George, 18 February 1803, IOL.

[34] Forrest, *A Voyage to New Guinea*, 310.

[35] Parliamentary Papers, 66; Joseph Conrad in *The Rescue* recounts how Jorgenson the old derelict captain ends his life in a blaze of glory on the shore of refuge near Karimata. He found himself surrounded by Iranun on an old mastless hulk, the *Emma*, which had been packed with arms and gunpowder by his friend Captain Lingard. Jorgenson, cigar in mouth, had managed to jump down the open hatchway of the powder magazine under the hostile eyes of the Iranun.

[36] Van der Kraan, *George Pockock King: Merchant Adventurer and Catalyst of the Bali War, 1846-1849*, 8.

[37] Parliamentary Papers, 21.

[38] "Adventures of C. Z. Pieters Among the Pirates of Maguindanao," 301-02.

[39] Parliamentary Papers, 110.

[40] Blake to Maitland, 13 August 1838, PRO, Admiralty 125/133.

[41] St. John, *Life in the Forests*, 212.

[42] Ibid., 209; Rutter, *The Pirate Wind Tales of the Sea Robbers of Malaya*, 46-47; R.H. Barnes, *Sea Hunters of Indonesia; Fishers and Weavers of Lamalera* (New York: Oxford University Press, 1996), 311; Marnie Bassett, *Realms and Islands The World Voyage of Rose De Freycinet in the Corvette URANIE 1817-1820 from her Journals and Letters and the Reports of Louis de Soulces de Freycinet Capitaine de Corvette* (London: Oxford University Press, 1962), 101-102.

[43] Forrest, *A Voyage to New Guinea*, 7.

[44] Parliamentary Papers, 67.

[45] Lt. W. Spiers to chief sec. to government at Fort William, 10 August 1822, IOL, F/4/714, no. 19495.

[46] Ibid., 14.

[47] Ibid.

[48] Ibid., 19.

[49] Deposition of Kreemon in Parliamentary Papers, House of Commons, 1852-1853, vol. LXI (5), "Burns Schooner Dolphin."

[50] Depositions of Sawal, one of the Dolphin's crew, and Sherif

Yassin, in Parliamentary Papers, House of Commons, 1852-1853, vol. LXI (55), "Burns Schooner Dolphin" Rutter, *The Pirate Wind Tales of the Sea Robbers of Malaya*, 260-74.

[51] Pryer to Dent, 7 June 1880, CO 874/192.

[52] Bulwer to the Earl of Carnarvon, 4 July 1874, CO 144/42.

[53] Governor of Straits Settlements to sec. to the government of India, 23 October 1863, FO, 71/1.

[54] Statement of John Dill Ross, enclosure 2 in despatch no. 1, Bulwer to Earl of Kimberley, January 1874, CO 144/42.

[55] Ross, still alive in the late 1920s, provided a very detailed account of this sea battle to Owen Rutter. Ross' oral recollections supplemented the narrative in his autobiography, *Sixty Years Life and Adventures in the Far East*. See Rutter, *The Pirate Wind Tales of the Sea Robbers of Malaya*, 275-82.

[56] Statement of Tibarcio Juan in Expediente 12, 4 October 1836, PNA, Mindanao/Sulu 1803-1890; No. 7, El Gobernador Capitan General a Señor Secretario de Estado, 4 June 1806.

[57] Ibanez y Garcia, *Mi Cautiverio Carta*, 13.

[58] Narrative of Haji Abdurahim in Notes of William Geoghegan on "Balangingi Piracy," 1-2.

[59] Statement of Francisco Thomas in Bonham to Maitland, 28 June 1838, PRO, Admiralty 125/133.

[60] Statements of Essu, Omar, Yusof and Ahmat in Bonham to Maitland, 28 June 1838, PRO, Admiralty 125/133.

[61] Statement of Juna Florentino in Relacion jurada de los individuos cautivos en la corbeta de Guerra Francesa Salina, PNA, Piratas 3.

[62] No. 49, El Goberbador Capitan General a Señor Secretario de Estado, 15 December 1838, AHN, Ultramar, 5155.

[63] Statements of Silammkoon, Tala Goa and Daniel in Bonham to Maitland, 28 June 1838, PRO, Admiralty 125/133.

[64] Forrest, *A Voyage to New Guinea*, 302.

[65] MF Ramo: Filipinas, Reel 3, Tomo 5, Expediente 3. Fols. 196b-198; Mallari, "Muslim Raids in Bicol, 1580-1792," 276.

[66] *Singapore Free Press* and *Mercantile Advertiser*, 24 May 1838.

[67] Statement of Tala Goa in Bonham to Maitland, 28 June 1838, PRO Admiralty 125/133.

[68] *Singapore Free Press* and *Mercantile Advertiser*, 24 May 1838.

[69] Ibid., 14 June 1838.

[70] Mundy, *Narrative Events in Borneo and Celebes Down to the Occupation of Labuan, from the Journals of James Brooke, esq. together with a Narrative of the Operations of H.M.S. Iris by Capt. Rodney Mundy*, vol. II, 359-63.

[71] Geoghegan, "Balangingi Samal," 28.

[72] Mundy, *Narrative Events in Borneo*, 188-91.

[73] Ibanez y Garcia, *Mi Cautiverio Carta*, 17.

[74] Parliamentary Papers, 96, 117-120; Mundy, *Narrative Events in Borneo*, 359-63.

[75] Geoghegan "Balangingi Samal," 20.

Chapter 11

[1] Charles Tilly, "Quantification in History, as seen from France," in Val. R. Lorwin and Jacob M. Price (eds.), *The Dimensions of the Past: Materials, Problems and Opportunities for Quantitative Work in History* (New Haven: Yale University Press, 1972), 94.

[2] Bonham to Maitland, 28 June 1838, PRO, Admiralty 125/133.

[3] Statement of Mahroon in Bonham to Maitland, 28 June 1838, PRO, Admiralty 125/133.

[4] Warren, *The Sulu Zone, 1768-1898*, xi-xvi, 252-55; *The Sulu Zone, The World Capitalist Economy and the Historical Imagination*, 29-50.

[5] Carlo Ginzburg, *Clues, Myths and the Historical Method* (Baltimore: Johns Hopkins University Press, 1989), 156.

[6] Warren, *The Sulu Zone, 1768-1898*, 215-51.

[7] See Expediente 12, 4 October 1836, PNA, Mindanao/Sulu, 1803-1890.

[8] Verklaringen von outvlugten personen uit de handen de Zeeroovers van 1845-1849, ANRI, Menado 37.

[9] Parliamentary Papers, House of Commons, 1851, vol. LVI, pt. I [1390], "Historical Notices upon the Piracies committed in the East Indies and upon measures taken for suppressing them, by the Government of the Netherlands within the last thirty years," abstracted from articles by

Cornets de Groot in the *Moniteur des Indies*, 112-13; Rutter, *The Pirate Wind Tales of the Sea-Robbers of Malaya*, 45-48.

[10] Ibanez y Garcia, *Mi Cautiverio Carta con motivo del que sufrio entre Los Moros Piratas Joloanos y Samalos en 1857*, 21.

[11] Ibid., 7-8.

[12] Ibid.

[13] Statement of Sabit in Bonham to Maitland, 28 June 1838, PRO, Admiralty 125/133.

[14] Parliamentary Papers, 66.

[15] Deposition of Si-Ayer, 7 November 1851, in Parliamentary Papers, House of Commons, 1852-1853, vol. LXI [55], "Burns Schooner Dolphin."

[16] Bonham to Maitland, 28 June 1838, PRO, Admiralty 125/133

[17] Statements of Nah Soo Hong, Francisco Thomas, Yusof Abdullah and Amat in Bonham to Maitland, 28 June 1838, PRO, Admiralty 125/133.

[18] Pieters, "Adventures of C. Z. Pieters among the Pirates of Maguindanao," 302; also Ibanez y Garcia, *Mi Cautiverio Carta*, 8.

[19] Jansen, "Aanteekeningen omtrent Sollok en de Solloksche Zeeroovers," 224; *Times*, 16 July 1862, CO 144/22.

[20] Ibanez y Garcia, *Mi Cautiverio Carta*, 21.

[21] Parliamentary Papers, 112-13.

[22] "Adventures of C. Z. Pieters among the Pirates of Maguindanao," 303.

[23] Jansen, "Aanteekeningen," 224; Ibanez y Garcia, *Mi Cautiverio Carta*, 10, 14; *Times*, 16 July 1862, CO 144/22.

[24] Ibanez y Garcia, *Mi Cautiverio Carta*, 15-16.

[25] Statement of Francisco Thomas in Bonham to Maitland, 28 June 1838, PRO, Admiralty 125/133; *Times*, 16 July 1862, CO 144/22.

[26] St. John, *Life in the Forests of the Far East*, vol. 2, 239.

[27] Forrest, *A Voyage to New Guinea and the Moluccas, 1774-1776*, 27, 304.

[28] Ibanez y Garcia, *Mi Cautiverio Carta*, 21.

[29] Statement of Francisco Thomas in Bonham to Maitland, 28 June 1838, PRO, Admiralty 125/133.

[30] Ibanez y Garcia, *Mi Cautiverio Carta*, 14.

[31] Extract from Presgraves Report on the Subject of Piracy, 5

December 1828, PRO, Admiralty 125/133.

32 "The Illanoon," extract from the *Singapore Free Press*, 6 April 1847, PRO, Admiralty 125/133.

33 Ibid.

34 Ibid.

35 Belcher, *Narrative Voyage of the H.M.S. Samarang, During the Years 1843-1846*, 406-07.

36 Rutter, *The Pirate Wind Tales of the Sea Robbers of Malaya*, 91.

37 Zuniga, *Estadismo de las Filipinas*, vol. I, 118-120.

38 No. 43, El Obispo de Nueva Caceres a Gobernador Capitan General, 16 October 1785, PNA, Ereccion de Pueblo, Camarines Sur, 1786-1873, VII.

39 No. 226, AGI, Filipinas 492, 22.

40 PNL MF Ramo: Filipinas 3, Tomo 5, Expediente 3, fol. 197.

41 Ereccion de Pueblo Camarines Sur, 1799-1820, folio 79-87, Partes sobre el arribo de varios pancos de Moros en los pueblos de Mambulao y Ragay de Camarines, 1805; Ereccion de Pueblo Albay, 1799-1864, tomo II, folio 123, alcalde mayor de Albay Tiburcio de Gorostiza to gobernador-general, Albay, 25 April 1820.

42 "The Illanoon," extract from the *Singapore Free Press*, 6 April 1847, PRO, Admiralty 125/133.

43 Deposition of Tay Song Que, 27 April 1843, in Parliamentary Papers, House of Commons, 1852, vol. 31 [1538], "Borneo Piracy."

44 "The Illanoon," extract from the *Singapore Free Press*, 6 April 1847, PRO, Admiralty 125/133.

45 St. John, *Life in the Forests of the Far East*, vol. 2, 236-37.

46 Robinson, Journal, 31 January 1842, 4 February 1842.

47 Memoir of Sooloo, IOL, Orme Collection, vol. 67, 128.

48 El Gobernador de Zamboanga a Gobernador Capitan General, 12 April 1769, PNA, Varias Provinces, Zamboanga; No. 226, II, AGI, Filipinas 492.

49 No. 226, II, AGI, Filipinas 492, 11; Montero y Vidal, *Historia General de Filipinas desde el descubrimiento de dichas Islas hasta nuestras dias*, vol. 2, 377.

50 Montero y Vidal, *Historia de las Filipinas*, vol. 2, 482.

51 Sultan Muyamad Alimudin a Gobernador D. Juan de Mir, 13 May 1781, PNA, Mindanao/Sulu 1769-1898; Barrantes *Guerras Piraticas*, 162.

[52] Parliamentary Papers, 105-06.
[53] Parliamentary Papers, 110.
[54] Ibanez y Garcia, *Mi Cautiverio Carta*, 10.
[55] Ibid., 11.
[56] Ibid., 18-20.
[57] Robinson, Journal, 4 February 1842; no. 338, Secretaria de Gobierno, 20 August 1863, PNA, Piratas 3; no. 12, 31 May 1845, AR, Kolonien 2669; no. 31, 24 March 1847, Kolonien 2602.
[58] Pieters, "Adventures of C. Z. Pieters among the Pirates of Maguindanao," 310-11.
[59] Ibid., 312.
[60] Thomas Jefferson Jacobs, *Scenes Incidents and Adventures in the Pacific Ocean, or the islands of the Australasian Seas, during the Cruise of the Clipper Margaret Oakley under Captain Benjamin Morrell* (New York: Harper and Bros., 1844), 336.
[61] Nicholas Loney, *A Britisher in the Philippines or the Letters of Nicholas Loney* (Manila: 1964), 64.
[62] St. John, *Life in the Forests of the Far East*, vol. 2, 209.
[63] Belcher, *Narrative Voyage of the H.M.S. Samarang, During the Years 1843-1846*, vol. I, 201-07.
[64] Statement of Ignacio Ambrocio, 29 August 1850, PNA, Piratas 3; extracts from the Journal of the barque Osprey in Col. Cavanagh to the secretary of the government of India, 28 January 1863, Fo 71/1; no. 12, 31 May 1845, AR Kolonien 2669; no. 31, 24 March 1847, Kolonien 2692.
[65] According to Mallari, the cutting of the Muslim ears dates to an earlier period when Maguindanao raiders plundered Albay province. According to oral tradition, the Bicolanos severed the ears of several Maguindanao raiders near Cagraray Island. See PNL HDP Albay, III-4, 1-2; Mallari, "The Maritime Response, 1793-1818," 488.
[66] Jansen, "Aanteekeningen," 222.
[67] Ibanez y Garcia, *Mi Cautiverio Carta*, 15.
[68] Jansen, "Aanteekeningen," 221.
[69] Rutter, *The Pirate Wind Tales of the Sea-Robbers of Malaya*, 21.
[70] Ibanez y Garcia, *Mi Cautiverio Carta*, 10.
[71] John Falconer, "The Eastern Seas," in David Cordingly (ed.),

Pirate Terror on the High Seas from the Caribbean to the South China Sea (Atlanta: Turner Publishing, 1996), 204.

[72] Ibanez y Garcia, *Mi Cautiverio Carta*, 21; Jansen, "Aanteekeningen," 22.

[73] Deposition of Si-Ayer, in St. John to Viscount Palmerston, 19 February 1852, Parliamentary Papers, House of Commons, Vol. XXI [1538] "Borneo Piracy"; Statements of Juan Apolonio and Diomicio Francisco, Expediente 12, 4 October 1836, PNA, Mindanao/Sulu, 1803-1890.

[74] Statement of Felix Feliciano in PNA, Ereccion de los Pueblos, Cebu 1818-1877.

[75] Fedor Jagor, *Travels in the Philippines* (Manila: Filipiniana Book Guild, 1965), 87; Ibanez y Garcia, *Mi Cautiverio Carta*, 16.

[76] Concas y Palau, "Nuestra Relaciones con Jolo," *Geographica de Madrid*, vol. 16 (1884), 204; extract from a letter from John Hayes to the resident of the Molucca Islands, 21 August 1801, IOL, P/242/42; Charles Gray to Samuel Hood Ingelfield, 31 May 1847, IOL, F/4/2262 (114837), 179; *Times*, 16 July 1862, CO 144/22.

[77] Statement of Amat in Bonham to Maitland, 28 June 1838, PRO, Admiralty 125/133.

[78] Statements of Amat and Yusuf in Bonham to Maitland, 28 June 1838, PRO, Admiralty 125/133.

[79] Statement of Nah Soo Hong in Bonham to Maitland, 28 June 1838, PRO, Admiralty 125/133.

[80] Parliamentary Papers, 119-20.

[81] Statement of Nazario de la Cruz in Relacion jurada de los cinco cautivos en la Falua de la division de la isla del Corregidor, 23 August 1845, PNA, Piratas 3.

[82] Statement of Jose Ruedas in Expediente 12, 4 October 1836, PNA, Mindanao/Sulu, 1803-1890.

[83] "Berigten omtrent den Zeeroof in den Nederlandsch-Indischen Archipel, 1857," 439.

[84] Parliamentary Papers, 112-13.

[85] Albert Bickmore, *Travels in the East Indian Archipelago* (London: John Murray, 1868), 320-21.

[86] Historical data on Lucbuan, HDP, Palawan.

[87] "Berigten omtrent den Zeeroof in den Nederlandsch-Indischen

Archipel, 1858," 304-05.

[88] Statement of Antonio Juan in Relacion jurada de los cinco cautivos venidos en la Falua de la division de la isla del Corrigidor de Albay a Gobernador Capitan General, 9 August 1836, PNA, Ereccion de Pueblo, Albay 1772-1831.

[89] Statement of Maria Damiani in Expediente 12, 4 October 1836, PNA. Mindanao/Sulu, 1803-1890.

[90] Verklaring van Chrishaan Soerma, 10 August 1846, ANRI, Menado 50.

[91] Pieters, "Adventures of C. Z. Pieters," 303.

[92] Statement of Francisco Sacarias in Expediente 12, 4 October 1836, PNA, Mindanao/Sulu, 1803-1890.

[93] Statement of Juan Pedro in Expediente 12, 4 October 1836, PNA, Mindanao/Sulu, 1803-1890.

[94] "The Illanoon," extract from the *Singapore Free Press*, 6 April 1847, PRO, Admiralty 125/133.

[95] Jansen, "Aanteekeningen," 229; "The Illanoon," extract from the *Singapore Free Press*, 6 April 1847, PRO, Admiralty 125/133.

[96] Jansen, "Aanteekeningen," 231.

[97] Statement of Francisco Sacarias in Expediente 12, 4 October 1836, PNA, Mindanao/Sulu, 1803-1890.

[98] Jansen, "Aanteekeningen," 231-32.

[99] Ibanez y Garcia, *Mi Cautiverio Carta*, 8-9.

[100] Jansen, "Aanteekeningen," 224, 228.

[101] Pieters, "Adventures of C. Z. Pieters," 302-303.

[102] Ibid.

[103] "Berigten omtrent den Zeeroof in den Nederlandsch-Indischen Archipel, 1858," 436.

[104] Diary of William Pryer, 11 March 1878, CO 74/67.

[105] Pieters, "Adventures of C. Z. Pieters," 303.

Chapter 12

[1] "The Illanoon," extract from the *Singapore Free Press*, 6 April 1847, PRO, Admiralty 125/133.

[2] MN Coleccion Enrile XIII, documento 9, II, 32; no. 82, Corregidor

de Camarines Sur a GCG, 4 September 1834, PNA, Ereccion de Pueblo, Camarines Sur 1831-1832, XI; Corregidor de Albay a GCG, 18 May 1836, PNA, Ereccion de Pueblo, Albay, 1772-1885, pt. I; no. 15 GCG a Señor Secretario de Estado, 26 May 1838, AHN, Ultramar 5155; no. 70, Gobernador Politico y Militar de Albay a GCG, 12 May 1841, PNA, Ereccion de Pueblo Albay, 1854-1891; no. 7, GCG a Señor Secretario de Estado, 31 December 1846, AHN, Ultramar, 5159; GCG a Señor Secretario de Estado, 20 October 1847, AHN, Ultramar 5161.

[3] No. 75, Alcaldia Mayor de la Provincia de Zambales a GCG, 1 July 1843, PNA, Ereccion de Pueblo Zambales, 1801-1844, pt. I; no. 135, GCG a Señor Secretario de Estado, 20 October 1836, AHN, Ultramar 52153; J. Farren to John Bidwell, 7 October 1847, PRO, FO, 72/732; GCG a Señor Secretario de Estado, 7 December 1827, AGI, Filipinas, 515; Farren to Earl of Aberdeen, 10 December 1844, PRO, FO, 72/663.

[4] No. 38, GCG a Señor Secretario de Estado, 20 August 1838, AHN, Ultramar 5155; no 49, GCG a Señor Secretario de Estado, AHN, Ultramar 5155.

[5] No. 100, Major Eales to the sultan of Sooloo, 16 January 1804, IOL, P/154.

[6] Enclosure 2, James Brooke to the Earl of Aberdeen, 31 March 1845, in Parliamentary Papers, House of Commons, 1851, vol. LVI, pt. I [1390], 'Historical Notices upon the Piracies committed in the East Indies and upon measures taken for suppressing them, by the Government of the Netherlands within the last thirty years,' abstracted from articles by Cornets de Groot in the *Moniteur des Indies*, 134-36.

[7] No. 7, partes pasados a la Capitania General sobre acontecimientos de Moros, PNA, Mindanao/Sulu, unclassified bundle; Manuel Baron a D. Jose Maria Halcon, 21 October 1836, PNA, Mindanao/Sulu, 1836-1897; Exp. 591, El Gobierno Militar y Politico de Zamboanga a GCG, 8 April 1838, PNA, Mindanao/Sulu 1838-1890, 17; Exp. 34, El Gobernador de Zamboanga a GCG, 15 February 1838, PNA, Mindanao/Sulu 1838-1885.

[8] Wilkes, "Jolo and the Sulus," 140-41.

[9] Hagemann, "Aanteekeningen omtrent een gedeelte der Oostkust van Borneo," 103; van Dewall, "Aanteekeningen omtrent de Noordoostkust van Borneo," 446-47.

[10] Warren, *The Sulu Zone, 1768-1898*, 105-06.

[11] Frake, "The Genesis of Kinds of People in the Sulu Archipelago," 323-25.

[12] No. 173, Gobernador Capitan General a Secretario de Estado, 15 October 1846, AHN, Ultramar, 5159.

[13] Expediente 12, Jayme Simo, subteniente de Marina Sutil, a GCG, 17 March 1845, PRO, FO, 72/684, 184-186; Bernaldez, *Resana historico de la guerra a sur Filipinas*, 151-53; Exp. 7, Gobierno Militar y Politico de Zamboanga a GCG, 17 August 1846, PNA, Mindanao/Sulu, 1838-1885; Farren to Palmerston, 27 December 1849, PRO, FO, 72/761.

[14] Expediente 12, Sobre haber salido la expedicion contra Balangingi, 17 February 1845, PNA, Mindanao/Sulu, 1836-1897.

[15] The Spanish first attempted to purchase a steamer from the English in 1844 with no success. No. 100, Vice-Admiral William Parker to Lord Ellenborough, 12 January 1844, IOL, F/4/2702.

[16] Letter from Gov.-Gen. Narciso Claveria to the Minister of War, 12 April 1845, PNA, Cartas, 1845, L. 75. no. 28, Seccion de Gobierno.

[17] For a detailed description of the fortifications at Balangingi see Gainzi, *Memoria y antecedentes sobre las expediciones de Balangingi y Jolo*; Pedro Muncariz a el Gobierno Politico y Militar de Zamboanga, 9 June 1847, PNA, Mindanao/Sulu, 1838-1885.

[18] J. Farren to Viscount Palmerston, 10 January 1848, PRO, FO, 72/749; Bernaldez, *Resana historico de la guerra a sur Filipinas*, 155. See also Claveria's report on the occupation of Balangingi, 28 February 1848, PNA, Cartas, 1847-1848.

[19] El Gobernador Capitan General a Señor Secretario de Estado, 28 February 1848, PNA, Cartas 1847-1848.

[20] Ibid.

[21] Santanina Rasul, 'The Samal Bangingih,' in Cojuangco, "The Samal Balangingi: An Experiment in Colonial Diaspora," 410-11.

[22] Emmanuel Baja, *The Philippine National Flag and Anthem* (Manila: Philippine Education Company, 1936), 34.

[23] El Gobernador Capitan General a Señor Secretario de Estado, 28 February 1848, PNA, Cartas 1847-1848.

[24] Ibid.

[25] Spanish copies of the letter are found in Montero y Vidal, *Historia de Filipinas*, vol. 3, 128-30; Bernaldez, *Resana historico de la guerra a sur*

Filipinas, p. 238; the translation is from Horacio de la Costa, *Readings in Philippine History*, (Manila: Bookmark, Inc., 1965), 208.

[26] El Gobernador Capitan General a Secretario de Estado, 28 February 1848, PNA, Cartas 1847-1848; Bernaldez, *Resana historico de la guerra a sur Filipinas*, 163; Extract from *Straits Times*, 7 March 1848, in J. Plumridge to H. Ward, 24 March 1848, PRO Admiralty 125/133.

[27] El Gobernador Capitan General a Secretario de Estado, 28 February 1848, PNA, Cartas 1847-1848; Extract from *Straits Times*, 7 March 1848, in J. Plumridge to H. Ward, 24 March 1848, PRO Admiralty 125/133.

[28] El Gobernador Capitan General a Señor Secretario de Estado, 28 February 1848, PNA, Cartas 1847-1848.

[29] PNA, Cartas 1847-1848, folios 71-77, Doc. 10; See also Margarita de los Reyes Cojuangco, *Kris of Valor The Samal Balangingi's Defiance and Diaspora* (Manila: Manison, 1993), 81-96.

[30] J. Farren to Viscount Palmerston, 29 February 1848, PRO, FO, 72/749; J. Farren to Viscount Palmerston, 28 January 1848, PRO, FO, 72/761; Diario de mi Commission a Jolo en al Vapor Magellenes, Jose Maria Peñaranda, 19 March 1848, PNA, Mindanao/Sulu, uncatalogued bundle.

[31] El Gobernador Capitan General a Sultan Mohammad Pulalon, 19 February 1849, PNA, Mindanao/Sulu, 1803-1890; Gobierno Militar y Politico de Zamboanga a Gobernador Capitan General, 21 November 1849, PNA, Piratas 3; J. Farren to Viscount Palmerston, 26 March 1849, PRO, FO, 72/761.

[32] El Gobernador Capitan General a Señor Secretario de Estado, 24 June 1851, AHN, Ultramar 5162.

[33] Jansen, "Aanteekeningen omtrent Sollok en de Solloksche Zeeroovers," 231.

[34] Gobierno Militar y Politico de Zamboanga a Gobernador Capitan General, 16 November 1852, PNA, Mindanao/Sulu, 1838-1885.

[35] St. John, *Life in the Forests of the Far East*, vol. 2, 186.

[36] Ibid., 237.

[37] El Gobernador Capitan General a Sultan Mohammad Pulalon, 19 February 1849, PNA, Mindanao/Sulu, 1803-1890.

[38] Warren, *The Sulu Zone, 1768-1898*, 194-95.

[39] Concas y Palau, 'Nuestras Relaciones con Jolo. Discourso

pronunciado en la Sociedad Geografica en 12 de Febrero de 1884,' *Revista General de Marina*, vol. 16 (1895), 204.

[40] Ibid., 211.

[41] Sultan Mohammad Pulalon a El Gobernador de Zamboanga, 16 June 1857, PNA, Mindanao/Sulu, uncatalogued bundle.

[42] Warren, *The Sulu Zone, 1768-1898*, 197, 199.

[43] Ibanez y Garcia, *Mi Cautiverio Carta con motivo del que sufrio entre Los Moros Piratas Joloanos y Samalos en 1857*, 12-18.

[44] El Gobernador de Zamboanga a el Gobernador Capitan General, 26 February 1845, PNA, Mindanao/Sulu, 1836-1887.

[45] Report of Julio de Tolosa, Secretary of State, 10 July 1858, PNA, Mindanao/Sulu, uncatalogued bundle.

[46] Warren, *The Sulu Zone, 1768-1898*, 195.

[47] Ibid., 197.

[48] Report of Julio de Tolosa, Secretary of State, 10 July 1858, PNA, Mindanao/Sulu, uncatalogued bundle; See Cojuangco, *Kris of Valor*, 124-27.

[49] Report of Julio de Tolosa, Secretary of State, 1859, PNA, Mindanao/Sulu, 1859, uncatalogued bundle.

[50] "Farewell Speech of Panglima Taupan," 1858 Zamboanga, PNA, Mindanao/Sulu, uncatalogued bundle; See Cojuangco, *Kris of Valor*, 280-81.

[51] Report of Julio de Tolosa, secretary of State, 15 September 1858, PNA, Mindanao/Sulu, uncatalogued bundle; See Cojuangco, "The Samal Balangingi," 280-81.

[52] Ibid., 281.

[53] Report of Julio de Tolosa, secretary of State, 15 September 1858, PNA, Mindanao/Sulu, uncatalogued bundle.

[54] Ibid., 31 May 1859, PNA, Mindanao/Sulu, uncatalogued bundle.

[55] Report of the alcalde mayor of Tondo, 10 June 1859, PNA, Mindanao/Sulu 1859, uncatalogued bundle.

[56] Report of Julio de Tolosa, secretary of State, 11 June 1859, PNA, Mindanao/Sulu, 1859, uncatalogued bundle.

[57] El Gobernador Capitan General a el Alcalde Mayor de Tondo, 15 June 1859, PNA, Mindanao/Sulu, 1859, uncatalogued bundle.

[58] Ibid., Report of Julio de Tolosa, 11 June 1859, PNA, Mindanao/Sulu 1859, uncatalogued bundle.

[59] El Gobernador Capitan General a el Alcalde Mayor de Tondo, 15

June 1859, PNA, Mindanao/Sulu, 1859, uncatalogued bundle.

[60] Ibid., Report of the alcalde mayor of Tondo, 18 June 1859, PNA, Mindanao/Sulu, uncatalogued bundle.

[61] Report of Julio de Tolosa, secretary of State, 12 October 1859, PNA, Mindanao/Sulu, 1859-1861.

[62] Report of Leonardo Castello y Castro, secretary of State, 28 April 1860, PNA, Mindanao/Sulu, 1860.

[63] Report of Julio de Tolosa, secretary of State, 12 October 1859, PNA, Mindanao/Sulu, 1859-1861.

[64] El Gobernador Capitan General a el Alcalde Mayor de Tondo, 15 June 1859, PNA, Mindanao/Sulu, 1859, uncatalogued bundle.

[65] Report of Julio de Tolosa, secretary of State, 18 April 1859, PNA, Mindanao/Sulu, uncatalogued bundle.

[66] Cojuangco, *Kris of Valor*, 137.

[67] El Gobernador Capitan General a el Alcalde Mayor de Tondo, 15 June 1859, PNA, Mindanao/Sulu, 1859, uncatalogued bundle.

[68] Report of Julio de Tolosa, secretary of State, 25 August 1859, PNA, Mindanao/Sulu, uncatalogued bundle.

[69] Report of Julio de Tolosa, secretary of State, PNA, Mindanao/Sulu 1860, uncatalogued bundle.

[70] Ibid.

[71] Ibid., 30 August 1859, PNA, Mindanao/Sulu, uncatalogued bundle.

[72] Ibid., 8 September 1859, PNA, Mindanao/Sulu 1859-1861, uncatalogued bundle.

[73] Testimony of Maria Manobo in PNA, Mindanao/Sulu, 1863-1894, uncatalogued documents.

[74] Cojuangco, *Kris of Valor*, 129-65.

[75] Report of Julio de Tolosa, secretary of State, 5 March 1860, PNA, Mindanao/Sulu, 1860, uncatalogued bundle; Soledad Ocasta, 'Historical Sketch of Barangay Dammang, Echague, Isabela,' in Cojuangco, "The Samal Balangingi," 347-47. Report of Julio de Tolosa, 13 August 1859, PNA, Mindanao/Sulu, 1859, uncatalogued bundle.

[76] Fray Buenaventura Campa, "Une Visita a las Rancherias de Ilongotes," in *El Correo Sino-Annomita o correspondencia de las missiones del Sagrado Orden de Predicadores en Formosa, China, Tung-*

King & Filipinas (Manila: Imprenta del Real Colegio de Santo Tomas, 1891), 25, 55.

[77] Statement of Hailan Kaligiran De Perez in Cojuangco, "The Samal Balangingis," 381.

[78] Report of Julio de Tolosa, secretary of State, 5 March 1860, PNA, Mindanao/Sulu, 1860, uncatalogued bundle; Soledad Ocasta, 'Historical Sketch of Barangay Dammang, Echague, Isabela,' in Cojuangco, "The Samal Balangingi," 344-47.

[79] Soledad Ocasta, 'Historical Sketch of Barangay Dammang, Echague, Isabela,' in Cojuangco, "The Samal Balangingi," 345.

[80] Ibid., 346.

[81] Statement of Hadji Jainudden Nuno and his wife Bai Sheika, 26 May 1985, in Cojuangco, "The Samal Balangingi," 369.

[82] Report of Rafael M. Caracciola, el Gobernador de Isabela a el Gobernador Capitan General, 10 September 1880, PNA, Gobierno General de Filipinas, 22, Folio 986/5, no. 956.

[83] Wendover, "The Balangingi Pirates," 325, 337-38; Majul, *Muslims in the Philippines: Past, Present and Future Prospects* (Manila: Convislam, 1971), 15.

[84] Statement of Hailan Kaligiran de Perez in Cojuangco, "The Samal Balangingi," 381-84.

[85] Wendover, "The Balangingi Pirates," 325, 337-38; Majul *Muslims in the Philippines*, 15.

[86] Wendover, "The Balangingi Pirates," 337-38.

[87] Ibid.

[88] Ibid.

[89] Majul, *Muslims in the Philippines*, 15.

[90] See Cojuangco, *Kris of Valor*, 27-38, 137-54.

Chapter 13

[1] Extracts from Journal of the barque *Osprey* in Colonel Cavanagh to sec. of the Government of India, 28 January 1863, PRO, FO, 71/1; Jansen, "Aanteekeningen omtrent Sollok en de Solloksche Zeeroovers," 231.

[2] El Gobernador Capitan General a Señor Ministro del Consejo, 20

July 1861, AHN, Ultramar 5184; Loney to Farren, 10 July 1861, PRO, FO 72/1017.

³ Concas y Palau, "Nuestra Relaciones con Jolo"–Discourso pronunciado en la Sociedad geografica en 12 Febrero de 1884, *Revista General de Marina*, vol. 16 (1895), 204.

⁴ Farren to the Earl of Clarendon, 9 March 1854, PRO, FO, 72/663.

⁵ Loney to Farren, 10 July 1861, PRO, FO 72/1017.

⁶ St. John, *Life in the Forests of the Far East*, vol. 2, 240.

⁷ No. 3, El Commandante de la Goleta, *Santa Filomena*, a Commandancia General de Apostadero de Filipinas, 23 July 1862, AHN, Ultramar 5190.

⁸ Ibid.; GCG a Señor Ministro de la Guerra y de Ultramar, 4 September 1862, AHN, Ultramar 5290; El Sultan de Jolo a D. Vincente Roca, 21 September 1862, AHN, Ultramar 5193; GCG a Señor Ministro de la Guerra y de Ultramar, 25 October 1862, AHN, Ultramar, 5192; CGC a Señor Presidente del Consejo de Ministros, 20 May 1863, AHN, Ultramar, 5194; Colonel Cavanagh to sec. to the government of India, 28 January 1863, PRO, FO, 71/1.

⁹ Mr. Ricketts to the Earl of Clarendon, 27 June 1870, PRO, FO, 72/1246; Gobierno Politico y Militar de la Isla de Mindanao a GCG, 28 July 1872, PNA, Pirates (1); Ricketts to the Earl of Derby, 28 January 1875, PRO, FO, 72/1423; no. 179, Gobierno Politico y Militar de la Isla de Mindanao a GCG, 2 December 1877, PNA, Mindanao/Sulu 1858-1897; no. 34 Gobierno Politico y Militar de Misamis a Gobernador Politico y Militar de Mindanao, 19 November 1880, PNA, Mindanao/Sulu, 1860-1898.

¹⁰ John Hay to Lord Clarence Paget, 25 March 1862, PRO, FO, 12/30; H.A. Reilly to Vice Adm. Sir John Hope, 3 February 1862; AR, Ministeria van Buitenlandsch Zaken 3268; no. 842, Kommandant de Zeemagt Uhlenbeck aan de Gouveneur-General van Nederlandsche Indie, 29 January 1872, AR-Schaarsbergen, Kolonien 2496; Captain Corbett to Rear-Adm. Kuper, 21 March 1863, CO, 144/22; Webb to Lord Russel, 24 October 1864, PRO, FO, 71/1; Pope Hennesey to Earl of Clarendon, 6 July 1869, CO, 144/29; *The Straits Times Overland Journal* 20, N. 471, 30 September 1879; Pryer to Treacher, 5 October 1881, CO, 874/229.

¹¹ Warren, "Slavery: Southeast Asia," in *A Historical Guide to World*

Slavery, ed. Drescher and Engerman, 85.

[12] Ibid., 85-86.

[13] Treacher to the Earl of Derby, 11 August 1877, CO, 144/49; Diary of William Pryer, 21 March 1878, CO, 874/67; 7 April 1878, CO, 874/187; 12 October 1878, CO, 874/68; and 17 October 1878, CO, 874/68; Pryer to Treacher, 5 October 1861, CO, 874/229.

[14] *The Straits Times Overland Journal* 20, N. 471, 30 September 1879; Den Gouveneur-General van Nederlandsche Indie aan den Minister van Kolonien, 22 February 1873, AR-Schaarsbergen, Kolonien 2565; Kommandant der Zeemagt aan zijne Excellentie der Gouveneur-General van Nederlandsche Indie, 9 August 1879, ANRI; Rapport van den Resident de Zuider en Ooster afdeeling van Borneo aan de Gouveneur-General van Nederlandsche Indie, 21 April 1880, in besluit no. 30, 3 June 1880, ANRI.

[15] Governor of north Borneo to governor of Sulu, 9 January 1892, in El Gobernador Politico y Militar de Jolo a GCG, 4 September 1890, PNA, Mindanao/Sulu, 1862-1898; C.V. Creagh to his Excellency the governor of Sulu, 27 December 1894, PNA, Isla de Borneo (2).

[16] Warren, *The North Borneo Chartered Company's Administration of the Bajau*, 52-58, 70-78.

[17] Mallari, "Muslim Raids in Bicol, 1580-1792," 257.

[18] Frake, "The Genesis of Kinds of People in the Sulu Archipelago," 314.

[19] Alfred Memmi, *The Coloniser and the Colonised*, London: Souvenir Press, 1974, 85.

[20] Michael Cullinane and Peter Xenos, "The Growth of Population in Cebu During the Spanish Era: Constructing a Regional Demography from Local Sources," in *Population and History the Demographic Origins of the Modern Philippines*, ed. Daniel F. Doeppers and Peter Xenos, Madison: University of Wisconsin, Center for Southeast Asian Studies 1998, 89.

[21] Mary Douglas, *Purity and Danger: An Analysis of Concepts of Pollution and Taboo*, London: Routledge and Kegan Paul, 1966; Peter Stallybass, and Allen White, *The Politics and Poetics of Transgression*, London: Methuen, 1986.

[22] Gov.-Gen. Narsico Claveria to the Minister of War, 12 April 1845, PNA, *Cartas 1845*, no. 28, Seccion Gobierno.

[23] Notes translated from the Spanish relative to the pirates on

Mindanao, PRO, Admiralty, 125/133.

[24] Mundy, *Narrative Events in Borneo and Celebes Down to the Occupation of Labuan, from the Journal of James Brooke, esq. Together with a Narrative of the Operations of HMS Iris*, vol. 2, 13-14.

[25] For a revolutionary critique of Western Literature and society and the ways in which it invented and sought to control the East see Edward Said, *Orientalism: Western Concepts of the Orient*, London: Routledge and Kegan Paul Ltd., 1978; Jonah Raskin, *The Mythology of Imperialism*, New York: Delta, 1971; Jerry Allen, *The Sea Years of Joseph Conrad*, London: Methuen, 1967; Norman Sherry, *Conrad's Eastern Sea*, Cambridge: Cambridge University Press, 1966.

[26] See Sherry, *Conrad's Eastern Sea*; G.J. Resink, "The Eastern Archipelago Under Joseph Conrad's Western Eyes," in *Indonesia's History Between the Myths*, The Hague: Van Hoeve, 1968, 305-324; James F. Warren, "Joseph Conrad's Fiction as Southeast Asian History Trade and Politics in East Borneo in the Late 19th Century," *Brunei Museum Journal* (1977), 21-34.

[27] See Cécile Parrish, *The Image of Asia in Children's Literature: 1814-1964*, Melbourne: Center for Southeast Asian Studies, Monash University, 1977.

[28] See Resink, "The Eastern Archipelago under Joseph Conrad's Western Eyes," 305-24.

[29] Joseph Conrad, *An Outcast of the Islands*, London: Penguin, 1975, 20-21.

[30] See Conrad, *An Outcast of the Islands*; *Almayer's Folly*, London: Penguin, 1976; *The Rescue*, London: J.M. Dent and Sons, 1924.

[31] Conrad, *The Rescue*, 223.

[32] Ibid., 296.

[33] Ibid., 297.

[34] Ibid., 164.

[35] Ibid., 200.

[36] In the Joseph Conrad Collection of the Beinecke Rare Book and Manuscript Library, Yale University, is a bill of lading dated 12 August 1884, for the S.S. Vidar of one Babalatchi sending 58 bags of dammar from Dongala to the Chinese trader Sing Jimmung in Singapore.

[37] Sherry, *Conrad's Eastern Sea*, 150.

38 Conrad, An Outcast of the Islands, 50.

39 Ibid., 20-21.

40 Conrad describes the Arabs as "treacherous" and a "venomous breed" in An Outcast of the Islands, particularly when focusing on the trade network and family of Sheik Abdullah, depicted as a man born to world commerce. He has lead a wandering life from the age of 17. Travelling as far as the Persian Gulf, he eventually returns to Southeast Asia at the age of 27 to take over the business interests of his dying father, "the rich Syed Selim bin Sali, the great Mohommedan trader of the Straits." While Daman in The Rescue is described as a "nervous figure in which lived the breath of the great desert haunted by his nomad, camel-riding ancestors." Conrad, An Outcast of the Islands, 86; The Rescue, 295.

41 Conrad, The Rescue, 293.

42 Ibid., An Outcast of the Islands, 33.

43 Warren, The Sulu Zone, The World Capitalist Economy and the Historical Imagination, 15.

44 Ibid., 25-26; Peter Burke, History and Social Theory, Oxford: Polity Press, 1992, 152.

45 Warren, The Sulu Zone 1768-1898 The Dynamics of External Trade, Slavery and Ethnicity in the Transformation of a Southeast Asian Maritime State, 252-55; The Sulu Zone, The World Capitalist Economy and the Historical Imagination, 9-50, 58-64.

46 Michael Southon, The Navel of the Perahu: Meaning and Values in the Maritime Trading Economy of a Butonese Village, Canberra: Research School of Pacific and Asian Studies, 1995, 22.

47 Robert Barnes, Sea Hunters of Indonesia: Fishers and Weavers of Lamalera, New York: Oxford University Press, 1996, 44; Christian Heersink, "Environmental Adaptations in Southern Sulawesi," in Environmental Challenges in Southeast Asia, ed. Victor T. King, London: Curzon, 1998, 103-04.

48 Stenross was astonished when Daruji, his boatbuilding informant, pointed to the photographs—a mnemonic device of the historian—and responded in an excited manner, "*ini dari zaman Lanun.*" He then asked Daruji how he knew about the Lanun period and people, and the extremely knowledgeable man replied, "In earlier times (Zaman Kuno) the

Lanun used to call regularly at Tamberu to obtain *sirih*." Daruji then explained that he used to hear about such matters from the old people of the village. This surprised Stenross somewhat, knowing the maritime raiding proclivities of the Iranun, and he told Daruji, 'that the Iranun were actually a much-feared people,' and suggested that perhaps the reason they did not harm the people of Tamberu was because they were fellow Muslims. Daruji replied that they were definitely not Muslims. Indeed, they could not possibly have been Muslims, because they were far too "wicked and cruel." He added that if the request of a 'Lanun' for sirih or betel nut was not immediately complied with, the man from whom it was requested, would be either slashed open on the spot with a sword, or taken away. The local people did not know where the 'Lanun' came from; all of those taken away were never returned. Report of interview with Daruji conducted on 4 January 2000, in Stenross to Warren, personal correspondence, 8 March 2000.

[49] Warren, *The Sulu Zone 1768-1898*, 174-81, 237-45; Rene B. Javellana, S.J., *Wood and Stone for God's Greater Glory Jesuit Art and Architecture in the Philippines*, Manila: Ateneo de Manila Press, 1991, 61-110; *Fortress of Empire Spanish Colonial Fortifications of the Philippines 1565-1898*, Manila: Bookmark, 1997.

[50] Forrest, *A Voyage to New Guinea and the Moluccas, 1771-1776*, 192-93.

[51] Scott, "The State and People Who Move Around," 3.

[52] Gavin Young, *In Search of Conrad*, London: Penguin, 1991, 254; Warren, *The Sulu Zone 1768-1898*, 85-86.

[53] Roger Keesing, "Asian Cultures?" *Asian Studies Review*, vol. 15, 2 (1991), 46.

[54] Ibid.

[55] Eric Wolf, *Europe and the People Without History*, Berkeley: University of California Press, 1982, 387.

[56] Comaroff and Comaroff, *Ethnography and the Historical Imagination*, 44. For a broad regional and theoretical consideration of population flows, particularly 'migrant,' identities and the nation-state in Southeast Asia see Filomeno V. Aguilar, Jr., "The Triumph of Instrumental Citizenship? Migrations, Identities and the Nation-State in Southeast Asia," *Asian Studies Review*, vol. 23, 3 (1999), 307-36.

GLOSSARY

Adat. Customary law.

Alcalde mayor. Governor of a province.

Alforean. A term applied to all peripheral people inhabiting the interior of the larger islands in the Molucca Sea.

Almojarifazgo. Import-export duty.

Amihan. Northeast monsoon.

Armadilla. Small coastal patrol squadrons of light sea craft created by the Spanish Colonial Government to thwart the Iranun and Balangingi raids.

Baju rantai. Chain-armor.

Baju. Shirt or clothes.

Balengkong. See barong.

Baluarte. Forts of wood, stone or earthwork.

Banyaga. A chattel-slave who was either the victim or the offspring of victims of slave raids.

Barangay. An administrative unit under Spanish rule, through which Filipino people paid tribute and owed compulsory corvee labor.

Barangayan. A Philippine sailing vessel up to 55 feet in length carrying two masts and worked by oars as well as by sails.

Barong. A broad heavy knife used in Malaysia, Indonesia and the Philippines as implement and weapon.

Baroto. A sampan or dugout canoe with or without outriggers employed as an auxiliary craft for inshore raiding.

Bora. Intricately dyed multicolored rattan Balangingi sleeping mat.

Brigantine. Two-masted vessel with square-rigged foremast and fore-and-aft rigged mainmast.

Buitengewesten. Dutch term for the 'outer islands'; area beyond Java.

Cabecera. A town or the capital of a parish: provincial capital.

Camarin. A large storehouse.

Canonero. Flat decked, shallow draught steam warship that was rigged as a schooner.

Caracao. Large, double ended sailing vessel, 60-80 feet long. The *caracao* was especially adapted for sailing in reef-filled waters and was commonly used by eastern Indonesians to defend themselves against the Iranun and Balangingi.

Castillo. (Philippines) an elevated enclosed lookout platform and defensive tower which gave an uninterrupted view of the sea.

Cautivo fugado. Christian captive who escaped from the Taosug, Iranun or Balangingi.

Cautivo. Captive: residents of Christian municipalities captured by Iranun and Balangingi in maritime raids

Chapa. Small Chinese brass coin commonly used as a form of currency throughout Southeast Asia.

Cohetes. Skyrockets.

Contrabandista. Smuggler.

Convento. Rectory, the residence of the priest, usually attached to a church.

Corregidor. Politico-military governor of a Province that had not been completely pacified or whose location was of strategic consequence.

Dammar. Resin obtained from tree especially of genus *agathis* or *thorea*.

Datu. Chief or aristocrat.

Degredados. The degraded ones.

Deportado. An individual who has been banished.

Duro. Spanish dollar.

Estado. A report or account.

Falua. Light, fast sailing antipiracy craft with a crew of 15 to 20. This was the most commonly used vessel in patrolling the coasts of the Philippines before the age of steam.

Frigate. Sailing warship next in size and equipment to ships of the line (carrying between 50 and 90 guns) with a full battery of up to 38 guns on the gundeck and, often, a light battery on the upper deck.

Garay. Balangingi maritime raiding vessel of the nineteenth century.

Ginjals. See lantanca and lela.

Gutta Percha. Greyish-black plastic substance got from the latex of various Bornean trees

Habagat. Southwest monsoon; the 'pirate wind.'

Haji. Honorific title for one who has made the pilgrimage to Mecca

Hakim. Judge.

Hukum-hukum laut. Maritime code of laws.

Imam. Leader of a mosque or *surau* organization.

Indio. Term used by the Spaniards to refer to the inhabitants of the Philippines.

Janggollan. Large double-stern Madurese transport *prahu*.

Jihad. Holy war.

Joanga. The large raiding vessel the Iranun used for long cruises. The *joanga* measured on the average 80-90 feet in length, and 20 feet wide amid ship.

Juru mudi/julmuri. Experienced officer; steersman.

Juru batu. Boatswain.

Kadi. Muslim judge.

Kakap. A sampan or dugout canoe with or without outriggers employed as an auxiliary craft for inshore raiding.

Kampilan. Iranun sword whose handle was long enough to be wielded with two hands.

Kampong ayer. Stilted village built out over the water.

Kangan. A bolt of coarse cotton cloth from China.

Kapal api. Steam ship.

Kapitan China. Headman of a Chinese community.

Kiapangtilihan. Bond slaves.

Kerajaan. The colonial Malayo-Muslim state.

Kima. Giant clam.

Kora-Kora. A long vessel used in the Moluccas with a high prow and higher stern, large deck house, outriggers, and propelled by oar and sail.

Kota. Fort.

Kris. Malay or Javanese dagger.
Lahar. Flow of volcanic mud.
La Muralla de Sangre. The Wall of Blood.
Lancha. Armed, flat boat of the *Marina Sutil,* antipiracy force.
Lancha. See *falua.*
Lanong. See *joanga.*
Lantanca. Long, heavy, brass swivel cannon which were esteemed as symbols of wealth and social status.
Laxamana. Malay title for admiral of the Royal fleet.
Lela (lella/Lelah). Various types of portable cannon; see *lantanca.*
Mangooray/mangoorap. The Samal-Iranun term for maritime raiding.
Marina Sutil. 'The light navy' or antipiracy force.
Mayan. Flat bottomed, small transport boat with a large flat stern and a single small mast.
Merantau. Drive outward from one's present situation to enhance new opportunities; warriors and traders off seeking their fortunes in distant lands and frontier settlements.
Mestizo. People of Spanish-Filipino or Chinese-Filipino ancestry.
Moro. A term used by the Spaniards in the Philippines to refer to the Muslims.
Musim lanun. The easterly wind which brought the Iranun cruising fleets from their strongholds, in the months between August and October.
Njai. Mistress.
Nakodah. Master of a sailing craft.
Negara. See *kerajaan.*
Orang Kaya. A commoner and a person of means.
Padi. Unhusked rice.
Padron. Tribute roll.
Paduakan. Bugis sailing vessel of between 20 and 50 tons burden, broad beamed with high sides.
Panchallong (pencalang). Java trader of the nineteenth century: a large *mayang* with a deck house.
Panco. Spanish term used to refer to the largest type of Muslim raiding craft (between 50 to 90 feet in length).
Panglima. A high-ranking noble.

Peso. The official Spanish currency in the Philippines.
Polo. A system of forced labor service.
Pontin. A large two-masted sailing vessel with square mat sails; undecked cargo boat.
Prahu. Malay for sailing craft.
Presidio. A garrisoned post; also a penal settlement.
Pueblo. A municipal district.
Raja muda. 'Vice-King' and heir apparent to the throne.
Raja. Generic term of Hindu origin for 'Ruler.'
Rantanker. See *lantanca and lela*.
Ratu Adil. 'Just Prince'; the Javanese Messiah prophesied by Djajabaja.
Remontado. Person with no fixed habitation. In the nineteenth century the term was used to describe people who fled to the mountains.
Renegado. Renegade, an apostate, especially from Christianity to Islam.
Ruma Bichara. The Sultanate's loosely organized council of ministers, composed of Royal datus and high-ranking aristocrats.
Saga-saga. Spear.
Sakay. Crew of a Balangingi *garay*.
Salisipan. Long narrow and low canoe-like vessel used as an auxiliary craft for maritime raiding.
Sarong. A piece of cloth the ends of which have been sewn together.
Schooner. Fore-and-aft rigged vessel with two or more masts.
Servicio Personal. Personal labor service.
Shahbandar. Harbormaster.
Sherif. An individual claiming descent from the prophet, Mohammed.
Sirih. Mild narcotic comprised of three ingredients; the nut of the areca palm, the leaf of the betel vine, and lime.
Surau. Building used for purposes of religious worship.
Telegrafista. Sentry and/or signalman who stood guard in the watchtowers and small forts in Philippine coastal towns.
Tope (toop). Three masted sailing freighter with tilted rectangular or fore-and-aft rig and lateral rudders.
Tributo. The tax collected by the Spanish colonial government from the indigenous inhabitants of the Philippines aged 16 to 60. A whole tribute (*tributo*) was composed of husband and wife and their children. The tributes collected in kind were many.

Tripang. Malay for sea cucumber. A major ingredient of Chinese cuisine.

Tusut. The genealogical lore and traditions of the Iban or Sea Dyaks of Borneo.

Ulama. A Muslim scholar; those learned in religion.

Vagamundos. Category of Filipinos who were not integrated within organized municipalities.

Vigia. In the Philippines, *vigia* was used interchangeably with *Castillo*, referring to a wooden watchtower.

Vinta. Outriggered sailing vessel of the Philippines varying in length from 15 to upward of 50 feet.

Visita. Ecclesiastical term for a small village serviced by a nonresident priest.

BIBLIOGRAPHY

Official Records

I. Spain
  A. Records of the Archive de Indias, Seville
   Seccion - Audiencia de Filipinas
   323 – Expediente sobre el numero de religioses, pueblos, y Iglesias que tener las Religiones de Santo Domingo, San Francisco, y San Augustin 1751-1753
   324 – Expediente sobre el numero de religiosos, pueblos, y Iglesias que tener las Religiones de Santo Domingo, San Francisco y San Augustin 1753-1754
   359-368 – Consultos, Decretos, Ordenes Originales 1770-1650
   370 – Remisiones el Consejo y Ministros 1775
   390 – Gobierno del Capitan General Don Simon Anda 1769-1780
   391 – Gobiernos de los Capitanes Generales D. Jose Vasco y Vargas y D. Felix Berenguer de Marquina 1776-1787
   489-521 – Duplicados de Gobernador 1769-1850
   Cartas y Expedientes 1751-1800:
   602 – Inventario de Cartas y Expedientes, 603A – 1751-1761; 603B – 1751-1761; 610 – 1765; 611 – 1765; 618 – 1768; 621 – 1769; 626 – 1770; 627 – 1770; 632 – 1772; 633 – 1772; 634 – 1773; 635 – 1773; 636 – 1774; 641 – 1777; 645 – 1777; 645 – 1779; 651 – 1782; 654 – 1785; 660 – 1790
   Expedientes Diarios 1700-1800:
   667 – Inventario de Expedientes Diarios; 669 – 1765-1767
   Expedientes y Instancias de Partes 1700-1800: 681 – 1761-1764;

685 – 1773-1775; 686 – 1776-1778; 687 – 1779-1780; 688 – 1781-1783; 690 – 1784-1785; 697 – Ynstancias sin curso 1800-1849

700 – Duplicados de Autoridades Particulares 1731-1759

860, 811, 829 – Duplicados de Superintendentes y Yntendentes de Ejercito y Real Hacienda 1821-1832

976-979 – Expediente del Consular y Comercio 1788-1832

1027 – Duplicados del Obispo de Cebu 1718-1830

1031 – Duplicades del Obispo de Nueva Segovia 1757-1829

1033 – Duplicados del Obispo de Nueva Cazeras 1715-1830

Seccion – Ministerio de Ultramar

557 – Indices de consultados, ordenes y representationes que dividen los Gobernadores Capitanes Generales 1787-1822

558 – Indices de consultados, ordenes y representaciones que dividen los Gobernadores Capitanes Generales 1823-1835

559 – Indices de consultados, ordenes y representaciones que dividen los Gobernadores Capitanes Generales 1836-1850

Expedientes y Instancias del partes 1769–1870; 587 – 1809-1810; 591 – 1815-1816; 592 – 1816-1817; 599 – 1825-1826; 604 – 1831-1870

Expediente del Real Hacienda:

624 – 1825-1827; 625 – 1828-1830

650 – Expedientes de Marina 1802-1825

657-664 – Expedientes de Navegacion, Industria y Comercio 1772-1835

682-684 – Cartas y Expedientes de los Arbispos y Cabildos 1773–1833

Seccion – Indiferente
1527 – Indiferente General

B. Records of the Archive Historico Nacional, Madrid
   Seccion – Ultramar, Gobierno de Filipinas
   Legajos 4542, 5153, 5155, 5157, 5159, 5161, 5162, 5163, 5164, 5165, 5166, 5167, 5172, 5173, 5180, 5182, 5184, 5186, 5188, 5190, 5191, 5192, 5193, 5194, 5195, 5197, 5198, 5199, 5200, 5217
   Seccion – Estado
   Estado 2845, caja 2

Estado 8461

C. Records of the Archive de Ministerio de Asuntos Exteriores, Madrid
Correspondencia Consulados Singapore 1848-1920
Legajo 2067 – 1848-1880; 2068 – 1881-1920

D. Records of the Museo Naval, Madrid
Coleccion Enrile
Tomo VII, Documento 14, folio 53-54; Documento 15, folio 55; Documento 16, folio 56
Tomo XIII, Documento 2, folios 27-39; Documento 9, folios 73-82; Documento 10, folios 83-88; Documento 13, folios 93-94
Tomo XVIII, Documento 31, folio 213
Coleccion Guillen
Tomo V, Documento 18; Documento 19, folios 40-43; Documento 26, folios 118-133; Documento 33, folios 167-185
Tomo VI, Documento 6, folios 80-91
Tomo XIII, Ms. 1740
Ms. 211. Diario de Navegacion del Capitan de Frigata de la Real Armada D. Jose Maria Halcon en su Navegacion de Manila a Jolo con la Galeota de S.M. 'La Olosea' y una division de Faluas. Comprende desde 10 Junio de 1836 y abraza noticias peculiares a comision extraordinaria que en calidad de plenipotenciario desenipeno cerca del Sultan de Jolo
Ms. 623. Pancos y otros embarcaciones de Filipinas por Nicolas Enrile, 1834

II. England
A. Records of the East India Company, India Office Library, London
Bengal Public Consultations - P/1/51, P/2/1, P/2/6, P/2/10, P/2/14, P/4/39, P/4/43, P/5/11, P/6/7, P/8/25, P/12/51, P/12/58, P/13/13, P/13/17, P/13/20, P/13/25
Bengal Secret Consultations P/140, P/154, P/166, P/167, P/236
Bengal Foreign Consultations P/165/76
Bombay Public Consultations P/341/33, P/341/35, P/341/37, P/341/38, P/341/39, P/341/40, P/341/41
Madras General Consultations P/242/42

Madras Military Consultations P/254/69, P/255/18
Madras Military and Secret Proceedings - P/251/51
Factory Records, Borneo (1648-1814) G/4/1
Factory Records, Java G/21/1, G/21/17, G/21/24, G/21/25, G/21/26, G/21/27, G/21/28, G/21/37, G/21/40, G/21/41, G/21/42
Factory Records, Straits Settlements vols. 1-3
Home Miscellaneous Series vols. 102, 105, 107, 108, 115, 116, 118, 119, 122, 128, 146, 165, 166, 169, 437, 795, 815
Marine Records L/Mar/6/98C, L/Mar/6/4561 and J, L/Mar/6/456T, L/Mar/6/537A and 537B, L/Mar/6/556E, L/Mar/6/570A, L/Mar/6/570B
Orme Collection vol. 67, 88
Board's Collections 19495 (714) vol. 96, p. 231; 77129 (1841) vol. 25, p. 1374; 86974 (1978) vol. 34, p.138; 95244 (2072) vol. 42, p. 788; 10277 (2146) vol. 50, p. 805; 113126 (2245) vol. 58, p. 329; 114837 (2262) vol. 59, p. 705; 121954 (2331) vol. 64, p. 670; 121955 (2331) vol. 64, p. 670; 124781 (2358) vol. 66, p. 676; 125401 (2363) vol. 67, p. 597; 135371, 135372 (2450) vol. 75, p. 1021; 140594 (2489) vol. 79, p. 1160
Raffles Minto Collection EUR.F.148/3, EUR.F.148/5, EUR.F.148/7, EUR.F. 148/37
Raffles Family Collection Mss. EUR.D.742/1, Mss. EUR.D.742/45

B. Public Records Office
Colonial Office Records
C.O.144. Labuan, Original Correspondence, 1844-1906, vols. l-81
C.O.874. British North Borneo Papers 1878-1915
Foreign Office Records
F.O.12.Borneo, 1842-1875
F.O.71. Sulu, 1848-1888, vols. 1-19
F.O.72. Spain, 72/663, 72/684, 72/708, 72/732, 72/749, 72/761, 72/795, 72/812, 72/853, 72/876, 72/904, 72/927, 72/1017, 72/1070, 72/1193, 72/1246, 72/1221, 72/1283, 72/1423,72/1477
Admiralty Records Adm. 125/133 – Sulu Piracy
Adm. 125/144 – Borneo Piracy
State Papers – Spain S/P/94/197, S/P/94/198

Egremont Papers PRO, 30/47/20/1

C. National Maritime Museum, Greenwich
   MAS/7. A series of 83 numbered letters received and written by Massie, captain of H.M.S. *Cleopatra* at Hong Kong and Singapore, from 15 August 1851-9 March 1852
   MAS/22. Journal of H.M.S. *Cleopatra* in East Indies kept by Massie while in command as captain 1851-1853

D. Jardine Matheson Archives, Cambridge University Library
   East Indies, B1/99, 100, 101, B4/4, C1/14

E. British Museum, London
   James Rennell, Journal of a Voyage to the Sooloo Islands and the Northwest Coast of Borneo, from and to Madras with descriptions of the islands, 1762-1763

F. Parliamentary Papers, House of Commons
   1850. Vol. LV (238), 3. Malay Piracy
   1851. Vol. LVI, Pt. 1 [1390], 1. 'Historical notices upon the piracies committed in the East Indies, and upon the measures taken for suppressing them, by the Government of the Netherlands, within the last thirty years.' Abstracted from articles by Comets de Groot in the *Moniteur des Indies*
   1851. Vol. LVI, Pt. 1 [1351], 123. Papers respecting the Operations against the pirates on the northwest coast of Borneo
   1852. Vol. XXXI [1538], 473. Borneo Piracy
   1852-1853. Vol. LXI (55), 235. Burn's schooner *Dolphin*

III. Netherlands
  A. Records of the Algemeen Rijksarchief, The Hague
     Kolonien Archief-Overgekomen Brieven
     No. 2922, 3144, 3205, 3259, 3281,3283, 3315, 3337, 3341
     Kolonien No. 1393, 1594, 2597, 2669, 2675, 2692, 2703,2710, 3200, 3089, 4168, 4351
     De Archieven van het Department van Buitenlandsche Zaken
     No. 3268. Correspondentie over de bestrijding der Zeerooverijen in den Soeloe (Solok) Archipel. 1 April 1862-25 July 1868.

B. Records of Auxiliary Repository, Schaarsbergen
Ministrie van Kolonien No. 1398, 2166, 2290, 2434, 2450, 2496, 2565, 3378, 5873, 6000, 6001

C. Papers of Het Koningklyk Instituut voor-taal-en Volkenkunde, Leiden
Ligtvoet Collection
H609A-III-Ligtvoet (A) Bestuur sambtenaar (aantekiningen omtrent Z.W. Celebes)

IV. The United States
A. Records of the United States National Archive, Washington, D.C.
The Papers of the Bureau of Insular Affairs
File 2689. Slavery and Slave Trade in the Philippine Islands (1901-1936)
File 3671. 'Protocols, Capitulations, Official Letters, Decrees, and Correspondence relating to Jolo and Mindanao, 1751-1896'
The Department of State
Consular Despatches, Manila 1817-1840
The Department of the Navy
Journal of Lieutenant Charles Wilkes aboard the *Vincennes* and the *Porpoise*, volume 3 (6 April 1841-15 May 1842)
Journal of William Briskoe, Armorer, aboard the *Relief* and the *Vincennes* (18 August 1838-23 March 1842)
Journal kept aboard the *Vincennes*, probably by R.P. Robinson, Purser's Clerk (6 April 1841-15 May 1842)

B. The Library of Congress, Washington, D.C.
The Leonard Wood Papers
Container 3: Diary, May 1902-31 January 1906
Containers 32-35: General Correspondence, 1903-1904
Containers 191, 192, 216, 239: Personal Correspondence
The Hugh L. Scott Papers
Containers 55-56: Official letters January 1900-1905

C. The Philips Library, Salem Peabody Museum, Salem, Massachusetts
Ship logs
656/1792/3, *Britannide*. Journal of a voyage from England to Port Jackson New South Wales in the years 1792, 1793 and 1794, and in 1795 in the ship *Britannide*, kept by K. Murray

656/1833A, *Albree*. Abstract log from Boston towards Calcutta, 16 July 1833-11 September 1833, kept by Gamaliel E. Ward. Included also: Memo of goods obtainable at Sooloo and a list of goods for the Sooloo Market

656/1835A, *Leonidas* Brig. Log of Brig *Leonidas* from 8 February 1836 to 23 September 1636; departure from Manila to neighboring ports and return

656/1837/39, *Logan*. Journal kept on board the ship *Logan* 1837-1838 by Mrs Alonzo Fallonsbee

Papers of William D. Waters 10654/*Leonidas*, Letter: soliciting trade between United States and Sooloo [no date]

Papers of James Devereux 10654/container 6

East India Marine Society *Lydia* (barque), Journal of Salem vessel from Manila to Samboangue [Zamboanga] and Guam from 20 October 1801 to February 1804 kept by William Haswell.

D. Blunt White Library, Mystic Seaport Museum

Letter Copy Book, December 1805-March 1806 kept by John Carlton, the Master of the Ship Putnam, VFM152, Manuscript Collection.

E. United States Senate Documents, United States Congress

1899-1900. 56th Congress. 1st Session, vol. IX, No. 136, Treaty with the Sultan of Sulu

1900-1901. 56th Congress. 2nd Session, vol. XV, No. 218, The People of the Philippines

V. The Philippines

A. The Records of the Philippine National Archives, Manila

Mindanao y Sulu

Bundles 1769-1898, 1774-1887, 1780-1896, 1803-1890, 1816-1898, 1836-1897, 1838-1885, 1838-1890, 1838-1891, 1839-1898, 1842-1897, 1847-1896, 1857-1895, 1857-1897, 1858-1897, 1860-1897, 1860-1898, 1861-1893, 1861-1896, 1861-1897, 1861-1899, 1862-1896 (2 bundles), 1864-1898, 1877-1895, 15 unclassified bundles

Piratas

Bundles I-III
Isla de Borneo
Bundles I-II
Chinos
Padron de Chinos, Jolo – 1892, 1893, 1894
Padron de Zamboanga – 1892
Cotabato, Davao, Jolo, Misamis 1878-1898
Varias Provincias
One bundle – Zamboanga
Memorias
Memoria de Zamboanga
Ereccion del Pueblo
Albay, 1772-1831, 1772-1836; 1772-1885, 1799-1864, 1834-1864; 1841-1891, 1843-1846
Camarines Sur, 1768-1837; 1781-1809, 1785-1837; 1786-1837, 1797-1859, 1799-1820, 1831-1882, bundle 67, No. 1-28
Tayabas, bundles 1, 2, 3, 1793-1857, pt. II
Zambales, 1804-1844, pt. I
Negros, 1854-1857
Ramo
Filipinas Microfilm, Reel 3
Cartas
1845, Seccion de Gobierno
1847-1848 Seccion de Gobierno

B. The Records of the Archives of the University of Santo Tomas, Manila
'Memoria sobre Mindanao y demas puntos del Sur,' Seccion Folletos, Tomo 117

C. Society of Jesus Archives of the Philippine Province, Quezon City
Series XIV – Zamboanga and Jolo
XIV – 9 Isabela
XIV – 10 Jolo
XIV – 23 Zamboanga Residence (l)

D. National Library of the Philippines
   Republic of the Philippines, Bureau of Public Schools, 'Historical Data Papers, unpublished MS
   Historical Data Papers for Albay, vols. I-IV; Camarines Sur, vols. I-IV; Camarines Norte; Catanduanes; Masbate, I-III; Romblon; Antique; Cebu; vols. I-IV; Bohol, vols. I-II; Samar, vol. VIII; Palawan; Surigao; Misamis Oriental; Zamboanga del Norte; Zamboanga del Sur

VI. Arsip Nasional Republik Indonesia, Jakarta
    Menado
    Files 37, 50, 166
    Riouw
    File 20/3
    Besluit, 9 August 1879, N. 22
    Besluit, 3 June 1880, No. 30

Collections

A. Beyer-Holleman collection of Original sources in Philippine Customary Law. Typescript, Library of Congress, Washington, D.C. and Philippine Studies Program, University of Chicago
   Paper No. 159, vol. I. General Introduction to the Papers on Moro Customary Law
   Paper No. 160, vol. I, no. 1. Major Charles Livingston, "Constabulary Monograph of Sulu" (1915)
   Paper No. 160, vol. I, no. 2. Ist Lieutenant A. Bruce Stephenson, "Constabulary Monograph of the District of Tawi-Tawi" (1916)
   Paper No. 161, vol. II, no. 8. Najeeb Saleeby, "The Moros" (1906)
   Paper No. 161, vol. II, no. 10. Howard Hickok, "Report of the 52nd Census District" (1903)
   Paper No. 161, vol. II, no. 11. K. Walker, "Report of the 53rd Census District" (1903)
   Paper No. 162, vol. VI, no. 16. Adolf Gunther, "Correspondence and Reports relating to the Sulu Moros" (Jolo and Manila, 1901-1903)

Paper No. 162, vol. XI, no. 19. John Whitaker, "Notes on the Yakan Moros" (1902)

Paper No. 162, vol. VI, no. 21. J. Mahoney, "Report of the Census of the Island of Basilan" (1903)

Paper No. 162, vol. VI, no. 23. Emerson B. Christie, "The Moros of Sulu and Mindanao"

Paper No. 162, vol. VI, no. 25. Emerson B. Christie, "The non-Christian Tribes of the Northern half of the Zamboanga Peninsula" (1903)

Paper No. 162, vol. VI, no. 26. F.P. Williamson, "The Moros between Buluan and Punta Flecha" (1903)

Paper No. 163, vol. VI, no. 28. L.W.V. Kennon, David P. Barrows, John Pershing and C. Smith, "Census Report Relating to the District of Lanao, Mindanao" (1903)

Paper No. 163, vol. VI, no. 34. Oscar J.W. Scott and Ira C. Brown, "Ethnography of the Magandanaos of Parang" (1908)

Paper No. 164, vol. VI, no. 49. "The Bates Treaty with the Sultan of Sulu"

Paper No. 164, vol VI, no. 50. "Conference of the Philippine Commission with the Sultan of Sulu and his adviser" (19, 20 and 26 July 1904)

Paper No. 164, vol. VI, no. 51. John J. Pershing, Leonard Wood and others, "Correspondence and Papers Relating to the Status of the Sultan of Sulu" (1904-1913)

Paper No. 164, vol. VI, no. 65. Vicente T. Zago, "The Sovereign Personality of the Sultan of Sulu" (1919)

Paper No. 165, vol. VI. John Garvan, "Papers on the Pagan People of Mindanao"

Paper No. 167, vol. VI. John Garvan, "Ethnography of the Manobo people of Eastern Mindanao"

B. John Neilson Conrad Collection, Oamaru, New Zealand
   Reed Papers
   Papers of the late Dr. J.G. Reed of Perak, Malaysia, relating to his research into the life of Joseph Conrad. Two notebooks, 1950-1951 correspondence, record of 13 April 1951 interview with

Mrs. C.C. Oehlers (Nelli Lingard) in Singapore, navigation charts and photographs

C. Haverschmidt Collection, Heerlen, Netherlands
Haverschmidt Papers
Records compiled 1951-1952 in Berau, Kalimantan Timor, Indonesia by Mr. R. Haverschmidt, late manager, N.V. Steenkolen Maatschappij Parapattan, Teluk Bajur, Berau. Interviews with elderly local residents (Sultan of Sambaliung, the Ratu of Gunung Tabor, Anang Dachlan Akay, Adji Bagian, Raden Ajub, and Kang Si Gok) in 'Statements of Residents'; a copy of 1904 deed of sale of Lingard house; a copy of chronology of events in Berau from 1800-1926 based on the chronicle of the Sultan of Gunung Tabor; copies of Netherlands government documents 1879-1933 pertaining to the Berau district.

D. Joseph Conrad Collection, Beinecke Rare Book and Manuscript Library, Yale University
Bill of Lading dated 12 August 1884, for the S.S. *Vidar*, of babalatchi a Dongala trader.

Newspapers

British North Borneo Herald and Official Gazette, 1883-1915 (Sandakan)
La Estrella de Manila, January-December 1848 (Manila)
Makassarsch Handelsblad, May 1868-1883 (Makassar)
Overland Singapore Free Press, 1847 (Singapore)
Singapore Chronicle, 1827, 1830-1833 (Singapore)
Singapore Chronicle and Commercial Register, 7 January 1837-30 September 1838 (Singapore)
Singapore Free Press and Mercantile Advertiser, February 1836-September 1838 (Singapore)
Singapore Daily Times, 1837 (Singapore)
Straits Times Overland Journal (1879), (Singapore)
Straits Times and Singapore Journal of Commerce, 1848, 1851-1853, 1883 (Singapore)

Dissertations

Ahmat bin Adam. "A Descriptive Account of the Malay Letters sent to Thomas Stamford Raffles in Malacca in 1810 and 1811 by the Rulers of the Indigenous States of the Malay Archipelago." M.A. diss., University of London, 1971.

Cheong, W.E. "Some Aspects of British Trade and Finance in Canton, With Special Reference to the Role of Anglo-Spanish Trade in the Eastern Seas, 1784-1834." Ph.D. diss., University of London, 1963.

Cojuangco, Margarita de los Reyes. "The Samal Balangingi: An Experiment in Colonial Diaspora." M.A. diss., University of Santo Tomas, 1986.

Cruikshank, R.B. "A History of Samar Island, the Philippines, 1768-1898." Ph.D. diss., University of Wisconsin, 1975.

De Jesus, Edilberto C. "The Tobacco Monopoly in the Philippines, 1782-1882." Ph.D. diss., Yale University, 1973.

Frake, Charles O. "Social Organization and Shifting Cultivation among the Sindangan Subanun." Ph.D. diss., Yale University, 1955.

Hunter, S.C. "English, German, Spanish Relations on the Sulu Question, 1871-1877." M.Sc. diss., University of London, 1963.

Julian, Elisa A. "British Projects and Activities in the Philippines, 1795-1805." Ph.D. diss., University of London, 1963.

Matheson, Virginia. "Tuhfat al Nafis." Ph.D. diss., Monash University, 1973.

Mednick, Melvin. "Encampment of the Lake: The Social Organization of a Moslem Philippine (Moro) People." Ph.D. diss., University of Chicago, 1965.

Nimmo, Harry Arlo. "The Structure of Bajau Society." Ph.D. diss., University of Hawaii, 1969.

Owen, Norman G. "Kabikolan in the Nineteenth Century: Socio-Economic Change in Provincial Philippines." M.A. diss., University of Michigan, 1976.

Reber, Anne L. "The Sulu World in the 18th and Early 19th Centuries: A Historiographical Problem in British Writings on Malay Piracy." M.A. diss., Cornell University, 1966.

Reynolds, John Keith. "Towards an Account of Sulu and Its Bornean

Dependencies, 1700-1878." M.A. diss., University of Wisconsin, 1970.
Surojo, A.M. Djuliati. "Perbudarkan di Indonesia pada abad XIX." Skripsi Sardjana. M.A. diss., Universitas Gadjah Mada, 1969.
Velthoen, Esther. "Of Chiefs and Warriors, A Historical Study of Precolonial Eastern Sulawesi 1650-1905." Ph.D. diss., Murdoch University, forthcoming 2001.
Warren, Carol A. "Bajau Consciousness in Social Change: The Transformation of a Malaysian Minority Community." M.A. diss., Australian National University, 1977.

Books

Abdullah bin Abdul Kadir. *The Hikayat Abdullah*, trans. A.H. Hill, *Journal Malaysian Branch Royal Asiatic Society* 28, no. 3 (1955).
Adas, Michael. *Machines as the Measure of Men: Science, Technology and Ideologies of Western Dominence*. Ithaca: Cornell University Press, 1989.
Ahmad, Kassim (ed.). *Kisah Pelayaran Abdullah*. Kuala Lumpur, 1960.
Allen, Jerry. *The Sea Years of Joseph Conrad*. London: Methuen, 1967.
Almeda, Fernando A., Jr. *Story of a Province: Surigao Across the Years*. Manila: Philippine National Historical Society, 1993.
Almeida, Anna. *A Lady's Visit to Manila and Japan*. London: Hurst & Blackett, 1863.
Andaya, Barbara Watson. *To Live as Brothers: Southeast Sumatra in the Seventeenth and Eighteenth Centuries*. Honolulu: University of Hawaii Press, 1993.
Andaya, Leonard. *The Kingdom of Johor, 1641-1728*. Kuala Lumpur: Oxford University Press, 1975.
Anderson, John. *Mission to the East Coast of Sumatra in 1823*. London: Oxford University Press, 1971.
Arenas, Rafael Dias. *Memoria sobre el Comercio y Navegacion de Las Islas Filipinas*. Cadiz: Imprenta de D. Feros, 1838.
Baja, Emmanuel. *The Philippine National Flag and Anthem*. Manila: Philippine Education Company, 1936.
Balandier, Georges. *Political Anthropology*. trans. A.M. Sheridan Smith. London: Penguin Press, 1970.

Balanza General del Comercio de las Islas Filipinas. Manila, 1853.
Balanza General del Comercio de las Islas Filipinas en 1845. Manila, 1854.
Balanza Mercantil de las Islas Filipinas correspondiente al ano de 1858. Manila, 1861.
Bandira, Datu and Datu Alang. *Iranun Sejarah Dan Adat Tradisi.* Kuala Lumpur: Dewan Bahasa Lan Pustaka, 1992.
Bankoff, Gregory. *Crime, Society and the State in the Nineteenth Century Philippines.* Quezon City: Ateneo de Manila University Press, 1996.
Banton, Michael, ed. *Political Systems and the Distribution of Power.* London: Tavistock Publications, 1965.
Baran, Paul. *The Political Economy of Growth.* London: 1957.
Baring-Gould, S., and Bampfylde, C.A. *A History of Sarawak under Its Two White Rajahs, 1839-1908.* London: Southeran, 1909.
Barrantes, Vicente. *Guerras Piraticas de Filipinas contra Mindanaos y Joloanos.* Madrid: Imprenta de Manuel H. Hernandez, 1878.
Barth, F., ed. *Ethnic Groups and Boundaries.* Boston, 1969.
Barnes, Robert. *Sea Hunters of Indonesia: Fishers and Weavers of Lamalera.* New York: Oxford University Press, 1996.
Bassett, Marnie. *Realms and Islands; The World Voyage of Rose de Freycinet in the Corvette URANIE 1817-1821 From her Journal and Letters and the Report of Louis de Saulces de Freycinet Capitaine de Corvette.* London: Oxford University Press, 1962.
Belcher, Edward. *Narrative of the Voyage of H.M.S. Samarang, During the Years 1843-1846.* 2 vols. London: Reeve, Benham & Reeve, 1848.
Berkhofer, Robert. *A Behavioral Approach to Historical Analysis.* New York: Free Press, 1969.
Bernaldez, Emilio. *Resana historico de la guerra a Sur de Filipinas, sostenida por las armas Espanoles contra los piratas de aquel archipielago, desde la conquista hasta nuestros dias.*Madrid: Imprenta del Memorial de Ingenieros, 1857.
Bickmore, Albert. *Travels in the East Indian Archipelago.* London: John Murray, 1868.
Blair, E.H., and Robertson, J.A. *The Philippine Islands, 1493-1898.* 55 vols. Cleveland: A.H. Clark Co., 1903-1919.
Blalock, Hubert M. *Toward a Theory of Minority Group Relations.* New York: John Wiley & Sons, 1967.

Blusse, Leonard. *Strange Company: Chinese Settlers, Mestizo Women and the Dutch in VOC Batavia*. Dordrecht: KITLV, 1986.

Bock, Carl. *The Headhunters of Borneo. A Narrative of Travel up the Mahakkam and down the Barito; Also Journeyings in Sumatra*. London: Sampson Low, 1882.

Bonney, R. *Kedah 1771-1821 The Search for Security and Independence*. Kuala Lumpur: Oxford University, 1971.

Bowring, John. *The Philippine Islands*. London: Smith, Elder & Co., 1859.

Boxer, Charles. *The Dutch Seabourne Empire 1600-1800*. London: Penguin Books, 1973.

Broersma, R. *Handel en Bedrijf in Zuid-en Oost Borneo*. The Hague: G. Noeff, 1927.

Brown, Donald. *Brunei: The Structure and History of a Bornean Malay Sultanate*. Brunei: Brunei Museum, 1970.

Brown, W. *Useful Plants of the Philippines*. 3 vols. Manila: Bureau of Printing, 1951.

Buckley, Charles B. *An Anecdotal History of Old Times in Singapore, 1819-1867*. Kuala Lumpur: University of Malaya Press, 1965.

Burke, Peter. *The French Historical Revolution: The Annales School 1929-1989*. Stanford: Stanford University Press, 1990.

_____. *History and Social Theory*. Oxford: Polity Press, 1992.

Casino, Eric. *Ethnographic Art of the Philippines: An Anthropological Approach*. Manila: 1973.

_____. *The Jama Mapun: A Changing Samal Society in the Southern Philippines*. Quezon City: Ateneo de Manila University Press, 1976.

Chaunu, Huguette and Pierre. *Seville et L'Atlantique, 1504-1650, Ports-Routes-Trafics*. 7 vols. Paris: Colin, 1955.

Chaunu, Pierre. *Les Philippines et le Pacifique des Iberiques (XVI, XVII, XYIII siecles)* Paris: Seupen, 1960.

Clodd, H.P. *Malaya's First British Pioneer: The Life of Francis Light*. London: 1948.

Coates, W.H. *The Old 'Country Trade' of the East Indies*. London: Imray, Laurie, Narie & Wilson, 1911.

Cohen, Ronald, and Service, Elman R., eds. *Origins of the State the*

Anthropology of Political Evolution. Philadelphia: Institute for the Study of Human Issues, 1978.

Cojuangco, Margarita de los Reyes. *Kris of Valor: The Samal Balangingi's Defiance and Diaspora*. Manila: Manisan, 1993.

Comaroff, John and Jean Comaroff. *Ethnography and the Historical Imagination*. Boulder: Westview Press, 1992.

Combes, Francisco S.J. *Historia de las Islas de Mindanao y Jolo*. Madrid, 1667.

Comyn, Tomas de. *State of the Philippines in 1810, Being an Historical, Statistical and Descriptive Account of the Interesting Portion on the Indian Archipelago*. Trans. with notes and preliminary discourse by William Walton. Manila: Filipiniana Book Guild, 1969.

Conrad, Joseph. *Almayers Folly*, London: Penguin, 1976.

_____. *An Outcast of the Islands*, London: Penguin, 1975.

_____. *The Rescue*. London: J.M. Dent and Sons, 1924.

Cook, Oscar. *Borneo: The Stealer of Hearts*. London: Hurst & Blackett, 1924.

Cooper-Cole, Fay. *The Bukidnon of Mindanao*. Chicago: Natural History Museum, 1956.

_____. *The Wild Tribes of Davao District, Mindanao*. Chicago: Field Museum of Natural History, Anthropological Series, vol. 12, no. 2, 1913.

Costa, Horacio de la. *Readings in Philippine History*. Manila: Bookmark, 1965.

Crawfurd, John. *A Descriptive Dictionary of the Indian Islands and Adjacent Countries*. London: Bradbury & Evans, 1856.

_____. *History of the Indian Archipelago, Containing an Account of the Languages, Religions, Institutions and Commerce of Its Inhabitants*. 3 vols. Edinburgh, 1820.

Cuadro General del Comercio Exterior de Filipinas con la Metropoli potencias extrangeras de Europa, America, Asia y Colonias de la Oceania en 1856. Manila, 1859.

Cushner, Nicholas. *Landed Estates in the Colonial Philippines*. New Haven: Yale Southeast Asian Studies, 1976.

Dalton, George, ed. *Primitive, Archaic and Modern Economies*. Garden City, N.Y.: Anchor Books, 1968.

Dalrymple, Alexander. *Oriental Repertory*. 2 vols. London, 1808.

Dampier, William. *A New Voyage Round the World*. 2 vols. Edited by John Masfield. London: E. Grant Ricardo, 1960.

_____. *A New Voyage Round the World*. London, 1697 reprint, with introduction by Sir Albert Gray, 1937.

Delano, Amasa. *A Narrative of Voyages and Travel in the Northern and Southern Hemispheres, Comprising Three Voyages Round the World; Together with a Voyage of Survey and Discovery, in the Pacific Ocean and Oriental Islands*. Boston: E.G. House, 1817.

Dery, Luis Camara. *From Ibalon to Sorsogon: A Historical Survey of Sorsogon Province to 1905*. Quezon City: New Day Publishers, 1991.

Despres, L.A., ed. *Ethnicity and Resource Competition in Plural Societies*. The Hague: Mouton, 1975.

Diaz-Trechuelo Spinola, M.L. *Arquitectura Espanola en Filipinas, 1565-1800*. Seville, 1959.

_____. *La Real Compania de Filipinas*. Seville, 1965.

Dobby, E.H. *Southeast Asia*. London: University of London Press, 1969.

Doeppers, Daniel F. and Peter Xenos. *Population and History: The Demographic Origins of the Modern Philippines*. Madison: University of Wisconsin, Center for Southeast Asian Studies, 1998.

Douglas, Mary. *Purity and Danger: An Analysis of the Concepts of Pollution and Taboo*. London: Routledge and Kegan Paul, 1966.

Dumont D'Urville, Jules Sebastian Cesar. *Voyages au pole sud et dans L'Oceanie sur les corvettes l'Astrolobe et la Zelee . . . pendant les annees 1837-1838-1839-1840*. 23 vols., Atlas, 7 vols. Paris: Gide et J. Baudry, 1841-1854.

Earl, George Windsor. *The Eastern Sens or Voyages and Adventures in the Indian Archipelago in 1832, 1833, 1834, Comprising a Tour of the Island of Java—Visits to Borneo, the Malay Peninsula, Siam; Also an Account of the Present State of Singapore with Observations on the Commercial Resources of the Archipelago*. London: W.H. Alien & Co., 1837.

El-Correo-Sino-Annamita o correspondencia de las Misiones del Sagrado Orden de Predicadores en Formosa, China, Tung-King y Filipinas. Vol. 25. Manila: Imprenta Del Real Colegio de Santo Tomas.

Escosura, Patricio de la. *Memoria sobre Filipinas y Jolo redactada en 1863 y 1864*. Madrid: Imprenta de Manuel G. Hernandez, 1882.

Espina, Miguel Angel. *Apuntos para hacer un libro sobre Jolo, entresacados de los escrito por Barrantes, Bernaldez, Escosura. Grancia, Giraudier, Gonzales, Parrado, Pagos y otros varios.* Manila: Imprenta de M. Perez, hijo, 1889.

Estadistica General del Comercio Exterior de las Islas Filipinas del ano de 1888. Manila, 1890.

Fardon, Richard. *Raiders and Refugees: Trends in Chamba Political Development 1750 to 1950.* Washington: Smithsonian Institution Press, 1988.

Fernandez, Pablo O.P. *History of the Church in the Philippines, 1521-1898.* Manila: National Book Store, 1979.

Finley, John P., and Churchill, William. *The Subanun: Studies of a Sub-Visayan Mountain Folk of Mindanao.* Washington, D.C.: Carnegie Institution of Washington, Publication No. 184, 1913.

Fischer, David Hackett. *Historians' Fallacies: Toward a Logic of Historical Thought.* New York: Harper & Row, 1970.

Foreman, John. *The Philippine Islands.* 2nd ed. New York: Charles Scribners, 1899.

Forrest, Thomas. *A Voyage from Calcutta to the Mergui Archipelago Lying on the East Side of the Bay of Sengal.* London, 1792.

_____. *A Voyage to New Guinea and the Moluccas from Balambangan: Including an Account of Maguindanao, Sooloo and Other Islands.* London: C. Scott, 1779.

Frank, Andre Gunder. *World Accumulation, 1492-1789.* London: MacMillan Press, 1978.

Freeman, Derek. *Report on the Iban.* London: The Athlone Press, 1970.

Fry, Howard. *Alexander Dalrymple and the Expansion of British Trade.* Royal Commonwealth Society, Imperial Studies No. 29, London: Cass, 1970.

Furber, Holden. *John Company at Work: A Study of European Expansion in India in the Late Eighteenth Century.* Cambridge: Harvard University Press, 1951.

Gainza, Francisco. *Memoria y antecedentes sobre las espediciones de Balangingi y Jolo.* Manila: Establecimiento tipografico del Colegio de Santo Tomas, 1851.

Garcia, Luiz de Ibanez. *Mi Cautiverio; carto que con motive del que sufrio entre los moros piratas Joloanos y Samales en 1857.* Madrid: G. Allhambra, 1859.

Garvan, John M. *The Manobos of Mindanao*. Memorial of the National Academy of Science, vol. 23, 1st Memoir. Washington, D.C., 1931.

Gazetteer of the Philippine Islands. 2 vols. Washington, D.C., 1902.

Geddes, W.R. *Nine Dayak Nights*. London: Oxford University Press, 1973.

Ginzburg, Carlo. *Clues, Myth and the Historical Method*. Baltimore: Johns Hopkins University Press, 1988.

Glamman, Kristof. *Dutch Asiatic Trade, 1620-1740*. The Hague: Nijhoff, 1958.

Gowing, Peter, and McAmis, Robert D., eds. *The Muslim Filipinos*. Manila: Solidaridad Publishing House, 1974.

Greenberg, Michael, *British Trade and the Opening of China, 1800-1842*. London: Cambridge University Press, 1951.

Gregori, F.A.A. *Aanteekeningen en Beshouwingen betrekkelijk de Zeeroovers en hunn rooverijen in den Indischen Archipel, alsmede aagaande Magindanao en de Soolo-Archipel*, 1844.

Guia de Forasteros en las Yslas Filipinas por el ano de 1843. Manila: Imprenta D. Miguel Sanchez, 1843.

Guia de Forasteros en las Yslas Filipinas por el ano de 1846. Manila: Imprenta de los Amigos del Pais, 1846.

Guia de Forasteros en las Yslas Filipinas para el ano de 1856. Manila: Imprenta de los Amigos del Pais, 1856.

Guia de Forasteros en las Yslas Filipinas para el ano de 1857. Manila: Imprenta de los Amigos del Pais, 1857.

Guillaume, Alfred. *Islam*. Baltimore: Penguin, 1954.

Guillelmard, F.H.H. *The Cruise of the Marchesa to Kamschatka and New Guinea, With Notices of Formosa, Liu-Kiu and Other Various Islands of the Malay Archipelago*. 2 vols. London: John Murray, 1886.

Gullick, J.M. *Indigenous Political Systems of Western Malaya*. London School of Economics Monographs on Social Anthropology No. 17. London: Athlone Press, 1958.

Handbook of the State of North Borneo, With a Supplement of Statistical and Other Useful Information. London: British North Borneo Chartered Co., 1934.

Hanks, Lucien M. *Rice and Man: Agricultural Ecology in Southeast Asia*. Chicago: Aldine, Atherton, 1972.

Hardy, Charles. *Register of Ships Employed in the Service of the Honourable*

United East India Company, 1707-1760, London, 1799.

Harlow, Vincent T. *The Founding of the Second British Empire, 1773-1793.* 2 vols. London: Longmans & Green Co., 1952.

Harrison, Tom and Barbara. *The Prehistory of Sabah.* Kota Kinabalu: Sabah Society, 1971.

Hatton, Joseph. *The New Ceylon, Being a Sketch of British North Borneo or Sabah.* London: Chapman & Hall, 1881.

Hendrick, Daniel R. *The Tools of Empire Technology and European Imperialism in the Nineteenth Century.* New York: Oxford University Press, 1989.

Horridge, Adrian. *The Prahu: Traditional Sailing Boat of Indonesia.* Singapore: Oxford University Press, 1985.

Horsburgh, James. *India Directory of Directions for Sailing to and from the East Indies, China, Australia, Cape of Good Hope, Brazil and the Interjacent Ports, Compiled Chiefly from the Original Journals of the Company Ships, and from the Observations and Remarks made during Twenty-one Years Experience Navigating in Those Seas.* 4th ed. London, 1836.

Hudson, A.B. *Padju Epat: The Ma'anyan of Indonesian Borneo.* New York: Holt Rinehart & Winston, 1972.

Hunter, Captain Charles. *The Adventures of a Naval Officer,* ed. Spencer St. John. London: 1905.

Hutterer, Karl L. ed. *Economic Exchange and Social Interaction in Southeast Asia: Perspectives from Prehistory, History and Ethnography.* Ann Arbor: Michigan Papers on South and Southeast Asia, 1978.

Ileto, Reynaldo Clemena. *Maguindanao 1860-1888: The Career of Dato Uto of Buayan.* Data Paper No. 82. Southeast Asia Program, Cornell University. Ithaca, N.Y., 1971.

Irwin, Graham. *Nineteenth Century Borneo: A Study in Diplomatic Rivalry.* Verhandelingen van het Koningklijk Instituut voor Taal-land-en Volkenkinde. deel XXV. The Hague: Martinus Nijhoff, 1955.

Jacobs, Thomas Jefferson. *Scenes, Incidents and Adventures in the Pacific Ocean, or the Islands of the Australasian Seas, during the Cruise of the Clipper Margaret Oakley under Captain Benjamin Morrell.* New York: Harper & Bros., 1844.

Jagor, Fedor. *Travels in the Philippines.* Manila: Filipiniana Book Guild, 1965.

Javellana, Rene B., S.J. *Fortress of Empire Spanish Colonial Fortifications of the Philippines 1565-1898*, Manila: Bookmark, 1997.

_____. *Wood and Stone for God's Greater Glory Jesuit Art and Architecture in the Philippines*. Manila: Ateneo de Manila University Press, 1991.

Kasaysayan: The Story of the Filipino People, vols. 1-10, Manila: Asia Publishing Company Limited, 1998.

Keppel, Henry. *The Expedition to Borneo of H.M.S. Dido for the Suppression of Piracy, With Extracts from the Journal of James Brooke, Esq., of Sarawak*. 3rd ed., 2 vols. London: Chapman & Hall, 1847.

_____. *A Visit to the Indian Archipelago in H.M.S. Maeander, With Portions of the Private Journal of Sir James Brooke, K.C.B.* London: Richard Bentley, 1853.

Kiefer, Thomas. *Tausug Armed Conflict: The Social Organization of Military Conflict in a Philippine Modern Society*. Philippine Studies Program, Research Series No. 7, University of Chicago. Chicago, Ill., 1969.

_____. *The Tausug: Violence and Law in a Philippine Moslem Society*. New York: Holt Rinehart & Winston, 1972.

Kolf, D.H. *Voyages of the Dutch Brig of War Dourga, through the Southern and Little Known Parts of the Moluccan Archipelago and the Previously Unknown Southern Coast of New Guinea Performed during the Years 1825 and 1826*, trans. George Windsor Earl. London: James Madden, 1840.

Kraan, Alfons Vander. *George Pokock King: Merchant Adventurer and Catalyst for the Bali War, 1846-1849*. Clayton: Monash University, no date.

Laarhoven, Ruurdje. *The Triumph of Moro Diplomacy: The Maguindanao Sultanate in the 17th Century*. Quezon City: New Day Publishers, 1989.

La Gironiere, Paul de. *Twenty Years in the Philippines*. Trans. and abridged by Frederick Hardman. London: Brown, Green, & Longmans, 1853.

Lannoy, P.J. *Iles Philippines De Luer situation Ancienne et Actualle*. Bruxelles: Delevingue et Callevaert, 1849.

Lasker, Bruno. *Human Bondage in Southeast Asia*. Chapel Hill: University of North Carolina Press, 1950.

Leach, E.R. *Political Systems of Highland Burma: A Study of Kachin Social Structure*. London: London School of Economics and Political Science, 1954.

Le Bar, Frank M., ed. *Ethnic Groups of Insular Southeast Asia.* Vol. I. New Haven: Human Relations Area Files Press, 1972.

_____, ed. *Ethnic Groups of Insular Southeast Asia.* Vol. II: *The Philippines and Formosa.* New Haven: Human Relations Area Files Press, 1975.

Lehman, F.K. *The Structure of Chin Society.* Urbana: University of Illinois Press, 1963.

Lenski, Gerhard E. *Power and Privilege: A Theory of Social Stratification.* New York: McGraw-Hill, 1966.

Lombard, Denys. *Le Sultanate d'Atjeh au temps d'Iskander Muda, 1607-1636.* Paris, 1967.

Loney, Nicholas. *A Britisher in the Philippines or the Letters of Nicholas Loney.* Manila: 1964.

Low, Hugh. *Sarawak: Its Inhabitants and Productions, Being Notes During a Residence in That Country with H.H. the Rajah Brooke.* London: Richard Bentley, 1848.

MacDonald, D. *A Narrative of the Early Life and Services of Captain D. MacDonald R.N. Embracing on Unbroken Period of Twenty-two Years Extracted from His Journal, and Other Official Documents.* 3rd ed., Weymouth, 1843.

McKenna, Thomas M. *Muslim Rulers and Rebels: Everyday Politics and Armed Separatism in the Southern Philippines.* Berkeley: University of California Press, 1998.

MacMicking, Robert. *Recollections of Manila and the Philippines During 1848, 1849 and 1850.* Manila: Filipiniana Book Guild, 1967.

Majul, Cesar A. *Muslims in the Philippines.* Quezon City: University of the Philippines Press, 1973.

_____. *Muslims in the Philippines: Past, Present and Future Prospects.* Manila: Convislam, 1971.

Mallari, Francisco, S.J. *Vignettes of Bicol History.* Quezon City: New Day Publishers, 1999.

Mallat, J. *Archipel de Soulou, ou description des groupes des Basilan, de Soulou et de Tawi-Tawi, suivie d'un vocabularie francais-malaise.* Paris: Imprimerie Pollet et compagnie, 1844.

_____. *Les Philippines; historie, geografie, moeurs, agriculture,* industrie et commerce des colonies Espagnoles dans L'Oceanie. 2 vols. Paris, 1846.

Marche, Alfred. *Luzon and Palawan*. Manila: Filipiniana Book Guild, 1970.

Marryat, Frank. *Borneo and the Indian Archipelago*. London: Longman, Brown, Green & Longman, 1848.

Mas, Sinibaldo de. *Estado de las Islas Filipinas en 1842*. 2 vols. Madrid: Imprenta de I. Sancha, 1843.

Meares, John. *Voyage Made in the Years 1788 and 1789 from China to the North-West Coast of America*. New York: N. Israel/Amsterdam Da Capo Press, 1967.

Meilink-Roelofsz, M.A.P. *Asian trade and European Influence in the Indonesian Archipelago Between 1500 and about 1630*. The Hague: Martinus Nijhoff, 1962.

Melville, Herman. *Moby Dick or the Whale*. Philadelphia: The Franklin Library: Franklin Center, 1977.

Memmi, Alfred. *The Coloniser and the Colonised*. London: Souvenir Press, 1974.

Milburn, William. *Oriental Commerce; Containing a Geographical Description of the Principal Places in the East Indies, China and Japan, with Their Produce, Manufactures, and Trade, Including the Coasting or Country Trade from Port to Port; Also the Rise and Progress of the Trade of the Various European Nations with the Eastern World, Particularly That of the English East India Company from the Discovery of the Passage Round Cape of Good Hope to the Present Period: With an Account of the Company's Establishments, Revenues, Debts, Assets, at Home and Abroad*. 2 vols. London: Black, Parry & Co., 1813.

Mills, L.A. *British Malaya, 1824-1867*. Kuala Lumpur: Oxford University Press, 1966.

Montero y Vidal, Jose. *Historia de la Pirateria Malayo Mahometano en Mindanao, Jolo y Borneo*. 2 vols. Madrid: Imprenta de M. Tello, 1888.

_____. *Historia General de Filipinas desde el descubrimiento de dichas Islas hasta nuestras dias*. 3 vols. Madrid: 1894-1895.

Moor, J.H., ed. *Notices of the Indian Archipelago and Adjacent Countries, Being a Collection of Papers Relating to Borneo, Celebes, Bali, Java, Sumatra,*

Nias, the Philippine Islands, Sulus, Siam, Cochin China, Malayan Peninsula. London: Cass, 1967 (first edition 1837).

Mouleon, Rafael. *Construccion Naveles: bajo un aspecto artestico por el restangador del Museo Naval, Catalogo descriptivo dos tomos*. 3 vols. Madrid, 1890.

Mundy, Rodney. *Narrative of Events in Borneo and Celebes down to the Occupation of Labuan, from the Journals of James Brook, esq., Together with a Narrative of the Operations of H.M.S. Iris by Capt. Rodney Mundy, R.N.* London: John Murray, 1848.

Nielson, Aage Krarup. *Mads Lange Til Bali*. Kobenhaven: Gyldendalske Bogforlag, Nordick Forlag, 1941.

Nimmo, Harra A. *The Sea People of Sulu: A Study of Social Change in the Philippines*. San Francisco: Chandler Publishing Co., 1972.

Olsen, Marvin, ed. *Power in Societies*. London: MacMillan, 1970.

Orosa, Sixto. *The Sulu Archipelago and Its People*. 2nd ed. Manila: New Mercury Printing Press, 1970.

Osborn, Sherard. *My Journal in Malayan Waters, or the Blockade of Quedah*. 3rd ed. London: Routledge, Warne & Routledge, 1861.

Owen, Norman G. *The Bikol Blend*. Quezon City: New Day Publishers, 1999.

_____. *Prosperity Without Progress: Manila Hemp and Material Life in the Colonial Philippines*. Berkeley: University of California Press, 1984.

Parrish, Cécile. *The Image of Asia in Children's Literature: 1814-1964*. Melbourne: Centre for Southeast Asian Studies, Monash University, 1977.

Parkinson, C. Northcote, ed. *Trade in the Eastern Seas, 1793-1813*. London: Cambridge University Press, 1937.

_____. *The Trade Winds: A Study of British Overseas Trade During the French Wars, 1793-1815*. London: George Allen & Unwin, 1948.

Patero, Santiago. *Sistema que conviene adopter para acabar con la pirateria que los mahometanos del Sultania de Jolo ejercen en el Archipielago Filipino por el capitan de la armada D. Santiago Paterno*. Madrid: Imprenta de Miguel Ginesta, 1872.

Pazos y Vela-Hidalgo, Pio A. de. *Jolo: Relato historico-militar desde descubrimiento por los Espanoles en 1578 a nuestros dias.* Burgos: Imprenta y esteotipia de Polo, 1879.

Perez, Elviro J. *Catalogo Bio-Bibliografico de las Religiosos Agustinos de la Provincia del Santisimo Nombre de Jesus de las Islas Filipinas desde su fundacion hasta nuestros dias.* Manila: Santo Tomas, 1901.

Phelan, John Leddy. *The Hispanization of the Philippines, Spanish Aims and Filipino Responses, 1562-1700.* Madison: University of Wisconsin Press, 1967.

Polanyi, Karl. Arensburg, Conrad M.; and Pearson, Harry W., eds. *Trade and Market in Early Empires.* Glencoe: The Free Press, 1957.

Polanyi, Karl. *Dahomey and the Slave Trade.* Seattle: University of Washington Press, 1966.

Pringle, Robert. *Rajahs and Rebels: The Ibans of Sarawak under Brooke Rule, 1841-1941.* Ithaca, N.Y.: Cornell University Press, 1970.

Quiason, Serafin D. *English "Country Trade" with the Philippines, 1644-1765.* Quezon City: University of the Philippines Press, 1966.

Raskin, Jonah. *The Mythology of Imperialism.* New York: Detta, 1971.

Reid, Anthony, ed. *The Last Stand of Autonomous States, 1750-1870 Responses to Modernity in the Diverse Worlds of Southeast Asia and Korea.* London: MacMillan 1997.

_____, *Southeast Asia in the Age of Commerce 1450-1680: Expansion and Crisis.* Vol. 2 New Haven: Yale University Press, 1993.

Renouard, Felix de Sainte-Croix. *Voyage Commercial et Politique aux Indes Orientales, aur Iles Philippenes, a la Chine, avec des nations Sur la Cochin chine et le Touquin, pendant les annees 1803, 1804, 1805, 1806 et 1807.* 3 vols. Paris: Clement, 1810.

Resink, G.J. *Indonesia's History Between the Myths: Essays in Legal and Historical Theory.* The Hague: Van Hoeve, 1968.

Reuk, Anthony de, and Knight, Julie, eds. *Caste and Race: Comparative Approaches.* London: J. & A. Churchill, 1967.

Robles, Eliodaro G. *The Philippines in the Nineteenth Century.* Quezon City: Malaya, 1969.

Ross, John Dill. *Sixty Years Life and Adventures in the Far East.* 2 vols. London: Hutchinsons, 1911.

Roth, Dennis, *The Friar Estates of the Philippines.* Albuquerque: University of New Mexico Press, 1977.

Ruibing, A.H. *Ethnologische studie betreffende de Indonesische Slavernij als Maatschappelijk verschijnsel.* Zutphen: W.J. Thieme & Co., 1937.

Rutter, Owen. *The Pirate Wind Tales of the Sea-Robbers of Malaya.* Singapore: Oxford University Press, 1986.

Said, Edward. *Orientalism.* London: Routledge and Kegan Paul, 1978.

Saleeby, Najeeb M. *Studies in Moro History, Law and Religion.* Dept. of the Interior, Ethnological Survey Publications. Vol. 4, pt. 1. Manila: Bureau of Public Printing, 1905.

Saleeby, Najeeb M. *The History of Sulu.* Manila: Filipiniana Book Guild, 1963.

Sandin, Benedict. *The Sea Dayaks of Borneo Before White Rajah Rule.* London: MacMillan, 1967.

Sather, Clifford. *The Bajau Laut Adaptation, History and Fate in a Maritime Fishing Society of South Eastern Sabah.* Kuala Lumpur: Oxford University Press, 1997.

Sears, Laurie, ed. *Autonomous Histories Particular Truths Essays in Honor of John Smail.* Madison: University of Wisconsin, Center for Southeast Asian Studies, 1993.

Service, Elman R. *Primitive Social Organization: An Evolutionary Perspective.* New York: Random House, 1962.

Sherry, Norman. *Conrad's Eastern Sea.* Cambridge: Cambridge University Press, 1966.

Singh, S.B. *European Agency Houses in Bengal, 1783-1833.* Calcutta: K. L. Mukhopadhyay, 1966.

Sonnerat, Pierre. *An Account of a Voyage to the Spice Islands, and New Guinea.* Paris: Bury St. Edmunds, Green, 1781.

——————. *A Voyage to the East Indies and China Performed by Order of Lewis XV between the Years 1774 and 1781.* Trans. Francis Magnus. Calcutta: Stuart & Cooper, 1788.

Sopher, David E. *The Sea Nomads: A Study Based on the Literature of the Maritime Boat People of Southeast Asia.* Memoir of the National Museum, No. 5. Singapore, 1965.

Sotoca, Maria Carmen Garcia. *Expedicion de Malespina: Catalogo de Grabados de la expedicion de Malespina.* Madrid, 1966.

Southon, Michael. *The Navel of the Perahu: Meaning and Values in the Maritime Trading Economy of a Butonese Village.* Canberra: Research School of Pacific and Asian Studies, 1995.

Spoehr, Alexander. *Zamboanga and Sulu: An Archeological Approach to Ethnic Diversity.* Ethnology Monograph No. 1., Dept. of Anthropology, University of Pittsburgh, Pittsburgh, 1973.

Stallybrass, Peter and Alan White. *The Politics and Poetics of Transgression,* London: Methuen, 1986.

Stapel, F.W., ed. *Corpus Diplomaticum Neerlands-Indicum.* Vol. 6. The Hague: Martinus Nijhoff, 1955.

Steinberg, David J., ed. *In Search of Southeast Asia: A Modern History.* New York: Praeger, 1971.

St. John, Horace. *The Indian Archipelago: Its History and Present State.* 2 vols. London: Longman, Brown, Green & Longman, 1853.

St. John, Spenser. *Life in the Forests of the Far East.* 2 vols. London: Smith Elder & Co., 1862.

Tarling, Nicholas. *Britain, the Brookes and Brunei.* London: Oxford University Press, 1971.

―――――――. *The Burthen, the Risk and the Glory: A Biography of Sir James Brooke.* Kuala Lumpur: Oxford University Press, 1982.

―――――――. *Piracy and Politics in the Malay World: A Study of British Imperialism in Nineteenth-Century Southeast Asia.* Singapore: Donald Moore, 1963.

―――――――. *Sulu and Sabah: A Study of British Policy Towards the Philippines and North Borneo from the Late Eighteenth Century.* Kuala Lumpur: Oxford University Press, 1978.

Tobing, Ph.O.L. *Hukum Pelajaran dan Perdagangan Ammana Gappa.* Jajasan Kebudajaan Sulawesi Selatan dan Tenggara. Makassar, 1961.

Travel Accounts of the Islands 1513-1787, by Tomes Pires, Pedro Ordenez de Cevallos, Francois Pyrard, Josis van Speilbergen, Pedro Cubero Sebastion, William Dampier, Alexander Dalrymple, Pierre de Pages, Captain Crozet, Guillaume Raynal, Thomas Forrest and De la Perouse. Manila: Filipiniana Book Guild, 1971.

Tregonning, K.G. *A History of Modern Sabah, 1881-1963.* Singapore: University of Malaya Press, 1965.

Tripathi, Amales. *Trade and Finance in the Bengal Presidency, 1793-1833.* Calcutta: Orient Longmans, 1956.

Trocki, Carl A. *Prince of Pirates: The Temenggongs and the Development of*

Johor and Singapore, 1784-1885. Singapore: Singapore University Press, 1977.

Van Leur, J.C. *Indonesian Trade and Society*. The Hague: Van Hoeve, 1967.

Veth, P.J. *Borneo's Wester-Afdeeling, Geographisch, Statistisch, Historisch, voorafgegaan door eene algemeene schets des ganschen eilands*. 2 vols. Norman, Zaltbommel, 1854-1856.

Wallace, Alfred Russel. *The Malay Archipelago: The Land of the Orang-Utan, and the Bird of Paradise. A Narrative of Travel with Studies of Man and Nature*. 2 vols. London: MacMillan, 1869.

Wallerstein, Immanuel. *The Modern World System: Capitalist Agriculture and the Origins of the European World Economy in the Sixteenth Century*. New York: Academic Press, 1974.

Warren, James Francis. *At the Edge of Southeast Asian History*. Quezon City: New Day Publishers, 1987.

_____. *The North Borneo Chartered Company's Administration of the Bajau, 1878-1909*. Papers in International Studies, Southeast Asia Series, no. 22. Athens, Ohio: Ohio University Center for International Studies, 1971.

_____. *The Sulu Zone 1768-1898*. Singapore: Singapore University Press, 1981.

_____. *The Sulu Zone the World Capitalist Economy and the Historical Imagination*. Amsterdam: VU University Press/CASA, 1998.

Wernstedt, Frederick L., and Spencer, J.E. *The Philippine Island World: A Physical, Cultural and Regional Geography*. Berkeley: University of California Press, 1967.

Wertheim W.F. *Indonesian Society in Transition: A Study of Social Change*. The Hague: Van Hoeve, 1959.

Wickberg, Edgar.*The Chinese in Philippine Life, 1850-1898*. New Haven and London: Yale University Press, 1965.

Wolf, Eric R. *Europe and the People Without History*. Berkeley: University of California Press, 1982.

Wolters, O.W. *The Fall of Srivijaya in Malay History*. Ithaca, N.Y.: Cornell University Press, 1970.

Woodward, David *The Narrative of Captain David Woodward and Four Seamen*. London: Dawsons, 1969.

Worcester, Dean C. *The Philippine Islands and Their People.* New York: MacMillan, 1898.
Wright, Leigh R. *The Origins of British Borneo.* Hong Kong: Hong Kong University Press, 1970.
Wrigley, E.A. *Population and History.* London: Weidenfeld & Nicolson, 1969.
Wu, C.L. *A Study of References to the Philippines in Chinese Sources from Earliest Times to the Ming Dynasty.* Quezon City: University of the Philippines, 1959.
Young, Gavin. *In Search of Conrad.* London: Penguin, 1991.
Yvan, Melchior. *Six Months Among the Malays and a Year in China.* London: James Blackwood, 1855.
Zuniga, Joachim Martinez de. *Estadismo de las Filipinas; a mis viajez por este pais.* 2 vols. Madrid: M. Minuesa de los Rios, 1893.

Articles

Abdul Latif bin Haji Ibrahim. "Padian, Its Market and the Women Vendors." *The Brunei Museum Journal* 2, no. 1 (1970): 39-51.
"Adventures of C. Z. Pieters among the Pirates of Maguindanao," *Journal of the Indian Archipelago and Eastern Asia* (1858), 301-312.
Aguilar, Filomeno V. "The Triumph of Industrial Citizenship? Migrations, Identities and the Nation–State in Southeast Asia," in *Asian Studies Review*, vol. 23, no. 3 (1999): 307-336.
Andre, E.M. "Slavery and Polygamy in the Sulu Archipelago," *The Independent*, 3220-222.
Appel, G.N. "Ethnographic Notes on the Iranun-Maranao (Illanun) of Sabah," *Sabah Society Journal* 5, no. 2 (1970): 77-82.
_____. "Social and Medical Anthropology of Sabah: Retrospect and Prospect," *Sabah Society Journal* 3, no. 7 (1968): 246-266.
_____. "Studies of the Tausug (Suluk) and Samal-Speaking Populations of Sabah and the Southern Philippines," *Borneo Research Bulletin* 1, no. 2 (1969): 21-22.
Asri J. Abubakar. "Muslim Philippines, With Reference to the Sulus, Muslim-Christian Contradictions, and the Mindanao Crisis," *Asian Studies* II, no. 1 (1973): 112-27.

Baradas, David. "Some Implications of the Okir, Motif in Lanao and Sulu Art," *Asian Studies* 6, no. 2 (1968): 129-168.

Barth, Frederick. "Ecologic Relationships of Ethnic Groups in Swat, North Pakistan," *American Anthropologist* 56 (1956): 1079-189.

Basset, D.K. "British Commercial and Strategic Interests in the Malay Peninsula During the late Eighteenth Century," in *Malayan and Indonesian Studies*, ed. J. Eastin and R. Roolvink. London: Oxford University Press, 1964.

Benda, Harry J. "The Structure of Southeast Asian History: Some Preliminary Observations," *Journal of Southeast Asian History*, 3, no. 1 (1962): 106-38.

"Berigten omtrent den Zeeroof in den Nederlandsch-lndischen Archipel, 1857," *Tijdschrift voor Indische Taal-, Land-en Volkenkunde, uitgegeven door her (Koninklijk) Bataviaasch Genootschap van Kunsten en Wetenschappen* 20 (1873): 302-326.

"Berigten omtrent den Zeeroof in den Nederlandsch-lndischen Archipel, 1857," *Tijdschrift voor Indische Taal-, Land-en Volkenkunde, uitgegeven door her (Koninklijk) Baraviaasch Genootschap van Kunsten en Wetenschappen* 18 (1868-1872): 435-457.

Black, I.D. "The Political Situation in Sabah on the Eve of Chartered Company Rule," *Borneo Research Bulletin* 3, no. 2 (1971): 62-65.

Blummentritt, Ferdinand. "Los Moros del Filipinas," *Boletin de la Sociedad geografica de Madrid* 23 (1892): 106-112.

Brassey, Lord. "North Borneo," *Nineteenth Century* (1887): 248-256.

Brown, D.E. "Brunei and the Bajau," *Borneo Research Bulletin* 3, no. 2 (1971): 55-58.

Butcher, John. "Recent Research in Southeast Asian History, and Another Look at the Question of Perspective," *Time Remembered* 2 (1978): 57-68.

Campbell, Capt. John F. "Pepper, Pirates and Grapeshot," in *American Neptune* 21, no. 4 (1961): 292-302.

Casino, Eric. "Jama Mapun Ethnoecology," *Asian Studies* 5 (1967): 1-32.

_____. "Some Notes on Sociopolitical Change among the Jama Mapun," *Borneo Research Bulletin* 3, no. 2 (1971): 65-66.

Cheong, W.E. "Changing the Rules of the Game (The India–Manila

Trade: 1785-1809)," *Journal of Southeast Asian Studies* 1, no. 2 (1970): 1-19.

Concas y Palau, Victor M. "Conferencia sobre las relaciones de Espana con Jolo," *Boletin de la Sociedad geografica de Madrid* 16 (1884): 400-24.

_____. "Nuestras relaciones con Jolo." Discurso pronunciado en la *geografica de Madrid* 16 (1884): 153-82.

_____. "Nuestras relaciones con Jolo." Discurso pronunciado en la Sociedad geografica en 12 de Febrero de 1884," *Revista General de Marina* 16 (1885): 55-70 (1885): 199-213.

_____. "Ocupacion de Tataan en la Isla de Taui-Taui," *Boletin de la Sociedad geografica de Madrid* 16 (1883): 307-310.

Curtin, Philip. "Field Techniques for Collecting and Processing Oral Data," *Journal of African History* 9, no. 3 (1968): 367-385.

Cullinane, Michael and Peter Xenos. "The Growth of Population in Cebu during the Spanish Era: Constructing a Regional Demography from Local Sources," in *Population and History The Demographic Origins of the Modern Philippines*, ed. Daniel Doeppers and Peter Xenos. Madison: University of Wisconsin, Center for Southeast Asian Studies, 1998, 71-138.

Dalrymple, Alexander. "Account of Some Natural Curiosities at Sooloo," in *An Historical Collection of the Several Voyages and Discoveries in the South Pacific Ocean*, vol. I. London, 1770.

Dalton, George. "Economic Anthropology," *American Behavioral Scientist* 20, no. 5 (1977): 635-56.

_____. "Karl Polanyi's Analysis of Long Distance Trade and His Wider Paradigm," in *Ancient Civilizations and Trade*, ed. J.A. Sabloff and C.C. Lamberg-Karlovsky, Albuquerque: University of New Mexico Press, n.d.

Dalton, J. "Makassar, The Advantages of Making It a Free Port," in *Notices of the Indian Archipelago and Adjacent Countries*, ed. J.H. Moor. London: Cass, 1967.

_____. "On the Present State of Piracy, amongst These Islands, and the Best Method of Its Suppression," in *Notices of the Indian Archipelago and Adjacent Countries*, ed. J.H. Moor. London: Cass, 1967.

_____. "Remarks on the Bugis Campong Semerindan," in

Notices of the Indian Archipelago and Adjacent Countries, ed. J.H. Moor. London: Cass, 1967.

_____. "Remarks on the Exports of Coti," in Notices of the Indian Archipelago and Adjacent Countries, ed. J.H. Moor. London: Cass, 1967.

Damsani, Maduh, Alawi Efren and Gerard Rixhon, "Four Folk Narratives from Mullung, a Tausug Storyteller," Sulu Sludies 1 (1972): 191-255.

Dery, Luis Camara. "Bikol History in Bikol Folklore: Documentary Evidence of five Bikol Oral Traditions," in Tracing from Solsogon to Sorsogon, ed. Reynaldo T. Jamoralin, Sorsogon: Sorsogon Arts Council, Inc. 1994.

Elkins, Stanley. "Slavery and Its Aftermath in the Western World," in Caste and Race: Comparative Approaches, ed. Anthony de Reuck and Julie Knight. London: J. and A. Churchill, 1967.

Falconer, John. "The Eastern Seas," in Pirates Terror on the High Seas from the Caribbean to the South China Sea," ed. David Cordingly. Atlanta: Turner Publishing, 1996, 188-211.

Frake, Charles O. "Abu Sayyaf Displays of Violence and the Proliferation of Contested Identities Among Philippine Muslims," in American Anthropoligist 100, No. 1 (1998): 41-54.

_____. "Cultural Ecology and Ethnography," American Anthropologist 63 (1962): 113-132.

_____. "The Eastern Subanun of Mindanao," in Social Structure of Southeast Asia, ed. G.P. Murdock. Viking Fund Publications in Anthropology No. 29. New York, 1960.

_____. "The Genesis of Kinds of People in the Sulu Archipelago," in Language and Cultural Description Stanford: Stanford University Press, 1980, 314-318.

_____. "Struck by Speech," in Law in Culture and Society, Chicago: L. Nader, 1969.

Fried, Morton H. "On the Evolution of Social Stratification and the State," in Culture in History, ed. S. Diamond. New York: Columbia University Press, 1960.

Garin y Sociats, Arturo. "Memoria sobre el Archipielago de Jolo," Boletin del la Sociedad geografica de Madrid 10 (1881): 110-133, 161-197.

Geoghegan, William. "Balangingi Samal," in Ethnic Groups of Insular

Southeast Asia, vol. 2, ed. Frank M. Le Bar. New Haven: Human Relations Area Files Press, forthcoming.

Hageman, J. "Aanteekeningen omtrent een gedeelte der Oostkust van Borneo," *Tijdschrift voor Indische Taal-, Land-en Volkenkunde, uitgegeven door het (Koninklijk) Bataviaasch Genootschap van Kunsten en Wetenschapen* 4 (1855): 71-106.

Harraway, Donna. "Situated Knowledges: The Science Question in Feminism and the Privilege of Partial Perspective," in *Simians, Cyborgs and Women: The Reinvention of Nature* New York: Routledge, 1991.

Harrison, Barbara. "Bird Caves of Idahan," *The Straits Times Annual* (1969), 91-94.

Harrison, Tom. "The Rennell Manuscript in the Brunei Museum," *Brunei Museum Journal* I (1969): 157-165.

_____. "The Unpublished Rennell Ms. A Borneo Philippine Journey, 1762-1763," *Journal Malaysian Branch, Royal Asiatic Society* 39, pt. 1 (1966): 92-136.

Heidhues Somers, Mary F. *Bangka Tin and Mentok Pepper: Chinese Settlement on an Indonesian Island* (Singapore: Institute Southeast Asian Studies, 1992).

Heersink, Christiaan. "Environmental Adaptations in Southern Sulawesi," in *Environmental Challenges in South-East Asia*, ed. Victor T. King. London: Curzon, 1988, 95-120.

Horsfield, Thomas. "Report on the Island of Banka," *Journal of the Indian Archipelago and Eastern Asia* 2 (1848): 299-336, 373-427, 705-25, 779-824.

Hunt, J. "Sketch of Borneo or Pulo Kalamantan, Communicated by J. Hunt Esq. in 1812 to the Honorable Sir T.S. Raffles, Late Lieut. Governor of Java," in *Notices of the Indian Archipelago and Adjacent Countries*, ed. J.H. Moor. London: Cass, 1967.

_____. "Sketch of Borneo or Sulo Kalamantan. Communicated by J. Hunt Esq. in 1812, to the Honorable Sir T. S. Raffles, Late Lieut. Governor of Java," in *Notices of the Indian Archipelago and Adjacent Countries*, ed. J.H. Moor, London: Cass, 1967.

_____. "Some Particulars Relating to Sulo in the Archipelago of Felicia,' in *Notices of the Indian Archipelago and Adjacent Countries*, ed. J.H. Moor. London: Cass, 1967.

Jansen, A.J.F. "Aanteekeningen omtrent Sollok en de Solloksche

Zeeroovers," *Tijdschrift voor Indische Taal-, Land-en Volkenkunde, uitgegeven door het (Koninklijk) Bataviaasch Geenootschap van Kunsten en Wetenschapen* 7 (1858): 212-39.

Keesing, Roger. "Asian Cultures?" in *Asian Studies Review* 15, no. 2 (1991): 43-50.

Kiefer, T.M. "Institutionalized Friendship and Warfare among the Tausug of Jolo" *Ethnology* 7 (1968): 225-44.

_____. "Modes of Social Action in Armed Combat: Affect, Tradition, and Reason in Tausug Private Warfare," *Journal of the Royal Anthropological Institute* 5 (1970): 586-96.

_____. "Parrang Sabbil: Ritual Suicide among the Tausug of Jolo," *Bidjdragen Tot de Taal, Land-en Volkenkunde* 129 (1973): 108-23.

_____. "Power, Politics and Guns in Jolo: The Influence of Modern Weapons on Tausug Legal and Economic Institutions," *Philippine Sociological Review* 15 (1967): 21-29.

_____. "Reciprocity and Revenge in the Philippines: Some Preliminary Remarks about the Tausug of Jolo," *Philippine Sociological Review*, 16 (1968): 124-31.

_____. "The Sultanate of Sulu: Problems in the Analysis of a Segmentary State," *Borneo Research Bulletin* 3, no. 2 (1971): 46-51.

_____. "The Tausug Polity and the Sultanate of Sulu: A Segmentary State in the Southern Philippines," *Sulu Studies* 1 (1972): 19-64.

Kottak, Conrad P. "Ecological Variables in the Origin and Evolution of African States: The Buganda Example," *Comparative Studies in Society and History* 14, no. 31 (1972): 351-80.

Kuder, Edward M. "The Moros in the Philippines," *Far Eastern Quarterly* 4, no. 2 (1945): 119-26.

Laarhoven, Ruurdje. "Lords of the Great River: The Maguindanao Port and Polity During the Seventeenth Century," in *The Southeast Asia Port and Polity Rise and Demise*, ed. J.K. Kathirithamby-Wells and John Villiers. Singapore: Singapore University Press, 1990, 161-86.

Lapian, Adrian B. "The Sealords of Berau and Mindanao: Two Responses to the Colonial Challenge," *Masyarakat Indonesia* 1, no. 2 (1974): 143-54.

Larkin, John. "The Place of Local History in Philippine Historiography," *Journal of Southeast Asian History* 8, no. 2 (1977): 306-17.

Leach, E.R. "Caste, Class and Slavery: The Taxonomic Problem," in *Caste and Race: Comparative Approaches*, ed. Anthony de Reuck and Julie Knight. London: J. and A. Churchill, 1967.
_____. "The Frontiers of Burma," *Comparative Studies in Society and History* 3 (1962): 48-67.
Lehman, F.K. "Ethnic Categories in Burma and the Theory of Social Systems," in *Southeast Asian Tribes, Minorities and Nations*, vol. 1, ed. P. Keinstader. Princeton: Princeton University Press, 1967.
Lenski, Gerhard E. "The Dynamics of Distributive Systems," in *Power in Societies*, ed. Marvin Olsen. London: MacMillan, 1970.
Lewis, Diane. "Growth of the Country Trade to the Straits of Malacca, 1760-1777," *Journal of the Malaysian Branch, Royal Asiatic Society* 47, no. 2 (1970): 1 14-30.
Leyden, Dr. "Sketch of Borneo," in *Notices of the Indian Archipelago and Adjacent Countries*, ed. J.H. Moor. London: Cass, 1967.
Linz, Juan J. "Five Centuries of Spanish History: Quantification and Comparison," in *The Dimensions of the Past: Materials, Problems and Opportunities for Quantitative Work in History*, ed. Val R. Lorwin and Jacob M. Price. New Haven: Yale University Press, 1972.
McKenna, Thomas, M. "The Defiant Periphery: Routes of Iranun Resistance in the Philippines," *Social Analysis* Vol. 35 (1994): 11-27.
Macknight, C.C. "The Nature of Early Maritime Trade: Some Points of Analogy from the Eastern Part of the Indonesian Archipelago," *World Archeology* 5, no. 2 (1973): 198-208.
Majul, Cesar A. "Chinese Relationships with the Sultanate of Sulu," in *The Chinese in the Philippines, 1570-1770*, ed. Alfonso Felix. Manila: Solidaridad Publishing House, 1966.
_____. "Islamic Influence in the Southern Philippines," *Journal of Sourheast Asian History* 7 (1976): 61-73.
_____. "Political and Historical Notes on the Old Sulu Sultanate," *Journal of the Malaysian Branch, Royal Asiatic Society* 36, pt. 1 (1965): 23-43.
_____. "The Role of Islam in the History of the Filipino People," *Asian Studies* 4 (1966): 303-15.
_____. "Succession in the Old Sulu Sultanate," *Philippine Historical Review* 1 (1965): 252-71.

Mallari, Francisco S.J. "Camarines Towns: Defenses Against Moro Pirates," *Philippine Quarterly of Culture and Society* 17, no. 1 (1989): 41-66.

_____. "The Maritime Response, 1793-1818," in *Philippine Studies*, vol. 34, (1986): 4-96.

_____. "Muslim Raids in Bicol, 1580-1792" in *Philippine Studies*, vol. 34 (1986): 257-86.

_____. "Peñaranda and the Bicol Defense System," in *Kinaadman* 14, no. 2 (1992): 105-22.

Medhurst, W. "British North Borneo," *Royal Colonial Institute* 16 (1884/85): 273-307.

Medina, Isagani R. "American Logbooks and Journals in Salem, Massachusetts on the Philippines, 1796-1897," *Asian Studies* 11, no. 1 (1973): 179-98.

Mednick, Melvin. "Some Problems of Moro History and Political Organization," *Philippine Sociological Review* 5 (1957): 39-52.

Moerman, M. "Accomplishing Ethnicity," in *Ethnomethodology*, ed. R. Turner. London: Penguin Books, 1974.

_____. "Who are the Lue?," *American Anthropologist* 67 (1965): 1215-230.

Montano, J. "Une Mission aux Iles Malaise," *Societe Geographic Bulletin* (1881), 465-83.

Montero y Gay, Claudio. "Conferencias sobre las Filipinas, pronunciados en 3 de Junie y 7 de Octubre de 1876," *Boletin de Sociedad geografica de Madrid* 1 (1876): 297-338.

Needham, Rodney. "Penan," in *Ethnic Groups of Insular Southeast Asia*, vol. 1, ed. Frank le Bar. New Haven: Human Relations Area Files Press, 1972.

Newbold, T. J. "Outline of Political Relations with the Native States on the Eastern and Western Coasts, Malayan Peninsular," in *Notices of the Indian Archipelago and Adjacent Countries*, ed. J.H. Moor. London: Cass, 1967.

Nimmo, Harry A. "Reflections on Badjau History," *Philippine Studies* 17 (1966): 32-59.

_____. "The Sea Nomads: Description and Analysis," *Philippine Studies* 15 (1967): 209-12.

_____. "Social Organization of the Tawi-Tawi Badjau,"

Ethnology 4 (1965): 421-47.

Nordholt, Henke Schulte, "The Mads Lange Connection," *Indonesia* 32, (1981): 14-48.

Phillips, James Duncan. "The Attack on the Marquis," in *American Neptune* 9, no. 4 (1949): 239-48.

Prentice, D. J. "The Linguistic Situation in Northern Borneo," in *Pacific Linguistic Studies in Honour of Arthur Capell*, ed. S.A. Wurm and D.C. Laycock. Pacific Linguistics. Canberra: Australian National University, 1970.

Pryer, William. "Diary of a Trip up the Kinabatangan," *Sabah Society Journal* 5, no. 2 (1970): 117-26.

_____. "Notes on Northeastern Borneo and the Sulu Islands," *Royal Geographical Society Proceedings* 5 (1883): 90-96.

_____. "On the Natives of North Borneo," *Royal Anthropological Institute of Great Britain and Ireland* 16 (1887): 230-36.

Reed, Robert T. "The Primate City in Southeast Asia: Conceptual Definitions and Colonial Origins," *Asian Studies* 10, no. 3 (1972): 283-321.

Rejeb, Lofti Ben. "Barbary's Character in European Letters, 1514–1830: An Ideological Prelude to Colonisation," *Dialectical Anthropology.* 6 (1982): 345-55.

Resink, G.J. "De Archipel voor Joseph Conrad," *Bijdragen tot de Taal- Land- en Volkenkunde* 115, pt. 11 (1959): 192-208.

_____. "The Eastern Archipelago Under Joseph Conrad's Western Eyes," in *Indonesia's History Between the Myths*, ed. G.J. Resink. The Hague: Van Hoeve, 1968.

Rixhon, Gerard. "Coordinated Investigation of Sulu Culture, Jolo, Sulu," *Borneo Research Bulletin* 5, no. 1 (1973): 19-21.

_____. "Mullung: A Taosug Storyteller," *Sulu Studies* 1 (1972): 172-90.

_____. "Ten Years of Research in Sulu, 1961-1971," *Sulu Studies* 1 (1972): 1-17.

Sather, Clifford. "Social Rank and Marriage Payments in an Immigrant Moro Community in Malaysia," *Ethnology* 6 (1967): 97-102.

_____. "Sulu's Political Jurisdiction over the Bajau Laut," *Borneo Research Bulletin* 3, no. 2 (1971): 58-62.

_____. "Tidong," in *Ethnic Groups of Insular Southeast Asia*, vol. 1, ed. Frank le Bar. New Haven: Human Relations Area Files Press, 1972.

_____, ed. "Traditional States of Borneo and the Southern Philippines," *Borneo Research Bulletin* 3, no. 2 (1971): 45-46.

Schlegel, Stuart. "Tiruray-Maguindanaon Ethnic Relations: An Ethnohistorical Puzzle," *Solidarity* 7, no. 4 (1972): 25-30.

Scott, James. "The Erosion of Patron-Client Bonds and Social Change in Rural Southeast Asia," *Journal of Asian Studies* 32, no. 1 (1972): 5-39.

_____. "The State and People who Move Around," in *International Institute Asian Studies Newsletter* 19, no. 3 (1999): 3, 45.

Shineberg, Dorothy. "The Sandalwood Trade in Melanesian Economics, 1841-1865," *Journal of Pacific History* 1 (1966): 129-46.

"Short accounts of Timor, Rotti, Savu, Solor," in *Notices of the Indian Archipelago and Adjacent Countries*, ed. J. H. Moor. London: Cass, 1967.

Singh, Ranjit D.S. "Brunei and the Hinterland of Sabah: Commercial and Economic Relations with Special Reference to the Second half of the Nineteenth Century," in *The Southeast Asian Port and Polity Rise and Demise*, ed. J. Kathiritamby-Wells and John Villiers. Singapore: Singapore University Press, 1990, 231-45.

Skertchly, Ethelbert Forbes. "Cagayan Sulu: Its Customs, Legends and Superstitions," *Asiatic Society of Bengal Journal* 65, pt. 3: 47-53.

Smail, John. "On the Possibility of an Autonomous History of Modern Southeast Asia," *Journal of Southeast Asian History* 2, no. 2 (1971): 72-102.

Soeri Soerato. "Tindjuan Singkat Tentang Pertumbuhan Badjak Laut Sulu,' *Buletin Sastra Universitas Gajah Mada* 1 (1970): 97-117.

Spoehr, Alexander. "An Archeological Approach to Ethnic Diversity in Zamboanga and Sulu," *Sulu Studies* 2 (1973): 95-101.

Stone, Richard L. "Intergroup Relations among the Tausogs, Samal, and Badjaw of Sulu," *Philippine Sociological Review* 10 (1962): 107-33.

St. John, Spenser. "Piracy in the Indian Archipelago," *Journal of the Indian Archipelago and Eastern Asia* 3 (1849): 251-60.

St. John Hart, E. "The Strange Story of a Little Ship," *The Wide World Magazine* (1906), 347-54.

"Sulu," *The Journal of the Indian Archipelago and Eastern Asia* 3, no. 7 (1849): 412.

Tarling, Nicholas. "British Policy in Malayan Waters in the 19th

Century," in *Papers on Malayan History*, ed. K.G. Tregonning. Singapore, 1962.

_____. "Consul Farren and the Philippines," *Journal of the Malaysian Branch, Royal Asiatic Society* 38, pt. 2 (1966): 258-73.

_____. "The Entrepot at Labuan and the Chinese." Reprinted from *Studies in the Social History of China and Southeast Asia*, ed. J. Chen and N. Tarling. London: Cambridge University Press, 1970, in *Sabah Society Journal* 5, no. 2 (1970): 101-16.

Terray, Emmanuel, "Long-Distance Exchange and the Formation of the State: The Case of the Abron Kingdom of Gyaman." *Economy and Society* 3 (1974): 315-45.

"The Piracy and Slave Trade of the Indian Archipelago," *Journal of the Indian Archipelago and Eastern Asia* 3 (1849): 581-88, 629, 636; 4 (1850): 45-52, 144, 162, 400-10, 617-28, 734-46; 5 (1851): 374-82.

Tilly, Charles. "Quantification in History, as Seen from France," in *The Dimensions of the Past: Materials, Problems, and Opportunities for Quantitative Work in History*, ed. Val R. Lorwin and Jacob M. Price. New Haven: Yale University Press, 1972.

Treacher, William. "Sketches of Brunei, Sarawak, Labuan and North Borneo," *Journal of the Straits Branch, Royal Asiatic Society* 20 (1889): 13-74; 21 (1890): 19-122.

Valera, J. "The Old Forts of Semporna," *Sabah Society Journal* I, no. 2 (1972): 40-41.

Van Capellan. "Berigt Aangaande den togt van Z.M. Schoener Egmond naar Berow, op de Oostkust van Borneo, in het najaar 1844," in *Bijdragen tot Kennis der Nederlandsche en vreemde Kolonien betrekklijk der vrijlating der slaven, 1844-1847*. Utrecht: Vanderpost, 1844-1847.

Van Dewall, H. "Aanteekeningen omtrent de Noordoostkust van Borneo," *Tijdschrift voor Indische Taal-, Land-en Volkenkunde, uitgegeven door het (Koninklijk) Bataviaasch Kunsten en Wetenschappen* 4 (1885): 423-58.

Van Hoevell, W.R. "Laboean, Serawak, de Noord-oostkust van Borneo en de Sulthan van Soeloe," *Tijdschrift voor Nederlandsche Indie* 11, pt. 1 (1849): 66-83.

Van Hoevell, W.R. "De Zeerooverijen der Soeloerezen," *Tijdschrift voor Nederlandsche Indie* 2 (1850): 99-105.

Van Marle, A. "De Rol van de Buitenlandse Avonturier," *Bijdragen en*

Mededelingen Betreffende de Geschiedenis Der Nederlanden 86, pt. 1 (1971): 32-39.

Van Sina, Jan. "Once Upon a Time: Oral Traditions as History in Africa," *Daedalus* (1971), 442-68.

Van Verschuer, F.H. "De Badjoo," *Nederlandsch Aadrijksckundig Genootschap* 7 (1883): 1-7.

Velthoen, Esther. "Armed Bands and Protection Rackets: 'Gangster' Politics in Eastern Sulawesi, 1700-1850," at the Conference, 'The Last Stand of Autonomous States in Southeast Asia and Korea, 1750-1870. Bali, 19-21 August 1994.

_____. "Wanderers, Robbers and Bad Folk: The Politics of Violence, Protection and Trade in Eastern Indonesia 1750-1870," *The Last Stand of Autonomous States, 1750-1870 Responses to Modernity in the Diverse Worlds of Southeast Asia and Korea*, ed. Anthony Reid, Houndmills: Macmillan, 1997, 367-88.

Vidrovitch, C. Coquery. "An African Mode of Production," *Critique of Anthropology* 4 (1975): 37-71.

Warren, James Francis. "Balambangan and the Rise of the Sulu Sultanate, 1772-1775," *Journal of the Malaysian Branch, Royal Asiatic Society* 50, pt. 1 (1977): 73-93.

_____. "Explorings and Reflections on Southeast Asian History," *Our Cultural Heritage*, ed. John Bigelow, Canberra: The Australian Academy of Humanities, 1998, 183-99.

_____. "Joseph Conrad's Fiction as Southeast Asian History: Trade and Politics in East Borneo in the Late Nineteenth Century," *The Brunei Museum Journal* (1977*)*, 21-34.

_____. "Looking Back on The Sulu Zone: State Formation, Slave Raiding and Ethnic Diversity in Southeast Asia," *Journal of Malaysian Branch of Royal Asiatic Society* 64, pt. 1 (1966): 21-33.

_____. "Sino-Sulu Trade in the Late Eighteenth and Nineteenth Centuries," *Philippine Studies* 25 (1977): 50-79.

_____. "Slave Markets and Exchange in the Malay World: The Sulu Sultanate, 1770-1878," *Journal of Southeast Asian Studies* 8, no. 2 (1977): 112-75.

_____. "Slavery in Southeast Asia," in *A Historical Guide to*

World Slavery, ed. Seymour Drescher and Stanley Engermann. New York: Oxford University Press, 1998, 80-87.

_____. "The Sulu Zone: Commerce and the Evolution of a Multi-Ethnic Polity, 1768-1898," *Archipel* 18 (1979): 223-29.

_____. "Who were the Balangingi Samal? Slave Raiding and Ethnogenesis in Nineteenth Century Sulu," *Journal of Asian Studies* 37, no. 3 (1978): 477-90.

Wendover, R.F. "The Balangingi Pirates," *Philippine Magazine* 38, no. 8 (1941): 323-38.

Wheatley, Paul. "Satjantra in Suvarnadvipa from Reciprocity to Redistribution in Ancient Southeast Asia," in *Ancient Civilisations and Trade*, ed. J.A. Sabloff and C.C. Lamberg Karlovsky. Albuquerque: University of New Mexico Press, 1975, 227-83.

Wickberg, Edgar. "Spanish Records in the Philippine National Archives," *Archivinia* 1, no. 1 (1968): 15-20, 30.

Windsor, G.E. "The Trading Ports of the Indian Archipelago," *Journal of the Indian Archipelago and Eastern Asia* 2 (1850): 283-51, 380-99, 483-93, 530-51.

Wong Lin Ken. "The Trade of Singapore, 1819-1869," *Journal Malaysian Branch Royal Asiatic Society* 33, pt. 4 (1960): 1-315.

Wortmann, J.R. "The Sultanate of Kutai, Kalimantan-Timur: A Sketch of the Traditional Political Structure," *Borneo Research Bulletin* 3, no. 2 (1971): 51-55.

Wright, Leigh. "The Lanun Pirate States of Borneo: Their Relevance to Southeast Asian History," Conference on Southeast Asian Studies, Kota Kinabalu, 22-26 November 1977.

Wulf, J. "Features of Yakan Culture," *Folk* 6 (1964): 52-72.

Bibliographical and Archival Guides

Guia de los Archives De Madrid: prologo del tenor D. Francisco Sintes y Obrador. Madrid: Direccion, General de Archives y Bibliotecas Servicio De Publicaciones del Ministerio de Educacion Nacional, 1952.

Jaquet, F.G.P. *Gids van in Nederland aanivezige Bronnen betreffende de geschiedenis van Asie en Oceanie, 1796-1949*; Vols. I-VII. Leiden: Konink-Lyk Instituut voor Taal-, Land-en Volkenkunde, 1968-1973.

Jaquet, F.G.P. 'Dutch Archive Material Relating to the History of Asia, 1769-1949,' *Southeast Asian Archives* 8 (1975): 10-36.

Lanzas Torres, Pedro. *Relacion Descriptivo de los Mapos, Planos, etc. de Filipinas existentes en Archivo de Indias.* Madrid, 1897.

Medina, Isagani. *Filipiniana Materials in the National Library.* Quezon City: University of the Philippines Press, 1972.

Retana, Wenceslao Emilio. *Aparato Bibliografico de la Historia General de Filipinos.* 3 vols. Madrid, 1906.

_____. *Bibliografia de Mindanao.* Madrid: Viuda de M. Minuesa de los Rios, 1894.

Robertson, James Alexander. *Bibliography of the Philippine Islands; Printed and Manuscript; Preceded by a Descriptive Account of the Most Important Archives and Collections Containing Philipiniana.* Cleveland, Ohio: Arthur H. Clark Co., 1908.

Sanchez Belda, Luis. *Guia del Archivo Historico Nacional,* Madrid, 1958.

Tello Leon, Pilar. *Mapos, Planos, y Dibujos de la Seccion de Estado del Archivo Historico Nacional.* Madrid: Direccion General de Archivos y Bibliotecas, 1969.

Tiamson, Aldfredo T. *Mindanao-Sulu Bibliography containing Published, Unpublished Manuscripts and Works in-Progress, A Preliminary Survey.* Davao City: Ateneo de Davao, 1970.

Van Der Chijs, J.A. *Inventaris van Stands Archief te Batavia (1602-1816).* Batavia: Landsdrukery, 1882.

INDEX

Aaro, Saadia, of Joloano warrior class, 225
Abdullah Sultan of Kedah, see Kedah.
Abdurahim, Haji, Balangingi storyteller, 295-6
Abubacal, son of Dando, 371
Agar-agar (seaweed), 139, 218, 270
Aguilar y Ponce de Leon, Rafael Maria (Governor of Philippines), and defense program, 103
Ajax (cruiser), and escaped slaves, 142
Ahmad, Rajah Ali Haji Ibn, on Iranun fleets, 180
Akil, Raja, advisor to Muntinghe, 89
Alcalde mayors, annual reports of, 72, 73, 343; corruption of, 189
Alforeans, 141, 210, 211, 222, 223
Alip, Panglima, 169, 172, 307, 360, 362
American traders, and cross-cultural trade, 36, 188, 189,190-94, 234, 276-81, 413
Amihan, northwest monsoon, 261
Ammunition, traded at Jolo, 52. See also Gunpowder.
Andaman Islands, targeted by maritime raiders, 54

An Outcast of the Islands (book), see Conrad.
Anti, Datu, 50
Australia, and cross-cultural trade, 188

Babalatchi, 396, 397, 398
Balambangan, 14, 36
Balangingi Island (map of) 147, 148-50; defeat at Fort de Sipac, 347, 348, 350-57
Balangingi Samal (ethnic group), vi, viii, ix, 4, 5, 15, 74, 94, 146, 147, 151-2, 357, 359, 379; and state sanctioned maritime raiding, 3 vi-vii, 2, 3, 145-6; and crews, 172; character and stereotypical images, 385-400; naval attacks on, 346-57, 360; defeat of, 5, 154, 343, 344-59; clemency from Spain, 369-370; settlements and bases, 27, 143-154; oral history of, 149-50; captives' statements, 151, 169; and steamboats, 154, 303, 344-5, 346, 349, 351, 352; and large scale expeditions, 167-207; raiding ships of, 244-8; diaspora of, 349, 372-8, 379; women and children at Sipac Fort, 352, 353-4, 355,

565

356; women and children as prisoners of Spanish, 359, 366, 367, 368; women sent to Cagayan, 371; deported to Cagayan, 370-72; and Tawi-Tawi pirates, 379; statements of Balangingi prisoners, 429-30
Baluarte, 102, 107
Banjarmassin, Sultan of, treaty with Dutch, 90
Banka (Bangka, Banca), 63, 67, 88, 93, 137, 138, 139, 141, 272-73, 338, 342; targeted by maritime raiders, 54, 62-3, 263, 266, 280, 284; and tin trade, 57, 62, 131; and captives, 340, 341
Banyaga (slaves), 35, 310-11, 311, 313, 323, 339, Appendix 4. See also Slaves,
Barangayanes (fleets of), defence against maritime raids, 106-7, 197
Barrantes, Vincente, nineteenth century historian, 81
Basco y Vargas, Governor, anti-'piracy' action, 100, 103, 113, 74, 49, 52, 356, 364
Basilo, Francisco, captured by Balangingi, 175
Batavia, 58, 124, 158, 267
Beckman, Captain of *De Vrede*, drowned, 315
Bees wax, as trading commodity, 33, 45
Belcher, Captain Edward, 116; on Iranun 42, 130, 131, 135, 160, 183-4, 187, 223, 259-60, 275, 331; on arms trafficking, 116, 187; and search for English woman captive, 323; *Narrative of the Voyage of H.M.S. Samarang, during the years 1843-1846* (book), 323; and Conrad, 392

Bella Carmen, transported Balangingi prisoners to Cagayan, 372
Bengal, and trade, 34, 58, 60, 87, 189, 190-91, 194, 250
Bengal, Bay of, and Iranun raiding, 16
Bermejo, Julian, on a 'just war', 110
Bernaldez, Emilio, on dangers of waters off Balangingi, 147; *Resana Historica de la Guerra al Sur de Filipinas* (book), 349; account of Claveria's defeat of Balangingi, 348-9
Bickmore, Albert, professor of natural history, 337
Bird's nest, vi, 2, 33, 59, 133, 140, 165, 181, 191, 257, 401, 405, 414
Blake, Edward, commander, hunter of Iranun, 146, 259
Blanco, Don Jose, 108
Bombay, 58
Bonham, George (Governor of the Straits Settlements), and captivity narratives, 19-20
Borneo, and the Iranun, 5, 20, 33-4, 43, 47, 54, 56, 74, 87, 90, 91, 95, 97, 99, 124-25, 130, 132-3, 136, 137, 140, 148, 150, 151, 153, 154, 155, 156, 159, 176, 179, 181, 186, 209, 215, 244, 255, 263, 314, 261, 267, 274, 275, 292-93, 304, 316, 345, 384
Bowditch, Nathaniel, Salem skipper, 279-80
Britain, and Sulu, vii; and trade rivalry and warfare, 8, 96; and China trade, vii, 11, 99, 401-3; and introduction of 'pirate cult,' 20; and problem of 'Malay piracy,' 85; and straits of Malacca, 93; and slave trade, 96, 310; intervention in politics of NW Borneo, 129; and regional capitalism, 382

British East India Company, 403; and trade with China, vii; trade rivalry and warfare, 7, 8, 9, 22, 36, 57, 58, 60, 61-2, 64, 65, 86, 87, 93-100; and sale of arms, 8; opium, 8; Thomas Forrest, 9-10, 14, 69; the Iranun, 15, 57, 65, 267
British, 11, 65, 70, 71, 97, 163, 267, 287-94, 304, 345, 364, 382, 383
Brooke, James, as 'white raja' of Sarawak, 97-100; merchant adventurer, 97; and the Iranun, 9, 14, 130, 136-7, 163, 177, 185, 215, 224, 245, 268, 275, 304, 306; and decay theory, 21; and maritime raiding, 43, 56, 122, 125; arrival in Singapore, 97; and Sultanate of Brunei, 97-100; antipiracy campaign, 99-100, 153; intervention in politics of NW Borneo, 129, 131; on ransom demands, 328; on pejorative labels for 'Moro,' 391; and Conrad, 392
Brunei, 74, 97, 98, 146, 181, 304, 344
Brunei, Sultanate of, disintegration of, vi, 37; and global-local trade, 9; and pre-European maritime raiding, 20; and James Brooke, 97-100, 130
Buayan Sultanate of, as precolonial state, 27, 28; and Maguindanao, 27; raided for slaves, 30; and trade, 30; and Ileto, 30; under military threat, 30; decline of, 32
Bugis, 1, 59, 67, 186-87, 209; trade threatened by Iranun, 4, 58-9, 64; and Forrest, 14; merchants, 33; and slave trade, 33, 34, 38; and cross-cultural trade, 36, 64
Burd, John, merchant adventurer, 188

Burias and Balangingi, settlements and bases, 74, 77, 79, 143-154, 179, 266
Burma, targeted by maritime raiders, 54, 238, 268

Cagayan, and banished captives, 370-71, 372-4, 376, 377; and women's stories, 17
Calcutta, 69, 92, 97, 191
Camarang, letter to the Sultan of Sulu, 352-3
Camarines, 47
Camphor, 2, 133
Camsa, Datu, son-in-law of Sultan Sharaf ud-Din, 50; involvement in maritime raiding, 50; trade rivalry, 50-51, expulsion from Sulu, 51
Canonero, 207, 380-81,
Canton Free Press, reports on anti-piracy, 93
Canton Repository, reports on anti-piracy, 93
Captives, 309-342, *See also* Slaves; treatment of, 314; and conditions on board slaving ships, 315-21; discipline and punishment of, 316-323; as rowers, 319-20; women, 321-3, 359, 363; and redemption by ransom, 323-331; health of, 334, 341; and escape, 337-8; division of, 339-41
Captivity narratives, 17-19, 166, 169, 217, 221, 309
Carlton, John, master of *Putnam*, 279-280
Carvello, Juan Portuguese master of *Constante*, 50
Castillo, Don Juan Miguel de, escaped slave, 76
Castillo, as fortification, 102, 204
Catholic Church, and maritime

raiding, 56; and village settlements, 117; demographics of, 117
Cattle, targeted by Iranun, 101, 145, 232
Cautivos fugados, see captivity narratives and historiography.
Ceramics, as trade commodity, 64
Cheribon, and Dutch East India Company, 37-8
Children, as victims of slave raiders, vi, 40, 80, 134-6, 295, 297; as workers, 126; captured at Sipac Fort, 352, 353-4, 355, 356, 363; imprisoned at Zamboanga and Fort Santiago, 366
China, and Britain vii, 99, 401-2; and Sulu, vii, xi; and patterns of consumption, x xi, 181; and global-local trade, 6, 33, 189, 234, 238, 342, 413
China trade, and maritime raiding, v, 3, 4, 14, 22, 24, 26, 33, 54, 59, 78, 79, 251, 276, 317, 366; and global-local trade, 9, 11, 13, 35, 36, 93-4, 181, 218-20; and the West, vii, 22, 34, 40, 85; and Iranun expansion, vii, 5, 32, 34,51, 60; and slavery, vii, 22, 33, 34, 38, 62, 96, 181; and founding of Singapore, 93
Chinese, as captives, 319, 342; nakodah, Tay Song Que, 326; tea, as global/local commodity, 35, 181, 194, 257, 401, 409, 401, 403; miners at Bangka, 62
Christian, churches targeted by maritime raiders, 56, 80; and coastal fortifications, 109, 112; and provision of arms, 114; people as slaves, 39
Christians, and Moros, 23-24

Christianization, of Philippines, 23, 72
Chronicle of the Netherlands East Indies, on rivalry and warfare with Iranun, 62-3
Cimarrones, as 'dangerous fugitives, 82
Cinnamon, as trade commodity, 33
Civilization, in conflict with Savagism, vii, 23
Class system, 35, 38
Claveria, Narcisco, Governor-General of Philippines, and steamboats, 122-3, 154, 380; attacks on Balangingi, 345-7, 349-352, 354-7, 358-9, 390-91
Cleopatra, H.M.S., 162-163
Coastal communities, terrorized by maritime raiders, 37, 93
Cochin China, targeted by maritime raiders, 54, 57
Cocoa, trade commodity, 64
Cojuangco, Margarita, *Kris of Valor* (book), 372, 374, 378
Colonial Marine, Dutch, 87-93
Colonial port cities, 124, 190, 226, 274
Colonial powers, and trade rivalry and warfare, vii
Colonialism's pirates, 379-385
Combes, Francisco, and rise of Maguindanao Sultanate, 31; silent on Balangingi origins, 146
Comyn, Tomas de (general manager of Compania Real), 223; on Filipino coastal defences, 109
Conception y Matos, Bishop Manuel de la, letter to King, 73
Congress of Vienna, 86
Conrad, Joseph, 391-400; *The Rescue* (book), 394-5, 399; *An Outcast of the Islands*, (book), 396, 398; and Babalatchi, 396-8, 397, 399

INDEX

Constante, frigate, 50
Contrabandistas, as enemies of Spaniards, 11. *See* Pirates, Piracy, Iranun.
Coral, as protective barrier, 164
Corvettes, and antipiracy efforts, 90
Cotabato, 36, 53, 65-9, 70, 74, 95, 100, 154, 220, 251, 255, 263
Cotabato Basin, flooding of, 25-26; homeland of Maguindanoan, 25-26, 28
Cotabato Sultanate, vi, 42-3, 54; and global-local trade, 6, 7, 9, 32, 35, 51; ascendancy of, 11, 30, 34; homeland of, 25-26; wealth in relation to, 25; statecraft in, 30; precolonial state, 27; and Maguindanao, 27, 28; as rival center of Dulawan, 28; and maritime strength, 32; and slave raiding, 33, 41; and sale of slaves, 33; relationship with Iranun, 42
Cotabato, Sultan of, granddaughter of, 48
Council of the Indies, and Muntinghe's plan, 90
Crew on raiding fleets, 171-3, 177-81, 208-37, 239, 242, 244, 245, 248, 257 , 258; origins of, 208-16; Iban in, 210-212, 214-15; warriors, 222-33; and violence, 222, 223, 224-7, 268, 271-72; provisions for, 232-236; discipline and punishment, 236-237
Cruickshank, R. B., on Iranun-Balangingi raids, 83-4
Cullinane and Xenos, demographic patterns and maritime raiding, 117; and 'Moro' label, 388
Cultural integration, 24, 217-8
Culture, exploration of, viii, xi in conflict, viii

Cygnet (British privateering vessel), 43

Daedelus, H.M.S., and destruction of Tempasuk, 130-131
Dalrymple, Alexander, accounts of, 14, 22, 50, 189-90, 221, 219, 229, 264, 265, 402
Dampier, William, accounts of, 14, 43-45
Dandells, G.G., Dutch administrator, 87
Dando, Palawan, 356, 358, 367, 373; wives captured at Sipac fort, 353, 367; captured by Spanish, 364-5; banished to Isabela, 365-6; Tainun, elderly mother of, 367, 368; Aleja Valentina, wife of, 368; Abubacal, son of, 371; Sabi, wife of, 368, 369; death of, 369
Daniel, Datu, Iranun warrior, 52, 173, 209, 248, 289, 299, 307, 430
Datus, 35, 166, 167, 168, 175
Defence, mangrove swamps as, 26, 41, 48-9, 164, 264; watchtowers, 49
Dery, Luis, 23, 101, 117, 118-120
De Vrede, Dutch cruiser, captured by Iranun, 315
Diana, steamboat, 78, 146, 179, 230, 262, 301-03, 335-6
Diaspora, of Balangingi Samal, 349, 372-8, 379
Din, Sultan Jamul-ud, 68
Domingo, Martin Santos, renegade, informer for Spanish, 367-8, 371-2
Dourga, Dutch brig of war, 181
Dowich (Malay *nakodah*), report on Iranun, 94
Du Buy, M., resident of Banka, 88
Dulawan, as rival center to Cotabato, 28
Dutch East Indies, and spice trade, 1; and straits of Malacca, 93

569

Dutch East India Company (VOC), 57, 139, 267, 403, 408; and trade with China, vii; and trade rivalry and warfare, vii, 7, 8, 37-8, 57, 65, 68, 86, 87-8, 131, 140, 157, 211, 345, 381

Dutch, 9, 14, 20, 21, 28, 33, 34, 41, 59, 67, 73, 86, 97, 155, 157, 173, 188, 190, 251, 256-7, 265, 276, 339, 382-4, 391, 395, 299, 310, 311, 405; and trade rivalry and warfare, vii, 4, 7, 8, 17, 23, 30, 31, 57-9, 60, 64, 65, 67-8, 70, 71, 91, 92-3, 99-100, 141, 142, 154-5, 157-9, 186-7, 267, 281, 282-7, 327, 359, 364; decline in Southeast Asia, 6, 10, 57; and Forrest, 9, 15

Dyak warriors, as Iranun crew, 213, 214

Edwards, Ebenezer (American whaler), and captivity narratives, 16, 19, 233, 289, 313, 318, 331, 336-7

Edwards, William, and Iranun violence, 333-4

Elcano, steam warship, 352

Empire building, 385-400

England, 15

English, 14, 28, 125, 166, 190, 379, 396, 405; and trade rivalry and warfare, vii-viii, 4, 23, 30, 60, 61-2, 160, 161, 251, 276, 282, 359, 388-9; and the Iranun, 6, 130, 327; and ascendancy of maritime raiding, 21; and global/local trade, 11, 33, 36; woman captive, 323

Enrile, Lt. Gen. Pascual, uncle of Peneranda, 115; community-based defense system, 116

Enterprise, American ship, 58

Essex, vessel of British East India Company, 14

Estados de las Islas Filipinas (book), See, Mas.

Esteban, D. Pedro (squadron leader of *Barangayanes*) 107-109

Ethnic Identity, vii, viii, x, 32, 41, 52, 141 209, 210-11, 225, 309-10; and *The Sulu Zone* (book), v

Europe, and patterns of consumption, x, 405, 413; trade as target of Iranun, 6; and trade with China, 35; and Taosog ascendancy, 35

Europe and *The People Without History* (book), see Wolf.

Europeans, 2, 3, 27, 268, 289, 319, 330, 335, 391-2, 398, 403, 415; and slaves, 33, 96, 310; and maritime raiding, 1, 4, 6, 10, 15, 326-8; trade rivalry and warfare, 33, 176, 283-4; as captives, 332

Faluas, cannon boats to counteract maritime raids, 49, 104, 206, 259, 334

Farquhar, (British Commander), on Iranun raiding, 70-71

Felix de Marquina, Don, on Iranun raiding, 103

Figuero, Rodriguez de, defeated Spanish captain, 30

Filipino, 232, 324, 328, 335; Christians and slave raiding, 106, 168, 342; officials and corruption, 116

Filipino renegades, 50, 170, 173, 174, 216-7, 260

Firearms, as trade commodities, 8

Fishers, targeted by Iranun, 93, 121; women as, 126

INDEX

Fishing, as way of life, 25
Flags and Pennants, 253-4, 350
Follansbee, Alonzo, 282
Follansbee, Mrs. Alonzo, passenger on *Logan*, 278
Forrest, Thomas, 9, 14, 66, 68, 69, 146, 234, 253, 255-6, 284, 299, 402, 407; and the Dutch, 11, 57, 154-5; and British East India Company, 9-10; as author and ethnographer, 9, 14-15, 16; as political emissary, 9-10, 15, 65; and *Tartar Galley*, 9, 14; and expansion of trade with China, 22; on the Iranun, 40, 42, 45, 48-51, 66 67-8, 72, 73, 76-7, 81, 144-5, 228, 232, 236-7, 264-5, 289-90; on eruption of Maketering volcano, 45-6, 126-8; on marriage alliances, 48; *Voyage to New Guinea* (book), 68; on production of salt, 220; on production of salt petre, 250-51; on Iranun raiding ships, 239-41, 241-2, 244, 245-6, 254-5, 257; meeting with Raja Muda, 240-41, 250, 251, and Iranun rowing song, 258, 320
Fortifications, in the Philippines, 73-4, 205; coastal defenses of Bishopric of Cebu, 421-24; Land and Sea defences of Albay Province, 425
Fox, British schooner, 252-3
Frake, Charles, and 'Moro' label, 23-24, 345, 387
Franklin, 280-81
Freycinet, Rose, smuggled aboard *Uranie*, 288
Friar soldiers, (*el padre capitan*), and fortifications, 106, 107-8, 405
Friars, 14, 73, 80-1, 84-5, 224
Frontiers, of desire, x

Fuerza sutil, reports of, 343

Gainza, Francisco OP, description of maritime raiders, 42
Garay, Balangingi boat, 18, 201, 245-8, 247, 249, 256, 261
Geohegan, William, anthropologist, 295-6
Ginsburg, Carlo, 311
Global economy, and *The Sulu Zone* (book), v; emerging, vi; and expansion of Sulu Sultanate, 51
Global-local trade, 9, 11, 13, 35, 36, 93-4, 181, 342. *See also* Trade
Gold, 45, 67-8, 83, 93, 273; and women miners, 126
Gomez de Careaga, Doña Maria Israel, donation to 'extirpate' Muslims, 102
Gresink, and Dutch East India Company, 37-8
Groot, Cornets de, on 'piracy,' 218
Gunboats, and antipiracy, 90
Gunpowder, 11, 37, 114, 183, 184
Guns, as trade commodity, 128, 183, 184, 250-51

Habagat, warm southwest monsoon, 'pirate wind,' 261
Hajis, treatment when captured, 314, 315
Halcon, Don Jose Maria, Spanish officer, 4, 146; and arms trade, 187; on Iranun fleet off Luzon, 259
Halmahera, targeted by maritime raiders, 54
Harraway, Donna, and historiography, 18
Haswell, William, 277
Hispanic Catholicism and 'civilizing agenda,' 100

Historiography, ix, 3, 5, 11-12, 13, 17, 20, 23, 309, 311; and ethnohistorical research, v, vii, ix, x, 6, 309, 311-13, 383-4, 411; and Anne Reber, 22; and decay theory, 21-23, 24; and Donna Harraway, 18; and ethnicity, viii, 309-10, 400-17; and oral history, 1, 16-18, 109, 112, 225, 376-377, 409; and problem of Malay 'piracy,' 21-24; and silences, 8, 12; and social statistics–ecclesiastical and civil, 117-20; and sources, ix, 12, 14 16, 176, 208, 222, 309; and *The Sulu Zone* (book). See Warren; and women, 17; captivity statements, 17-19, 78, 309; Eurocentric, 13-14

History of Sulu (book), 149. See also Saleely.

Hunt, J., Lieutenant Governor of Java, 16, 189-90; account of, 14, 183; report to Raffles, 16, 183; and slave raids, 51-52; on Tontoli, 71, 155

Iban, as warriors and crew for Iranun, 210-212, 214-15, 222, 223, 237, 319

Ibanez y Garcia, Luis de (Lieutenant Colonel), Mi Cautiverio: Carta que con motivo del que sufrio entre los Piiratas Joloanos y Samales en 1857 (captivity narrative), 16, 19, 233, 270-71, 295, 306313-14, 316, 318, 320, 321, 328-30, 332, 333, 341, 360-61; Captured by Tumugsuc, 314, 360

Ida'han Tribes, trade rivalry and warfare, 132, 134-6

Illana Bay, eastern extremity of Iranun heartland, 26, 32, 41, 42, 48-9, 74, 138, 165, 179, 224, 263, 276

Ileto, Ray, on Buayan, 30; on rise of Cotabato Sultanate, 30; on slavery, 31; on Lutaos, 31

Illanoon, images of, 16. See also Iranun

Illanun. See Iranun.

Imams, treatment when captured, 314

India trade, as target of Iranun, 5

Indonesia, and maritime raiding, 1, 34, 85, 224, 358, 383; and decline of Dutch control, 6

Iranun Age, 1-24 25-40

Iranun (ethnic group) of Mindanao, demographics of and geography of, ii, vi, 5, 27, 32, 197, 198, 202, 238; Age of, 25-40; and British East India Company, 15, 57, 65; Maranao relations, 44-47; and children, 134-6; and Dutch, 65, 68, 71; and Earl, 135; and ethnicity, 41-2, 141, 155, 309-10; and Europe, 6; and fishing, 218-20; and Sulu World, 41-52; and Forrest, 15; and raiding fleets, squadrons and crews, 171-3, 176-181, 208-37, 269, 271-308; and Singapore, 64; and violence, 222, 223, 224-7, 268, 271-2, 331-3, 335-7; and women, 131, 135; as maritime raiders, vi, vii 1-2, 6-7, 47, 61-3, 80; as pirates, viii, 8, 43, 141; ascendancy and expansion of, 5, 6, 8, 10, 25, 27, 53; boat building, 254-5; captives of, 309-342; escape from capture, 337-8; expeditions of, 164-207; flags and pennants of, 253-4; impact of steamboat on, 92, 97, 122, 154, 163; impact of volcanic eruption on, 45-7, 126-8; in the Philippines, 72-85, 100; marginalization of, ix, 4, 80; prizes

572

and booty, 180-181, 183, 184-5, 211, 212, 214; raiding routes and navigation, 261-6; raiding ships of, 238-266; reputation of, 2, 16, 222, 223, 224-6; settlements and bases, 44, 124-163; social organization and hierarchy of raiding fleet, 165-6, 170, 175-6; trade rivalry and warfare, 1, 2-4, 7, 9, 10, 1,1 57, 60, 62-4, 64-71 72-85, 86-93, 108-9, 120, 134-6, 142, 143-4, 146; warriors, 222-33; weapons, 11, 229-232, 242, 244, 248, 250-52, 268, 331

Iron, as trade commodity, 134

Islam, conversion to, 173-4, 216, 307, 410

Ismail, Raja, assault on Dutch garrison, 58-9

Israel, Mohammad, trade rivalry and warfare, 50-51, 133-4

Jambi Sultanate, at risk from raids, 93

Java Sea, targeted by maritime raiders, 54

Java, 72, 91, 138, 269, 274; and British East India Company, 15; and Dutch East India Company, 37; antipiracy tactics in, 88; and Forrest, 14

Javellana, Rene (Jesuit historian) on Philippine defense net, 107; on Samal Balangingi warship, 260-61

Javanese, as slaves, 52

Jesusa, merchant ship, 367

Jihad (holy war), 24

Joanga, 50, 53, 54, 60, 66, 80, 88, 238, 239, 242-5, 243, 250, 301; and long-range expeditions, 164, 170, 242

Jolo, seat of Sulu Sultanate, 11, 26, 33, 36-7, 38, 39, 49-50, 52, 74, 102, 150-51, 154, 161, 162, 183-84, 186, 189, 196, 219, 251, 255, 261, 288, 289-90, 376; and slave trade, 326, 327, 330; and Balangingi diaspora, 356

Josefita, transport ship for Balangingi prisoners sent to Cagayan, 371

Kakap. See Salisipan

Kaligeran de Perez, Hailan, and oral history of Balangingi, 149-50

Kapal api, see steamboats.

Kedah Sultanate, targeted by maritime raiders, 57, 93

Kedah, Abdullah Sultan of, and British East India Company, 61-2

Kema, destruction of, 68

Kent, Chancellor, definition of piracy, 2- 3

Keppel, Henry, Capt., commander of *Dido*, 99-100; on Samal identity, 153; and Iban and Iranun raiding, 214, 244-5, 276; and Conrad, 392

Kerajaan (Malayo-Muslim State), 24. See also Malayo-Muslim State.

Kestrel, H.M.S. (British steam gunboat), 163, 384-5

Kinabatangan, Sherif Abu of, on the Iranun, 160

King, George Pockock, merchant adventurer, 180, 188, 284-5

Kling, Raden and fortification, 64

Kolek Trengannu, cruising *prahu* used by Dutch marine, 90

Kolff, M. D.H., antipiracy report of, 88, 139, 181, 244-5; and arms trade, 187

Kora-Kora, 89, 206

Koran. See Qur'an

Koyang, antipiracy vessel, 89-90

Kris of Valor (book), See Cojuangco.

Kudrat, Sultan, rise of, 30

Lange, Mas, merchant adventurer, 188
La Politica, on lack of defense for remore villages, 117
Laarhoven, Ruurdje, on geography of Mindanao, 26; on sociopolitical organization of Maguindanao Sultanate, 30-31; and slavery, 31; on Lutaos, 32; on ethnicity, 41; on Iranun autonomy, 42
Labor, and redistributive economy, 22
Lanao Lake, boundary of Iranun heartland, 25-26, 41, 43
Lanchas, armed flat boats to counteract maritime raids, 104
Lanong, heavily armed *prahus*, 58, 60, 198, 238, 239, 269. See also *Joanga*.
Lanun, 1; dreaded by Christians, 81. See also Iranun.
Laut, Datu (Iranun lord) on maritime raiding, 43-4; alliance with Usman, 130
Leonides, Spanish brig, 190, 192, 330
Life in the Forests of the Far East (book), 135-6. See also St. John.
Light, Francis, founder of British East India Company in Penang, 11; rivalry and warfare, 61-2
Linga, 90, 140, 142, 180, 181, 280
Lingard, Conrad's protagonist, 392-3, 394-6
Liverpool, 333-4
Lizzie Webber, brig, 293-4
Lloyd's Returns, 273
Local community defense, Philippines, 110-112
Logan, 278, 282
Lutaos, as sea raiders and traders, 31-2

Luzon, and maritime raiding, 54,56, 72, 73, 76, 78-9, 80-81, 101, 103, 104, 106, 117, 118, 143, 145, 146, 176, 178, 300, 386, 411
Lydia, Salem barque, 277-8

Magallanes, steam warship, 352
Maguindanao, 25, 27-28, 34, 36, 41, 47, 67, 70, 154, 191, 224
Maguindanao lords, 34, 38, 251
Maguindanao Sultanate, 28
the 'golden age' of, 30-34, 36, 46, 47; and Sultan Kudarat, 30; and Islamic leadership, 30; trade rivalry and warfare, 31; and trade with Europe, 33; and contact with China, 35; and British East India Company, 36
Maguindanaon, ethnic group of Cotabato Basin, 25; use of label, 66
Maharajah (next in rank to *Panglima*), 165, 166
Mah Daut (Malay *nakodah*), report on Iranun, 94
Mah Roon (alias Mah Sandar), 310, 429-30; on fleet size, 177, 209
Mahmud, Sultan, and Dutch in Riau, 58, 59; and recorded exploits of Iranun, 138
Majul, Cesar, and Sulu 'piracy,' 21; and decline theory, 23; and Spanish colonization, 23 and *The Muslims in the Philippines* (book), 24; and *jihad* (holy war), 24
Makassar, 4, 63, 72, 124, 186, 209, 267, 273, 293, 322; as raiding target, 5, 27, 54, 67; as European colonial port, 33, 96; and Dutch East India Company, 37-8; Straits of as regional trade route, 86, 244; and Woodward, 58

INDEX

Maketering Volcano eruption of, and Iranun diaspora, 45-7, 50, 126-8; and growth of trade, 133

Malacca, Straits of, trade rivalry and warfare, vii, 1, 9, 15, 53, 57, 58-64, 87, 92-3, 126, 137, 138, 139, 141, 143, 151, 178, 180, 183, 187, 244, 269, 274, 281, 412; decline of Dutch control, 6; and Presgrave, 16; regional trade route, 86, 244; and British, 93, 166; and trade losses, 94

Malaya, 19, 146, 214

Malayo-Muslim, world, vii, 24, 32, 81; and Presgrave, 16; as maritime state, xi, 13; and pre-European maritime raiding, 20; and decay theory, 21-22

Malay Peninsula, 1, 57, 87, 93, 180, 214, 304

Malays, 21, 42, 53, 64, 325; as slaves, 62, 317, 335

Malaysia, 85

Malfalla, Datu, brother-in-law of Muda, journal, 257-8, 263

Mallari, Francisco S.J., on maritime raids, 56, 73, 101, 262; demographic patterns and maritime raiding, 117

Mallet, Jean, *The Philippines*, (book) on friar-soldier leadership, 110.

Mamburao, destruction of, 78-9, 143-4

Mampawa, Sultan of, treaty with Dutch, 90

Mangroves, as protective barrier, 26, 41, 48-49, 164, 264; as non-state space, 47

Manila, and maritime raiding, v-vi, 73, 77, 78, 100, 104, 109, 115, 124, 143, 145, 189, 192-93, 262, 267, 277, 306, 327, 348, 364, 368, 369, 379; trade rivalry and warfare, vii, 11, 75-6, 78, 101-2, 124-25, 174; as trading center, 4; and coastal trade, 82; as metropolitan city, 96; and trade with Sulu, 102, 251; as administrative capital, 50, 275, 346, 354, 355, 366

Maranao speaking Iranun, home of, 25, 41, 44, 45, 47; and migration, 26; and state formation, 27; impact of lack of trade concerns on, 28

Marasan, Raja, beheaded by Dutch, 92

Maria Fredericka, schooner captured by Iranun, 181, 285-6, 332

Marina sutil (light navy), 103, 195

Marivales, impact of Iranun on, 77

Markang, Raja, beheaded by Dutch, 92

Marriage, as strategic alliance, 47-8, 50, 67, 139, 155, 166, 174, 257; as assimilation process, 170, 174, 323, 410; destroyed by captivity, 322

Maruda, Iranun bases in, 99-100, 126-137, 150, 221, 263; regional boundaries of, 133; escaping captives, 311; destruction of, 345

Mas, Sinibaldo, *Estados de las Islas Filipinas* (book), 390-91

Matalissi, slave owner, 161

Matappiz, fugitive wife of Misul, 373-4

McKenna, Thomas, and flooding of Cotabato basin, 25

Meares, John, Capt., 275-6; on defense of Filipino coast, 112

Mecca, 58

Mednick, Melvin, and the Maranao, 27; on Maguindanao and Sulu Sultanates, 28, 166

575

Melampus (frigate) and expedition against Iranun, 159
Melville, Herman, *Moby Dick* (book), 281-2
Memmi, Alfred, and the 'mark of the plural,' 387
Menado, 67, 72, 93, 146, 254, 338, 339; (Dutch Resident of), account of Sulu piracy, 170, 227, 339
Merantau, and crews, 212
Merchant shipping, terrorized by maritime raiders, 37
Mexican, troops in Philippines, 79
Mexico, 79, 143
Migration, caused by Maketering eruption, 128
Mi Cautiverio: Carta que con motivo del que sufrio entre los Piiratas Joloanos y Samales en 1857 (captivity narrative). *See* Ibanez y Garcia.
Mindanao, 15, 19, 24, 26, 34, 38, 42, 45, 71, 87, 108, 109, 116, 124-25, 137, 139, 140, 141, 143; homeland and base of Iranun, 5, 14, 25, 27, 47, 49, 101, 155, 173, 179, 189, 230, 232, 244, 250, 254, 260, 276, 325, 375, 377, 387; and British East India Company, 10; and slaves, 315; and Spanish, 23, 385; and mangrove, 25; and maritime raiding, 54, 72, 74, 82-5, 175, 182, 238, 259, 363, 406; and Forrest, 15
Mindanao-Sulu Region, 14, 24, 31, 53, 61; geography of, 25, 27; and change, 13; and orally-transmitted women's stories, 17
Minerva, American barque, 330
Moby Dick (book). *See* Melville
Moluccas, Spice Islands, 1, 26, 35, 273; and Forrest, 9, 15, 69; and political instability, 9; and British East India Company, 10; and maritime raiders, 11, 54, 57, 60, 137, 141, 151, 154, 156, 158-9, 176, 178, 261, 262, 359; as source of slaves, 34; expulsion of Dutch from, 68; British occupation of, 7; Iranun raiding in, 64-72, 210
Monsoon wind systems, importance to Iranun, 27, 67, 124, 261-6, 342
Moro, 11, 12, 13; as ethnic label, 23-24, 41; as religious label, 23-24; as pejorative label, 16, 23, 385-90; as myth of savage, 23, 389-400; piracy, 72, 73; dreaded by Christians, 81
'Moro-wars cycle,' and historiography, 23
Mother of pearl, 192, 218, 219, 221
Muda, Raja (Maguindanao riverine lord), 43, 210, 263, 332; his daughter, 48; and raiding expedition, 66-67; and strategic marriage alliances, 67, 257; meeting with Forrest, 240-41, 250, 251
Munitions, as trade commodity, 4, 129, 139
Mundy, Captain, description of Pandassan, 132, 253, 305-06
Muntinghe, M. H. W., antipiracy report, 88, 139-40, 141-2, 159; and plan, 89, 90, 93; on pejorative labels for 'Moro,' 391
Museo Naval, Madrid, 256, 257
Musim lanun (the Iranun season: months of August, September and October), 2, 168, 261
Myth of savage, 389

Nakodahs, (headmen of trading vessel), 50, 66, 167, 168-9, 170, 171
Napoleon, defeat of, 86.

INDEX

Narrative of the Voyage of H.M.S. Samarang, during the years 1843-1846 (book). See Belcher
Negara, (Malayo-Muslim state), 24. *See also kerajan.*
Netherlands East Indies, see Dutch East Indies.
New Guinea, and Forrest, 9, 15, 58; targeted by maritime raiders, 54, 222, 260, 261, 273
Nipa, as trade commodity, 134
No-Jula, second generation in exile, 377
Norris, Sir W., recorder of Singapore, 253
Norzagaray, Governor-General, and prefabricated steam boats, 380
Nuku, Prince of Tidore, 65, 69, 211, 408; insurrection of, 142
Nuno, Haji Datu, youngest son of Taupan, 374-6
Nuyla, youngest wife of Taupan, 367, 369, 375

Omar, Haji, ambassador of the Sultan of Tidore, 68; and destruction of Kema, 68; the Tuan Hadji in Forrest's *Voyage to New Guinea* (book), 68
Opium, as trade commodity, 4, 34, 64, 193, 267, 268, 337, 403; and Tausog datus, 37
Orang kaya (local leader), 165, 167, 169, 214, 357
Orang Kaya Kullul, 209, 221, 228, 298-9, 303-4, 307-08, 314, 315
Orang timor (people from the east), 140-141
Orang tua, (elderly leader), 171
Owen, Norman, on maritime raids, 101; on demographic patterns and maritime raiding, 117

Pahar un-Din, Sultan of Cotabato, 67
Palembang Sultanate, at risk from raids, 62, 93
Pancos, description of, 73
Pandassan, torching of, 132
Pangeran, Syed Hassen Habassy, informer, 89
Panglima (highest ranking political leader), 165, 166, 168, 175, 357 taken prisoner by Dutch, 92
Pannisil, captive of Iranun, 310
Pariden, Datu, 300-01
Pearls, as trade commodities, 133, 157, 167, 192, 218, 229, 344; harvesting of, 219
Penang, as trading center, 4, 5, 59, 60, 61, 96, 124, 260, 267; trade rivalry and warfare, 5,11, 61-2
Peneranda, Jose Maria (Spanish army engineer), and coastal fortifications, 115-6
Penjajap (*gubang* or *panco*), principal craft, 239-241, 251, 253, 258-9, 269
Pepper (black gold), 279, 280
Perouse, de la impact of Iranun on Marivales, 77
Philippines, 78, 79, 103, 110-123, 224, 260-61, 343, 355, 358, 363, 366, 379-81, 406-7, 412; contemporary ethnic tensions, viii, 411; and maritime raiding, 1, 4, 11, 27, 31, 34, 38, 53, 54, 56, 72-85, 102, 121, 143-6, 154, 176, 178, 209, 217, 222, 224, 232-3, 240, 250, 265, 266, 269, 345, 349, 357, 386; and slaves, 34, 38, 39, 174, 183, 208-9, 297, 322, 383, 405; living conditions in, 40, 216; civil and religious authorities of, 79, 189; financial burden of maritime

577

raiding on, 101-2; coastal villages and fortifications, 109, 112, 113, 143, 403, 421-425; and changing demographics, 117-21, 426-8
Pieters, Cornelius Zacharias (Captain), captivity narratives, 19, 285-6, 317, 318, 330-1, 342
Piracy, x, 1, 86; definition of, 2-4, 21-23, 370; rising incidence of, 15; and world capitalist economy, 22; as 'lack of civilization,' 370
Piracy and Politics in the Malay World (book), 151. See also Tarling
Piratas (Iranun), enemy of Spaniards, 11. See also Pirates, Piracy, Iranun.
Pirates, 4, 6, 43; definition of, 2-4
Pontianak, Sultan of, treaty with Dutch, 90
Porcelain, 79
Portuguese, 20, 36, 190
Praetorious, M., resident of Palembang, 88
Prahus, 1, 4, 197, 248, 254, 309, 343; Iranun and Balangingi, 38; as home of Iranun, 43, 72; fleets of, 53-4, 60, 71, 79; and raiding expeditions, 66-7; Visayan war, 79; under attack, 86; used by Dutch antipiracy patrols, 87-8, 90; as protection for trade vessels, 91
Presgrave, Edward, comments on 'piracy,' 4-5, 16, 64
Product and fate, 401
Pula Nea, captive of Iranun, 310
Pulangi River (Rio Grande de Mindanau), and Maguindanao homeland, 28, 32, 257; homeland of Cotabato Sultanate, 25, 28, 41; geographical situation of, 26
Putnam, Salem ship, 279-80

Qur'an, 171, 226, 244, 306, 377

Raffles, Sir Stamford, and Iranun and Balangingi, 14, 43, 186; and 'piracy,' 15; and Hunt's report, 16, 51-2, 183; and decay theory, 21; empire and trade, 99, 186, 191; on pejorative labels for 'Moro,' 391; and Conrad, 392
Raiding Ships, 238-266
Raiding routes and navigation, 261-6
Raiding and conflict, 267-208
Rajah, and hereditary rulership, 166, 167, 168
Raman, Panglima, in partnership with Iranun, 62
Rattan, 2, 133
Rauws, Lt., and ransom, 235, 327
Reber, Anne, on decay theory, 22
Redistributive economy, and labor, 22
Reina de Castilla, steam warship, 352
Religious festivals, and maritime raids, 81, 322
Religious orders, and maritime raiding, 80, 328; and coastal defenses, 106, 107-8, 109-10, 112
Religious zealotry, and cultural transformation, 24
Remontados, 82, 122
Rennell, James, as navigator and cartographer, 14, 15; accounts of 14-15, 230, 401; and expansion of trade with China, 22; on slaves and prestige, 39; on Iranun ethnicity, 41-2 49-50
Representation, and historiography, 20
Resana Historica de la Guerra al Sur de Filipinas (book). See Bernaldez.
Resink, G. J., professor of Indonesian history, 393-4
Reteh, 59, 60, 61, 64, 74, 126, 137-43, 152, 242, 267

Riau Islands plundered by slave raiders, 1, 58, 59, 180, 181; and Dutch, 7, 58-9, 140, 187; trade rivalry and warfare, 93, 142, 179, 276

Riau-Lingga, Sultanate, at risk from slave raiding, 93

Riau, Prince of, and Iranun raiding, 91-2

Rice, as trade commodity, 33, 38, 64, 67-8, 133, 134, 145, 150, 151, 157, 180, 188; plunder of, 84, 121, 273; harvests, 100, 121

Ringdove, English warship, 253

Rio Grande River, *see* Pulangi River.

Rodriguez, Gregorio (Augustinian Provincial), report on sea borne defences, 105

Ross, John Dill, Capt, owner of *Lizzie Webber*, 293-4

Rowing song, 258

Royal Navy, and 'antipiracy' action 93, 96, 99-100, 131-132; and support for Brooke, 98

Royalist, Brooke's yacht, 44, 98-9, 253

Rutter, Owen, *The Pirate Wind* (book), 226; and 'Vikings of the seas,' 226; on Belcher's search for female English slave, 323

Sabah, and pre-European maritime raiding, 20

Sabi, wife of Dando, 368; death of, 369

Sabit, captive of Iranun, 314-5

Sago, as trade commodity, 94, 150, 157

Saleely, Najeed, *History of Sulu*, (book), 149

Salisipan (*kakap*) a sampan or dugout canoe, 200, 238, 239, 241-2, 249, 250, 253, 261

Salt, as trade commodity, 134, 184; production of, 219, 220-21

Salted fish, as trade commodity, 134

Samal, 150, 165, 168-170, 178, 208, 218, 220, 231, 245; and procurement of slaves, 19, 38, 175; and state formation, 27; demographics, 32; and ethnic identity, 152, 153

Samal Balangingi, 17, 35, 54

Samal Laut, 203

Samar, impact of maritime raiding on, 83-4

Samarang H.M.S., frigate, 183

Sambas, Sultan of, treaty with Dutch, 90; report on *Sea Flower* incident, 90-91

Sandin, Benedict, *The Sea Dayaks of Borneo before White Rajah Rule* (book), 215

Sangir Island, targeted by maritime raiders, 54

San Joseph, Manila galleon, 78-9, 143-4

Santa Maria, Augustine, evidence of, 183

Sarah and Elizabeth (whaler), 233, 288-9, 313, 318, 331; destruction of, 19

Sarangani, Raja of, emissary of the Sultan of Cotabato, 70

Sarawak, White Rajah of, *see* Brooke.

Sarawak, 44, 97, 98; targeted by maritime raiders, 55

'Savage,' and Empire building, 385-400; and stereotypical images, 385-400; myth of, 389-400

Savagism, in conflict with civilization, viii, 23

Sea cucumber. *See tripang*.

Sea Flower, British East India Company vessel, 90-91

Sharaf ud-Din, Sultan, father-in-law of Datu Camsa, 50
Si-Ayer, deposition of, 125, 161-2, 181, 210, 270, 316-317, 334
Siak Sultanate, at risk from raids, 93
Siam. *See* Thailand.
Silammkoom, prisoner of Balangingi, 169, 228, 253, 299, 429
Silk, as trade commodity, 79
Si Mirantau, Iranun chief of Tuaran, 128
Silver, as trade commodity, 83
Silveria, Maria, wife of Martin Santo Domingo, 368
Sindrah, captive of Iranun, 310
Singapore, 5, 15, 16, 39, 92-3, 97, 177, 186, 187, 208, 251, 302; as colonial port and commercial center, 64, 96, 124, 153, 186, 188, 251, 267, 293, 326; and trade rivalry and warfare, v-vi, vii, 15-16, 20, 27, 64, 93, 96-7, 99, 130, 146, 153, 186-7, 262, 272, 359, 383; and antipiracy decisions, 92-3; demand for slaves, 96, 186-7; and Bonham, 20
Singapore Chronicle, 191, 212
Singapore Free Press, and 'antipiracy' campaign, 100
Singapore Free Press and Mercantile Advertiser, description of a prahu, 248, 302
Singapore Journal of Commerce, 193
Sipac Fort, 334, 347, 348, 350-57, 362
Si-Tabak, Sultan, Iranun lord, 128
Slave markets, colonial involvement with, 33, 73
Slave raiding, as a vocation, 1, 2; and Iranun motivation, 6; on Buawan, 30; and population growth, vi, 33; staging points for, 37; in Thailand, 61; in the Philippines, 72, 73; abolition of, 384
Slavery, vi, x, xi; integrated with global-local trade, 24; integrated with maritime raiding, 24
Slaves, as trade commodities, 4, 7, 33, 37, 52, 62, 95, 96, 129, 138, 139, 151, 162, 167, 183, 187, 212, 214, 310; labor force, 1, 22, 23, 31, 33, 34, 38, 40, 62, 74, 80, 126, 155, 169, 170, 175, 208-10, 258, 310, 413; acquisition of, 30, 31, 34, 62, 257; as captured cargo, 33, 59, 237; marketing of, 38, 160; ownership of, 38, 39; and political power, 38-39; and status of, 39; Chinese, 62; Javanese, 62; Malays, 62; taken from Sulawesi, 71; escaped and rescued, 76, 78, 142, 144; as hostages, 130; and assimilation, 170, 216, 217; and sugar as product and fate, 401
Somes, M.A. (master of *Minerva*), 330, 331
Sopher, David, and dispute with Combes, 31
South China Sea, and maritime raiding, 15, 54, 59, 61, 94, 137, 138, 164, 166, 184, 212, 267, 302, 364, 383; and Royal Navy action, 99-100, 179
Southeast Asia, and patterns of consumption, x; mainland as boundary of Iranun, 1; as entrepot for China trade, 8-9; and change, 13
Southern Philippines, heartland of 'piracy,' 20
Southern Mindanao, extremity of Iranun heartland, 26
Spain, as colonial power, 1, 385; trade rivalry and warfare, 93, 100-

01; and steamboats, 122-3; and Empire building, 385-400
Spanish, 13, 17, 23, 34, 36, 41, 45, 72, 81, 125, 154, 173, 174, 190, 256-7, 310-13, 327, 329, 338, 344, 345, 349-51, 363, 405; and the Iranun, 4, 6, 11, 41, 101-2, 130, 240, 242, 251; and trade rivalry and warfare, 8, 23, 31, 72, 78, 82-3, 102-6, 114-5, 122, 267, 346, 383, 387-90; and introduction of 'pirate cult,' 20; and economic independence with Mindanao, 28; and Balangingi, 346, 347, 349-352, 354-7, 358-9, 369, 372, 377, 390-91; use of women and children as hostages, 363, 364, 366-9
Spices, as trade commodity, 4, 79
Spice Islands, and maritime raiding, v-vi, 31; and the Dutch, 9
St. John, Spencer, on Iranun weaving, 134; on Ida'han women, 135; *Life in the Forests of the Far East* (book), 135-6; on oral history, 160; on Iranun, 166-7, 178, 229, 274, 288, 289, 326; and Wyndham, 192-3, 210, 223, 241; on Iranun and Iban crew members, 214, 215; on Sipac survivors, 356, 360; on steam warships, 380
State, formation x, xi, 35, 181, 182
Steamboats, as instruments of Empire, 92, 97, 122, 154, 163, 180, 209, 216, 303, 344-5, 346, 349, 351, 352, 356, 357, 380-81, 390; as tools of 'Colonialism's pirates,' 280-81
Stokbroo, Lt. captured by Iranun, 315
Straits Times, 193

Subsistence agricultural workers, women as, 126
Sukut, captive of Iranun, 310
Sulawesi, 9, 47, 53, 58, 69, 124-25, 156, 158, 176, 208, 209, 211-12, 412; as safe haven for Iranun, 5, 57; and British East India Company, 10; and Dutch East India Company, 37; trade rivalry and warfare, 60, 87, 91, 151, 154, 159, 160, 180, 251-2, 258, 261, 262, 266, 269, 274, 282, 364, 386; and Forrest, 15; Iranun raiding in, 64-72
Sulu, 15, 19, 25, 34, 71, 74, 85, 87, 95, 124-25, 148, 152, 154, 219, 238, 342; and interactions with China and the West, xi, 22, 293, 344-5; homeland and main base of Iranun, 5, 17, 100, 101, 102, 155, 173, 179, 181, 182, 228, 230, 232, 251, 254, 334, 340, 360; as entrepot, 7; and slaves, 33, 39, 185, 274, 315, 323, 325; naval attack on, 346; world in conflict, 369, 387; and forrest, 15
Sulu Archipelago, as home of Iranun and Balangingi, 13, 49, 255; geographical location, 26; map of, 29; and Iranun expansion, 34; and pivotal position in global trade, 36; Cultural-ecological setting, 218
Sulu Mindanao Region, and 'piracy,' v
Sulu Sea, as border zone, xi; as heartland of 'piracy,' 20; currents of, 26
Sulu, Sultan of, 83, 129, 166, 293
Sulu Sultanate, vii, 5, 11, 23, 27, 28, 35-36, 48, 51, 102, 122, 152, 164-5, 183, 191, 276, 363, 413; and

slavery, vi, 189, 384, 411; and global-local trade, 6, 9, 10, 11, 22, 192; and British East India Company, 10, 15; and world capitalist economy, 13, 22, 79, 383; and Taosog, 27, 35; ascendancy of, 11, 22, 24, 34, 36; and maritime raiding, 37, 54, 70, 101-2, 260; statements of fugitive captives, 431-32, 433-448

Sulu Zone, 26, 37; and historiography, v, 21; and cultural and social forms, 6

Sumatra, and the Iranun, 5, 37, 47, 59, 87, 124-25, 139, 140, 141, 176, 209, 222, 238, 267, 274; and British East India Company, 10; and Forrest, 14; and the pepper trade, 279

Sunda, Straits of, regional trade route, 86

Sungailiat, attacked by Iranun, 62-3

Syed, Ali, and attack on Siam (Thailand), 61

Tabuddin, son of Datu Camsa, 50

Tainun, elderly mother of Dando, 367, 368

Tala Goa, 172-3, 221, 228, 253, 299, 302, 303-04, 306-07, 317, 335-6, 430

Tamu, system of reciprocity and exchange, 134

Tarling, Nicholas, and decay and decline theory, 20-21; questioning term 'pirate,' 21; and China trade, 22; *Piracy and Politics in the Malay World* (book), 151.

Tartar Galley (vessel), 9, 14-15, 67, 258

Taupan, Panglima Julano (celebrated Balangingi leader), x, 16-17, 120, 253, 271, 313, 314, 328-30, 295, 308, 332, 341, 356, 358-9, 360, 364-5, 367, 373; wives and children captured at Sipac Fort, 353, 363, 364, 367; lead Balangingi resistance against Spanish, 361-64; captured by Spanish, 363, 364-5, 366; banished to Cagayan, 365, 371; Nuyla, youngest wife of, 367, 369, 375; death of, 372; Taynan, woman of, 318; Haji Datu Nuno, alias, Antonio de la Cruz, youngest son of, 374-6

Tausog, 19, 27, 37, 39, 70, 154; coastal chiefs and world capitalist economy, 22; and state formation, 27; expansion of, 28, 35, 357; class system, 35; and geographical/ecological destiny, 35; and trade expansion, 34, 191; China trade with, 35; and importance of slaves, 38; as enemy of Maguindanao, 70; and Rennell's reports, 14

Tausog datus, and relationships with Iranun and Balangingi, 49-50, 355

Tawi-Tawi, 359, 360, 362, 379, 384

Taynan, woman of Taupan, 318

Telegrafistas (Signal crew), 107

Tempasuk, and maritime raiders, 5, 64-7, 74, 223, 253, 276, 305, 311, 323; Iranun maritime bases in, 54, 60, 64, 99, 126-137, 138, 140, 141, 143, 164-6, 179, 210, 242, 267; destruction of, 345; as mini-state, 128

Ternate, 31, 69, 70, 141, 283

Testimonio, of fugitive captives, 16

Textiles, as trade commodities, 8, 34, 45, 64, 79, 134, 193, 267, 403; and Tausog datus, 37

Thailand, targeted by maritime

raiders, 1, 54, 61, 212, 268, 296, 317
The Eastern Seas (book), see Earl
The Muslims in the Philippines (book), see Majul
The Pirate Wind (book), see Owen
The Philippines (book), see Mallet
The Rescue (book), see Conrad
The Sea Dayaks of Borneo before White Rajah Rule (book), see Sandin.
The State of the Philippines (book) on 'Moro' piracy, 101
The Sulu Zone (book), see Warren.
The Sulu Zone, The World Capitalist Economy and the Historical Imagination (book), see Warren.
Thomas, Francisco, 12 year old captive, 39, 150, 177, 296, 320
Tidore, 69
Timber, as trade commodity, 64, 133
Timor, 16, 57, 275, 287, 288, 327
Tin trade, 4, 57, 131; and rivalry between Dutch and Iranun, 58, 60, 64; and Chinese miners, 62; and women miners, 126
Tobacco, as trade commodity, 134, 376; and deportados labour, 370-71, 372, 374; as agent of change, 370
Tobello (seafaring group), vii, 69, 88, 141-42, 154, 209, 210, 211; and ethnicity, 152
Tobias, M.J.H. commissioner of Borneo, antipiracy report of, 88, 90-91, 168; on pejorative labels for 'Moro,' 391
Tobungku, Iranun settlements and bases on, 57, 65, 69, 142, 154-163, 210
Tontoli, 141; Iranun settlements and bases on, 71, 74, 154-163, 177, 179, 210, 276; and ethnicity, 152

Tortoise shell, as trade commodity, 157, 191, 192, 193, 194, 221
Trade commodities, agar-agar (seaweed), 139, 218, 270; birds' nest, 2, 33, 59, 133, 140, 165, 181, 191, 257, 401, 405, 414; camphor, 2, 133; cattle, 101, 145; ceramics, 64; Chinese tea, 35, 181, 194, 257, 401, 403, 414; cinnamon, 33; cocoa, 64; gold, 45, 67-8, 83, 93, 273; gunpowder, 37, 52, 183, 184; iron, 134; luxury goods, 38; opium, 4, 34, 37, 64, 193, 267, 268, 339, 403; mother of pearl, 192, 194, 218, 219, 221; munitions, 4, 129, 139; nipa, 134; pearls, 133, 15, 167, 192, 218, 21, 229, 344, 401; pepper (black gold), 279, 280; porcelain, 79; rattan, 2, 133; rice, 33, 38, 64, 67-8, 100, 133, 134, 145, 150, 151, 157, 180, 188, 273; sago, 94, 150, 157; salt, 134, 184, 219, 221; salted fish, 134; sharks fin, 401; silk, 79; silver, 83; slaves, 4, 7, 33, 37, 61, 62, 95, 96, 138, 139, 151, 167, 183, 186-7, 257, 258, 310; spices, 79; timber, 64, 133, 134; tin, 4, 57, 58, 60, 62; textiles, 45, 134, 193, 267, 403; tobacco, 134; tortoise shell, 157, 191, 192, 193, 194, 221; *tripang*, 33, 59, 133, 139, 157, 162, 165, 167, 181, 191, 218, 219-20, 221, 257, 270, 344, 401, 405, 414; wax, 33, 45, 133, 162; weapons and war stores, 37, 38, 65, 83, 128, 138, 183, 184, 186-7, 189, 190-1, 193, 194, 267, 403, 414
Trade, interconnections, 5; competition, 7; integration with maritime raiding, 24, 267-8; and

583

slavery, 24, 34; as preoccupation of sultanates, 28; consolidated at Cotabato, 32; global-local, 22, 33-34, 52, 267-8; as source of livelihood in Sulu Sultanate, 35; and status, 38-9; and patterns of consumption, 96

Tripang, the harvest of, vi, 18, 219-20, 221, 270; as trade commodity, 33, 59, 133, 139, 157, 162, 165, 167, 181, 191, 194, 218, 257, 344, 401, 405, 414; as provisions, 232, 234

Trophies, heads as, 210, 211-2, 214

Tuan Haji, Forrest's guide, 58; 'great pirate,' 59; navigator of *Tartar Galley*, 67; marriage alliance with Rajah Mudu's family, 67; rowing song, 258

Tubug, as Iranun harbor, 48; ruined by volcanic eruption, 46-7

Tufhat al-Nafis, (Malay language history of Riau), Bugis Epic, 138; and Iranun raiding in Malacca Straits, 58, 59, 180

Tulawie, Rene, and oral history of Sipac Fort, 353-4

Tulisanes, and migrants, 122

Tumugsuc (chief), 271, 356, 373; capturer of Ibanez y Garcia, 314, 318, 341; wives captured at Sipac Fort, 353, 367; capture by Spanish, 364-5; banished to Nueva Vizcaya, 365, 371

Tunku, Iranun settlements and bases on, 154-163

Uranie, and Rose Freycinet, 288

Usman, Sherif, Lord of Maruda Bay, 98, 132, 182, 184; married to sister of Raja Muda, 129; and commodity procurement, 129; and slave trade, 129-30; and Brooke, 130, 137; alliance with Laut, 130

Usop, Pangeran, and James Brooke, 98, 130

Valentina Aleja, wife of Dando, 368

Van Leur, J.C., and 'Asia-centric history,' 13

Velocipede, Wyndham's schooner, 192, 193

Velthoen, Esther, and slave raiding alliances, 69; on Tontoli, 155; on Tobello, and oral history, 156

Vidar, S.S., 393

Vikings of Asia, ix

Vinta (armed outriggered craft), 103, 220

Vietnam, 1, 212, 260, 267

Violence, 222, 223, 224-7, 268, 271-72, 273-308, 331-3, 335-7, 351

Visayan Sea, and maritime raiding, 16, 72, 74, 277; as trade route, 82

Visayas and Visayans, targeted by maritime raiders, 54, 74, 80-81, 83, 84, 102, 104, 106, 109, 110, 144, 145, 152, 174, 208-9, 210, 261, 270, 312, 319, 331, 343, 361, 381; impact of maritime raiding on, 82

Voyage to New Guinea (book). See Forrest

VOC, targeted by Iranun, 131. See also Dutch East India Company.

Vogel, Spanish planter and administrator, 373, 376

Volcanic eruptions, and diaspora, 26, 32-33, 45-6

War stores, and economic statecraft, 37; exchanged for slaves, 96, 129-30; difficulty in obtaining, 114

INDEX

Wallace, Alfred, Victorian naturalist, *The Malay Archipelago* (book), 273

Ward, Gamaliel, captain of *Leonidas*, 190, 192, 193, 194

Warren, James Francis, *The Sulu Zone* (book), v, ix, x, 6, 11, 13, 38, 383, 411; and world capitalist economy, 22; *The Sulu Zone, The World Capitalist Economy and the Historical Imagination* (book), ix; on Balangingi ethnicity, 152

Watchtowers, as line of defense, 49

Wax, 133, 162

Weapons, and the Iranun, 11, 242, 244, 248, 250-52, 267, 268, 331, 403; and Tausog datus, 37; as trade commodity, 34, 37, 38, 65, 83, 128, 138, 183, 184, 186-7, 189, 190-1, 193, 194, 414; trading and Forrest, 66; of mass destruction, 356

Werble, Sali, 225

West, the, and interactions with Sulu and China, xi and global-local trade, 6

White, John, Capt., master of *Franklin*, 280-81

Wilkes, Charles (American Naval Commander), on slaves, 39, 192, 343

Windsor, George Earl, (private trader), description of archipelago, 4; *The Eastern Seas* (book) 4, 95-6; report on maritime raiding, 94-5; on slave trade, 96; on Iranun women, 135; on Iranun and Iban, 214; on American traders, 192

Woodward, David, chief mate of *Enterprise*, castaway on Sulawesi, 58-9

Wolf, Eric, *Europe and the People Without History* (book), 12, 411

Wolf, warship, 302

Women, and maritime raiders, vi, 80, 112, 126, 131, 135, 237, 278, 280, 291, 295, 297, 321; drawn into global Chinese market economy, 9; oral history and 17; as mothers, 23; as captives and slaves, 40, 71, 203, 204, 291, 310, 321; as Iranun wives, 43, 131; and strategic marriage alliances, 47-8, 67, 129, 166; married to slaves, 170, 173-4; as consorts, 171; captured at Sipac Fort, 352, 253-4, 355, 356, 363, 364, 366-9

Wong, Lin Ken, on Iranun raiding in straits of Malacca, 94.

World Capitalist Economy, and Iranun and Balangingi, 2, 24, 40, 85, 181, 342, 401; and development in Asia, 5; and Sulu Sultanate, 13, 35; and slaves, 22, 181

World Commerce. *See* World Capital Economy

Wyndham, William (merchant adventurer), 160, 178, 192, 193-4, 210, 241, 275, 287-9, 331, 349; married to a mestiza, 192; description of Iranun, 223; and the transport of gunpowder, 251

Zamboanga, 26, 30, 49, 68, 74, 150, 192, 196, 277, 312, 326, 328, 339, 344, 346-7, 351, 354, 362, 364-8, 375-6, 377, 378, 382

Zephyr, Dutch schooner of war, 273

Zuñiga, Joachin Martinez de, report on impact of Iranun, 84, 323-4